NITA HEWITT RUTKOSKY
Pierce College at Puyallup
Puyallup, Washington

JUDY DWYER BURNSIDE
College of DuPage
Glen Ellyn, Illinois

JOANNE MARSCHKE ARFORD
College of DuPage
Glen Ellyn, Illinois

Developmental Editor Lisa McGowan
Copy Editor Patricia Brown
Proofreader Jennifer Anderson
Indexer Nancy Sauro
Cover Designer Bolger Publications/Creative Printing
Text Designer Shepherd Inc.
Desktop Publisher Jennifer L. Wreisner

Registered trademarks—Microsoft, DOS, and Windows are registered trademarks of Microsoft Corporation. IBM is a registered trademark of IBM Corporation.

Permissions—Microsoft Publisher clip art is used by permission of Microsoft Corporation. The following people have generously given permission to use their materials: Dane and Mary Beth Luhrsen, Ride Safe Inc., Warrenville, Illinois; Edward Hospital, Marketing Department, Naperville, Illinois; Edward Cardiovascular Institute, Naperville, Illinois; Floyd Rogers, Butterfield Gardens, Warrenville, Illinois; Four Corners Artists Ltd., Naperville, Illinois; and Crowe, Chizek, and Co. LLT. Material has been excerpted from *Microsoft Word 7* by Nita Hewitt Rutkosky, Paradigm Publishing Inc., 1997; *Telecommunications: Systems and Applications* by Robert Hendricks, Leonard Sterry, and William Mitchell, Paradigm Publishing Inc., 1993; and from *Effective Teaching: The Cornerstone of Quality Education* by James Foran, Paradigm Publishing, Inc., 1990.

Acknowledgments—The authors and publisher wish to thank the following instructors for their technical and academic assistance:

- George Behr, Just Perfect by George, Fountain Valley, California
- Deborah C. Clear, Virginia Highlands Community College, Abingdon, Virginia
- Denise Hayward, Consultant, Odessa, Texas
- Kay E. Stephan, University of Akron–Wayne College, Orrville, Ohio
- Nancy Stanko, College of DuPage, Glen Ellyn, Illinois
- Peggy Maas, College of DuPage, Glen Ellyn, Illinois

Dedication— To my husband, Michael, and my children, Audrey, Ryan, and Ian.—Nita Rutkosky

To my parents, Albert and Roberta Dwyer, and my children, Brandon and Cassie.—Judy Burnside

To my husband, Frank, and our children, Rachel, Lisa, and Kaitlin.—Joanne Arford

---

Library of Congress Cataloging-in-Publication Data
Rutkosky, Nita Hewitt
Advanced Microsoft Word 7 : desktop publishing / Nita Hewitt Rutkosky, Judy Dwyer Burnside, Joanne Marschke Arford.
p. cm.
Includes index.
ISBN 1-56118-901-4 (text only). — ISBN 1-56118-902-2 (text with 3.5" disk)
1. Microsoft Word for Windows. 2. Word processing. 3. Desktop publishing.
I. Burnside, Judy Dwyer. II. Arford, Joanne Marschke. III. Title.
Z52.5.M523R877 1996 96-25140
652.5'5369—dc20 CIP

Text + 3.5" disk: ISBN 1-56118-902-2
Order number: 05271

© 1997 by Paradigm Publishing Inc.
Published by **EMC**Paradigm
875 Montreal Way
St. Paul, MN 55102
(800) 535-6865
E-mail publish@emcp.com

All rights reserved. Making copies of any part of this book for any purpose other than your own personal use is a violation of the United States copyright laws. No part of this book may be used or reproduced in any form or by any means, or stored in a database retrieval system, without prior written permission of Paradigm Publishing Inc.

Printed in the United States of America
10 9 8 7 6 5 4 3 2 1

CONTENTS

* This feature appears in each chapter.

PREFACE

Microsoft Word, one of the best-selling word processing programs for microcomputers, includes a wide variety of desktop publishing features. The scope and capabilities of these features have expanded with each new version of Word. *Advanced Microsoft Word 7: Desktop Publishing* is designed to address specific desktop publishing features included in Microsoft Word 7 for Windows 95, along with general desktop publishing concepts.

Word's desktop publishing features allow the user to create very professional-looking documents. Desktop publishing eliminates the need for a typesetter and page designer, greatly reducing the cost of publishing documents. Desktop publishing produces immediate results and offers the computer user the ability to control the production from beginning to end.

Advanced Microsoft Word 7: Desktop Publishing is designed to be used by students already familiar with word processing. This textbook focuses on advanced Word features along with desktop publishing terminology and concepts. Most of the key desktop publishing concepts addressed in this textbook are presented in chapter 1. Applications of these key concepts are presented in the remaining 11 chapters. The applications are designed to develop skills in critical thinking, decision making, and creativity. Many applications in this textbook are designed to reinforce collaborative learning in planning, designing, and evaluating business documents. In numerous applications, basic information is given for a task just as it may be given in a real life situation.

The text contains three units with a total of 12 chapters. Each chapter contains the following elements:

- Performance objective
- Desktop publishing concepts
- Word features used
- Desktop publishing pointers used to reinforce concepts
- Word and desktop publishing terms and definitions
- Hands-on exercises interspersed within each chapter demonstrating key concepts and features
- Chapter summary
- Commands review
- Student study guide (Check Your Understanding)
- Hands on computer applications (Skill Assessments)
- Additional applications promoting collaborative learning as well as individual creativity (Creative Activity)

In addition, a unit objective summarizes the key goals emphasized in each unit. Each unit also ends with a Performance Assessment that evaluates students' mastery of both the desktop publishing concepts and the Word skills presented in the unit.

SCANS (Secretary's Commission on Achieving Necessary Skills) standards emphasize the integration of competencies from the areas of information, technology, basic skills, and thinking skills (see the back of the first page of each unit). The concepts and applications material in this book have been designed to coordinate with and reflect this important interdisciplinary emphasis. In addition, learning assessment tools implement the SCANS standards. For example, the end-of-chapter exercises called Skill Assessments reinforce acquired skills while providing practice in decision making. A Performance Assessment at the end of each unit offers simulation exercises that require students to demonstrate their understanding of the major skills and technical features taught in the unit's chapters within the framework of creativity, decision making, and writing. Optional exercises related to SCANS standards are included in the Performance Assessment and in selected Skill Assessments.

Students who successfully complete this course will have achieved the following competencies:

- Use basic type-oriented design techniques available with Microsoft Word 7 to enhance the readability of multiple-page, portrait, or landscape documents such as letterheads, business cards, personal documents, flyers, brochures, promotional documents, charts, transparencies, presentational materials, newsletters, reports, and manuals.

- Enhance the visual appeal of business and personal documents with variable page layouts using standardized type and graphic design techniques along with Word templates and clip art.
- Use Microsoft Word 7 to manage desktop publishing files and document templates.

READ THIS BEFORE YOU BEGIN

Using Microsoft Word 7 for Windows 95

Whether you are using the stand-alone version of Microsoft Word 7 or using Word within Microsoft Office for Windows 95, the following information is important to your success in using Word to complete the exercises in this textbook:

System Requirements

- Personal computer with at least a 486 processor; a Pentium processor is recommended
- At least 8 megabytes of RAM
- Large capacity hard disk or file server; the minimum amount of free disk space needed is 28 megabytes; more may be needed depending on the type of installation and your system's configuration
- Windows 95
- Super VGA or higher graphics adapter compatible with Windows 95; high-resolution monitor is preferable
- At least a 1.44 floppy disk drive or a double- or quad-speed CD-ROM drive
- 4 megabytes or more of free disk space at all times for temporary files
- Mouse (not all features are available through the keyboard)
- Laser printer or good quality inkjet printer supported by Windows 95; color printer if available

Word Folders/Directories

By default, Word is installed in a folder (or directory) named *Winword*. The default pathname to this folder is *C:\MSOffice\Winword*. The *Winword* folder contains the essential files and subfolders (containing additional files) necessary to run Word 7.0. The *MSOffice* folder contains additional folders (directories), such as *Clipart* and *Templates*, that contain files that are necessary to complete the exercises in this textbook. The *Clipart* folder contains clip art images that can be inserted into documents. The *Templates* folder contains all the template document files available through Word.

Installing Microsoft Word 7

To properly install Word, please refer to the Word documentation (or Microsoft Office documentation) and to the information that follows.

Microsoft Office for Windows 95 provides three installation options:

1. Typical—Microsoft Office will be installed with the most commonly used options.
2. Compact—Microsoft Office will be installed with the minimum necessary options.
3. Custom—Microsoft Office will be installed with only the selected options.

The best approach to installing Office is to choose the Custom option. With the Custom option, you can install other components in addition to the default options that are included in a Typical installation. To successfully complete the exercises in this textbook, the following components, in addition to the default options already selected, need to be included in a Custom installation:

1. Select the *Microsoft Word* option and change this option to include:
   a. All selections from the *Wizards, Templates, and Letters* component (*Faxes, Letters, Memos, Reports, Forms, More Wizards, Newsletters, Press Releases, Publications, Résumés, Table Wizard, Sample Letters*, and *Macro Templates*).
   b. All selections from the *Proofing Tools* component (*Hyphenation, Grammar, Thesaurus, and Find All Word Forms*).
   c. The *Online Help* selection included as part of the *Online Help* option.

   d. The *Text with Layout Converter* selection included as part of the *Text Converters* option.

2. Select the *Office Tools* option and change this option to include the following (some of these items may already be selected):
   a. *Spelling Checker*
   b. *WordArt*
   c. *Microsoft Graph 5.0*
   d. *ClipArt Gallery*
   e. *Clip Art*
3. Select the *Microsoft PowerPoint* option and change this option to include:
   a. *Online Help for Microsoft PowerPoint*
   b. *Design Templates*
4. Select the *Converters, Filters, and Data Access* option and change this option to include C*onverters and Graphic Filters.*

Adding Additional Word Options

If Microsoft Word 7 for Windows 95 has already been installed on your computer, you may install the additional features listed above by completing the following basic steps (refer to the Word documentation for more specific information):

1. At the Desktop, double-click the *My Computer* icon.
2. At the My Computer window, double-click the Control Panel folder.
3. At the Control Panel window, double-click the *Add/Remove Programs* icon.
4. At the Add/Remove Programs Properties dialog box, click Install.
5. At the next screen, insert the Word or Microsoft Office setup disk in the appropriate drive.
6. Follow the steps provided by the Install Wizard to install additional features.

Defaults

All default formatting settings, such as font, margin settings, line spacing, and justification; toolbars; templates; and directories used in this textbook are based on the assumption that none of the original defaults have been customized after installation.

Using This Book

As you work through the desktop publishing information presented in this textbook, you need to be aware of the following important points:

- Instructions for all features and exercises emphasize using the mouse. Where appropriate, keyboard or function key presses are added as an alternative.
- As you complete exercises, view the completed figure following each exercise to see what the document should look like.
- Be aware that the final appearance of your printed documents depends on the printer you use to complete the exercises. Your printer driver may be different than the printer driver used for the exercises in this textbook. Not all printer drivers interpret line height the same, nor do they all offer the same font selections. Consequently, you may have to make some minor adjustments when completing the exercises in this book. For instance, if you need to select a different font than the one stated in the instructions, you may need to change the type size to complete the exercise in the space allotted. Or you may need to adjust spacing between paragraphs or specific blocks of text. As you will see in the chapters that follow, creating desktop published documents is a constant process of making small adjustments to fine-tune your design and layout.

Most of the fonts specified in the exercises are common fonts, but it is possible that some of the fonts used may not be supported by your printer. In that case, you will need to select an alternate font. When substituting another font, your documents may look slightly different from what you see in this text. Minor adjustments may need to be made on your part to accommodate a different font.

Using the Graphics Data Disk

Some Word 7 users may have more clip art available in the Picture dialog box or the Microsoft ClipArt Gallery than others. If you installed Word 7 as a stand-alone version, you will have approximately 95 clip art images available for your use. If you installed Word 7 as part of Microsoft Office, you may have additional clip art images available in the Microsoft ClipArt Gallery. The Microsoft ClipArt Gallery may also include clip art from other Microsoft software currently loaded on your hard drive.

Some exercises in this textbook use Microsoft clip art images that are not included with Word 7. To accommodate all users of this textbook, these additional clip art images are included on a separate graphics data disk with your textbook. To copy these files into the Clipart directory so they will be available when you access the Insert Picture dialog box (make sure you change the Files of type to All Files (*.*) at the Insert Picture dialog box), complete the steps below. (Since your computer setup may be different or you may be operating on a network, check with your instructor before completing the following steps):

1. Load Microsoft Windows Explorer.
2. Place your graphics data disk in Drive A (or whatever drive you are using to access your student data disk).
3. Double-click 3½ Floppy (A:) to display all the graphic file names.
4. Choose Edit, then Select All.
5. Choose Edit, then Copy.
6. Double-click Msdos _6_22 (C:).
7. Double-click MSOffice.
8. Double-click Clipart.
9. Choose Edit, then Paste.

The steps to add graphic files to the Microsoft ClipArt Gallery are included in Chapter 9.

Using the Data Disk

Advanced Microsoft Word 7: Desktop Publishing is packaged with two student data disks containing prekeyed documents and some extra graphics that you will use to complete various exercises. The most efficient and easiest approach is to copy the student data disk files into their own directory on the hard drive or network file server. When a file needs to be opened, open the file from the directory holding the data disk files instead of repeatedly reinserting the student data disk.

The remaining disk space on the student data disk will not be enough to store all the exercises in this textbook. To be on the safe side, allow at least 10 extra disks to completely store all the exercises in this textbook. Your instructor may suggest that you delete specific exercise files once you have turned in the documents and they have been graded. Check with your instructor.

PHOTO CREDITS

The following photo credits are courtesy of:

Page		Page	
3	Hewlett Packard Company	311	Peter Fox/Apple Computer, Inc.
73	Micron Electronics, Inc.	355	Micron Electronics, Inc.
177	Hewlett Packard Company	405	Frank Pryor/Apple Computer, Inc.
227	Apple Computer, Inc.	443	Dave Martinez/Apple Computer, Inc.
277	Apple Computer, Inc.	489	Intel Corporation

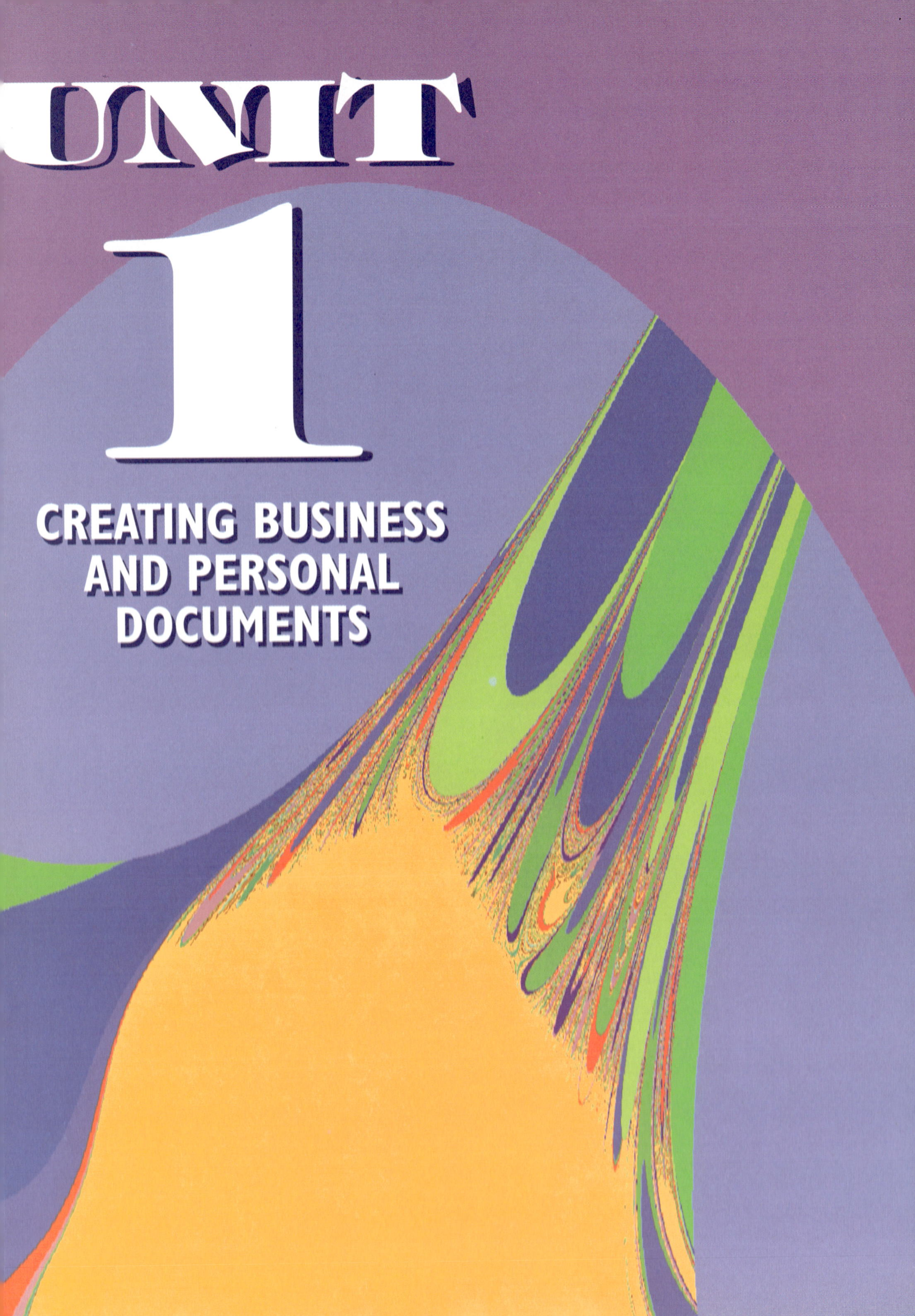
UNIT
1
CREATING BUSINESS
AND PERSONAL
DOCUMENTS

In this unit, you will learn to define and incorporate desktop publishing concepts in the design and creation of business and personal documents.

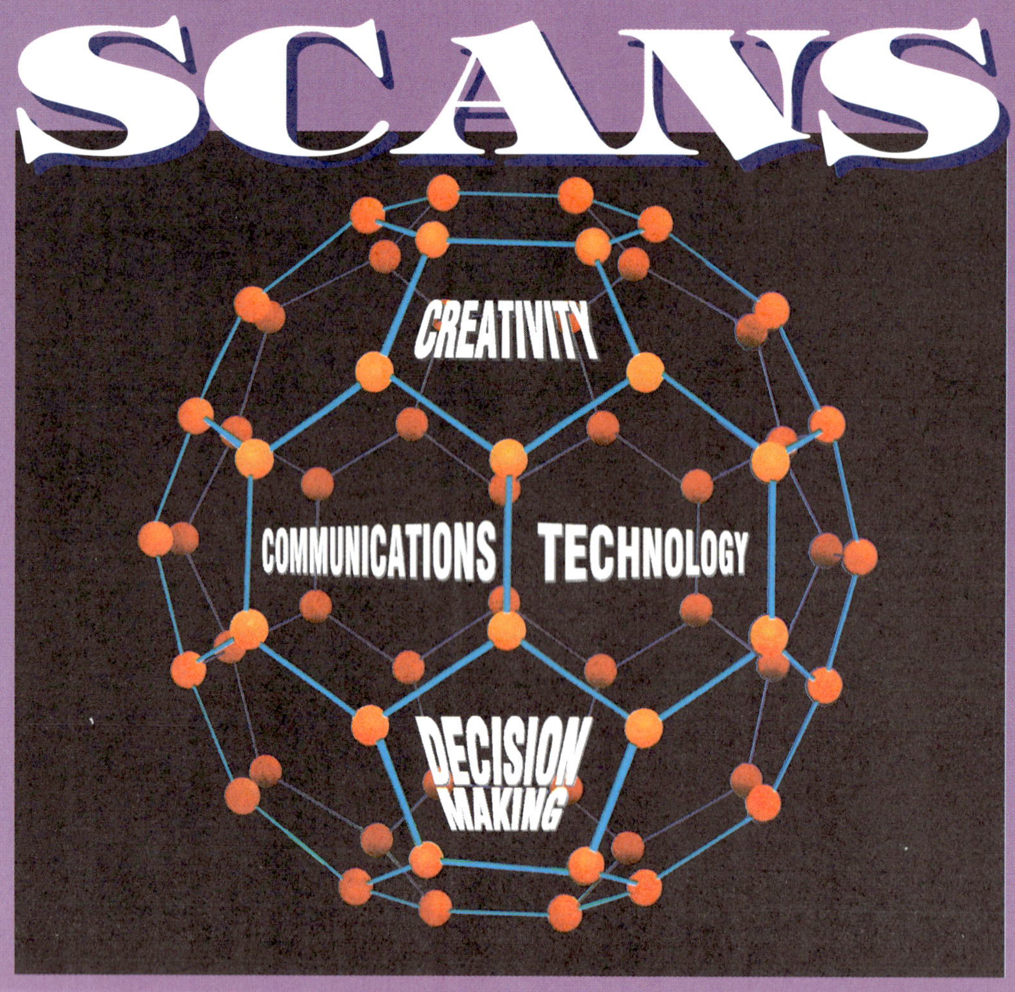

1 UNDERSTANDING THE DESKTOP PUBLISHING PROCESS

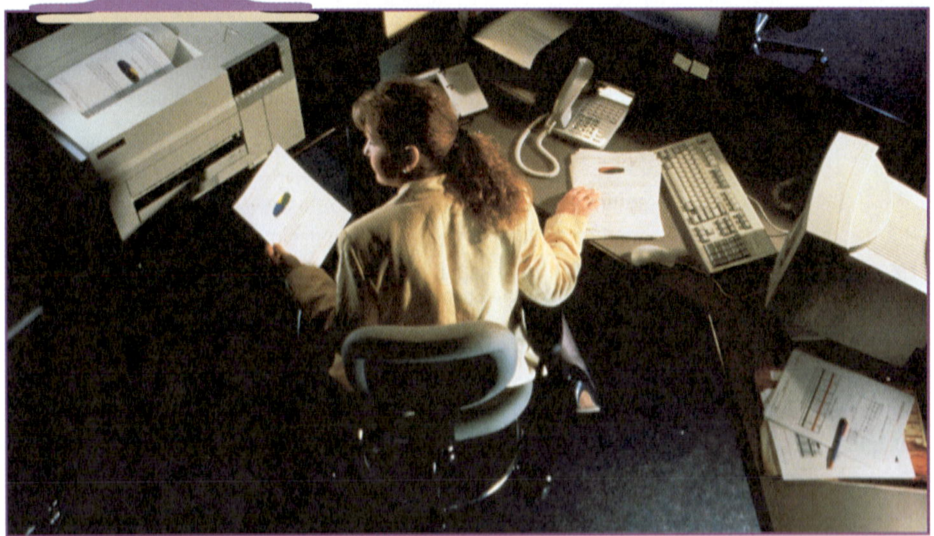

PERFORMANCE OBJECTIVE

Upon successful completion of chapter 1, you will be able to evaluate design elements in a desktop published document for the appropriate use of focus, balance, proportion, contrast, directional flow, consistency, color, and page layout.

DESKTOP PUBLISHING CONCEPTS

Planning
Designing
Focus
Thumbnail sketch
Balance
Symmetrical design
Asymmetrical design
Proportion
Contrast
White space
Directional flow
Consistency
Color
Page layout
Grid

WORD FEATURES USED

Open file
Open a document as Read-Only
Save
Save As
Close
Print
Templates
Viewing multiple pages

Defining Desktop Publishing

Since the 1970s, microcomputers have been an integral part of the business environment. Businesses use microcomputers and software packages to perform a variety of tasks. Until recently, the three most popular types of software purchased for microcomputers were word processing, spreadsheet, and database.

During the past decade, another type of software program called *desktop publishing* has gained popularity with microcomputer users. With the introduction of the laser printer and its ability to produce high-quality documents, desktop publishing software became the fastest growing microcomputer application of the 1980s, and its widespread use continues into the 1990s. Desktop publishing involves using desktop publishing software or word processing software with desktop publishing capabilities, a computer system, and a printer to produce professional-looking documents. The phrase "desktop publishing," coined by Aldus Corporation president Paul Brainard, means that publishing can now literally take place at your desk.

Until the mid-1980s, graphic design depended almost exclusively on design professionals. But desktop publishing changed all that by bringing graphic design into the office and home. Faster microprocessors, improved printer capabilities, an increased supply of clip art, and CD-ROMs continue to expand the role of desktop publishing. Everything from a flyer to a newsletter can be designed, created, and produced at a computer.

In traditional publishing, several people may be involved in completing the publication project. This may be costly and time-consuming. With the use of desktop publishing software, one person may be performing all of the tasks necessary to complete a project, greatly reducing the costs of publishing documents. The two approaches have a great deal in common. Both approaches involve setting goals, planning and organizing content, analyzing layout and design, arranging design elements, typesetting, printing, and distributing the project.

Desktop publishing can be an individual or a combined effort. As an individual effort, desktop publishing produces immediate results and offers you the ability to control the production from beginning layout and design to the end result—printing and distribution. However, desktop publishing and traditional publishing work well together. A project may begin on a desktop, where the document is designed and created, but an illustrator may be commissioned to create some artwork, or it may end up at a commercial printer for printing and binding.

Initiating The Desktop Publishing Process

The process of creating a publication begins with two steps—planning the publication and creating the content. During the planning process, the desktop publisher must decide on the purpose of the publication and the intended audience. While the design of a publication is important, the content of a publication must get the intended message to the reader.

Planning the Publication

Initial planning is probably one of the most important steps in the desktop publishing process. During this stage, the following items must be addressed:

- **Clearly identify the purpose of your communication.** The more definite you are about your purpose, the easier it will be for you to organize your material into an effective communication. Are you trying to provide information? Are you trying to sell a product? Are you announcing an event?

DTP POINTERS
Consider your audience when planning your publication.

- **Assess your target audience.** Whom do you want to read your publication? Are they employees, co-workers, clients, friends, or family? What will your target audience expect out of your publication? Do they expect a serious, more conservative approach or an informal, humorous approach?
- **Determine in what form your intended audience will be exposed to your message.** Will your message be contained in a brochure enclosed in a packet of presentation

materials for a company seminar? Or will your message be in the form of a newspaper advertisement, surrounded by other advertisements? Will your message be in the form of a business card that is to be distributed when making sales calls? Or will your message be tacked on a bulletin board?

- **Decide what you want your readers to do after reading your message.** Do you want your readers to ask for more information? Do you want some kind of a response? Do you want your readers to be able to contact you in person or over the telephone?
- **Collect examples of effective designs**. Decide what you like and do not like. Try and determine why one design is more appealing than another. What elements attract your attention? Let the designs you like be a catalyst for developing your own ideas.

Creating the Content

The most important goal in desktop publishing is to get the message across. Design is important because it increases the appeal of your document, but content is still the most important consideration. Create a document that communicates the message clearly to your intended audience.

In analyzing your message, identify your goals and start organizing your material. Establish a hierarchy of importance among the items in your communication. Consider what items will be important to the reader, what will attract the reader's attention, and what will spark enough interest for the reader to go on. Begin to think about the format or layout you want to follow. Clear and organized content combined with an attractive layout and design contribute to the effectiveness of your message.

Designing The Document

If the message is the most significant part of a communication, why bother with design? A well-planned and relevant design sets your work apart from others, and it gets people to read your message. Just as people may be judged by their appearance, a publication may be judged by its design. Design also helps organize ideas so the reader can find information quickly and easily. Whether you are creating a business flyer, letterhead, or newsletter, anything you create will look more attractive, more professional, and more convincing if you take a little extra time to design it. When designing a document, you need to consider many factors:

DTP POINTERS
Take the time to design!

- What is the intent of the document?
- Who is the intended audience?
- What is the feeling the document is meant to elicit?
- What is the most important information and how can it be emphasized?
- What different types of information are to be presented and how can these elements be distinguished and kept internally consistent?
- How much space is available?
- How is the document going to be distributed?

Answering these questions will help you determine the design and layout of your communication.

Thumbnail Sketch: A rough sketch used in planning a layout and design.

An important first step in planning your design and layout is to prepare a *thumbnail sketch*. A thumbnail sketch is a miniature draft of the document you are attempting to create. As you can see in figure 1.1, thumbnail sketches let you experiment with alternative locations for such elements as graphic images, ruled lines, columns, and borders.

FIGURE 1.1

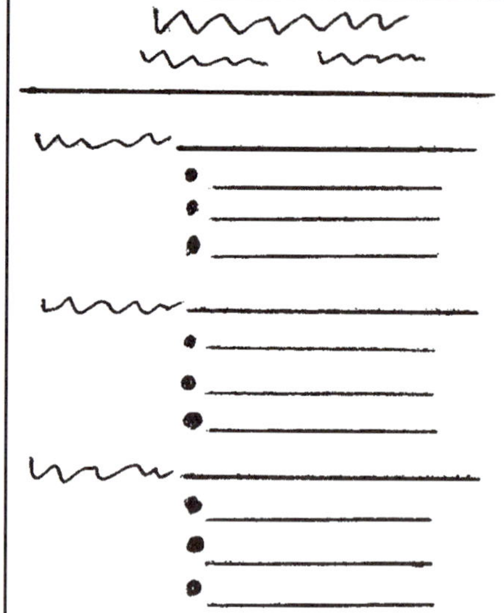

A good designer continually asks questions, pays attention to details, and makes well-thought-out decisions. Overdesigning is one of the most common tendencies of beginning desktop publishers. Design should be used to communicate, not decorate. Consider examples A and B in figure 1.2. Which example attracts your attention, entices you to read on, and would most likely cause you to act?

FIGURE 1.2

PRIVATE
MUSIC LESSONS

Contact Kim Diehl at:

The Music Store
(708) 555-7867

A

B

Although there are no hard-and-fast rules on how to arrange elements on a page, there are some basic design principles that can be used as guidelines to help you get started. To create a visually attractive and appealing publication, some concepts to consider are focus, balance, proportion, contrast, directional flow, consistency, and color.

Creating Focus

The *focus* on a page is an element that draws the reader's eyes. Focus is created by using elements that are large, dense, unusual, and/or surrounded by white space. Two basic design elements used to create focus in a document are:

Focus: An element that draws the reader's eyes.

- Titles, headlines, and subheads created in a larger and bolder typeface
- Graphic elements such as ruled lines, clip art, photographs, illustrations, logos, or images created with a draw program or scanned into the computer

Titles, Headlines, and Subheads. Untrained desktop publishers often create publications that are essentially typewritten documents that happen to be set in proportional type. Focus is difficult to create on a typewritten page because of the limitations of type size and positioning. With desktop publishing features, however, choice of typeface, type size, and positioning are highly flexible.

In a text-only document, primary focus is usually created by using large or bold type for titles and headings, surrounded by enough white space to contrast with the main text. *White space* is the background where no text or graphics are located. The amount of white space around a focal element can enhance its appearance. The size of a headline in proportion to surrounding text is an indicator of its importance. A headline or title set in a larger type size is easily identified and immediately informs the reader of the nature of the publication. A well-designed headline not only informs, but it also attracts the reader's attention. It can play a big part in whether a reader continues reading your publication. A title/headline needs to be precisely stated and easily understood. *Legibility* is of utmost importance. Readers must be able to clearly see and read the individual letters in the headline/title. The impact of your headline/title as a focal element in your document is affected by your selection of an appropriate font (typeface, type size, and type style), the alignment of the text, and the horizontal and vertical white space surrounding the text.

White Space: Background space with no text or graphics.

Legibility: The ease with which individual characters are recognized.

In any type of communication—a semi-annual report, company newsletter, advertising flyer, or brochure—subheads can be used to provide a secondary focal element. A headline may be the primary focal element used to attract the reader's attention, but the subheads may be the key to luring the reader in. Subheads provide order to your text and give the reader further clues about the content of your publication. Content divided by subheads appears more manageable to the reader's eye and lets the reader focus in on a specific area of interest. Like titles and headlines, subheads need to be concise, legible, and easy to understand. Selecting an appropriate font, spacing above and below the subhead, length, and alignment must be taken into consideration also.

Look at document A in figure 1.3. Can you find any focal element? Does any particular location on the page attract your attention? Now look at document B. Are your eyes drawn to a certain spot on the page? The headline, set in a larger and bolder type, definitely serves as a primary focal point. Your eyes are immediately drawn to the headline and an important question is answered for the reader; namely, what is this all about? After viewing the headline in figure 1.4, what area of the page are your eyes drawn to next? Notice how subheads set in a type bolder and larger than the body text but smaller than the heading provide secondary focal points on the page.

FIGURE 1.3

Desktop Publishing Newsletter

November 1995 **Volume 2, No. 5**

Knowledge Is Power!

How can one have the up-to-date knowledge needed to keep on the cutting edge of desktop publishing? One way to have knowledge is to read some of the periodicals, newsletters, and books now available that address all aspects of desktop publishing.

Two basic types of periodicals are available. The first type is based on technological development to communication arts. These periodicals contain useful information about current and new products. The second type contains knowledge of technique, style, and applications.

Many newsletters and books are available. Listed below are some magazines, newsletters, and books that can help you as a desktop publisher.

Publish is a monthly magazine with information of interest to those involved in all areas of print and multimedia productions. The focus is on print design and production and addresses emerging technologies.

PC Publishing covers information on desktop publishing and presentation graphics for those using IBM and compatibles. Each issue addresses specific subjects with in-depth discussion.

Desktop Communications covers hardware/software, design, typography, and useful tips. Industry professionals provide extensive knowledge from their experience.

WordPerfect Magazine is a practical periodical dedicated to WordPerfect users and published by WordPerfect Corporation. It contains how-to graphic design and typographic guidance.

Before and After, a bimonthly newsletter, gives down-to-earth advice with graphic design and desktop typography.

Newsletters from the Desktop by Roger Parker has tips on saving time and money on design and layout.

The Makeover Book has 101 design solutions for desktop publishers. "Before" and "after" examples are given to show you how to make your documents more interesting and persuasive.

Training Techniques

Two types of training are available for those just beginning in desktop publishing.

The first type is a content-based program. This program is based on a typical college program and the information is presented in a classroom situation. Instructional books and videos are frequently utilized.

Skill-based training is another type of training. This training is useful to businesses as skill-based training produces capable people quickly. Productive skills are put to use on the type of job the person will be expected to fulfill.

Both types of training produce workers with equal productivity and confidence. The best equipment is wasted if people are not trained to use it efficiently. Good training, regardless of which type, is essential to desktop publishing.

A

Desktop Publishing Newsletter

November 1995 **Volume 2, No. 5**

Knowledge Is Power!

How can one have the up-to-date knowledge needed to keep on the cutting edge of desktop publishing? One way to have knowledge is to read some of the periodicals, newsletters, and books now available that address all aspects of desktop publishing.

Two basic types of periodicals are available. The first type is based on technological development to communication arts. These periodicals contain useful information about current and new products. The second type contains knowledge of technique, style, and applications.

Many newsletters and books are available. Listed below are some magazines, newsletters, and books that can help you as a desktop publisher.

Publish is a monthly magazine with information of interest to those involved in all areas of print and multimedia productions. The focus is on print design and production and addresses emerging technologies.

PC Publishing covers information on desktop publishing and presentation graphics for those using IBM and compatibles. Each issue addresses specific subjects with in-depth discussion.

Desktop Communications covers hardware/software, design, typography, and useful tips. Industry professionals provide extensive knowledge from their experience.

WordPerfect Magazine is a practical periodical dedicated to WordPerfect users and published by WordPerfect Corporation. It contains how-to graphic design and typographic guidance.

Before and After, a bimonthly newsletter, gives down-to-earth advice with graphic design and desktop typography.

Newsletters from the Desktop by Roger Parker has tips on saving time and money on design and layout.

The Makeover Book has 101 design solutions for desktop publishers. "Before" and "after" examples are given to show you how to make your documents more interesting and persuasive.

Training Techniques

Two types of training are available for those just beginning in desktop publishing.

The first type is a content-based program. This program is based on a typical college program and the information is presented in a classroom situation. Instructional books and videos are frequently utilized.

Skill-based training is another type of training. This training is useful to businesses as skill-based training produces capable people quickly. Productive skills are put to use on the type of job the person will be expected to fulfill.

Both types of training produce workers with equal productivity and confidence. The best equipment is wasted if people are not trained to use it efficiently. Good training, regardless of which type, is essential to desktop publishing.

B

FIGURE 1.4

Desktop Publishing Newsletter

November 1995 **Volume 2, No. 5**

Knowledge Is Power!

How can one have the up-to-date knowledge needed to keep on the cutting edge of desktop publishing? One way to have knowledge is to read some of the periodicals, newsletters, and books now available that address all aspects of desktop publishing.

Two basic types of periodicals are available. The first type is based on technological development to communication arts. These periodicals contain useful information about current and new products. The second type contains knowledge of technique, style, and applications.

Many newsletters and books are available. Listed below are some magazines, newsletters, and books that can help you as a desktop publisher.

Publish is a monthly magazine with information of interest to those involved in all areas of print and multimedia productions. The focus is on print design and production and addresses emerging technologies.

PC Publishing covers information on desktop publishing and presentation graphics for those using IBM and compatibles. Each issue addresses specific subjects with in-depth discussion.

Desktop Communications covers hardware/software, design, typography, and useful tips. Industry professionals provide extensive knowledge from their experience.

WordPerfect Magazine is a practical periodical dedicated to WordPerfect users and published by WordPerfect Corporation. It contains how-to graphic design and typographic guidance.

Before and After, a bimonthly newsletter, gives down-to-earth advice with graphic design and desktop typography.

Newsletters from the Desktop by Roger Parker has tips on saving time and money on design and layout.

The Makeover Book has 101 design solutions for desktop publishers. "Before" and "after" examples are given to show you how to make your documents more interesting and persuasive.

Training Techniques

Two types of training are available for those just beginning in desktop publishing.

The first type is a content-based program. This program is based on a typical college program and the information is presented in a classroom situation. Instructional books and videos are frequently utilized.

Skill-based training is another type of training. This training is useful to businesses as skill-based training produces capable people quickly. Productive skills are put to use on the type of job the person will be expected to fulfill.

Both types of training produce workers with equal productivity and confidence. The best equipment is wasted if people are not trained to use it efficiently. Good training, regardless of which type, is essential to desktop publishing.

Graphic Elements. Graphic elements provide focus on a page and can enhance the overall appearance of a publication. Graphic elements, such as ruled lines, pull quotes, sidebars, clip art, illustrations, photos, charts, graphs, diagrams, and tables, can be used effectively to establish focus in your document.

When considering using a graphic element as a focal point, remember the following two points:

- **Communicate; don't decorate.** Let your message dictate the use of graphic elements. Does the graphic element enhance your message or does it overshadow your message? Is it relevant, meaningful, and appropriate? Do not use it if you find yourself saying, "It doesn't really add to the message, but I just like the looks of it."
- **Less is best.** Simplicity rules. Owning a CD-ROM with 10,000 clip art images does not mean that you should find as many pictures as you can to insert into your document. One simple, large, and effective graphic image provides more impact than using several smaller images. Your goal is to provide focus. Too many images create visual confusion for the reader.

DTP POINTERS

- Graphics should enhance your message, not decorate the page.
- Keep your design simple.

If all other factors are equal, publications containing graphic elements will be noticed and perused before text-only publications. The flyer illustrated in figure 1.5 uses two graphic clip art images, one of a paint splatter and one of an artist, as focal points. The impact of the paint splatter image is enhanced by the use of color. The impact of the artist is emphasized as a solid black silhouette. Both of these images are very effective and relate well to the message within the flyer. The use of gray shading behind the picture of the artist creates the look of a framed portrait, further enhancing the graphic image and its use as a focal point. The varying typeface, type size, and density accent the information's order of importance and establish secondary focal points on the page.

FIGURE 1.5

Four Corners
Artists, Ltd.
Studio/Gallery

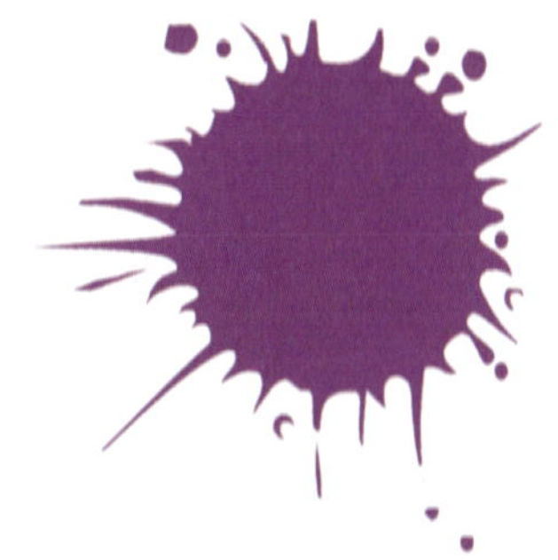

- Colored Pencil Drawing
- Mixed Media
- Watercolor
- Oil Painting
- Open Workshop

190 East Fifth Avenue • Naperville, IL 60563 • (708) 555-6787

6 Sessions • $60.00

Creating Balance

Balance:
The equal distribution of design elements on a page.

Symmetrical Design:
Balancing elements of equal weight on a page.

Asymmetrical Design:
Balancing contrasting elements on a page.

Balance is attained by equally distributing the weight of various elements, such as blocks of text, graphic images, headings, ruled lines, and white space on the page. Balance can be symmetrical or asymmetrical. A *symmetrical design* contains similar elements of equal proportion or weight on the left and right sides and top and bottom of the page. Contemporary design favors *asymmetrical balance*, which is a balance of dissimilar elements on a page, such as two smaller blocks of text with one larger graphic image. Asymmetrical design is more flexible and visually stimulating. In asymmetrical design, balance is created by moving, resizing, and positioning opposing elements on a page with enough contrast to be noticeable.

The FOUR CORNERS flyer in figure 1.5 illustrates an asymmetrical design that achieves balance through the use of contrasting elements. The shaded rectangular box enclosing the headline, *Four Corners Artists, Ltd. Studio/Gallery*, provides opposing balance to the square box containing the purple paint splatter set on a contrasting white background. Even though these two boxes and their contents are different, the weight of these contrasting elements provides a pleasing balance. The box containing the high-contrast black and white artist image effectively balances the shaded box to the right containing a bulleted listing of services offered. Although the last box on the right is narrower, balance is achieved with high contrast bullets, dense type, and white space. The type size is smaller than the main heading but large enough to distribute more weight down the length of the column. An appropriate amount of white space in and around each line of text in this column adds weight and balance to the column itself.

As you can see, a block of text set in a larger and denser type can be used to offset a graphic image. A number of small graphic images can balance a large graphic or large headline. A small graphic or small block of type surrounded by white space can have the same weight as a large graphic or block of body text.

On single-page display publications, beginning designers have a tendency to set everything centered and, for multipage publications, to set everything in even, gray columns.

This type of design is a carryover from typewriter formatting. When learning to take advantage of the great expressiveness that type and graphics can convey, viewing pages that will face each other when opened (called a two-page spread) as one unit is essential. Balance must be achieved among the elements on both pages.

Providing Proportion

Proportion:
Sizing elements in relation to one another.

When designing a communication, think about all the parts as they relate to the big picture. Readers tend to view larger elements as more important. Proportionally size the visual elements in your publication according to their importance. This way you can make sure your readers see the most important information first. Readers also are more likely to read a page where all the elements are in *proportion* to one another. Appropriate typeface and type size selection for headlines, subheads, and body text can set the proportional standards for a document.

When viewing the documents in figure 1.6, look at the headline size in proportion to the body text. Think about this relationship when selecting the type size for any headlines, subheads, and body text.

FIGURE 1.6

TOO LARGE!

When designing a page, think about all the parts as they relate to the big picture. Readers tend to view larger elements as more important.

Proportionally size the visual elements in your publication according to their importance. This way you can make sure your readers see the most important information first.

Readers also are more likely to read a page where all the elements are in proportion to one another. Appropriate typeface and type size selection of headlines, subheads, and body text can set the proportional standards for a document.

A

TOO SMALL!

When designing a page, think about all the parts as they relate to the big picture. Readers tend to view larger elements as more important.

Proportionally size the visual elements in your publication according to their importance. This

B

JUST RIGHT!

When designing a page, think about all the parts as they relate to the big picture. Readers tend to view larger elements as more important.

Proportionally size the visual elements in your publication according to their importance. This way you can make sure your

C

White space is also important in establishing proportion in your document. Margins that are too narrow create a typing line that looks long in relation to the surrounding white space. Too much white space between columns makes the line length look short. Too little space between columns makes the text harder to read. Excess white space between lines of text creates gaps that look out of proportion to the type size. Not enough white space between lines of text makes the text hard to read. Proportion must be achieved consistently throughout your whole project. A whole, integrated, unified look is established when elements are in proportion to one another.

Creating Contrast

Contrast is the difference between different degrees of lightness and darkness on the page. More conservative and formal types of documents, such as an annual report, a legal contract, a research paper, or minutes from a meeting, will have less visual contrast than an advertising flyer, a newsletter, or an announcement. Text with a low level of contrast gives an overall appearance of gray to your page. While appropriate for some situations, a higher level of contrast is visually stimulating and can serve to keep your reader's interest longer. Sharper contrast enables the reader to distinctly identify and read all the elements on the page.

Contrast: The difference in degrees of lightness and darkness.

Consider using contrast as a way to achieve some emphasis or focus. High contrast in graphics can create a powerful image or focal point. A solid black image against a solid white background produces a sharp contrast. A graphic image in varying shades of gray or a watermark can also create contrast on a lower level. Depending on the colors used in the image, a color graphic can provide great contrast. Graphic rules, whether gray shaded or 100% black, can also provide visual contrast when used alone, as part of a heading, or as a visual separator in your text.

Headlines and subheads set in a larger and denser type can help to create contrast on an otherwise "gray" page. Using a reverse technique for a headline or subheadings, such as white text on a black background, can create a higher level of contrast.

Special characters used as bullets to define a list of important points, such as •, ■, ▼, ◆, ●, ✦, ★, ❑, ➢, ☞, ✔, or ✧, not only serve as organizational tools, but they also contribute visual contrast to your page. Placing these special characters in a bolder and larger type size provides a higher level of contrast. Look at the quill pen tip bullets in figure 1.5. These high-contrast symbols help to neatly organize the services offered, provide visual contrast, and add weight and emphasis to each item listed.

DTP POINTERS

- To create contrast, set heads and subheads in larger, denser type than the text.
- Use bullets to organize information and add visual contrast.
- Use plenty of white space to convey an open feeling.

White space is an important tool in achieving contrast. A more open and light feeling is projected with the increased use of white space on a page. A more closed and darker feeling is projected when use of white space is limited. Think of white space as the floor space in a room. The more furniture and accessories in the room, the more closed or crowded the room becomes. Rearranging or removing some of the furniture can free up more floor space, producing a more open and lighter feeling. Your page design, like a room, may need to have some elements rearranged or removed to supply some visually contrasting white space.

The use of color in a heading, a logo, a graphic image, a ruled line, or as a background can also add to the contrast level on a page. When using more than one color, select colors that provide a pleasing contrast, not colors that provide an unpleasant conflict. In addition, consider whether the color(s) being used increase or decrease the legibility of your document. Color may look nice, but it will confuse the reader if there is not enough contrast to easily identify the text. Look at the examples in figure 1.7. The level of contrast is obvious in the first two figures. In example C, notice how the text is more difficult to read with the shaded background. Use high contrast for the best legibility.

FIGURE 1.7

LOW CONTRAST

Consider using contrast as a way to achieve some emphasis or focus. High contrast in graphics can create a powerful image or focal point. A solid black

A

HIGH CONTRAST

Consider using contrast as a way to achieve some emphasis or focus. High contrast in graphics can create a powerful image or

B

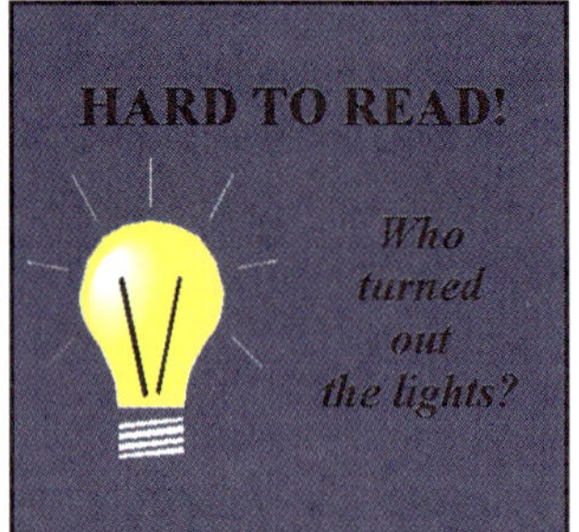

HARD TO READ!
Who turned out the lights?

C

Creating Directional Flow

Directional Flow: A pattern that leads the reader's eye down a page.

Directional flow on a page is created by a pattern that leads the reader's eyes. This pattern can be established with the use of ruled lines, lines of type, or paths created by the placement of focal elements.

By nature, graphics and display type (larger than 14 points) act as focal elements that attract the eye as it scans a page. Directional flow is created by positioning focal elements on a page so that the eye moves from one focal point to the next.

Strictly symmetrical design (all elements centered) is static because there is little directional flow, except down the visual center. If the design is asymmetrical but balanced, dynamic flow can be created with the placement of focal elements and white space, leading the eye through the text and to particular words or images that the designer wishes to emphasize. Focal elements may include a well-designed headline, logo, subheadings, ruled lines, graphic images, boxes with text inside, a chart, reverse text, or a shaded background.

When scanning a page, the eye tends to move in a Z pattern. The eye begins at the upper left corner of the page, moves to the right corner, then drops down to the lower left corner, and finally ends up in the lower right corner of the page. In text-intensive publications such as magazines, newspapers, and books, visual landmarks are set in these positions. In an advertisement, the lower right corner is often where important information, such as a company name, address, and phone number, is placed.

The Low Income Housing flyer shown in figure 1.8 positions elements on the page to provide directional flow down the page. The title, serving as the focal element, is located in the upper left corner of the page, where the reader's eye is most likely to look first. The subheadings and bulleted items draw the eye down the page. The date and location of the conference, positioned in the lower left corner of the page, draw the reader's eye along the bottom and to the right with additional information about the conference. The name and telephone number of a contact person is positioned in the lower right corner of the page where the reader's eye is likely to stop.

The Z pattern is only a guideline. Since there are no hard-and-fast rules, not all designs fit exactly into this pattern. Take another look at the art studio/gallery flyer in figure 1.5. The eyes are drawn to the vivid purple paint splatter in the upper right corner. The eyes then gravitate to the left toward the headline and down toward the artist image. The eyes are then led to the right—the direction the artist is facing. The quill pen tip bullets help to supply the directional flow to the right and down the column, ending in the lower right corner.

FIGURE 1.8

LOW INCOME HOUSING...

A conference on rural/urban low income housing issues for nonprofit sponsors, owners, and developers of low income housing; housing advocates; lenders and funders; state and local government officials; and other housing professionals.

FEATURED SPEAKERS

- RENÉ LECLAIR
  Former President, National Low Income Housing Coalition
- LEI CHOUN
  Director, National Rural Housing Coalition
- CYNTHIA SIKES
  President, National Low Income Housing Coalition

WORKSHOPS

- Building Partnerships
- Housing Finance & Housing Trust Fund
- Housing Preservation & SROs
- Housing Special Populations
- Innovative Low Income Housing Programs
- Rural and Farmworker Housing
- Transitional Housing & Housing for the Homeless

sponsor:
Pierce County Association
for Community Economic Development

November 2-4, 1996
POINT DEFIANCE INN
TACOMA, WASHINGTON

complete conference information to follow • for more information call Jean Ramirez (206) 555-2344

Just as headlines and subheads set in larger and bolder type create focal points for your reader, they also serve as direction markers. The reader knows when to start and stop and what comes next. Directional flow can also be aided by vertical and horizontal ruled lines. Ruled lines are effective for drawing the eye across or down the page. Text alignment can also affect directional flow. Left-aligned text is the easiest to read, with all lines aligning on the left side, leaving the right margin ragged or uneven. The reader has no difficulty finding the beginning of each line. With right-aligned text—text with a ragged left margin because all lines align on the right—and centered text—text centered around a specific point, leaving both margins ragged—the reader has to spend more time finding the beginning of each line. Headers and footers, text that appears repetitively at the top or bottom of each page, also contribute to directional flow in a publication. Chapter name, chapter number, title of a report, and page numbering are common items included in headers or footers. These page identifiers direct the reader to specific locations in a document.

DTP POINTERS
Center align only small amounts of text.

As in the design of balanced pages, the design of pages with good directional flow is best accomplished by experimenting with variable placement of elements on the page. Position elements on the page so the reader is directed to information in a logical order. For single-page display publications, you can consider each element, or group of elements, as a separate focus in establishing directional flow on the page. For multipage publications, you can consider body text and white space as the landscape in which focal elements are set to establish directional flow.

Establishing Consistency

Uniformity among specific design elements establishes a pattern of consistency in your document. Design elements such as margins, columns, typefaces, type sizes, spacing, alignment, and color should remain consistent throughout a document to achieve a degree of unity. In a single-page or multipage publication, consistent elements help to integrate all the individual parts into a whole unit. In a multipage publication, consistency provides the connecting element between the pages. Repetitive, consistent elements can also lend identity to your document and provide the reader with a sense of familiarity.

Consider the consistent components of this textbook. Find the first page of each chapter. The chapter title and chapter number are consistent in typeface, type size, color, and position throughout the book. This consistency lets you easily identify the end of one chapter and the beginning of the next. Look at the top, bottom, and side margins on each page. For the most part, they are consistent throughout the book. Notice the headings and subheadings. Consistency exists in the typeface, size, color, and position. Examine the footers on the odd and even pages. They are consistent in their placement on the page and in the information they supply. You, as the reader, become familiar with the footers as consistent elements and depend on them for the information they provide. Glance at the captions identifying the illustrations throughout this book. The figure numbering format is consistent in every chapter. The end of the chapter sections, such as Chapter Summary, Check Your Understanding, and Skill Assessments, are also unifying elements that appear at the end of each chapter.

DTP POINTERS
- Consistency establishes unity within a document.
- Inconsistency confuses and frustrates the reader.

Inconsistency can confuse and frustrate the reader. Reader frustration can lead to a reduction in your readership. Consider the following scenario. In this textbook, what if the chapter number on the chapter opening page was placed at the top of the page in one chapter, at the bottom of the page in the next, and somewhere on the left side of the page in the next chapter? What if the margins were different from page to page? What if the headings and subheadings changed typeface, size, color, and position from chapter to chapter? What if a footer existed in one chapter that contained the chapter name, number, and page number and then was changed to a header in the next chapter? What if some figure captions were positioned at the bottom left, outside the border, while some captions were positioned at the top right, inside the border? Does this scenario totally confuse you? Of course it does! Consistency not only establishes unity *within* a chapter (or a newsletter, or an advertisement), but it also establishes unity *among* the chapters (or series of newsletters or advertisements).

When trying to design consistent parts of a publication, keep it simple and distinct. Simplicity is important since consistent elements are repetitive elements. Elaborate repetitive elements, such as a chapter opening page, have their place but can be distracting. Unfortunately, simple, consistent elements can sometimes be boring. Make your consistent elements distinct as well. The use of color can set some consistent elements apart. Page numbering in color, a color horizontal ruled line in a header, a color background for a reverse text heading, or color subheadings are all ways to achieve distinct consistency. Distinctiveness can also be achieved with black and white. A solid black ruled line in a header, a reverse text heading, or a contrasting typeface and type size are also effective.

Using Color

Color is a powerful tool in communicating a message and portraying an image. Color on a page can help organize ideas and highlight important facts. Publications that use color appropriately have a professional look. Color can be used to create focus, organize information, organize documents, and add emphasis to bar graphs and pie charts. Color can even elicit an emotional response from the reader.

If a color printer is not available, consider using color paper to complement your publication. Color paper can match the tone or mood you are creating in your document. Orange paper used for a Halloween flyer is an inexpensive alternative to color graphics and text. Your audience will recognize the theme of the flyer by associating the paper color with the event. The color paper provides contrast and adds vitality and life to the publication.

DTP POINTERS
Use color to create focus, organize ideas, and emphasize important facts.

You can also turn plain white documents into colorful, attention-grabbing documents by purchasing preprinted letterheads, envelopes, brochures, or presentation packets from paper supply companies. Color, emphasis, and contrast can all be achieved through an assortment of colorful page borders, patterned and solid color papers, as well as gradient color, marbleized, and speckled papers. Many of these paper suppliers provide free catalogs and offer inexpensive sample paper packets.

Laser printers are becoming more affordable, but the color laser printer remains rather expensive. A less expensive alternative is the ink jet color printer. Color is provided by a color ink cartridge. The copy may be slightly damp when first removed from the printer. The resolution can be improved by using specially designed ink jet paper. Some ink jet printers are capable of achieving near-photographic quality with a resolution of 720 dpi (dots per inch).

Another option for color is to send your formatted copy to a commercial printer for color printing. You can get almost any color you want from a commercial printer, but it increases the cost of the project.

Here are a few guidelines to follow when using color in documents:

- Use color sparingly—less is best! Limit your use of colors to two or three, including the color of the paper.
- Remember that the message is most important; color can add emphasis and style, but do not let color overpower the words!
- Text printed with light colors is difficult to read. Use light colors for shaded backgrounds or watermarks. Black text is still the easiest to read.
- Color can be used to identify a consistent element.
- Remember to use color to communicate, not decorate!

DTP POINTERS
Use color sparingly.

Opening, Saving, Closing, And Printing A Document

When a document has been saved, it can be opened with the Open option from the File drop-down menu. To open a previously saved document, complete the following steps:

1. At a clear editing window, choose File, then Open; click the Open button on the Standard toolbar; or press Ctrl + O.
2. At the Open dialog box, key the name of the document to be opened; or double-click the document name.
3. Choose OK or press Enter.

Opening a Document as Read-Only

Another option exists that eliminates the risk of saving over the original copy of a document. This option is known as Open Read Only. The words *Read-Only* will appear in the Title Bar when a document is opened as a read-only document. You may read the document or make changes to it. However, when a read-only document is saved with the Save command, Word leads you to the Save As dialog box so you can enter a new name for the document. This option protects the original copy of a document from being saved with any changes. Many of the documents you will open from your student data disk will be retrieved as Open Read Only files. To open a document as read-only, complete the following steps:

1. Choose File, then Open; click the Open button on the Standard toolbar; or press Ctrl + O.
2. At the Open dialog box, click the desired filename.
3. Click the Commands and Settings button located at the upper right corner of the dialog box.
4. From the drop-down menu that displays, click Open Read Only.
5. After reading or making changes to the file, choose File, then Save.
6. Click OK at the dialog box that displays the message, "This file is read-only."
7. At the Save As dialog box, key a name for the document, then choose OK.

Saving a Document

When you have created a document, the information will need to be saved. Windows 95 and Word 7.0 for Windows 95 allow you to use much longer filenames than in the past. A Word document name can be from 1 to 255 characters in length. A document filename can contain letters and/or numbers, as well as spaces. By default, Word assigns the first sentence in the document as the filename. You may accept this as the filename or key your own filename. If you do not include an extension to a document name, Word automatically adds the extension *.doc*. Even though longer filenames are available in Word 7.0 for Windows 95, make filenames as concise as possible. A variety of methods can be used to save a document:

- Clicking the Save button on the Standard toolbar
- Clicking File, then Save
- Pressing the Alt Key, the letter F for File, then the letter S for Save
- Pressing Ctrl + S

You should save periodically to avoid losing your work if a power or system failure occurs. This is particularly important when creating desktop published documents that involve many steps.

Saving a Document with Save As

The Save As option is used to save a previously created document with a new name. Give the document a new name immediately after opening and before editing. This reduces the risk of saving over an original document. To do this, choose File, then Save As.

Closing a Document

When a document is saved with the Save or Save As option from the File menu, the document is saved on the disk and remains in the document window. To remove the document from the screen, choose File, then Close. When you close a document, the document is removed from the screen and a blank screen is displayed. At this screen, you can open a previously saved document, create a new document, or exit the Word program.

If you choose Close before the document has been saved for the first time, a prompt will appear asking you if you want to save the changes to your document. If you choose Yes, the Save As dialog box will be displayed. Key the desired filename and then click the Save button. The document will be saved and cleared from the screen. If the document has already been saved and you choose Yes to save the changes, the Save As dialog box will not be displayed. The document changes will be saved and cleared from the document editing window.

Printing a Document

There are basically two methods for printing a document. To immediately print the document displayed in the document screen, click the Print button on the Standard toolbar. The document is sent directly to the printer. You can also print from the Print dialog box. The Print dialog box lets you print the whole document, the current page, a specific range of pages, selected text, or a specific number of hard copies. To use this method, choose File, then Print; or press Ctrl + P.

Evaluating Documents

Up to this point, you have learned the importance of carefully planning and designing your publication according to the desktop publishing concepts of focus, balance, proportion, contrast, directional flow, and consistency. In exercise 1, you will evaluate the document illustrated in figure 1.9. You will open a copy of the *Document Analysis Guide*, which is saved to your student data disk as *document analysis guide.doc*. The *Document Analysis Guide* will be used to analyze your intentions, decisions, and any processes you used in designing and creating your desktop documents. In addition, a *Document Evaluation Checklist* has been saved to your student data disk as *document evaluation checklist.doc*. The focus of this evaluation tool is directed toward the finished document. Both forms will be used to analyze your own documents, existing commercial publications, and/or other students' desktop publications.

FIGURE 1.9

Skyline Communications, Inc.

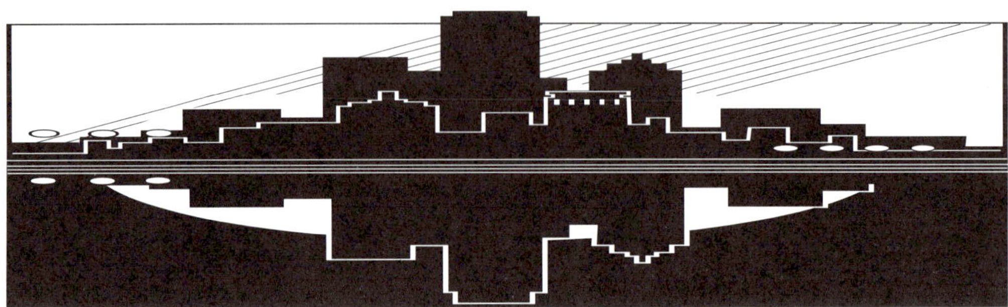

For 1997, we are offering three different formats to meet your scheduling needs:

- One-day hands-on workshops
- One-day seminars
- One-day conferences

Networking

"Establishing Relationships"

- One-day seminar
- Morris Inn, Rosemont
- May 15, 1997

Presentations

"Using Word for Windows 95"

- One-day conference
- Palmer House, Chicago
- June 6, 1997

Team Building

"Building Trust and Mutual Respect"

- One-day hands-on workshop
- Holiday Inn, Lisle
- June 19, 1997

Managing Time

"How to Get Things Done"

- One-day seminar
- Hyatt, Oak Brook
- June 19, 1997

Read over the enclosed information for details, times, and fees.
Mail or fax the attached reservation form.

Skyline Communications, Inc. ∨ 73 West 22nd Street ∨ Oak Brook, IL 60555 ∨ (708) 555-5647 ∨ Fax: (708) 555-6521

Evaluating a Document

Evaluate the flyer illustrated in figure 1.9 by completing the following steps:

1. Open as a read-only document *document analysis guide.doc* from your student data disk. This file is the *Document Analysis Guide.*
2. Print one copy of the *Document Analysis Guide.*
3. Close *document analysis guide.doc.*
4. Turn to figure 1.9 in your textbook.
5. Complete an analysis of the flyer in figure 1.9 by writing a short answer to the questions in the *Document Analysis Guide.*
6. When completed, fill in the exercise number, located at the top of the guide, as c01ex01.

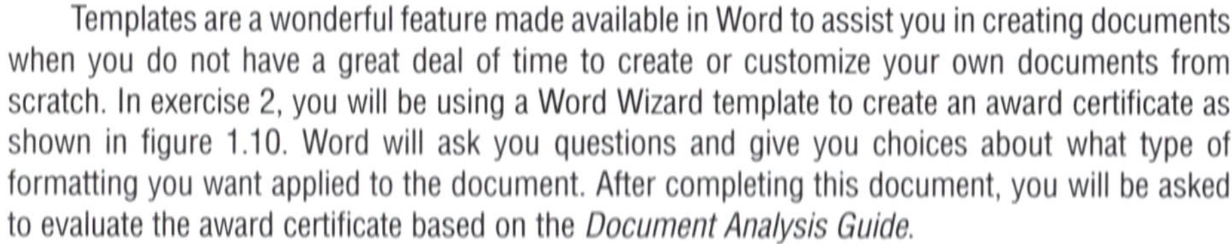

Templates are a wonderful feature made available in Word to assist you in creating documents when you do not have a great deal of time to create or customize your own documents from scratch. In exercise 2, you will be using a Word Wizard template to create an award certificate as shown in figure 1.10. Word will ask you questions and give you choices about what type of formatting you want applied to the document. After completing this document, you will be asked to evaluate the award certificate based on the *Document Analysis Guide.*

Producing an Award Certificate with a Word Template

1. Open as a read-only document *document analysis guide.doc* from your student data disk.
2. Print one copy and then close *document analysis guide.doc.*
3. At a clear editing screen, create the award certificate illustrated in figure 1.10 using the Jazzy-style Award Wizard template by completing the following steps:
   a. Choose File, then New; or press Ctrl + N.
   b. At the New dialog box, click the Other Documents tab. (If the Other Documents tab does not display at the New dialog box, Word was installed with a standard installation and some components that you need have not been installed. Refer to the Preface and a Word reference manual to add uninstalled components.)
   c. At the New dialog box with the Other Documents tab selected, double-click Award Wizard.
   d. When Word asks what style award you want to create, choose Jazzy, then choose Next.
   e. At the next screen, make sure Portrait is selected as the printing orientation, select No to answer the question concerning paper with a preprinted border on it, and then choose Next.
   f. At the next screen, key **Gail Holtmeyer** as the name of the award recipient and **Desktop Publishing Award** as the title of the award, then choose Next.
   g. At the next screen, key **Mary Uhrick** as one of the people who will sign the award, and then click Add. Key **Joseph Valentino** as the name of the second person who will sign the award, and then click Add. If any names are already listed at this screen, select each name, then click Remove. Choose Next when done.
   h. At the next screen, make sure Presented by: is selected, then key **Impact Designs, Inc**. as the name of the group that is presenting the award, and then choose Next.
   i. At the next screen, key **March 6, 1997** as the date for the award. As additional text to be included on the award, key **Awarded for Proficiency in Designing**, and then press Enter. Key **and** and then press Enter. Key **Creating Desktop Publishing Documents** and then choose Next.
   j. At the next screen, choose Finish.

4. When the award is generated and displayed on the screen, choose File, then Page Setup.
5. At the Page Setup dialog box, select the Margins tab.
6. Change the top margin to 0.33 inches, the bottom margin to 0.67 inches, then choose OK.
7. Save the award as c01ex02, award.
8. Print and then close c01ex02, award.
9. Complete the analysis form and attach it to the front of the award certificate. Fill in the exercise number as c01ex02, award.

FIGURE 1.10

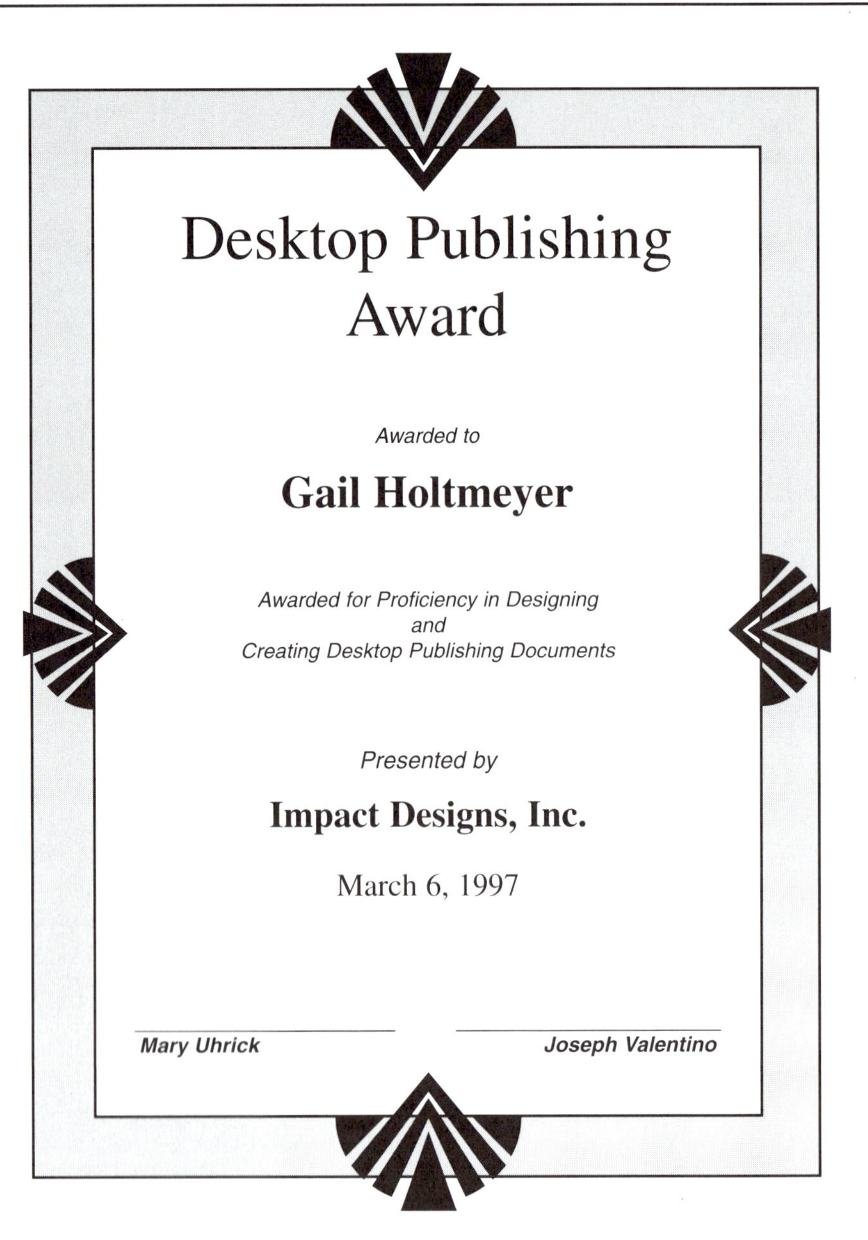

Creating A Page Layout

Planning your margins is one of the first steps in designing a page layout. Using wider margins is an excellent way to add white space or breathing room around text and graphics. Margins can also be a means of creating consistency in your document. Use the same margin settings throughout your entire publication. To apply an asymmetrical design to your document, try varying the width of your margins to create a more interesting use of white space. The width of your margins is also dependent on the type size you have chosen to use. Large type sizes demand wider margins.

DTP POINTERS
Use the same margin settings throughout your entire publication.

In addition to establishing margins for your page layout, you also need to consider the amount of text needed to express your message, the paper size desired, and the number of pages you plan to use. If you are producing a multipage publication, remember that basic elements such as margins, headers and footers, page numbers, and borders should stay consistent from page to page. Typically, when you work at a computer, you are creating and viewing one page at a time. In designing a page layout for a multipage document, think in terms of what is called a *two-page spread* or a *two-page layout.* Pages that are viewed opposite each other when opened, as in a book or brochure format, need to be looked upon as one unit. Remember that your readers will see both pages at the same time so certain elements must remain consistent.

In Word 7.0 for Windows 95, you can view your document in a two-page spread. To do this, make sure the viewing mode is Page Layout, then click the Zoom Control button on the Standard toolbar. At the drop-down menu that displays, click Two Pages. The pages appear in reduced size, but you should be able to see placement of elements, the use of white space, and certain consistencies (or inconsistencies!) between the two pages.

Word also lets you view more than two pages at a time. To do this, choose View, then Zoom. At the Zoom dialog box, select Many Pages. Click the monitor icon under Many Pages and then click the number of pages you want to display. If you click the first page icon, one page will be displayed. If you click the second page icon, two pages will be displayed at once. If you click the third page icon, three pages will be displayed at once, and so on. The Preview box shows the number of pages that will be displayed together horizontally across the screen at one time. Click OK when done. Notice the two-page and six-page spreads illustrated in figures 1.11 and 1.12.

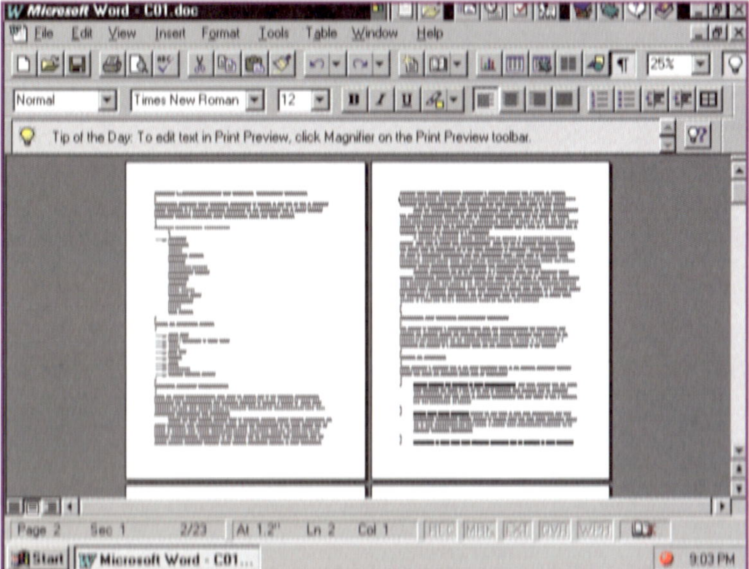

FIGURE 1.11

Two-Page Spread View

FIGURE 1.12

Six-Page Spread View

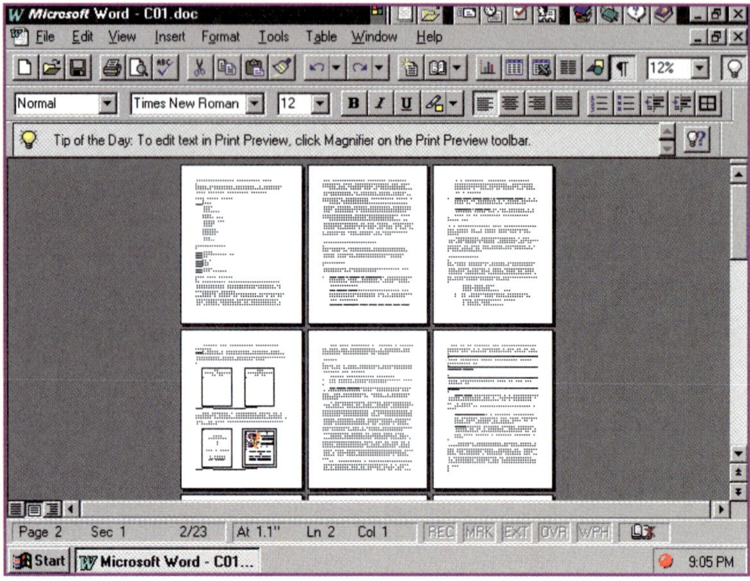

Gutter:
The white space between columns.

In planning page layout, a column format is commonly used. Laying out text in columns adds visual interest and makes the text easier to read. The *gutter*, which is the space between columns, creates additional contrasting white space and serves as a separator between the columns. Text in full justification needs more column space than left-justified text. Also, text created in a larger type size demands more space between the columns than text in a smaller type size.

The line length of each column affects the readability of your publication. Long lines of text are difficult to read because your eye can get lost reading along the line or trying to get to the next line. As a general rule, lines should be under 70 characters long but no less than 30 characters in length.

Too many columns can decrease readability and confuse your readers. In portrait orientation (when the paper's short side is the top of the paper), use no more than three columns on standard-sized paper. With a landscape orientation (when the paper's long side is the top of the paper), you can use four or five columns on standard-sized paper.

Grid:
The underlying structure of a document.

In determining the exact placement of columns and varying elements on the page, a *grid* is a helpful tool. A grid is the underlying structure of a document. In some software programs, a grid appears on the screen as a non-printing framework to assist you in laying out the page. A grid can be created on a sheet of paper using a ruler and pencil. Notice the grid illustrated in figure 1.13. A grid consists of vertical and horizontal lines to be used as a guide in the placement of elements on the page. Grids enable the desktop publisher to be consistent with the location of elements and the size of columns. However, the number of columns actually used does not have to match the number of columns in the grid as long as the underlying framework is maintained. For example, notice the three-column layout with the clock graphic in figure 1.13. Even though you can only see two columns, it has an underlying structure of three columns. Notice the grid lines in the background.

The centered one-column page layout is commonly used for more formal, conservative documents such as letters, a financial report, a legal document, or a wedding invitation. Multicolumn layouts, whether equal or unequal, include such items as sales brochures, advertisements, résumés, and newsletters.

FIGURE 1.13

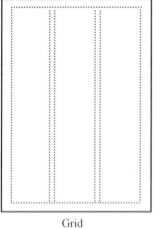

Grid

One-Column Layout

Two-Column Layout

Three-Column Layout

Three-Column Layout (Left column equal to twice the width of the third column—notice the extended grid)

Three-Column Layout (Right column equal to twice the width of the first column)

Two-Page Spread

Using Word 7.0 For Windows 95 In Desktop Publishing

Microsoft Word, one of the best-selling word processing programs for microcomputers, includes a wide variety of desktop publishing features. The scope and capabilities of these features have expanded with each new Word version. Word 7.0 for Windows 95 is a highly visual program providing an efficient means of editing and manipulating text and graphics resulting in professional-looking documents. Some of the desktop publishing features include a wide variety of fonts and special characters; drawing, charting, and text design capabilities; graphics, graphic manipulation, and image editing tools; predesigned templates; template wizards, and much more.

Putting It All Together

DTP POINTERS
Experiment with different layouts and designs.

Design can be learned by studying good design and by experimentation. Analyze what makes the design and layout unique and try using the same principles or variations in your publications. Take advantage of the special design and layout features that Word 7.0 for Windows 95 has to offer. Take time to design. Layout and design is a lengthy process of revising, refining and making adjustments. And above all else, *EXPERIMENT, EXPERIMENT, EXPERIMENT!* Start with small variations from the default formats to create designs that are attractive and visually interesting.

The rest of the chapters in this book will take you through the steps for creating specific business and personal desktop publishing applications, such as letterheads, business cards, résumés, flyers, brochures, charts, and newsletters. In addition to step-by-step directions for completing the applications using Word 7.0 for Windows 95, each application will introduce guidelines relevant to that particular application as well as reinforce the design concepts introduced in this chapter.

Remember: **Take the time to design!**
Communicate; don't decorate!
Less is best!

Creating a Portfolio

Begin a portfolio of the documents you will create in the exercises and assessments throughout this book. Exercises marked with the portfolio icon should be included in your job-hunting portfolio. These documents have been chosen to show a prospective employer a wide range of your desktop publishing skills. You may also include some documents from the chapter and unit assessments. Since the assessments are less structured than the exercises, your creativity can really shine.

You will create a title page for your portfolio in the Unit 3 Performance Assessments. As an optional assignment, you may create a table of contents after completing Unit 3. Your instructor will determine a due date for your portfolio. If possible, purchase plastic protector sheets for your documents and a binder to hold them.

Chapter Summary

- When creating a publication, clearly define your purpose, assess your target audience, establish where your audience will see your message, and decide what outcome you are expecting.
- Effective design involves planning and organizing content. Decide what items are most important to the reader. Design concepts such as focus, balance, proportion, directional flow, consistency, and the use of color are essential to creating a visually attractive publication.
- Focus can be created by using large and/or bold type, such as for titles and subheads; by using graphic elements, such as ruled lines, clip art, and photographs; and by using color for emphasis.
- Balance on a page is created by equally distributing the weight of elements on a page in either a symmetrical or asymmetrical manner. Symmetrical design balances similar elements of equal proportion or weight on the left and right sides and the top and bottom of the page. Asymmetrical design balances contrasting elements of unequal proportion and weight on the page.
- In establishing a proportional relationship among the elements on a page, think about all the parts as they relate to the total look. Proportionally size the visual elements in your publication according to their importance.
- Contrast is the difference between varying degrees of lightness and darkness on the page. A higher level of contrast is visually stimulating and can serve to keep your reader's interest longer. Sharper contrast enables the reader to distinctly identify and read all the elements on the page.
- Directional flow can be produced with ruled lines, type, or paths created by the placement of elements. A reader's eye tends to scan a page in a Z pattern.
- In determining page layout, consider the width of the margins, the amount of text in the message, the desired length of the publication, and the desired paper size.
- Pages that are viewed opposite each other when opened, as in a book or brochure format, need to be looked upon as one unit.
- Most documents are laid out in some type of a column format ranging from one column to several columns.

Commands Review

	Mouse	Keyboard
Open dialog box	File, Open; or click the Open button on the Standard toolbar	Ctrl + O
Open document as Read-Only	File, Open, click desired filename, click Commands and Settings button, then click Open Read Only	
Save dialog box	File, Save; or click the Save button on the Standard toolbar	Ctrl + S

Save As dialog box	File, Save As	
Close a document	File, Close	
Print a document	File, Print; or click the Print button on the Standard toolbar	Ctrl + P
Templates (New dialog box)	File, New, then click desired tab	
Viewing multiple pages	View, Zoom, Many Pages, then click the monitor button below and select the number of pages	

Check Your Understanding

Terms: Match the terms with the correct definitions by writing the letter of the term on the blank line in front of the correct definition.

A. Asymmetrical design
B. Balance
C. Consistency
D. Contrast
E. Desktop publishing
F. Directional flow
G. Focal point
H. Grid
I. One-column
J. Proportion
K. Symmetrical design
L. Thumbnail sketch
M. Traditional publishing
N. White space

_______ **1.** Areas in a document where no text or graphics appear.

_______ **2.** Page design containing similar elements of equal weight distributed evenly on the page.

_______ **3.** Process of creating publications with the cooperation of several people, each performing specific tasks.

_______ **4.** An element that draws the reader's eye to a particular area in the document.

_______ **5.** The difference between varying degrees of lightness and darkness on the page.

_______ **6.** Pattern established by the use of ruled lines, lines of type, or paths created by the placement of focal elements.

_______ **7.** Process where one person can accomplish the tasks of several people by using a computer, a software program, and a printer to design, create, and print a document.

_______ **8.** A preliminary rough draft of the layout and design of a document.

_______ **9.** Uniformity among specific design elements in a publication.

_______ **10.** The sizing of various elements so that all parts relate to the whole.

_______ **11.** Contemporary design where balance is created by positioning opposing elements on the page with enough contrast to be noticeable.

_______ **12.** The underlying structure of a page layout.

_______ **13.** Common page layout used for more formal, conservative documents.

Skill Assessments

Assessment 1

In this skill assessment, you will launch a *presentation* project. The purpose of this assignment is to acquaint you with outside sources on desktop publishing and Word features, concepts, tips, and techniques. Specific instructions are provided for you in the document named *presentation.doc*, on your student data disk. To print this document, complete the following steps:

1. Open as a read-only document *presentation.doc* from your student data disk.
2. Print one copy and then close *presentation.doc*.

Begin researching a topic for your presentation. You may use any one of the many desktop publishing and Word resources available at your local library or bookstore. Some suggestions include *Inside Microsoft Word 95,* published by The Cobb Group; *Working Smarter with Microsoft Word*, published by OneOnOne Computer Training; *Word for Windows Design Companion*, written by Katherine Shelly Pfeiffer and published by Ventana Press; *Publish* magazine; *PC Publishing*; and the *Makeover Book* and *The Presentation Design Book*, both published by Ventana Press. You may also consider demonstrating a unique technique or tip you have discovered while using Word. Your instructor will notify you of a scheduled date for your presentation.

Assessment 2

The information highway is littered with good and bad documents. Looking critically at as many publications as you can will give you a sense of what works and what does not. In this skill assessment, find three different examples of documents—flyers, newsletters, résumés, brochures, business cards, announcements, certificates, etc. Evaluate these documents according to the desktop publishing concepts discussed in this chapter using the *Document Analysis Guide* located on your student data disk. To do this, complete the following steps:

1. Open as a read only document *document analysis guide.doc* from your student data disk.
2. Print three copies of this form and then close *document analysis guide.doc*.
3. Complete the evaluation forms and attach them to the front of each example document. Write the exercise number as c01sa02 on the front of each form.

Assessment 3

In this assessment, you will evaluate a poorly designed flyer according to the items listed on the *Document Analysis Guide* located on your student data disk. On a separate piece of paper, list three suggestions to improve this flyer.

1. Open as a read-only document *document analysis guide.doc* on your student data disk.
2. Print one copy, then close *document analysis guide.doc*.
3. Open as a read-only document *four seasons.doc* on your student data disk.
4. Print one copy, then close *four seasons.doc*.
5. Complete the *Document Analysis Guide* and name the exercise c01sa03.

Creative Activity

You have been asked to create flyers for the situations described below. Draw two thumbnail sketches, using lines, boxes, and rough drawings to illustrate the placement of text and graphics on the page. You decide how to include focus, balance, proportion, contrast, white space, directional flow, and consistency in your thumbnail sketches. Be sure to consider the purpose and target audience for each situation. Designate areas in your sketches for such items as time, date, location, and response information.

Situation 1: Annual office golf outing

Situation 2: Software training seminar

Label your sketches as c01ca01.

2 PREPARING INTERNAL DOCUMENTS

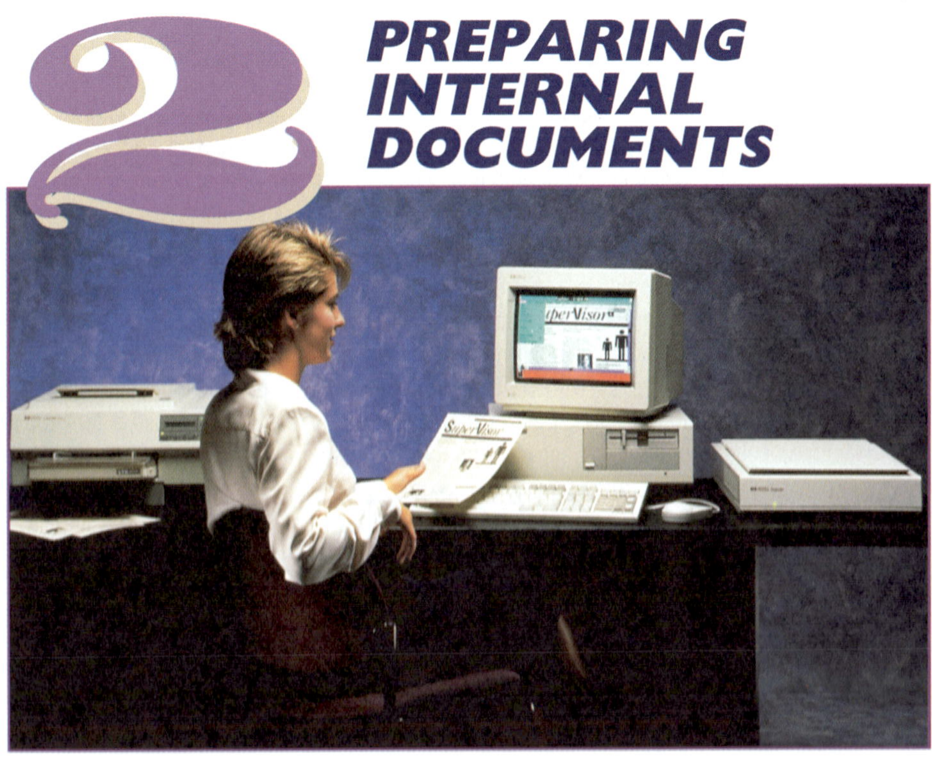

PERFORMANCE OBJECTIVE

Upon successful completion of chapter 2, you will be able to produce internal business documents such as memos, agendas, press releases, and fax cover sheets with a variety of typefaces, type styles, type sizes, and special symbols.

DESKTOP PUBLISHING CONCEPTS

Font Selection
Typeface
Type size
Type style
Readability
Spacing after end-of-sentence punctuation
Using special characters and symbols
Em dash
En dash
Quotation marks
Apostrophe
Watermark
Bullets

WORD FEATURES USED

Templates
Wizards
Special characters
Smart Quotes
AutoFormat
Headers and Footers
Watermark

Understanding Basic Typography

A document created on a typewriter generally contains uniform characters and spacing. A typeset document may contain characters that vary in typeface, size, and style and that are laid out on the page with variable spacing.

In this chapter, you will produce internal business documents using Word's Template feature and produce and format your own business documents. An important element in the creation of internal business documents such as memos, agendas, and press releases is the font used to format the text. Information on the elements of a font as well as how to choose a font is presented in this chapter. You will use this information to prepare documents in this chapter as well as documents presented in the remaining chapters. To choose a font for a document, you need to understand basic typography and the terms that apply.

As you learned in chapter 1, a professional graphic designer considers many factors when creating a document, including the intent of the document, the audience, the feeling the document is to elicit, and the important information that should be emphasized. These factors help the graphic designer determine the layout of the document and the type specifications. With Word, which contains desktop publishing features, these decisions can be made by the originator of the document rather than a graphic designer. The person creating the document chooses the type specifications, determines the layout, and produces the final product.

Before selecting the type specifications to be used in a document, the terms used in desktop publishing need to be defined. Terms that are used to identify the type specifications are typeface, type size, and type style.

Choosing a Typeface

Typeface: A set of characters with a common design and shape.

A *typeface* is a set of characters with a common general design and shape. One of the most important considerations in establishing a particular mood or feeling in a document is the typeface. For example, a decorative typeface may be chosen for invitations or menus, while a simple block-style typeface may be chosen for headlines or reports. Choose a typeface that reflects the content, your audience expectations, and the image you want to project.

Baseline: An imaginary horizontal line on which type characters rest.

There are characteristics that distinguish one typeface from another. Type characters rest on an imaginary horizontal line called the *baseline.* From this baseline, parts of type may extend above the baseline and/or below the baseline. Figure 2.1 illustrates the various parts of type.

FIGURE 2.1

Parts of Type

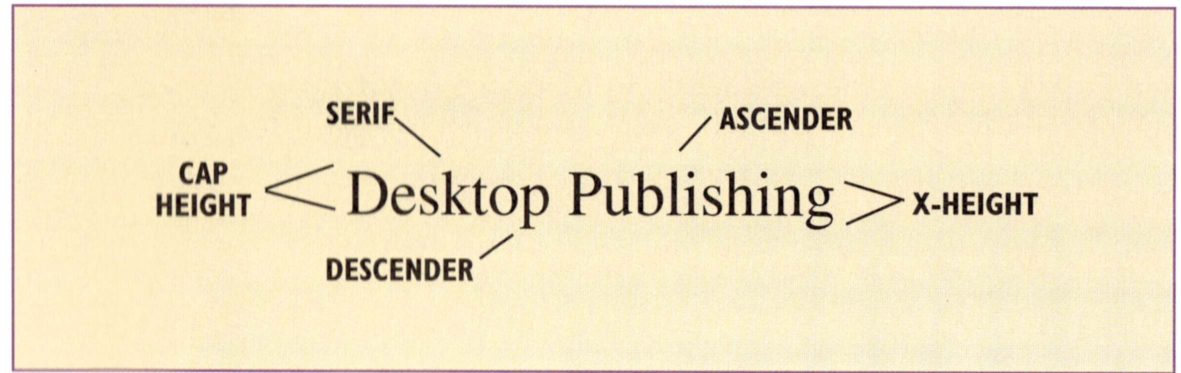

The *x-height* is the height of the main body of the lowercase characters and is equivalent to the lowercase *x*. The cap height is the distance between the baseline and the top of capital letters. Ascenders are the parts of lowercase characters that rise above the x-height, and descenders are parts of characters that extend below the baseline. *Serifs* are the small strokes at the ends of characters.

x-Height:
Height of lowercase x.

Serif:
A small stroke at the end of a character.

There are many typefaces, and new designs are created on a regular basis. A variety of typefaces are popular with desktop publishing programs, including Arial, Times New Roman, Bookman Old Style Bold, Garamond, Century Gothic, Impact, Matura MT Script Cap, and more.

Typefaces are either monospaced or proportional. A monospaced typeface allots the same amount of horizontal space for each character and is rarely used in professional publications. Courier is an example of a monospaced typeface. Proportional typefaces allow a varying amount of space for each character. For example, the lowercase letter *i* takes up less space than an uppercase *M*. Also, different proportional typefaces take up different amounts of horizontal space. The same sentence in Times New Roman, for example, takes up less horizontal space when set in the same size Century Gothic.

Proportional typefaces are divided into two main categories: serif and sans serif. As mentioned earlier, a serif is a small stroke at the edge of a character. Traditionally, a serif typeface is used with documents that are text intensive (documents that are mainly text, such as business letters) because the serifs help move the reader's eyes across the page.

A *sans serif* typeface does not have serifs (*sans* is French for *without*). Sans serif typefaces are often used for headlines and advertisements that are not text intensive. In modern designs, sans serif typefaces may also be used for body text. Figure 2.2 shows examples of serif typefaces. Figure 2.3 shows examples of sans serif typefaces.

Sans Serif:
Without a small stroke at the end of a character.

FIGURE 2.2

Serif Typefaces

Book Antiqua

Bookman Old Style Bold

Footlight MT Light

Garamond

Century Schoolbook

Times New Roman

FIGURE 2.3

Sans Serif Typefaces

Arial
Arial Narrow
Arial MT Black
Arial Rounded MT Bold
Century Gothic
Impact
Kino MT

The field of desktop publishing has a set of general guidelines, or conventions, that provide a starting point for designing documents. A guideline for selecting typefaces is to use no more than two different typefaces in the same document. Too many typefaces and styles give the document a disorderly appearance, confuse the reader, and take away from the content of the document.

DTP POINTERS
- Use a sans serif font for headings
- Use a serif font for text-intensive documents

For publications, especially those that are not text intensive, one typeface with different type sizes and type styles used to distinguish elements is usually adequate. To emphasize headings and other important elements, a typeface that is distinct from the body text typeface may be used. Display type (titles and headings) are sometimes set in a sans serif typeface and the body text in a serif typeface, since the uniform strokes of a sans serif typeface give the appearance of greater density than a serif typeface. For example, an Arial typeface may be used for headlines, headings, and subheadings, with a Garamond typeface used for the text within the body. Fonts such as Arial MT Black, Braggadocio, Colonna MT, Impact, and Wide Latin would be good choices for display text. Script fonts resemble handwriting and are frequently used in formal documents, such as invitations and social announcements. Avoid using all caps with script fonts because they will not be legible. Figure 2.4 displays fonts that match the mood and tone of your message.

FIGURE 2.4

Fonts That Match the Tone of Your Message

Calling All Students!	**Braggadocio**
25th Anniversary	*Brush Script MT Italic*
Four Corners Art Gallery	Matura MT Script Cap
FUNFEST '97	**Impact**
DESIGN 2000	DESDEMONA
Antique Auction	Colonna MT
Line Dancing Classes Available	**Playbill**

Choosing a Type Size

Type size is defined by two categories: pitch and point size. *Pitch*, a measurement used for monospaced typefaces, is the number of characters that can be printed in one horizontal inch. (For some printers, the pitch is referred to as cpi, or characters per inch. For example, the font Courier 10 cpi is the same as 10-pitch Courier.) The pitch measurement can be changed to increase or decrease the size of the characters. The higher the pitch measurement, the smaller the characters. The lower the pitch number, the larger the characters. Figure 2.5 shows examples of different pitch sizes in Courier typeface:

Pitch: The number of characters that can be printed in 1 horizontal inch.

FIGURE 2.5

Varying Courier Pitch Sizes

12-pitch Courier

10-pitch Courier

8-pitch Courier

Proportional typefaces can be set in different sizes. The size of proportional type is measured vertically in units called *points* (measured vertically from the top of the ascenders to the bottom of the descenders). A point is approximately 1/72 of an inch. The higher the point size, the larger the characters. When keying a point measurement in a Word dialog box, you must use the abbreviation *pt* to indicate a point increment.

Point Size: A vertical measurement; a point is approximately 1/72 of an inch.

There are common point sizes used in typesetting. Some common sizes are 6, 8, 9, 10, 11, 12, 14, 18, 24, 36, and 48. These sizes date back to the time when typesetters cut blocks of wood for each character in a particular typeface, size, and style. The use of standard sizes reduced the number of wood blocks required. Figure 2.6 shows Garamond and Arial typefaces in a variety of point sizes:

FIGURE 2.6

Varying Garamond and Arial Point Sizes

8-point Garamond	8-point Arial
12-point Garamond	12-point Arial
18-point Garamond	18-point Arial
24-point Garamond	24-point Arial

Choosing a Type Style

Within a typeface, characters may have a varying *type style*. The standard style of the typeface is referred to as *Roman* for some typefaces and as *regular* for others. In addition to the standard style, other styles include *bold*, *italic*, and *bold italic*. Figure 2.7 illustrates the four main type styles in 12-point type.

Type Style: Variations of the basic type design, including regular or normal, bold, and italics.

FIGURE 2.7

Type Styles in 12-Point Type

Times New Roman Regular	Arial Regular
Times New Roman Bold	**Arial Bold**
Times New Roman Italic	*Arial Italic*
Times New Roman Bold Italic	***Arial Bold Italic***
Century Schoolbook Regular	Century Gothic
Century Schoolbook Bold	**Century Gothic Bold**
Century Schoolbook Italic	*Century Gothic Italic*
Century Schoolbook Bold Italic	***Century Gothic Bold Italic***

Choosing A Font

Font: A particular typeface in a specific style and size.

The term *font* describes a particular typeface in a specific style and size. Some examples of fonts include 10-point Arial, 12-point Times New Roman Bold, 12-point Century Gothic Italic, and 14-point Book Antiqua Italic. What fonts you have available depends on the printer and soft fonts or cartridges you are using.

Choosing a Printer Font

The printer that you are using has built-in fonts. These fonts can be supplemented with cartridges and/or soft fonts. The built-in fonts and the supplemental fonts are referred to as printer fonts. The types of fonts you have available with your printer depend on the type of printer you are using, the amount of memory installed with the printer, and the supplemental fonts you have. A font cartridge is inserted directly into the printer and makes more fonts accessible. To install a font cartridge, refer to the documentation that comes with the cartridge.

Soft fonts are available as software on disk or CD-ROM. Before you can use soft fonts, the fonts must be installed. More than likely, several TrueType soft fonts were installed with Microsoft Word. These fonts are displayed in the Font dialog box. In addition, some other fonts may be listed in the Font dialog box. These fonts are a shared resource from other Windows-based software programs already installed on your hard drive. You will use many TrueType typefaces as you create documents in this book. If your printer does not support a font or size you are using to format your text, Word may substitute the closest possible font and size.

To see what fonts you have available and their appearance, print a table containing all the fonts displayed in the Font dialog box or Font list box by accessing a macro named *FontSampleGenerator*. Locating this macro is a somewhat complicated task. To access the macro, you would complete the following steps:

1. At a clear document screen, choose File, then Templates.
2. At the Templates and Add-ins dialog box, click the Organizer button.
3. At the Organizer dialog box, click the Macros tab.
4. Click the Close File button at the left side of the dialog box. (The button name will change to Open File.)
5. Click the Open File button.
6. At the Open dialog box, click the down-pointing triangle at the right side of the Look in text box.
7. From the drop-down menu that displays, click Msoffice.
8. In the Look in list box, double-click Winword, then double-click Macros.
9. When the contents of the macro folder are displayed, double-click Macros7.
10. At the Organizer dialog box with the Macros tab selected, click *FontSampleGenerator* in the In Macros7 list box.
11. Click Copy. (The *FontSampleGenerator* macro has now been copied into the Normal.dot template.)
12. Click Close to remove the Organizer dialog box.
13. At a clear document screen, choose Tools, then Macro.
14. At the Macro dialog box, click *FontSampleGenerator* in the Macro name list box, then click the Run button.
15. At the Font Sample Generator dialog box, click OK.
16. The Font Sample Generator will provide a table with samples of all the fonts that are available. Print the table and then close the document without saving it.

Using the Font Dialog Box

The fonts available with your printer and with Word are displayed in the Font list box at the Font dialog box. To display the Font dialog box shown in figure 2.8, choose Format, then Font or click the down-pointing triangle to the right of the Font list box at the Formatting toolbar.

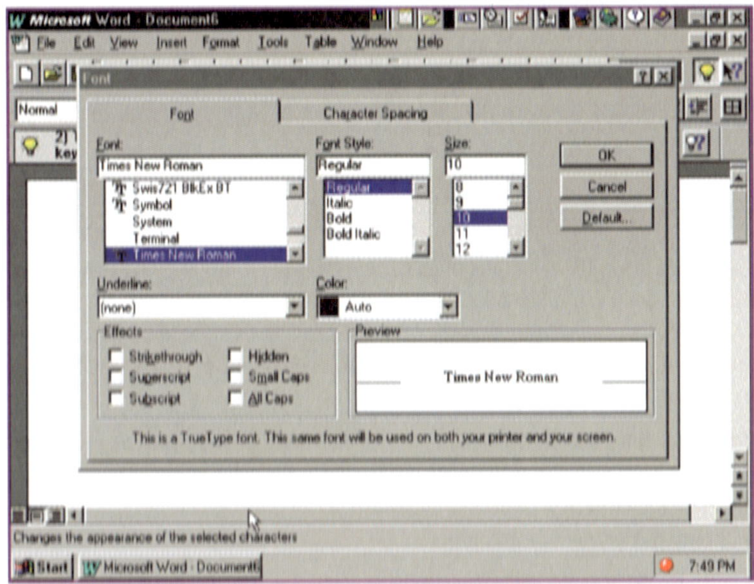

FIGURE 2.8

Font Dialog Box

Changing the Default Font

Each printer defaults to a specific font. The default font setting dictates the font Word defaults to every time the program is loaded or a new blank document is opened. The default font is 10-point Times New Roman. To change this, choose Format, then Font. At the Font dialog box, select the new defaults you want to use, then click the Default button. At the dialog box stating that the change will affect all new documents based on the NORMAL template, click Yes. (The Normal template will be explained later in this chapter).

When you exit Word for Windows, you may see a message box asking whether you want to save changes to Word for Windows. At this message box, choose Yes. When you change the default font, the change is in effect for all documents you create. Font selections made within a document through the Font dialog box will override the default font settings for the current document only.

For this textbook, use 12-point Times New Roman as the default font. Make this change to the default font following instructions in the previous paragraph.

Changing Typefaces

The Font list box at the Font dialog box displays the typefaces available with your printer. The printer or printers you install determine what fonts are available. An HP LaserJet printer, for example, may include CG Times, Times New Roman, Palatino, Bookman, and Avant Garde.

DTP POINTERS

- Use a typeface that reflects the tone of the document.
- Text set in a large, dense font adds weight, balance, and contrast to a document.

An icon may display before the typefaces in the Font list box. TrueType fonts are identified with the TT icon. TrueType typefaces are *graphically* generated and may take a little longer to print. The fonts that display without a preceding icon are usually non-scalable fonts, printer-generated fonts, or various other types of fonts.

To choose a typeface in the Font list box, select the desired typeface, then choose OK or press Enter. You can also double-click the desired typeface. When you select a typeface in the Font list box, the Preview box in the lower right corner displays the appearance of the selected typeface. A message at the bottom of the Font dialog box provides information about the type of font selected. Often documents created in Word are keyed first and then formatted later. In these instances, you need to select the text first then change the font and any of its attributes.

In addition to the Font dialog box, a typeface can be chosen from the Font drop-down menu. To display this drop-down menu, click the down triangle to the right of the Font list box on the Formatting toolbar. To choose a typeface from the list, click the desired typeface. As you choose typefaces, Word displays the most recently chosen typefaces at the top of the drop-down menu.

Changing Type Size

The Size list box at the Font dialog box displays a variety of common type sizes. Decrease point size to make text smaller or increase point size to make text larger. To select a point size, click the desired point size. You can also key a specific point size. To do this with the mouse, position the arrow pointer on the number immediately below Size, click the left mouse button, then key the desired point size.

In addition to the Font dialog box, you can use the Font Size button on the Formatting toolbar to change type size (third button from the left). To change the type size with the Font Size button, click the Font Size button, and then from the drop-down menu that displays, click the desired point size or key a point size.

The point size of selected text can also be increased by one point by pressing Ctrl +]. The shortcut key combination to decrease the point size is Ctrl + [.

Changing Type Style

The Font Style list box at the Font dialog box displays the styles available with the selected typeface. As you select different typefaces, the list of styles changes in the Font Style list box. To choose a type style, click in the check box next to the desired style in the Font Style list box.

Selecting Underlining

To use the underline feature in the Font dialog box, first select any desired text, then at the Font dialog box, click the down-pointing triangle to the right of the Underline list box. From the list that displays, select one of the following choices: (none), Single, Words Only, Double, or Dotted.

Changing Effects

The Effects section of the Font dialog box contains a variety of options that can be used to create different character formatting, such as Strikethrough, Superscript, Subscript, Hidden, Small Caps, and All Caps. To choose an effect, click the desired option. The text in the Preview box will reflect the change. If the text already exists, select the text before applying these formatting options.

DTP POINTERS
Use italics or small caps to emphasize text instead of all caps or underlining.

Changing Font Color

Select the text you want to change to another color. At the Color section of the Font dialog box, click the down-pointing triangle to the right of the Color list box. At the drop-down list, select a font color that will enhance the appearance of your document.

Bold

Italic

Underlining

Highlighting

Enhancing Text Using the Formatting Toolbar

In addition to the character enhancements available to you in the Font dialog box, the appearance of your text can also be changed using bold, italics, underlining, and highlighting from the Formatting toolbar. Highlighting lets you call attention to a specific area of text. Click any one of these features, then key your text; or if the text already exists, select the text you want to format then click the buttons that correspond with the formatting you want to apply.

You can also use the following keyboard commands to activate formatting commands: Ctrl + B for bold, Ctrl + I for italics, and Ctrl + U for underlining. To change the color of the highlighting, click the down-pointing triangle to the right of the Highlighting button. At the drop-down list of colors that displays, click the desired color.

Spacing Punctuation

When keying a document in a monospaced font, such as Courier, end-of-sentence punctuation, such as the period, exclamation point, and question mark, is followed by two spaces. When creating a document set in a proportional typeface, space only once after end-of-sentence punctuation as well as after a colon (except a colon used to indicate a ratio, such as 1:3). Proportional type is set closer and extra white space at the end of sentences is not needed. If the extra white space is added, the text will appear blotchy.

With Word's Replace feature, you can search for ending punctuation followed by two spaces and replace it with the same punctuation followed by one space. Choose Edit, then Replace. At the Find What text box of the Replace dialog box, key a period then press the space bar twice. At the Replace With text box, key a period then press the space bar once. Click the Find Next button, then click the Replace button. To automatically replace all occurrences of the correction, click the Replace All button.

DTP POINTERS
When using proportional fonts:

- Space once after end-of-sentence puncutation.
- Do not use the space bar to align text.

Viewing Format Settings

Word displays text as you will see it when printed. To check the formatting of a particular character or paragraph, click the Help button on the Standard toolbar (first button from the right). When the insertion point becomes a question mark, click the text you want to check. A callout will appear on the screen with details about paragraph and font formatting. When you finish checking your text, press ESC. You can also remove the callout by clicking in the document screen outside the callout. Click the Help button again to deactivate it.

Creating A Memo With A Word Template

Template: A preformatted document layout that can be used again and again.

Every document created in Word is based on a *template.* When you create a document at a clear document window, you are using the default template. This default template, called the *Normal.dot* template, establishes the formatting for the document, including margins, tabs, font, etc.

Time spent designing and formatting basic documents is not productive. You can save time by creating a variety of documents using Word's predesigned templates, such as agendas, awards, brochures, business reports, calendars, fax cover sheets, letters, memos, newsletters, résumés, and more. To display the types of templates available, choose File, then New. The predefined templates are organized on different tabs in the New dialog box as shown in figure 2.9.

FIGURE 2.9

New Dialog Box with the Memos Tab Selected

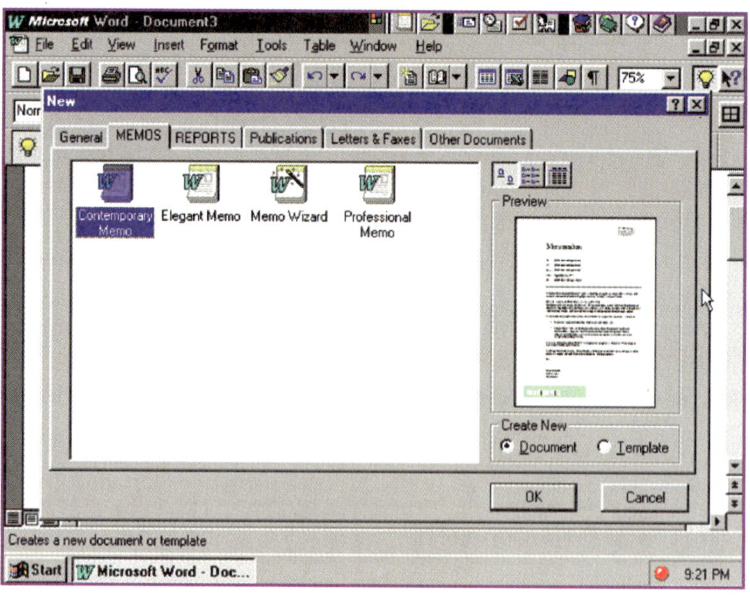

If you select the Memos tab, Word displays Memo icons representing *Contemporary Memo, Elegant Memo,* and *Professional Memo* templates. Figure 2.10 shows the three types of memo templates and the formatting used for each. The use of consistent formatting within each category lends a harmonious, professional appearance to your documents. For instance, use the same category of template for a cover letter, résumé, and follow-up letter to show consistency.

FIGURE 2.10

Memo Templates

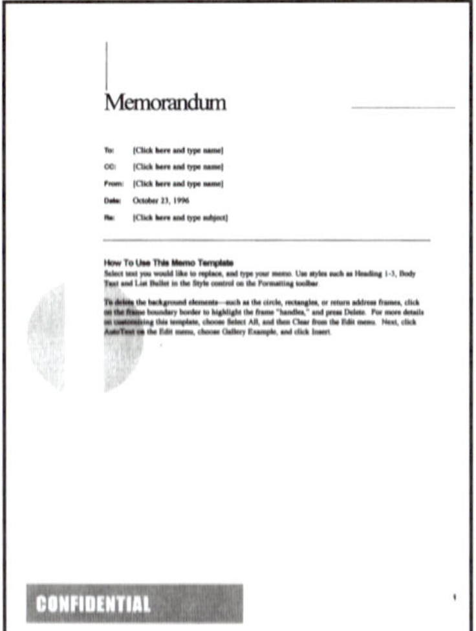

Memorandum

To: [Click here and type name]
CC: [Click here and type name]
From: [Click here and type name]
Date: October 23, 1996
Re: [Click here and type subject]

How To Use This Memo Template
Select text you would like to replace, and type your memo. Use styles such as Heading 1-3, Body Text and List Bullet in the Style control on the Formatting toolbar.

To delete the background elements—such as the circle, rectangles, or return address frames, click on the frame boundary border to highlight the frame "handles," and press Delete. For more details on customizing this template, choose Select All, and then Clear from the Edit menu. Next, click AutoText on the Edit menu, choose Gallery Example, and click Insert.

CONFIDENTIAL

1

CONTEMPORARY

INTEROFFICE MEMORANDUM

TO: [CLICK HERE AND TYPE NAME]
FROM: [CLICK HERE AND TYPE NAME]
SUBJECT: [CLICK HERE AND TYPE SUBJECT]
DATE: OCTOBER 23, 1996
CC: [CLICK HERE AND TYPE NAME]

HOW TO USE THIS MEMO TEMPLATE

Select text you would like to replace, and type your memo. Use styles such as Heading 1-3, Body Text and List Bullet in the Style control on the Formatting toolbar. For more details on customizing this template, choose Select All, and then Clear from the Edit menu. Next, click AutoText on the Edit menu, choose Gallery Example, and click Insert.

NOTE: This memo contains "click-here-and-type" features that make creating memos easier. To fill in the top portion of the memo, click and type between the brackets as indicated.

ELEGANT

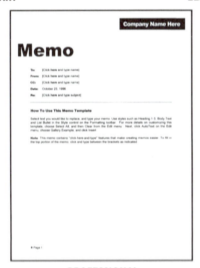

PROFESSIONAL

If Word was preloaded on your computer or if you completed a regular installation of Word on your own computer, some of the templates used in this text may not appear in the New dialog box. See the Preface for a listing of Word's templates. If these templates do not display in the New dialog box, see the Preface for adding these templates.

To choose a template, select File, then New. Depending on the template you choose, you will be presented with a screen or a dialog box requesting specific information. The Wizard templates will assist you in creating distinctive documents through the answers you provide at the on-screen prompts.

The memo templates contain "Click **here** and type" features that make creating memos easier. To fill in areas containing this prompt, click and then key text between the brackets. Select the placeholder text in the memo body location, then key your memo. Prompts will suggest that you use styles such as Heading 1-3, Body Text, and List Bullet in the Style button on the Formatting toolbar. For more details on customizing this template, choose Select All, and then Clear from the Edit menu. Next, click AutoText on the Edit menu, choose Gallery Example, and then click Insert.

Each tab in the New dialog box corresponds to the name of a subfolder (subdirectory) in the template folder (directory). To change the folder Word uses for templates, choose Tools, then Options. At the Options dialog box, click the File Locations tab. At the Options dialog box with the File Locations tab selected, choose Modify, then choose a new template folder.

Readability: The ease with which a person can read and understand groups of words.

When choosing a font for a memo, readability of the document should be considered. *Readability* is the ease with which a person can read and understand groups of words. In a text-intensive document such as a memo, readability is a primary consideration since multiple paragraphs of text are set in large blocks of type. Generally, a serif typeface in approximately 12-point size is appropriate in the body of the memo.

Earlier in this chapter, you learned about choosing fonts. In the template documents, Word chooses fonts for each template. Word may use more than one font within a template document to add variety to the document. In the Contemporary Memo template, Word sets the text after the headings and the body text in 10-point Times New Roman, which is a serif typeface.

Each of the memo templates is distinctive in design. The Contemporary memo attracts attention through the use of a lightly shaded geometric shape in the left margin and subtle gray vertical and horizontal lines that tend to lead the reader's eyes down and over to the right margin. Also, the placement of the shaded box containing the word "CONFIDENTIAL" in the bottom left corner of the memo balances the darker and stronger weight of the word "Memorandum" in the top left corner of the memo. This is a good example of asymmetrical design—the left margin is wider than the right margin and the left side of the memo is balanced with the weight of the body text.

The Elegant memo is subtle in overall appearance. It uses a quiet, simple approach to all formatting. This template uses the Garamond font, which is a serif typeface with a somewhat formal, elegant appearance.

The Professional memo uses the Arial font, which is a sans serif typeface. The overall appearance of the Professional memo is plain and straightforward. Although this memo format is very conservative in nature, the larger MEMO title is balanced by the reverse text box in the upper right corner. The overall characteristics of these template types remain consistent from one template to another.

Creating a Professional Memo with a Word Template

1. At a clear document window, create a memo with the text shown in figure 2.11 using the Professional Memo template by completing the following steps:
   a. Choose File, then New.
   b. At the New dialog box, select the MEMOS tab.
   c. At the New dialog box with the MEMOS tab selected, double-click the Professional Memo icon. (The document template will display in the preview box.)
   d. Key **Denver First Bank & Trust** in the text frame located in the upper right-hand corner.
   e. Select **Denver First Bank & Trust**, change the text alignment to center by clicking the Center button (eighth button from the right) on the Standard toolbar, then click the Italic button on the Standard toolbar.
   f. Select *Memo* and change the font color by choosing Format, then Font. At the Font dialog box, click Color, then select Dk Gray at the drop-down list.
   g. At the memo heading, *To:*, position the arrow pointer inside the text [Click **here** and type name], click once, then key **All Supervisors**.
   h. Point, click, then key **Your name** in place of [Click **here** and type name] at the *From:* heading.
   i. Select, then delete the entire line at *CC:*.
   j. Make sure the date defaults to the current date.
   k. Point, click, then key **Relationship Building Workshop** at the *Re:* heading.
   l. Read the sample text in the body of the memo template, then select and delete the sample text. Key the text shown in figure 2.11. Key your initials in all caps in place of XX.

m. Select the headings and heading text, then change the font to 12-point Arial Rounded MT Bold.

n. Select the body text of the memo and change the font to 11-point Book Antiqua.

2. Save the completed memo and name it c02ex01, bank memo.
3. Print and then close c02ex01, bank memo.

FIGURE 2.11

Denver First Bank & Trust

Memo

To: **All Supervisors**

From: **Your Name**

Date: **March 9, 1997**

Re: **Relationship Building Workshop**

The Human Resources Department is offering the second of a two-part training series for improving work relationships. Titled "Intergroup Relationship Building," the workshop is scheduled for Tuesday, May 24, from 9:30 a.m. to 12:30 p.m. in Room 208.

The workshop will use simulation to engage participants in a cross-group experience to illustrate how groups have different rules for interaction and how group stereotypes are developed and reinforced. The simulation will be followed by a discussion on how dynamics influence individuals. Focusing on the work setting, the workshop will provide specific suggestions for improving unit/departmental work relations and tips for individuals interacting with other work groups.

To participate in the Intergroup Relationship Building workshop, contact the Human Resources Department at extension 1445.

xx:c02ex01, bank memo

• Page 1

Using the Memo Wizard

Word provides a Memo Wizard that guides you through the steps of creating a memo using any of the predesigned memo templates as shown in figure 2.10. The on-screen prompts will guide you through the process of creating a memo according to your specifications. The wizard will also include tips that will give you advice on making certain selections. To use the Memo Wizard, choose File, then New. Select the MEMOS tab, then double-click the Memo Wizard icon.

Creating a Memo with the Memo Wizard

1. At a clear document window, use the Memo Wizard to create a memo with the text in figure 2.12 by completing the following steps:
   a. Choose File, then New; or click the New button on the Standard toolbar; or press Ctrl + N
   b. At the New dialog box, select the MEMOS tab.
   c. Double-click the Memo Wizard icon.
   d. At the prompt, "Do you want to include a heading?" Click Yes.
   e. In the heading text box, key **Hospital Memorandum**, then click Next>.
   f. At the prompt to include a distribution list, click No, then click Next.
   g. Click inside the check boxes to include Date, To, From, and Subject. Key the current date if it does not display. Key **Susan Howard** in the text box to the right of From, then click Next>.
   h. Click in the check box to include the Writer's Initials. Key **Your initials**, then click Next>.
   i. At the prompt, "Which items would you like in the header after the first page?" do not click any boxes. At the prompt, "Which items would you like in the footer for all of the pages?" click in the check box to include the Date, then click Next>.
   j. At the prompt, "Which style would you like?" click Contemporary, then click Next>.
   k. Click Finish.
   l. Point, click, then key **All Hospital Staff** in the text box to the right of To.
   m. Point, click, then key **Children and Hospital Week** in the text box to the right of Re.
   n. Point, click, then key the memo text shown in figure 2.12.
   o. Select the memo text from the heading *Date:* to the end of the memo, then change the font to 11-point Century Schoolbook.
2. Save the completed memo and name it c02ex02, memo wizard.
3. Print and then close c02ex02, memo wizard.

FIGURE 2.12

hospital memorandum

Date: March 3, 1997

To: All Hospital Staff

From: Susan Howard

RE: Children and Hospital Week

The week of April 14 through 18 has been set aside to pay particular attention to the unique needs of children in the health care setting. The hospital has adopted the theme "Commitment to Caring." This theme reflects the belief that all children and families deserve the best health care possible and that health care should be family-centered and developmentally appropriate.

To celebrate this special week, Chicago Mercy Hospital is sponsoring the Children's Health and Safety Fair on Friday, April 18, from 9:00 a.m. to 3:30 p.m. at the Health Center. The fair will include a bicycle rodeo, fire safety demonstration, and car seat checkup. The fair provides the perfect opportunity for children and families to become better acquainted with hospital and medical equipment.

The intent of the Children's Health and Safety Fair is to teach children good safety habits and to dispel fears if they should ever be admitted to the hospital. Everything children do at the fair will be hands-on, and they will be helped by professional hospital staff.

xx:c02ex02, memo wizard

Formatting A Memo

In exercises 1 and 2, you used Word's template feature to create formatted memos. A memo can also be created and formatted at a clear editing window. Use the default margin settings of 1-inch top and bottom margins, and 1.25-inch left and right margins. Double space between the memo headings at the beginning of the document. Triple space between the last memo heading and the body text. Single space the body text, but double space between paragraphs. Double space before the reference initials.

Memos are internal business documents that are conservative in nature. Do not let the font selection interfere with the message you are trying to convey. Generally, choose a serif typeface of approximately 12-point type size for text-intensive information, such as paragraphs in the body of a memo. Some typefaces you may want to use for memos include Book Antiqua, Century Schoolbook, Footlight MT Light, Garamond, and Times New Roman.

Adding Symbols And Special Characters To A Document

DTP POINTERS
Special characters add visual contrast to a document.

You can insert many symbols and special characters into your Word documents. Symbol fonts such as Monotype Sorts, Wingdings, and Symbol include decorative characters that may display in the form of bullets, stars, flowers, and more. Other symbol fonts may be built into your printer. For example, most PostScript printers include Zapf Dingbats. Interesting and useful symbols are also available in [normal text] fonts (Times New Roman, Braggadocio, Colonna MT, Kino MT, etc.). In addition, other character sets may be available from other software installed on your hard drive.

Special characters can also be used to add interest and originality to documents. ANSI symbols are the regular character set that you see on your keyboard plus many more characters, including a copyright symbol, registered trademark symbol, scientific symbols, and foreign language characters such as umlauts (¨) and tildes (˜). Special characters include em and en dashes, smart quotes, ellipses, non-breaking hyphens, and more. These characters are used to add a polished, professional look to your documents.

Inserting Symbols Using the Symbol Dialog Box

To insert symbols using the Symbol dialog box with either the Symbols tab or the Special Characters tab selected as shown in figures 2.13 and 2.14, complete the following steps:

1. Position the insertion point in the document where you want the symbol to display.
2. Choose Insert, then Symbol. (The Symbol dialog box will appear.)
3. Select either the Symbol tab or the Special Characters tab.
4. At the Font list box, select the font for which you want to see the symbols.
5. Click a symbol to see it enlarged. You can press the arrow keys to move around the screen. If a shortcut key combination is available for a particular symbol, it will appear to the right of the Font text box. (You can use these shortcut keys instead of the mouse.)
6. Click the Insert button. (At the Symbol dialog box, you can choose Insert to insert the symbol in the document and not close the dialog box. This might be useful if you are inserting more than one symbol in the document at the same time.)
7. Click Close.

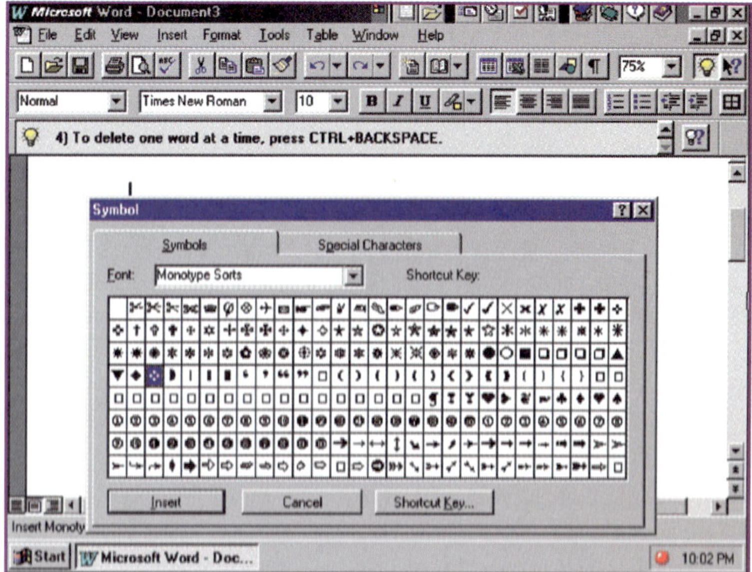

FIGURE 2.13

Symbol Dialog Box at the Symbols Tab

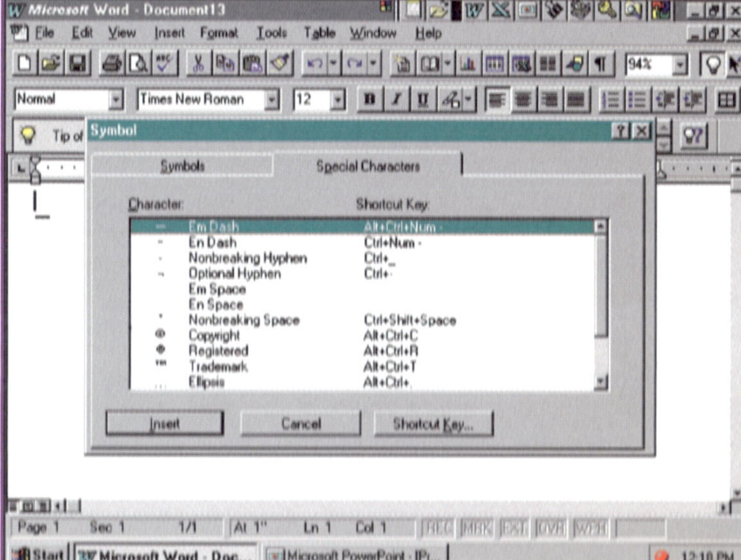

FIGURE 2.14

Symbol Dialog Box at the Special Characters Tab

Inserting Special Characters Using the Keyboard

Three techniques in Word may be used to access special characters and symbols. One method is to choose Insert, then Symbol, then select the Symbols or Special Characters tab. Select the special character that you want to use in your document then click the Insert button then the Close button, or double-click the desired character.

You can also insert special characters from the Symbol dialog box using the keyboard. To do this, press the up, down, left, or right arrow key until the desired character is selected, then press Alt + I. Press Enter to close the Symbol dialog box.

Special characters can also be added by using shortcut keys. The shortcut keys are listed in the Symbol dialog box. For example, to insert a copyright symbol in a document, you would press Alt + Ctrl + C. To create é (as in résumé) hold down the Ctrl key, press the single quotation mark key, press the "e" key, then release the Ctrl key and the symbol will display.

Assigning a Shortcut Key to a Symbol

If you frequently use a particular symbol, you may want to assign a shortcut command to the symbol for faster accessing. For instance, assume you are working in a local hospital and you are in charge of all promotional documents for Healthy Heart Week. You frequently use a heart symbol from one of the character sets.

Assign a shortcut command to this symbol by choosing Insert, then Symbol. At the Symbol dialog box, choose the Symbols tab. Choose the Monotype Sorts font from the Font list, then click the heart symbol located in the fifth row and the second to the last column. Click the Shortcut Key. At the Customize dialog box, key the combination of Alt + H (Word will prompt you if this key combination has already been used), click Assign, then choose Close. From now on you can access the heart symbol by simply pressing Alt + H.

Creating Em and En Dashes

The Symbol dialog box with the Special Characters tab selected contains two symbols that are used with proportional type—an em dash and an en dash. An em dash (—) is as long as the point size of the type and is used in text to indicate a pause in speech. An em dash is created on a typewriter by typing two hyphens. In typesetting, an em dash is one character. An em dash can also be created at the keyboard by pressing Alt + Ctrl + Num -. An en dash (–) indicates a continuation, such as 116–133 or January–March, and is exactly one-half the width of an em dash. An en dash can be inserted at the keyboard by pressing Ctrl + Num -.

Using Smart Quotes

In typesetting, the open quotation mark is curved upward (“) and the close quotation mark is curved downward (”) The quotation mark used on the standard keyboard creates a vertical mark ("). This is commonly used in documents created on a typewriter but is not appropriate for typesetting. In typesetting, the vertical mark is used to indicate inches.

DTP POINTERS
Use vertical quotation marks only to indicate inches.

The Smart Quote option in the AutoFormat feature is on by default and causes quotation marks entered around text to change to proper open and close quotation marks. Additionally, AutoFormat automatically converts single quotation marks around text to the proper open and close quotation marks and inserts the appropriate symbol for an apostrophe (’).

To display the AutoFormat dialog box, choose Tools, then Options. At the Options dialog box, select the AutoFormat tab. In the Show Options section of the dialog box, click AutoFormat As You Type. Click inside the text boxes that correspond with the features you want replaced as you type.

Using Word Text Layers In Documents

In exercise 3, you will customize a memo by adding a watermark for visual appeal. A basic understanding of the unique three-level layering of text, pictures, and drawing objects in Word will be helpful in understanding how to create watermarks in documents.

Word has three basic layers you can use when creating a document. You may think of a document created in Word as a sandwich. Document text exists in the middle layer or text layer. This layer is the one you may be most accustomed to working with in word processing. Word also has two additional layers that include the drawing layer above the text and the layer below the text layer.

If an object is drawn using a button on the Drawing toolbar in a document containing text, the object is positioned above the text. It can also be positioned below the text. If you want the text in the document to wrap around the object, it must be framed. Placing text or pictures in a frame prepares them to exist in the text layer. The frame causes the surrounding text to wrap around the item and makes it easier to move the item around the screen.

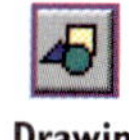

Drawing

You can also use a text box when you want to place text or a graphic below or above the text layer. Unlike a frame, text does not wrap around a text box because text or graphics displayed in a text box does not lie in the document text layer. A text box does not automatically resize when you add more text. You can manually resize the text box to fit the contents. Several of these features will be discussed in greater detail in later chapters.

Adding a Watermark for Visual Appeal

Adding a watermark to a memo is a simple, quick way to add visual appeal to a document. A *watermark* is a lightened image that displays behind text on a page. Traditionally, a watermark is a design impressed in high-quality paper stock. This design can be seen more clearly when the paper is held up to the light.

Watermark: A lightened graphic or text image displayed behind text on a page.

One of the easiest ways to create a watermark, that will automatically appear on every page of your document, is to insert the image or text you want to use in the watermark into a header or footer. Placing the watermark into a header or footer automatically positions the object in the appropriate layer below the text layer. To access the Header and Footer pane, choose View, then Header and Footer. If you need to edit the watermark image, double-click on the image to access the Header and Footer pane or choose View, then Header and Footer.

The watermark is not confined to the area at the top or bottom of the page where a typical header or footer is found. By placing the text or image into a text box, you can move it anywhere on the page. To create a text box, display the Drawing toolbar by clicking the Drawing button on the Standard toolbar (fifth button from the right), then click the Text Box button on the Drawing toolbar as shown in figure 2.15. Drag the crosshair on the page to draw a text box that will hold a graphic image. You can later size and position the text box more precisely by accessing the Size and Position tab at the Drawing Object dialog box.

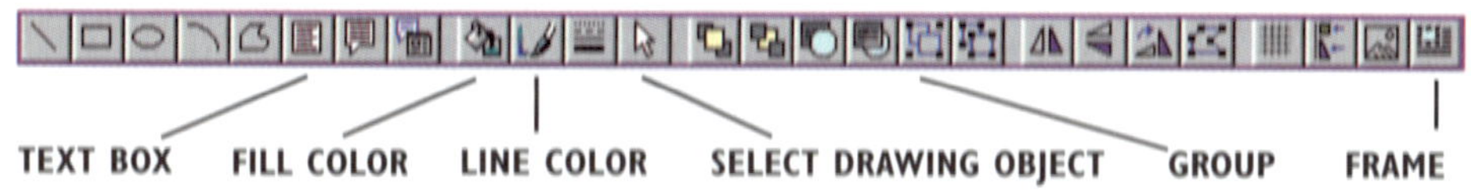

FIGURE 2.15

Drawing Toolbar

If a text box was created in a previous document, the Fill and Line settings will default to the previous document settings. Remember to change these settings if they interfere with the ones you want to apply to the current document. To change the text box fill, choose Format, then Drawing Object. At the Drawing Object dialog box, select the Fill tab as shown in figure 2.16. Select fill color and pattern choices at the Fill dialog box, then choose OK or press Enter. Additionally, you can change the fill by clicking the Fill Color button on the Drawing toolbar as shown in figure 2.15.

To change the Line Color, choose Format, Drawing Object, then select the Line tab and make line color choices at the Line dialog box. Alternatively, you can click the Line Color button on the Drawing toolbar as shown in figure 2.15.

FIGURE 2.16

Drawing Object Dialog Box

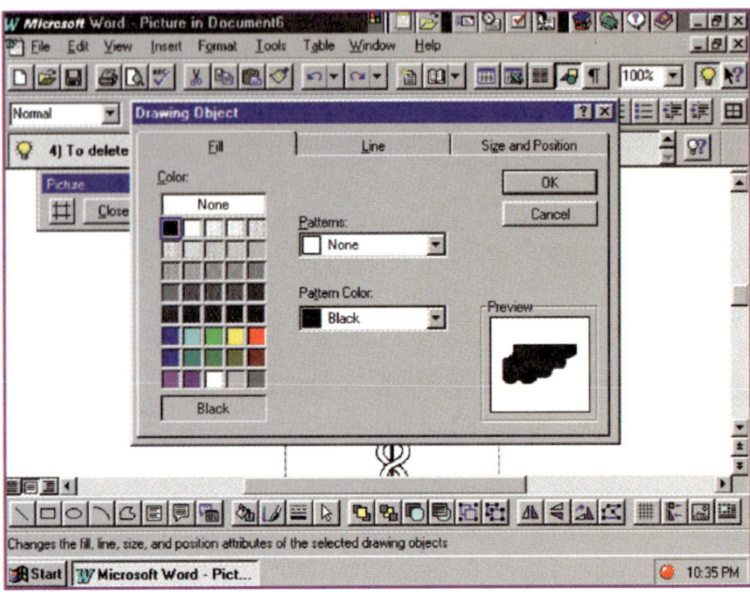

Position the insertion point inside the text box, then insert a graphic image by choosing Insert, then Picture. Click the down-pointing triangle to the right of the Look in text box and select the folder or disk where your graphic files are located. Select a graphic file from the list box that displays at the Insert Picture dialog box. Choose OK or press Enter to close the Insert Picture dialog box.

If a graphic watermark overpowers the text in the document, you can lighten it. To lighten a graphic image, double-click the image to access Word's graphic editor, Microsoft Word Picture, as shown in figure 2.17. Many clipart images are made up of different segments and varying colors or shades. If you are creating a watermark and you want to change each segment with different percentages of a color or shade, you must select each segment individually or press the Shift key while selecting similarly colored segments.

FIGURE 2.17

Microsoft Word Picture

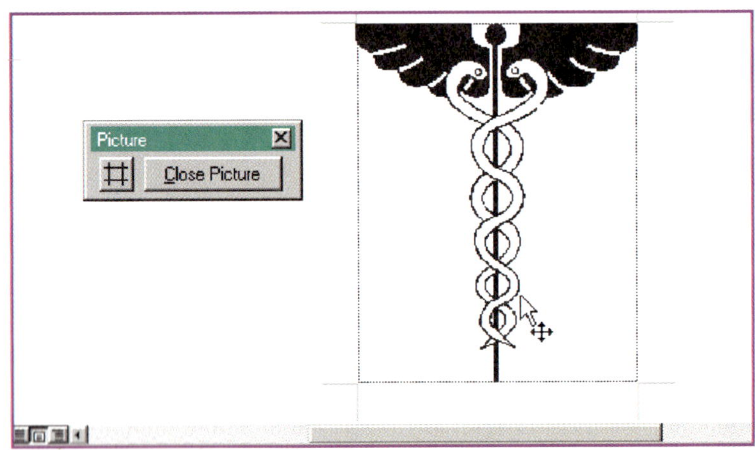

Select Drawing Object

If you prefer to lighten the image using just one color or percentage of shading for the entire image, click the Select Drawing Object button on the Drawing toolbar (twelfth button from the left). Draw a dashed box around the entire image by dragging the crosshair along the perimeter of the grid of the image, then release the left mouse button. When you release the mouse, the image will display with handles distinguishing each segment of the image. Click the Group button on the Drawing toolbar (tenth button from the right). This groups the individual segments together as one unit. (More information will be presented in chapter 5 on using various buttons on the Drawing toolbar.)

Double-click anywhere on the image to access the Drawing Object dialog box as shown in figure 2.16. Change the fill and line colors, patterns, or pattern colors at the Fill tab or the Line tab of the Drawing Object dialog box. Alternatively, click the Fill Color and Line Color buttons on the Drawing toolbar. (You may need to experiment with the settings to find the right color or shade.) See figure 2.15 for the Select Drawing Object and Group buttons on the Drawing toolbar.

If text is used as a watermark, lighten the text by choosing a lighter color or shade at the Color drop-down list of the Font dialog box.

To create a watermark in a header or footer and change the watermark shading, you would complete the following steps:

1. On the Standard toolbar, click the Drawing button to display the Drawing toolbar (fifth button from the right).
2. Choose View, then Header and Footer.
3. Click the Switch Between Header and Footer button to move to the header or footer pane (first button on the left of the Header and Footer toolbar).
4. Enter the text or graphic you want. If you are inserting text, key the text within the dashed area of the header or footer pane. If you are inserting a graphic, you would complete the following steps:
   a. Click the Text Box button on the Drawing toolbar, then drag to create a box in which to insert an image.
   b. Choose Insert, then Picture.
   c. At the Insert Picture dialog box, double-click the graphic you want to insert.
5. To lighten the watermark image, you would complete the following steps:
   a. Double-click the image to access Microsoft Word Picture.
   b. If you want to apply different shades or colors to several segments of an image, double-click each section of the image to change the color at the Drawing Object dialog box. Change the color, pattern, and pattern color at the Fill tab. Change any lines at the Line tab, and adjust the size and position of the image at the Size and Position tab; or click the Fill Color or Line Color buttons on the Drawing toolbar. If you want to uniformly change the shade or color of the entire image, click the Select Drawing Objects button on the Drawing toolbar, group the image, then change the fill color.
   c. Click OK to close the Drawing Object dialog box.
   d. Click the Close Picture button at the top of Microsoft Word Picture.
6. Click Close on the Header and Footer toolbar.

Switch Between Header and Footer

Creating a List in a Memo

You can insert a special character as a bullet preceding a list by using one of the following methods. One method involves inserting a special character from the Symbols dialog box, pressing the Tab key, then keying the text. Word automatically converts your text to a Bullet List item when you press Enter, if the Automatic Bulleted Lists feature has been turned on. To check if this feature has been turned on, choose Tools, then Options. At the Options dialog box, select the AutoFormat tab. Make sure a check mark appears in the check box preceding the Automatic Bulleted Lists in the Apply As You Type section of the dialog box. This method works only if the Automatic Bulleted Lists feature has been turned on. In addition, this feature will not work if you press the Enter key twice after each line to create a double space between each entry. Press Shift + Enter to create a blank line. The Enter key will actually turn off the Automatic

Bulleted Lists feature. After the list has been keyed, additional formatting can be applied to the selected list. For instance, a paragraph indentation may be applied to the text by accessing the Paragraph dialog box.

A second method for inserting a special character as a bullet is available at the Bullets and Numbering dialog box. More information on bullets will be provided in the next section of this chapter.

Creating a Memo with a Watermark and Special Symbols

1. At a clear document window, create the memo shown in figure 2.18 by completing the following steps:
   a. Key the memo headings and the information after the headings shown in figure 2.18. To create the special é, select the "e" in *Medard,* then press the Shortcut Key command (Ctrl + ', E), or complete the following steps:
      (1) Choose Insert, then Symbol.
      (2) At the Symbol dialog box, select the Symbols tab.
      (3) Select [normal text] in the Font text box. (To do this, click the down-pointing triangle at the right side of the text box. At the drop-down menu that displays, click the down-pointing triangle in the scroll bar until *[normal text]* displays, then click *[normal text].*)
      (4) Click the é symbol located in the sixth column, eighth row.
      (5) Click Insert, then Close.
   b. After keying the headings, press the Enter key three times.
   c. Retrieve the memo body text from a file on your student data disk by completing the following text:
      (1) Choose Insert, then File.
      (2) At the Insert File dialog box, click the down-pointing triangle to the right of the Look in text box and select the drive where your student data disk is located.
      (3) At the list box, double-click the file, *medical memo text.*
   d. Key your reference initials in caps.
   e. Select the memo headings and heading text (To: etc.) and change the font to 12-point Century Schoolbook Bold. (Add or delete tabs to align the text.)
   f. Select the memo body text and change the font to 11-point Century Schoolbook.
   g. Create the watermark by completing the following steps:
      (1) Display the Drawing toolbar by clicking the Drawing button on the Standard toolbar (fifth button from the right on the Standard toolbar).
      (2) Choose View, then Header and Footer.
      (3) Click the Text Box button on the Drawing toolbar (sixth button from the left).
      (4) Position the crosshair in the memo approximately an inch from the left margin between the Subject line and the first line of the first paragraph, hold down the left mouse button and drag the crosshair to within 1 inch of the right margin and downward toward the bottom of the memo, then release the left mouse button. (Refer to figure 2.18 for approximate size and location.)
      (5) If a fill other than white displays in the text box, choose Format, then Drawing Object. Select the Fill tab. Change the current settings to Color: None; Patterns: None; and Pattern Color: White. Choose OK to close the

dialog box. Or click the Fill Color button on the Drawing toolbar and select None (see figure 2.16 for the Fill Color button).

(6) If a border displays around the text box, choose Format, then Drawing Object. Select the Line tab. Select None in the Line section. Choose OK or press Enter. Or click the Line Color button on the Drawing Toolbar and select None (see figure 2.15 for the Line Color button.)

(7) With the insertion point positioned inside the text box, choose Insert, then Picture.

(8) At the Insert Picture dialog box, make sure *Clipart* displays in the Look in text box, then double-click *Medstaff* in the Name list box.

(9) Lighten the image to create a watermark by completing the following steps:

- **(a)** Double-click the image to open Microsoft Word Picture.
- **(b)** Click the Select Drawing Objects button on the Drawing toolbar (twelfth button from the left), then drag the crosshair around the grid that displays at the perimeter of the image. (A dashed box will display.)
- **(c)** Click the Group button on the Drawing toolbar (tenth button from the right) to group the selected segments into a single graphic element.
- **(d)** Choose Format, then Drawing Object; double-click the image; or click the Fill Color button on the Drawing toolbar.
- **(e)** At the Drawing Object dialog box, select the Fill tab.
- **(f)** Change the Color to 15% Gray by choosing the gray color in the second row and first column of the Color palette. (If you clicked the Fill button, select the first gray box in the second row of the color palette.)
- **(g)** Click OK to close the Drawing Object dialog box.
- **(h)** Click the Close Picture at Microsoft Word Picture.

(10) Click the Close button on the Header and Footer toolbar.

h. Choose File, then Print Preview. If the watermark is too light or too dark, you may need to select a different shade of gray. To edit the watermark, choose View, then Header and Footer. To change the color, complete steps similar to steps 9a through 9h. Click the Close button at the Preview toolbar.

2. Save the memo and name it c02ex03, medical memo.

3. Print and then close c02ex03, medical memo.

FIGURE 2.18

DATE: **March 7, 1997**

TO: **Fred Médard**

FROM: **Juliette Danner**

SUBJECT: **PREOPERATIVE PROCEDURES**

At the last meeting of the medical team, concern was raised about the structure of preoperative procedures. In light of recent nationwide occurrences in some city hospitals, members of the team decided to review written procedures to determine if additional steps should be added. A meeting of the surgical team has been set for Tuesday, March 25. Please try to arrange surgical schedules so a majority of the surgical team can attend this meeting.

Please review the following items to determine where each should be positioned in a preoperative surgical checklist:

- ✔ Necessary operative forms are signed—admissions and consent for surgery.
- ✔ Blood tests have been completed.
- ✔ Blood type is noted in patient chart.
- ✔ Surgical procedure has been triple-checked with patient and surgical team.
- ✔ All allergies are noted in patient chart.
- ✔ Anesthesiologist has reviewed and initialed patient chart.

I am confident that the medical team will discover that the preoperative checklist is one of the most thorough in the region. Any suggestions made by the medical team will only enhance a superior checklist.

xx:c02ex03, medical memo

Inserting Bullets

Bullets

Bullets can be inserted in a document at the Bullets and Numbering dialog box or with the Bullets button on the Standard toolbar. To insert a bullet with the Bullets button, position the insertion point where you want the bullet to appear or anywhere within a paragraph that you want preceded by a bullet, then click the Bullets button. A bullet is inserted at the left margin of the line or paragraph where the insertion point is positioned. By default, a small circle bullet is inserted in the document. This can be changed at the Bullets and Numbering dialog box shown in figure 2.19. When a bullet is inserted with this dialog box, the insertion point is also automatically indented to the first tab setting to the right. Each time you press the Enter key in the document, another bullet or the next number in the sequence is inserted in the document.

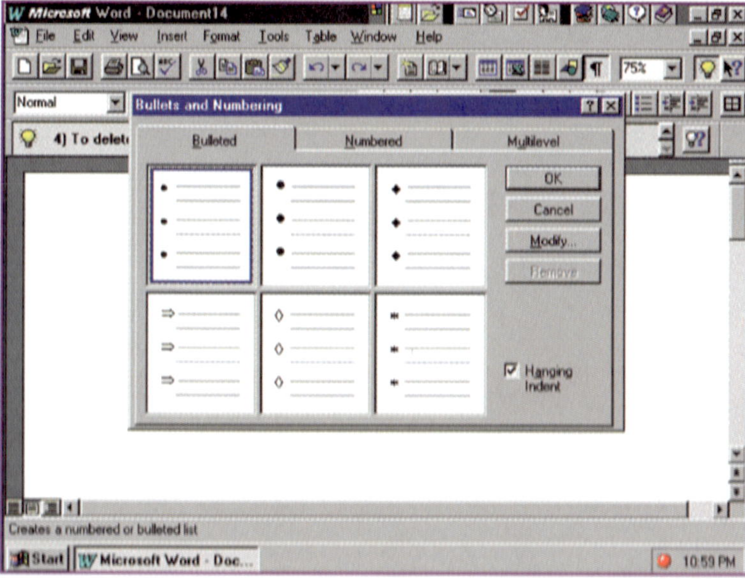

FIGURE 2.19

Bullets and Numbering Dialog Box

To display the Bullets and Numbering dialog box, choose Format, then Bullets and Numbering. The Bullets and Numbering dialog box contains three tabs: Bulleted, Numbered, and Multilevel. If you click the Modify button at the right side of the dialog box, the Modify Bulleted List dialog box displays. At this dialog box, you can select different bullet characters, colors, point sizes, and character alignment. For instance, to insert a different bullet character, click the Bullet button in the Modify Bulleted List dialog box, then select a character at the Symbol dialog box.

Word can also create numbered and bulleted lists automatically. When you create a list with a number, asterisk, or a symbol followed by punctuation such as a period, or followed by a hanging indentation from the Paragraph dialog box, Word automatically inserts a number, asterisk, or symbol in front of each item when you press the Enter key.

DTP POINTERS

- Use bullets to organize lists.
- Use special characters as customized bullets to add interest and contrast.

Creating Text in a Watermark

DTP POINTERS
Use spot color to add contrast and impact to a document.

As discussed earlier in this chapter, a watermark is created most easily in a header or footer because the watermark is automatically positioned below the text layer. In exercise 4, you will create two watermarks from text created in a header pane and in a footer pane. Instead of reducing the shading in the Drawing Objects dialog box, you will change the color of the text to a light gray in the Font dialog box.

Creating a Memo with Text in a Watermark

1. At a clear editing window, create the memo shown in figure 2.20 by completing the following steps:
   a. Press the Enter key five times.
   b. Key the memo headings and the information after the headings as shown in figure 2.20. To create the special symbol ö, press the Shortcut Keys, Ctrl + :, then O, or complete the following steps:
      (1) Choose Insert, then Symbol.
      (2) At the Symbol dialog box with the Symbols tab selected, select [normal text] in the Font list box.
      (3) Click the ö symbol in the last row and the tenth column from the right.
      (4) Click Insert and then click Close.
      (5) Complete similar steps to create the ñ. (The ñ symbol is located in the [normal text] font, last row, fourteenth column from the left.)
   c. Press the Enter key three times.
   d. Key the first paragraph of text in the memo, then press Enter twice.
   e. Create the heart bullet by completing the following steps:
      (1) Choose Format, then Bullets and Numbering.
      (2) At the Bullets and Numbering dialog box, select the Bulleted tab.
      (3) Click the Modify button.
      (4) At the Modified Bulleted List dialog box, click the Bullet button in the Bullet Character section.
      (5) At the Symbol dialog box, select Monotype Sorts in the Symbols Font list box.
      (6) Click the heart symbol located in the fifth row and the second to the last column, then click OK.
      (7) At the Modify Bulleted List dialog box, make the following changes:
         (a) Change the Color option to Red.
         (b) Change the Alignment of List Text: option to Centered.
         (c) Change the Distance from Indent to Text: option to 0.50 inches.
         (d) Insert a check mark in the Hanging Indent check box. (To do this, click inside the check box.)
         (e) Click OK.
   f. After inserting the first heart bullet, key the remaining paragraphs in the body of the memo in figure 2.20. Press Shift + Enter to create a blank line between each paragraph in the list, then press Enter to activate the bullet feature. (Pressing the Enter key twice will turn off the special character.) Use the en and em dashes from the Symbol dialog box with the Special Characters tab selected. Press the Enter key twice after the last paragraph.
   g. Select the headings and heading text and change the font to 14-point Arial Bold. Add or delete tabs as necessary to align the text.

h. Select the memo body text including the bulleted list and change the font to 14-point Footlight MT Light Regular.
i. Create two watermarks by completing the following steps:
   (1) Choose View, then Header and Footer.
   (2) At the Header pane, change the font to 32-point Arial MT Black and the Color option to Lt Gray.
   (3) Key **Healthy ♥ Heart ♥ Week**. To insert the heart symbol, complete the following steps:
      (a) Display the Symbol dialog box with the Symbols tab selected.
      (b) Choose the Monotype Sorts font.
      (c) Click the heart symbol located in the fifth row and the second to the last column.
      (d) Click Insert, then Close.
   (4) Select **Healthy ♥ Heart ♥ Week**, then click the Copy button on the Standard toolbar.
   (5) Click the Switch Between Header and Footer button on the Header and Footer toolbar.
   (6) With the insertion point positioned in the Footer pane, click the Paste button on the Standard toolbar.
   (7) Click the Close button on the Header and Footer toolbar.
j. Key your reference initials and the exercise number in 11-point Footlight MT Light a double space below the last paragraph.

2. Save the memo and name it c02ex04, heart memo
3. Print and then close c02ex04, heart memo.

FIGURE 2.20

Healthy ♥ Heart ♥ Week

DATE: **March 12, 1997**

TO: **Audra Schöenbeck**

FROM: **Marcus Cañete**

SUBJECT: **HEALTHY HEART WEEK**

Chicago Mercy Hospital will celebrate Healthy Heart Week from April 13–19. During this week, the hospital will sponsor several workshops on how to improve the quality of life by improving the quality of a person's heart. These workshops are free and will be open to the general public. When the times and locations are determined, I will let you know. In the meantime, as a buildup to Healthy Heart Week, I would like you to add the following information to next week's newsletter:

- ♥ One high blood pressure reading does not necessarily mean a person has high blood pressure—a problem is indicated when a person has several high blood pressure readings.
- ♥ High blood pressure usually has no symptoms. The only way to know for sure is to have it checked.
- ♥ A normal blood pressure reading is 120/80. If the top number (called the *systolic*) consistently exceeds 140, or if the bottom number (called the *diastolic*) consistently exceeds 90, a person should be working with a physician to lower his or her blood pressure.

xx:c02ex04, heart memo

Healthy ♥ Heart ♥ Week

Preparing An Agenda

Before a meeting in a business, an agenda is generally prepared that includes such information as the name of the group or department holding the meeting; the date, time, and location of the meeting; and the topics to be discussed during the meeting. In Word, an agenda can be created with the Agenda Wizard or created at a clear document screen.

Preparing an Agenda with a Template

Word contains one Agenda Wizard. The wizard creates an agenda form that could be used by the person chairing the meeting and/or by the person taking the minutes of the meeting. The Agenda Wizard is very comprehensive and includes information such as a description of the meeting; date, time, and location of the meeting; who called the meeting; the facilitator, note taker, timekeeper, and attendees; and a place for meeting notes and more.

The Agenda Wizard will automatically compute the amount of time you have allotted for an agenda topic into a time schedule. For instance, suppose you have allotted one hour for discussion of an agenda topic. Word will record the time in the agenda as 9:00–10:00 AM. The Agenda Wizard will also ask if you would like additional sheets provided for note-taking during a meeting.

Preparing an Agenda with the Agenda Wizard

1. At a clear document screen, create the agenda shown in figure 2.21 using Word's Agenda Wizard by completing the following steps:
   a. Choose File, then New.
   b. At the New dialog box, select the Other Documents tab.
   c. Double-click the Agenda Wizard icon.
   d. At the Agenda Wizard, make sure the Boxes style is selected, then click Next>.
   e. Select the current date in the Date text box, then key **April 22, 1997**.
   f. Select the current time in the Starting time text box, key **8:30 a.m.**, then click Next>.
   g. Select the current text in the Type the title or main topic of your meeting text box, then key **Quality Care Project Establish Data Gathering Timeline**. Select the text in the Type the location text box, key **Room 208**, then click Next>.
   h. At the next screen, exclude the following headings by clicking inside the check box to remove the check mark: *Please read*: and *Special notes:*.
   i. Click Next>.
   j. At the next screen, exclude the following names on the agenda by clicking inside the check box to remove the check mark: *Meeting called by:*, *Timekeeper:*, *Observers:*, and *Resource persons:*.
   k. Click Next>.
   l. At the next screen, key the following information in the sections listed below:

Agenda topic:	Person responsible:	Minutes allocated:
1 **Meeting Overview**	**Becky Peterson**	**30**
2 **Introduce Facilitator**	**Stanley Barnett**	**10**
3 **Quality Care Timeline**	**Gail Zinn, Consultant**	**90**
4 **Area Reports and Discussion**	**Ellen Heitz, Hui Lenzi, Geoffrey Benn, Wendy Mitaki**	**60**
5 **Summary**	**Becky Peterson**	**20**

m. Click Next>.
n. At the next screen, click Next>. (You do not want to change the order of the agenda.)
o. At the next screen, click No to include a form for recording minutes, then click Next>.
p. Click Finish.

2. At the document window, key the following information in the sections listed below:

Type of meeting:	**Committee meeting**	Note taker:	**Katrina O'Dell**
Facilitator:	**Gail Zinn, Consultant**		
Attendees:	**Hospital Timeline Committee members**		
Please bring:	**Area summaries**		

3. Save the agenda and name it c02ex05, agenda wizard.
4. Print and then close c02ex05, agenda wizard.

FIGURE 2.21

Quality Care Project
Establish Data Gathering Timeline

April 22, 1997
8:30 AM to 12:00 PM
Room 208

Type of meeting:	Committee meeting	**Note taker:**	Katrina O'Dell
Facilitator:	Gail Zinn, Consultant		
Attendees:	Hospital Timeline Committee members		
Please bring:	Area summaries		

----- Agenda Topics -----

1. Meeting Overview	Becky Peterson	8:30-9:00 AM
2. Introduce Facilitator	Stanley Barnett	9:00-9:10 AM
3. Quality Care Timeline	Gail Zinn, Consultant	9:10-10:40 AM
4. Area Reports and Discussion	Ellen Heitz, Hui Lenzi, Geoffrey Benn, Wendy Mitaki	10:40-11:40 AM
5. Summary	Becky Peterson	11:40-12:00 PM

Other information

Creating An Agenda Using Tables

In some situations, you may not need the comprehensive agenda created by the Agenda Wizard. An agenda can be prepared at a clear document screen with side-by-side columns similar to a parallel-column approach. Word does not include a parallel-column feature where text is grouped across a page in rows. However, the same effect can be accomplished by using a table to format an agenda as shown in figure 2.22.

Side-by-Side Columns: Column format that groups text horizontally across the page in rows.

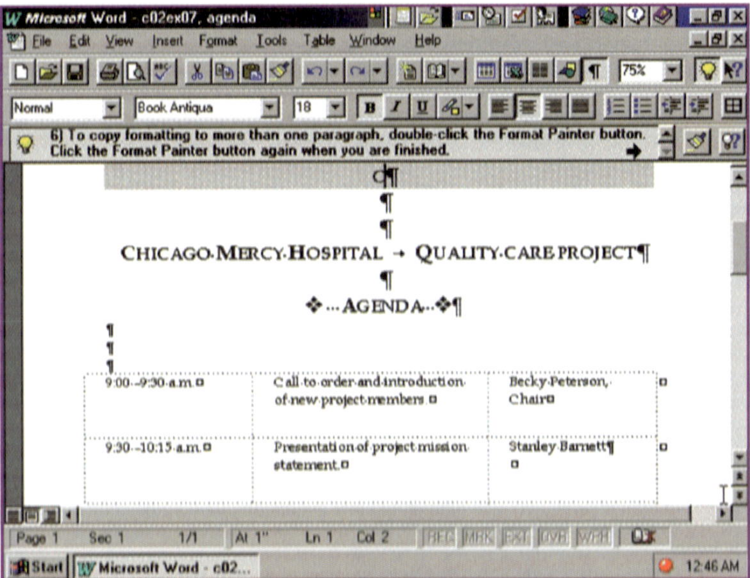

FIGURE 2.22

Agenda Created in a Table

A table can be created with the Insert Table button on the Standard toolbar (eighth button from the right) or the Table option from the Menu bar.

Insert Tables

To create an agenda similar to the one shown in figure 2.23, create a table with three columns and six rows. The number of rows will depend on the number of entries in your agenda. To create a table using the Insert Table dialog box, you would complete the following steps:

1. Choose Table, then Insert Table.
2. At the Insert Table dialog box, key **3** in the Number of Columns text box.
3. Choose Number of Rows.
4. Key **6**.
5. Choose OK or press Enter.

Entering Text in a Table

Information in a table is keyed in cells. A *cell* is the intersection between a row and a column. With the insertion point positioned in a cell, key or edit text as you would normal text. Move the insertion point to other cells with the mouse by positioning the arrow pointer in the desired cell, then clicking the left mouse button. If you are using the keyboard, press Tab to move the insertion point to the next cell or press Shift + Tab to move the insertion point to the previous cell. If you want to move the insertion point to a tab stop within a cell, press Ctrl + Tab.

Cell: The intersection between a row and a column in a table.

If the insertion point is located in the last cell of the table and you press the Tab key, Word adds another row to the table. If you have added too many rows to your table, select the unwanted rows then press Delete. When all the information has been entered into the cells, move the insertion point below the table and, if necessary, continue keying the document, or save the document in the normal manner.

Preparing an Agenda with Tables

1. At a clear document screen, create the agenda shown in figure 2.23 by completing the following steps:
   a. Change the left and right margins to 1 inch.
   b. Change the font to 18-point Book Antiqua Bold and turn on Small Caps.
   c. Press the Enter key four times.
   d. Click the Center alignment button on the Standard toolbar.
   e. Key **Chicago Mercy Hospital**, press Tab, and then key **Quality Care Project**.
   f. Press Enter twice, and then key ❖ **Agenda** ❖. (Insert the ❖ symbol at the Symbol dialog box with the Monotype Sorts font selected. The symbol is located in the fourth row, third column. Press the space bar three times before and after *Agenda*.)
   g. Press Enter three times, then click the Align Left button on the Standard toolbar. Change the font size to 12 points.
   h. Create a table to hold the agenda text by completing the following steps:
      (1) Choose Table, then Insert Table.
      (2) At the Insert Table dialog box, change the number in the Number of Columns text box to 3.
      (3) Change the number in the Number of Rows text box to 6.
      (4) Click OK.
      (5) At the document screen with the insertion point positioned inside the table, choose Table, then Cell Height and Width.
      (6) At the Cell Height and Width dialog box, select the Column tab.
      (7) Change the Width of Column 1 to 2 inches.
      (8) Click the Next Column button at the bottom of the dialog box.
      (9) Change the Width of Column 2 to 2.8 inches.
      (10) Click the Next Column button.
      (11) Change the Width of Column 3 to 2 inches.
      (12) Change the Space Between Columns to 0.5 inches.
      (13) Select the Row tab.
      (14) Change the Height of Rows 1–6 to At Least and change the At measurement to 54 pt.
      (15) Click OK.
   i. At the table, press Shift + Tab until the insertion point is positioned in the first cell.
   j. Key **9:00–9:30 a.m.** in the first cell, then press Tab. (Use the en dash between the times).
   k. Key **Call to order and introduction of new project members.**, then press Tab.
   l. Continue keying the text and pressing Tab until the agenda is completed.
   m. Choose Table, then Select Table. Change the font to 12-point Book Antiqua.
   n. Position the insertion point in the first column of the table, then choose Table, then Select Column. Click the Bold button.
   o. Position the arrow pointer below the table, then click the left mouse button.
   p. Change the font to 18-point Book Antiqua Bold, then press Enter two times.
   q. Click the Center alignment button on the Standard toolbar.
   r. Create the three symbols (❖), spacing three times between each.
   s. Press Enter three times.
   t. Add the bottom border to the agenda by completing the following steps:
      (1) Display the Borders toolbar. (To do this, click the Borders button on the Formatting toolbar—the right-most button.)
      (2) Click the down-pointing triangle in the Shading button on the Borders toolbar.
      (3) From the drop-down menu that displays, click 30%.
   u. Press Ctrl + Home to move the insertion point to the top of the page.

v. Create the border at the top of the agenda by completing steps t2 and t3.

2. Save the agenda and name it c02ex06, table agenda.
3. Print and then close c02ex06, table agenda.

FIGURE 2.23

CHICAGO MERCY HOSPITAL **QUALITY CARE PROJECT**

❖ **AGENDA** ❖

9:00–9:30 a.m.	Call to order and introduction of new project members.	Becky Peterson, Chair
9:30–10:15 a.m.	Presentation of project mission statement.	Stanley Barnett
10:15–11:00 a.m.	Determination of project goals timelines.	Katrina O'Dell, Geoffrey Benn, and Wendy Mitaki
11:00–11:45 a.m.	Brainstorming on public relations activities.	Ellen Heitz and Hui Lenzi
11:45-12:00 Noon	Scheduling of next project meeting.	Becky Peterson, Chair
12:00 Noon	Adjournment.	Becky Peterson, Chair

Preparing A Press Release

A press release is prepared by a business for submission to a public agency such as a newspaper. It announces something special or new that is being offered by the business, or it may announce accomplishments or promotions of business people. In exercise 7, you will be creating a press release for Chicago Mercy Hospital announcing the construction of a new pediatrics wing.

Word contains three press release templates: Contemporary, Elegant, and Professional Press Releases. In exercise 7, you will create a press release with the Elegant Press Release template.

Preparing a Press Release

1. At a clear document screen, create the press release shown in figure 2.24 using a Word template by completing the following steps:
   a. Choose File, then New.
   b. At the New dialog box, select the Publications tab.
   c. Double-click the Elegant Press Release icon.
2. Read the information below the heading *HOW TO CUSTOMIZE THIS PRESS RELEASE* located in the body of the Elegant Template screen.
3. Select the default name located at the upper left corner of the press release, then key **CHICAGO MERCY HOSPITAL**.
4. Select the default text and then key the following information in the specified areas: (Include superscripted text as shown in the address.)

Address:	**708 North 42nd Street** **Chicago, IL 63209** **Phone (312) 555-2200** **Fax (312) 555-2086**
Contact:	**Your Name**
Phone:	**(312) 555-2200**
For Immediate Release:	**9 AM EDT, March 12, 1997**

5. Select the text from the heading *HOW TO CUSTOMIZE THIS PRESS RELEASE* to the end of the document, then key the text shown in figure 2.24.
6. Save the press release and name it c02ex07, press release.
7. Print and then close c02ex07, press release. (If your printer does not print the shaded area to your satisfaction, click the text area, then choose Format, and then Borders and Shading. At the Paragraph Borders and Shading dialog box, select a new shade or pattern, and then choose OK. Be sure to select the two different shaded areas.)

FIGURE 2.24

CHICAGO MERCY HOSPITAL

708 North 42nd Street
Chicago, IL 63209
Phone 312-555-2200
Fax 312-555-2086

Press Release

Contact: Your Name
Phone: (312) 555-2200

FOR IMMEDIATE RELEASE
9 AM EDT, March 12, 1997

NEW PEDIATRICS WING

Chicago, Illinois—Chicago Mercy Hospital announces a $3-million project to build a pediatrics wing on the north side of the hospital. Construction will begin at the end of this month and will be completed by the end of the year. The new wing will include 50 patient rooms and 10 family rooms, a children's physical therapy unit, and three operating rooms equipped with the latest medical technology. In a recent interview, Terry Kasuski, chief executive officer for Chicago Mercy, stated, "The construction of the new pediatrics wing reflects our strong commitment to providing the highest possible quality medical care to children in our community."

-End-

Preparing A Fax Cover Sheet

In the fast-paced business world of the 1990s, many businesses need to send information rapidly to customers, clients, or other businesses. To do this, many businesses use facsimile machines (faxes) to send information over telephone lines. When sending a fax, a cover sheet generally accompanies the fax identifying the name of the person to receive the fax, the subject of the fax, and the number of pages.

Word contains three fax cover sheet templates: Contemporary Fax, Elegant Fax, and Professional Fax. In exercise 8, you will be creating a fax cover sheet using the Contemporary Fax template.

Creating a Fax Cover Sheet

1. At a clear document window, create the fax cover sheet shown in figure 2.25 using a Word template by completing the following steps:
   a. Choose File, then New.
   b. At the New dialog box, select the Letters & Faxes tab.
   c. Double-click the Contemporary Fax icon.
   d. Point and click at the prompts that are similar to [Click **here** and type name]. Key the following information at each specific prompt:

(Upper right corner)	
[Click **here** and type address]	**1308 East River Street**
	St. Paul, MN 55101
	Fax: (612) 555-6901
To:	**Marie Finney**
Fax:	**(312) 555-4711**
From:	**Your name**
Date:	**Current date**
Re:	**Legal Contract**
Pages (including cover sheet):	**14**
CC:	**Kathy Nixon, Kevin Cohen, John Shea**

   e. Place a (✔) in the check boxes corresponding to Urgent, Please Reply, and Please Recycle. (The ✔ will replace the check box symbol.) Use the check mark symbol from the Symbol dialog box with the Monotype Sorts font selected. The symbol is located in the first row and the eighth column from the right. (You may want to make a shortcut command for this symbol or use Copy and Paste.)
   f. Key the following in the Notes section:

      Please read the legal document, sign both copies, then return one copy to me. Thank you.

2. Save the fax cover sheet and name it c02ex08, fax cover.
3. Print and then close c02ex08, fax cover.

FIGURE 2.25

1308 East River Street
St. Paul, MN 55101
Fax: (612) 555-6901

facsimile transmittal

To:	Marie Finney	**Fax:**	(312) 555-4711
From:	Your name	**Date:**	October 23, 1996
Re:	Legal Contract	**Pages:**	14
CC:	Kathy Nixon, Kevin Cohen, John Shea		

✓ Urgent ☐ For Review ☐ Please Comment ✓ Please Reply ✓ Please Recycle

Notes: Please read the legal document, sign both copies, then return one copy to me. Thank you.

CONFIDENTIAL

Chapter Summary

- A font consists of three characteristics: typeface, type style, and type size.
- The term *typeface* refers to the general design and shape of a set of characters.
- The typeface used in a document establishes a particular mood or feeling.
- Characteristics that distinguish one typeface from another include x-height, cap height, height of ascenders, depth of descenders, and serifs.
- A serif is a small stroke on the edge of characters. A sans serif typeface does not have serifs.
- Typefaces are either monospaced or proportional. Monospaced typefaces allot the same amount of horizontal space to each character, while proportional typefaces allot a varying amount to each character.
- Pitch is the number of characters that can be printed in one horizontal inch. The higher the pitch, the smaller the characters.
- Point size is a vertical measurement and is approximately 1/72 of an inch. The higher the point size, the larger the characters.
- Printer fonts are the built-in fonts and the supplemental fonts that are available to your printer. Supplemental fonts can be added to your printer in cartridge form or as soft fonts.
- At the Font dialog box, you can change the typeface, type size, and type style of text.
- For text set in a proportional typeface, space once after end-of-sentence punctuation.
- A number of template documents are provided by Word that can be used to produce a variety of documents. The default template document is the *Normal.dot.*
- A number of memo templates are available including Contemporary, Elegant, and Professional. A memo wizard is also available that guides you through the creation of a memo.
- A watermark is a lightened image that can be added to a document to add visual interest.
- One of the easiest ways to create a watermark in Word is to insert the watermark into a header or footer.
- Special symbols can be inserted in a document at the Symbol dialog box with the Symbols tab or the Special Characters tab selected.
- Bullets can be inserted in a document at the Bullets and Numbering dialog box or with the Bullets button on the Formatting toolbar.
- Word contains an agenda template that can be used to prepare an agenda.
- Tables can be used when formatting an agenda into side-by-side columns.
- Three press release templates are available in Word—Contemporary, Elegant, and Professional Press Releases.
- Three fax cover sheet templates are available in Word—Contemporary, Elegant, and Professional Faxes.

Commands Review

	Mouse/Keyboard Codes
Font dialog box	Format, Font; or press Ctrl + D
New dialog box	File, New
Header and Footer	View, Header and Footer
Drawing Object dialog box	Format, Drawing Object
Symbols dialog box	Insert, Symbol
AutoFormat	Choose Tools, Options, then select AutoFormat tab.
Bullets and Numbering dialog box	Format, Bullets and Numbering
Insert Table dialog box	Table, Insert Table

Check Your Understanding

Terms: Match the terms with the correct definitions by writing the letter of the term on the blank line in front of the correct definition.

A.	Baseline	**F.**	Cap height	**K.**	Type style
B.	Monospaced	**G.**	Point size	**L.**	Sans serif
C.	Serif	**H.**	x-height	**M.**	Typeface
D.	Descenders	**I.**	Roman	**N.**	Ascenders
E.	Point	**J.**	Proportional	**O.**	Font

_______ **1.** A set of characters with a common design and shape.

_______ **2.** Imaginary horizontal line on which text rests.

_______ **3.** Height of the main body of the lowercase characters and equivalent to the lowercase *x*.

_______ **4.** Distance between the baseline and the top of capital letters.

_______ **5.** Parts of lowercase characters that rise above the x-height.

_______ **6.** Parts of characters that extend below the baseline.

_______ **7.** Approximate distance from the top of the ascenders to the bottom of the descenders.

_______ **8.** A small stroke at the edge of characters.

_______ **9.** A typeface that does not contain serifs.

_______ **10.** Approximately 1/72 of an inch.

_______ **11.** Varying style of a typeface, including bold and italic.

_______ **12.** A typeface in a specific size and style.

True/False: Circle the letter T if the statement is true; circle the letter F if the statement is false.

T F 1. Proportional typefaces allot the same amount of horizontal space for each character in a typeface.

T F 2. An em dash is used to indicate a duration of time.

T F 3. When text is set in a proportional typeface, space once after end-of-sentence punctuation.

T F 4. The default template document is the *Main* template.

T F 5. Click the New button on the Standard toolbar to display the New dialog box.

T F 6. A watermark exists in the text layer of a document.

T F 7. Choose Format, then Bullets and Numbering to display the Bullets and Numbering dialog box.

T F 8. Press the Tab key to move the insertion point to the next cell in a table.

Skill Assessments

Assessment 1

1. At a clear document screen, create a memo using one of the memo templates or the memo wizard. Include the following information in the memo heading:

   To: **Amanda Wong**
   From: **Your name**
   Date: **Current date**
   Re: **Outpatient Survey**

2. Key the text shown in figure 2.26 in the memo.
3. Add an appropriate watermark.
4. Save the completed memo and name it c02sa01, survey memo.
5. Print and then close c02sa01, survey memo.

FIGURE 2.26

For the past six months, the members of the Outpatient Survey Team have been preparing a survey to gather data on the quality of patient care in the Outpatient Clinic. The information gathered from this survey will help us make positive changes in the services offered by the clinic. We are also interested in why patients choose the Outpatient Clinic rather than the traditional Surgical Unit.

Please read the enclosed survey and let me know what you feel should be changed or added. I would like to present the final draft of the survey to the team by next week. I will schedule a meeting with you later in the week to get your feedback.

XX:c02sa01

Enclosure

Assessment 2

1. At a clear document screen, create the agenda shown in figure 2.27 with the following specifications:
   a. Change the top margin to 1.5 inches and the left and right margins to 1 inch.
   b. Change the font to 24-point Colonna MT Bold.
   c. Set a right tab at 6.5 inches.
   d. Key ✧✧✧ **L. & D. INC.** (Create the special symbol ✧ at the Symbol dialog box with the Wingdings font selected. The symbol is located in the sixth row, seventh column.)
   e. Press Tab, then key **AGENDA ✧✧✧**.
   f. Press Enter twice, then key **BOARD OF DIRECTORS MEETING** centered.
   g. Turn off bold, change the alignment to Left Align, press Enter twice, then change the font to 14-point Book Antiqua.
   h. Create a table with three columns and seven rows. Adjust each column width to 2.22 inches with 0.15 inches in between. Change the Height of Rows 1 through 7 to At Least and At 56 points.
   i. Key the agenda text shown in figure 2.27.
   j. Position the arrow pointer below the table, click the left button, then press Enter three times.
   k. Change the font to 24-point Colonna MT Bold, then center and key the remaining symbols.
2. Save the agenda and name it c02sa02, board agenda.
3. Print and then close c02sa02, board agenda.

Optional: Insert an appropriate watermark that will enhance the appearance of the agenda.

FIGURE 2.27

✧✧✧ L. & D. INC. AGENDA ✧✧✧

BOARD OF DIRECTORS MEETING

8:00–8:15 a.m.	Introduction of Members	Scott Ingram, Chief Executive Officer
8:15–9:30 a.m.	Discussion of expansion into Canada	Suzanne Reiser, Director of Facilities Planning
9:30–10:15 a.m.	Discussion of expansion into Europe	Ryan Keyes, Assistant Director of Facilities
10:15–10:45 a.m.	Break	Refreshments served
10:45–11:30 a.m.	Review of short-term and long-term goals for 1997	Lucinda White, Vice President
11:30–12 :15 p.m.	Short-term and long-term goal setting for 1997	Francis Lewellyn, President
12:15 p.m.	Adjournment	Scott Ingram, Chief Executive Officer

Creative Activity

Situation: You work for a desktop publisher called Desktop Designs located at 4455 Jackson Drive, Raleigh, NC 27613; phone: (277) 555-2864; fax: (277) 555-2880; http://www.desktop.com. You have been asked by your supervisor to develop a press release describing the services performed by Desktop Designs. Use a Word template to create this press release and include the following information:

- Desktop Designs has been operating in the Raleigh area for over 12 years.
- The employees of Desktop Designs have over 30 years of combined graphics design and typesetting experience.
- The company provides a variety of services, including creating personal documents such as cover letters, résumés, invitations, programs, cards, envelopes and labels; creating business documents such as letterheads, envelopes, business cards, forms, logos, and slides; and creating promotional and marketing documents such as newsletters, flyers, and brochures.
- The company is open Monday through Saturday from 7:00 a.m. to 6:00 p.m.

After creating the press release, save it and name it c02ca01, press release. Print and then close c02ca01, press release.

3 CREATING LETTERHEADS, ENVELOPES, AND BUSINESS CARDS

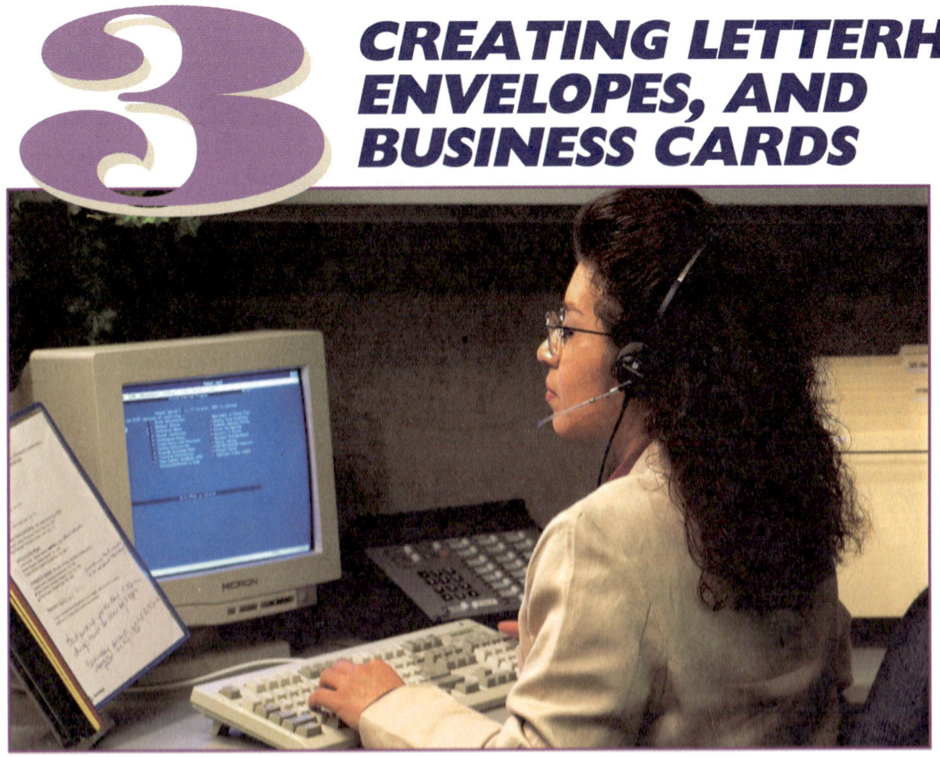

PERFORMANCE OBJECTIVE

Upon successful completion of chapter 3, you will be able to produce business letterheads, envelopes, and business cards using a variety of templates, fonts, and ruled lines.

DESKTOP PUBLISHING CONCEPTS

Identifying purpose
Design
Appropriate font selection
Templates
Styles
Use of horizontal and vertical lines
Exact placement of elements on a page
Kerning
Tracking
Graphic images

WORD FEATURES USED

Letter template
Template styles
Letter Wizard
Drawing Object Fill
Fonts
Drawing toolbar
Borders toolbar
Borders and shading
Frames
Symbols
Template folder
Automatic and manual kerning
Character spacing
Envelopes and Labels feature
AutoText
Picture
Business card label definition

In this chapter, you will produce business letterheads, envelopes, and business cards using your own design and creative skills as well as Word's Template feature. While Word provides a variety of letter templates to choose from, they do not meet the needs of all situations. Information on how to customize an existing template and how to create your own design and layout from scratch are presented in this chapter. Ruled lines, kerning (the spacing between specific pairs of letters), and tracking (character spacing), along with Word's Envelopes and Labels, Frames, and AutoText features, are also discussed.

Identifying The Purpose Of Letterheads

In planning your letterhead, clearly identify its purpose. While the content of a letter may vary, the purpose of any letterhead is generally the same—to convey information, to establish an identity, and to project an image.

Conveying Information

Consider all the necessary information you want to include in your letterhead. Also, consider what items your readers expect to find in your letterhead. Although the information provided may vary, letterheads commonly contain the following:

- name of company or organization
- logo
- very brief business philosophy statement, marketing statement, or slogan
- address
- shipping or mailing address, if different from street address
- telephone number, including area code (include actual numbers if your phone number incorporates a catchy word as part of the number; include extra phone numbers, such as a local number and/or an 800 number, if any)
- fax number, including area code
- e-mail address

The information in a letterhead supplies the reader with a means of contacting you in person, by phone, or by mail. Leaving out an important component in your letterhead can affect your company's business and project a careless attitude.

Establishing an Identity

DTP POINTERS
A letterhead conveys information, establishes an identity, and projects an image.

Oftentimes a business relationship is initiated through one or more business letters. For example, a buyer from one company may write to another company inquiring about a certain product or asking for a price list; a real estate agent may send out a letter explaining his or her services to residents in surrounding communities; or, your volunteer organization may send thank-you letters to local businesses. Whatever the reason for the letter content, a letterhead with a specific design and layout helps to establish your organization's identity. When readers are exposed to the same pattern of consistent elements in your letterhead over a period of time, they soon begin to establish a certain level of familiarity with your organization's name, logo, colors, etc. Your letterhead is recognizable and identifiable. You can further emphasize your company's identity by using some of the design elements from your letterhead in your other business documents. Many direct mail paper suppliers offer a whole line of attractively designed color letterheads, along with coordinating envelopes, business cards, brochures, postcards, note cards, disk labels, and more. All you have to do is design and lay out your letterhead text to complement the existing design and then print on the preprinted papers. Purchasing a coordinating line of preprinted papers can save on the high costs of professional designing and printing. It also provides a convenient way to establish your identity among your readers. Some paper suppliers offer a sample kit of their papers for purchase at a reasonable price. This is a great opportunity to see and feel the papers and to test some of them in your printer.

Projecting an Image

Along with establishing an identity, you need to think about the image that identity projects to your readers. As mentioned in chapter 1, assess your target audience. Who are your readers? Whom do you want to be your readers? What image do you want to project and what image do your readers expect you to project? Pretend that you have a folded letter in your hand from a bank. Without even looking at the letter, what image do you expect that letter to portray? Pretend, again, that in your other hand you have another folded letter from an old country inn. Without looking at that letter, what image comes to your mind? Are the two images the same or different? Most likely, you expect the bank's image to be more serious, conservative, formal, and businesslike. And you probably expect the old country inn's image to be more casual, informal, comfortable, and cozy. Figures 3.1 and 3.2 show examples of company names in different fonts.

DTP POINTERS
Printing on high-quality paper presents a professional image.

First Bank of Dupage

First Bank of DuPage

FIGURE 3.1

Which Typeface Best Projects the Image of a Bank?

Salem Country Inn

Salem Country Inn

FIGURE 3.2

Which Typeface Best Projects the Image of a Country Inn?

However, giving your readers what they expect can sometimes lead to boredom. Your challenge is to create a design that gives the readers what they expect and, at the same time, sets your letterhead apart from the rest.

Printing your letterhead on high-quality paper may add to the cost, but it certainly presents a more professional image. An off-white, ivory, cream, or gray paper is a better choice than plain white. You may have to go to a commercial printer to purchase this kind of paper. Many print shops let you buy paper by the sheet, along with matching envelopes.

Using Word's Letterhead Templates

As discussed in chapter 2, Word includes a variety of predesigned template documents, including letterheads. At the New dialog box, select the Letters & Faxes tab to display the following Word letter templates:

Letter Wizard.wiz (Helps you create a letter)
Contemporary Letter.dot
Elegant Letter.dot
Professional Letter.dot

DTP POINTERS
Establish identity and consistency among your internal and external business documents.

Notice that the descriptive letterhead names coordinate with the descriptive names for the memo and fax templates introduced in Chapter 2. This is an easy way for you to establish identity and consistency among both your internal and external business documents. For example, select Professional for your memo, fax, and letter template choices and all your documents will have matching elements. Even though you can view a template in the Preview box at the New dialog box, printing samples of your template documents lets you see firsthand what is available. The body of the template document also contains some valuable user information. To create a business letter based on the Professional Letter template, complete exercise 1.

Creating a Letter Using Word's Professional Letter Template

1. At a clear document screen, create the business letter shown in figure 3.3 using the Professional Letter template by completing the following steps:
   a. Choose File, then New.
   b. At the New dialog box, select the Letters & Faxes tab.
   c. Make sure that Document is selected in the Create New section and then double-click the Professional Letter icon in the Letters & Faxes tab (or click the template name, then click OK).
   d. Select Company Name Here, then key **Chicago Mercy Hospital**.
   e. Position the I-beam (not the arrow pointer) anywhere in the prompt that reads [Click **here** and type return address], click once to select this section, then key the following in the return address location:

      780 North 42nd Street
      Chicago, IL 63209
      (312) 555-2035
      Fax: (312) 555-2086

   f. Position the I-beam anywhere in the prompt that reads [Click **here** and type recipient's address], click once to select this section, then key the following as the inside address:

      Sylvia Hensley, M.D.
      Quality Care Program Director
      Allenmore Clinic
      1005 Seventh Avenue
      Chicago, IL 65145

   g. Position the I-beam anywhere in the prompt that reads [Click **here** and type recipient's name], click once to select this section, then key **Dr. Hensley** in the salutation location.
   h. Select the placeholder paragraph below the salutation, then key the body of the letter as shown in figure 3.3. (*Note:* Press the Enter key once after each paragraph, except the last paragraph. The Professional Letter template contains a paragraph spacing code that moves the insertion point down the appropriate amount of space when the Enter key is pressed.)
   i. After keying the body of the letter, create the complimentary close by completing the following steps:
      (1) Position the I-beam anywhere in the prompt that reads [Click **here** and type your name], click once to select this section, then key your name.

(2) Position the I-beam anywhere in the prompt that reads [Click **here** and type job title], click once to select this section, then key **Health Care Director**, then press Enter.
(3) Key your initials followed by **:c03ex01, letter**, then press Enter once.
(4) Select *Normal* from the Style list box located on the left side of the Formatting toolbar, and then press Enter. (This step is included to correct a spacing error problem in this template.)
(5) Key **Attachments**.

2. Save the completed letter and name it c03ex01, letter.
3. Print and then close c03ex01, letter.

FIGURE 3.3

Chicago Mercy Hospital

780 North 42nd Street
Chicago, IL 63209
(312) 555-2035
Fax: (312) 555-2086

April 2, 1996

Sylvia Hensley, M.D.
Quality Care Program Director
Allenmore Clinic
1005 Seventh Avenue
Chicago, IL 65145

Dear Dr. Hensley:

I am excited about the potential benefits of a community-oriented health care program and look forward to working with you. Attached is a copy of the letter of intent that we submitted for the health care program. Also attached is the response we received notifying us that we had been selected to receive further consideration for this special funding.

There is a meeting on May 10, from 1:30 to 3:00 p.m., in the conference room at Chicago Mercy Hospital. If you cannot personally attend the meeting, please send a designated representative from your clinic. After the meeting, we will pull together a work group to define the particular health care issues to be proposed in our grant application.

If you have any questions or comments on the attached material or the process being contemplated, please give me a call at 555-2035.

Sincerely,

(Your name here)
Health Care Director

xx:c03ex01, letter

Attachments

Understanding Template Styles

A template may include several components, such as styles, text, graphics, AutoText entries, and macros. As mentioned in the previous chapter, Word automatically bases a new document created at a blank screen on the *Normal.dot* template. This template initially contains five styles, including one called the *Normal* style. The Normal style contains formatting instructions to use 10-point Times New Roman as the font, English (US) as the language, flush left alignment, single spacing, and Widow/Orphan Control. Word automatically applies the Normal style to all paragraphs in your documents unless you give it other formatting instructions. Depending on the type of document that is being created, some templates often have additional styles. For example, the Professional Letter template used to create a letter in exercise 1 contains many styles. Styles are included for the body text, closing, date, enclosure, inside address, reference initials, salutation, and more. For example, if you open *c03ex01, letter*, and position the insertion point within the inside address, the Style box on the Formatting toolbar displays *Inside Address* as shown in figure 3.4. This means that a style named *Inside Address*, containing formatting instructions for the inside address, has been applied to this section of text. Additionally, if the insertion point is positioned in other sections of text in *c03ex01, letter*, you will see different style names displayed in the Style box on the Formatting toolbar. You may override any style formatting instructions by selecting text and making the desired changes at the normal editing window or by modifying the style itself. Styles are discussed in greater detail in Chapter 6.

FIGURE 3.4

Style Box on the Formatting Toolbar

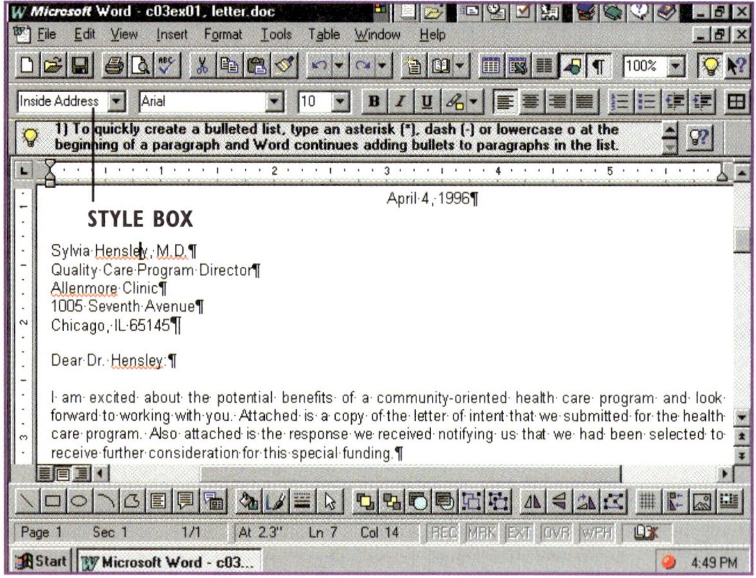

Using the Letter Wizard

Word provides a Letter Wizard that guides you through the steps for creating a letter. You may create a business letter, a personal letter, or a letter based on one of the 15 prewritten letters that are included in the Word program using either the Professional, Contemporary, or Elegant Letter template. You may use the prewritten letters as written, or you may change them to fit your situation. The Letter Wizard also gives you the opportunity to make an envelope or label for the letter being created.

Word's User Info feature is a way to store the name, initials, and address of the primary user of your Word program. Word automatically inserts this information in specific documents, such as letters, memos, and résumés, that are constructed with a Wizard. For example, the

Letter Wizard uses the Name listed in User Info in any of the letter closings it helps you create. However, it does not use this information if you select one of the letter templates from the New dialog box instead of using the Letter Wizard to create your letter. Word uses the Mailing Address from User Info as the default return address on envelopes. The Initials are used in conjunction with Word's Annotation feature—a feature that lets you leave notes to yourself or others in your document.

After constructing a document with a wizard or template, you can customize that document by adding or replacing text, inserting or replacing graphic images, and including formatting instructions to fit your needs. Complete exercise 2 to create a Contemporary letter using the Letter Wizard and a prewritten letter. You will then customize the letter by changing the shading of some of the graphic elements included in the template.

Creating a Contemporary Letter with the Letter Wizard and a Prewritten Letter

1. At a clear document screen, enter User Info by completing the following steps:
   a. Choose Tools, then Options.
   b. At the Options dialog box, select the User Info tab.
   c. Key your name at the Name list box. (Do not take the time to change the Initials or Mailing Address. This information will not be used by the Letter Wizard.)
   d. Click OK.
2. Use the Letter Wizard to create the business letter shown in figure 3.5 using the Contemporary Letter style and a prewritten letter by completing the following steps:
   a. Choose File, then New.
   b. At the New dialog box, select the Letter & Faxes tab.
   c. Make sure that Document is selected in the Create New section, then double-click the Letter Wizard icon in the Letters & Faxes tab (or click the wizard, then click OK).
   d. At the Letter Wizard dialog box, make sure Select a prewritten business letter is selected, then choose Next.
   e. In the Select the letter you want list box, select *Thank you: for applying*, then click Next.
   f. Make sure that Plain paper is selected, then click Next.
   g. Key the recipient's name and address as follows:

      Mr. George Peraza
      Assistant Director, Health Services
      Chicago Mercy Hospital
      780 North 42nd Street
      Chicago, IL 63209

   h. Select any existing text in the return address, key the return address as follows, then click Next:

      (Your name here)
      Director of Human Resources
      Worldwide Health Services
      893 Renquist Avenue
      Chicago, IL 65068

i. Select Contemporary as the letter style, then click Next.
j. Make sure that Just display the letter is selected, then click Finish.

3. Complete the Contemporary Letter document created by the Letter Wizard by completing the following steps:
   a. Position the I-beam pointer anywhere in the prompt [Type Company Name], click once to select it, then key **Worldwide Health Services**.
   b. In the salutation, position the I-beam anywhere in the prompt that reads [Name], click once to select it, then key **Mr. Peraza**.
   c. In the first paragraph in the body of the letter, select *Costoso, Ltd*, click the Underline button on the Formatting toolbar to turn underline off, then key **Worldwide Health Services**.
   d. In the second paragraph of the letter, select *one year*, turn underline off, then key **six months**.
   e. Position the insertion point after *Human Resources Manager* in the letter closing, press Enter, then key **XX:c03ex02, letter**.
   f. Scroll down to the gray shaded rectangle located at the bottom of the document. Position the mouse pointer inside the rectangle until it displays as an I-beam, click once to display the text box that exists in this area, then key **Serving those in need around the globe!** (If the slogan displays on two lines, select the text box containing the slogan, then use the sizing handle located at the right side of the box to increase the width of the box.)
4. Darken the gray shading in the rectangular boxes located at the top and bottom of the Contemporary Letter document by completing the following steps:
   a. Position the I-beam pointer in the gray shaded rectangle containing the company name at the top of the letter until it turns into an arrow with a four-pointing arrow attached, then click once. (This selects the box and displays sizing handles.)
   b. Choose Format, then Drawing Object.
   c. At the Drawing Object dialog box, select the Fill tab.
   d. In the Color section, click 25% gray (second row, third box from the left), then click OK.
   e. Position the I-beam pointer in the gray shaded rectangle located at the bottom of the letter until it turns into an arrow with a four-pointing arrow attached, then click once. (This selects the box and displays sizing handles.)
   f. Repeat the steps in 4b through 4d to darken the gray shading to 25%.
5. Darken the gray shading in the globe graphic image by completing the following steps:
   a. Position the I-beam pointer on any part of the globe graphic image until it turns into an arrow with a four-pointing arrow attached, then double-click the left mouse button. (This inserts the globe into Microsoft Word Picture where the image can be edited.)
   b. Position the mouse pointer at the left side of the globe, then click once to select it.
   c. Choose Format, then Drawing Object; or right-click once then select Format Drawing Object from the shortcut menu.
   d. At the Drawing Object dialog box, select the Fill tab.
   e. In the Color section, click 25% gray (second row, third box from the left), then click OK.
   f. Select the right side of the globe and repeat steps 5c through 5e.
   g. Click Close Picture in the Picture dialog box to return to your document.
6. Save the completed letter and name it c03ex02, letter.
7. Print and then close c03ex02, letter.

FIGURE 3.5

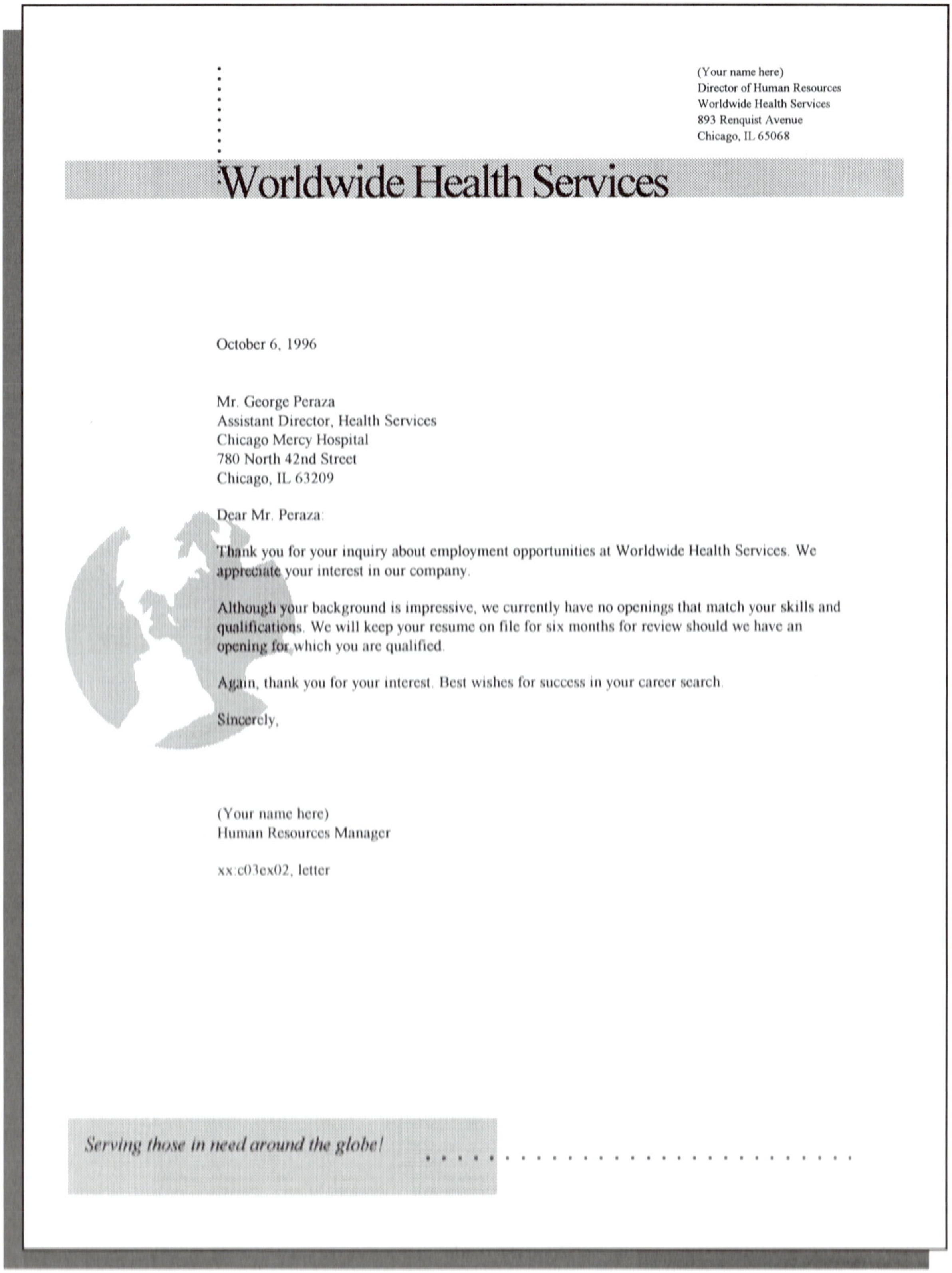

(Your name here)
Director of Human Resources
Worldwide Health Services
893 Renquist Avenue
Chicago, IL 65068

Worldwide Health Services

October 6, 1996

Mr. George Peraza
Assistant Director, Health Services
Chicago Mercy Hospital
780 North 42nd Street
Chicago, IL 63209

Dear Mr. Peraza:

Thank you for your inquiry about employment opportunities at Worldwide Health Services. We appreciate your interest in our company.

Although your background is impressive, we currently have no openings that match your skills and qualifications. We will keep your resume on file for six months for review should we have an opening for which you are qualified.

Again, thank you for your interest. Best wishes for success in your career search.

Sincerely,

(Your name here)
Human Resources Manager

xx:c03ex02, letter

Serving those in need around the globe!

The Letter Wizard remembers the choices you made during the letter creation process. It automatically uses these same choices the subsequent times you select the Letter Wizard. By simply changing the recipient's name and address, you can create similar but personalized letters.

After printing the Contemporary style business letter created in exercise 2 (figure 3.5), compare it with the Professional style business letter created in exercise 1 (figure 3.3). In exercise 1 (Professional style), the company name, set in 16-point Arial Black, provides the only real focal point on the page. The reader is able to readily identify the name of the company. Notice how this focal element draws the reader's eyes to the natural starting position for reading (upper left corner of the page) and initiates the directional flow in the letter. The larger and bolder company name leads the eye to the block of text containing the return address, set in 7-point Arial. The date, inside address, body text, and closing continue to direct the flow down the page. Word's Professional style letter is very straightforward and conservative in its layout and design.

In contrast, the letter created in exercise 2 employs more contemporary design elements. The eye is immediately drawn to the gray shaded text box containing the company name, which is set in 30-point Times New Roman. The text box provides directional flow to the right side of the page. The globe watermark acts as a secondary focal point that draws the eye back over to the left side of the page and to the body text. The gray shaded text box located in the bottom left corner of the page leads the reader down to the bottom of the page and over to the right. The horizontal dotted line provides a finishing touch, leading the reader to the bottom right corner of the page. Can you visualize a form of the Z directional flow pattern mentioned in Chapter 1 in this letter's design and layout? Consistent elements are exemplified by the repeated use of the same typeface, the gray shaded text boxes, the gray shading of the watermark, and the dotted lines. This letter utilizes several examples of asymmetrical design. The vertical dotted line along with the accompanying white space to the left help to balance the block of text containing the return address. Also note that the white space provided by the wider left margin and the globe watermark extending into the left margin counterbalance the larger block of letter text. In addition, the horizontal dotted line and the surrounding white space located at the bottom of the page serve as balancing contrasting elements to the gray shaded box containing the slogan.

DTP POINTERS
Asymmetrical design adds interest and impact.

Word's template documents are definitely an easy and convenient way to create a variety of professional-looking documents, but they cannot meet the needs of all people, companies, or organizations in all situations. However, templates can serve as the framework for creating customized documents. A document created from a template can be individualized, an existing template can be edited permanently, or a whole new template can be created from an existing document or from scratch. Designing your own letterhead is also possible. Designing your own letterhead lets you create your own identity and image while cutting costs at the same time. In upcoming exercises, you will have the chance to create a letterhead from scratch and to convert the letterhead into a template.

Designing Your Own Letterhead

When it comes to designing a letterhead, you might ask yourself, "Isn't this where the commercial printer takes over? Doesn't everyone have their letterhead designed and created by a commercial printer?" Obviously, a lot of businesses have their letterheads created professionally. However, there are distinct cost-saving advantages to creating your own letterheads.

Smaller businesses and newly created businesses may not have the financial resources to purchase a letterhead designed by a graphic designer and created by a printer. Not only is a custom design costly, but using more than one color on a page adds to the expense (and black is counted as one color!). With the lower-cost laser and color ink jet printers available today and your Word software, you can create very professional-looking letterheads at a much lower cost. In addition, when working with a commercial printer, you would probably be required to meet a minimum purchase order. If you produce your own letterhead, you can print any amount you need and save yourself the upfront costs of purchasing a large number of letterheads. Also, as long as you have a supply of paper (and your equipment is not temperamental!), your letterhead is always only a few keystrokes away. Second sheets to go along with your letterhead are readily available, too. All things considered, designing and producing your own letterhead is a cost-effective alternative to having it created through an outside source.

Designing and producing your own letterhead takes some time and practice. When you have completed the planning stage for your letterhead and you are actually ready to "create" the design, get out pencil and paper and make some thumbnail sketches. This is a great way to experiment with your layout and design without your software interfering with the creative process, as we all know it can from time to time!

DTP POINTERS
Designing takes time and practice.

When creating your thumbnail sketches and, ultimately, your letterhead, think of the following design concepts as presented in chapter 1:

- *Focus:* What is the focal point(s) in your letterhead? What is the most important information? What is the least important information? Is there more than one focal element? If so, is there a natural progression from one to the other?
- *Balance:* Is your layout and design symmetrical (similar elements distributed evenly on the page, such as a horizontally centered layout)? Or is it asymmetrical (dissimilar elements distributed unevenly on the page in such a way as to balance one another out)?
- *Proportion:* Are the design elements used in proportion to one another? Is the type size of the company name in proportion to the company logo? To the other letterhead information? To the type size that will be used for the body text? Is the size indicative of importance?
- *Contrast:* Are there varying degrees of lightness and darkness? Is there enough surrounding white space assigned to darker elements on the page? Does the typeface used in the letterhead provide a complementary contrast to the typeface that will be used in the body text? Does the use of color provide a pleasing contrast?
- *Directional flow:* Are the design elements strategically placed to create a natural flow of information? Is the reader able to logically progress from the more important information to the less important information? Do text, special characters, ruled lines, and graphic images direct the flow rather than impede the flow of information?
- *Consistency:* Are there any elements of your page layout and design that are consistent? Is a particular typeface consistently used in your letterhead even though it may vary in type size, type style, or color? Is one color repeated sparingly to emphasize important or distinctive elements (called "spot" color)? Is there some repeating element that ties the letterhead to subsequent pages, such as a ruled horizontal line that is repeated as a footer on each page?
- *Color:* Does the use and intensity of color relate proportionally to the importance of the item? Is color used sparingly to provide emphasis and contrast? Does the color used meet readers' expectations?

Creating Horizontal and Vertical Ruled Lines Using Word Draw

Ruled Lines: Horizontal or vertical lines.

Word has a feature that lets you set horizontal and/or vertical lines anywhere on a page. In addition, you can adjust the length and width, color, and shading of the lines. In typesetting, these horizontal and vertical lines are called *rules, ruling lines,* or *ruled lines* to distinguish them from lines of type. Horizontal and vertical ruled lines are used in a document to guide readers across and/or down the page, to separate one section of text from another, to separate columns of text, or to add visual interest.

DTP POINTERS
Ruled lines act as boundaries to surrounding text.

Remember that ruled lines act as boundaries to the surrounding text. A thicker line serves as more of a barrier than a thinner line. For example, a thin vertical line separating columns of text tends to keep the reader's eyes from jumping over to the next column. Alternately, a thicker ruled line between columns tends to tell the reader that the information in one column is entirely separate from the information in the next column. Keep this same idea in mind when considering using ruled lines with headings. Ruled lines should be placed above the heading rather than below the heading. This way the reader knows that the heading belongs to the text that follows it. In addition, when using ruled lines, be consistent in their purpose and their appearance.

Use Word's Draw program to create horizontal and vertical ruled lines. To use the Draw program, the Drawing toolbar must be displayed. The Drawing toolbar is one of the predefined toolbars provided by Word. To turn on the display of the toolbar, choose one of the following methods:

Drawing

- Click the Drawing button on the Standard toolbar.
- Choose View, then Toolbars, click Drawing (this inserts a check mark in the check box), then choose OK or press Enter.
- Position the arrow pointer in any gray area of any currently displayed toolbar, click the right mouse button, then click Drawing at the drop-down menu.

When you select the Drawing toolbar, the toolbar appears at the bottom of the screen above the Status bar. The Drawing toolbar and the names of each button are shown in figure 3.6.

FIGURE 3.6
Drawing Toolbar

LINE
RECTANGLE
ELLIPSE
ARC
FREEFORM
TEXT BOX
CALLOUT
FORMAT CALLOUT
FILL COLOR
LINE COLOR
LINE STYLE
SELECT DRAWING OBJECTS
BRING TO FRONT
SEND TO BACK
BRING IN FRONT OF TEXT
SEND BEHIND TEXT
GROUP
UNGROUP
FLIP HORIZONTAL
FLIP VERTICAL
ROTATE RIGHT
RESHAPE
SNAP TO GRID
ALIGN DRAWING OBJECTS
CREATE PICTURE
INSERT FRAME

To insert a straight horizontal or vertical ruled line in a document using the Drawing toolbar, first change the viewing mode to the Page Layout viewing mode. If you do not, Word will prompt you to change to Page Layout when you click a button on the Drawing toolbar. Click the Line button (the first button) on the Drawing toolbar. Position the crosshairs at the desired starting point of your horizontal or vertical line. To create a perfect horizontal or vertical line, hold down the Shift key and the left mouse button, drag the mouse horizontally or vertically to create the line length of your choice, then release the mouse button and the

Shift key when done. (Ragged or imperfect lines are created when the Shift key is not pressed during the drawing process.) This same procedure may also be used to create perfect diagonal lines at 30-, 45-, or 60-degree angles. To display the crosshairs continuously to draw additional lines, double-click on the Line button, and then draw any number of lines. Click anywhere on the page or click a button on the Drawing toolbar to discontinue line drawing.

In typesetting, the thickness of a line, called its *weight*, is measured in points. Word defaults to a line thickness of 0.75 points. You can select different line styles and weights from the Line Style palette, shown in figure 3.7, that displays when you click the Line Style button (the eleventh button from the left) on the Drawing toolbar.

Weight: Describes the thickness of a line.

FIGURE 3.7

Line Style Options

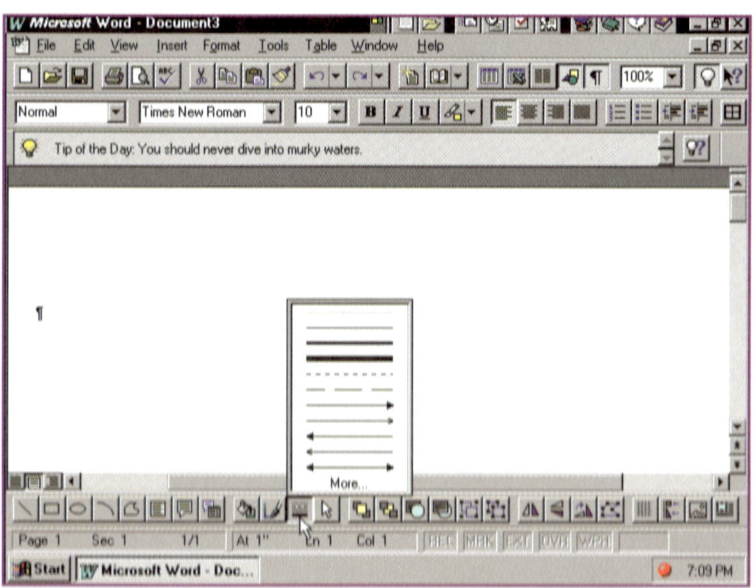

To have more control over the appearance of your line, you can select More from the Line Style palette to display the Drawing Object dialog box. From this dialog box with the Line tab chosen, you can enter a point measurement to determine the weight (thickness) of a horizontal or vertical ruled line. The most recent line weight and line style information is used as the default for the next line you choose to draw. For example, if you just drew a red line, the next line drawn will also be red unless you change the color. When entering a point measurement, key the point number followed immediately by *pt*. The letters *pt* tell Word that the number is a point measurement. Figure 3.8 shows horizontal ruled lines at varying point sizes (weights).

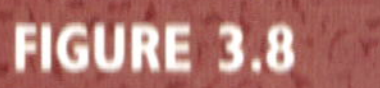

FIGURE 3.8

Varying Weights of Horizontal Lines

To change the color of a horizontal or vertical line created with the Line button, use the Drawing toolbar. Click the Line Color button (the tenth button from the left) on the Drawing toolbar to display the Line Color palette, shown in figure 3.9. Or you can change the line color by accessing the Drawing Object dialog box. Your most recent line color choice is used as the default for the next line you choose to draw.

FIGURE 3.9

Line Color Palette Options

Horizontal or vertical ruled lines created in Draw, called *objects*, can be customized. To edit or change an object, you must first select it. To do this, position the I-beam pointer on the line to be edited until it turns into an arrow pointer with a four-headed arrow attached, and then click the left mouse button. This causes the line to be selected and to display with sizing handles (square boxes) at each end of the line. Once the line is selected, you can use the mouse to change the length and location of the line. To change the length of the line, position the arrow pointer on either sizing handle (depending on the direction you want to increase or decrease the line) until it turns into cross hairs. Hold down the Shift key and the left mouse button, drag the cross hairs in the appropriate direction until the line is the desired length, and then release the mouse button. The length of a line may be controlled more precisely at the Drawing Object dialog box. To do this, position the I-beam pointer on the line until it turns into an arrow with a four-headed arrow attached, and then double-click the left mouse button. At the Drawing Object dialog box, choose the Size and Position tab. Key the desired length of the line in the Width list box. You can also access the Drawing Object dialog box by selecting the line first, then choosing Format, and then Drawing Object.

To change the location of the line with the mouse, position the I-beam pointer on the line until it turns into an arrow with a four-headed arrow attached. Hold down the left mouse button, drag the outline of the object to the new location, then release the mouse button. To have more precise control over the line's location on the page, you can also change the location of a line at the Drawing Object dialog box. With the Size and Position tab selected, you can specify the distance you want the object positioned horizontally from the margin, page, or column. You can also specify the vertical distance for the object relative to the margin, page, or paragraph. Using either method places a line at a specific location on the page. If surrounding text is edited, the line location may need to be readjusted.

To change the thickness or weight of the line, you must access the Drawing Object dialog box. To do this with the mouse, position the I-beam pointer on the line until it turns into an arrow with a four-headed arrow attached, and then double-click the left mouse button. At the Drawing Object dialog box, make sure the Line tab is selected, then key the desired thickness in the Weight list box.

Creating Horizontal Lines Using the Borders Toolbar

Borders

Word's Borders feature can be used to add horizontal or vertical lines in headers and/or footers, as well as to any other text. Every paragraph you create in Word contains an invisible frame. (Remember that a paragraph may contain text or it may only consist of a hard return.) A border can be added to the frame that appears around a paragraph. In addition, a border can be added to specific sides of a paragraph. Consequently, you can add a border above or below a paragraph to create a horizontal line. A ruled line created with the borders feature stays with the paragraph that was current when the feature was applied.

To create a border, click on the Borders button on the Formatting toolbar to display the Borders toolbar and its options, as shown in figure 3.10. The Line Style option, located at the left side of the Borders toolbar, contains a variety of choices for changing the thickness or style of the border. You can make the border line thicker or choose a double, dotted, or dashed line. You can even select different line styles for specific sides of the border. Select the Top Border button to create a horizontal line above the current paragraph or select the Bottom Border button to insert a horizontal line below the current paragraph. Select the left Border button to insert a vertical line on the left side of the current paragraph, or select the right Border button to insert a vertical line on the right side of the current paragraph. For example, you can add a line below text in a header or add a line above text in a footer. This line acts as a graphic element that separates the header/footer text from the rest of the text and adds visual appeal to the document.

You can further customize a border by choosing Format, then Borders and Shading. With the Borders tab selected at the Borders and Shading dialog box, additional options exist to change the border line color, the border location, the border style, and the distance between border and text. The length of a horizontal line created with the Borders feature can only be adjusted from the right side. To do this, position the insertion point in the paragraph that contains the border, then drag the right margin marker on the Ruler Bar to the left until the line is the desired length. Even though you can create a variety of customized horizontal and vertical lines with the Borders feature, you have more flexibility when creating lines with the Draw program. The Draw program has the ability to create both horizontal and vertical lines, to change the color of a line, to easily change the size of a line, and to place a line at an exact location on a page.

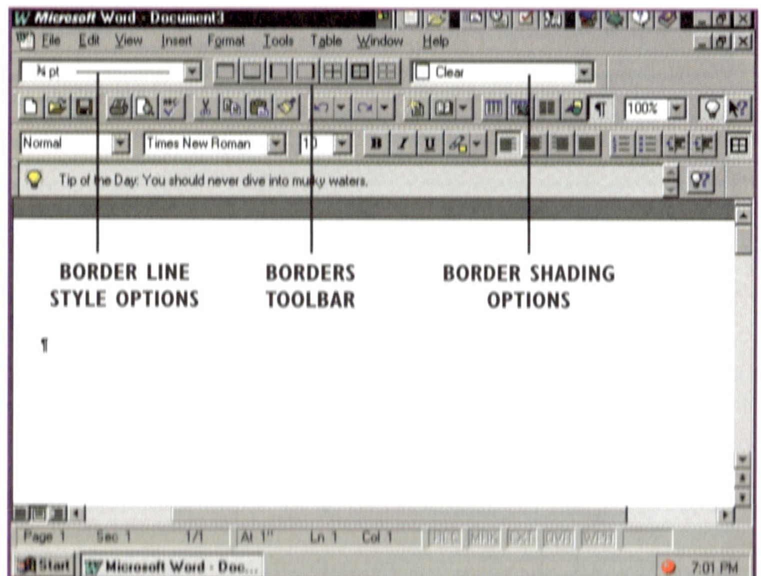

FIGURE 3.10

Borders Toolbar

Placing Text At Specific Locations On A Page Using The Frame Feature

When creating desktop-published documents, there is often a need to place design elements at specific locations on a page. The Enter key and the space bar are ways of moving the insertion point on the page, but they may not give you the exact location desired. For example, pressing the Enter key one time after a line of text or a design element may not allow enough white space, but pressing Enter two times may allow too much white space. Adjustments to the spacing before and after a paragraph (or hard return) can be made at the Paragraph dialog box; however, paragraph spacing adjustments affect vertical spacing of text only. The space bar and the tab function in Word can place text in specific locations horizontally across the page, but have no effect on vertical placement. In addition, the tab function works best with text as opposed to graphic elements.

DTP POINTERS
Use the frame feature to place design elements at specific locations in the text layer.

Word has a great formatting feature, known as a *frame*, that enables you to place design elements, including text, at precise locations on a page. When an item is enclosed in a frame, you can drag the frame to a different position in the document using the mouse, or you can specify a measurement at the Frame dialog box. This feature is extremely useful in desktop publishing because it lets you align design elements on a page, allows just the right amount of white space around elements, and helps fit text and other design elements into a specific amount of space (called copy fitting) on a page.

DTP POINTERS
A text box operates in the drawing layer and can be layered, flipped, or rotated.

A frame may seem similar to a text box, which is created through the Drawing toolbar. However, there are some important differences. As mentioned in chapter 2, text automatically wraps around a frame but not around a text box. A frame resizes itself when text is added or deleted, whereas a text box does not. The biggest advantage of using a text box instead of a frame is that a text box is created in the drawing layer and is considered a drawing object. Therefore, a text box (whether it contains text or a picture) can be placed above or below the main text (created in the text layer) in a Word document. A frame is created in the text layer and cannot be layered in front of or behind other text, objects, or frames. Because a text box is a drawing object, the text box itself (not the contents) can be flipped or rotated. A frame cannot be flipped or rotated.

Framing Text

A frame can be inserted around selected text or a picture. The frame is sized automatically to the text or picture. To insert a frame around existing text, change the viewing mode to Page Layout, select the text to be framed, then choose Insert, then Frame. When you insert a frame, the frame is automatically selected so that you can size and position it if necessary. A selected frame displays with a border of diagonally slanting lines and black square sizing handles as shown in figure 3.11.

FIGURE 3.11

A Selected Frame

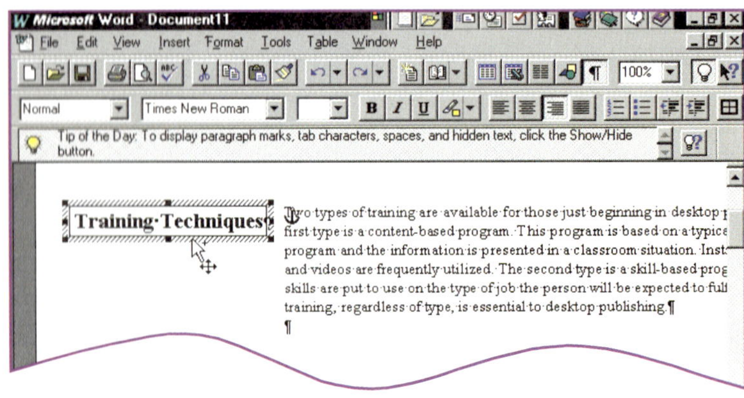

A frame inserted around selected text assumes the size of the text. If text is inserted or deleted, the frame changes to accommodate the text size. The frame inserted around text contains a single-line border around all sides. A frame inserted around a picture does not contain border lines.

Drawing a Frame

When framing text or a picture, the frame is positioned around the object you are framing. In addition to framing an object, you can draw a frame in a document. You can draw a frame in a document to hold a spot for something to be inserted, such as a photograph, or you can draw a frame in a specific location in a document then insert text or a picture. To draw a frame in a document, change to the Page Layout viewing mode, then choose Insert, then Frame. Position the arrow pointer, which displays as cross hairs, where you want the top left corner of the frame to appear, hold down the left mouse button, drag the outline of the frame to the location where you want the lower right corner of the frame to appear, then release the mouse button.

Sizing a Frame

The size and position of a frame can be changed using the mouse or options in the Frame dialog box. With either method, you must first select the frame. To do this, position the I-beam pointer on any line of the frame until it becomes an arrow pointer with a four-headed arrow attached, then click the left mouse button. This selects the frame and adds sizing handles to the frame.

Using the Mouse.

Once the frame has been selected, you can use the mouse in combination with the sizing handles to change the size of the frame. To make a frame wider or thinner, position the arrow pointer on the middle sizing handle at the left or right side of the frame until it turns into a double-headed arrow pointing left or right. Hold down the left mouse button, drag the double-headed arrow to the left or right until the frame is the desired size, then release the mouse button. Complete similar steps using the middle sizing handles at the top or bottom of the frame to make the frame taller or shorter. Change both the width and the height of the frame at the same time with the corner sizing handles.

If you change the size of a frame around a picture using the sizing handles, the size of the picture is also changed. However, when a frame around text is changed, the size of the text does not change.

Using Options in the Frame Dialog Box.

If you want to precisely size a frame, use options from the Frame dialog box shown in figure 3.12. To display this dialog box, select a frame, then choose Format, then Frame.

FIGURE 3.12

Frame Dialog Box

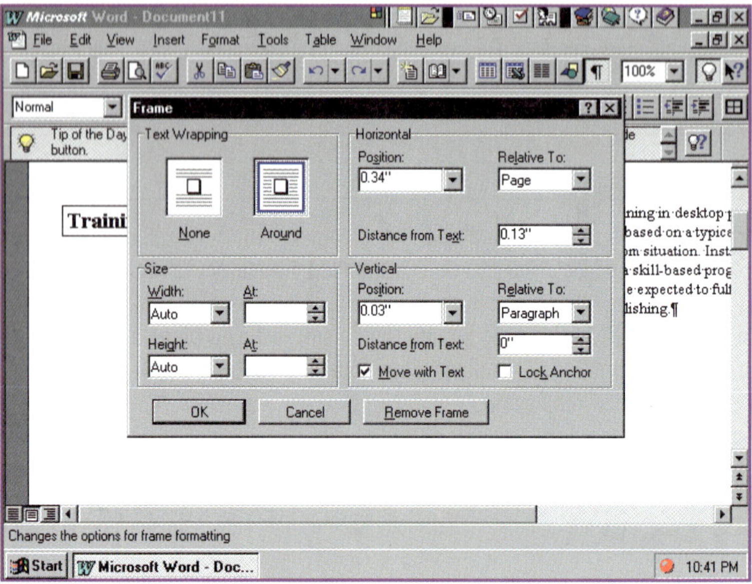

With options in the Size section of the Frame dialog box, you can enter specific measurements for the width and height of the frame. If you have not sized the frame at the document screen, the Width and Height options have a default setting of Auto.

If you want to specify an exact width measurement for a frame, choose Width. From the drop-down menu that displays, choose *Exactly*. Choose At, then key the desired measurement. If you are using the mouse, you can click the up- or down-pointing triangle after the At text box to specify the width measurement.

Make changes to the Height option in a similar manner. By default, the height is determined automatically either by the amount of text in the frame or the size of the picture.

If you change the size of a frame surrounding a picture at the Frame dialog box, the picture size does not change. After changing the size of the frame, you can then use the sizing handles around the picture to change the size of the picture to fill the frame.

Positioning a Frame at a Specific Location on the Page

Using the Mouse.

DTP POINTERS
Change the display to whole page when repositioning a frame.

One of the biggest advantages to framing text or a picture is the ability to reposition the frame in the document. To reposition framed text using the mouse, position the I-beam pointer on any side of the text frame (for a framed picture, position the I-beam inside the picture) until it turns into an arrow pointer with a four-headed arrow attached. Hold down the left mouse button, drag the outline of the frame to the desired location, then release the mouse button.

When repositioning text or a picture in a frame, changing the page display to Whole Page is helpful so that you can see the entire page on the screen. Select the frame, reposition it, then return the display back to 100%.

Using Options from the Frame Dialog Box.

To precisely position a frame on a page, use options from the Frame dialog box. When a frame is inserted around text or a picture, the frame is automatically positioned horizontally at the left side of the document. This horizontal position can be changed with the Position option in the Horizontal section of the Frame dialog box. When you choose Position, a drop-down menu displays with *Left*, *Right*, *Center*, *Inside*, and *Outside* options. Where the frame is positioned when choosing one of these options is determined by the setting at the Relative To: option.

If Relative To: is set at *Margin*, choosing *Left* in the Position option aligns the frame horizontally at the left margin, *Right* aligns the frame at the right margin, *Center* aligns the frame between the left and right margins, *Inside* aligns the frame inside the margin and *Outside* aligns the frame outside the margin.

If Relative To: is set at *Page*, choosing *Left* in the Position option aligns the frame horizontally at the left edge of the page, *Right* aligns the frame at the right edge of the page, *Center* aligns the frame between the left and right edges of the page, *Inside* aligns the frame at the left side of odd-numbered pages and the right side of even-numbered pages, and *Outside* aligns the frame at the right side of odd-numbered pages and the left side of even-numbered pages.

If Relative To: is set at *Column*, the Position options will align the frame relative to the columns.

Use the Distance from Text option to specify the amount of space you want to appear between the frame and the text on the left and right sides.

At the Relative To: option in the Vertical section of the Frame dialog box, you can specify if you want the frame positioned relative to the page, margin, or paragraph.

Choose *Top*, *Bottom*, or *Center* at the Position option in the Vertical section to determine the position of the frame in relationship to the page, margin, or paragraph. You can also enter an exact measurement in the Position text box if *Top*, *Bottom*, or *Center* are not appropriate choices.

Anchoring a Frame

By default, a frame is anchored to the nearest paragraph. When a frame is inserted in a document, an anchor symbol displays to the left of the paragraph to which the frame is anchored. If a frame is repositioned, the anchor moves to the paragraph closest to the frame. To view this anchor, click the Show/Hide ¶ button on the Standard toolbar to turn on the display of nonprinting characters, and then select the frame.

Anchor: A connection between a frame and the nearest paragraph that causes the frame to move with the paragraph.

A frame always appears on the same page as the paragraph to which it is anchored. By default, if you move a paragraph to which a frame is anchored, the frame moves with the paragraph. If you want a frame to stay in a specific spot and not move with the paragraph to which it is anchored, you would choose Format, then Frame to display the Frame dialog box, then remove the check mark from the Move with Text option and the Lock Anchor option.

A frame's anchor can be moved to another paragraph without moving the frame itself. Consequently, a frame can be anchored to a paragraph that is not the nearest paragraph to the frame. To move an anchor, make sure the Page Layout viewing mode and the display of nonprinting characters is turned on, then select the frame. Position the I-beam pointer on the anchor icon until the pointer turns into an arrow with a four-headed arrow attached. Hold down the left mouse button, drag the anchor icon to the desired paragraph, then release the left mouse button. When you move an anchor icon, the frame does not move. However, if the paragraph containing the anchor is moved to another page, the frame will move also.

Wrapping Text Around a Frame

By default, text in a document will wrap around a frame. If you do not want text to wrap around a frame in a document, display the Frame dialog box, then choose None in the Text Wrapping section. If you had turned off wrapping and then decided to turn it back on, choose Around.

Removing a Frame

To remove a frame around text or a picture, select the frame or picture, display the Frame dialog box, then choose Remove Frame. The frame is removed leaving the text or the picture. To delete a frame and its contents, select the frame, then press the Delete key.

Customizing a Frame Border

By default, a frame inserted around text and an empty frame contain a single-line border around all sides. A frame inserted around a graphic/picture defaults to no borders. However, a border can be added or removed around a frame at any time through the Paragraph Borders and Shading dialog box or the Borders toolbar.

To customize or add a border to framed text or a framed picture, position the insertion point inside the frame and click the left mouse button once to select the framed object. Choose Format, then Borders and Shading. With the Borders tab selected, choose Box or Shadow in the Presets section to add a border. If desired, change the border line weight or style by selecting one of the choices in the Style list box. To change the color of the border, click the down-pointing triangle in the Color section and make a selection from the drop-down menu of color choices.

DTP POINTERS
Customize borders by changing the line style, thickness, color and location.

A border can be further customized by adding or deleting a border line from specific sides of a frame. At the preview page in the Border section of the dialog box, you can add or remove a border line. To do this, position the arrow pointer on the side of the preview page where you want to add or remove a border, then click the left mouse button. The line style may be changed for specific sides of the frame in a similar manner.

Many of the same changes can be made to a frame border by using options on the Borders toolbar. Options for changing the border line color and to create a shadow style border are not available through the Borders toolbar.

In addition, shading can be added to framed text. With the Shading tab selected at the Paragraph Borders and Shading dialog box, choose an option in the Shading list box to add shading or a pattern. With the Foreground option, you can select the color of the dots or lines that make up the shading pattern. Choose Background to select a color option for the background color of the shading pattern. In the Shading list box, choose Clear to apply the selected background color. Choose Solid to apply the selected foreground color. Creating custom colors at the Paragraph Borders and Shading dialog box is also possible. For example, to create a purple color, choose Format, then Borders and Shading. At the Borders and Shading dialog box, select the Shading tab. Click the down-pointing arrow in the Foreground list box, then select red. In the Shading list box, select 50%. Click the down-pointing arrow in the Background list box and select blue. The Preview box will display the resulting color.

Similarly, framed text can be shaded by clicking the down-pointing triangle in the Shading list box on the Borders toolbar and then making a selection.

Creating a Letterhead with Horizontal and Vertical Lines Using the Frame Feature

1. At a clear document screen, create the letterhead shown in figure 3.13 by completing the following steps:
   a. Change the left margin to 2.25 inches and the right margin to 1 inch.
   b. Press Enter twice.
   c. Key the following text, pressing Enter the number of times indicated:

Desktop (press Enter)
Design (press Enter twice)
568 Pine Street (press Enter)
St. Louis, MO 63131 (press Enter)
(314) 555-8755 (press Enter)
Fax: (314) 555-8758

d. Select *Desktop Design*, then change the font to 24-point Arial Bold.
e. Select the address, phone number, and fax number, then change the font to 10-point Arial.
f. Insert a frame around the letterhead text so that it can be positioned within the left margin by completing the following steps:
   (1) Change to the Page Layout viewing mode.
   (2) Choose Edit, then Select All. (This selects the entire document.)
   (3) Choose Insert, then Frame.
g. Size and position the framed text by completing the following steps:
   (1) Click the Zoom Control button on the Standard toolbar, then change the display to Whole Page.
   (2) With the frame already selected, choose Format, then Frame.
   (3) In the Size section of the Frame dialog box, key **1.5** in the At list box under the Width option.
   (4) Key **9.6** in the At list box under the Height option in the Size section.
   (5) In the Horizontal section of the Frame dialog box, select the current choice, key **0.25** in the Position list box, and make the position Relative To: Page.
   (6) In the Vertical section, key **0.75** in the Position list box and make the position Relative To: Page.
   (7) Make sure there is no check mark in the Move with Text check box, then click OK.
   (8) Click the Zoom Control button, then change the display to 100%. Use the vertical scroll bar to bring the text into view if necessary.
h. Insert the horizontal line by completing the following steps:
   (1) Click the Drawing button on the Standard toolbar to display the Drawing toolbar; or position the arrow pointer anywhere within the Standard toolbar, click the right mouse button once, then select Drawing from the drop-down menu.
   (2) Click the Line Style button on the Drawing toolbar, then select the fourth line style from the top (the thickest solid line) in the Line Style palette.
   (3) Click the Line Color button on the Drawing toolbar and make sure the line color selected is black.
   (4) Click the Line button on the Drawing toolbar. Position the cross hairs at the beginning of the blank line between the company name and address, hold down the Shift key and the left mouse button, drag the mouse across to the other side of the frame, then release the mouse button.
i. Adjust the size and position of the horizontal line by completing the following steps:
   (1) Position the I-beam on the horizontal line until it turns into an arrow with a four-headed arrow attached, then double-click the left mouse button.
   (2) At the Drawing Object dialog box, select the Size and Position tab.
   (3) In the Position section of the Drawing Object dialog box, change the Horizontal position to 0.25" From Page.
   (4) In the Size section, change the Width of the line to 1.53", then click OK.

j. Customize the borders of the frame by completing the following steps:
   (1) Click inside the framed text area to select it.
   (2) Choose Format, then Borders and Shading.
   (3) At the Borders and Shading dialog box, select the Borders tab.
   (4) In the Border preview box, click the top, bottom, left, and right borders as displayed to remove the borders from the frame.
   (5) In the Line Style list box, select the single line labeled 2¼ pt. The changed right border will automatically display in the Border preview box as long as it was the last border to be removed. If the border does not appear on the correct side in the preview box, click any side of the box in the Border preview box to turn a border on or off for that specific side.
   (6) Choose OK.
   (7) Click outside of the frame and use Print Preview to view the entire document.

2. Save the letterhead and name it c03ex03, ddletterhead.
3. Print and then close c03ex03, ddletterhead.

FIGURE 3.13

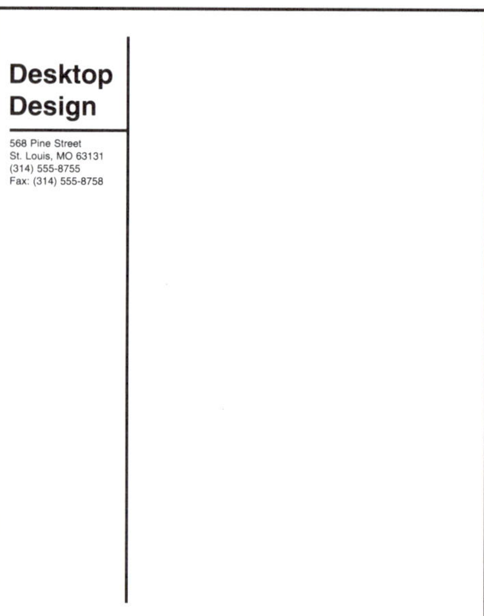

In exercise 4, you will create another letterhead and use the Frame feature to position elements on the page.

Creating a Letterhead Using Varying Type Sizes, Ruled Lines, and Frames

1. At a clear editing window, create the letterhead shown in figure 3.14 by completing the following steps:
   a. Change the left and right margins to 1 inch.
   b. Create the text in the letterhead by completing the following steps:
      (1) Key the following text. To insert the bullet, choose Insert and Symbol, select the *Symbols* tab, change the Font to Wingdings, and insert the round bullet in the third row, eighth column from the right. Press Enter where indicated:

JOHNSON (press Enter)
FURNITURE COMPANY (press Enter)
Providing comfort • since 1930

(2) Select **JOHNSON**, change the font to 30-point Arial Rounded MT Bold, and change the color to red.
(3) Select **FURNITURE COMPANY** and change the font to 14-point Arial Rounded MT Bold. (The right alignment of the text will be adjusted in a later exercise.)
(4) Select **Providing comfort • since 1930** and change the font to 10-point Arial Rounded MT Bold.

c. Insert a frame around the first line of text and adjust the text wrapping by completing the following steps:
(1) Change to the Page Layout Viewing mode.
(2) Select *JOHNSON*, choose Insert, and then Frame. (The remaining text moves to the right of the frame.)
(3) With the frame selected, choose Format, then Frame.
(4) In the Text Wrapping section, choose None, then click OK.

d. Remove the border around the frame by completing the following steps:
(1) With the frame still selected, choose Format, then Borders and Shading.
(2) At the Borders and Shading dialog box, select the Borders tab.
(3) Click None in the Presets section, then click OK.

e. Insert and position a frame around the second line of text by completing the following steps:
(1) Select *FURNITURE COMPANY*, choose Insert, and then Frame. (The framed text overlaps the previous frame.)
(2) With the frame selected, choose Format, then Frame.
(3) At the Frame dialog box, choose None in the Text Wrapping section.
(4) Change the Horizontal Position to Left Relative To: Margin.
(5) Change the Vertical Position to 1.38 inches Relative To: Page.
(6) Click OK.

f. Create a double line border under *FURNITURE COMPANY* by completing the following steps:
(1) With the frame still selected, choose Format, then Borders and Shading.
(2) At the Borders and Shading dialog box, make sure the Borders tab is selected.
(3) In the Border preview box, click on the left, right, top, and bottom border to remove them from the frame. (Make sure you remove the bottom border last.)
(4) In the Line section, select the 2¼ pt double line from the Style list box.
(5) Click the down-pointing triangle under the Color option, then select blue from the Line Color palette.
(6) Click OK.

g. Insert and position a frame around the third line of text by completing the following steps:
(1) Select *Providing comfort • since 1930*, choose Insert, and then Frame. (The framed text overlaps the first frame.)
(2) With the frame selected, choose Format, then Frame.
(3) At the Frame dialog box, choose None in the Text Wrapping section.
(4) Change the Horizontal Position to Left inches Relative To: Margin.

(5) Change the Vertical Position to 1.73 inches Relative To: Page.
(6) Click OK.
(7) Follow steps 1d(1) through 1d(3) to remove the default frame border.

h. Create the footer containing the horizontal line, address, and phone and fax numbers displayed at the bottom of the page by completing the following steps:
(1) Choose View, then Header and Footer.
(2) Click the Switch Between Header and Footer button (the first button) on the Header and Footer toolbar to switch from the Header pane to the Footer pane.
(3) Click the Page Setup button (eighth button from the left) on the Header and Footer toolbar.
(4) At the Page Setup dialog box, select the Margins tab.
(5) Key **0.75** inches in the Footer text box in the From Edge section of the Page Setup dialog box, then click OK. (This change ensures that the footer will not fall in a printer's unprintable zone.)
(6) At the Footer pane, press the Enter key once.
(7) Key the following address and phone and fax numbers shown in figure 3.14 according to the following specifications:
(a) Change the justification to Center.
(b) Change the font to 9.5-point Arial Rounded MT Bold Italic.
(c) Use the bullet from the Wingdings font as indicated in step 1a(4).
(d) Space once before and after each bullet.
(e) Select each bullet and remove italics formatting.

4302 Garden Avenue
Salem, Oregon 97326
(509) 555-3200
Fax: (509) 555-3201

(8) Position the I-beam pointer in the blank line above the address, then select Format, then Borders and Shading.
(9) At the Borders and Shading dialog box, select the Borders tab.
(10) Click the bottom border of the preview page in the Border section of the dialog box.
(11) Select the 2¼ pt single line from the Line Style list box, then change the Line Color to blue.
(12) Click OK to close the dialog box.
(13) Click Close on the Header and Footer toolbar.

2. Save the document and name it c03ex04, Johnson ltr.
3. Print and then close c03ex04, Johnson ltr.

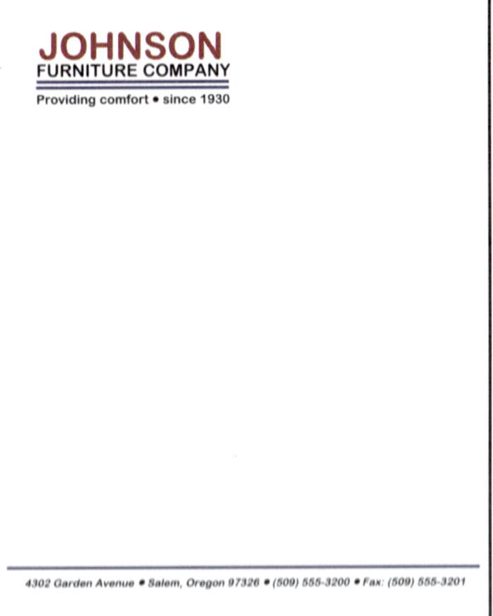
JOHNSON
FURNITURE COMPANY
Providing comfort • since 1930

4302 Garden Avenue • Salem, Oregon 97326 • (509) 555-3200 • Fax: (509) 555-3201

FIGURE 3.14

Review the letterheads created in exercises 3 and 4. What is the focus? Is the design symmetrical or asymmetrical? How is balance achieved on the page? Are the type sizes in proportion to each other? Does the type size indicate a logical order of importance? How is directional flow established? What elements provide contrast? If color was used, was it used effectively? Can you identify any consistent elements? Are any elements out of alignment? Continually asking yourself these kinds of questions will help develop your sense of design and layout.

Using The Template Feature To Produce Individualized Documents

Word's Template feature can make your task of producing individualized documents easier. A document created from a template can be customized once it is displayed in the document window, a new template can be created based on an existing template, the template itself can be modified permanently, an existing Word document can be converted to a template, or a new template can be made from scratch. For example, if you like the design of the Contemporary Letter template but would like to change the location of the world graphic and to change the font for the letterhead and body text, you have three choices—the document can be revised when it is displayed in the editing window, a new template based on the Contemporary Letter template can be created, or the original Contemporary Letter template can be permanently modified.

DTP POINTERS
Templates can provide the framework for creating customized documents.

If you choose to revise the document created by the template, you would select the Contemporary Letter template, replace the text markers with the appropriate information for your letter, and then make the graphic location and font changes when the document is displayed in the document window. You would then save and name the document as normal. The changes you make only affect the current document on the screen. No changes will be made to the original Contemporary Letter template. It will still be available for you to use over and over again.

Your second alternative, creating a new template based on the Contemporary Letter template, keeps the original template intact in addition to creating a new modified template for your future use. This process is accomplished by opening the original template file, making the desired changes, then saving the template to the default template folder with a new name. To do this, you would complete the following steps:

1. Choose File, then Open
2. At the Open dialog box, click the down-pointing triangle to the right of the Look in: option and change to the folder that contains the desired template files. If you are using a stand-alone version of Word, the default location of the template files is most likely *C:\Winword\Templates.* If you are using Office or Office Professional, the default location for the template files should be *C:\MSOffice\Templates.*
3. At the Templates folder, make the *Letters & Faxes* folder active, then change the Files of type option at the bottom of the dialog box to *Document Templates.*
4. Double-click the filename of the template you want to modify; in this case, *Contemporary Letter*, or select the filename, then click Open.
5. With the original template displayed on the screen, use any of Word's features to make the desired changes.
6. Choose File, then Save As.
7. Change to the folder where you want to save your template (for example, the *Letters & Faxes* folder), then key a new name in the File name list box. Do not key an extension as part of the filename. Word automatically adds a *.dot* extension to a template.

As a result of following this procedure, a new template now exists in your template folder that resembles the Contemporary Letter template. To use the new template, choose File, then New. Select the appropriate tab, such as Letters & Faxes, and the new template you just created is listed with the other available templates. This new template has all the characteristics of the original template except for the changes that were made. This method will not change the original Contemporary Letter template. Both templates are available to use as often as you like. This approach is preferable to making permanent changes to any of Word's original templates.

DTP POINTERS
Avoid editing Word's predesigned templates.

To modify an original template permanently, follow the same steps as above; however, name the edited template with the same name as the original template. For instance, to edit the *Contemporary Letter.dot*, follow steps 1 through 7 above but name the changed template *Contemporary Letter.dot* instead of giving the file a new name. The original Contemporary Letter template is now altered and will reflect these changes every time you access it. CAUTION: Avoid modifying the templates provided by Word. This approach is not recommended since many of the Word templates might be difficult to recreate.

A template can also be created from any existing Word document. If you have documents that you have already created, you can easily make any one of them into a Word template. To do this, you would complete the following steps:

1. With the document you want to change into a template displayed on your screen, delete any unnecessary text, graphics, and/or formatting. Leave only the text, graphics, and formatting instructions that you want available every time you use the template.
2. Choose File, then Save As.
3. At the Save As dialog box, change the Save as type option to *Document Template.*
4. Change to the folder containing your template files.
5. Replace any existing name in the File name text box with a name for your new template. Word automatically adds a *.dot* extension to the template.
6. Choose Save to save the new template. This new template will now be listed with the other available Word templates.

Since the existing templates that come with the Word program cannot satisfy all needs, creating a template from scratch is possible. At a clear editing window, create the desired document from scratch and then follow the steps above to save it as a template.

A letterhead would benefit from being converted into a template. Since your letterhead helps to establish an identity for your organization, it will probably stay the same for quite a long period of time. Converting your letterhead into a template ensures that your letterhead is always available in its original form. If the letterhead is mistakenly rearranged while keying the letter content, the original template can be opened again to start anew. For more efficiency, you can even include styles, AutoText entries, field codes, macros, and more in your template letterhead. (See the Word Reference Manual for including these items in your template.)

Creating a Template from an Existing Word Document

1. Convert the Johnson letterhead created in exercise 4 into a template by completing the following steps:
   a. Open c03ex04, Johnson ltr.doc.
   b. Choose File, then Save As.
   c. In the Save As dialog box, change the Save as type option at the bottom of the dialog box to *Document Template.*
   d. Click the down-pointing triangle to the right of the Save in: option, then change to the folder that contains the desired template files. If you are using a stand-alone version of Word, the default location of the template files is most likely *C:\Winword\Templates.* If you are using Office or Office Professional, the default location for the template files should be *C:\MSOffice\Templates.* If you are working on a network, consult your instructor as to the location of the template files.
   e. At the Templates folder, make sure the *Letters & Faxes* folder is active.
   f. Replace the existing filename in the File name text box with **(your last name), letterhead**. Word automatically adds a *.dot* extension to the template. (Ordinarily, a filename like *Company letterhead.dot* might be more appropriate; however, in a classroom situation, students would be replacing each other's templates in the *Letters & Faxes* folder if each student did not use a unique filename.)
   g. Choose Save to save the new template.
2. Close the document. (Ask your instructor about deleting this template from the template folder at the end of this chapter.)

Refining Letter And Word Spacing

Certain refinements such as kerning and tracking make your letterhead or any other document look more professional.

Kerning Character Pairs

The process of decreasing or increasing the white space between specific character pairs is called *kerning*. Kerning is used only on headlines and other blocks of large type. Generally, the horizontal spacing of typefaces is designed to optimize body text sizes (9- to 13-point). At larger sizes, the same relative horizontal space appears "loose," especially when uppercase and lowercase letters are combined. Kerning visually equalizes the space between characters and is especially important at large point sizes (14-point and larger).

Decreasing or increasing white space between specific character pairs.

Figure 3.15 illustrates character pair kerning set in 18-point Times New Roman Bold. As you can see, kerning results in very minor but visually important adjustments.

FIGURE 3.15

Character Pair Kerning

WA (kerned)	**Ta (kerned)**
WA (not kerned)	**Ta (not kerned)**
Ty (kerned)	**Vi (kerned)**
Ty (not kerned)	**Vi (not kerned)**

DTP POINTERS
Kern when the type size exceeds 14 points.

Kerning can be accomplished automatically or manually in Word by selecting the Character Spacing tab at the Font dialog box as displayed in figure 3.16. If the automatic kerning feature is turned on, Word adjusts the space between specific letter pairs above a specific point size. For example, some common character pairs that may be automatically kerned are *Ta, To, Ty, Vi,* and *WA*. The amount of kerning for specific character pairs is defined in a kerning table, which is part of the printer definition. The printer definition is a preprogrammed set of instructions that tells the printer how to perform various features. Word contains printer definitions for hundreds of printers. When a printer is selected during installation of Word, a file containing the particular printer definition is copied to the folder specified for printer files. Word has defined kerning tables for some fonts but not for all fonts. You may want to print some of the character pairs listed as kerned and not kerned in large point sizes (14-point and larger) to see if your printer definition supports kerning. To turn on the automatic kerning feature, you would complete the following steps:

1. If the text to be kerned has not been keyed yet, go to the next step. If the text to be kerned already exists, select the text first.
2. Choose Format, then Font.
3. At the Font dialog box, select the Character Spacing tab.
4. Click the check box to the left of the Kerning for Fonts option to insert a check mark.
5. In the Points and Above text box, use the up and down arrows to specify the minimum point size for kerning to take effect; or key the desired point size.
6. Click OK.

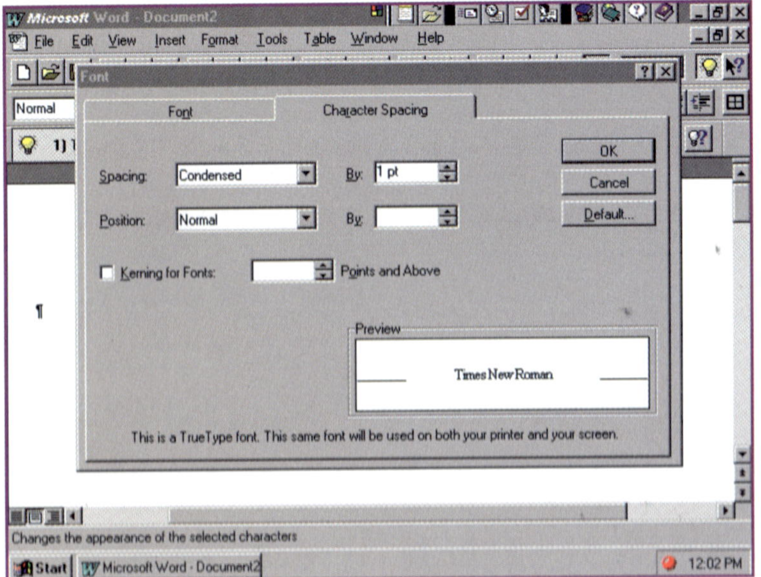

FIGURE 3.16

Font Dialog Box with Character Spacing Tab Selected

If you choose to manually kern letters, you make the decision as to which letters to kern. Manual kerning can also be used to increase or decrease space between letters if legibility is a problem or if a special effect is desired. To manually kern a specific pair of letters, you would complete the following steps:

1. Select the pair of characters you want to kern.
2. Choose Format, then Font.
3. At the Font dialog box, select the Character Spacing tab.
4. Click the down-pointing triangle in the Spacing list box, then select Expanded (if you want to increase the spacing between the selected character pair) or Condensed (if you want to decrease the spacing).
5. In the By: list box, click the up- or down-pointing triangle to specify the amount you want to increase or decrease the character spacing of the selected character pair.
6. Click OK.

Tracking Text

In typesetting, equally reducing or increasing the horizontal space between all characters in a block of text is called *tracking*. Tracking affects all characters, while kerning affects only specific character pairs. The purpose of tracking is the same as kerning: to produce more attractive, easy-to-read type.

Tracking: Equally reducing or increasing the horizontal space between all characters in a block.

Like kerning, tracking adjustments in Word are also made at the Font dialog box with the Character Spacing tab selected as shown in figure 3.16. At this dialog box, you can reduce or increase spacing between characters. Figure 3.17 specifies what occurs with each option.

FIGURE 3.17

Character Spacing Options

Normal	The default setting chosen by the program or the printer as the best spacing between words and letters.
Condensed	Condenses the spacing between all characters in a block of text by the number of points specified by the user.
Expanded	Expands the spacing between all characters in a block of text by the number of points specified by the user.

In Word, condensing or expanding character spacing affects all spacing in a block of text, including the spaces between words. Generally, in typesetting, if the character spacing is adjusted, then the space between words is also adjusted. However, the amount of space specified between characters and the amount of space specified between words does not have to be the same. The headings shown in figure 3.18 are set in 24-point Garamond Bold. The first heading is set at the default character spacing of Normal. The character spacing for the text in the second heading was condensed by 1 point and the space between each word was condensed by 0.5 points.

FIGURE 3.18

Tracking Example

DESKTOP PUBLISHING IN THE 90s
DESKTOP PUBLISHING IN THE 90s

Tracking (reducing character spacing) is usually done on headings and subheadings. While reducing character spacing on body text allows more text in the same amount of space, the text appears more dense and can be more difficult to read. On the other hand, reducing the character spacing of italicized text can give it the appearance of script, as illustrated in figure 3.19.

FIGURE 3.19

Tracking Example

The text in this paragraph is set in 11-point Book Antiqua Italic. The character spacing is set at the default of ***Normal****.*

The text in this paragraph is set in 10-point Book Antiqua Italic. The character spacing is ***Condensed By: 0.5 pt****.*

DTP POINTERS
Kern and track headings and subheadings.

In typesetting, headings and subheadings are almost always tracked and then kerned. Look at the Johnson letterhead originally created in exercise 4 and used to create a template in exercise 5. The letters on the right side of the letterhead would look much better if they were aligned as evenly as those on the left side. In exercise 6, you will correct the alignment problem in your template using kerning and tracking.

Kerning and Tracking Text in a Letterhead

1. At a clear document screen, kern and track the text in the Johnson letterhead as shown in figure 3.20 by completing the following steps:
   a. Choose File, then Open.
   b. At the Open dialog box, change the Files of type option at the bottom of the dialog box to *Document Templates.*
   c. Choose Look in, then change to the folder that contains the Johnson Letterhead template file. (If you are using a stand-alone version of Word, the location is most likely to be *C:\Winword\Templates\Letters & Faxes.* If you are using Office or Office Professional, the location is most likely to be *C:\MSOffice\Templates\Letters & Faxes.*)
   d. At the Templates folder, double-click *(your last name), letterhead.*
   e. Kern *JOHNSON* by completing the following steps:
      (1) Select *JOHNSON.*
      (2) Choose Format, then Font.
      (3) At the Font dialog box, select the Character Spacing tab.
      (4) Click the check box to the left of Kerning for Fonts to insert a check mark. Make sure that the Points and Above text box displays 30.
      (5) Click OK.
   f. Kern and track *FURNITURE COMPANY* by completing the following steps:
      (1) Select *FURNITURE COMPANY.*
      (2) Display the Font dialog box with the Character Spacing tab selected.
      (3) Click the check box to the left of Kerning for Fonts to insert a check mark. Make sure that the Points and Above text box displays 14.
      (4) In the Spacing list box, click the down-pointing triangle, then select *Condensed.*
      (5) In the By: text box, change the point specification to 0.5 pt.
      (6) Click OK.
   g. Track *Providing comfort • since 1930* by completing the following steps:
      (1) Select *Providing comfort • since 1930.*
      (2) Display the Font dialog box with the Character Spacing tab selected.
      (3) In the Spacing list box, click the down-pointing triangle, then select *Condensed.*
      (4) In the By: text box, change the point specification to 0.3 pt.
      (5) Click OK.
2. Save the template with the same name, *(your last name), letterhead,* then close the document.
3. Print a copy of your kerned and tracked letterhead by completing the following steps:
   a. Choose File, then New.
   b. At the New dialog box, select the Letters & Faxes tab.
   c. Double-click *(your last name), letterhead;* or select the template, then click OK.
   d. Save the document as c03ex06, kern&track.
   e. Print and then close c03ex06, kern&track.

FIGURE 3.20

Creating Envelopes

DTP POINTERS
Use your company's letterhead as the starting point for the design of your other business documents.

Let your company's letterhead be the starting point for the design of your other business documents. An envelope designed in coordination with a letterhead is another way of establishing your identity with your target audience. Using some of the same design elements in the envelope as in the letterhead contributes to continuity and consistency among your documents. These same elements can be carried over into memos, faxes, business cards, invoices, and brochures.

Creating the Content

As in a letterhead, there is certain information that must be included on the front of an envelope. Include all necessary information so your correspondence reaches its intended destination, such as:

Return Address:

- Logo
- Name
- Address
- Mailing address if different
- Optional: Company motto or slogan
- Optional: Telephone (include area code) and fax number

Recipient's Address:

- Name
- Title (only if you really know it)
- Company name
- Street address
- City, State, ZIP (check a ZIP Code directory if necessary)

Designing Your Own Envelope

If you decide to design your own envelope, consider the size of the envelope to be used. Any design elements will most likely be located on the left side of the envelope, concentrated in the upper left corner. Hence, your design area is much smaller than that of a letterhead.

DTP POINTERS
Consider the actual size of your design area.

When planning your design, remember that the envelope design does not have to be an exact replica of the letterhead. Select enough common elements for your design so a link is established in the viewer's eyes between the two documents. For example, using the same typeface and type styles in a smaller type size and repeating a graphic element on a smaller scale may be just enough to establish that link. Size the fonts used on the envelope so they are in proportion to those used in the letterhead. Restrain from making the design too large or overpowering. The design should not interfere in any way with the recipient's name and address.

Using Word's Envelope Feature

Word has a very convenient Envelope feature that makes creating envelopes easy. The Envelope feature lets you insert the return address, the delivery address, a United States Postal Service Postnet Bar Code, and Facing Identification Marks (FIMS) that identify different kinds of Courtesy Reply Mail. Additional Envelope options allow the user to change fonts for the delivery and return addresses, adjust the placement of the return or delivery addresses on the envelope, print the envelope, or add the envelope to the document currently displayed in the editing window. The envelope size defaults to a 4⅛-inch by 9½-inch #10 business envelope, but the envelope size definition can be changed, or you can create your own custom-size envelope definition. Names and addresses for both the return and delivery addresses can be stored in Word's Address Book feature for later use.

If you have a letter currently displayed in the editing window when accessing the Envelope feature, the inside address from the letter is automatically inserted in the Delivery Address section of the Envelopes and Labels dialog box. In addition, an address may automatically display in the Return Address section. A return address will automatically display if an address has been entered in User Info. To access User Info, choose Tools, then Options. At the Options dialog box, select the User Info tab. Any address that displays in the Mailing Address section in the User Info tab will automatically appear in the Return Address section of the Envelopes and Labels dialog box. Entering an address at this dialog box is useful if the return address will remain the same for the majority of your correspondence. You can change a return address at the Options dialog box with the User Info tab selected or in the Envelopes and Labels dialog box.

After the delivery address and the return address have been filled in, the envelope can either be printed or added to the current active document. If Add to Document is chosen, Word adds the envelope to the beginning of the current active document. The program numbers the envelope as page 0. If you add the envelope to a blank document and then save the envelope, a blank page will be saved with your envelope and ejected from the printer when printing the envelope.

Word determines the feed method for envelopes and the feed form as shown in the Feed section of the Envelopes and Labels dialog box (with the Envelopes tab selected). If this method does not work for your printer, choose the correct feed method and feed form at the Envelope Options dialog box with the Printing Options tab selected. Feed methods are visually displayed at the dialog box. You can also determine if the envelope is fed into the printer face up or face down.

To use the Envelope feature and to include your own design for the envelope, key the delivery address and the return address, add the envelope to the document, and then create the design. If you are taking the time to design an envelope, convert it to a template so you can use it over and over again.

Designing and Creating an Envelope Template Using the Envelope Feature

1. At a clear document screen, create an envelope template as shown in figure 3.21 to coordinate with the JOHNSON letterhead created in exercise 4 by completing the following steps:
   a. Choose Tools, Envelopes and Labels.
   b. At the Envelopes and Labels dialog box, select the Envelopes tab.
   c. In the Return Address section, key the following (if a default return address already exists, select it before keying the new address):

      JOHNSON
      FURNITURE COMPANY
      4302 Garden Avenue
      Salem, Oregon 97326

   d. Choose Options.
   e. At the Envelope Options dialog box, select the Envelope Options tab.
   f. Click Font in the Return Address section and change the font to Arial Rounded MT Bold.
   g. Click OK.
   h. At the Envelope Options dialog box, choose Close.
   i. At the Envelopes and Labels dialog box, click Add to Document.
   j. Answer No to saving the new return address as the default. (The screen will display with the insertion point in the return address position. The page number in the status line will display as *Page 0.* A blank page will also be included following the envelope because the envelope was added to a clear document screen.)
   k. Add a round bullet and a space before the street address as shown in figure 3.21 by completing the following steps:
      (1) Position the insertion point to the left of *4302 Garden Avenue.*
      (2) Choose Insert, then Symbol.
      (3) At the Symbol dialog box, select the Symbols tab.
      (4) Change the Font to Wingdings, then select the round bullet in the third row, eighth column from the right.
      (5) Choose Insert, then Close.
      (6) Press the space bar once.
   l. Add a space and a bullet to the end of the address as shown in figure 3.21 by completing the following steps:
      (1) Position the insertion point to the right of the ZIP Code, then press the space bar once.
      (2) Follow the steps 1k(2) through 1k(5) above to insert the bullet.
   m. Format *JOHNSON* by completing the following steps:
      (1) Change to the Page Layout viewing mode.
      (2) Select *JOHNSON.*
      (3) Display the Font dialog box, then change the point size to 26 and the color to red.
      (4) With the Font dialog box still displayed, select the Character Spacing tab, then change the Spacing to Expanded By: 0.4 pt.
      (5) Choose OK to close the dialog box.

n. Insert a frame around *JOHNSON* and adjust the text wrapping by completing the following steps:
   (1) With *JOHNSON* still selected, choose Insert, then Frame. (The remaining lines of text move to the right.)
   (2) With the frame selected, choose Format, then Frame.
   (3) In the Text Wrapping section, choose None.
   (4) Choose OK to close the dialog box.
o. Remove the border around the frame by completing the following steps:
   (1) With the frame still selected, choose Format, then Borders and Shading.
   (2) At the Borders and Shading dialog box, select the Borders tab.
   (3) Click None in the Borders Presets section.
   (4) Click OK to close the Borders and Shading dialog box.
p. Format *FURNITURE COMPANY* by completing the following steps:
   (1) Select *FURNITURE COMPANY.*
   (2) Display the Font dialog box, then change the point size to 13 points.
   (3) With the Font dialog box still displayed, select the Character Spacing tab, then change the Spacing to Condensed By: 0.9 pt.
   (4) Choose OK to close the dialog box.
q. Insert and position a frame around *FURNITURE COMPANY* by completing the following steps:
   (1) With *FURNITURE COMPANY* still selected, choose Insert, then Frame. (The current frame will overlap the previous frame.)
   (2) With the frame still selected, choose Format, then Frame.
   (3) In the Frame dialog box, choose None in the Text Wrapping section.
   (4) Change the Horizontal Position to Left and Relative To: Margin, then change the Vertical Position to 0.58 inches and Relative To: Page.
   (5) Choose OK to close the dialog box.
r. Create the double-line border under *FURNITURE COMPANY* by completing the following steps:
   (1) With the frame still selected, choose Format, then Borders and Shading.
   (2) At the Borders and Shading dialog box, select the Borders tab.
   (3) In the Border preview box, click on the left, right, top, and bottom borders to delete them. In the Line Style section, select the 2¼ pt double line for the bottom border.
   (4) Change the Color of the double line to blue.
   (5) Choose OK to close the dialog box.
s. Format ● *4302 Garden Avenue* by completing the following steps:
   (1) Select ● *4302 Garden Avenue.*
   (2) Display the Font dialog box, then change the style to Bold Italic and the point size to 10.
   (3) With the Font dialog box still displayed, select the Character Spacing tab, then change the Spacing to Expanded By: 1 pt.
   (4) Choose OK to close the dialog box.
   (5) Select the first bullet and remove the Italics formatting.
t. Insert and position a frame around the street address by completing the following steps:
   (1) With ● *4302 Garden Avenue* still selected, choose Insert, then Frame. (The current frame will overlap the first frame.)
   (2) Choose Format, then Frame.
   (3) In the Frame dialog box, select None in the Text Wrapping section.
   (4) Change the Horizontal Position to Left and Relative To: Margin, then change the Vertical Position to 0.9 inches and Relative To: Page.
   (5) Choose OK to close the dialog box.
u. Remove the border around the frame by completing the following steps:
   (1) With the frame still selected, choose Format, then Borders and Shading.

(2) At the Borders and Shading dialog box, select the Borders tab.
(3) Choose None in the Borders Presets section.
(4) Choose OK to close the dialog box.

v. Format *Salem, Oregon 97326* ● by completing the following steps:
(1) Select Salem, *Oregon 97326* ●.
(2) Display the Font dialog box, then change the style to Bold Italic and the point size to 10.
(3) With the Font dialog box still displayed, select the Character Spacing tab, then change the Spacing to Expanded By: 0.8 pt.
(4) Choose OK to close the dialog box.
(5) Select the second bullet and remove the Italics formatting.

w. Insert and position a frame around the city, state, and ZIP Code by completing the following steps:
(1) With *Salem, Oregon 97326* ● still selected, choose Insert, then Frame. (The current frame will overlap the first frame.)
(2) Choose Format, then Frame.
(3) In the Frame dialog box, select None in the Text Wrapping section.
(4) At the Frame dialog box, change the Horizontal Position to Left and Relative To: Margin, then change the Vertical Position to 1.03 inches and Relative To: Page.
(5) Choose OK to close the dialog box.

x. Remove the border around the framed text by completing the following steps:
(1) With the frame still selected, choose Format, then Borders and Shading.
(2) At the Borders and Shading dialog box, select the Borders tab.
(3) Choose None in the Borders Presets section.
(4) Choose OK to close the dialog box.
(5) Click to the right of the frame to see the overall results.

2. Save your envelope as a template by completing the following steps:
   a. Choose File, then Save As, and change the Files of type: option to *Document Templates (*.dot)*.
   b. Make the *Other Documents* template directory active. (If this directory is not automatically displayed as one of the selections, change to the appropriate directory. The path to this directory is most likely *C:\Winword\Templates\Other Documents* or *C:\MSOffice\Templates\Other Documents.*)
   c. In the File name text box, name the template **(your last name), Johnson envelope**.
   d. Click Save or press Enter.
   e. Close the envelope template.
3. Open a copy of your envelope template and insert a delivery address by completing the following steps:
   a. Choose File, New, and then select the *Other Documents* tab.
   b. Double-click on *(your last name), Johnson envelope.dot*; or select the envelope template and click OK.
   c. With the envelope template document displayed on the screen, press the down arrow until the insertion point displays inside another frame located in the delivery address position. (This frame exists when an envelope is produced using the Envelopes and Label feature.)
   d. Key the following address:

      Mr. Vincent Martinez
      Carter Furniture Company
      1232 North Randolph Street
      Chicago, IL 60631

4. Save and name the document c03ex07, Johnson env.
5. Print the page containing the envelope and then close c03ex07, Johnson env.

FIGURE 3.21

Mr. Vincent Martinez
Carter Furniture Company
1232 North Randolph Street
Chicago, IL 60631

Adding Graphics To An Envelope

In addition to including text in a return address, a clip art image, a company logo, a graphic created using Word's drawing tools, or an image created using WordArt can also be included. You can have professional-looking envelopes at a very low cost. One method of doing this is to use Word's Envelope feature as in exercise 7, insert a graphic image, then save the document as a template that you can use over and over again. Another method is to use the Envelope feature as well as the AutoText feature.

Using AutoText

AutoText allows you to quickly and easily store commonly used text and/or graphics, including any associated formatting, and to insert them into documents whenever you need them. The AutoText entries remain in memory for future use after you exit the document and turn the computer off. The AutoText feature is useful for items such as addresses, a company logo, lists, standard text, a closing to a letter, or any other text that you use on a frequent basis.

DTP POINTERS
Use the AutoText feature to store commonly used text and/or graphics.

Saving an AutoText Entry

To save an AutoText entry, key the desired text and apply any desired formatting. Select the text, then choose Edit, then AutoText. At the AutoText dialog box, either accept the default name assigned to the AutoText entry or key a new name. Try to name the AutoText entry something that is short but indicative of the entry contents. After determining the entry name, choose Add.

When you save selected text as an AutoText entry, the formatting applied to the text is also saved. If you are saving a paragraph or paragraphs of text that have paragraph formatting applied, make sure you include the paragraph mark with the selected text. To make sure the paragraph mark is included, turn on the display of nonprinting characters before selecting the text.

Inserting an AutoText Entry

An AutoText entry can be inserted into a document by pressing the shortcut key, F3, or accessing the AutoText dialog box. To insert an AutoText entry and all of its associated formatting with the shortcut key, key the name given to the AutoText entry, then press F3. To insert an entry and all its associated formatting using the AutoText dialog box, choose Edit, then AutoText. Select the AutoText entry in the Name list box, then choose Insert. If you cannot remember the name of a desired entry at the AutoText dialog box, click each entry in the Name list box and view the contents in the Preview box.

To insert an AutoText entry without the associated formatting, display the AutoText dialog box, choose Plain Text, select the AutoText entry in the Name list box, then choose Insert. When you choose Plain Text, the entry is inserted in the document at the location of the insertion point and takes on the formatting of surrounding text.

Editing an AutoText Entry

An AutoText entry can be edited by inserting the entry in a document, making any necessary changes, then saving it again with the same AutoText entry name. When Word asks if you want to redefine the AutoText entry, choose Yes.

Deleting an AutoText Entry

An AutoText entry can be removed from the AutoText dialog box. To do this, display the AutoText dialog box, select the entry name from the Name list box, then click the Delete button. In a lab situation, check with your instructor about deleting AutoText entries after you are finished with them. Deleting them would allow other students the opportunity to create their own entries.

Creating an Envelope Using the AutoText and Envelope Features

1. At a clear document screen, create an AutoText entry to be used as the return address of an envelope as shown in figure 3.22 by completing the following steps:
   a. Choose Tools, then Envelopes and Labels.
   b. At the Envelopes and Labels dialog box, select the Envelopes tab.
   c. Position the insertion point in the Return Address text box. (If a default return address already exists, select it first before keying the new address.) Key the following address:

      The Music Store
      1301 North Market Street
      Akron, OH 44201

   d. Click Add to Document. Choose No when you are asked if you want to save the address as the default. (The screen will display with the insertion point in the return address position. The page number in the status line will display as *Page 0*. A blank page will also be included following the envelope because the envelope was added to a clear document screen.)
   e. With the insertion point positioned at the beginning of the first line of the address, choose Insert, then Picture.
   f. At the Insert Picture dialog box, double-click *Notes* in the Name list box; or select *Notes*, then click OK.
   g. Press Enter to move the company name below the picture.
   h. Position the I-beam pointer on the notes image, then click once to select it.
   i. Choose Format, then Picture.
   j. At the Picture dialog box, change the Width and Height to 65% in the Scaling section by clicking the down-pointing triangles in each text box or by keying the amount.

k. Choose OK to close the dialog box.
l. Position the arrow pointer to the right of the notes image, then click once to deselect it.
m. Format the address text by completing the following steps:
   (1) Change to the Page Layout viewing mode.
   (2) Select the company name, then change the font to 20-point Kino MT Bold Italic.
   (3) Select the street address and the city, state, and zip, then change the font to 14-point Kino MT Bold Italic.
   (4) Select all three lines of the address (do not include the graphic), then choose Insert, then Frame.
   (5) Choose Format, then Borders and Shading.
   (6) At the Borders and Shading dialog box, select the Borders tab.
   (7) Select None in the Presets section.
   (8) Choose OK to close the dialog box.
   (9) Choose Format, then Frame.
   (10) At the Frame dialog box, change the Width to 1.95 inches in the Size section.
   (11) Change the Horizontal Position to 0.5 inches Relative To: Page.
   (12) Choose OK to close the dialog box.
n. Save the return address and graphic image as an AutoText entry by completing the following steps:
   (1) Press Ctrl + Home.
   (2) Select the address text by holding down the Shift key, then pressing the down arrow key two times. The notes image and the entire address should be selected. (Selecting with the mouse causes some problems in this situation.)
   (3) Choose Edit, then AutoText.
   (4) At the AutoText dialog box, key **music address** in the Name text box, then click Add. (If you are asked if you want to redefine the AutoText entry, choose Yes.)
   (5) Close the document without saving it.
o. Create an envelope using the AutoText entry you just created for the return address by completing the following steps:
   (1) At a clear document screen, display the Envelopes and Labels dialog box with the Envelopes tab selected.
   (2) Make sure the Delivery Address and the Return Address text boxes are empty. If not, delete any existing text.
   (3) Click Add to Document.
   (4) With the insertion point located in the return address section of your envelope, key **music address** then press F3.

2. Save the envelope as c03ex08, music env.
3. Print and then close c03ex08, music env. (Check with your instructor about printing on an actual envelope or standard-size paper. Your printer will eject a blank sheet of paper after printing the envelope due to the envelope being added to a blank document. Insert the blank paper back into the printer for future use.)

FIGURE 3.22

The Music Store
1301 North Market Street
Akron, OH 44201

Creating Business Cards

Business cards eliminate the unprofessional and sometimes awkward scribbling of your name, address, and telephone number on whatever piece of paper you can find. A business card represents you and your company and projects an organized, professional image. A business card is one of your best marketing opportunities.

DTP POINTERS
Using coordinating design elements in your business documents establishes identity and consistency.

A business card usually includes your name, title, company name, address, e-mail address, telephone number, and fax number. You can also include a one-sentence description of your business, philosophy, or slogan. To further establish your identity and to stay consistent with your other business documents such as letterheads, envelopes, etc., include the same company logo or symbol in reduced size. Also, continue to use the same typefaces and colors used in your other business documents. Most business cards are created with sans serif typefaces because the characters are easier to read. The type sizes vary from 12 to 14 points for key words and 8 to 10 points for telephone and fax numbers. Vary the appearance by using bold, italics, or small caps.

Business cards should be printed on high-quality cover stock paper. Specially designed full-color papers and forms for creating business cards more easily and professionally are available at office supply stores and paper companies. Printing your own business cards saves you the expense of having to place a large minimum order with an outside printer. This is especially helpful to a new small business. You may decide to design your own card and then take it to a professional printer to be printed in larger quantities.

Using Word's Labels Feature to Create Business Cards

Although Word does not include a template for creating business cards, you can use Word's business card label definition when designing and creating your own business cards. To automatically create a full sheet of business cards with the same information on each card, you would complete the following steps:

1. Choose Tools, then Envelopes and Labels.
2. At the Envelopes and Labels dialog box, select the Labels tab.

3. Key the information and/or insert any AutoText entry you want to appear on the business cards/labels in the Address text box.
4. Choose Options.
5. At the Label Options dialog box, select *Avery Standard* in the Label Products list box, then choose *5371 Business Card* or *8371 Business Card* from the Product Number list box.
6. Choose OK or press Enter.
7. At the Envelopes and Labels dialog box, make sure Full Page of the Same Label is selected, then choose New Document.

There is no difference between these two business card label definitions. The difference occurs in the actual product when you purchase these brand-name items at an office supply store—the *5371* is made to be used in a laser printer and the *8371* is made to be used in an ink jet printer.

When you select a label, information about that label is displayed in the Label Information section of the Label Options dialog box, including the type, height, width, and page size. (In this case, each business card will be 3½ inches by 2 inches. The sheet containing the business cards will be 8½ inches by 11 inches.) To further customize your business card label selection, choose Details from the Label Options dialog box. The Business Card 5371 (or 8371) Information dialog box appears. The Preview box displays a label with the margins, pitch measurements, and height and width indicated. At this dialog box, you can customize the top and side margins, vertical and horizontal pitch, the label height and width, and the number of labels across and down the label page.

When you change any of the predefined settings of a label listed in the Product Number list box, you are actually creating a new label definition. Remember that these labels are actually cells in a table. If you change the margin settings in a label, you are really changing where the cell begins in relation to the edge of the paper. You are not changing the margins within each label or cell—that is, the area between the edge of the label and the beginning of the address. In this instance, the label definition will produce 10 business cards—two columns of labels with five rows in each column.

As an alternative method for creating your business cards, you can leave the Address text box empty, then choose New Document and a full page of blank label forms will be displayed at the document screen. You can then create the first business card/label at the document screen and copy it to the rest of the label forms.

You will create 10 business cards in exercise 9 using the Avery 5371 Business Card label definition. Before accessing the Labels feature, you will create one business card in a frame at a clear editing window. You will then select the business card text to be an AutoText entry. To actually create the 10 business cards, you will access the Envelopes and Labels dialog box, insert the AutoText entry, and create a full sheet of business cards. Consider using this label definition to create membership cards, name tags, coupons, place holders, or friendly reminders. However, keep in mind that working with text or pictures that are in the text layer when using the label definitions is much easier. Objects or text from the drawing layer (anything created using the Drawing toolbar) can be used; however, the process is very time-consuming and cumbersome.

Creating a Business Card Using Word's Envelopes and Labels Feature and AutoText

1. At a clear document screen, create the business cards shown in figure 3.23 using the Avery 5371 Business Card label definition by completing the following steps:
   a. Choose Insert, and then Frame.
   b. Position the cross hairs on the insertion point at the left margin, then draw a frame approximately 3.5 inches wide and 2 inches high. (Do not worry about being exact; you will adjust the frame size in step f.)
   c. Choose Format, then Borders and Shading, and then select the Borders tab.
   d. Choose None in the Presets section, then click OK.
   e. Choose Format, then Frame.
   f. At the Frame dialog box, change the Width to 3.4 inches and the Height to 1.8 inches.
   g. Choose OK to close the dialog box.
   h. Insert and size the graphic border by completing the following steps:
      (1) Click once inside the frame to position the insertion point in the upper left corner.
      (2) Choose Insert, then Picture.
      (3) At the Insert Picture dialog box, double-click *Travel* in the Name list box; or select *Travel*, then click OK.
      (4) Click once inside the graphic border to select it.
      (5) Choose Format, then Picture.
      (6) At the Picture dialog box, change the Width to 3.3 inches and the Height to 0.44 inches in the Size section.
      (7) Choose OK to close the dialog box.
   i. Adjust the paragraph spacing and justification to place the name on the card in the appropriate location by completing the following steps:
      (1) Choose Format, then Paragraph.
      (2) At the Paragraph dialog box, select the Indents and Spacing tab.
      (3) Key **20** in the After text box in the Spacing section.
      (4) Choose OK to close the dialog box.
      (5) Press Enter once and the insertion point will advance 20 points rather than the amount of a regular hard return.
      (6) Click the Center button on the Formatting toolbar.
      (7) Change the font to 16-point Kino MT Bold, then key **Linda Urban**.
      (8) Change the font to 12-point Kino MT Italic.
      (9) Change the paragraph spacing back to 0 pt After by following steps (1) through (4) above.
      (10) Press Enter once, then key **Travel Consultant**.
   j. Adjust the paragraph spacing, justification, font, and tab positions to place the address, phone, and fax numbers in the appropriate location by completing the following steps:
      (1) Change the paragraph spacing to 24 pt After by following the steps in i(1) through i(4) above.
      (2) Press Enter once, then change the justification back to left.
      (3) Change the font to 10-point Kino MT Regular.
      (4) Choose Format, then Tabs.
      (5) At the Tabs dialog box, select Clear All.
      (6) Set left tabs at 0.13 inches, 2.25 inches, and 2.38 inches, then click OK. (You may need to make minor adjustments to the last two tab settings.

Make sure the text fits on the lines as shown in figure 3.23.)

(7) Press the Tab key once, then key **6300 Kingery Highway**.

(8) Press the Tab key once, then key **Phone: (708) 555-1203**.

(9) Change the paragraph spacing to **0 pt** After, then press Enter once.

(10) Press the Tab key once, then key **Willowbrook, IL 60514**.

(11) Press the Tab key twice, then key **Fax: (708) 555-0647**.

k. As a precaution, save your document and name it c03ex09, card AutoText.

l. Create an AutoText entry from the business card text by completing the following steps:

(1) With the graphic and text framed, choose Edit, then Select All. (This selects all of the frame contents.)

(2) Choose Edit, then AutoText.

(3) At the AutoText dialog box, key **travel card** in the Name text box, then click Add. (If you are asked if you want to redefine the AutoText entry, choose Yes. Any AutoText Entry with the same name will automatically be replaced with your newly created AutoText entry.)

m. Close c03ex09, card AutoText.

n. At a clear document screen, create 10 business cards using the Envelopes and Labels feature and your AutoText entry by completing the following steps:

(1) Choose Tools, then Envelopes and Labels.

(2) At the Envelopes and Labels dialog box, select the Labels tab.

(3) Choose Options, then make sure that Avery Standard is displayed in the Label Products: list box.

(4) In the Product Number: list box, select 5371 - Business Card (or 8371 - Business Card), then click OK.

(5) At the Envelopes and Labels dialog box, delete any existing text in the Address text box. Key **travel card** then press F3 to insert the AutoText entry.

(6) Make sure Full Page of the Same Label is selected, then click New Document.

(7) Use Print Preview to make sure your document will print correctly. Depending on your printer's unprintable zone and the margins set in the business card's label definition, the printing on the bottom row of the business cards may be cut off. One easy way to avoid this is to fool your printer into thinking your document is going to be printed on a longer piece of paper. To do this, complete the following steps:

(a) Choose File, then Page Setup.

(b) In the Page Setup dialog box, select the Paper Size tab.

(c) In the Paper Size list box, select Legal and then click OK.

2. Save the document with the name c03ex09, business card.

3. Print and then close c03ex09, business card. The grid lines displayed on the screen will not automatically print with the business cards. To print the grid lines, complete the following steps:

(a) Choose Table, then Select Table.

(b) Choose Format, then Borders and Shading.

(c) Select the Borders tab.

(d) In the Presets section, select Grid.

(e) In the Line Style section, choose the ¾ pt fine dotted line.

(f) Make sure the inside grid lines display in the Border Preview box. If not, click once in the center of the box to display the internal grid lines.

(g) Click OK.

FIGURE 3.23

Linda Urban
Travel Consultant

6300 Kingery Highway
Willowbrook, IL 60514

Phone: (708) 555-1203
Fax: (708) 555-0647

Linda Urban
Travel Consultant

6300 Kingery Highway
Willowbrook, IL 60514

Phone: (708) 555-1203
Fax: (708) 555-0647

Linda Urban
Travel Consultant

6300 Kingery Highway
Willowbrook, IL 60514

Phone: (708) 555-1203
Fax: (708) 555-0647

Linda Urban
Travel Consultant

6300 Kingery Highway
Willowbrook, IL 60514

Phone: (708) 555-1203
Fax: (708) 555-0647

Linda Urban
Travel Consultant

6300 Kingery Highway
Willowbrook, IL 60514

Phone: (708) 555-1203
Fax: (708) 555-0647

Linda Urban
Travel Consultant

6300 Kingery Highway
Willowbrook, IL 60514

Phone: (708) 555-1203
Fax: (708) 555-0647

Linda Urban
Travel Consultant

6300 Kingery Highway
Willowbrook, IL 60514

Phone: (708) 555-1203
Fax: (708) 555-0647

Linda Urban
Travel Consultant

6300 Kingery Highway
Willowbrook, IL 60514

Phone: (708) 555-1203
Fax: (708) 555-0647

Linda Urban
Travel Consultant

6300 Kingery Highway
Willowbrook, IL 60514

Phone: (708) 555-1203
Fax: (708) 555-0647

Linda Urban
Travel Consultant

6300 Kingery Highway
Willowbrook, IL 60514

Phone: (708) 555-1203
Fax: (708) 555-0647

Chapter Summary

- A letterhead contains a specific design and layout that helps establish an organization's identity with a target audience. Designing your own letterhead can be a less costly alternative to having it designed and produced through a professional printer.
- A number of letter templates are available, including Contemporary, Elegant, and Professional. A Letter Wizard is also available that guides you through the creation of a business letter.
- Template documents may contain several styles that automatically format a specific section of text.
- Ruled lines act as boundaries to the surrounding text. Ruled lines can be used in a document to create a focal point, draw the eye across or down the page, separate columns and sections, or add visual appeal. The thickness of a line is measured in points.
- In the text layer, design elements can be placed at exact horizontal and/or vertical locations on the page by using the frame feature. Paragraph spacing can also be used to vertically position elements on the page.
- An existing template document can be customized once it is displayed at the document screen. Any changes made only affect the document displayed on the screen, leaving the template available in its original format.
- A template can be edited permanently by opening a template from the template folder. If changes are made and the template is saved with the same name, the template will reflect those changes every time it is used.
- A new template can be created that is based on an existing template. The new template will have all the characteristics of the original template except for any changes made. A new template can also be created from an existing Word document or from scratch.
- Kerning is the process of decreasing or increasing the white space between specific character pairs and is used on headlines and other blocks of large type.
- Tracking is the equal reduction or enlargement of the horizontal space between all characters in a block of text.
- When creating a design for an envelope, select enough common elements so a link is established in the viewer's eyes between the letterhead and the envelope.
- Use the AutoText feature to save and insert frequently used text and/or graphics.
- Business cards are another way to establish identity among a target audience. Establish an identifying connection between a business card and a letterhead by repeating some of the design elements from the letterhead.

Commands Review

	Mouse/Keyboard
New dialog box to access a template	File, New, select desired tab
Letter Wizard	File, New, Letters & Faxes tab

User Info	Tools, Options, User Info tab
Change font	Format, Font; or click the Font list box, Type Size list box, and/or character formatting buttons on the Formatting toolbar
Drawing Object dialog box	Format, Drawing Object
Display Drawing toolbar	Click Drawing button on Standard toolbar; or right-click Standard toolbar, select Drawing; or View, Toolbars, select Drawing, then press Enter
Borders toolbar	Click the Borders button on the Formatting toolbar; or right-click Standard toolbar, select Borders; or View, Toolbars, select Borders; press Enter
Paragraph Borders and Shading dialog box	Format, Borders and Shading
Create Header/Footer	View, Header and Footer, click Switch Between Header and Footer to display Footer pane
Draw a frame	Insert, Frame, position cross hairs and draw frame
Insert frame around selected text	Select text, choose Insert, Frame
Size and position a frame	Select frame, choose Format, Frame
Default template folder	File, Open, Look in:, *C:\Winword\Templates* (stand-alone version) or *C:\MSOffice\Templates* (Office or Office Professional version)
Kerning (Character spacing specific pairs of characters)	Format, Font, Character Spacing tab, Kerning for Fonts, enter Points and Above:
Tracking (Character spacing)	Format, Font, Character Spacing tab, Spacing, enter point By: amount in point increments
Envelopes and Labels dialog box	Tools, Envelopes and Labels, select Envelopes or Labels tab
Symbol dialog box	Insert, Symbol
Insert Picture dialog box	Insert, Picture
Scale, crop, and size a picture	Select picture, choose Format, Picture
AutoText dialog box	Edit, AutoText
Insert AutoText entry	Edit, AutoText, select entry in Name list box; or key name of AutoText entry at document screen and press F3

Check Your Understanding

Terms: In the space provided at the left, indicate the correct term.

_____________ **1.** This feature guides you through the steps for creating a business letter using any of the available letter templates.

_____________ **2.** This term refers to the decreasing or increasing of white space between specific character pairs.

_____________ **3.** In typesetting, the thickness of a line is called its weight and is measured in this.

_____________ **4.** A customized horizontal or vertical ruled line can be created using this feature.

_____________ **5.** This term refers to the equal reduction or enlargement of the horizontal space between all characters in a block of text.

_____________ **6.** When saving a document as a template into the template folder, Word automatically adds this extension.

_____________ **7.** Turn on kerning for specific point sizes and above at this dialog box.

_____________ **8.** This feature allows you to store commonly used text and/or graphics along with their formatting.

_____________ **9.** Use this type of paper size definition when designing and creating your own business cards.

Concepts: Answer the following questions in the space provided.

1. What is the purpose of a letterhead?

2. What information might be contained in a letterhead?

3. Define the User Info feature. What other Word features does it affect?

4. When creating your own letterhead, design concepts presented in chapter 1 such as focus, balance, and proportion should be considered. What are some other design concepts that should be considered?

5. Name two methods of creating lines in Word. Explain advantages or disadvantages of using one method over the other.

6. Explain the difference between using a frame and using a text box.

Skill Assessments

Assessment 1

1. You have decided to open your own restaurant. Design a letterhead for your business that will be used for a mailing to introduce your business to the community. Include the following information:

Company Name:	**You decide on the name depending on the picture/graphic that you incorporate into your design.**
Name of owner:	**Use your own name and include *Owner* or *Proprietor* as your title.**
Slogan:	**You decide on a slogan.**
Address:	**250 San Miguel Boulevard** **Mission Viejo, CA 92691**
Phone:	**(714) 555-8191**
Fax:	**(714) 555-8196**

2. Create a thumbnail sketch(es) of your proposed letterhead incorporating the following elements:
   a. Create an asymmetrical design.
   b. Incorporate appropriate and proportional typeface, type size, and type style selections.
   c. Turn on kerning and use tracking (condensing or expanding character spacing) if necessary.
   d. Include ruled lines using either the Borders feature or the Draw feature; you decide on the placement, thickness, and color.
   e. Include one of the following pictures/graphics: *Coffee.wmf*, *Dinner1.wmf*, *Dinner2.wmf*, *Drink.wmf*, *Server.wmf*, or *Wine.wmf*.
   f. Use special characters if appropriate.
   g. Incorporate some color if a color printer is available.
3. Save the document and name it c03sa01, restaurant ltrhd.
4. Print and then close c03sa01, restaurant ltrhd.
5. As a self-check for your design, print a copy of *document analysis guide.doc* from your student data disk and answer the questions on the form. Name the exercise c03sa01, restaurant ltrhd.
6. Attach the *Document Analysis Guide* to the hard copy of the letterhead.

Assessment 2

1. Design an envelope to be used with the letterhead created in assessment 1. Include some consistent elements that demonstrate continuity from the letterhead to the envelope. Include the following specifications:
   a. Create a thumbnail sketch(es) of your proposed envelope design.
   b. At a clear editing window, use the automatic envelope feature and add the envelope to the blank document.
   c. Use the same typeface(s) as in your letterhead. Pay attention to size and proportion.
   d. Turn on automatic kerning and adjust character spacing if necessary.
   e. Use the same colors in the envelope as in your letterhead.
   f. Create an AutoText entry of the return address and use it to create an envelope.
2. Save and name the document c03sa02, restaurant env.
3. Print and then close c03sa02, restaurant env.

Assessment 3

1. Create a page of business cards to coordinate with the letterhead and envelope created in assessments 1 and 2. Even though a business card does not have to be an exact replica of your letterhead, include some consistent identifying elements that link the two documents together. Include the following specifications when creating the business cards:
   a. Create a thumbnail sketch(es) of your proposed business card design and layout.
   b. Use the Labels feature and the Avery 5371 (or 8371) business card label definition.
   c. Use the same typeface(s) used in your letterhead. You decide on size and proportion.
   d. Kern and track if necessary.
   e. If you used color in your letterhead, use it here also.
   f. Keep your text and graphics in the text layer so you can create an AutoText entry that will work easily in the Envelope & Labels feature. If you are having difficulty incorporating the AutoText entry into the label/business card, you may have to add a blank sheet of label forms to a clear document screen, create the business card in the first label form, and then copy it to the rest of the labels.
5. Save and name the business cards as c03sa03, restaurant buscard.
6. Print and then close c03sa03, restaurant buscard.

Creative Activity

Find an example of a letterhead from a business, school, volunteer organization, etc. Redesign the letterhead using the desktop publishing concepts learned so far. On a separate sheet, key the changes you made and why. Evaluate your letterhead using the *Document Analysis Guide, document analysis guide.doc,* located on your student data disk. Name the revised letterhead c03ca01. Submit a thumbnail sketch, the original letterhead (or a copy), the revised letterhead, and the *Document Analysis Guide.*

CREATING PERSONAL DOCUMENTS

PERFORMANCE OBJECTIVE

Upon successful completion of chapter 4, you will be able to create résumés, calendars, personal address labels, and certificates.

DESKTOP PUBLISHING

Templates	Character spacing	Scaling
Balance	Rules	Cropping
Consistency	Kerning	
Em and en dashes	Leading	

WORD FEATURES USED

Résumé template	Calendar Wizard	AutoText
Résumé Wizard	Watermark	Scaling
WordArt	Text boxes	Cropping
Tables	Drawing toolbar	Award Wizard
Border lines	Pictures	
Format Painter	Labels	

In this chapter, you will produce personal documents using Word's templates and wizards and create and format your own personal documents. You will use other Word features such as WordArt, tables, text boxes, labels, and more to produce résumés, calendars, address labels, and certificates. In addition, you will apply basic desktop publishing concepts of planning document content, maintaining consistency, and achieving balance through the use of graphic images, border lines, and column placement.

Creating A Résumé

A résumé is a summary of your qualifications, skills, and experiences. The main purpose of a résumé is to convince a prospective employer to grant you an interview and, ultimately, employment. Before creating your résumé, consider researching the prospective company and tailoring your résumé to what the company is seeking. Different types of business people respond differently to the same résumé. The kind of résumé that might catch an advertising executive's eye might not appeal to the personnel director of a bank.

Planning a Résumé

As you learned in chapter 1, plan your document (résumé) with a goal in mind. Take time to identify your objectives, employment experiences, qualifications, and skills. Then decide how to design your résumé to highlight the qualifications you want to emphasize. With this information in mind, categorize your qualifications by creating appropriate section headings (titles) for your résumé. Arrange the headings in the order important to you and to the job you are seeking. The order of these headings is important, because it will benefit you to showcase your best qualifications. You should refer to an up-to-date reference manual for additional information on résumés and sample résumés.

Composing your résumé in clear, concise language is important. Many sources suggest that you limit your résumé to one page. However, you might need more than a page depending on the extent of your work experience and the job you are seeking.

The information you provide about your business experience is usually presented in reverse chronological order (most current first and then working backwards). This approach is useful in demonstrating your employment growth.

Most résumés are prepared in a traditional format with the section headings keyed at the left margin and pertinent information keyed to the right of the headings. This is easily accomplished with the use of side-by-side columns created in tables or a wide left margin with the headings back-tabbed into the left margin.

Word provides three résumé templates and one résumé wizard, each serving as partially completed forms or frameworks for your résumé. You will be creating résumés in the upcoming exercises using these templates, WordArt, and tables.

Designing a Résumé

Typically, résumés are conservative in design. The design of your résumé depends on the type of employment you are considering and the image you want to portray. Think about focus, balance, and consistency in designing your résumé as you would consider these concepts in preparing all documents. You are the focus of this résumé! So the heading with your name, address, and telephone number should be emphasized in a larger font with bold, small caps, or italics used to add visual interest.

DTP POINTERS

- Limit the use of all caps in résumés.
- Do not use underlining.
- Use no more than 2-3 typefaces.
- Use kerning when type size exceeds 14 points.

Many résumés use the italics version of a serif typeface in a larger type size for headings. Using the italics version can soften the effect between the headings and the body text. Avoid using all caps in the section headings—you may want to use small caps in place of all caps. Also, do not use underlining to emphasize—underlining is a dated practice.

Your choice of typefaces and type sizes will lend consistency to your document. All of the section headings should use the same typeface and type size. Remember to turn on kerning if the point size exceeds 14 points. A general rule is to limit your use of typefaces to two to three per document. In a résumé, two typefaces are sufficient. Consider using these typefaces for body text: Times New Roman, Garamond, Century Schoolbook, or Book Antiqua. For headings, you can choose any of these suggestions: Arial, Century Gothic, Impact, or Britannic Bold. Times New Roman or other serif typefaces can also be used in résumé headings.

You may vary the design of your résumé by using *rules* (border lines) between the different sections. White space, section titles, and rules can be added to a résumé to assist in organizing information, to aid in directional flow, and to create balance. The placement of headings on the left side of a résumé with sufficient amount of white space balances a heavier right side that includes more text. Also, use bullets to create attractive lists. Bullets are good tools for organizing facts and they give the reader rest from text-intensive copy.

Rules: Horizontal or vertical lines used to separate text or to set off page elements.

The main purpose of a résumé is to sell yourself to a prospective employer. This is serious business and your résumé should be conservative, neat, organized, concise, and truthful. If you are interested in varying the design so your résumé stands out from the crowd, carefully incorporate some creativity. One approach that adds a unique touch is to rotate the heading of your résumé.

Choosing and Placing Section Headings

Begin your résumé by deciding which section headings are appropriate and in which order they should appear. Most résumés include these essential parts:

- Heading—Name, Address, Telephone Number, Fax Number, e-mail Address
- Career Objective
- Work Experience
- Education
- Special Skills or Achievements
- Interests
- References

Carefully plan your career objective and position this statement at the beginning of your résumé. Typically, the career objective is composed of one or two statements about the kind of job you want and what you can contribute to the company interviewing you. The career objective gives the résumé a sense of direction. Do not make your goal statement so vague that it is meaningless.

Your work experience history usually follows the career objective. In the work experience section, list your responsibilities, contributions, and special achievements. Many companies give the most weight to relevant job experiences. This is a crucial section of your résumé. This is where you want to sell yourself by emphasizing your strengths in dealing with people, problem-solving skills, goal-setting abilities, and more.

Educational history is usually listed next on the résumé, although the exact location may vary depending on the length of your professional experience and the strength of your educational achievements. If you recently completed school and have very little work experience, your education is probably your best achievement and should be listed before job experience. As you gain work experience, your education may be less important to a prospective employer.

The next essential heading may be special skills, achievements, or interests. This area could include your membership in any professional organizations, community, or volunteer organizations.

A current trend in writing résumés is to eliminate the last category—references. If you decide to include references, you must ask permission to use someone's name as a reference before making that information available. Another choice is to simply state, "References will be furnished upon request."

When printing a professional-looking résumé, use conservative colors for the paper such as light gray, white, or cream. A good quality bond paper is also recommended. Print your résumé using a laser printer or high resolution quality ink jet printer. Avoid using a dot matrix printer.

Choosing A Résumé Template

DTP POINTERS
Consistency is important in designing documents that are meant to be used together.

Word's predefined résumé templates contain text, formatting, border lines, bullets, and styles. The résumé templates vary slightly in design and layout. The differences are primarily in typefaces, type sizes, appearance attributes (bold and italics), and rules.

Word includes three résumé templates from the same template family discussed earlier—Contemporary, Elegant, and Professional. If you use the Professional Résumé template, use the Professional Letter template to create a cover letter. Consistency is important in designing documents that are meant to be used together. Take the time to view each version as illustrated in figure 4.1 and note the subtle variations in each.

FIGURE 4.1

Résumé Template Types

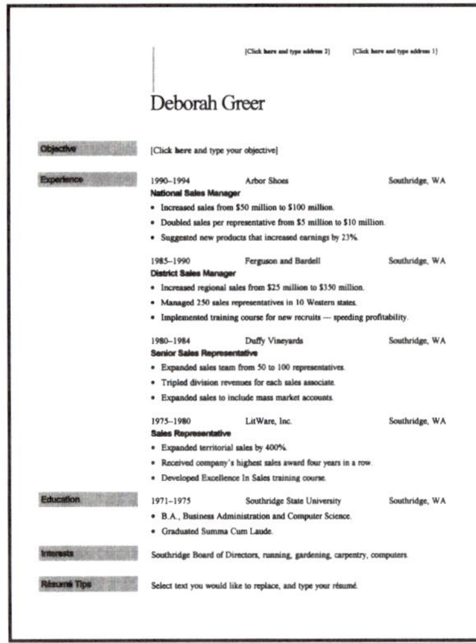

[Click here and type address 2] [Click here and type address 1]

Deborah Greer

Objective [Click **here** and type your objective]

Experience 1990–1994 Arbor Shoes Southridge, WA
National Sales Manager
- Increased sales from $50 million to $100 million.
- Doubled sales per representative from $5 million to $10 million.
- Suggested new products that increased earnings by 23%.

1985–1990 Ferguson and Bardell Southridge, WA
District Sales Manager
- Increased regional sales from $25 million to $350 million.
- Managed 250 sales representatives in 10 Western states.
- Implemented training course for new recruits — speeding profitability.

1980–1984 Duffy Vineyards Southridge, WA
Senior Sales Representative
- Expanded sales team from 50 to 100 representatives.
- Tripled division revenues for each sales associate.
- Expanded sales to include mass market accounts.

1975–1980 LitWare, Inc. Southridge, WA
Sales Representative
- Expanded territorial sales by 400%.
- Received company's highest sales award four years in a row.
- Developed Excellence In Sales training course.

Education 1971–1975 Southridge State University Southridge, WA
- B.A., Business Administration and Computer Science.
- Graduated Summa Cum Laude.

Interests Southridge Board of Directors, running, gardening, carpentry, computers.

Résumé Tips Select text you would like to replace, and type your résumé.

CONTEMPORARY

RICH ANDREWS

OBJECTIVE
[Click **here** and type objective]

EXPERIENCE
1990–1994 Arbor Shoe Southridge, SC
National Sales Manager
- Increased sales from $50 million to $100 million.
- Doubled sales per representative from $5 million to $10 million.
- Suggested new products that increased earnings by 23%.

1985–1990 Ferguson and Bardell Southridge, SC
District Sales Manager
- Increased regional sales from $25 million to $350 million.
- Managed 250 sales representatives in 10 Western states.
- Implemented training course for new recruits — speeding profitability.

1980–1984 Duffy Vineyards Southridge, SC
Senior Sales Representative
- Expanded sales team from 50 to 100 representatives.
- Tripled division revenues for each sales associate.
- Expanded sales to include mass market accounts.

EDUCATION
1971–1975 Southridge State University Southridge, SC
- B.A., Business Administration and Computer Science.
- Graduated Summa Cum Laude.

INTERESTS
Southridge Board of Directors, running, gardening, carpentry, computers.

RÉSUMÉ TIPS
Select text you would like to replace, and type your résumé.

12345 MAIN STREET • ANY CITY, STATE 12345-6789 • PHONE (123) 456-7890
123 ANY STREET • ANY CITY, STATE 12345 • PHONE (123) 456-7890

ELEGANT

[Click here and type address 1] [Click here and type address 2]

Max Benson

Objective [Click **here** and type objective]

Experience 1990–1994 Arbor Shoe Southridge, SC
National Sales Manager
- Increased sales from $50 million to $100 million.
- Doubled sales per representative from $5 million to $10 million.
- Suggested new products that increased earnings by 23%.

1985–1990 Ferguson and Bardell Southridge, SC
District Sales Manager
- Increased regional sales from $25 million to $350 million.
- Managed 250 sales representatives in 10 Western states.
- Implemented training course for new recruits — speeding profitability.

1980–1984 Duffy Vineyards Southridge, SC
Senior Sales Representative
- Expanded sales team from 50 to 100 representatives.
- Tripled division revenues for each sales associate.
- Expanded sales to include mass market accounts.

1975–1980 LitWare, Inc. Southridge, SC
Sales Representative
- Expanded territorial sales by 400%.
- Received company's highest sales award four years in a row.
- Developed Excellence In Sales training course.

Education 1971–1975 Southridge State University Southridge, SC
- B.A., Business Administration and Computer Science.
- Graduated Summa Cum Laude.

Interests SR Board of Directors, running, gardening, carpentry, computers.

Résumé Tips Select the text you would like to replace, and type your résumé.

PROFESSIONAL

The Contemporary design is straightforward and uses clean lines. The section titles are set in Arial typeface; the text is set in Times New Roman. The gray vertical line located at the top of the résumé points to the name on the résumé and promotes a downward directional flow. The shaded boxes used in the section titles maintain consistency through percent of shading and text formatting. Styles are very important in each of the templates since they reduce time and effort in formatting the résumés. These styles are used consistently in all the résumé templates—Objective, Section Title, Company Name, Job Title, Institution, and Achievement styles. In addition, an asymmetrical design is consistent among the résumé templates.

The Elegant template design is a compromise between the Contemporary and Professional templates. Garamond was selected for the document typeface. Rules help to organize the text and aid directional flow. Again, styles play an important role in formatting the entire template. The name was emphasized by using expanded character spacing. The expanded information at the bottom of the résumé balances the name at the top of the page.

The design and layout of all of the elements in the Professional Résumé template are basic and predictable. Two sans serif typefaces, Arial Black and Arial, are used throughout the entire résumé. The "no frills" approach to the formatting of this résumé is shown through the lack of shaded boxes or lines around the section titles, the simple and plain formatting of the name, and the use of square bullets that complement the blocked look of the Arial typeface.

Using the Résumé Wizard

The Résumé Wizard assists you in creating a customized, personal résumé based on your answers to various built-in prompts within the Wizard. The Wizard saves time and effort since most of the formatting has been completed for you. Figure 4.2 illustrates the first screen that appears after selecting the Résumé Wizard at the New dialog box with the Other Documents tab selected. Notice the on-screen selections and descriptions.

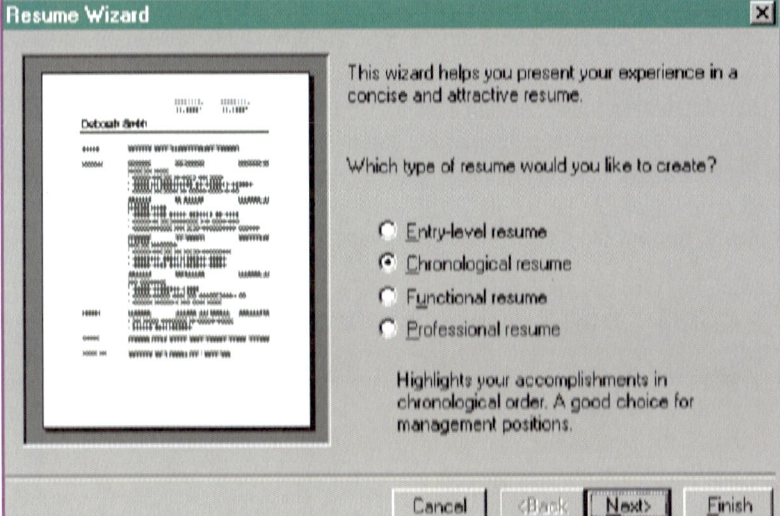

FIGURE 4.2

Résumé Wizard

Accessing a Résumé Template or Wizard

To use a résumé template, choose File, then New. At the New dialog box, select the Other Documents tab. Select one of the three résumé templates or the Résumé Wizard that displays. Double-click the résumé icon that corresponds with the style you want to use or click the icon once and press Enter or click OK. Key your résumé information and then save it when completed. You can save the résumé as a document or as a template.

Customizing Résumé Templates

Word's templates include placeholder (sample) text that shows what the finished document will look like. Placeholder text also makes it easier to insert your own information into the template. You simply select the placeholder text and replace it with your personal information. Avoid deleting the paragraph symbol at the end of the sample text; formatting codes in the styles are embedded in the paragraph symbols. The correct formatting is already in place. Placeholder text also offers helpful tips on using the template.

Word templates also contain "click-**here**-and-type" features that make creating a résumé easier. For instance, to include an objective in a résumé based on a template, position the arrow pointer on **"here"**, click once, then key your objective statement.

As previously mentioned, Word résumé templates include many styles. Styles are useful because they apply a whole group of formats in one step. If you decide to edit a style, all the changes you make will automatically apply to all occurrences of that style in your document. With the Style command from the Format menu or the Style box on the Formatting toolbar, you can apply the styles that come with Word, or you can create your own styles. In the next exercise, you will apply preexisting styles to text. More information on creating styles will be presented in a later chapter.

DTP POINTERS
- Use an en dash to indicate a duration or range.
- Use an em dash to indicate a change of thought.

Applying Desktop Publishing Guidelines to a Résumé

When creating a résumé, remember to use typographical symbols for en and em dashes. An en dash is used in place of a hyphen indicating a duration or range, such as 1991–1993. Use an em dash to indicate a change of thought or where a period is too strong and a comma is too weak.

DTP POINTERS
Use consistent ending punctuation in a résumé.

When using bullets to list items in a résumé, be consistent with ending punctuation. If the bulleted items consist of phrases, do not key a period at the end of the phrase. However, if the bulleted items are stated as complete sentences, key a period at the end of each sentence. Consistency is important, so try not to mix phrases and complete sentences together as bulleted items. Reword the items if necessary to maintain consistency.

EXERCISE 1

Creating a Résumé Using the Elegant Résumé Template

1. Create the résumé shown in figure 4.3 by completing the following steps:
   a. Choose File, then New.
   b. At the New dialog box, select the Other Documents tab.
   c. Double-click the Elegant Résumé template icon.
   d. Click the Show/Hide ¶ button on the Standard toolbar to display spaces, tabs, and paragraph symbols in the document. This will be helpful in deleting and replacing text.
   e. Select *RICH ANDREWS.*
   f. Key your name in place of *RICH ANDREWS.*
   g. Click once on the prompt, [Click **here** and type objective], then key **To work in an Accounting/Business position that offers opportunities for advancement.**
   h. Select the placeholder text in the Experience section. Key the following text under the Experience section title:

      Key **1994–Present** (use an en dash). Press tab if necessary to align. Key **Patterson, McNichols, & Company**; press Tab if necessary, then key **Manchester, MO**. (Press the down arrow key to position the insertion point on the next line.)
      Accountant
      Responsible for accounts receivable.
      Responsible for all basic accounting functions: coding and distribution of invoices, classifying transactions, and processing orders.
      Responsible for preparation of tax forms.

      Key **1993**, press Tab if necessary, key **Case Foods, Inc.**; press Tab if necessary, then key **Springfield, MO**.
      Accounting Clerk—Cooperative Education

Responsible for data entry into computer system.
Responsible for product orders for regional representatives.

Key **1992**; press Tab if necessary, key **Morris Insurance Company**; press Tab if necessary, then key **St. Louis, MO**.
Accounting Clerk—College Summer Internship
Responsible for billing and receiving payments from multi-state area.
Revised and updated accounts.
Assisted in telephone survey.

i. Select the placeholder text in the Education section. Key the following text under the Education section title:

   Key **1991–1993** (use an en dash); press Tab if necessary, key **Hadley University**; press Tab if necessary, then key **Springfield, MO**.
   Bachelor of Science Degree, Accounting Major.
   Phi Kappa Phi Honor Society.
   Cum Laude, GPA 3.85/4.0.

j. Press Enter twice. (The second Enter will turn off the bullet feature.)
k. Key **1989–1991**; press Tab, key **Westlake Community College**; press Tab, then key **Manchester, MO**.
l. Apply the *Institution* style to the last line by completing the following steps:
   (1) Select the text in step k.
   (2) Click the down-pointing triangle to the right of the Style box on the Formatting toolbar (first button from the left).
   (3) Click the *Institution* style from the Style drop-down list.
   (4) Position the insertion point at the end of the line.
m. Press Enter.
n. Key the following text (a bullet should display automatically when the Enter key is pressed):

   Associate Degree, Accounting Major.
   Tennis Team.

o. Select the placeholder text in the Interests section. Key the following text under the Interests section title:

   Hadley University Student Government Representative; running; tennis; and computers.

p. Select and then delete Résumé Tips. (This text may appear on the next page.)
q. Position the insertion point and click anywhere in the first address line at the bottom of the résumé template. The text has been inserted in a frame and formatted with a style named *Address 2*. (Notice *Address 2* in the Style list box when the insertion point is located anywhere in the formatted text.) Delete the placeholder text in this line, leaving the bullet symbol between the street address and city and between the zip code and telephone number. If you should accidentally delete the bullet, insert the • symbol by turning on the Num Lock function (the first key in the top row of the key pad on your keyboard) and using the shortcut key command, Alt + 0149 (hold down the Alt key), insert a blank space before and after the symbol. Key the following text:

   531 PINELAND AVENUE • MANCHESTER, MO 63011 • PHONE (314) 555-5946

r. Turn off the Num Lock key if you used it to create bullets in step q.
s. Select and then delete the framed text formatted with the *Address 1* style.

2. Save the document with the name c04ex01, template resume.
3. Print and then close c04ex01, template resume.

FIGURE 4.3

YOUR NAME HERE

OBJECTIVE

To work in an Accounting/Business position that offers opportunities for advancement.

EXPERIENCE

1994–Present	Patterson, McNichols, & Company	Manchester, MO

Accountant

- Responsible for accounts receivable.
- Responsible for all basic accounting functions: coding and distribution of invoices, classifying transactions, and processing orders.
- Responsible for preparation of tax forms.

1993	Case Foods, Inc.	Springfield, MO

Accounting Clerk—Cooperative Education

- Responsible for data entry into computer system.
- Responsible for product orders for regional representatives.

1992	Morris Insurance Company	St. Louis, MO

Accounting Clerk—College Summer Internship

- Responsible for billing and receiving payments from multi-state area.
- Revised and updated accounts.
- Assisted in telephone survey.

EDUCATION

1991–1993	Hadley University	Springfield, MO

- Bachelor of Science Degree, Accounting Major.
- Phi Kappa Phi Honor Society.
- Cum Laude, GPA 3.85/4.0.

1989–1991	Westlake Community College	Manchester, MO

- Associate Degree, Accounting Major.
- Tennis Team.

INTERESTS

Hadley University Student Government Representative; running; tennis; and computers.

531 PINELAND AVENUE • MANCHESTER, MO 63011 • PHONE (314) 555-5946

Designing Your Own Résumé

As mentioned earlier in this chapter, most résumés are conservative in layout and design. In exercise 2, you will be creating a résumé that will probably stand out from the crowd. The heading is created in WordArt, rotated 90 degrees, and then framed. This design is sure to catch a prospective employer's eye. In addition, you will use the Format Painter button, which automatically "paints" formatting codes to other areas of text in the résumé created in exercise 2.

DTP POINTERS
Use a rotated box to create contrast and focus.

Format Painter

Using WordArt to Rotate Text

With WordArt, you can create many special effects, such as conforming text into 36 different shapes in addition to rotating, slanting, and curving text. WordArt enables you to change the font, style, size, alignment, and character spacing of the text. You can also enhance text by adding shadows, outlines, colors, and fills. As you can see, WordArt is a comprehensive program.

WordArt is an OLE-based (object linking and embedding) add-in program. Because WordArt is built within Word for Windows, it cannot be run by itself. WordArt can, however, be used by other Windows programs that support OLE.

When using WordArt, you are creating text and applying special effects chosen from the WordArt toolbar or menu bar. Text created in WordArt does not appear in a window of its own; the WordArt menus and buttons actually replace Word menus and buttons.

WordArt images can be treated as pictures inserted into a Word document. The object moves with the text that surrounds it. You can also size, crop, or scale the object by choosing Format, then Picture. A border can be added to the object by choosing Format, then Borders and Shading. A frame can also be added to the picture by choosing Format, then Frame, or by clicking the Insert Frame button on the Drawing toolbar (last button from the left). One advantage to framing the picture is that you can move the frame and the picture is automatically moved with it. A text box can be rotated at 90-degree intervals, but the text within the box will not rotate. Therefore, WordArt is needed to rotate text.

To enter WordArt, you would position the insertion point where you want the WordArt object to appear, then choose Insert, then Object. At the Object dialog box, with the Create New tab selected, you would double-click *Microsoft WordArt 3.0 (2.0)* in the Object Type list box. The Object dialog box with the Create New tab selected is shown in figure 4.4. If you double-click *Microsoft WordArt 3.0 (2.0)*, the text entry box displays in the document screen as shown in figure 4.5.

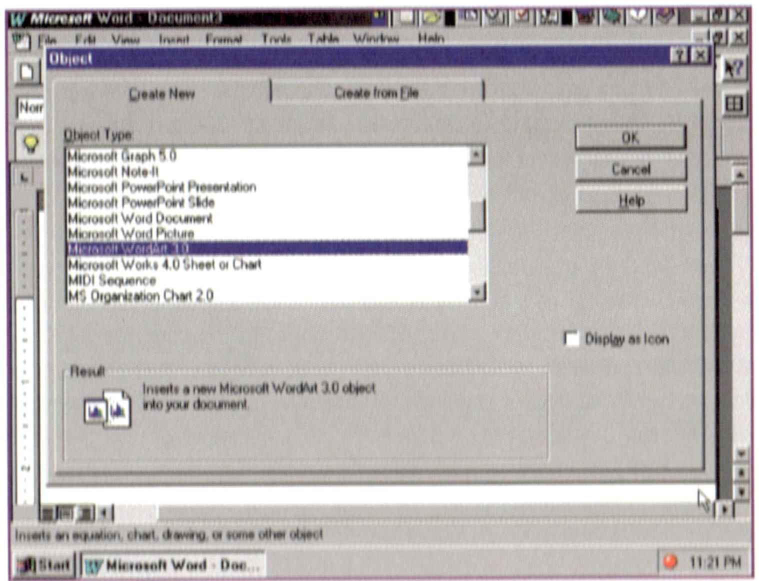

FIGURE 4.4
Object Dialog Box with Microsoft WordArt 3.0 Selected

FIGURE 4.5

WordArt Screen

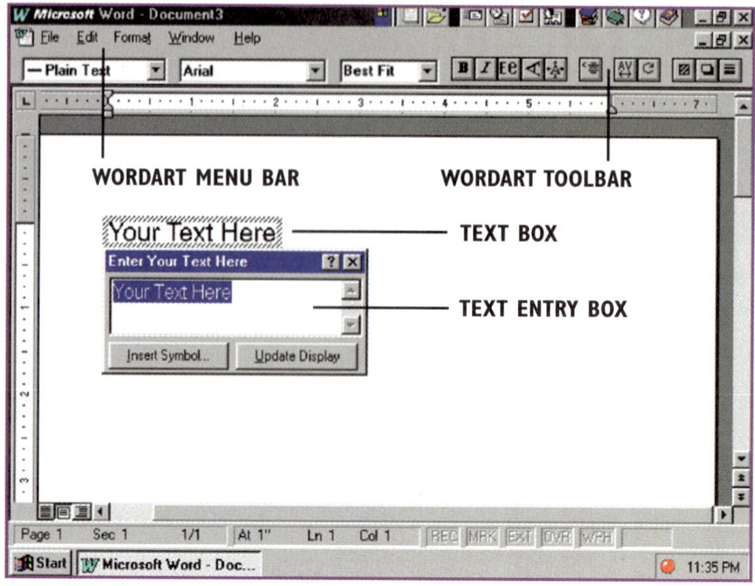

Entering Text in WordArt

When you first enter WordArt, the insertion point is positioned in the Enter Your Text Here text entry box. The words *Your Text Here* display in the text entry box and are selected. Key your text in the text entry box and the original words are removed. Press the Enter key if you want to move the insertion point to the next line. Text in the WordArt text box is center aligned by default. Also, by default WordArt applies the Arial font to text.

To view how the text will display in the text box, choose the Update Display button at the right side of the text entry box. By default, WordArt uses *Best Fit* when displaying text in the text box. This setting fits your text into the default two-inch WordArt box. The size of the box adjusts to the size of your text.

If you want to insert a symbol in the text entry box, choose the Insert Symbol button at the bottom of the text entry box. With the Insert Symbol dialog box displayed, click the desired symbol then choose OK to close the dialog box.

Editing WordArt Text

To edit a WordArt object, double-click the object and the Enter Your Text Here dialog box and WordArt toolbar and the menu bar will appear. Or select the object at your document window, then choose Edit, WordArt 3.0 (2.0) Object, then select either Edit or Open. If you choose Edit, the WordArt toolbar, menu bar, and text entry box will appear. If you choose Open, the WordArt 3.0 (2.0) dialog box will appear.

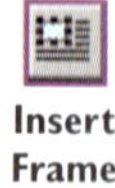

Insert Frame

To change the size of the WordArt object without changing its proportions, select the image, then hold down the Ctrl key as you drag one of the corner sizing handles inward to reduce the size or outward to increase the size of the image. To resize an object nonproportionally, drag a side sizing handle. You can also resize a WordArt object by selecting the object, choosing Format, then Picture. To position a WordArt object, choose Format, then Frame; right click to access the Shortcut Menu, then select Frame Picture; or click the Insert Frame button on the Drawing toolbar. Once the object has been framed, drag it to another location.

To exit WordArt, click in the working area of your page outside the Enter Your Text Here box. The Standard toolbar, menu bar, and your WordArt image will appear in your document.

Applying Special Effects to WordArt Text

The WordArt toolbar includes the buttons shown in figure 4.6.

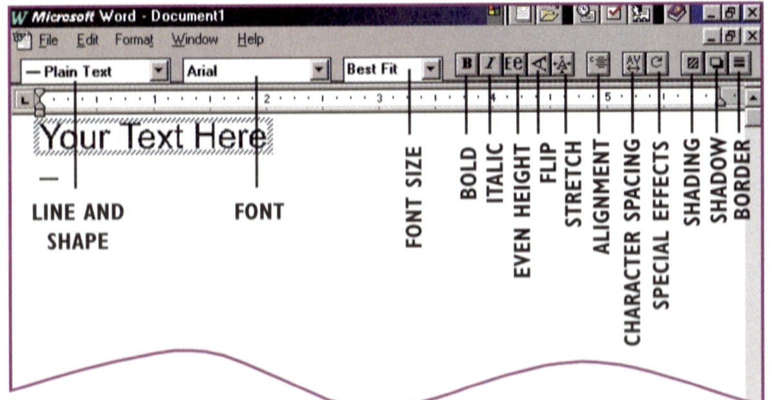

FIGURE 4.6

WordArt Toolbar Buttons

Each of the buttons on the WordArt toolbar can accomplish the tasks listed in figure 4.7.

FIGURE 4.7

Buttons on the WordArt Toolbar

Name of Button	What the Button Can Do
Line and Shape	Conforms text to a variety of shapes.
Font	Changes fonts (Arial is the default).
Font Size	Changes font sizes (Best Fit is the default).
Bold	Applies bold to text.
Italics	Applies italics to text.
Even Height	Makes all the letters the same size.
Flip	Flips each letter on its side at 90 degrees.
Stretch	Stretches text vertically and horizontally to fit the box where the text is located.
Alignment	Aligns and justifies text in six different ways (center is the default).
Character Spacing	Increases and decreases spacing between characters. Kerning can be turned on or off.
Special Effects	Rotates text and slants or curves text.
Shading	Adds shading, pattern, or color to text.
Shadows	Adds a shadow to each character.
Border	Adds a border around each letter.

WordArt can be used to create logos and interesting signs. You can select a shape from the Shapes list and your text will conform to this shape. Figure 4.8 shows the wide range of shapes that are available in WordArt. You will work more with these shapes in chapter 5.

FIGURE 4.8

Line and Shape Palette

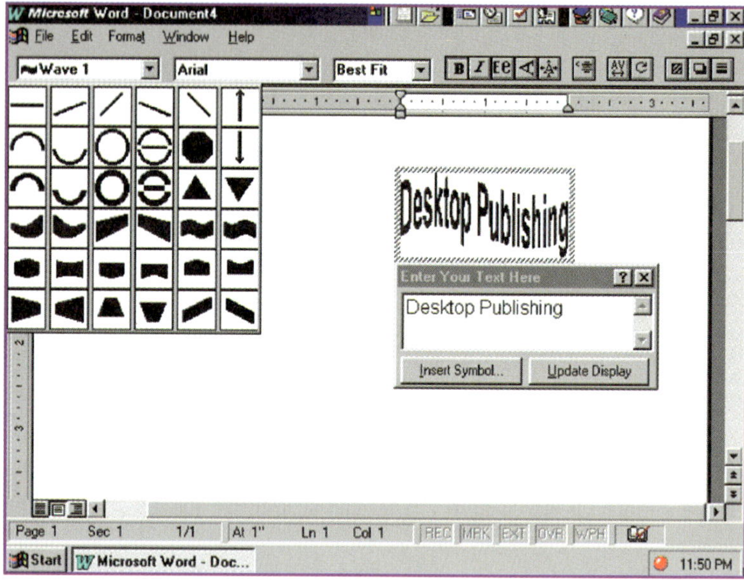

Rotating Text

With the Special Effects button on the WordArt toolbar, you can rotate, arc, and slant text. The Special Effects dialog box, shown in figure 4.9, will display if you click the Special Effects button on the WordArt toolbar (fourth button from the right). Enter a degree of rotation in the Rotation text box or click the up- or down-pointing triangles. To rotate the image upside-down, change the rotation to 180 degrees. In exercise 2, you will rotate the text 90 degrees.

FIGURE 4.9

Special Effects (Rotating Text at 90 Degrees)

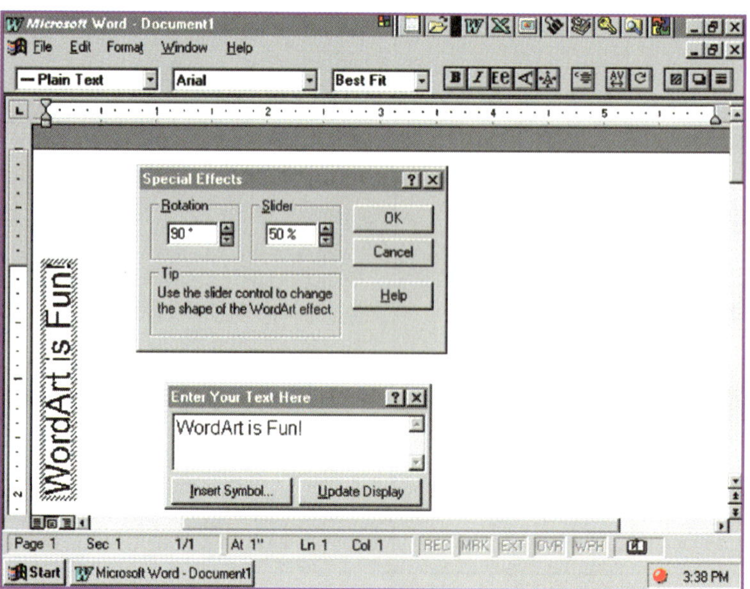

Using Format Painter in a Résumé

You will be using a Word feature called Format Painter to copy or "paint" formatting codes from one section heading to the rest of the section headings in a résumé. To use the Format Painter, you would complete the following steps:

1. Position the insertion point on the text that has the formatting you want to copy.
2. Click the Format Painter button on the Standard toolbar (tenth button from the left—it looks like a paintbrush). Double-click if you want to format more than one occurrence.
3. Select the text to which you want the format applied using the mouse. (The I-beam pointer displays with a paintbrush attached.) When you release the mouse button, the text will take on the new formatting.
4. Click the Format Painter button again to turn the feature off if you double-clicked the Format Painter button to format more than one occurrence.

The keyboard can also be used to apply formatting to text. To do this, select the text containing the formatting to be applied to other text, then press Ctrl + Shift + C. Select the text to which you want to apply the formatting, then press Ctrl + Shift + V.

To remove all character formatting, select the text that has the formatting you want to remove, then press Ctrl + space bar.

Creating a Résumé with Rotated Text

1. At a clear document window, create a résumé with rotated text as shown in figure 4.10 by completing the following steps:
   a. Change the top margin to 0.75 inches. Change the bottom, left, and right margins to 0.50 inches. (If the prompt *One or more of the margins are set outside the printable zone...* appears, choose the Fix button and then click OK.)
   b. Choose Insert, then Object.
   c. At the Object dialog box, select the Create New tab.
   d. In the Object Type list box, double-click *Microsoft WordArt 3.0 (2.0)*.
   e. Create the rotated text in WordArt by completing the following steps:
      (1) With the insertion point positioned in the text entry box, key **NANCY WEBER**, then press Enter.
      (2) Key **204 Shanahan Court, Wheaton, IL 60153**, then press Enter.
      (3) Key **(708) 555-8960**.
      (4) Click the Update Display button.
      (5) At the WordArt toolbar, click the down-pointing triangle to the right of the Font button, then select Garamond at the drop-down list.
      (6) Click the Font Size button, then change the size from *Best Fit* to 24 points.
      (7) Click the bold and italic buttons on the WordArt toolbar.
      (8) Click the Alignment button (sixth button from the right on the WordArt toolbar) and make sure Center alignment is selected.
      (9) Click the Spacing Between Characters button (fifth button from the right). At the Spacing Between Characters dialog box, make the following changes:
         (a) Change the tracking to Loose.
         (b) Make sure the setting Automatically Kern Character Pairs is turned on.
         (c) Click OK to close the Spacing Between Characters dialog box.
      (10) Click the Special Effects button (fourth button from the right). At the Special Effects dialog box, change the Rotation to 90 degrees, then click OK to close the Special Effects dialog box.

(11) Click outside the text entry box to remove the text entry box from the document window.
(12) Change the size of your WordArt object by choosing Format, then Picture. At the Picture dialog box, make the following changes:
(a) Change the Width in the Size section to 1.6 inches.
(b) Change the Height in the Size section to 9.5 inches.
(c) Click OK to close the dialog box.

f. Create the vertical line to the right of the rotated text by completing the following steps:
(1) Display the Borders toolbar by clicking the Borders button on the Formatting toolbar (last button at the right).
(2) At the Borders toolbar, click the down-pointing triangle to the right of the Line Style button, then click *1½ pt.*
(3) Click the Right Border button (fifth button from the left) on the Borders toolbar. (A vertical line positioned to the right of the WordArt text should appear in the document window.)
(4) Make sure the WordArt image is selected (eight selection handles should appear at the top, bottom, and sides of the image).
(5) Choose Insert, then Frame.
(6) Choose Format, then Frame. At the Frame dialog box, change the Horizontal Distance from Text to 0.3 inches (this setting creates the left margin for the body text), then choose OK to close the dialog box.

g. Click outside the WordArt image to deselect it. (The insertion point should be positioned at the top of the page and to the right of the WordArt image.)
h. Key **PROFESSIONAL OBJECTIVE**, then press Enter.
i. Key **Provide word processing software installation and support for small- to medium-sized businesses.**, then press Enter twice. (Use a regular hyphen.)
j. Select *Professional Objective*, then change the font to 16-point Garamond Bold Italics and turn on small caps.
k. Position the insertion point at the beginning of the line *Provide word processing...*
l. Choose Format, then Paragraph.
m. At the Paragraph dialog box, select the Indents and Spacing tab. Make the following changes:
(1) Change the Left Indention setting to 0.25 inches.
(2) Change the Spacing Before to 6 points (6 pt).
(3) At the Line Spacing box, select *At Least* and change the At setting to 11 points.
(4) Click OK to close the Paragraph dialog box.

n. Press Ctrl + End.
o. Key **WORK EXPERIENCE** (without any formatting), then press Enter. (You will use the Format Painter after all the section titles have been keyed into the document.)
p. Choose Insert, then File.
q. At the Insert File dialog box, select the drive where your student data files are located. Double-click the file *para01* in the list box or key **para01** in the File name text box. Click OK to close the Insert dialog box.
r. Key **EDUCATION**, then press Enter.
s. Insert *para02* from your student data disk by following steps similar to steps p. and q.
t. Key **INTERESTS AND ACTIVITIES**, then press Enter.
u. Insert *para03* from your student data disk.
v. Key **REFERENCES**, then press Enter.
w. Insert *para04* from your student data disk.

2. Use the Format Painter to format the section titles by completing the following steps:
a. Position the insertion point anywhere on the already formatted section title *Professional Objective.*

b. Double-click the Format Painter button on the Standard toolbar. (The I-beam pointer will display with a paint brush attached.)
c. Select each remaining section title one at a time using the mouse. (This applies the formatting.)
d. Click once on the Format Painter button to turn off the feature.

3. Save the résumé and name it c04ex02, rotated resume.
4. Print and then close c04ex02, rotated resume.

FIGURE 4.10

NANCY WEBER
204 Shanahan Court, Wheaton, IL 60153
(708) 555-8960

PROFESSIONAL OBJECTIVE

Provide word processing software installation and support for small- to medium-sized businesses.

WORK EXPERIENCE

Bayman Computer Consultants, Downers Grove, IL
Computer Systems Consultant, August 1993–Present

- Provides word processing software installation, implementation, and technical support for various firms in Illinois, Indiana, and Michigan.

Computer Solutions, Naperville, IL
Office Manager, November 1990–June 1993

- Supervised and trained office staff in Microsoft Office Professional.
- Established and supervised production of office procedures manual.
- Created and implemented automated accounts payable system.

College of DuPage, Glen Ellyn, IL
Part-time instructor in Office Careers Department, September 1992–Present

- Taught Microsoft Word for Windows 6.0, Microsoft Word for Windows 95, and PowerPoint for Windows 95.

EDUCATION

North Central College, Naperville, IL
1993–Present
Courses include Mastering the Internet, Windows 95, and Desktop Publishing using Microsoft Word for Windows 95.

College of DuPage, Glen Ellyn, IL
1991-1992
Courses include Word 6.0 and Graphic Design.

Western Michigan University, Kalamazoo, MI
Master's Degree in Business Administration—August 1990
Bachelor's Degree in Business Education—December 1989
Pi Omega Pi Honorary
President's Honor Roll

INTERESTS AND ACTIVITIES

Chicago Area Business Education Association
National Secretaries Association

REFERENCES

References available upon request.

Creating A Résumé Using Side-By-Side Columns

In Word you can create two types of columns: newspaper columns (also called snaking columns) and side-by-side columns (also referred to as parallel columns). Newspaper columns are frequently used for text in newspapers, newsletters, and magazines, and are created by choosing Format, then Columns or by clicking the Columns button on the Standard toolbar.

Side-by-side columns group text horizontally across the page in rows and are commonly used in an agenda, résumé, itinerary, script, or address list. Side-by-side columns are created by inserting a table into a document using either the Insert Table button on the Standard toolbar (eighth button from the right) or the Table option from the menu bar.

To create a résumé using the table feature, you may want two columns and possibly six rows. The number of rows will depend on the number of section titles needed in your résumé. To create a table using the Insert Table dialog box, choose Table, then Insert Table. At the Insert Table dialog box, specify the desired number of rows and columns, then choose OK to close the dialog box. To create a table using the Insert Table button on the Standard toolbar, position the arrow pointer on the Insert Table button, hold down the left mouse button, drag down and to the right until the desired number of rows and columns are selected (and display at the bottom of the grid), then release the mouse button.

Creating a Résumé in a Table

1. At a clear document window, create the résumé shown in figure 4.11 using a table by completing the following steps:
   a. Change the top margin to 0.75 inches, the bottom margin to 0.5 inches, and the left and right margins to 1 inch.
   b. Display the Font dialog box with the Character Spacing tab selected, then turn on Kerning at 14 points and above.
   c. Create and format a table by completing the following steps:
      (1) Position the arrow pointer on the Insert Table button on the Standard toolbar, hold down the left mouse button, drag down and to the right until two columns and eight rows are selected in the grid (and *8 x 2 Table* displays below the grid), then release the mouse button.
      (2) Change the width of the two columns by completing the following steps:
         (a) Choose Table, then Cell Height and Width.
         (b) At the Cell Height and Width dialog box, select the Column tab.
         (c) Change the Width of Column 1 to 2.25 inches.
         (d) Change the Space Between Columns to 0.5 inches.
         (e) Click the Next Column button, then change the Width of Column 2 to 4.75 inches.
         (f) Click OK or press Enter.
   d. Position the insertion point in the first cell, then insert the round bullet symbol as shown in figure 4.11 by completing the following steps:
      (1) Choose Insert, then Symbol.
      (2) At the Symbol dialog box, select the Symbols tab.
      (3) In the Font text box, select Wingdings from the drop-down list.
      (4) Click the round bullet symbol located in the fifth row and the sixteenth column.
      (5) Click Insert three times, then click Close.
      (6) Insert a blank space between each symbol.

(7) Press Tab.

e. Click the Align Right button (seventh button from the right) on the Formatting toolbar, key **Diane Anderson**, then press Tab twice.

f. Click the Right Align button on the Formatting toolbar, key **1414 Cleveland Avenue • St. Joseph • MI 49605** (use the same symbol as in step d), then press Tab twice.

g. Click the Right Align button, key **(616) 555-4476 • Fax (616) 555-7032**, then press Enter twice.

h. Position the insertion point in the selection bar in front of the first row, then click to select the first row.

i. Change the font to 36-point Footlight MT Light Bold, then click inside any cell to deselect the first row.

j. Select *Diane Anderson.* Change the character spacing by completing the following steps:

   (1) Choose Format, then Font.

   (2) At the Font dialog box, select the Character Spacing tab.

   (3) Click the down-pointing triangle to the right of the Spacing text box, then select *Expanded* from the drop-down list.

   (4) Key **3** in the By text box.

   (5) Turn on Kerning at 14 points and above.

   (6) Click OK to close the dialog box.

k. Select *1414 Cleveland...*, then change the font to 13-point Footlight MT Light. While still selected, display the Font dialog box with the Character Spacing tab selected. Click the down-pointing triangle to the right of the Position text box, select *Lowered*, then key **16** in the By text box. Choose OK to close the Font dialog box.

l. Select *(616) 555-4476...*, then change the font to 13-point Footlight MT Light.

m. Press Tab.

n. Key **Career Objective**, then press Tab.

o. Insert the document named *para05* at the Insert File dialog box.

p. Press Tab, key **Experience**, then press Tab.

q. Insert *para06*, then press Tab.

r. Key **Education**, then press Tab.

s. Insert *para07*, then press Tab.

t. Key **Interests**, then press Tab.

u. Insert *para08*, then press Tab.

v. Key **References**, then press Tab.

w. Key **References available upon request.**, then press Tab twice.

x. Click the Align Right button on the Formatting toolbar, then insert three symbols like the ones created at the beginning of the résumé. Insert a blank space between each symbol.

y. Select the three symbols in step x, then change the Font to 36-point Footlight MT Light Bold.

z. Select the first section title, *Career Objective*, then change the font to 16-point Footlight MT Light Bold. Format the remaining section titles by completing the following steps:

   (1) Position the insertion point on any character in the title *Career Objective*.

   (2) Double-click the Format Painter button on the Standard toolbar.

   (3) Select each of the remaining section titles.

   (4) Click once on the Format Painter button to turn off this feature.

2. Save the résumé and name it c04ex03, table resume.
3. Print and then close c04ex03, table resume.

FIGURE 4.11

Diane Anderson

1414 Cleveland Avenue • St. Joseph • MI 49605
(616) 555-4476 • Fax (616) 555-7032

Career Objective

Seeking an executive assistant position utilizing my knowledge and experience in word processing, desktop publishing, and office management.

Experience

McMann Printing Company, St. Joseph, MI
1988–Present
Executive Secretary
Responsibilities and duties include:

- Manage correspondence and all travel arrangements and accommodations for executives.
- Compile and graph financial data for weekly management meetings.
- Prepare desktop documents for presentations, forms, graphs, etc.
- Create monthly newsletter.
- Instruct various personnel in Microsoft Word 7.0 and desktop publishing.

Case, Newman, and Company, CPA, South Bend, IN
1978–1987
Office Supervisor
Responsibilities and duties included:

- Typed monthly and quarterly financial reports.
- Performed word processing, typing, filing, and general office duties; set appointments.
- Coordinated company meetings and social functions.
- Designed and created seminar pamphlets, flyers, invitations, evaluation forms, and transparencies.
- Created office and staff procedures manual.

Education

Indiana Vocational & Technical Institute, South Bend, IN
Associate Degree in Secretarial Science—August 1987
Lake Michigan Community College, Benton Harbor, MI
Word Processing Certificate—March 1993

Interests

Office Careers Advisory Committee, Lake Michigan College
National Secretaries Association, Lake Michigan Chapter
St. Joseph Chamber of Commerce, Secretary

References

References available upon request.

Creating A Personal Calendar

A calendar can be one of the most basic tools of organization in your household. No desk at home or at work is complete without a calendar to schedule appointments, plan activities, and serve as a reminder of important dates and events.

A calendar can also be used as a marketing tool in promoting a service, product, or program. For example, a schedule of upcoming events may be keyed on a calendar to serve as a reminder to all the volunteers working for a charitable organization, or the calendar could be sent to possible donors to serve as a daily reminder of the organization.

You will create and customize your own calendars using Word's Calendar Wizard. If you want to create your own calendar from scratch without the help of the Calendar Wizard, you may want to start by creating a table using Word's Table feature.

Using the Calendar Wizard

The Calendar Wizard helps you create monthly calendars. Three basic styles of calendars are available: Boxes and borders, Banner, and Jazzy. See figure 4.12 for an illustration of the different styles.

FIGURE 4.12

Calendar Wizard Template Types

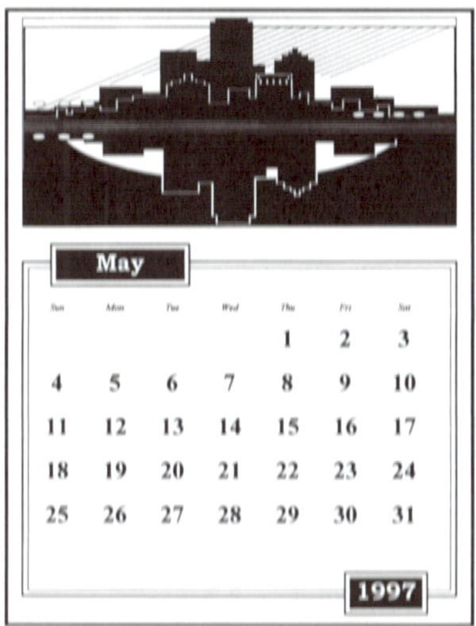

BOXES AND BORDERS

BANNER

JAZZY

To access the Calendar Wizard, choose File, then New. Select the Other Document tab, then select the Calendar Wizard template. Proceed with making choices from the prompts built into the template. Continue clicking on the Next> button to advance to the next screen. Click Finish when the calendar is complete.

If you choose to add a picture to your calendar when prompted in the Calendar Wizard, the default picture is a city landscape (*Cityscpe*). This picture is inserted in a placeholder, so you can easily replace it with a different image. After using the Calendar Wizard, select the existing picture, then press Delete. To replace the image, choose Insert, then Picture, or Insert, then Object, depending on the source of your graphic. To edit the image, double-click the picture to open *Microsoft Word Picture*. Choose Format, then Drawing Object. At the Drawing Objects dialog box make changes to the fill, line, size, or position of the picture. Use the Drawing toolbar to make further changes.

To avoid having a calendar that looks like everyone else's, consider the following suggestions: select a different graphic from the default, add text near important dates, add a watermark, scan a photograph, or print on color or preprinted papers.

Understanding Template Formatting

If you plan to customize a calendar that was created from a template, understanding how the template was formatted in Word can be helpful. Turning on the Show/Hide ¶ button and using the Help button on the Standard toolbar will provide helpful formatting information. The Show/Hide ¶ button is the fourth button from the right on the Standard toolbar and it displays symbols indicating where text was spaced, indented, tabbed, or placed in paragraphs.

When you click the Help button (first button from the right on the Standard toolbar), the arrow pointer displays with a question mark attached. Position the arrow pointer on the text containing formatting that you want to view, then click the left mouse button. The formatting information will appear near the text as a callout. Click once on the Help button to turn off this feature.

In exercise 4, the Calendar Wizard sets up the calendar using tabs. Understanding this formatting will help you add text within the calendar. In this case, text added below the dates on the calendar will have to be inserted into text boxes and dragged to the desired locations as shown in figure 4.13.

If the bottom line of your document does not print, you may have to make adjustments to your document to compensate for the unprintable zone of your particular printer. For instance, if the bottom line of the calendar created in exercise 4 does not print properly, you will have to make adjustments in the formatting of that document. The easiest solution is to reduce the top and/or bottom margins. If the margins cannot be changed, experiment with moving the text up or reducing the length of the document. See the steps listed below exercise 4 for suggestions on making adjustments to a calendar based on a template.

FIGURE 4.13

Using Text Boxes in a Calendar

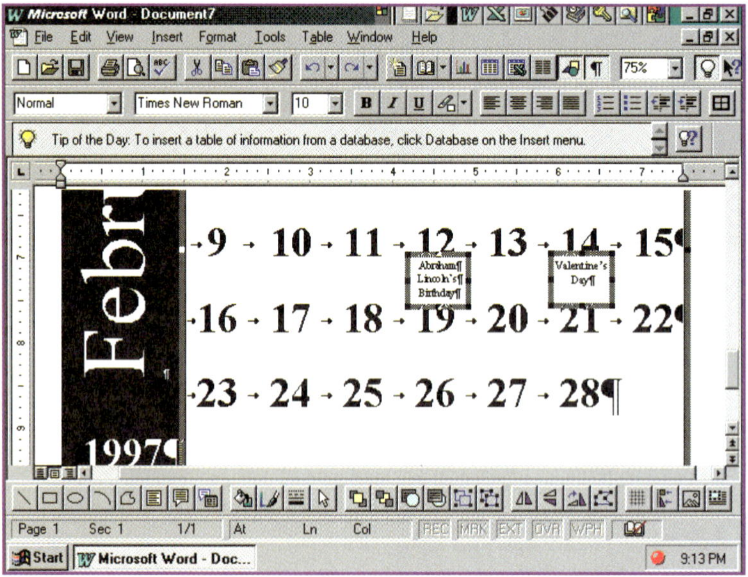

Using Calendar Wizard and Adding a Graphic

1. Add a picture to a calendar as shown in figure 4.14 by completing the following steps:
   a. Choose File, then New.
   b. At the New dialog box, select the Other Documents tab.
   c. Double-click the Calendar Wizard icon.
   d. Choose Portrait orientation for your calendar.
   e. Click Next>.
   f. Choose the Banner style.
   g. Click Next>.
   h. Choose Yes to leave room for a picture in your calendar.
   i. Click Next>.
   j. Select **February** in the Start and End text boxes. Key **1997** in both Year text boxes.
   k. Click Next>.
   l. Click Finish.
2. At the document window, select then delete the placeholder picture (*Cityscpe*). (You will know the picture has been selected when eight sizing handles display in the inside border of the picture. Be careful not to select the frame instead of the border around the picture. The frame should remain once the picture has been deleted. If you accidentally remove the frame you can undo the deletion by clicking the Undo button on the Standard toolbar or you can draw another frame by clicking the Insert Frame button on the Drawing toolbar [last button from the left], or choosing Format, then Frame.) Insert another picture by completing the following steps:
   a. With the insertion point positioned in the frame, choose Insert, then Picture.
   b. At the Insert Picture dialog box, double-click *Houses* at the Name list box.
3. Insert text below designated dates in the calendar by completing the following steps:
   a. Display the Drawing toolbar by clicking the Drawing button on the Standard toolbar (fifth button from the right).
   b. Click the Text Box button on the Drawing toolbar (sixth button from the left).
   c. Drag to create a text box below February 12 as shown in figure 4.13. (Be careful that the box does not cut off the sides of the calendar or the days of the week; resize the box if necessary by dragging the double-pointed arrow). If a border displays around the box, click the Line Color button on the Drawing toolbar (tenth button from the left), then select None. If the shading in the text box is a color other than white, click the Fill Color button on the Drawing toolbar (ninth button from the left) and select None.
   d. Change the font to 9-point Times New Roman.
   e. Click the Center button on the Formatting toolbar, then key **Abraham Lincoln's Birthday** in the text box created in step 3c under February 12.
   f. Click the Text Box button on the Drawing toolbar and drag to create another text box below February 14.
   g. Center align and key **Valentine's Day** at 9-point Times New Roman under February 14.
   h. Select *Valentine's Day* and change the font color to red.
   i. Click the Text Box button on the Drawing toolbar and drag to create another text box below February 19.

j. Center align and key **President's Day** at 9-point Times New Roman under February 19.
k. Create another text box under February 22.
l. Center align and key **George Washington's Birthday** at 9-point Times New Roman under February 22.
m. Create a text box below February 3. Draw this text box to be about 0.45 inches square. Insert the picture *Realest* into this small box.
n. Create a text box below the picture in step 3m. Center align and key **Call for a Free Appraisal** at 9-point Times New Roman.
o. Click the Text Box button on the Drawing toolbar and drag to create a box below the last week as shown in figure 4.15. (Be careful to keep the text box within the border of the calendar.)
p. Change the alignment to Center.
q. Key **Forecast Realty** in the text box created in step o, then press Enter.
r. Key **Predicting a Successful Move for You**, then press Enter.
s. Key **450 South Ashton Avenue**, press the space bar twice, create the ❖ symbol, then press the space bar twice. (Insert the ❖ symbol by choosing Insert, then Symbol. At the Symbol dialog box, change the font to Monotype Sorts, then select the ❖ symbol in the fourth row and the third column.)
t. Key **Nashville, TN 37201**, press the space bar twice, insert the ❖ symbol, press the space bar twice, then key **(901) 555-1000**.
u. Select *Forecast Realty*, then change the font to 22-point Arial MT Black (or Arial Bold) and the font Color to Dk Gray.
v. Select *Predicting a Successful Move for You*, then change the font to 12-point Times New Roman Bold Italic. Choose Format, then Paragraph. At the Paragraph dialog box, select the Indent and Spacing tab. Change the Spacing Before to 4 pt to allow for more leading between the lines. Click OK to close the dialog box.
w. Select *450 South Ashton Avenue...* then change the font to 10-point Arial MT Black (or Arial Bold). Choose Format, then Paragraph. At the Paragraph dialog box, select the Indent and Spacing tab. Change the Spacing Before to 6 pt to allow for more leading between the lines. Click OK to close the dialog box.
x. Adjust the sizing and position of the frame as needed.

4. Save the document and name it c04ex04, house calendar.
5. Print and then close c04ex04, house calendar.

If the bottom line of the calendar does not print, you may need to adjust the length of the calendar so the bottom line will not be positioned within the unprintable zone defined by your printer. To make adjustments to exercise 4, complete the following steps:

1. Click to select *1997* in the reversed text box located on the left side of the calendar.
2. Choose Format, then Drawing Object.
3. At the Drawing Object dialog box, select the Size and Position tab.
4. Change the Height to 0.9 inches in the Size section.
5. Click OK or press Enter to close the Drawing Object dialog box.
6. Click the thin black border line that surrounds the calendar.
7. Choose Format, then Drawing Object.

8. At the Drawing Object dialog box, select the Size and Position tab.
9. Change the Height to 6.1 inches in the Size section.
10. Click OK or press Enter to close the Drawing Object dialog box.
11. If the text box containing the real estate company name and address overlaps onto the bottom border of the text box edited in step 9, you may need to select it and move it up slightly away from the bottom border. Choose File, then Print Preview. If the lines do not display, continue to experiment with different settings until the entire document is visible. Print when the document is complete.

FIGURE 4.14

February

1997

Sun	*Mon*	*Tue*	*Wed*	*Thu*	*Fri*	*Sat*
						1
2	**3**	**4**	**5**	**6**	**7**	**8**
9	Call for a Free Appraisal **10**	**11**	**12** Abraham Lincoln's Birthday	**13**	**14** Valentine's Day	**15**
16	**17**	**18**	**19** President's Day	**20**	**21**	**22** George Washington's Birthday
23	**24**	**25**	**26**	**27**	**28**	

Forecast Realty

Predicting a Successful Move for You

450 South Ashton Avenue ✧ Nashville, TN 37201 ✧ (901) 555-1000

FIGURE 4.15

Creating a Text Box below the Calendar Dates

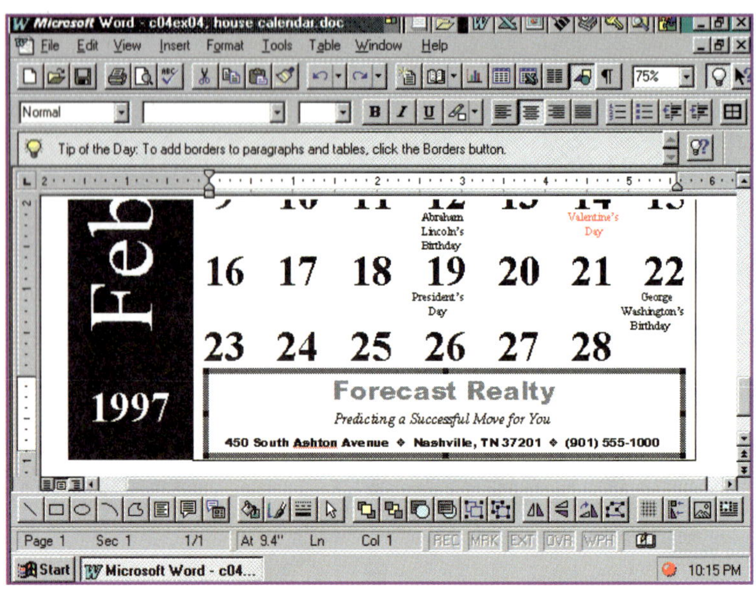

Customizing a Calendar by Adding a Watermark

DTP POINTERS
Reduce watermark shading to improve readability of text.

A calendar is a perfect document in which to use a watermark. The watermark adds visual interest to a calendar. It can also be used to promote a theme or identity to a person or an organization. Two important considerations when using a watermark in a calendar, or any other document, are that the shading of the picture or object can be lightened to improve the readability of the text, and that the picture or text you select relates to the subject of the document.

EXERCISE 5

Using Calendar Wizard and Adding a Watermark

1. Create a calendar with a watermark as shown in figure 4.16 by completing the following steps:
   a. Choose File, then New.
   b. At the New dialog box, select the Other Documents tab.
   c. Double-click the Calendar Wizard icon.
   d. Choose Portrait orientation for your calendar, then click Next>.
   e. Choose the Boxes and borders style, then click Next>.
   f. Choose No at the question asking if you want to leave room for a picture, then click Next>.
   g. Select *June* in the Start and End text boxes. Key **1997** in both Year text boxes, then click Next>.
   h. Click Finish.
2. Insert text within the calendar by completing the following steps:
   a. Display the Drawing toolbar.
   b. Click the Text Box button on the Drawing toolbar.
   c. Drag the outline of the text box below June 4, then create another text box and drag it under June 6 as shown in figure 4.16. (Be careful that the boxes do not cut off the sides of the calendar or the days of the week; resize the boxes if necessary by dragging the double-pointed arrow).
   d. Make sure that the text box fill is white and there is no border line on either text box. Eliminate any fill or border line by completing the following steps:
      (1) Choose Format, then Drawing Object.

(2) At the Drawing Object dialog box, select the Fill tab.
(3) At the Color section, click the rectangle box above the color palette. (This box contains the word *None.*)
(4) Make sure *None* is displayed in the Patterns text box and *White* is displayed in the Pattern Color text box.
(5) Choose the Line tab at the Drawing Object dialog box, then select None.
(6) Choose OK to close the dialog box.

e. Change the font to 10-point Times New Roman.
f. Center align, then key the following text in the text box created in step 2c.

Volunteer at School Picnic 11:00 a.m.	June 4
Last Day of School!	June 6

g. Click the Text Box button on the Drawing toolbar, then drag the crosshair below each date listed below to create text boxes to hold the following information. Center align, then key the following information under the correct dates using 10-point Times New Roman:

Kaitlin Gymnastics 9:00 a.m.	June 9
Dentist Appointment 10:00 a.m.	June 13
Swim Team Meeting 7:00 p.m.	June 17
Summer Solstice	June 21
Car Appointment 8:00 a.m.	June 23

3. Create a watermark for your calendar by completing the following steps:
   a. Choose View, then Header and Footer.
   b. Click the Text Box button on the Drawing toolbar.
   c. Drag the crosshair into the calendar and create a box about a half inch from the calendar border. (The box will not fit inside the header and footer pane.)
   d. Choose Insert, then Picture.
   e. At the Insert Picture dialog box, make sure Clipart displays in the Look in text box. Double-click *Summer* in the Name list box.
   f. Reduce the shading by completing the following steps:
      (1) Double-click the *Summer* image. (This opens *Microsoft Word Picture.*)
      (2) Click the upper portion of the picture to select the yellow area.
      (3) Choose Format, then Drawing Object.
      (4) At the Drawing Object dialog box, select the Fill tab.
      (5) At the Drawing Object dialog box with the Fill tab selected, change the Color to White. (Select the first white box in the first row.) At the Patterns drop-down list, select 30%. At the Pattern Color drop-down list, select Yellow.
      (6) Click OK to close the Drawing Object dialog box.
      (7) Click the lower section of the picture to select the blue area.
      (8) Reduce the blue shading by following steps similar to those in 3f3 through 3f6.
      (9) Click the Close Picture button to close *Microsoft Word Picture.*
   g. Click Close at the Header and Footer toolbar.
4. Choose File, then Print Preview. Make sure all the lines around the calendar display. If the bottom line of the text box containing the year does not appear, click the text box to select it and drag the box up slightly until it is almost even with the double border surrounding the calendar. Choose Close to close Print Preview.
5. Save the document and name it c04ex05, watermk calendar.
6. Print and then close c04ex05, watermk calendar.

FIGURE 4.16

Sun	Mon	Tue	Wed	Thu	Fri	Sat
1	2	3	4 Volunteer at School Picnic 11:00 a.m.	5	6 Last Day of School!	7
8	9 Kaitlin Gymnastics 9:00 a.m.	10	11	12	13 Dentist Appointment 10:00 a.m.	14
15	16	17 Swim Team Meeting 7:00 p.m.	18	19	20	21 Summer Solstice
22	23 Car Appointment 8:00 a.m.	24	25	26	27	28
29	30					

June 1997

Creating Personal Return Address Labels

Return address labels are convenient and cost efficient to use at home as well as at the office. Whether paying a huge stack of bills, addressing holiday cards, or volunteering to mail a hundred PTA newsletters, the convenience of having preprinted return labels is worth the little time it takes to create them. Instead of purchasing personalized return labels through a stationery store or printing company, you can create your own return labels using Word's label feature. Word includes a variety of predefined label definitions that coordinate with labels that can be purchased at office supply stores.

When purchasing labels, be careful to select the appropriate labels for your designated printer. Labels are available in sheets for laser and ink jet printers and tractor-feed forms for dot matrix printers. Carefully follow the directions given with your printer to insert the forms properly into the printer.

Return labels can be created using two different methods—creating labels individually and copying them using the label feature or creating labels using a data source and the merge feature. In exercise 6, you will be creating labels using a label definition and inserting a graphic. Merge will be used in a later chapter.

Using a Predefined Label Definition

As mentioned in chapter 3, Word's Label feature allows you to print a full page of labels using the same name or a single label. After keying your name and address at the Address box of the Labels dialog box, you may want to change the font or apply other text attributes. To do so, select your name and address, then click the right mouse button to access the Shortcut menu or press the Shortcut key if it is available on your keyboard. At the Shortcut menu, select Font from the drop-down list. At the Font dialog box, click any of the text attributes displayed.

Word includes a great many label definitions for mailing labels, file labels, disk labels, and many more in addition to return address labels. The label definitions coordinate with frequently used labels you can purchase at most office supply stores. So before creating your own label definition, be sure you have scrolled through the predesigned labels available in Word.

Adding a Graphic to a Label

To personalize your return labels, you may want to add a graphic image or create a fancy initial letter. There are several methods for adding a graphic to a return address label. For instance, you may insert a paragraph indentation command into a cell, key the address text, then draw a text box next to the address and insert a graphic by choosing Insert, then Picture. A second method involves splitting the cell (label) into two cells and placing the graphic in one cell and the address text in the other. A third method would involve drawing two text boxes within a cell and inserting a graphic in one and the address in the other. However, all of these methods are quite time-intensive.

To more fully utilize Word's label feature, which is efficient in creating numerous labels, consider the following method, which uses WordArt, AutoText, and the Labels feature.

Creating the Address in WordArt

First, create the label content at a clear document window. Insert a graphic image into your document—the graphic will display at its default size. Create your return address text in Microsoft WordArt by choosing Insert, then Object. At the Object dialog box, make sure the Create New tab is selected, then select *Microsoft WordArt 3.0 (2.0)* in the Object Type list box. Key your address in the *Enter Your Text Here* dialog box. Choose a font from the Font drop-down list, then click the Align Left button on the WordArt toolbar. Click anywhere in your document to exit WordArt. Your graphic and address text will appear side by side as shown in figure 4.17.

FIGURE 4.17

Return Address Label Content

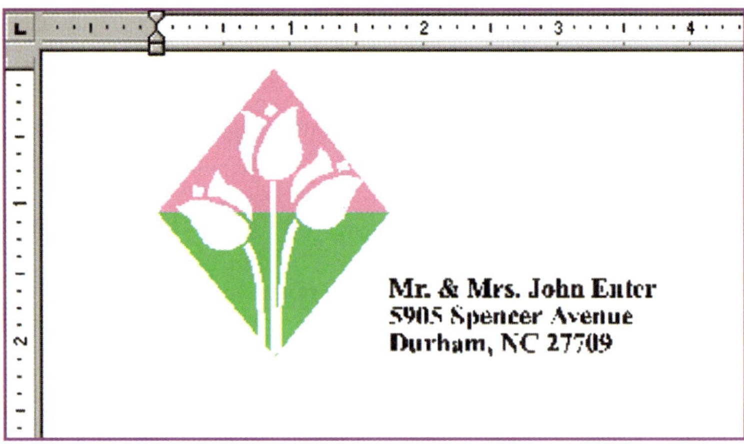

Sizing the Graphic and Address

In exercise 6, you will be selecting the Avery 5160 label definition, which is a frequently used label. This definition creates thirty labels on one sheet. In addition, the size of each label is l inch high and 2.63 inches wide. Usually the graphic and address text are too big to fit into this standard label size. Therefore, you will need to scale and crop the graphic and text to fit into each label. When determining how to size a graphic and text for a label, look at the label dimensions, then size your graphic and text to allow for enough white space that printing will not occur past the label boundaries.

Sizing Handles: Eight small black squares that appear at each corner and along the sides of an area that surrounds a selected drawing object.

Cropping: Eliminating unwanted portions of a picture.

Scaling: Reducing or enlarging an image to fit into a specific area.

When you select a picture, eight small black boxes called *sizing handles (*or *selection handles)* appear if you are in the Page Layout viewing mode. These handles appear at each corner and along the sides of an area that surrounds a selected drawing object. The handles provide you with control over cropping and scaling an image. *Cropping* a picture eliminates unwanted portions of the picture as shown in figure 4.18. Word crops pictures when you drag on a handle while holding down the Shift key.The arrow pointer changes to a cropping tool. When you select a picture to crop it, watch the arrow pointer. If you see a two-headed diagonal arrow, you can size or crop the picture proportionately using the corner handles. If a two-headed horizontal or vertical arrow displays, you can crop the picture disproportionately. You can also add more white space around a bordered picture by holding down the Shift key as you pull the image side handles away from the center.

Scaling is reducing or enlarging an image to fit a specific area as shown in figure 4.18. Word will compute the percentages to increase or decrease an image at the Picture dialog box. However, you can also use the sizing (selection) handles to scale the items by holding down the Ctrl key as you drag one of the handles. If you drag a corner handle (any one of four), you enlarge or reduce the image proportionately. If you drag on a side, top or bottom handles, Word will enlarge or reduce the graphic disproportionately.

ORIGINAL PICTURE

SCALED PICTURE

CROPPED PICTURE

FIGURE 4.18

Scaling and Cropping a Picture

To scale the *Spring* graphic shown in figure 4.17, click to select the image, then choose Format, and then Picture. At the Picture dialog box, key -0.25 inches in the Right text box in the Crop From section of the dialog box. This setting will create more white space between the graphic and the address text. Notice the original sizes of the graphic at the bottom of the box. The picture defaults to a width of 1.74 inches and a height of 2.1 inches. The height of the label is one inch, therefore, key 0.75 inches in the Height text box in the Size section. Click inside the Width text box of the Scaling section and a percentage will automatically display in the Height text box in the Scaling section. Now, key that same percentage into the Width text box (your insertion point is already located there). The settings are in proportion to the original measurements as shown in figure 4.19.

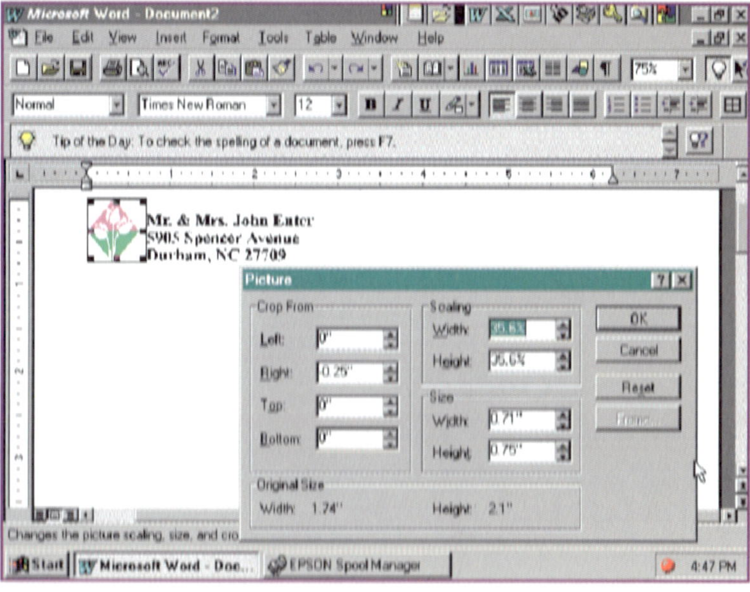

FIGURE 4.19

Picture Dialog Box (Sizing Graphic)

To scale the WordArt text (address) shown in figure 4.17, click to select the address, then choose Format, and then Picture. At the Picture dialog box, notice the original sizes at the bottom of the box. The WordArt text defaults to a width of 2.0 inches and a height of 0.65 inches. Key 1.50 inches in the Width text box in the Size section of the dialog box. Click inside the Height text box of the Scaling section and a percentage will automatically display in the Width text box. Key that same percentage into the Height text box. The settings are in proportion to the original measurements as shown in figure 4.20.

FIGURE 4.20

Picture Dialog Box (Sizing WordArt Text)

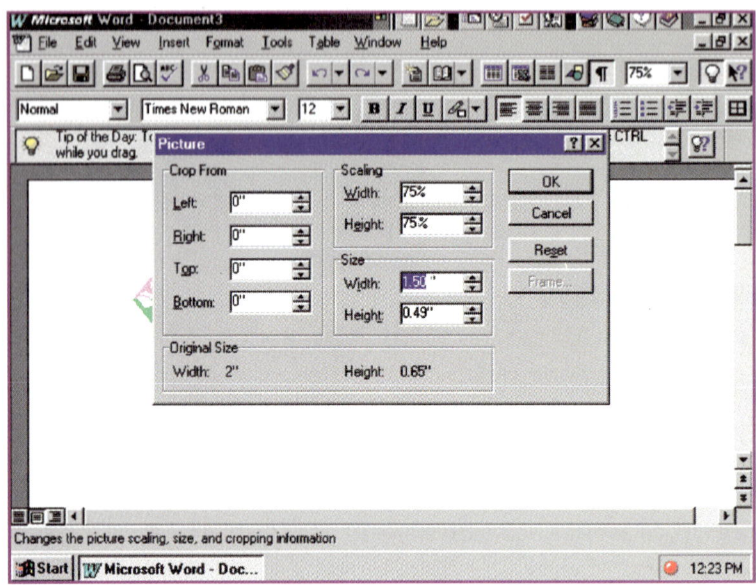

Creating the Labels

In exercise 6, you will save the graphic and WordArt text (address) as an AutoText entry and then retrieve it in the Envelopes and Labels dialog box. To do this, choose Tools, then Envelopes and Labels at a clear document window. At the Envelopes and Labels dialog box, select the Labels tab, then click the Options button. At the Label Options dialog box, select the label, *5160 - Address* from the Product Number list box, then click OK. With the insertion point positioned in the Address text box, key the name you gave to the AutoText entry (as shown in figure 4.21), then press F3. Click the New Document button in the Envelopes and Labels dialog box. All thirty labels on the sheet should include a graphic and an address.

FIGURE 4.21

AutoText Entry in Address Box

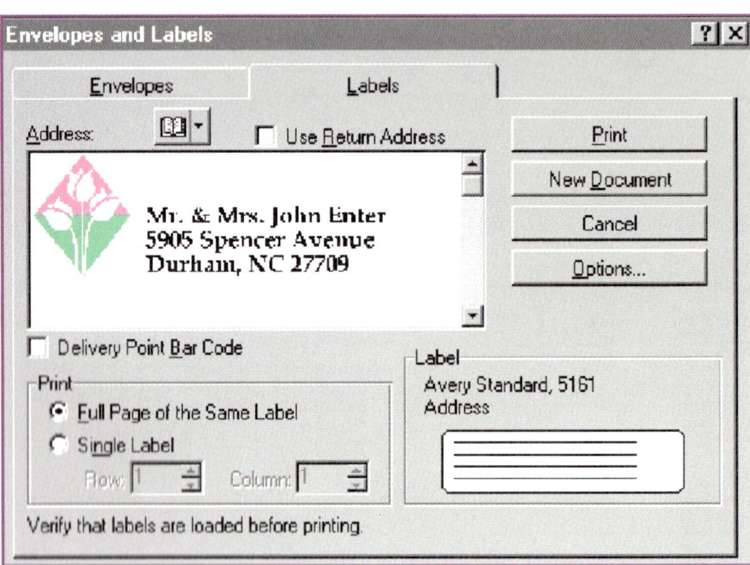

Using WordArt and a graphic in the labels feature produces an attractive, customized sheet of return address labels. However, the WordArt and graphic objects are actually OLE objects that cause the label file to become huge. To view the size of your document, click File, then Properties. At the Properties dialog box, select the Statistics tab. Facts about your document will display. Notice the size of the document file you created. You may be amazed to see that the file is approximately 550,000 bytes. This document will take up an enormous amount of hard drive space or disk space. Consider printing the document, then not saving it. Your WordArt text and graphic have been saved as AutoText files. These files will remain accessible for use in later applications. However, if you are creating documents in a lab situation, be sure to consult your instructor on whether you should delete your AutoText entries.

Personal Return Address Labels with a Graphic

1. At a clear document window, create the contents (picture and address) that will be used in a sheet of return address labels as shown in figure 4.22, by completing the following steps:
    a. Choose Insert, then Picture.
    b. At the Insert Picture dialog box, double-click *Spring* in the Name list box.
    c. With the insertion point positioned at the bottom right of the picture, choose Insert, then Object.
    d. At the Object dialog box, make sure the Create New tab is selected, then select *Microsoft WordArt 3.0 (2.0)* in the Object Type list box.
    e. Choose OK or press Enter.
    f. With the insertion point positioned in the text entry box, complete the following steps:
        (1) Key **Mr. & Mrs. John Enter**, then press Enter.
        (2) Key **5905 Spencer Avenue**, then press Enter.
        (3) Key **Durham, NC 27709**.
        (4) Click the Update Display button.
        (5) Select Book Antiqua at the Font drop-down list.
        (6) Click the Bold button on the WordArt toolbar.
        (7) Click the Alignment button on the WordArt toolbar (sixth button from the right), then select Left from the drop-down list.
    g. Click outside the text entry box to remove the box.
2. At the document window, scale the picture object so it will fit into a designated label by completing the following steps: (The label definition that will be used in this exercise creates a label that measures 1 inch high by 2.63 inches wide.)
    a. Select the picture, then choose Format, then Picture.
    b. At the Picture dialog box, key **-0.25** in the Right text box in the Crop From section. (This setting will increase the white space between the picture and the address text).
    c. Key **0.75** inches in the Height text box in the Size section.
    d. Click inside the Width text box in the Scaling section and 35.6 percent will automatically display in the Height text box.
    e. Key **35.6** percent in the Width text box in the Scaling section (your insertion point is already there).
    f. Click OK to close the Picture dialog box.
3. At the document window, scale the WordArt address text so it will fit into a designated label by completing the following steps:
    a. Select the WordArt address text, then choose Format, then Picture.
    b. At the Picture dialog box, key **1.5** in the Width text box in the Size section.
    c. Click inside the Height text box in the Scaling section and 75% will automatically display in the Width text box.

d. Key **75** in the Height text box in the Scaling section (your insertion point is already there).
e. Click OK to close the Picture dialog box.

4. Insert the graphic and WordArt address text into AutoText by completing the following steps:
   a. Using the mouse, select by dragging the picture and the WordArt address text, then choose Edit, then AutoText.
   b. At the AutoText dialog box, key **Spring Address** in the Name text box, then click the Add button.
5. At the document window where you created the AutoText entry, close without saving.
6. At a clear document window, create a sheet of labels by completing the following steps:
   a. Choose Tools, then Envelopes and Labels.
   b. At the Envelopes and Labels dialog box, select the Labels tab.
   c. Click the Options button to the right of the Address text box.
   d. At the Label Options dialog box, select *5160 - Address* from the Product Number list box.
   e. Click OK to close the Label Options dialog box.
   f. At the Envelopes and Labels dialog box, make sure the insertion point is positioned in the Address text box, key **Spring Address**, then press F3. (The AutoText entry should display in the Address text box.)
   g. Make sure that Full Page of the Same Label is selected in the Print section of the Envelopes and Labels dialog box.
   h. Click the New Document button to the right of the Address text box. (Your address labels should copy to each label on the sheet).
7. Save the document and name it c04ex06, address labels. (If you are concerned about disk space, you may want to print the document and not save it.)
8. Print and then close c04ex06, address labels. (Check with your instructor to find out whether you should delete the AutoText entry created with this document.)

FIGURE 4.22

Mr. & Mrs. John Enter
5905 Spencer Avenue
Durham, NC 27709

Mr. & Mrs. John Enter
5905 Spencer Avenue
Durham, NC 27709

Mr. & Mrs. John Enter
5905 Spencer Avenue
Durham, NC 27709

Mr. & Mrs. John Enter
5905 Spencer Avenue
Durham, NC 27709

Mr. & Mrs. John Enter
5905 Spencer Avenue
Durham, NC 27709

Mr. & Mrs. John Enter
5905 Spencer Avenue
Durham, NC 27709

Mr. & Mrs. John Enter
5905 Spencer Avenue
Durham, NC 27709

Mr. & Mrs. John Enter
5905 Spencer Avenue
Durham, NC 27709

Mr. & Mrs. John Enter
5905 Spencer Avenue
Durham, NC 27709

Mr. & Mrs. John Enter
5905 Spencer Avenue
Durham, NC 27709

Mr. & Mrs. John Enter
5905 Spencer Avenue
Durham, NC 27709

Mr. & Mrs. John Enter
5905 Spencer Avenue
Durham, NC 27709

Mr. & Mrs. John Enter
5905 Spencer Avenue
Durham, NC 27709

Mr. & Mrs. John Enter
5905 Spencer Avenue
Durham, NC 27709

Mr. & Mrs. John Enter
5905 Spencer Avenue
Durham, NC 27709

Mr. & Mrs. John Enter
5905 Spencer Avenue
Durham, NC 27709

Mr. & Mrs. John Enter
5905 Spencer Avenue
Durham, NC 27709

Mr. & Mrs. John Enter
5905 Spencer Avenue
Durham, NC 27709

Mr. & Mrs. John Enter
5905 Spencer Avenue
Durham, NC 27709

Mr. & Mrs. John Enter
5905 Spencer Avenue
Durham, NC 27709

Mr. & Mrs. John Enter
5905 Spencer Avenue
Durham, NC 27709

Mr. & Mrs. John Enter
5905 Spencer Avenue
Durham, NC 27709

Mr. & Mrs. John Enter
5905 Spencer Avenue
Durham, NC 27709

Mr. & Mrs. John Enter
5905 Spencer Avenue
Durham, NC 27709

Mr. & Mrs. John Enter
5905 Spencer Avenue
Durham, NC 27709

Mr. & Mrs. John Enter
5905 Spencer Avenue
Durham, NC 27709

Mr. & Mrs. John Enter
5905 Spencer Avenue
Durham, NC 27709

Mr. & Mrs. John Enter
5905 Spencer Avenue
Durham, NC 27709

Mr. & Mrs. John Enter
5905 Spencer Avenue
Durham, NC 27709

Mr. & Mrs. John Enter
5905 Spencer Avenue
Durham, NC 27709

Creating A Certificate

Certificates are generally used to show recognition and promote excellence. Some suggested uses include: diplomas, warranties, special event awards, program completion awards, and special offer documents.

There are many ways to create distinctive, professional-looking certificates. Award Wizard prompts you to key information about the recipient and an area of recognition. The Award Wizard includes four different styles of award templates: Formal, Modern, Decorative, and Jazzy (see figure 4.23). If none of these templates fit your needs, you can create a certificate by using one of Word's graphic borders and incorporating ornate fonts such as Brush Script MT Italic, Colonna MT, or Matura MT Script Cap. More information on using Word's graphic borders in documents will be provided in chapter 5.

The template used to create the certificate in exercise 7 contains many layers to create the unique border around the certificate. You will be instructed to create a watermark to add interest to this document, but you will not be able to create the watermark in a header or footer as previously instructed in earlier exercises. A text box will be drawn into the document, a picture will be inserted into the text box, and the picture shading will be adjusted to create an appealing and effective watermark. However, you will click the Send Text Behind button on the Drawing toolbar (eleventh button from the right) to move the watermark below the text layer instead of using a header or footer, which automatically positions the image behind the text layer.

Send Text Behind

If you need to edit the watermark image after it has been sent behind the text layer, click the Select Drawing Object button (twelfth button from the left) on the Drawing toolbar. An upward pointing arrow displays on the button. The template used in exercise 7 includes many text boxes and frames around the text; therefore, carefully click an area between the text boxes to access the text box where the watermark exists.

An appropriate choice of high-quality bond paper or parchment paper is recommended for a certificate, along with a conservative choice of colors, such as natural, cream, off-white, light gray, or any light marbleized color. Preprinted border paper is available through many mail-order catalogs and office supply stores. Word's Award Wizard includes a prompt asking if you want to create an award using preprinted paper. If you decide to use this special paper, you will want to answer Yes at the built-in prompt. The Award Wizard will adjust formatting to compensate for the preprinted form.

FIGURE 4.23

Award Wizard Template Types

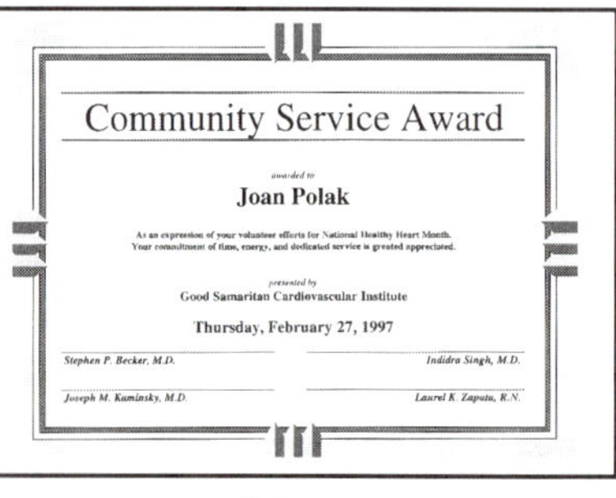

FORMAL

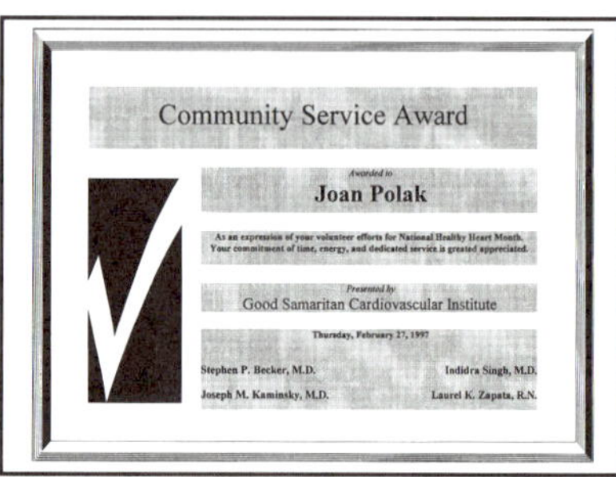

MODERN

JAZZY

DECORATIVE

Using the Award Wizard

1. Use the Award Wizard to create the certificate shown in figure 4.24 by completing the following steps:
   a. Choose File, then New.
   b. At the New dialog box, select the Other Documents tab.
   c. Double-click the Award Wizard.
   d. At the first prompt, choose Jazzy style for this certificate, then click Next>.
   e. At the next screen, choose Landscape orientation for your certificate and click No to using preprinted border paper.
   f. Click Next>.
   g. At the next screen, key **Joan Polak** as the recipient of the award. Key **Community Service Award** as the type of award, then click Next>.
   h. At the next screen check to see if there are any names displayed in the list box above the Add button. If there are, select each name, then click the Remove button to eliminate each unwanted name. Key the following names in the list box below the Add button, clicking the Add button after keying each name: **Stephen P. Becker, M.D.**, (click the Add button), **Indidra Singh, M.D.**, (click the Add button), **Joseph M. Kaminsky, M.D.**, (click the Add button), and **Laurel K. Zapata, R.N.**, (click the Add button).
   i. Click Next>.
   j. At the next screen, make sure the radio button for Presented by is selected. If there is an entry in the Presented by box, delete it. In the Presented by text box, key **Good Samaritan Cardiovascular Institute**, then click Next>.
   k. At the next screen, key **Thursday, February 27, 1997** as the date of the award. At the additional information text box, key **As an expression of your volunteer efforts for National Healthy Heart Month.** (press Enter) **Your commitment of time, energy, and dedicated service is greatly appreciated.**
   l. Click Next>.
   m. Click Finish.
2. Click the down-pointing triangle to the right of the Zoom Control button (third button from the right) on the Standard toolbar, then select 50% from the drop-down menu.
3. Add a watermark to the award certificate by completing the following steps:
   a. Display the Drawing toolbar.
   b. Click the Text Box button on the Drawing toolbar.
   c. Drag the crosshairs into the calendar and create a text box to hold the watermark. Begin drawing the text box at the second "m" in Community to the "w" in Award and end drawing the text box at the first line of signatures. (Usually a Header or Footer is used to create a watermark in a document, but because of the layered formatting in this template, creating the watermark in a text box and positioning it below the text layer using the Drawing toolbar is easier.)
   d. Make sure the text box fill is set at None and the border line is set at None.
   e. Choose Insert, then Picture.
   f. At the Insert Picture dialog box, make sure Clipart displays in the Look in text box. Double-click *Heart* in the Name list box.
   g. Double-click the picture to open *Microsoft Word Picture*, then make the following changes to the picture:
      (1) Double-click the top half of the picture again to display the Drawing

Object dialog box. (A portion of the heart will display in the preview box of the Drawing Object dialog box.)

(2) At the Drawing Object dialog box, select the Fill tab.

(3) Change the fill Color to white (click the white color in the first row and the second column), change Patterns to 30% (at the Pattern drop-down list), and the Pattern Color to Dk Red (at the Pattern Color drop-down list).

(4) Click OK to close the Drawing Object dialog box.

(5) Double-click the bottom half of the picture to display the other half of the heart picture in the preview box of the Drawing Object dialog box.

(6) Change the color of this section of the picture by completing steps similar to steps 3f2 through 3f4.

(7) Click the Close Picture button at *Microsoft Word Picture*.

(8) Resize the heart picture, if necessary. (To do this, click the arrow pointer on one of the sizing handles. Position the arrow pointer on a sizing handle until it turns into a double-pointing arrow, hold down the left mouse button, drag to the desired location, then release the mouse button.)

h. At the document window, click the heart picture to select it.

i. Click the Send Behind Text button on the Drawing toolbar (eleventh button from the right).

j. The gray fill in the border is preventing the watermark from showing through the text layer. Complete the following steps to change the fill color in the border:

(1) Double-click the gray border of the certificate.

(2) At the Drawing Object dialog box, select the Fill tab.

(3) Change the fill Color to *None* by clicking inside the rectangle box above the color palette (contains the word *None*). Do not change the Patterns or Pattern Color. (The gray shaded border will be replaced with a white border—this cannot be avoided.)

(4) Click OK to close the Drawing Object dialog box.

(5) Deselect the border by clicking outside the selected area.

4. Choose File, then Print Preview. If any one of the borders around the certificate does not display in the preview screen, make an adjustment for the unprintable zone of your printer by changing the size and position of the border. (To do this, double-click on the border at the document screen, then select the Size and Position tab at the Drawing Object dialog box. Key an increment less than the original setting. View the document at Print Preview before printing. Experiment with other settings if necessary.)

5. Save the document and name it c04ex07, heart certificate.

6. Print and then close c04ex07, heart certificate.

FIGURE 4.24

Community Service Award

Awarded to

Joan Polak

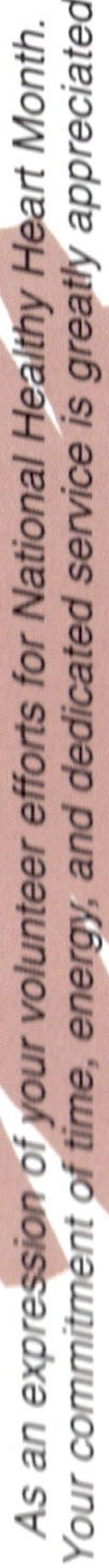

As an expression of your volunteer efforts for National Healthy Heart Month.
Your commitment of time, energy, and dedicated service is greatly appreciated.

Presented by

Good Samaritan Cardiovascular Institute

Thursday, Februrary 27, 1997

Stephen P. Becker, M.D.	*Indidra Singh, M.D.*
Joseph M. Kaminsky, M.D.	*Laurel K. Zapata, R.N.*

Chapter Summary

- Most current résumés use these essential parts: Heading, Career Objective, Work Experience, Education, Special Skills, Interests, and References.
- Em and en dashes are used in place of keyboard hyphens and dashes.
- WordArt can be used to rotate the heading text in a résumé.
- Use Format Painter to copy formatting from one area of text to another.
- Side-by-side columns (tables) can be used to create résumés.
- Word provides a Calendar Wizard that guides you through the steps of creating monthly calendars in either portrait (narrow) or landscape (wide) orientation.
- Watermarks, pictures, special characters, shading, and text can be added to a calendar to enhance its appearance and add to its effectiveness. Reducing the shading of a watermark in a calendar improves the readability of the calendar text.
- Adjustments may be necessary in the size and position of document elements to compensate for the unprintable zone of a particular printer.
- Address labels are created by selecting a predefined label definition at the Envelopes and Labels dialog box.
- Customized address labels that include a picture can be created using WordArt, AutoText, and the Labels feature.
- Scaling is a method used to reduce or enlarge the size of an object to fit a specific area. Word scales objects using the Picture dialog box. Cropping eliminates unwanted areas of an object. Objects can be cropped by dragging a sizing handle while pressing the Shift key.
- Word's Award Wizard includes four different styles of award templates: Formal, Modern, Decorative, and Jazzy.

Commands Review

Résumé Templates & Wizard	File, New. Select Other Documents tab at New dialog box
Rules	Display Borders toolbar, click Left Border or Right Border button; or choose Format, Borders and Shading, Borders tab
Format Painter	Click Format Painter button on Standard Toolbar
WordArt	Insert, Object, select Create New tab at Object dialog box, choose *Microsoft WordArt 3.0 (2.0)*
Side-by-Side Columns	Tables, Insert Table; or click Insert Table button on Standard Toolbar
Picture	Insert, Picture
Text Box	Text Box button on Drawing Toolbar
Frame	Insert, Frame; or click Insert Frame button on Drawing toolbar
Watermark	View, Header and Footer. At the Header and Footer pane, create a text box. Click Insert, Picture, Object, or key text. Reduce shading at *Microsoft Word Picture*, Drawing Object dialog box, and Fill or Line tabs.
Labels	Tools, Envelopes and Labels
AutoText	Edit, AutoText

Check Your Understanding

True/False: Circle the letter T if the statement is true; circle the letter F if the statement is false.

T F **1.** Use border lines (rules) to organize or separate text in a résumé.

T F **2.** References must always be listed in a résumé.

T F **3** All bulleted items in a list should be punctuated with a period.

T F **4.** Daily, weekly, monthly, and yearly calendars can be created using the Calendar Wizard.

T F **5.** When rotating a text box, the text or picture inside the box rotates with the box.

T F **6.** The Format Painter changes the intensity of color in a picture.

T F **7.** A watermark image can be inserted into a calendar through a built-in prompt in the Calendar Wizard.

T F **8.** To reduce the shading in a watermark, open *Microsoft Word Picture* and make changes to the fill, pattern, and pattern color of the picture at the Drawing Object dialog box.

T F **9.** To add a graphic image to a return address label, position the image inside the label by framing it.

T F **10.** AutoText stores selected text and graphics temporarily in the document where they are created as AutoText entries.

T F **11.** The Award Wizard is located in the New dialog box with the Publications tab selected.

T F **12.** To scale an image at the Picture dialog box, enter one desired measurement and Word will automatically compute the percentages to increase or decrease the image.

Concepts: Answer the following questions in the space provided.

1. What is the main purpose of a résumé?

2. What essential parts are contained in most current résumés?

3. What are the two page orientations used in the Calendar Wizard?

4. What are the three descriptive types of résumé templates?

5. Why would you add a watermark to a document? What are two important considerations to keep in mind when using a watermark in a document?

Skill Assessments

Assessment 1

1. At a clear document window, create your own résumé using any one of the three techniques discussed in this chapter. You may use one of Word's résumé templates or wizard or you may create a résumé using a rotated text box or side-by-side columns. Prepare your career objective with a particular job in mind, or look in your local newspaper for employment ads and tailor your résumé toward one job description that interests you. Arrange the sections of your résumé according to your particular qualifications.
2. Save your completed résumé and name it c04sa01, personal resume.
3. Print and then close c04sa01, personal resume.

Assessment 2

You are in charge of preparing certificates for the all sports awards at Kennedy Junior High. Create a generic certificate that can be used for any sports category. Create the certificate based on the following specifications:

1. Use the Award Wizard and select the Modern award style in Portrait orientation.
2. Key the following information at the appropriate prompts:

Awarded to:	**Annika Johansson**
Title of award:	**All Sports Award for 1997**
Names to sign:	**Maureen Grier, Principal**
	Eric Gohlke, Coach
	David Hollander, Coach
	Alice Feeney, Coach
Presented by:	**Kennedy Junior High**
Date:	**June 3, 1997**
Award text:	**This certificate is awarded** (press Enter)
	for sportsmanship and outstanding accomplishments in sports at (press Enter)
	Kennedy Junior High for 1997.

3. Delete the existing check mark picture.
4. Create a frame in place of the check mark and insert the picture, *Sports*. (The size of the sports picture and frame should be approximately the same size as the check mark picture it replaces.)
5. If you are using a color printer, add the Dk Blue color to the text *All Sports Awards for 1997* and *Kennedy Junior High* in the Presented by text box.
6. Save the completed certificate and name it c04sa02, sports award.
7. Print and then close c04sa02, sports award.

Assessment 3

1. Use the Calendar Wizard to create a calendar similar to the one shown in figure 4.25 with the following specifications:
   a. Use the Calendar Wizard to create a calendar for September, 1997.
   b. Select the Banner style in Landscape orientation.
   c. Insert *Computer* as a picture while using the Wizard or insert it as a watermark after completing the wizard.
   d. Insert the calendar text in text boxes created under the designated dates. Be sure to change the text box fill to *None* at the Drawing Object dialog box with the Fill tab selected. (This will allow the watermark to show through the text layer.) Make sure the text box line color is set at *None.*
   e. If you create a watermark, insert the picture into a text box created in a Header and Footer pane. Reduce the shading of the picture at *Microsoft Word Picture.*

Change each section of the picture at the Drawing Object dialog box with the Fill tab selected. Adjust the shading of each section of the picture by changing the Fill Color to white and the Pattern to 30%. Do not change the Pattern Color.

f. Key the company name, address, and phone/fax numbers in a text box or frame created below the last week of the calendar. Include the following formatting changes: font, character spacing (expand), type size, and font color.

2. Make sure all the lines around the calendar print by choosing File, then Print Preview. (If any one of the vertical or horizontal lines does not display, make adjustments for the non-printable zone of your particular printer. Position the arrow pointer on one of the calendar border lines and click to select the text box. Choose Format, then Drawing Object. At the Drawing Object dialog box, select the Size and Position tab. Change the Width to 8.4 inches in the Size section of the dialog box. Experiment to find the appropriate settings.)
3. Save the calendar and name it c04sa03, business calendar.
4. Print and then close c04sa03, business calendar.

FIGURE 4.25

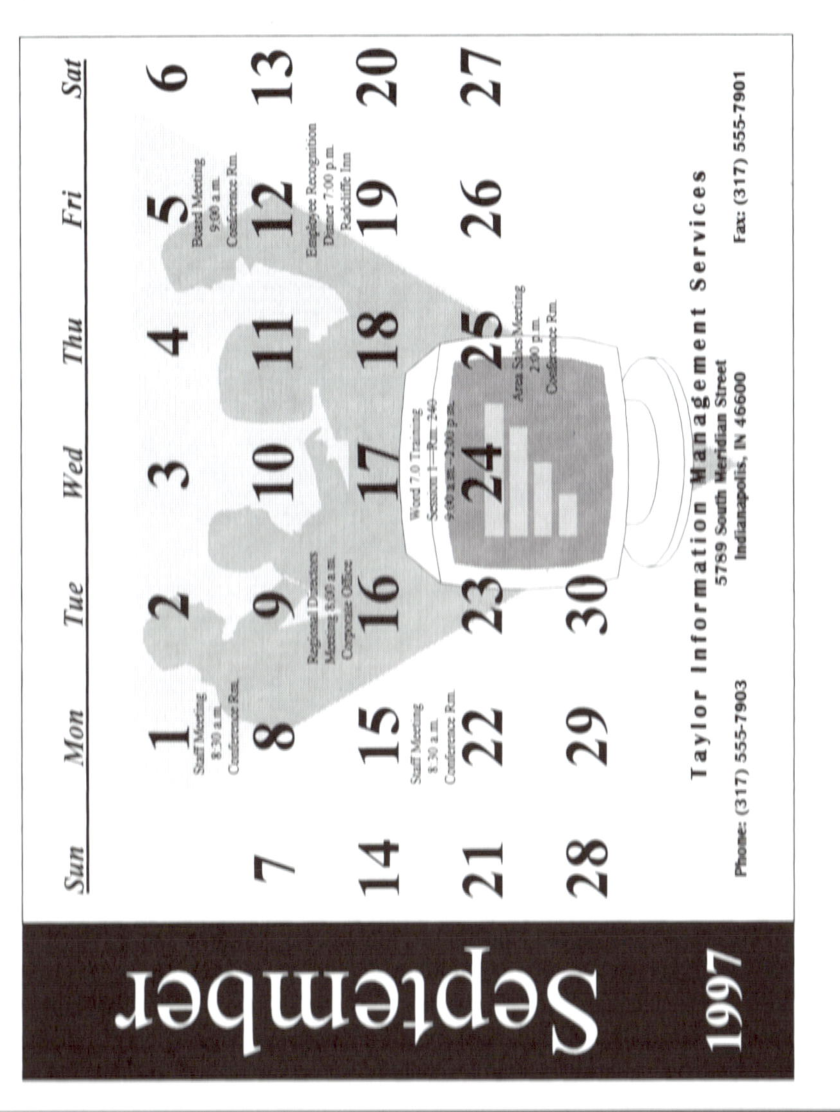

Assessment 4

1. Create a sheet of personal return address labels using your name and address. Include a picture of your choice. Use the Avery Standard *5160 - Address* label definition. Size the picture and address to fit into the label dimensions of 1 inch in height and 2.63 inches in width.
2. Save the address labels as c04sa04, personal labels. (If the document is too large, do not save it.)
3. Print and then close c04sa0a4, personal labels.

UNIT 1 PERFORMANCE *Assessment*

In this unit you have learned to define and incorporate desktop publishing concepts in the design and creation of business and personal communications.

Assessment 1

1. Use the Professional Memo template to create the memo shown in figure U1.1 with the following specifications:
   a. Key **Alpine Ski Company** in the shaded box in the upper right corner of the memo. Change the shading color in the box to Dk Blue. (To do this, choose Format, then Borders and Shading. Select the Shading tab and click the Dk Blue color at the drop-down list at the Foreground color text box.)
   b. Key the heading text and body text as shown in figure U1.1. Key the Canadian and European locations at the left margin, unformatted. (You will format them after the memo text is keyed.) Use shortcut commands to create the letters with accents. (For instance, to create **é** hold down the Ctrl key, press the single quotation mark key, press the "e" key, then release the Ctrl key and the symbol should display.) Refer to the following list:

      è = Ctrl + ` + e
      à = Ctrl + ` + a
      é = Ctrl + ´ + e
      î = Ctrl + ^ + i (^ is the shift of 6, release Shift when keying the "i")
      ü = Ctrl + : + u (release Shift when keying the "u")
      ç = Ctrl + , + c

   c. Key your reference initials in capital letters a double space below the last paragraph. Include the document name **u01pa01, ski memo**.
   d. Select the heading, *Memo*, then change the font color to Dk Blue.
   e. Select the three Canadian locations, Lac-Frontière, Quebec, etc., then apply bullets. To do this, display the Bullets and Numbering dialog box (Format, then Bullets and Numbering). At the Bullets and Numbering dialog box, choose the Modify button. At the Modify Bulleted List dialog box, choose the Bullet button. At the Symbol dialog box, choose the bullet in the seventh row, second to the last column. Choose OK to close the Symbol dialog box. At the Modify Bulleted List dialog box, change the Color to Dk Blue. Choose OK to close the dialog box.
   f. With the three Canadian locations still selected, change the left paragraph indentation to 0.25 inches.
   g. Format the three Europe locations as you did in steps 1e and 1f.

h. Create the graphic image to the right of the memo heading text by drawing a frame, then inserting the picture *Winter*.

i. Delete the footer containing the page number by completing the following steps:

   (1) Choose View, then Header and Footer; or double-click the footer in the document window.

   (2) At the header pane, click the Switch Between Header and Footer button, the first button on the Header and Footer toolbar.

   (3) At the first page footer pane, select the bullet symbol and Page 1, then press Delete.

   (4) Click the Close button on the Header and Footer toolbar.

2. When the memo is completed, save it and name it u01pa01, ski memo.
3. Print and then close u01pa01, ski memo.

Optional: Open the memo (*u01pa01, ski memo*) as completed in assessment 1. Choose a different bullet for the bulleted items. Create a watermark at the bottom of the page using the picture *Confiden.*

Alpine Ski Company

Memo

To: Maggie Rivière, Vice President

From: (your name)

CC: Martin Schoenfeld, Senior Vice President

Date: (current date)

Re: Company Expansion

The board of directors has agreed to consider expanding the company into Canada and/or Europe. The following locations in Canada are being considered:

- Lac-Frontière, Quebec
- Pointe-à-la-Frégate, Quebec
- St. Benoît, Quebec

Several of the board members feel that Canada should be our first choice. They are, however, not ruling out Europe. The following locations in Europe are being considered:

- Mühldorf, Germany
- Alençon, France
- Zürich, Switzerland

A site selection committee is being formed to assess the viability of each site. I would like you to be a member of this committee. Members will be asked to visit a specific site to gather information. I would like you to fly to Pointe-à-la-Frégate, Quebec, next week to gather information on land prices, availability of workers, educational facilities, and the general economic situation. Please let me know as soon as possible if you will be available to visit Pointe-à-la-Frégate.

xx:u01pa01, ski memo

FIGURE U1.1

Assessment 2

1. At a clear document screen, use the Letter Wizard to create a business letter as shown in figure U1.2 with the following specifications:
   a. Select the prewritten letter labeled *collection letter: 30 days past due.*
   b. Create the letter on plain paper.
   c. Send the letter to:
      Mr. Daniel Harrigan
      Harrigan Construction Company
      413 Pinecrest Road
      Scarborough, ME 04210
   d. Key the return address as:
      370 Brighton Avenue
      Portland, ME 04102
      Phone: (207) 555-3777
      Fax: (207) 555-3780
   e. Select Contemporary as the letter style.
   f. Just display the letter without making an envelope or mailing label.
   g. Change the font of the company return address, phone, and fax number to 10-point Garamond.
   h. Click in the company name location, change the font to 30-point Garamond Bold, then key **Portland Electric Supply** as the company name.
   i. Change the fill of the rectangular drawing object (shaded rectangle) that encloses the company name to a medium light blue according to the following specifications:
      (1) Select blue as the Color (first column, sixth row).
      (2) Change the Patterns to 60%.
      (3) Select white as the Pattern Color.
   j. Position the insertion point to the left of the date. Select from the date through the end of the postscript (P.S.) text, then change the font to 12-point Garamond.
   k. Make the following replacements in the prewritten letter text:

Salutation	=	**Mr. Harrigan**
Invoice #	=	**1546** (remove underlining)
Amount	=	**$1,027.39** (remove underlining)

   l. Select the globe graphic image, then choose Insert, then Picture. At the Insert Picture dialog box, double-click *Lightblb.*
   m. Change the fill of the rectangular drawing object (shaded rectangle) at the bottom of the page to a medium light blue by repeating steps i1 through i3 above. (*Note:* There are three drawing objects located in this area. To select the correct object, make sure you position the mouse pointer on the edge of the shaded rectangle to select it.)
   n. Insert and appropriately position a slogan in the blue shaded rectangle at the bottom of the page by completing the following steps:

(1) Position the I-beam in the middle of the blue shaded rectangle, then click once to select the slogan text box.
(2) Position the insertion point to the left of the first paragraph symbol in the text box. (Click the Show/Hide & on the Standard toolbar to display the nonprinting paragraph symbols.)
(3) Format the text box (drawing object) so that it is 3 inches wide.
(4) Change the font to 13-point Garamond Italic, then key **Offering the highest quality in electrical supplies!** as the slogan. (The slogan should fit on one line. If it wraps, decrease the point size.)
(5) Position the text box horizontally 0.6 inches from the left edge of the page and vertically 9.88 inches from the top edge of the page.

5. Save the completed letter and name it u01pa02, electric letter.
6. Print and then close u01pa02, electric letter.

Optional: Open u01pa02, electric letter and rewrite the letter in a more firm tone of voice. Include information that the account is more than four months past due and payment is due immediately. After rewriting the letter, save it as u01pa02, optional. Print and then close u01pa02, optional.

370 Brighton Avenue
Portland, ME 04102
Phone: (207) 555-3777
Fax: (207) 555-3780

Portland Electric Supply

(current date)

Mr. Daniel Harrigan
Harrigan Construction Company
413 Pinecrest Road
Scarborough, ME 04210

Dear Mr. Harrigan:

This is a reminder about invoice number 1546 for $1,027.39, which is now over 30 days past due. If there is a problem with this invoice, please call me at once so we can correct it.

Thank you for your business and for your prompt attention to this matter.

Sincerely,

(Your name here)
Account Representative

P.S. If your payment is already in the mail, please accept our thanks and disregard this notice.

Offering the highest quality in electrical supplies!

FIGURE U1.2

Assessment 3

1. You work for a company named Design 2000 that specializes in ergonomically designed offices. Your company works hard to create designs that provide maximum worker comfort. Create a letterhead and envelope for Design 2000. Include the following information in your letterhead design:

Slogan	=	**(Make up a slogan for your company.)**
Address	=	**300 Sun Drive**
	=	**Tucson, AZ 96322**
Phone	=	**(304) 555-2344**
Fax	=	**(304) 555-2345**

   Include the following in the letterhead and envelope design:
   a. Create a thumbnail sketch or sketches of your proposed letterhead and envelope design and layout.
   b. Create an asymmetrical design.
   c. Incorporate appropriate and proportional typeface, type size, and type style.
   d. Turn on kerning for 14 points and above.
   e. Use tracking (condensing or expanding character spacing) if necessary.
   f. Use one or more horizontal or vertical ruled lines in any length or thickness that fits into your design.
   g. You may use special characters or a graphic image if appropriate.
   h. Use some color if a color printer is available.
2. Save the letterhead and name it u01pa03, letterhead.
3. With the letterhead still displayed on the screen, create a coordinating envelope by completing the following steps:
   a. Display the Envelopes and Labels dialog box with the Envelopes tab selected.
   b. Delete any text in the Delivery Address and Return Address text boxes.
   c. Display the Envelope Options dialog box (with the Envelope Options tab selected) and make sure the Envelope Size list box displays *Size 10 (4⅛ x 9 ½ in)*.
   d. Add the envelope to your document (your letterhead) and create a return address for Design 2000 that incorporates some of the same design elements as your letterhead. You decide what information from your letterhead will also be included in the envelope return address.
4. Save the document containing the envelope and name it u01pa03, ltr&env.
5. Print and then close u01pa03, ltr&env.

Optional: Print *document analysis guide.doc* located on your student data disk and use it to evaluate your finished document.

Assessment 4

1. At a clear document window, create the résumé shown in figure U1.3 following the handwritten specifications.
2. Insert *para09*, *para10*, and *para11* from your student data disk following each appropriate heading.
3. Save the résumé and name it u01pa04, rotated resume.
4. Print and then close u01pa04, rotated resume.

Optional: Assume you are a personnel director and the résumé prepared in u01pa04 has landed on your desk for review. Write a critique of this résumé by considering the following points:

- Appropriate layout and design?
- Consistency in heading?
- Headings in proper order?
- Appropriate choice of fonts, type sizes, and type styles?
- Career Objective—clear? vague? restrictive?
- Proper punctuation?
- Job Experience—clear? specific? descriptive?
- Education—thorough? too lengthy? appropriate?
- References—more information needed? delete?

When your critique is complete, label the assignment as u01pa04x, optional.

Margins: Top 0.75", Bottom 0.5"

Distance from text 0.3" (Frame)

Use WordArt - rotate text at 90 degrees — *24 point Britannic Bold* — *Center Align*

Christine M. Garvey

2689 Kingsley Blvd. • Ann Arbor, MI • 49153

Phone (616) 555-6514 • Fax (616) 555-2341

Symbol (14th row, 11th column)

Size as picture - 1.6" width, 9.5" length

Professional Objective

16 point Britannic Bold

Position with a growth-oriented company in need of a person with word processing, desktop publishing, secretarial, and administration skills.

Use Format Painter — *3 point after (spacing) Line Spacing at least 11 pt*

Work Experience

0.25" Left Indentation

Murdock Communications Consultants, Lansing MI 49293
Office Manager, August, 1993–Present

- Proficient in use of Microsoft Office Professional for Windows 95 to create documents, monthly statements, annual reports, and monthly newsletters.

Bullet Button 0.25" from Indent to Text

Lansing Community College, Lansing, MI 49283
Part-time Instructor in Office Careers Department, September 1993–Present

- Currently teaching Microsoft Word 7.0 for Windows 95 and Desktop Publishing using Microsoft Word 7.0 for Windows 95.

Creative Computer Solutions, Ann Arbor, MI 49283
Office Manager, November 1990–June 1993

- Supervised and trained office staff in Microsoft Word 6.0 for Windows and Microsoft PowerPoint.
- Responsibilities included routine secretarial functions: e.g., word processing, assisting calls, maintaining filing system, and scheduling travel arrangements.

16 point Britannic Bold
Paragraph - Indents + Spacing Tab
0" Left + Right Indentations
After Spacing - 3 pt, Line Spacing at least 11 pt

Education

Lansing Community College, Lansing, MI 49293
1993-Present

- Computer courses—Windows 95, Internet for Educators, Creating Your Own WWW Page.
- Accounting courses—Cost Accounting.

University of Michigan, Ann Arbor, MI 49283
1991-1992

- Desktop publishing using Microsoft Word 7.0 for Windows 95.

Western Michigan University, Kalamazoo, MI 49122
Bachelor's Degree in Business Education—December 1987
Pi Omega Pi
President's Honor Roll

Interests and Activities

Michigan Area Business Education Association
National Secretaries Association

Insert Frame

Border Style 3/4 pt double line

References

References available upon request.

Text Stud Da Disk para

Text Stud Da Disk para

Text Stud Da Disk para

FIGURE U1.3

Assessment 5

1. At a clear document window, create a calendar for your employer, Harbor Realty as shown in figure U1.4. The calendar should include office-related events and client appointments for May 1997. Your employer is extremely busy, with a full client load and a real estate class to teach at your local community college. Perhaps your calendar will help your employer stay organized and informed.
   a. Select the Calendar Wizard and choose the Jazzy style in portrait orientation.
   b. Create the calendar for May 1997.
   c. Determine an appropriate typeface and type size for the text to be inserted in the calendar. Apply color to the text if appropriate.
   d. For added interest, include a picture or watermark that relates to the real estate theme. Include a "catchy" phrase that correlates to the picture and the real estate theme. If you create a watermark, be sure to reduce the shading to increase the readability of the text.
   e. Include the real estate agency's name, address, telephone number, and fax number somewhere on the calendar. Use the following information:

      Harbor Realty, 34 Saybrooke Lane, Chatham, MA 03270, Telephone: (508) 555-9402, Fax: (508) 555-5900.

   f. Include the following information in the calendar along with any special characters or pictures you may want to add.

May 1	**8:00 a.m. Staff Meeting**
May 6	**Office Golf Outing**
May 9	**2:00 p.m. Open House**
May 11	**Mother's Day**
May 14	**7:00 p.m. Award Dinner**
May 19	**Seminar in San Diego**
May 23	**9:00 a.m. Real Estate Class**
May 26	**Memorial Day**

2. Save the calendar and name it u01pa05, harbor calendar.
3. Print and then close u01pa05, harbor calendar.

Harbor Realty
34 Saybrooke Lane
Chatham, MA 03270
Telephone: (508) 555-9402
Fax: (508) 555-5900

Sun	Mon	Tue	Wed	Thu	Fri	Sat
				1 8:00 a.m. Staff Meeting	2	3
4	5	6 Office Golf Outing	7	8	9 2:00 p.m. Open House	10
11 Mother's Day	12	13	14 7:00 p.m. Award Dinner	15	16	17
18	19 Seminar in San Diego	20	21	22	23 9:00 a.m. Real Estate Class	24
25	26 Memorial Day	27	28	29	30	31

Harbor Realty—A Leader on the East Coast

1997

FIGURE U1.4

UNIT

PREPARING PROMOTIONAL DOCUMENTS

In this unit, you will learn to plan, design, and create promotional documents including flyers, brochures, and presentation materials.

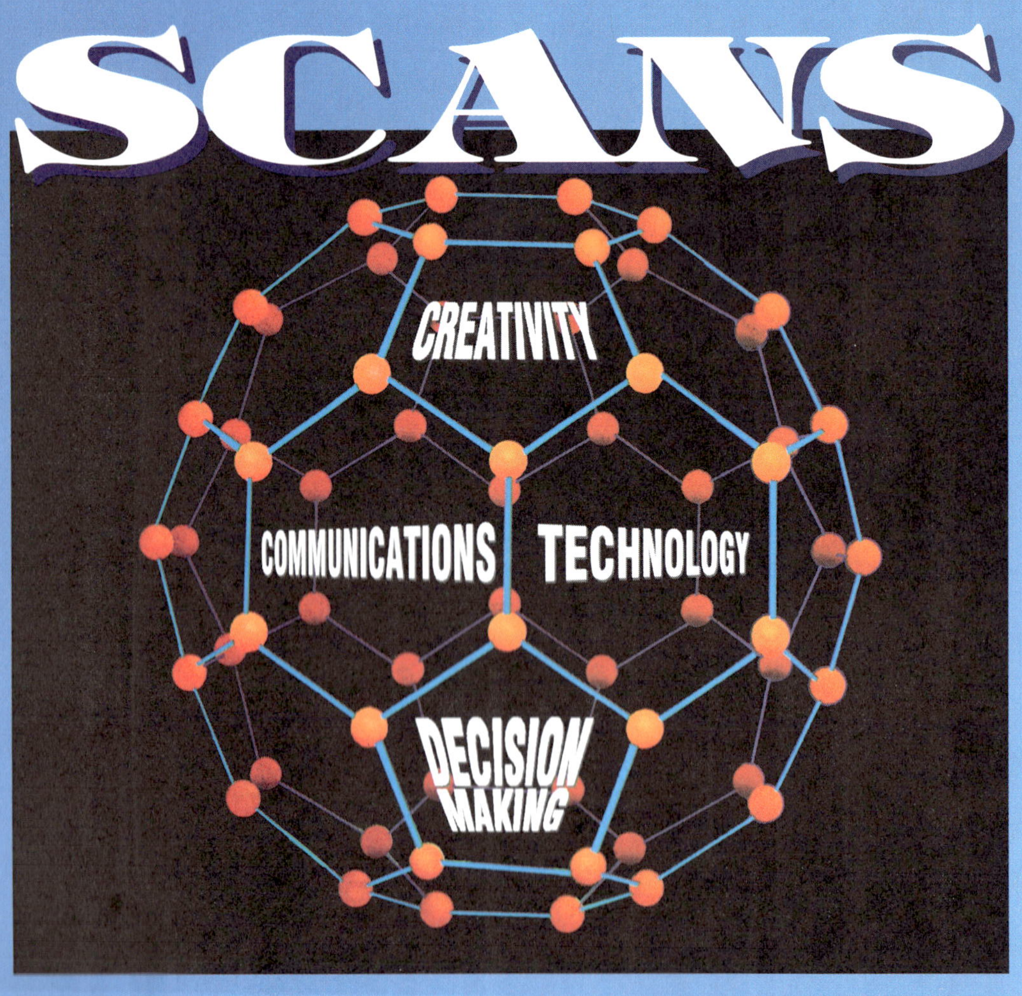

5 PREPARING PROMOTIONAL DOCUMENTS

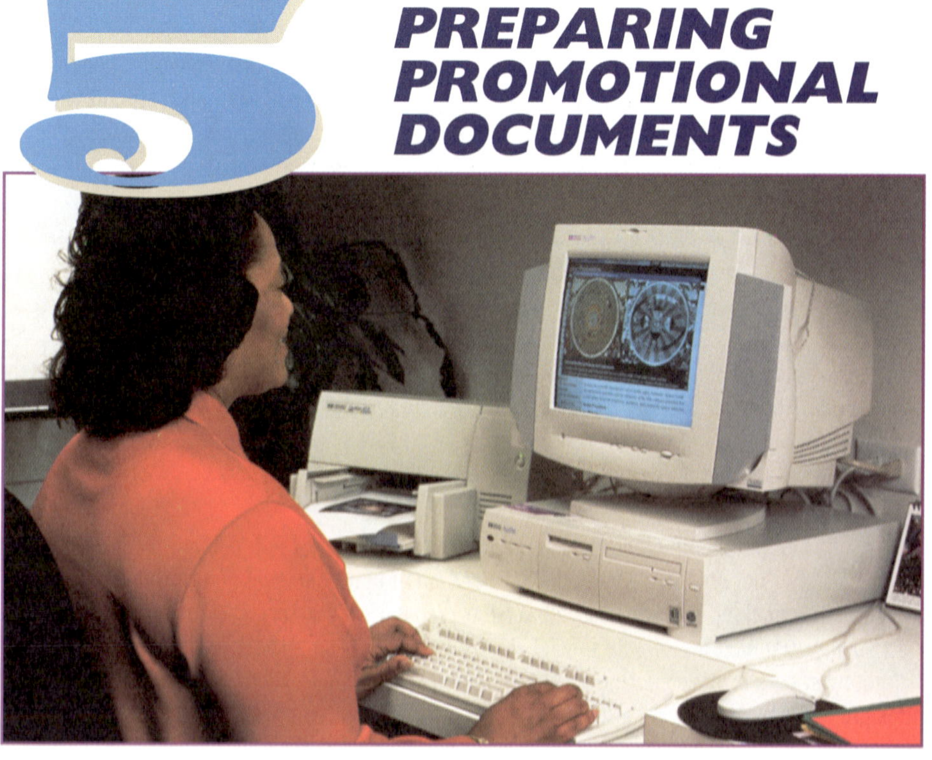

PERFORMANCE OBJECTIVE

Upon successful completion of chapter 5, you will be able to produce promotional documents such as flyers and announcements using WordArt, Microsoft Word Picture editor, and Word's Drawing Toolbar along with frames, text boxes, pictures, lines, freeform objects, callouts, and borders.

DESKTOP PUBLISHING CONCEPTS

Identifying purpose	Directional flow	White space
Focus	Consistency	Kerning
Balance	Color	Leading
Proportion	Design and layout	Graphic images
Contrast	Thumbnail sketch	

WORD FEATURES USED

Pictures	Text boxes	Callouts
WordArt	Drawing objects	Grouping and ungrouping objects
Symbols	Frames	Aligning objects
Rotating text	Shapes	Fill and line colors
Character spacing	Lines	
Drawing toolbar		

In this chapter, you will produce flyers and announcements for advertising products, services, events, classes, and more using your own design and layout ideas with the help of Word features. First, you will review basic desktop publishing concepts for planning and designing promotional documents. Then, you will incorporate fonts, graphics, borders, objects, and watermarks into your documents to increase their appeal. Finally, more complex and powerful features such as

WordArt, Microsoft Word Picture, and the Drawing toolbar will be introduced to further enhance the appeal of your publications. Information, suggestions, and examples are provided in this chapter to stimulate your interest and creativity so you will be able to produce effective promotional documents.

Planning And Designing Promotional Documents

As you learned in chapter 1, planning your document is a basic desktop publishing concept that applies to flyers and announcements as well as to other publications. Clearly define your purpose and assess your target audience. Besides assessing your needs and your approach, consider your budget as well. Flyers and announcements are generally considered one of the least expensive means of advertising.

DTP POINTERS
Prepare a thumbnail sketch.

DTP POINTERS
White space creates a clean page that is easy to read.

Start thinking about what elements are needed to produce a document that gets results. A successful document attracts the reader's attention and keeps it. In designing your document, consider how you can attract the reader's eye: by using eye-catching headlines, displaying graphics that create impact, or using color for emphasis or attention. Flyers and announcements provide enormous opportunities for creative freedom within the parameters of design concepts. To grab attention, you may consider using BIG graphics, uncommon typefaces, and a lot of white space. Use a thumbnail sketch as a tool to guide you in creating a visually pleasing and effective document. Figure 5.1 illustrates a flyer that attracts attention through the use of varying fonts and font attributes.

FIGURE 5.1

Sample Flyer (All Text)

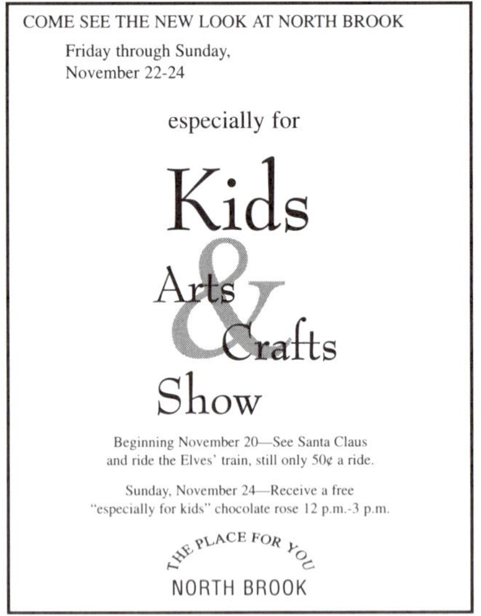

Once you have finished a document, look at the document from a distance to make sure that the important information is dominant.

DTP POINTERS
With text-intensive material:

- Vary type sizes and styles.
- Use varying shades of black and white as well as color.

Choosing Fonts for Headlines

Text-intensive material is usually not appropriate for flyers or announcements unless you vary the typefaces, type sizes, and type styles as shown in figure 5.1, otherwise your reader probably will not take the time to read it. In designing this type of publication, careful selection of fonts and type sizes is important. Select typefaces that match the tone of the document and type sizes that stress important information. For instance, avoid choosing a typeface that is characteristically formal, such as Brush Script MT Italic, if you are creating a flyer advertising a garage sale. For a strong headline you might want to use Braggadocio, Impact, or Arial MT Black, all of which demand attention. For a casual appearance, consider using Century Gothic, Arial, or Kino MT.

A headline should be a dominant visual element, set significantly larger than the words that follow. Standard headlines are usually 36 to 48 points in size. However, depending on your document, the headline may even exceed 72 points. The font size drop-down lists in the Font dialog box and on the Formatting toolbar display type sizes that range from 2 to 72 points. To use a type size greater than 72 points, key the setting in the Font Size text box in the Font dialog box or key the setting in the Font Size text box on the Formatting toolbar, then press Enter. Select all existing text before changing the type size.

DTP POINTERS
Turn on kerning.

Besides increasing the point size for headlines, you may want to change the shading and/or color of the font. Depending on your needs, you may choose a large, thick typeface and change the shading to a desired percentage of black at the Font dialog box. Or, you may choose a font color by clicking the down-pointing triangle to the right of the Color text box, then select a specific color from the Color drop-down list. Existing text in a document must first be selected. See figure 5.2 for examples of different typefaces. Notice that all of the examples are keyed in the same type size, but the amount of horizontal space they occupy varies greatly.

DTP POINTERS
Use color consistently within a document.

FIGURE 5.2

Type Variations and Color Choices

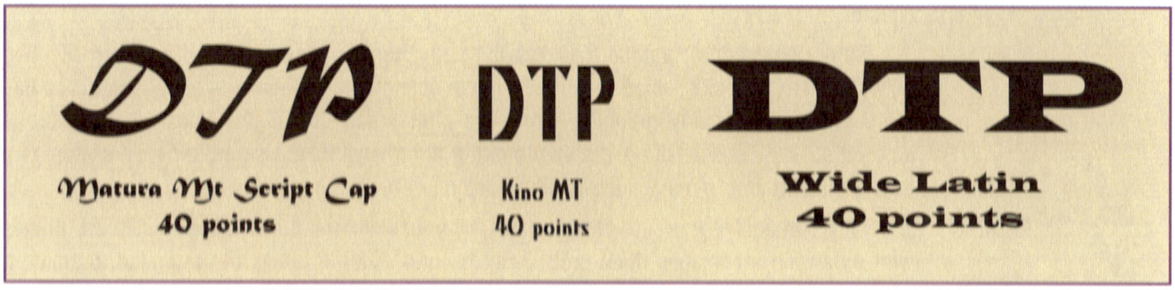

DTP	DTP	DTP
Matura Mt Script Cap 40 points	Kino MT 40 points	Wide Latin 40 points

Using WordArt for Headlines

Consider the impact that text can have, as shown in figure 5.3. The name of the font used in this example is *Impact* and when used with a WordArt shape in a green color you can imagine the impact this heading will have—a big savings in dollars! Wise use of text in publications can have a forceful effect on how the message is communicated. A flyer with a large, colorful headline is an eye-catching way to announce an event or advertise a product or service.

FIGURE 5.3

WordArt for Emphasis

50% Off Sale!

WordArt can change text into graphics and since WordArt is based on text, fonts are very important in creating interesting text designs. The fonts that are available for use in WordArt applications include Windows fonts, Word program fonts, printer fonts, and any other soft fonts you may have added to your computer. In addition, you have the option of including symbols with your WordArt text. WordArt will be discussed later in this chapter.

Using Graphics for Emphasis

DTP POINTERS
- Choose images that relate to the message.
- Leave plenty of white space.

Graphics can add excitement and generate enthusiasm for a publication. However, they are effective only if the image relates to the subject of the document. Graphics could be the key to attracting the attention of your audience. Word provides many graphics images and borders, but you may also consider other sources. If you purchased Word for Windows 95 as part of Microsoft Office Professional for Windows 95, you have access to Microsoft ClipArt Gallery. The ClipArt Gallery is a tool for organizing and previewing clip art. In addition, you have access to hundreds of images within the ClipArt Gallery. To access these graphics, choose Insert, then Object. At the Create New tab, select Microsoft ClipArt Gallery in the Object Type list box, then click OK.

Once a clip art image is inserted into your document, you can move it, resize it, and change its colors. You can use the Drawing toolbar and the graphic editor, Microsoft Word Picture, to disassemble the image, group and ungroup segments of the image, and change colors. The Drawing toolbar and Microsoft Word Picture will be discussed in greater detail later in this chapter.

Before selecting a graphic, decide what your theme or text will be. If you are deciding between many graphics, select the simplest. A simple graphic demands more attention and has more impact. Too many graphics can cause clutter and confusion. Also, use a generous amount of white space. Use a graphic to aid in directional flow. Use a thumbnail sketch as a tool in guiding you to make decisions on position, size, and design.

DTP POINTERS
Do not overuse clip art; use one main visual element per page.

Also consider using clip art as a basis for your own creations. Combine clip art images with other clip art images, then crop, size, or color different areas of the image to create a unique look. In addition, you can add a frame to the image and add a border, shade, or color to the frame as shown in figure 5.4.

FIGURE 5.4

Example of a Shaded Frame and the Paragraph Borders and Shading Dialog Box—Shading Tab

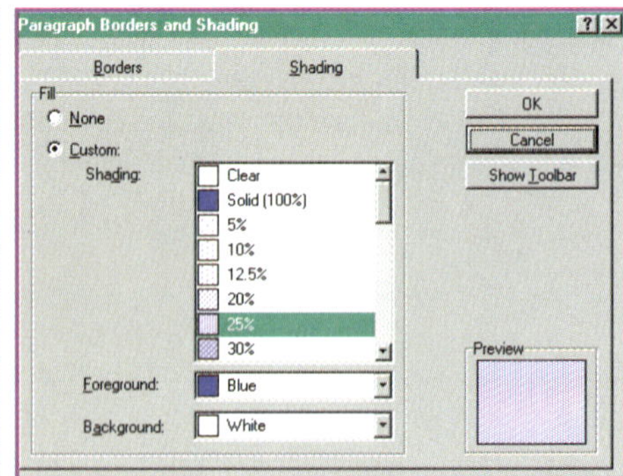

The bordered and shaded frame in figure 5.4 is larger than the bordered picture inside it, creating a double border. To create this effect, you would complete the following steps:

1. In Page Layout view, choose Insert, then Frame.
2. Draw a frame approximately 2 inches high by 2½ inches wide.
3. Choose Format, then Borders and Shading.

4. At the Paragraph Borders and Shading dialog box, select the Shading tab.
5. Choose Custom in the Fill section.
6. Select 25% at the Shading drop-down list.
7. Select Blue at the Foreground drop-down list.
8. Select White at the Background list.
9. Choose OK or press Enter.
10. With the insertion point positioned inside the frame, choose Insert, then Frame, then draw another frame inside the first frame that is 1 inch high by 1½ inches wide.
11. Insert the picture, *Books* (choose Insert, Picture, then double-click *Books*).
12. Select the book picture, then click Format, then Borders and Shading.
13. Select the Borders tab at the Picture Borders and Shading dialog box.
14. Click the Box in the Presets section.
15. Select 3 pt in the Style list.
16. Click the down-pointing arrow to the right of the Color text box and select the color Blue.
17. Choose OK or press Enter.
18. If necessary, drag the picture to the middle of the blue border.

Using Color in Promotional Documents

Color is a powerful tool in communicating information. Color elicits feelings, emphasizes important text, attracts attention, organizes data, and/or creates a pattern in a document. Color focuses a reader's attention, but use color sparingly or it will lose its power. The colors you choose should reflect the nature of the business you represent. Someone in an artistic line of work would use bolder, splashier colors than someone creating documents for a business dealing with finance. Additionally, men and women often respond differently to the same color. Always identify your target audience in planning your documents and think about the impact color will have on your audience.

DTP POINTERS
Color can create a mood.

Choose one or two colors for a document and stick with them to give your page a unified look. Use "spot color" in your document by using color only in specific areas of the page. Also pick up a color from your graphic in your text.

Many of the Word graphic images included in this program are created in color. In Word everything you key onto a page can be printed in color. You can choose from millions of different colors depending on your monitor and color printer. You have the capability to alter graphic images and the distribution of their colors through Microsoft Word Picture and the Drawing Object dialog box.

DTP POINTERS
Use spot color to attract the reader's eye.

Many flyers and announcements are prepared on personal computers and printed on either white or color paper and duplicated on a copy machine to help keep costs down. A color printer or color copier adds to the cost but can help the appeal of the document. If you are using a color printer, limit the color to small areas so it attracts attention but does not create visual confusion. As an inexpensive alternative to printing in color, use color paper or specialty papers to help get your message across. Specialty papers are predesigned papers used for brochures, letterheads, postcards, business cards, certificates, etc. and can be purchased through most office supply stores or catalog paper supply companies such as *Paper Direct* and *Quill*. Be sure to choose a color that complements your message. Choose colors that match the theme of your document—orange for Halloween, green for spring, yellow for summer, or blue for water and sky.

When working in desktop publishing and using Word for Windows 95 you may encounter terms used in explaining color. Here is a list of color terms along with explanations:

- *Brightness* or *value* is the amount of lightness or darkness in a color.
- *Color Wheel* is a device used to illustrate color relationships.
- *Complementary Colors* are colors directly opposite each other on the color wheel, such as red and green, which are among the most popular color schemes.
- *CYMK* is an acronym for cyan, yellow, magenta, and black. A color printer combines these colors to create different colors.
- *Dither* is similar to halftone. It is a method of combining several different-colored pixels to create new colors.
- *Gradient* is a gradual varying of color.
- *Grayscale* is a range of shades from black to white.
- *Halftone* is a process of taking basic color dots and combining them to produce many other colors. Your print driver can use halftoning to produce more shades of color.
- *Hue* is a variation of a color, such as green-blue.
- *Pixel* is each dot in a picture or graphic.
- *Resolution* is the number of dots that make up an image on a screen or printer. The higher the resolution, the higher the quality of the print.
- *Reverse* is a black background and white foreground or white type against a colored background.
- *RGB* is an acronym for red, green, and blue. Each pixel on your color monitor is made up of these three colors.
- *Saturation* is the purity of a color. A color is completely pure, or saturated, when it is not diluted with white. Red, for example, has a high saturation.

Adding Rules, Borders, And Shading To Text And Pictures

As discussed in chapter 3, ruled lines can be used in a document to create a focal point, draw the eye across or down the page, separate columns and sections, or add visual appeal. Rules are generally thought of as single vertical, horizontal, or slanted lines in various line styles. Borders are generally used to frame text or an image with more than one side. Rules and/or borders can be drawn using the Line button or the Rectangle button on the Drawing toolbar, clicking on specific line buttons on the Borders toolbar, or using the Paragraph Borders and Shading dialog box. In addition, picture borders are available in Word and accessed as any other picture image. A few of the many picture borders in Word include: *hcorner.wmf, hdecobox.wmf, hmedeval,wmf, hplaque.wmf,* and *hpresbox.wmf.* Rules can even be created using a series of special symbols, as shown in figure 5.5.

FIGURE 5.5

Using Symbols to Create a Ruled Line

Borders, like ruled lines, can be used to customize text, create interest, and attract attention to a headline in an announcement or flyer. When a border is added to a paragraph(s) of text, the border expands as text is inserted. To access the Borders toolbar, click the Borders button (first button from the right) on the Formatting toolbar. The first option at the left side of the Borders toolbar, the Line Style option, contains a variety of choices for thickness or style of the border. The next seven buttons contain options to apply borders to the top, bottom, left, right, inside, outside, and no border. With choices from the Shading options on the Borders toolbar, shading can be added to a paragraph or selected paragraphs. Shading can be applied from 5 to 90 percent of the color. In addition, patterns can be applied to wider borders, as shown in figure 5.6.

DTP POINTERS
Your heading should be large enough to grab and hold the reader's attention.

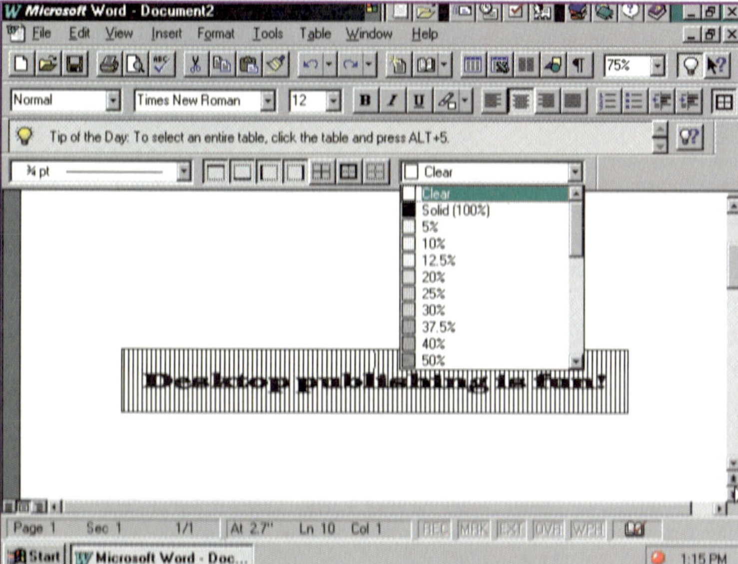

FIGURE 5.6

Borders Toolbar Shading List

If you want to further customize a border, use options from the Paragraph Borders and Shading dialog box. To display this dialog box, choose Format, then Borders and Shading. At the Paragraph Borders and Shading dialog box with the Borders tab selected, choose Box or Shadow in the presets section to add a border. If a paragraph contains a border and you want to remove it, choose None at the Paragraph Borders and Shading dialog box.

You can change the color of the border line with the Color option at the Paragraph Borders and Shading dialog box. To change the border line color, choose Color, then select a color from the drop-down menu.

Shading can be added to the area within the border with options on the Borders toolbar or at the Paragraph Borders and Shading dialog box with the Shading tab as shown in figure 5.4. Choose an option in the Shading list box to add shading inside a border, as shown in figure 5.6.

DTP POINTERS
Bold text in shaded boxes to increase readability.

With the Foreground option, you can select the color of the dots and lines that create the shading pattern. Choose Background, then select a color option for the background color of the shading pattern. In the Shading list box, choose Clear to apply the selected background color. Choose solid to apply the selected foreground color. To print reverse text (white text on black or color background) choose White for the Foreground color and Black for the Background color, as shown in figure 5.7. Color can be effective in promotional documents by organizing information, creating focus and emphasis, producing contrast, and providing balance among other design elements. The reversed text in figure 5.7 creates a high degree of contrast.

DTP POINTERS
Use contrast to add interest and impact.

FIGURE 5.7

Creating Reversed Text in the Borders and Shading Dialog Box

Desktop Publishing Using Word for Windows 95

In addition, graphic borders can be sized and positioned around text, pictures, and objects to add interest, organization, and balance to other design elements. Edit graphic (picture) borders at the Picture dialog box.

Creating Announcements

Announcements communicate or inform an audience of upcoming events. They may promote interest in events, but do not necessarily promote a product or service. For instance, you may have received an announcement for course offerings at your local community college or an announcement of an upcoming community event, sporting event, concert, race, contest, raffle, or a new store opening. Announcements, like flyers, are an inexpensive means of advertising.

Creating a Seminar Announcement with Text in Frames

1. At a clear document window, create the seminar announcement in figure 5.8 by completing the following steps:
   a. Change to Page Layout viewing mode.
   b. Click the Show/Hide ¶ button on the Standard toolbar to turn this feature on.
   c. Turn on Kerning at 14 points and above.
   d. Make sure 12-point Times New Roman is the default font, key **McGuire, Sullivan,** then press Enter. Key **& Murphy, Inc.**, then press Enter four times.
   e. Press Ctrl + E or click the Center button on the Standard toolbar.
   f. Key **Check Your Calendar and Reserve a Date!**, then press Enter five times.
   g. Key **1997 Summer Events**, then press Enter five times.
   h. Key **MSM Investment Seminars**, then press Enter three times.
   i. Key the following: **Friday, June 6**, press Enter; **Friday, June 13**, press Enter; **Friday, June 20**; then press Enter three times.
   j. Press Ctrl + L or click the Align Left button on the Standard toolbar.
   k. Key **Followed by...**, then press Enter four times.
   l. Press Ctrl + E or the Center button on the Standard toolbar. Key the following: **Dinner and a performance of**, press Enter; **the musical "Show Boat"**; then press Enter four times.
   m. Press Ctrl + L or click the Align Left button on the Standard toolbar. Key **Seminars are being held in our Chicago office on the dates listed above. Seminar attendees, along with their spouse or one guest, will be invited to join us for dinner and a performance of "Show Boat."**, then press Enter three times.
   n. Press Ctrl + E or click the Center button on the Standard toolbar, then key **More details and registration information will be forthcoming.**
   o. Format the seminar by completing the following steps:
      (1) Select *McGuire, Sullivan, & Murphy, Inc.*, then change the font to 22-point Colonna MT Bold.

(2) Select *Check Your Calendar and Reserve a Date!*, then change the font to 22-point Footlight MT Light Bold Italic in small caps.
(3) Select *1997 Summer Events*, then change the font to 20-point Footlight MT Light Bold.
(4) Create a shaded box around *1997 Summer Events* as shown in figure 5.8 by completing the following steps:
  (a) Select *1997 Summer Events* along with one paragraph symbol above and below it.
  (b) Choose Format, then Borders and Shading.
  (c) Select the Borders tab and make sure None is selected in the Presets section.
  (d) Select the Shading tab. At the Fill section, click Custom, then select 25% at the shading drop-down list.
  (e) Change the Foreground color to Dk Green and the Background color to White.
  (f) Click OK or press Enter.
(5) Select *MSM Investment Seminars*, then change the font to 26-point Colonna MT Bold.
(6) Format the list of dates by completing the following steps:
  (a) Select the list of dates, then choose Format, then Bullets and Numbering.
  (b) At the Bullets and Numbering dialog box, make sure the Bulleted tab is selected, then choose the diamond-shaped bullet in the first row of the third column.
  (c) Click OK or press Enter to close the dialog box.
  (d) With the bulleted text still selected, change the font to 18-point Footlight MT Light.
  (e) With the bulleted text still selected, press Ctrl + L or press the Align Left button on the Standard toolbar, then choose Insert, then Frame.
  (f) Size the frame to fit close to the list of dates. To do this, position the insertion point on the right border of the frame, drag the double-headed arrow close to the text, then release the mouse.
  (g) With the frame selected, choose Format, then Frame.
  (h) At the Frame dialog box, change the Text Wrap to None, the Horizontal Position to Center at the Position drop-down list, then click OK.
  (i) If a border appears around the frame, display the Borders toolbar then click the No Border button (eighth button). If shading appears in the frame, select Clear in the Shading list box on the Border toolbar.
(7) Select *Followed by...*, then change the font to 16-point Footlight MT Light Italic.
(8) Select *Dinner and a performance of the musical "Show Boat"*, change the font to 18-point Footlight MT Light Bold, and change the font color to Dk Green at the font Color drop-down list.
(9) Create a border above and below *Dinner and a performance of the musical "Show Boat"* as shown in Figure 5.8 by completing the following steps:
  (a) Select *Dinner and a performance of the musical "Show Boat"* along with the paragraph symbol above and below the text.
  (b) Insert a frame.
  (c) Display the Borders toolbar.
  (d) If a border appears around the frame, click the No Border button on the Borders toolbar.
  (e) With the frame still selected, click the down-pointing triangle to the right of the Line Style button on the Borders toolbar, then select the *¾ pt* double line from the drop-down list.

(f) With the frame still selected, click the Top Border and Bottom Border buttons on the Border toolbar.

(10) Select the entire paragraph that begins *Seminars are being…*, then change the font to 14-point Footlight MT Light.

(11) Select *More details and registration information will be forthcoming*, then change the font to 11-point Footlight MT Light Bold Italic.

2. Save the document as c05ex01, seminar announce.
3. Print and then close c05ex01, seminar announce.

FIGURE 5.8

McGuire, Sullivan,
& Murphy, Inc.

Check Your Calendar and Reserve a Date!

1997 Summer Events

MSM Investment Seminars

◆ Friday, June 6
◆ Friday, June 13
◆ Friday, June 20

Followed by…

Dinner and a performance of
the musical "Show Boat"

Seminars are being held in our Chicago office on the dates listed above. Seminar attendees, along with their spouse or one guest, will be invited to join us for dinner and a performance of "Show Boat."

More details and registration information will be forthcoming.

Creating A Logo

In exercise 2, you will create a logo and apply it to the seminar announcement produced in exercise 1. A *logo* is a unique design that may be made up of combinations of letters, words, shapes, symbols, or graphics that serve as an emblem for an organization or for a product. As discussed earlier, AutoText entries can include frequently used phrases, pictures, graphic letterheads, graphics of digitized signatures, logos, or symbols. If you frequently use a company logo in your documents, you may want to save the logo as an AutoText entry. The logos in figure 5.9 were created using the Ellipse button on the Drawing toolbar, a Word picture, and WordArt to configure text.

Logo:
A unique design that serves as an emblem for an organization or for a product.

FIGURE 5.9

Logo Examples

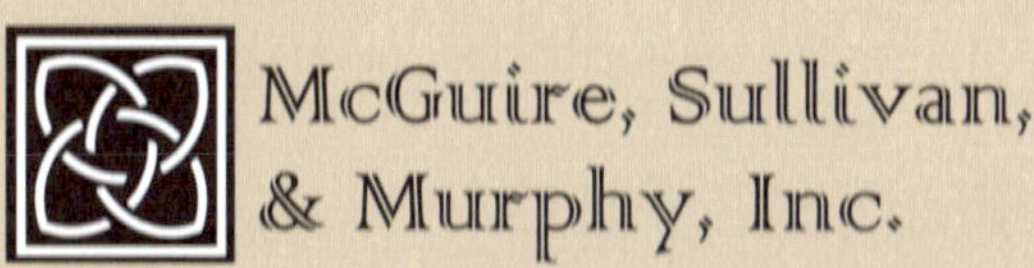

Customizing a Seminar Announcement Using a Logo, Graphic Image, and Border

1. At a clear document window, open c05ex01, seminar announce.
2. Save the document with Save As and name it c05ex02, seminar update.
3. Change to Page Layout viewing mode.
4. Click the Show/Hide ¶ button on the Standard toolbar to turn this feature on.
5. Create a logo and insert it into the document shown in figure 5.10 by completing the following steps:
   a. Select *McGuire, Sullivan, & Murphy, Inc.*, then insert a frame.
   b. Size the frame to fit close to the text by positioning the mouse pointer on the right border line until it turns into a double-headed arrow, drag the line toward the text, then release the mouse button.
   c. If a border line appears around the frame, delete the border by clicking the No Border button on the Borders toolbar. (To display the Borders toolbar, click the Borders button on the Standard toolbar.)
   d. With the insertion point positioned to the right of *McGuire, Sullivan, & Murphy, Inc.*, choose Insert, then Picture.
   e. At the Insert Picture dialog box, double-click *Celtic.*
   f. Select the picture, then insert a frame.
   g. Double-click the picture to access Microsoft Word Picture.
   h. Position the arrow pointer on the black area of the image, then double-click. The entire black area of the image should be selected and the Drawing Object dialog box should display.
   i. Select the Fill tab.
   j. At the Color palette, select the dark green color in the seventh row of the third column. Click OK to close the Drawing Object dialog box.
   k. Click the Close Picture button to close Microsoft Word Picture.

l. Drag the logo to the left of the company name as shown in figure 5.10.
m. Click to select the frame around McGuire, Sullivan, etc., then drag the frame to the right of the Celtic picture as shown in figure 5.10.
n. With the frame in step m still selected, choose Format, then Frame. Click the None box in the Text Wrapping section. Choose OK or press Enter.

6. Insert the graphic logo and text into AutoText by completing the following steps:
   a. Select the graphic logo.
   b. Choose Edit, then AutoText.
   c. At the AutoText dialog box, key **McGuire Logo** in the Name text box.
   d. Click the Add button.
   e. Select the framed company text to the right of the graphic logo.
   f. Complete steps similar to steps 6b through 6d. However, name the AutoText entry **McGuire Text**.
7. Insert a check mark symbol as shown in figure 5.10 by completing the following steps:
   a. Position the insertion point at the beginning of the line, *Check Your Calendar....*
   b. Choose Insert, then Symbol.
   c. At the Symbol dialog box, select the Symbols tab.
   d. Select *Monotype Sorts* at the Font drop-down list.
   e. Click the check mark symbol in the first row and the eighth column from the right.
   f. Click Insert, then Close.
8. Insert a graphic image as a paragraph divider as shown in figure 5.10 by completing the following steps:
   a. Select the frame around *Dinner and a performance of the musical "Show Boat"*, then delete the two horizontal border lines above and below the text by clicking the No Border button on the Border toolbar.
   b. Position the insertion point on the second paragraph symbol below *Dinner and a performance...* and choose Insert, then Picture.
   c. At the Insert Picture dialog box, double-click *Divider1*. (Remove any blank lines that interfere with positioning the *Divider1* as shown in figure 5.10.) Make sure the last line displays at the bottom of the page. (Remove any blank lines if necessary.)
9. Create a border around the entire document by completing the following steps:
   a. Display the Drawing toolbar.
   b. Click the Line Color button (tenth button from the left) on the Drawing toolbar, then select the Dk Green color square from the color palette.
   c. Click the down-pointing triangle to the right of the Zoom Control text box, then click Whole Page.
   d. Click the Rectangle button (second button from the left) on the Drawing toolbar.
   e. Drag the crosshairs to draw a rectangular border beginning at the left corner of the document and ending in the right corner approximately ¾ inch from the edge of the paper.
10. Display the document in Print Preview to make sure all the text appears on the page and the design elements appear in proportion.
11. Save the document with the same name (c05ex02, seminar update).
12. Print and then close c05ex02, seminar update.

FIGURE 5.10

✓*CHECK YOUR CALENDAR AND RESERVE A DATE!*

1997 Summer Events

MSM Investment Seminars

◆ Friday, June 6
◆ Friday, June 13
◆ Friday, June 20

Followed by…

Dinner and a performance of
the musical "Show Boat"

Seminars are being held in our Chicago office on the dates listed above. Seminar attendees, along with their spouse or one guest, will be invited to join us for dinner and a performance of "Show Boat."

More details and registration information will be forthcoming.

Creating Flyers

DTP POINTERS
The upper left corner is usually read first.

Flyers are generally used to advertise a produce or service that is available for a limited amount of time. Frequently, you may find flyers stuffed in a grocery bag; attached to a mailbox, door handle, or windshield; placed in a bin near an entrance; or placed on a countertop for prospective customers to carry away. Examples of businesses that use flyers for advertising services include lawn maintenance companies, babysitters, window washers, cleaning services, realtors, dentists, doctors, lawyers, and more. As you can see, this form of advertising is used by just about anyone.

Typically, flyers are one of the least expensive forms of advertising. The basic goal of a flyer is to communicate a message at a glance, so the message should be brief and to the point. For the flyer to be effective, the basic layout and design should be free of clutter—without too much text or too many graphics. Have the information arranged so it is easy to understand.

DTP POINTERS
Consider your audience when choosing type size.

As you learned in chapter 1, use white space generously to set off an image or text. Also, consider directional flow in placing elements on a page. The left corner is usually read first. Consider your audience when choosing type sizes. The older your audience, the larger the print might need to be. Most important, always prepare a thumbnail sketch, which is like thinking on paper, before beginning a project.

Creating a Flyer Using a Graphic Border

In exercise 3, you will create a flyer using a Word graphic border and insert text inside the border. Compare figure 5.11 to figure 5.12. Which flyer attracts your attention and pulls you in to read the text? Of course, figure 5.12 communicates more effectively because of the relevant graphic border and the varied typefaces, type styles, and type sizes. How many typefaces can you find in this document? (There are only two typefaces used in this flyer—Brush Script MT and Book Antiqua.)

A graphic border is inserted into a document like any other picture. Choose Insert, then Picture. Size and position a graphic border using the sizing handles or use the Drawing Object dialog box.

Creating a Flyer Using a Graphic Border

1. At a clear document window, create the flyer in figure 5.12 by completing the following steps:
   a. Change to Page Layout viewing mode.
   b. Make sure the default font is 12-point Times New Roman.
   c. Turn on Kerning at 14 points and above.
   d. Choose Insert, then Picture.
   e. At the Insert Picture dialog box, double-click *Nouvflwr* from the Name list.
   f. Insert a frame around the picture. (To do this, select the picture then choose Insert, then Frame.)
   g. With the picture still selected, change the width and height of the picture by completing the following steps:
      (1) Choose Format, then Picture.
      (2) At the Picture dialog box, choose Width in the Size section of the dialog box, then key **6**.
      (3) Position the insertion point in the Height text box in the Scaling section, then key **159.1** percent. (This percentage should have displayed in the Width text box in the Scaling section.)
      (4) Click OK or press Enter.

h. With the picture still selected, change Format, then Frame. Click the down-pointing triangle to the right of the Position text box in the Horizontal section, and select Center. Change the Vertical Position to Center. Make sure the Horizontal and Vertical positions are Relative to Margin. Choose OK or press Enter.
i. Deselect the picture. (You may need to zoom to a smaller percentage to be able to deselect the picture.)
j. Display the Drawing toolbar. (To do this, click the Drawing button on the Standard toolbar—fifth button from the right.)
k. Create the text box inside the graphic border by completing the following steps:
   (1) Click the Text Box button on the Drawing toolbar.
   (2) Drag the crosshair inside the graphic border, then create a box about ½ inch from all sides of the graphic border.
   (3) If the text box has a border, remove the border by clicking the Line Color button on the Drawing toolbar and selecting None.
l. Key the following text in 12-point Times New Roman:
   Details by Design, press Enter.
   Residential and, press Enter.
   Commercial, press Enter.
   Design, press Enter five times.
   Think Spring!, press Enter two times.
   Plan a new look for your home or office—complete design service available, press Enter two times. (Use an em dash.)
   Space planning and consultation with trained professionals, press Enter five times.
   Call today for an appointment, press Enter.
   (614) 555-0898, press Enter two times.
   25 W. Jefferson • Columbus, OH • 43201, (create the bullet symbol by pressing the Num Lock key on the keypad to turn it on, holding down the Alt key, keying 0149 on the keypad, then turning off the Num Lock key).
m. Select *Details by Design*, then change the font to 36-point Brush Script MT. Click the Align Right button on the Standard toolbar.
n. Select *Residential and Commercial Design*, then change the font to 16-point Book Antiqua Bold Italic and the font Color to Dk Gray. Click the Align Right button on the Formatting toolbar.
o. Deselect the text.
p. Select all the text from *Think Spring!* to the end of the document, then click the Center button on the Standard toolbar.
q. Select *Think Spring!*, then change the font to 28-point Brush Script MT.
r. Select the next two paragraphs, then change the font to 14-point Book Antiqua.
s. Select *Call today for an appointment (614) 555-0898*, then change the font to 14-point Book Antiqua Bold Italic.
t. Select *25 W. Jefferson • Columbus, OH • 43201*, then change the font to 12-point Book Antiqua Bold Italic and the font Color to Dk Gray.
u. Resize the text box if necessary.

2. Save the document and name it c05ex03, graphic border.
3. Print and then close c05ex03, graphic border.

Optional: Add color to the flowers in the graphic at Microsoft Word Picture by changing the fill and lines.

FIGURE 5.11

Flyer Before

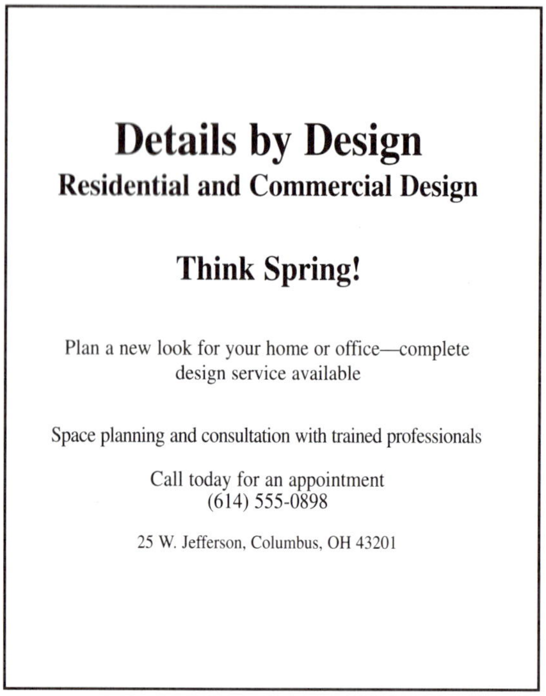

Details by Design
Residential and Commercial Design
Think Spring!
Plan a new look for your home or office—complete design service available
Space planning and consultation with trained professionals
Call today for an appointment
(614) 555-0898
25 W. Jefferson, Columbus, OH 43201

FIGURE 5.12

Flyer After

Details by Design
Residential and Commercial Design
Think Spring!
Plan a new look for your home or office—complete design service available
Space planning and consultation with trained professionals
Call today for an appointment
(614) 555-0898
25 W. Jefferson • Columbus, OH • 43201

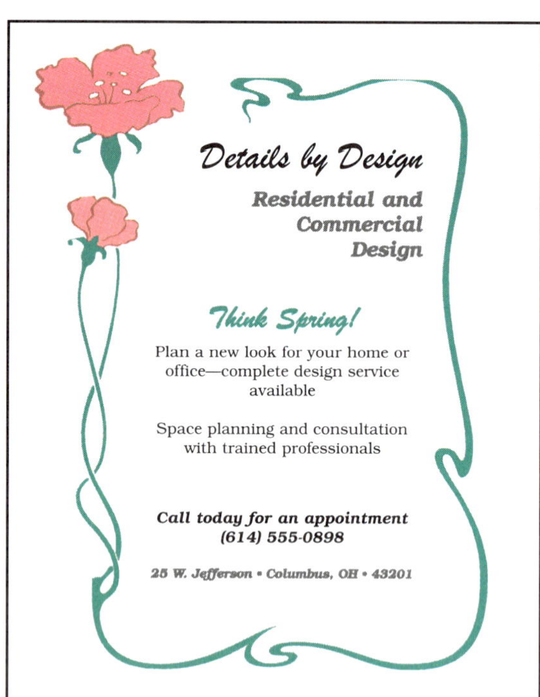

Using WordArt In Announcements And Flyers

As discussed earlier in chapter 4, WordArt can distort or modify text to create a variety of shapes. This is useful for creating company logos and headings. It is especially useful for headlines in flyers and announcements. The shapes can exaggerate the text to draw in an audience. Many flyers that advertise sales use this feature to emphasize a discount and persuade an audience to act on the message. WordArt enables you to change fonts, type styles, and alignment. You can also add a border, shadow, or shading to your text to increase its impact. After creating the text, you can save it, insert it into a current document, or use it as a watermark.

WordArt includes 36 different shapes that you can use to pour text into, as shown in figure 5.13. Some shapes produce different results depending on how many lines of text you key into the text entry box in WordArt. When you are deciding on which shape to use, experiment with several to find the right effect.

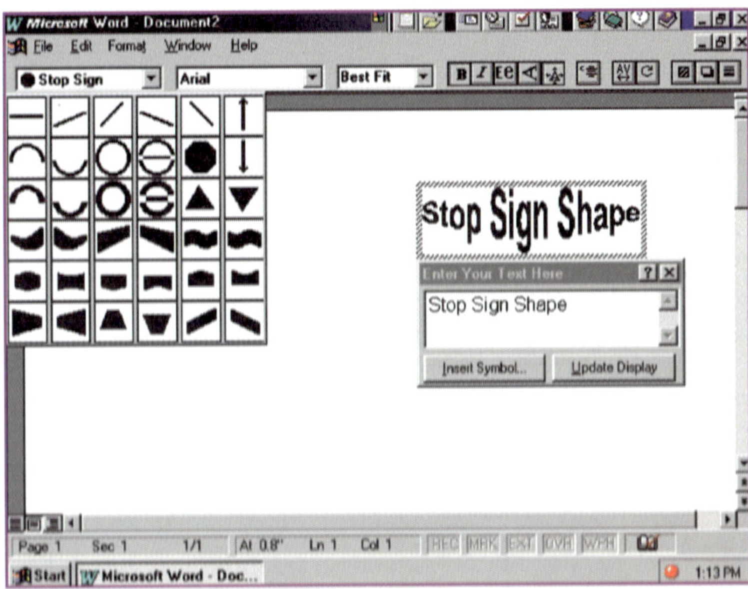

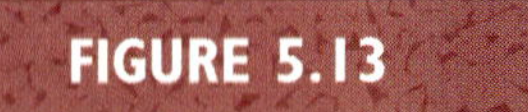

WordArt Line and Shape Palette

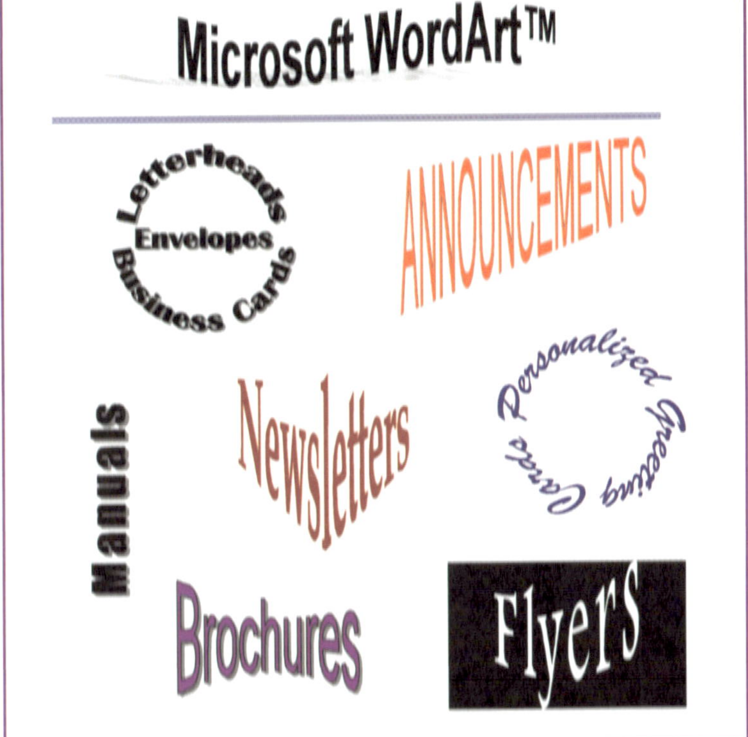

FIGURE 5.14

Examples of WordArt Shapes

To shape text, complete the following steps:

1. Choose Insert, then Object.
2. At the Insert dialog box, select the Create New tab.
3. At the Object Type list, double-click Microsoft WordArt 3.0 (2.0).
4. Key your text into the Enter Your Text Here dialog box.
5. Click the Update Display button at the bottom of the text entry box.
6. Click the down-pointing triangle to the right of the Line and Shape text box on the WordArt toolbar.
7. At the Line and Shape palette, click a shape that complements your text.
8. Click the down-pointing triangle to the right of the Font text box to select a different font. (Choose a font that matches the tone of the document.)
9. Click the Font Size button to select a different point size for your text. (*Best Fit* is the default and is usually sufficient for most text.)
10. Click any of the special effects buttons on the WordArt toolbar to enhance your text. See figure 5.15 for the WordArt toolbar.
11. Click in the document screen outside the text entry box to remove the text entry box.
12. Select the WordArt object, then frame it by choosing Insert, then Frame; or, by clicking the Insert Frame button (second to the last button) on the Drawing toolbar.

FIGURE 5.15

WordArt Toolbar

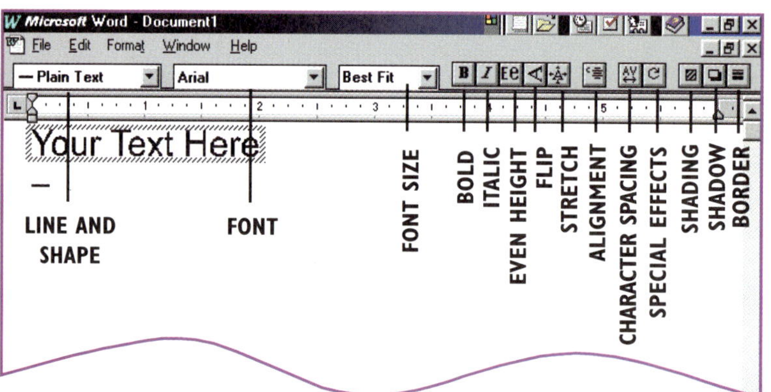

As discussed earlier in chapter 4, WordArt is an OLE-based program (object linking and embedding). Any time you embed an object into your document, you are increasing the size of that document substantially. Keep this in mind if your hard drive or disk drive space is limited.

A WordArt object moves with the text that surrounds it. You can size, crop, move, copy or add a border to a WordArt object by using the same techniques you use to edit a picture. Inserting a frame around a WordArt object or inserting the object into a text box so you can move it freely on the page is a good idea.

Creating Watermarks from WordArt

Shading

WordArt objects can be inserted into documents as watermarks: lighten the color of the WordArt text at the Shading dialog box, then insert the text into a text box in a header and footer pane. The Shading button is the third button from the right on the WordArt toolbar. At the Shading dialog box, a palette of fill colors and fill patterns will display in the Style section of the dialog box as shown in figure 5.16. Additionally, color choices can be made at the Foreground and Background color lists in the Color section of the Shading dialog box.

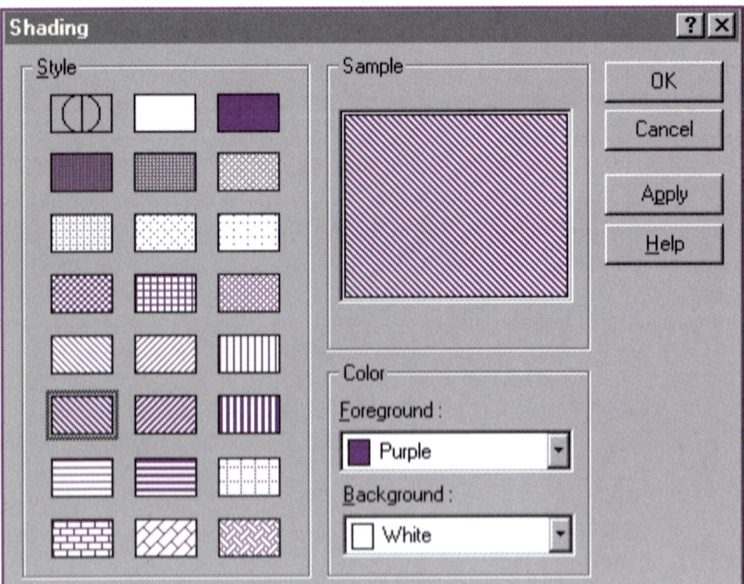

FIGURE 5.16

WordArt's Shading Dialog Box

To create a WordArt watermark, complete the following steps:

1. Choose View, then Header and Footer.
2. Display the Drawing toolbar.
3. Click the Text Box button on the Drawing toolbar, drag the crosshairs into the header or footer pane, then draw a box at a desired size to accommodate the WordArt text.
4. With the insertion point located in the text box, choose Insert, then Object.
5. At the Object dialog box with the Create New tab selected, choose Microsoft WordArt 3.0 (2.0).
6. Key your text into the Enter Your Text Here dialog box.
7. Shape and enhance your text using the buttons on the WordArt toolbar.
8. Reduce the value of the color you have decided to use in your text by clicking the Shading button. Experiment with selecting colors and patterns from the Style palette as well as from the Foreground and Background color lists. When you are satisfied with a lightened color, click OK or press Enter.
9. Click in the document screen outside the text entry box to remove the text entry box.
10. At the header or footer pane, drag the text box to a desired location. If you decide to change the size of the text box, WordArt will adjust to the box size if you click the Stretch button on the WordArt toolbar (seventh button from the right).
11. Click the Close button on the Header and Footer toolbar.

DTP POINTERS
Reduce watermark shading to 20-25% of the original image.

Creating a Flyer Using WordArt

1. At a clear screen create the flyer in figure 5.17 by completing the following steps:
   a. Open *Jazz*. This document is located on your student data disk.
   b. Save the document with Save As and name it c05ex04, jazz flyer.
   c. Change to Page Layout viewing mode.
   d. Make sure the default font is 12-point Times New Roman.
   e. Turn on Kerning at 14 points and above.

f. Create the heading, *Jazz Festival 1997* as shown in figure 5.17 by completing the following steps:
   (1) Position the insertion point above the jazz graphic, then choose Insert, then Object.
   (2) At the Object dialog box make sure the Create New tab is selected, then double-click Microsoft WordArt 3.0 (2.0) in the Object Type list box.
   (3) Key **Jazz Festival 1997** in the text entry box.
   (4) Choose Update Display.
   (5) Click the down-pointing triangle to the right of the Line and Shape button on the WordArt toolbar.
   (6) Click the last shape from the left in the fourth row (*Wave 2).*
   (7) Click the down-pointing triangle to the right of the Font text box, then select Wide Latin. (The Font Size text box should display *Best Fit.*)
   (8) Click the Stretch button (seventh button from the right) on the WordArt toolbar. (The text will display in a 2-inch square box and appear a little distorted.)
   (9) Click the Shading button (third button from the right) on the WordArt toolbar.
   (10) At the Shading dialog box, select the second box in the second row of the Style box.
   (11) In the Color section, change the Foreground color to Blue. Change the Background color to Maroon. Choose OK or press Enter.
   (12) Click the Shadow button on the WordArt toolbar (second button from the right).
   (13) At the Shadow dialog box, select the fourth box from the left. (This box is located in the Choose a Shadow section.)
   (14) Click the down-pointing arrow to the right of the Shadow Color textbox and select the color Pumpkin.
   (15) Choose OK or press Enter.
   (16) Click in the document screen outside the text entry box to remove the text entry box.
   (17) With the object selected, insert a frame.
   (18) With the object selected, change the size of the object by choosing Format, then Picture.
   (19) At the Picture dialog box, change the Width to 7.25 inches and the Height to 0.75 inches. (These options are located in the Size section of the dialog box.)
   (20) Choose OK or press Enter.
   (21) Drag the object to a location similar to figure 5.17. If necessary, remove any borders around the frame.
   (22) Deselect the text box.

g. Create the subheading *A Summer Event by the Lake,* as shown in figure 5.17, by completing the following steps:
   (1) Display the Drawing toolbar.
   (2) Click the Insert Frame button (last button) on the Drawing toolbar.
   (3) Drag the crosshairs below the *Jazz* graphic image, then draw a frame approximately 0.65 inches high and 3.5 inches wide. If necessary, remove any borders around the frame.
   (4) Choose Insert, then Object.
   (5) At the Object dialog box make sure the Create New tab is selected, then double-click Microsoft WordArt 3.0 (2.0) in the Object Type list box.
   (6) Key **A Summer Event by the Lake** in the text entry box.
   (7) Choose Update Display.

(8) Click the down-pointing triangle to the right of the Line and Shape button on the WordArt toolbar, then click the fourth shape in the fifth row—Deflate (Bottom).

(9) Click the down-pointing triangle to the right of the Font text box, then select Arial MT Black (or Arial Black). (The Font Size text box should display *Best Fit.*)

(10) Click the Stretch button (seventh button from the right) on the WordArt toolbar. (The text will display in a 2-inch square box and appear a little distorted.)

(11) Click the Shading button (third button from the right) on the WordArt toolbar.

(12) At the Shading dialog box, select the second box in the second row of the Style box.

(13) In the Color section, change the Foreground color to Blue. Change the Background color to Maroon.

(14) Click the Shadow button, select the third box from the left, and select the color Pumpkin. Choose OK or press Enter.

(15) Click in the document screen outside the text entry box to remove the text entry box.

(16) With the object selected, change the size of the object by choosing Format, then Picture.

(17) At the Picture dialog box, change the Width to 3.50 inches and the Height to 0.65 inches. (These options are located in the Size section of the dialog box.)

(18) Choose OK or press Enter.

(19) With the object selected, choose Format, then Frame.

(20) At the Frame dialog box, click the down-pointing triangle to the right of the Position text, then select *Center.* (This option is in the Horizontal section.) Click OK or press Enter.

(21) Deselect the object.

h. Create the "Featuring" heading to the left of the flyer message in figure 5.17 by completing the following steps:

(1) Draw a frame approximately 1.75 inches in width and 1.75 inches in height. Remove any border around the frame.

(2) Access WordArt.

(3) Key **Featuring** in the text entry box, then change the font to Arial.

(4) Select the *Slant up* shape in the fifth column of the sixth row.

(5) Format *Featuring* as above in steps g10 through g15.

(6) Make sure *Featuring* is positioned near the message as shown in figure 5.17.

i. Create the "Featuring" heading to the right of the flyer message completing steps similar to steps h1 through h6, except select the *Slant Down* shape in the Line and Shape palette in WordArt. (This shape is the last one displayed in the Line and Shape palette.)

2. Save the document again with the same name (c05ex04, jazz flyer).
3. Print and then close c05ex04, jazz flyer.

Optional: Recreate the jazz flyer using the same text and graphic image, but use an asymmetrical design and layout. You may use different lines and shapes to configure your headings. You may also use lines or symbols to help create a different directional flow. Name this exercise c05ex04x, jazz flyer.

FIGURE 5.17

Jazz Festival 1997

A Summer Event by the Lake

July 12-20, 1997

Grant Park
Michigan Avenue
Chicago

Featuring

Blue Grass Jazz
Jazz Express
Duke Mitchell Duo
Jazzettes
Low Country Jazz
and more...

Working In A Document's Layers

Before discussing the functions of the Drawing toolbar, it is helpful to understand the layering of Word documents. Document text exists in the middle layer or text layer. Word also has two additional layers: the drawing layer above the text and the layer below the text layer. You can move any object, picture, or text between these layers. Word *pictures* are images that are inserted into either the document layer or the header and footer text layer. *Drawing objects* are rendered above or below the text layer in the drawing layers.

To work in this sandwich-type environment, you can position items in a text box to place them above or below the text layer. Placing text, objects, or pictures in frames prepares them to exist in the text layer. The frame causes the surrounding text to wrap around the item and it makes it easier to move it around the screen. Work in Page Layout view when working between the various layers of a document.

Pictures: Images that are inserted into the document layer—or into the text layer if inserted in a header or footer.

Drawing Objects: Images rendered above or below the text layer in the drawing layer.

Illustrating the Three Layers of a Document

The illustration in figure 5.18 is an example of a picture placed in the document text layer. The picture was inserted at the insertion point and resized at the Picture dialog box. Notice that the text does not wrap around the image because the picture was not framed.

FIGURE 5.18

Object in the Text Layer (No Wrap)

When a picture is framed as in figure 5.19, text automatically wraps around the frame. A frame was used to position the graphic at a specific location in the document. When a frame is inserted, it appears as a box. You must switch to page layout view to see the correct layout of your framed item. Once you add a frame, you can change its position or size it by dragging the frame's sizing handles or editing the frame at the Frame dialog box.

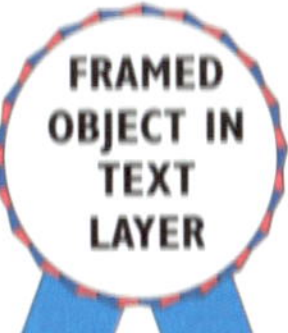

FIGURE 5.19

Framed Object in the Text Layer (Wrap Around)

FIGURE 5.20

Object in the Drawing Layer Above the Text Layer

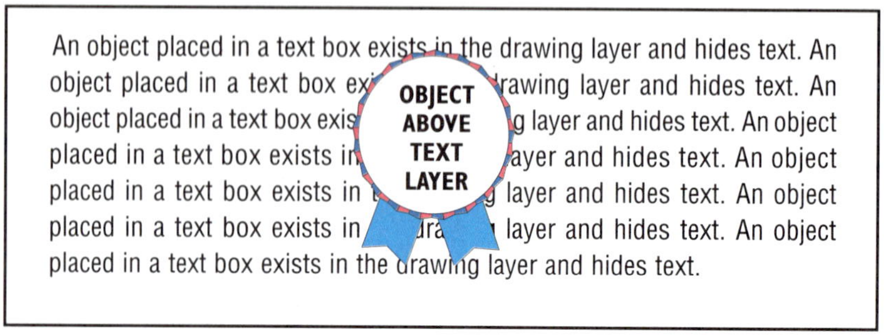

An object placed in a text box exists in the drawing layer and hides text. An object placed in a text box ex rawing layer and hides text. An object placed in a text box exis g layer and hides text. An object placed in a text box exists in ayer and hides text. An object placed in a text box exists in layer and hides text. An object placed in a text box exists in dra layer and hides text. An object placed in a text box exists in the drawing layer and hides text.

OBJECT ABOVE TEXT LAYER

FIGURE 5.21

Object Layered Below the Text Layer

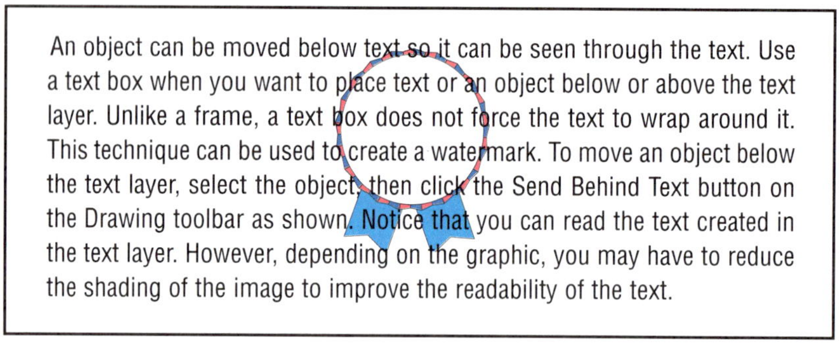

An object can be moved below text so it can be seen through the text. Use a text box when you want to place text or an object below or above the text layer. Unlike a frame, a text box does not force the text to wrap around it. This technique can be used to create a watermark. To move an object below the text layer, select the object, then click the Send Behind Text button on the Drawing toolbar as shown. Notice that you can read the text created in the text layer. However, depending on the graphic, you may have to reduce the shading of the image to improve the readability of the text.

Positioning Text In Documents

Using Frames to Position Text, Pictures, and Objects

As mentioned in chapter 3, frames work in the text layer to position blocks of text or graphics. When text or an object is enclosed in a frame, you can drag the frame to a different position in the document, or you can specify a position at the Frame dialog box. Text outside the frame flows around the frame. Empty frames may be inserted in a document to hold a spot open for a graphic element to be inserted later. A frame automatically resizes as you add text; but you can also resize the frame manually by dragging the sizing handles in the frame.

Be sure to change to Page Layout view before inserting a frame. Changing the page display periodically to view all the design elements in relation to the whole page is also helpful. To change the page display, click the Zoom Control button (third button from the right) on the Standard toolbar, then select a workable setting. In addition, preview your documents before printing them by choosing File, then Print Preview.

Using Text Boxes to Position Text, Pictures, and Objects

Use a text box when you want the text box contents to appear above or below the document text layer. Text does not wrap around a text box because text displayed in a text box does not lie in the document text layer. For instance, a watermark can be inserted in a text box so it will be positioned below the text layer. A text box does not automatically resize when you add more text; you must manually resize the text box to fit the contents. A text box is very versatile because you can format, flip, move, rotate, or layer it using buttons on the Drawing toolbar. Edit a text box as an object at the Drawing Object dialog box.

Using The Drawing Toolbar

Word's Draw program is a complete vector-based drawing program buried within Word. Word for Windows 95 makes it easier to include drawings in your documents. With the Drawing toolbar, you can create a drawing without leaving your document window. With Word's Drawing tools, you can draw shapes, draw freehand, and create and customize text. Be sure to change the viewing mode to Page Layout when using the Drawing toolbar. The objects that you create using the buttons on the Drawing toolbar can be moved anywhere on the page by simply dragging them.

Displaying the Drawing Toolbar

To display the Drawing toolbar, click the Drawing button (fifth button from the right) on the Standard toolbar; or, choose View, then Toolbars, then select Drawing from the Toolbars list. Alternatively, you can right-click on the gray area between the buttons on any toolbar to access the Drawing toolbar from a drop-down list. Figure 5.22 displays the Drawing toolbar with callouts to identify each button. Unlike the other toolbars, the Drawing toolbar displays at the bottom of the screen.

FIGURE 5.22

Drawing Toolbar

Each button on the Drawing toolbar performs a specific function. Browse through the pictures and buttons depicting their functions in figure 5.23.

FIGURE 5.23

Drawing Toolbar

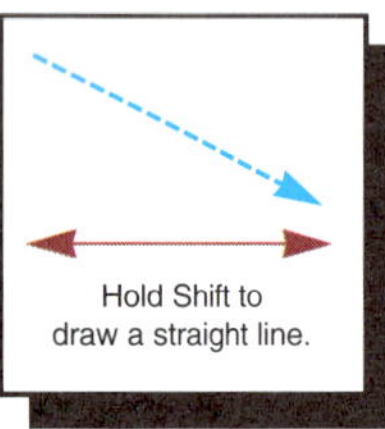

Line

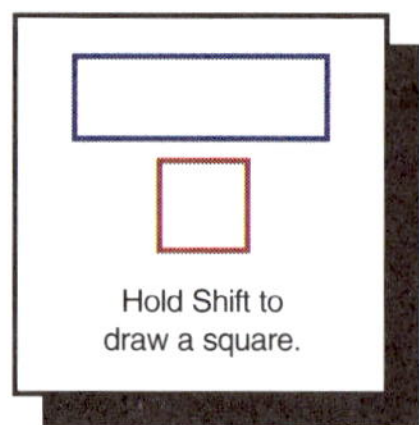

Rectangle

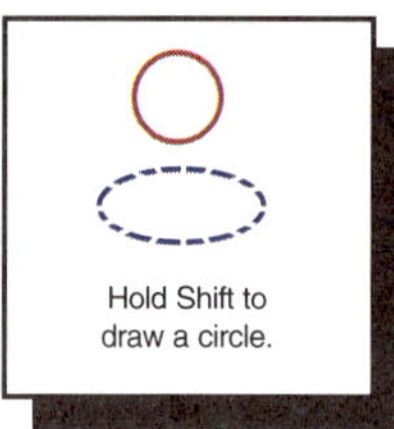

Ellipse

Arc

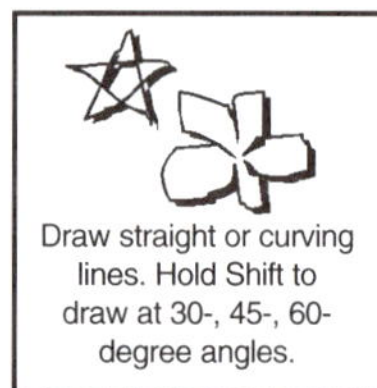

Freeform

Text Box

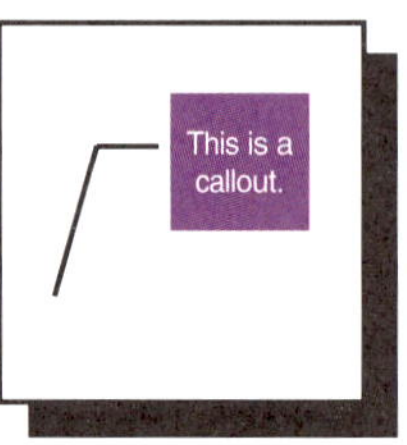

Callout

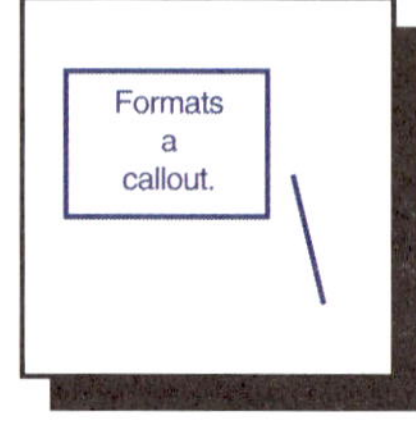

Format Callout

Fill Color

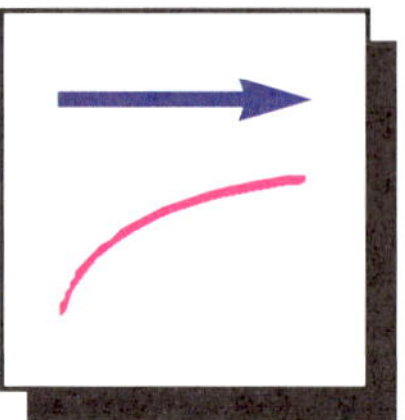

Line Color

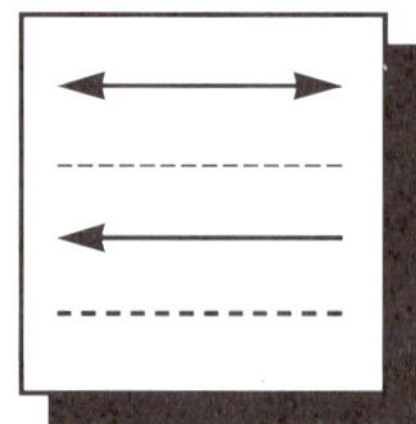

Line Style

Select Drawing Object

Bring to Front

Drawing Toolbar

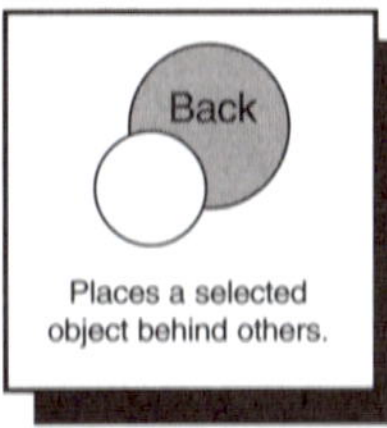

Places a selected object behind others.

Send to Back

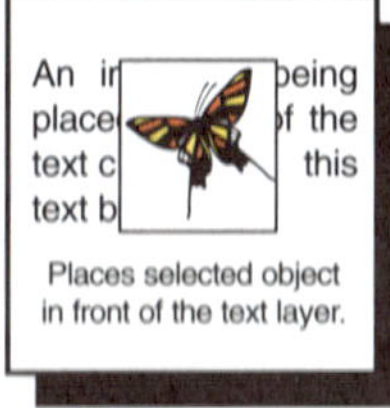
Places selected object in front of the text layer.

Bring in Front of Text

Sends selected objects behind the text layer.

Send Behind Text

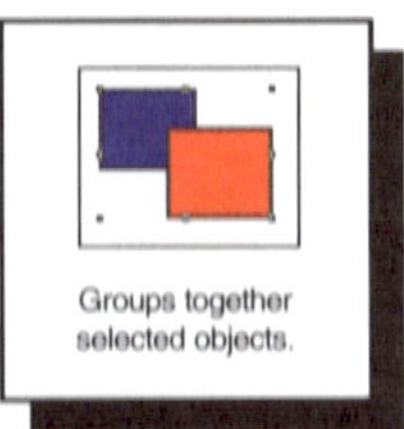
Groups together selected objects.

Group

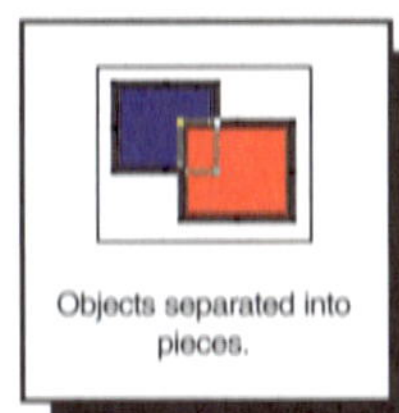
Objects separated into pieces.

Ungroup

Flip Horizontal

Flip Vertical

Rotate Right

Reshapes a free-form or polygon

Reshape

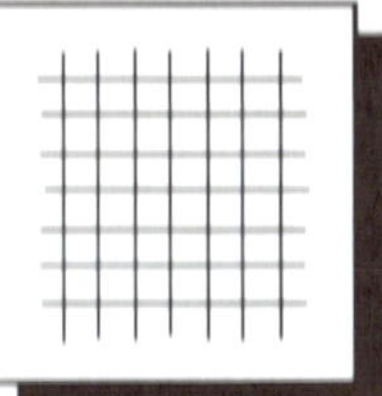

Snap to Grid

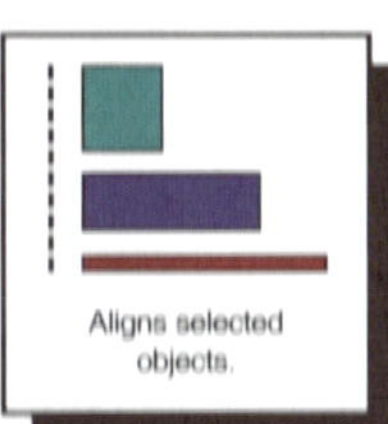
Aligns selected objects.

Align Drawing Objects

Inserts a picture container.

Create Picture

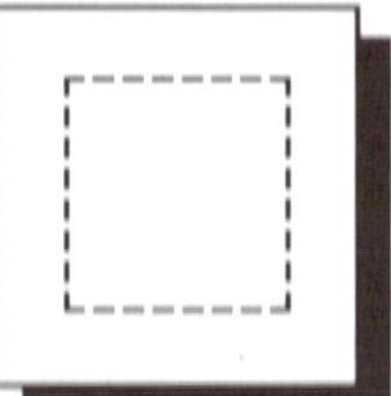

Insert Frame

Drawing Shapes

The first five buttons on the Drawing toolbar create drawing shapes and are illustrated in figure 5.23. They include: Line, Rectangle, Ellipse, Arc, and Freeform. Refer to figure 5.23 as you read the following information about each button.

Creating Lines

The Line button enables you to draw straight vertical or horizontal lines or lines at 30-, 45-, or 60-degree angles if the Shift key is held down. Select your line, then use the sizing handles to size it. Move the line around the screen while the line is selected, and the arrow pointer displays as a four-headed arrow. While the line is selected, you can hold down the Ctrl key and drag a copy of the line to another location. Use the Line Style and Line Color to customize your lines. You can draw a triangle by drawing three lines. If you want to draw more than one line, double-click the Line button. After drawing all necessary lines, click the Line button again to deactivate it.

Drawing Rectangles and Squares

The Rectangle button is used to draw rectangles or to draw squares if the Shift key is held down. Use the Fill Color, Line Color, and Line Style buttons to customize your shape. Or, double-click on the shape and customize it at the Drawing Object dialog box, where you can change the Fill, Line, or Size and Position of the shape. A Shadow or Round Corners can be added at the Line tab. Select, then drag your shape anywhere on the screen. Copy the shape by selecting it, then holding down the Ctrl key while dragging it to a new location; or use the Copy and Paste commands from the Edit menu. In addition, you can select your shape and rotate it at 90-degree increments by clicking the Rotate Right button (sixth button from the right) on the Drawing toolbar.

Drawing Ellipse Shapes

The Ellipse button enables you to create an oval shape, or a circle if you hold down the Shift key. Customize the shape by using the Fill Color, Line Color, Line Style, etc. buttons on the Drawing toolbar or double-click on the object to access the Drawing Object dialog box. You can add text within an ellipse by drawing a text box to hold the text within the shape. Figure 5.24 illustrates various shapes with text boxes containing text. (Text color is changed at the Font dialog box.)

FIGURE 5.24

Text Inside Shapes

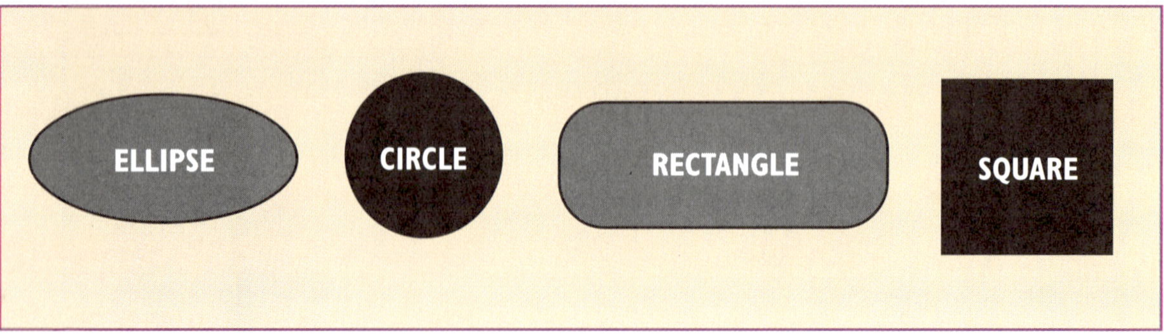

Drawing Arc Shapes

Use the Arc button to draw arcs and wedges. An arc has no fill; a wedge is an arc filled with color or a pattern. Be sure to select None as the fill if you simply want an arc. Hold down the Shift key as you draw an arc to create a circular arc. Hold down the Ctrl key to draw your shape from the center. Customize by using buttons on the Drawing toolbar or by accessing the Drawing Object dialog box.

Drawing Freeform Shapes

You can draw straight-line polygons and curving freeform shapes using vertical or horizontal line segments, or if you hold down the Shift key, you can create these segments in 30-, 45-, or 60- degree angles. A *polygon* is a closed plane figure having three or more angles and straight lines, for example, a hexagon or pentagon.

Polygon: A closed plane figure having three or more angles and straight lines.

Position your insertion point where you want to start drawing, then drag to draw curved lines or click to make straight lines. Double-click where you want the line to end. You can add fill and pattern to these shapes by using the Drawing Object dialog box or the Fill Color button on the Drawing toolbar. Press the Esc key to cancel the last line segment you created in a polygon shape.

Using Text Boxes

Use a text box when you want the text box contents to appear above or below the document text layer. Text does not wrap around a text box because text displayed in a text box does not lie in the document text layer. For instance, a watermark can be inserted into a text box at the header or footer pane where it is positioned below the text layer, and it becomes easy to move around the screen. Text boxes are very useful in desktop publishing because they can contain text as well as pictures and they can be positioned anywhere on the page—in a margin, in the text, or behind text.

Creating Callouts

Callouts help explain illustrations used in documents. A callout can display as a box with a border and fill or as text only. You can insert text or a picture in a callout. Using the Drawing Object dialog box or various buttons on the Drawing toolbar, you can customize and layer a callout like any other drawing object.

Formatting a Callout

You can change callout specifications through the options available in the Format Callout dialog box shown in figure 5.25. To access this dialog box, click the Callout button (eighth button from the left) on the Drawing toolbar. You can also display the Format Callout dialog box by displaying the Drawing Object dialog box (double-click the callout), selecting the Size and Position tab, then clicking the Callout button. You can choose from four different callout formats and customize by choosing from the options displayed in the box.

FIGURE 5.25

Format Callout Dialog Box

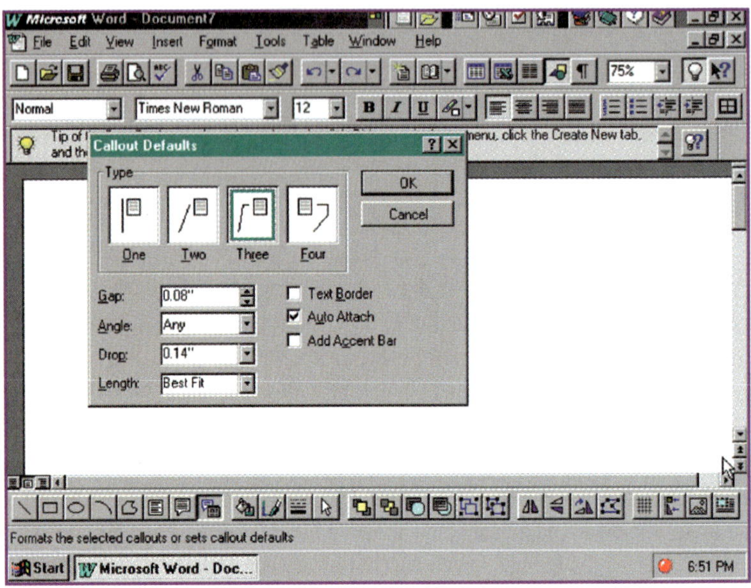

In exercise 5, you will create a flyer for the grand opening of a video store. You will open a partially completed document, then complete the document to make it an effective, attention-getting flyer. Maroon and bright yellow are two dominant colors in the graphic image. These colors are used throughout the flyer to establish a connection to the graphic and to attract attention at a glance. WordArt was used to configure *Grand Opening* in a shape that emphasizes grandness and excitement. You will create a map to provide detailed directions to the video store.

Creating a Flyer with a Map, Picture, WordArt, and Shapes

1. Create the video flyer shown in figure 5.26 by completing the following steps:
   a. Open *Grand Opening* from your student data disk.
   b. Save the document with Save As and name it c05ex05, video flyer.
   c. Change to Page Layout view.
   d. Display the Drawing toolbar by clicking the Drawing button (fifth button from the right) on the Standard toolbar.
   e. Display the Borders toolbar by clicking the Borders button (first button from the right) on the Formatting toolbar.
   f. Flip the movie picture located in the left corner of the flyer by completing the following steps:
      (1) Double-click the picture to enter Microsoft Word Picture.
      (2) At Microsoft Word Picture, click the Select Drawing Object button (twelfth button from the left) on the Drawing toolbar.
      (3) Position the crosshair in the upper left corner of the image grid, hold down the left mouse button and drag the dashed box to the lower right corner of the image grid, then release the mouse button. (When the mouse is released, the graphic will be displayed in numerous segments.)
      (4) Click the Group button (tenth button from the right) on the Drawing toolbar. (The graphic will display as one unit.)
      (5) Click the Flip Horizontal button (eighth button from the right) on the Drawing toolbar.
      (6) Click Close Picture button. Deselect the image.
   g. Select the heading, *Show It Again Video* and change the font to 28-point Braggadocio.

h. Create the ellipse shape as shown in figure 5.26 by completing the following steps:
   (1) Click the Ellipse button (third button from the left) on the Drawing toolbar.
   (2) Drag the crosshair to the upper right corner of the flyer. Draw an ellipse shape approximately 0.5 inches in height by 1 inch in width. (You can verify the size at the Size and Position tab of the Drawing Object dialog box.)
   (3) Select the ellipse shape, then click the Fill Color button (ninth button from the left) on the Drawing toolbar. Select the maroon color box in the seventh row and the fifth column of the color palette.
   (4) Click the Line Color button (tenth button from the left) on the Drawing toolbar and select None.
   (5) Deselect the ellipse shape.

i. Create the yellow rectangular shape as shown in figure 5.26 by completing the following steps:
   (1) Click the Rectangle button (second button from the left) on the Drawing toolbar.
   (2) Drag the crosshair to the upper right corner of the flyer and to the right of the ellipse shape. Draw a rectangular shape approximately 1.40 inches in width by 0.60 inches in height. (Verify this setting at the Size and Position tab of the Drawing Object dialog box.)
   (3) Select the rectangular shape, then click the Fill Color button on the Drawing toolbar. Select the yellow color in the sixth row and the fourth column.
   (4) Click the Line Style button (eleventh button from the left) on the Drawing toolbar, then click the third line style from the top of the Line Style list box.
   (5) Click the Line Style button again, then click More at the bottom of the Line Style list box.
   (6) At the Drawing Object dialog box, select the Line tab, then click the check box to the left of Round Corners. Click the down-pointing arrow to the right of Color and select Black.
   (7) Choose OK or press Enter.

j. Select the yellow rectangular shape and drag it near the ellipse shape as shown in figure 5.26.

k. With the yellow shape still selected, click the Send to Back button (eleventh button from the right) on the Drawing toolbar. (The rectangular shape should be positioned behind the maroon ellipse shape as shown in figure 5.26.) Deslect the shape.

l. Configure the text, *Grand Opening*, in WordArt by completing the following steps:
   (1) Double-click *Grand Opening* to enter WordArt.
   (2) Click the down-pointing triangle to the right of the Line and Shape text box on the WordArt toolbar.
   (3) At the Line and Shape drop-down palette, select the Deflate (Top) shape box in the fifth row and the sixth column.
   (4) Change the font to Britannic Bold. Make sure the font size is set at *Best Fit*.
   (5) Click the Stretch button (seventh button from the right) on the WordArt toolbar.
   (6) Click the Character Spacing button (fifth button from the right) on the WordArt toolbar. At the Spacing Between Characters dialog box, select Tight in the Tracking section. Choose OK or press Enter.
   (7) Click the Shading button (third button from the right) on the WordArt

toolbar. At the Shading dialog box, click the down-pointing arrow to the right of the Foreground text box and select Maroon from the drop-down list. Select White at the Background text box. Choose OK or press Enter.

(8) Click the Shadow button (second button from the right) on the WordArt toolbar. Select the third box from the left. Change the Shadow Color to Silver. Choose OK or press Enter.

(9) Click outside the text entry box to close WordArt. Deselect the heading.

m. Select the bulleted items. (Do not include the last paragraph marker.) Change the font to 28-point Britannic Bold.

n. Create the text in the yellow rectangle shape at the bottom left corner of the flyer by completing the following steps:

(1) Click the Text Box button on the Drawing toolbar. Drag the crosshair into the yellow rectangle shape located at the bottom of the page and draw a box approximately 1.85 inches in width and 0.50 inches in height.

(2) Double-click on the border of the text box created in step n.(1). At the Drawing Object dialog box, select the Line tab. Click to remove the check mark near Round Corners. Click None in the Line section. Choose OK or press Enter.

(3) With the insertion point positioned inside the text box, click the Center align button on the Formatting toolbar, change the font to 14-point Braggadocio, then key **Show It Again Video** in the text box. Deselect the text box.

o. Create the map in the bottom right corner of the flyer as shown in figure 5.26 by completing the following steps:

(1) Click the Insert Frame button on the Drawing toolbar.

(2) At the bottom right corner of the flyer, drag the crosshair to draw a frame approximately 3 inches in width by 1.75 inches in height. (You can verify this size at the Frame dialog box.)

(3) Select the frame, then click the Create Picture button (second button from the right) on the Drawing toolbar. (Creating the map in Microsoft Word Picture ensures that the map streets and symbols will remain in place within the frame when the frame is moved inside the document.)

(4) At Microsoft Word Picture, click the Line Color button on the Drawing toolbar and select Black. Click the Line Style button on the Drawing toolbar and select the second line from the top of the list. Click the Line button (first button from the left) on the Drawing toolbar. Hold down the Shift key as you drag the crosshair from the center of the top border downward to the center of the bottom border as shown in figure 5.26.

(5) Click the Arc button (fourth button from the left) on the Drawing toolbar. Drag an arc from the upper section of the left border downward toward the right border as shown in figure 5.26. (If a fill displays with the arc, click the Fill Color button on the Drawing toolbar, then select None.)

(6) Click the Rectangle button (second button from the left) on the Drawing toolbar. Draw a small rectangle just below the intersection of the vertical and arc lines as shown in figure 5.26.

(7) Select the rectangle, then click the Fill Color button on the Drawing toolbar and select Black. Deselect the rectangle.

(8) Click the Text Box button on the Drawing toolbar. Draw a small text box above the arc as shown in figure 5.26. (This box will hold *Main*). Click the Fill Color button on the Drawing toolbar, then select None. If a border appears around the text box, click the Line Color button on the Drawing

toolbar and select None. (A light gray dotted box will display around *Main*. This box will not display in the document.)

(9) Position the insertion point inside the text box, change the font to 10-point Times New Roman Bold, then key **Main**. If necessary, drag the box to the right of the arced line as shown in figure 5.26.

(10) Create another text box similar to the box containing *Main* and position the box to the left of the vertical line that was created earlier. See figure 5.26 for correct placement of the text box. If a fill or border displays, select None at each setting. Change the font to 10-point Times New Roman Bold and key **Ogden** in this text box.

(11) Click the Format Callout button (eighth button from the left) on the Drawing toolbar. Select Two in the Type section and click inside the check boxes to turn on Text Border and Auto Attach. Choose OK or press Enter.

(12) Click the Callout button (seventh button from the left) on the Drawing toolbar, then drag the crosshair down and to the right beginning at the bottom of the black box. If a black line and border does not display, click the Line Color button on the Drawing toolbar and select Black.

(13) Resize the text box in the callout by dragging the double-headed arrow which displays when you position the arrow pointer on the sizing handles.

(14) Position the insertion point inside the callout box, change the font to 10-point Times New Roman Bold, then key **Show It Again**.

(15) With the callout selected, click the Fill Color button on the Drawing toolbar and select Yellow. Deselect the callout.

(16) Click the Close Picture button to exit Microsoft Word Picture.

(17) To display a border around the frame, click the Outside Border button on the Borders toolbar. (If the bottom line of the map does not display, select the frame around the map and drag the sizing handle in the center of the bottom line upward slightly; or select the map and move the entire map upward slightly.)

p. Insert the compass graphic into the map by completing the following steps:

(1) Click the Insert Frame button (first button from the right) on the Drawing toolbar, then drag the crosshair to the top right corner of the map and draw a frame that is approximately 0.5 inches square.

(2) With the insertion point inside the box, choose Insert, then Picture.

(3) At the Insert Picture dialog box, make sure Clipart displays in the Look in text box. Double-click Compass in the Name list.

(4) Choose OK or press Enter.

(5) If a border displays around the compass image, click the Line Color button on the Drawing toolbar and select None.

(6) Resize and position the image as shown in figure 5.26.

(7) Deselect the image.

2. Change the Zoom Control to Whole Page and make sure all the design elements display as shown in figure 5.26. Select and drag any elements that are not properly positioned in the flyer.
3. Save the document again with the same name (c05ex05, video flyer).
4. Print and then close c05ex05, video flyer.

FIGURE 5.26

Show It Again
Video

GRAND OPENING

• Rent two videos, get one FREE

• FREE popcorn—opening day

• Great selection

Show It Again
Video

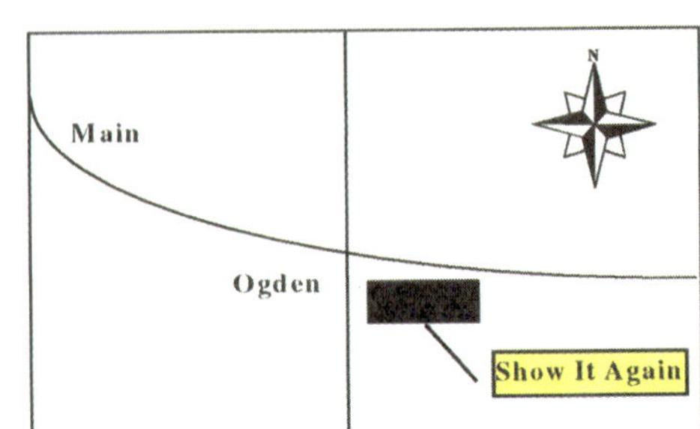

N
Main
Ogden
Show It Again

Choosing Fill Color, Line Color, and Line Style

Use the Fill Color, Line Color, and Line Style buttons to access various palettes. From these palettes you can apply color and different line styles to your selected, enclosed objects. However, keep in mind that the choices you make become the new defaults. When you select the next object and use any of these buttons or the Drawing Object dialog box, the previous settings will display.

When using the Line Style palette, remember that a point is equal to 1/72 of an inch. Line width is measured in points. You can key your own measurement for a line width in the Drawing object dialog box. A 36-point line is ½ inch wide.

Selecting a Drawing Object

If a document screen contains more than one object, you can select several objects at once using the Select Drawing Object button. To use this feature, click the Select Objects button, then position the crosshairs in the upper left corner of the area containing the objects, hold down the left mouse button, drag the outline to the lower right corner of the area containing the objects, then release the mouse button. The selected objects are now connected. If you move one object, you move all the objects. Also, you can now group or ungroup the selected objects or use the align feature on the Drawing toolbar to align the objects in relation to one another or to the page. If you use the Select Drawing Object feature on a graphic while in Microsoft Word Picture, you can group the image then use the Flip Horizontal, Flip Vertical, and Rotate Right button on the Drawing toolbar because the image becomes an object once it is edited in Microsoft Word Picture.

You can also select several objects by holding down the Shift key as you select each object. The Select Drawing Object is also helpful in selecting text, objects, or pictures that are positioned in different layers of the document.

Moving an Object Front/Back

Objects created using the Drawing toolbar can overlap. With the Bring to Front and Send to Back buttons, you can bring an object to the front or move it to the back of another object. Selecting a front object and clicking the Send to Back button causes the object to move behind another object. Selecting this object again and clicking the Send to Front button moves it back in front. (You could also click the Undo button on the Standard toolbar.)

Moving an Object in Front or Behind Text

If you create an object in a document containing text, the object will default to displaying in the text layer. This will result in the object covering the text. To have both the text and object display, click the Send Behind Text button on the Drawing toolbar. The object can also be moved back in front of the text by clicking the Bring in Front of Text button. This technique can be used to create watermarks. However, a watermark created in a header or footer has the advantage of being positioned automatically in the appropriate layer and appearing on more than one page.

Grouping and Ungrouping Objects

Grouping objects fuses them together as one object. To group objects, click the Select Drawing Objects button on the Drawing toolbar. Position the crosshairs in the upper left corner of the area containing the objects, hold down the left mouse button, drag the outline to the lower right corner of the area containing the objects, then release the mouse button. Click the Group button on the Drawing toolbar.

For instance, if you insert a picture into your document and want to flip the image so it faces the opposite direction, you will need to group all the sections of the image together so they will rotate as a single object. If the image is detailed, with many angles, lines, colors, etc., you cannot rotate it without grouping it first. Also, you cannot use the Flip Horizontal button on the Drawing toolbar until the picture becomes a drawing object. Therefore, you will want to edit the image in Microsoft Word Picture and group all the sections of the picture. Click the Select Drawing Objects button on the Drawing toolbar, then draw a box around the image. Next, click the Group button on the Drawing toolbar, then click the Flip Horizontal button to invert the image. Finally, click the Close button in Microsoft Word Picture.

To ungroup a group of objects or sections of a picture, select the objects, then click the Ungroup button on the Drawing toolbar.

Flipping and Rotating an Object

Use the Flip Horizontal and Flip Vertical buttons on the Drawing toolbar to flip the display of a selected object. The Flip Horizontal button reverses left and right. The Flip Vertical button reverses top and bottom. The Rotate Right button rotates the shape or object 90 degrees to the right. If you rotate a text box, the box rotates but the text within it does not—use WordArt to rotate text. Bring a picture into Microsoft Word Picture to rotate it as an object.

Reshaping an Object

Nodes: Small black squares that connect line segments in a shape or object.

A freeform object or a polygon shape is created by line segments connected by small black squares called *nodes*. When you select an object then click the Reshape button on the Drawing toolbar, the nodes display at the intersection of the line segments. For example, a triangle is composed of three straight line segments connected by three nodes. You can drag any of these nodes to reshape the object or you can drag any of the sizing handles.

Using Snap to Grid

The drawing grid is an invisible grid of lines that is helpful in aligning drawing objects and drawing straight lines. It acts as a magnet attracting your crosshairs as you draw lines at certain increments. At the Snap to Grid dialog box, you can change the spacing between the horizontal and vertical lines that make up the grid lines. You can temporarily turn the Snap to Grid feature on or off by pressing Alt as you move or draw an object.

The Snap to Grid feature is especially useful when creating vertical and horizontal lines in a document or form. After creating the first line, turn on the Snap to Grid feature and specify the amount of space you want between the lines. The next line you create or copy will automatically snap to that specific increment. Turn off the Snap to Grid feature when you are finished with it.

You can specify a specific location in your document where you want the Snap to Grid feature to be used by keying an increment in the Horizontal Origin and/or Vertical Origin text boxes in the Snap to Grid dialog box.

Aligning Drawing Objects

When you align objects with each other, they line up on the side you specify in the Align dialog box. You can align a single object with the page. To align objects with each other, you must select more than one object. To align objects, select the objects using the Select Drawing Objects button on the Drawing toolbar by dragging a box around them, or individually select each object while holding down the Shift key. Once the objects are selected, you can click the Align button on the Drawing toolbar. At the Align dialog box, select your vertical and horizontal alignment choice.

Creating a Picture

Within Word, a graphic editor exists known as Microsoft Word Picture. You can invoke the graphic editor by clicking the Create Picture button on the Drawing toolbar or by double-clicking on any metafile graphic, which includes all the Word clip art files. Within Microsoft Word Picture, you can group and ungroup objects then customize them by moving certain sections of an object, changing the object's fill with color, shading, or patterns, and changing the line style, thickness, or color. Microsoft Word Picture can be referred to as a graphic editor or a picture container. Because Draw is a vector-based program, all the graphics accepted in this program are created by incorporating five shapes. These shapes are: lines, arcs, ellipses, rectangles, and polygons. Figure 5.27 illustrates the Microsoft Word Picture screen. After a picture has been grouped, you can also use the Flip Horizontal or Flip Vertical buttons to alter the image.

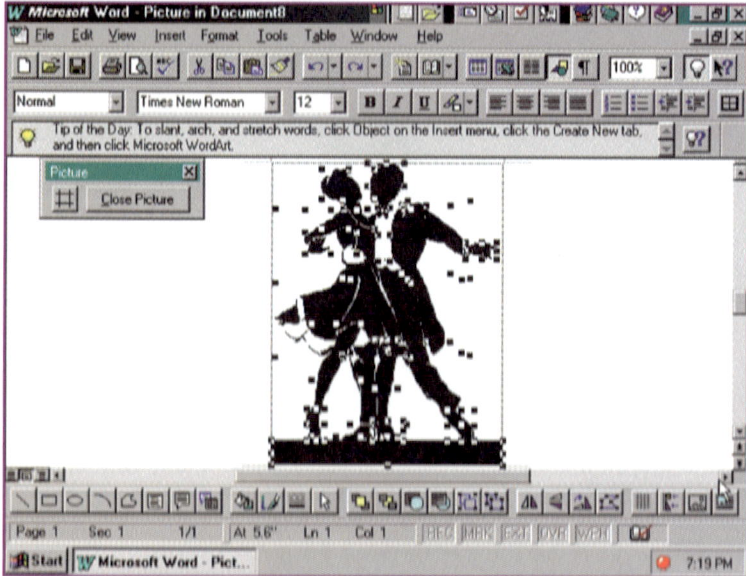

FIGURE 5.27

Ungrouped Picture in Microsoft Word Picture

Inserting a Frame

A frame is used to position text, pictures, or objects in a specific location in a document text layer. When a frame is added to text in a document, the text outside the frame wraps around the frame. As you add text or a picture to a frame, the frame will automatically resize to fit the text or image or you can resize it by dragging the sizing (selection) handles. To frame an object, select the object, then click the Insert Frame button on the Drawing toolbar.

In exercise 6, you will create an office workshop announcement with a clip-off section at the bottom of the document. This document shows a conservative, professional layout and design. The colors selected are navy and gray, which are safe colors to choose for a business document. The triangle shape in the picture and in the symbols in the reversed box aid directional flow in this document.

Office Technology Workshop Announcement

1. At a clear document window, create the Office Technology Workshop announcement as shown in figure 5.28 by completing the following steps:
   a. Change the Top, Left, and Right margins to 1 inch and the Bottom margin to 0.5 inches. (Choose the Fix button if one of the margins is outside the printable area.)
   b. Change to Page Layout viewing mode.
   c. Turn on Kerning at 14 points and above.
   d. Display the Drawing toolbar and the Borders toolbar.
   e. Insert and size the graphic image as shown in figure 5.28 by completing the following steps:
      (1) Choose Insert, then Picture.
      (2) At the Insert Picture dialog box, double-click *Computer.*
      (3) Select the picture.
      (4) Insert a frame around the picture by clicking the Insert Frame button on the Drawing toolbar.
      (5) With the picture still selected, choose Format, then Picture.
      (6) At the Picture dialog box, change the Width to 2 inches and the Height to 1.75 inches. (These settings are in the Size section.)
      (7) Choose OK or press Enter. Deselect the Frame.
   f. Create the heading in a frame as shown in figure 5.28 by completing the following steps:
      (1) Click the Insert Frame button on the Drawing toolbar, then drag the crosshairs to the right of the graphic image. Create a box that is approximately 4 inches wide by 1.5 inches high. (To verify this size, choose Format, then Frame. At the Frame dialog box, key the exact settings in the Size section of the dialog box.) If the frame displays with a border, click the No Border button on the Borders toolbar to remove it. Or, if the box displays with a fill color, click the down-pointing triangle to the right of the Shading text box in the Borders toolbar, then select Clear.
      (2) Change the font to 24-point Wide Latin Bold and the font Color to Dk Blue.
      (3) Select the Character Spacing tab, then change the Spacing to Expanded By 4 pt. Choose OK or press Enter.
      (4) Key **Office Technology Workshop** as shown in figure 5.28. Resize and move the box if necessary. Deselect the frame.
   g. Create the navy box by completing the following steps:
      (1) With the insertion point located just below the graphic image, change the font to 14-point Book Antiqua Bold.
      (2) Press the Enter key twice.
      (3) Click the Show/Hide ¶ button on the Standard toolbar to turn this feature on.
      (4) Key **Friday, April 25 ▼ Western Michigan University ▼ Kalamazoo, MI.** (The down-pointing triangle symbol can be found in the Monotype Sorts character set as the first symbol in the fourth row of the Symbol dialog box.)
      (5) Press Enter 4 times.
      (6) Select *Friday, April 25 ▼ Western Michigan University ▼ Kalamazoo, MI,* along with the paragraph marker above and below this line.
      (7) Click the Center button on the Formatting toolbar.
      (8) Choose Format, then Borders and Shading.

(9) Select the Shading tab.
(10) Click Custom in the Fill section.
(11) Click the down-pointing triangle to the right of the Foreground text box, then select White.
(12) Click the down-pointing triangle to the right of the Background text box, then select Dk Blue.
(13) Choose OK or press Enter.
(14) Select *Friday, April 25* ▼ *Western Michigan University* ▼ *Kalamazoo, MI*, then turn on Bold and Small Caps at the Font dialog box.

h. Move your insertion point down two lines, make sure the font is 14-point Book Antiqua, turn on bold and italics, then key **Featuring Sessions on:**.

i. Press Enter 8 times. (This is necessary so the insertion point will be in the correct location to insert text from a file after creating the ellipse shapes.)

j. Create the ellipse shapes by completing the following steps:
(1) Click the Ellipse button on the Drawing toolbar.
(2) Drag the crosshairs into the document window to create an ellipse shape as shown in figure 5.28 (position the ellipse shape about a double space below *Featuring Sessions on:*). The shape should be approximately 3.25 inches wide and 1.5 inches high. (To verify this size, select the shape, then choose Format, then Drawing Object. At the Drawing Object dialog box, select the Size and Position tab. In the Size section, make sure the Height is approximately 1.5 inches and the Width is 3.25 inches.
(3) Select the Fill tab.
(4) At the color palette in the Color section, select the Lt Gray box in the last row of the palette (second from left).
(5) Select the Line tab, then select None.
(6) Choose OK or press Enter.
(7) Select the ellipse shape, hold down the Ctrl key, drag the ellipse shape to the right of the original, release the mouse button first then the Ctrl key. (A copy of the original ellipse shape should display.)

k. Align the two ellipse shapes vertically by completing the following steps:
(1) Click the Select Drawing Objects button on the Drawing toolbar.
(2) Draw a box around both ellipse shapes.
(3) Click the Align Drawing Objects button on the Drawing toolbar.
(4) At the Align dialog box, choose Top in the Vertical section of the dialog box; also, make sure the Relative to Each Other option is selected.
(5) Choose OK or press Enter.
(6) Click the Select Drawing Objects button again to deactivate it.
(7) Deselect the ellipse shapes.

l. Create the text inside the ellipse shapes by completing the following steps:
(1) Click the Text Box button on the Drawing toolbar, then drag the crosshairs into the first ellipse shape. Create a box that is approximately 2.5 inches wide and 0.5 inches high.
(2) If the fill color in the text box defaults to a color other than Lt Gray, change the fill to match the ellipse shape. (Change the fill at the Drawing Object dialog box.)
(3) With the insertion point positioned inside the text box, change the font to 12-point Arial Bold.
(4) Click the Center button on the Formatting toolbar.

(5) Key **Microsoft Office Professional for Windows 95** as shown in figure 5.28. (If the text does not appear centered in the ellipse shape, select the box, then drag it to an appropriate location.)
(6) Deselect the text box.
(7) Create the text inside the second ellipse shape by completing steps similar to steps l1 through l6. Key **Desktop Publishing Using Microsoft Word 7.0 for Windows 95** as shown in figure 5.28. (Make your text box a little larger than the one in the first ellipse.)

m. Insert a document from your student data disk by completing the following steps:
(1) Move the insertion point to the end of the document.
(2) Choose Insert, then File.
(3) At the Insert File dialog box, double-click *Technology Workshop*.

n. Click the down-pointing triangle to the right of the Zoom Control text box in the Standard toolbar. Change the page display to Whole Page. Select then drag any design elements that appear out of balance. The ellipse shapes should be positioned between *Featuring Sessions on*: and the Agenda text. Change the page display to 75%.

o. Create the clip-off section of the announcement as shown in figure 5.29 by completing the following steps:
(1) Create a text box (use the Text Box button on the Drawing toolbar) approximately 6.5 inches wide by 1.75 inches high in the area below the agenda text. (If the box defaults to a color other than white, choose Format, then Drawing Object. At the Drawing Object dialog box, select the Fill tab. Select the white box in the first row and second column of the Color palette in the Color section. Select the Size and Position tab and verify the size of your text box. Select the Line tab and make sure None is selected in the Line section. Choose OK or press Enter.)
(2) With the insertion point positioned inside the text box, insert the scissors symbol from the Wingdings character set. This symbol is the second symbol in the first row.
(3) Press the space bar once.
(4) Click the Line button on the Drawing toolbar.
(5) Drag the crosshairs into the text box, then hold down the Shift key, and draw a line after the scissors symbol. The line should be approximately 6.25 inches long. (If the line is a color other than black, click the Line Color button on the Drawing toolbar and select Black.)
(6) With the line still selected, click the Line Style button on the Drawing toolbar and select the dotted line, which is the fifth choice from the top in the Line Style drop-down list.
(7) Move the insertion point to the right of the scissors symbol.
(8) Change the font to 12-point Book Antiqua.
(9) Press Enter twice.
(10) Key **To reserve your place, please return this form by Monday, April 19.**
(11) Press Enter twice.
(12) Key **Name:**
(13) Press Enter twice.
(14) Key **Organization:**
(15) Press Enter twice.

(16) Key **Telephone:**
(17) Click the Line button on the Drawing toolbar.
(18) Create a line approximately 5.5 inches long. (Notice in figure 5.28 that the line begins approximately 0.5 inches to the right of *Name:*. Hold down the Shift key as you drag to create a straight line.)
(19) With the line still selected, click the Line Style button on the Drawing toolbar, then select the second line from the top.
(20) Click the Snap to Grid button on the Drawing toolbar.
(21) At the Snap to Grid dialog box, click in the check box to turn on the Snap to Grid feature, then change the Vertical Spacing to 0.44 inches.
(22) Choose OK or press Enter.
(23) Select the line next to *Name:*.
(24) Hold down the Ctrl key and drag a copy of the first line next to *Organization:*.
(25) Hold down the Ctrl key and drag another copy of the first line to *Telephone:*.
(26) Turn off the Snap to Grid feature.
(27) Select all three lines by clicking on each line while holding down the Shift key.
(28) Click the Align Drawing Objects button on the Drawing toolbar.
(29) At the Align dialog box, click Right in the Horizontal section. Make sure Relative to Each Other is selected.
(30) Choose OK or press Enter.
(31) Deselect the three lines.

2. Change the Zoom to Whole Page and make sure all the design elements are in proportion to the entire page and similar in layout to figure 5.28.
3. Save your document and name it c05ex06, technology workshop.
4. Print and then close c05ex06, technology workshop.

FIGURE 5.28

Office Technology Workshop

FRIDAY, APRIL 25 ▼ WESTERN MICHIGAN UNIVERSITY ▼ KALAMAZOO, MI

Featuring Sessions on:

Microsoft Office Professional for Windows 95

Desktop Publishing Using Microsoft Word 7.0 for Windows 95

Agenda:

9:30 – 10:00 a.m.	Registration	Room 3Q, Instructional Center
10:00 – 12:00 p.m.	Microsoft Office Professional for Windows 95	*Presenter: Ron Kapler*
12:00 – 1:00 p.m.	Complimentary lunch	Sponsored by WMU
1:00 – 3:00 p.m.	Desktop Publishing Using Microsoft Word 7.0 for Windows 95	*Presenter: Margo Godfrey*

✂ ....

To reserve your place, please return this form by Monday, April 19.

Name: ______________________________

Organization: ______________________________

Telephone: ______________________________

Chapter Summary

- Flyers and announcements are generally considered one of the least expensive means of advertising. Clearly define your purpose and assess your target audience before preparing a flyer or announcement. Flyers are generally used to advertise a product or service that is available for a limited amount of time. An announcement communicates or informs an audience of upcoming events.
- When creating headlines for flyers or announcements, select typefaces that match the tone of the document and type sizes that stress important information. A headline should be a dominant visual element, set significantly larger than the words that follow.
- Graphics added to a flyer or announcement can add excitement and generate enthusiasm for the publication. A simple graphic demands more attention and has more impact than a complex one.
- Use color in a publication to elicit a particular feeling, emphasize important text, attract attention, organize data, and/or create a pattern in a document. Limit the color to small areas so it attracts attention but does not create visual confusion.
- Use WordArt to distort or modify text to create a variety of shapes. In WordArt, you can change fonts, type size, and alignments as well as add shading, shadow, and borders to text.
- Create your own shapes and images using Word's Drawing toolbar. You can draw shapes, draw freehand, and create and customize text.
- When using the Drawing toolbar, change the viewing mode to Page Layout.
- A text box can be used to position text, pictures, or objects above or below the text layer. A text box does not automatically resize for additional content. Document text does not wrap around a text box.
- With buttons on the Drawing toolbar, you can add fill color or patterns to an enclosed object, change thickness and color of the line that draws the object, and change the position of the object.
- Callouts can be created with the Callout button on the Drawing toolbar. A callout can be customized at the Format Callout dialog box.
- When objects overlap, use the Bring to Front and Send to Back buttons on the Drawing toolbar. You can also move an object in front or behind text.
- With the Group button on the Drawing toolbar, you can group two or more objects or sections of an object together as a single object. You can also ungroup objects or sections of an object using the Ungroup button.
- With the drawing grid turned on, an object is pulled into alignment with the nearest intersection of grid lines.
- Selected items can be aligned with options from the Align dialog box.
- Frames can be used to position text, pictures, or objects in the text layer of a document. Text outside the frame wraps around the frame. A frame resizes to adjust to additional text or a larger image.

Commands Review

Command	Mouse/Keyboard
WordArt	Insert, Object, Create New tab, double-click Microsoft WordArt 3.0 (2.0)
AutoText	Edit, AutoText
Microsoft Word Picture	Double-click picture; Insert, Object, Create New tab, then select Microsoft Word Picture in Object Type list; click Create Picture button on the Drawing toolbar; or double-click on graphic in document window.
Display Drawing Toolbar	Click Drawing button on Standard toolbar; position arrow pointer in gray area of any displayed toolbar, click right mouse button, click Drawing; or click View, Toolbars, select Drawing, then press Enter

Check Your Understanding

Terms: Match the terms with the correct definitions by writing the letter (or letters) of the term on the blank line in front of the correct definition.

A.	Announcement	**H.**	Pixel
B.	Flyer	**I.**	Nodes
C.	Resolution	**J.**	Drawing toolbar
D.	Thumbnail	**K.**	Frame
E.	WordArt	**L.**	Microsoft toolbar
F.	Text box	**M.**	Logo
G.	Reverse	**N.**	Polygon

_______ **1.** With this Word feature, you can distort or modify text to create a variety of shapes.

_______ **2.** A rough sketch of the design and layout of your document.

_______ **3.** Small black squares that connect line segments.

_______ **4.** A black background and white foreground or white type against a color background.

_______ **5.** Each dot in a picture or graphic.

_______ **6.** This box positions text, pictures, or objects in a specific location in a document text layer.

_______ **7.** The number of dots that make up an image on a screen or printer.

_______ **8.** This type of document communicates or informs an audience of an upcoming event.

_______ **9.** This toolbar includes buttons that are used to create shapes and pictures, format callouts, add fill, position pictures and text, group and ungroup objects, align objects, and insert frames.

_______ **10.** A unique design that may be made up of combinations of letters, words, shapes, or graphics that serve as an emblem for an organization or a product.

_______11. This box positions text, pictures, or objects in the layer above or below the text layer.

_______12. A closed plane figure having three or more angles and straight lines.

True/False: Circle the letter T if the statement is true; circle the letter F if the statement is false.

T F 1. A complex graphic demands more attention and has more impact than a simple graphic.

T F 2. Generally, the upper right side of a document is read first.

T F 3. To Display the Drawing toolbar, choose Tools, then Draw.

T F 4. The Drawing toolbar displays at the bottom of the screen.

T F 5. Be sure the viewing mode is Normal when using the buttons on the Drawing toolbar.

T F 6. A Word document contains three levels: the text layer, a layer above the text, and a layer below.

T F 7. To draw a square shape using the Rectangle button on the Drawing toolbar, hold down the Ctrl key as you draw the shape.

T F 8. To reverse a selected object from top to bottom, click the Flip Horizontal button on the Drawing toolbar.

T F 9. Once objects have been grouped, they cannot be ungrouped.

T F 10. If you rotate a text box, the box rotates but the text does not.

T F 11. Hold down the Shift key and select each object you want to align using the Align Drawing Objects button on the Drawing toolbar.

T F 12. Text automatically wraps around a text box.

Skill Assessments

Assessment 1

You are volunteering in the office of your son's junior high school and are well known for your desktop publishing skills. You have been asked to create a flyer advertising a writing workshop in April.

1. Create a flyer and include these elements:
   a. The headline *Writing is for Everyone.*
   b. A line that reads *Parents and Students in Grades 7–9....*
   c. A line that reads *Make writing a family affair at a special workshop.*
   d. The following bulleted items in your choice of bullet style:

      Explore creative writing
      Attend dynamic sessions
      Participate in writing a short story
      Meet with the authors
      Celebrate learning
      Visit the library display
      Enjoy refreshments

Shop at the Book Fair
Win a door prize

e. Location, date, and time of the workshop, which is *Spring Hill Junior High School, Friday, April 25, 1997, from 2 to 4 p.m.*
f. The slogan *Milton School District...a great place to learn!*

2. Consider creating a thumbnail sketch to help you organize your ideas. Be creative. Use any desktop publishing features you have learned to produce an appealing flyer. You might want to include the clip art image *Books* in the document. (This graphic contains a fountain pen so you can assume it is relevant to the subject.)
3. Save the document and name it c05sa01, writing flyer.
4. Print and then close c05sa01, writing flyer.
5. At a clear document window, open *document evaluation checklist.doc.*
6. Print one copy of the form.
7. Evaluate your flyer according to the guidelines on the form. Attach the form to the back of c05sa01, writing flyer.

Assessment 2

You are working in the Dallas office of Universal Packaging Company. Your company is well known for its involvement in environmental issues. On April 21, several Dallas businesses will offer free seminars, flyers, brochures, etc. in an effort to promote public awareness and involvement in Earth Day 1997. Complete the following task:

1. Create the document as shown in figure 5.29 with the handwritten specifications.
2. Save the document and name it c05sa02, earth day.
3. Print and then close c05sa02, earth day.

FIGURE 5.29

Recyclewmf, Width 0.75"
Height 0.75"
(Group + change to DK Green)

36 pt Wide Latin

Celebrate Earth Day

Paragraph Borders and Shading - Shading tab - Shading (Solid), Foreground (DK Green), Background (White)

28 pt Arial Rounded MT Bold

"Recycle ⇨ Reuse ⇨ Reduce"

Symbols Wingdings (13th symbol in bottom row)

Dr. Michael Goodman, Speaker — 18 pt Arial Bold Expand 2 pt

Professor of Environmental Studies
University of Texas — 14 pt Arial

Rotate text 90 degrees in WordArt
36 pt Wide Latin

April 21, 1997

Recyclewmf
Width 1", Height 1"
(Group + change color to DK Green)

Left Align
16 pt Arial Bold

Monday, April 21, 1997
10:00 a.m. and 2:00 p.m.

Right Align
16 pt Arial Bold

Corporate Plaza West
San Antonio Drive, TX

Use Align Drawing Object button on Drawing Toolbar to Align Shapes

12 pt Arial Italic

Sponsored by:

14 pt Arial Rounded Mt Bold, Bold

Universal Packaging Company

9 pt Arial Bold

Printed on recyclable paper — 9 pt Arial Bold Italic

Ellipse Shape
DK Gray Border, Lt Gray Fill

Picture
3.75" width, 2.0" Height

continent.wmf

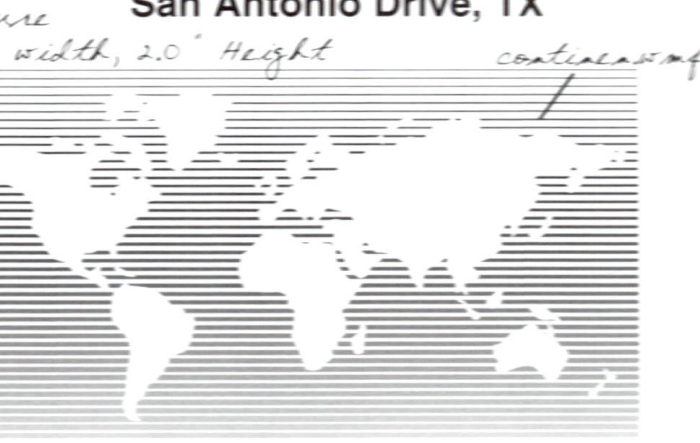

Assessment 3

Spring is here! This is a busy season for window and housecleaning companies. You are the owner of the Atomic Window Cleaning Service, and you need an advertising flyer for your company. All the details are listed here:

1. Create an advertising flyer for your cleaning service that includes the following:
   a. Your name, address, and phone number.
   b. Will offer 10% off with this flyer.
   c. Will clean windows, mirrors, chandeliers, and more.
   d. Provide commercial, industrial, and high-rise services.
   e. Have a seasonal program with a 10% discount.
   f. Are fully insured.
   g. Give free estimates.
   h. Have 5 years of experience.
   i. Provide glass and screen replacement.
   j. Offer quick, quality, professional service.
2. Provide a clever slogan or headline for your flyer.
3. Use any Word features such as WordArt, Drawing Toolbar, Text Boxes, Frames, Expanded or Condensed Character Spacing, Lines, Shapes, Callouts, Fill Color, Line Color, Pictures, Watermarks, Borders, Fonts, etc. to enhance your flyer.
4. Use appropriate fonts, type sizes, and type styles.
5. A suggested picture is *Atomengy*.
6. Use your imagination! Have fun!
7. Save the flyer and name it c05sa03, atomic flyer.
8. Print and then close c05sa03, atomic flyer.
9. At a clear document window, open *document evaluation checklist.doc.*
10. Print one copy of the form.
11. Evaluate your flyer according to the guidelines on the form.

Optional: Choose a business you have always dreamed of owning and create a flyer to advertise your grand opening. Or, if you are currently employed, create an announcement of an upcoming company event or a flyer advertising your company's product or service.

Assessment 4

You are employed at Smith & Barney, a regional accounting firm in Atlanta, GA. You have volunteered to coordinate the annual office golf outing. You scheduled the date at a local golf course and are now ready to create an announcement to send to all the employees. You need a reply from the employees interested in attending, so include a response form at the end of the announcement. Design an announcement using the following guidelines and text:

- Prepare and hand in a thumbnail sketch.
- Use appropriate fonts—vary the size and style of each.
- Use at least one special character.
- Use a vertical or horizontal line, graphic border, or page border (optional).
- Use a graphic image, WordArt text, or a watermark (text or graphic).
- Use color if it is available.

Include the following information:

- Date: June 21, 1997.
- Reply needed by May 30, 1997.
- Kendall Pointe Golf Course.
- Tee-Off Times—Beginning 9:00 a.m. (every 15 minutes).
- Set up your own foursome or you will be assigned to a group.
- Provide your handicap.
- Indicate whether you are going to stay for dinner.
- Dinner: 7:00 p.m. in the Kendall Pointe Clubhouse.
- Sign up for Prize Raffle.
- Prizes will be awarded for low gross score, low net, low front nine, low back nine, longest drive, and closest to the pin.

Save your document and name it c05sa04, golf outing.
Print and then close c05sa04, golf outing.

Creative Activity

Collect three examples of flyers and/or announcements and evaluate them according to the guidelines presented in the document, *document evaluation checklist.doc.* You may use any of the flyers and announcements that you started collecting in chapter 1. Include at least one example of a flyer or announcement that demonstrates poor layout and design; no graphic or one that does not relate to the subject; poor use of fonts, sizes, and styles; and a message that is unclear. Complete the following steps:

1. Open *document evaluation checklist.doc.*
2. Print three copies of the form.
3. Complete and attach an evaluation form to each publication.
4. Re-create one of the flyers incorporating your own ideas and formatting. You do not have to reconstruct the poor example. However, the poor example will show the greatest amount of improvement.
5. A few possible suggestions for improving your document are to include appropriate fonts, sizes, and styles; reverse; WordArt; special characters; color paper; color graphics, watermarks and/or text; horizontal or vertical lines; borders and shading; rotate, scale, size, reduce shading, etc.; and/or Microsoft Word Picture to change the colors or patterns in a graphic image or object.
6. Create a thumbnail sketch first.
7. Format and key the document.
8. Save your document and name it c05ca01, example flyers.
9. Print and then close c05ca01, example flyers.

6 CREATING BROCHURES

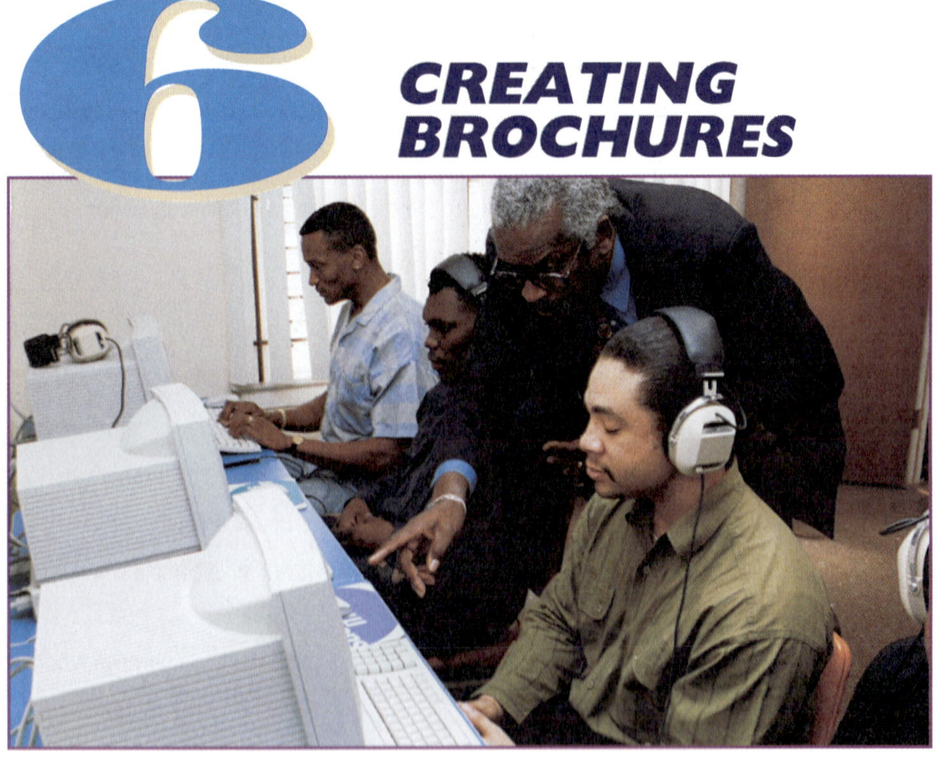

PERFORMANCE OBJECTIVE

Upon successful completion of chapter 6, you will be able to create brochures using a variety of page layouts and design techniques.

DESKTOP PUBLISHING CONCEPTS

Determining size and type of paper
Types of brochure folds
Dummy
Newspaper columns
Reverse text
Screens
Color
Styles
Templates
Drop caps

WORD FEATURES USED

Paper size
Margins
Columns
Frames
Styles
Brochure template
Paragraph spacing
Indents
Tabs
Alignment
Drop caps
Drawing toolbar
Text boxes
Picture editor

In this chapter, you will be introduced to different methods for creating your own brochures. You will use the Columns feature and the Word brochure template to create brochures. Purpose, content, paper selection, brochure folds, page layout, design considerations, and desktop publishing concepts are also discussed.

Planning A Brochure

As mentioned in chapter 1, a very important step in initiating the desktop publishing process is to clearly identify the purpose of your communication. Consequently, defining purpose is as important to the creation of a brochure as it is to the creation of any other publication.

Defining the Purpose

A brochure can inform, educate, promote, or sell. Identify the purpose in the following examples:

- A city agency mails brochures to the community explaining a local recycling program.
- A doctor displays brochures on childhood immunizations in the patient waiting room.
- A car salesperson hands out a brochure on a current model to a potential buyer.
- A new management consulting firm sends out brochures introducing its services.
- A professional organization mails brochures to its members about an upcoming convention.

If you found yourself thinking that some brochures have more than one purpose, you are correct. For example, the goal of a brochure on childhood immunizations may be to inform and educate, while the goal of a brochure on a new car model may be to inform and promote the sale of the product.

In addition, a brochure may be another means of establishing your organization's identity and image. Incorporating design elements from your other business documents into the design of your brochure reinforces your image and identity among your readers.

Determining the Content

Before creating the actual layout and design of your brochure, determine what the content will be. Try to look at the content from a reader's point of view. The content should include the following items:

- A clearly stated description of the topic, product, service, or organization
- A description of the people or company doing the informing, educating, promoting, or selling
- A description of how the reader will benefit from this information, product, service, or organization
- A clear indication of what action you want your audience to take after reading the brochure
- An easy way for readers to respond to the desired action, such as a fill-in form or detachable postcard

Determining the Size and Type of Paper

Brochures are usually printed on both sides on an assortment of paper stocks. The paper stock may vary in size, weight, color, and texture, and it can also have defined folding lines.

Brochures can be folded in a number of different ways. The manner in which a brochure is folded determines the order in which the panels are set on the page and read by the recipient. The most common brochure fold is called a *letter fold.* It is also known as a *trifold* or *three-panel brochure.* The letter fold and other common folds, as shown in figure 6.1, are referred to as *parallel folds*. All of the folds run in the same direction. *Right-angle folds* are created by pages that are folded at right angles to each other, such as the folds in a greeting card. Standard-size 8½-by-11-inch (landscape orientation) paper stock can easily accommodate a letter fold, accordion fold, and single fold. Standard legal-size paper, 8½-by-14 inches, can be used to create a brochure with a map fold or a gate fold. Different paper sizes can be used to create variations of these folds. In addition, folds do not always have to create equal panel sizes. Offsetting a fold can produce an interesting effect.

Parallel Folds: All folds run in the same direction.

Right-Angle Folds: Folds created by pages folded at right angles to each other.

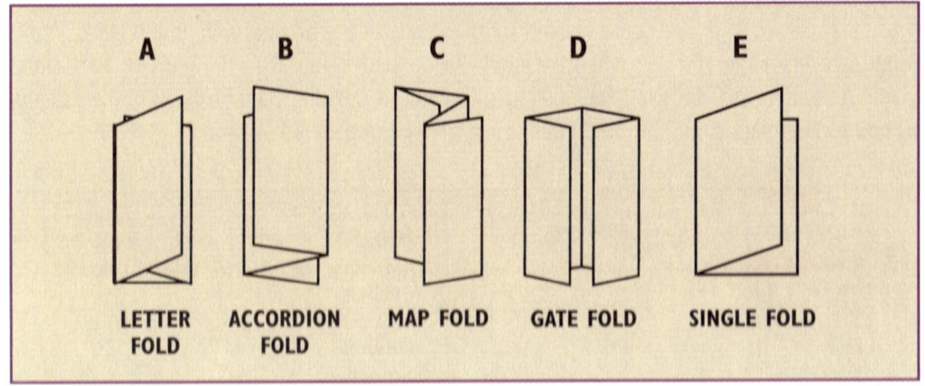

FIGURE 6.1

Brochure Folds

The type of paper selected for a brochure affects the total production cost. When selecting the paper stock for a brochure, consider the following cost factors:

- Standard-size brochures, such as a three-panel brochure created from 8½-by-11-inch paper stock or a four-panel brochure created from 11-by-14-inch paper stock, are easily enclosed in a #10 business envelope.
- Standard-size brochures designed as self-mailers satisfy postal regulations and are, therefore, less costly to mail.
- Nonstandard-size paper stock may be more expensive to purchase and to mail.
- Higher-quality paper stocks are more expensive to purchase.
- Heavier weight papers are more costly to mail.
- Color paper is more costly than standard white, ivory, cream, or gray.
- Predesigned paper stock is more expensive than plain paper stock.

While cost is an important issue when choosing paper stock, also take into account how the brochure will be distributed, how often it will be handled, and the image you want to project. If you plan to design the brochure as a self-mailer, take a sample of the paper stock to the post office to see if it meets USPS mailing regulations. If you expect your target audience to keep your brochure for a period of time or to handle it often, plan to purchase a higher-quality, heavier paper stock. By the same token, choose a paper within your budget that enhances the image you want to leave in the reader's mind.

If you intend to print the brochure yourself, run a sample of the paper you intend to use through your printer. Some papers are better suited for laser and ink jet printers than others. If you are unsure about what type of paper to purchase, take a master copy of your brochure to a printer for advice on the best type of paper for the situation. You can also take your brochure to a print shop and have it folded on their folding equipment.

Understanding a Basic Brochure Page Layout

Panels: Sections separated by folds in a brochure page layout.

A brochure page (defined by the dimensions of the paper stock) is divided into sections called *panels.* At least one fold separates each panel. Folds create distinct sections to place specific blocks of text. For example, a three-panel or letter-fold brochure layout actually has six panels available for text—three panels on one side of the paper and three more panels on the other side. The way a brochure is folded determines the order in which the panels are read by the recipient. The correct placement of text depends on understanding this order. As illustrated in figure 6.2, panels 1, 2, and 3 are located on the inside of the brochure, counting left to right. Panel 4 is the page you see when the cover is opened. Panel 5 is the back of the folded brochure, which may be used for mailing purposes, if desired. Panel 6 is the cover of the brochure. The main content of the brochure is focused in panels 1, 2, and 3.

FIGURE 6.2

Letter-Fold Panel Layout

PANEL 1 (inside)	PANEL 2 (inside)	PANEL 3 (inside)

PANEL 4 (first flap viewed when cover is opened)	PANEL 5 (back/ mailing)	PANEL 6 (cover)

Dummy: A mock-up that is positioned, folded, trimmed, and/or labeled as the actual publication.

To avoid confusion about the brochure page layout and the panel reference numbers, create a mock-up or *dummy* of your brochure. A dummy is folded in the same manner as the actual brochure and is particularly useful since brochures can be folded in a number of different ways. A brochure or a dummy can be created using Word's Columns, Table, or Frame features. These features can be used to create brochures, programs, booklets, cards, tickets, bookmarks, and more. For example, for a standard-size three-panel brochure, the actual page size is 8½-by-11 inches positioned in a landscape orientation. The page is then divided into three columns using the Columns feature or into three columns and one row when using the Table feature. Or three frames could be sized and positioned on the page to represent three panels. Although each method has its advantages and disadvantages, the Columns feature requires the least adjustments. Consequently, having a solid understanding of the Columns feature is necessary to create a brochure, a dummy of your brochure, or to use the brochure template provided by Word.

Understanding Newspaper Columns

Newspaper Columns: Text in this type of column flows up and down in the document.

The types of columns used to create a brochure are commonly referred to as *newspaper columns* or *snaking columns.* Newspaper columns are commonly used for text in newspapers, newsletters, brochures, and magazines. Text in these types of columns flows up and down in the document as shown in figure 6.3. When the first column on the page is filled with text, the insertion point moves to the top of the next column on the same page. When the last column on the page is filled with text, the insertion point moves to the beginning of the first column on the next page.

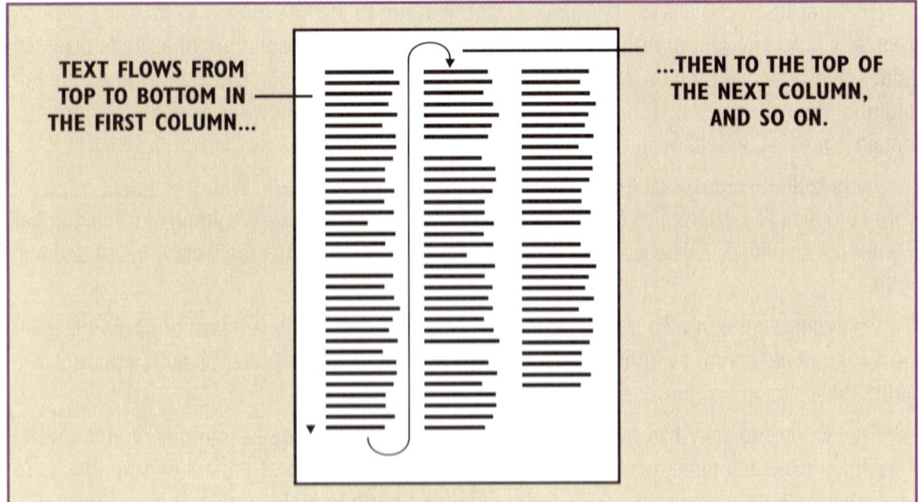

FIGURE 6.3

Newspaper Columns

A document can include as many columns as there is room for on the page. Word determines how many columns can be included on the page based on the page width, the margin settings, the size of the columns, and the spacing between columns. Column formatting can be assigned to a document before the text is keyed or it can be applied to existing text.

Creating Newspaper Columns of Equal Width

To easily create newspaper columns of equal width using the Columns button on the Standard toolbar, you would complete the following steps:

Columns

1. Change the viewing mode to Page Layout to see the columns display side by side.
2. Position the arrow pointer on the Columns button.
3. Hold down the left mouse button, drag the mouse down and to the right highlighting the desired number of column displays, then release the mouse button.

DTP POINTERS
Use Page Layout View to display columns side by side.

Even though only four column icons display, you can continue dragging towards the right to select a greater number of columns. Columns of equal width can also be created using the options at the Columns dialog box.

Creating Columns of Unequal Width

While the Columns button on the Standard toolbar is useful for creating columns of equal width, you must use the Columns dialog box to create columns of unequal width. To create columns with options at the Columns dialog box, you would complete the following steps:

DTP POINTERS
Be consistent when varying column widths within a document.

1. Change the viewing mode to Page Layout to see the columns displayed side by side.
2. Choose Format, then Columns.
3. At the Columns dialog box, select One, Two, Three, Left, or Right in the Presets section; or key the desired number of columns in the Number of Columns text box.
4. Click the Equal Column Width check box to disable this option.
5. In the Width and Spacing section, find the column number(s) you want to change, then enter the desired column widths and spacing between columns in the corresponding Width and Spacing text boxes.
6. Choose OK or press Enter.

The first three choices of One, Two, or Three in the Presets section will result in columns of equal width. The Left and Right options will result in unequal columns of a predetermined width. If you choose the Left option, the right column of text will be twice as wide as the left column of text. Choose the Right option if you want the left column twice as wide. The options contain a preview box showing what the columns will look like.

By default, the Equal Column Width option contains a check mark. With this option selected, Word automatically determines column widths and the spacing between columns for the number of columns specified. This check mark must be removed in order to create columns of unequal width.

By default, columns are separated by 0.5 inches of space. The amount of space between equal or unequal column widths can be increased or decreased with the Spacing option in the Width and Spacing section.

The dialog box only has room to display measurements for three columns. If you specify more than three columns, a vertical scroll bar displays to the left of the column numbers. To view other column measurements, click the down-pointing triangle at the bottom of the scroll bar.

Column widths and spacing can also be changed with the column markers on the horizontal ruler. To do this, you would complete the following steps:

1. Choose View, then Ruler to display the horizontal ruler.
2. Position the arrow pointer in the middle of the column marker on the horizontal ruler until it turns into a double-headed arrow pointing left and right.
3. Hold down the left mouse button, drag the column marker to the left or right to make the column wider or narrower, then release the mouse button.

If the columns are of equal width, changing the width of one column changes the width of all columns. If the columns are of unequal width, changing the width of a column only changes that column.

Varying Column Formatting Within the Same Document

By default, column formatting is applied to the whole document. If you want to create different numbers or styles of columns within the same document, the document must be divided into sections. For example, if a document contains a title, you may want the title to span the top of all the columns rather than be included within the column formatting. To span a title across the tops of columns, you would complete the following steps:

1. Key and format the title.
2. Position the insertion point at the left margin of the first line of text to be formatted into columns.
3. Display the Columns dialog box, then change the Apply To option at the bottom of the Columns dialog box from *Whole Document* to *This Point Forward.*

When the *This Point Forward* option is selected, a section break is automatically inserted in your document. Column formatting is then applied to text from the location of the insertion point to the end of the document or until other column formatting is encountered.

In addition to the method just described, you can manually insert the section break before accessing the Columns dialog box by choosing Insert, then Break. At the Break dialog box, choose Continuous, choose OK or press Enter, and then access the Columns dialog box.

If you decide to include text that is not to be formatted into columns after the text that is formatted in columns, you must change the column format to one column and then select the *This Point Forward* option. You can also insert a section break through the Break dialog box and then use the Columns button on the Standard toolbar to create one column.

Specific text can also be formatted into columns in a document by first selecting the text in the document, then using the Columns button on the Standard toolbar or the options from the Columns dialog box.

If you want to remove column formatting, position the insertion point in the section containing columns and change the column format to one column either by using the Columns button on the Standard toolbar or the Columns dialog box.

Inserting a Column and/or Page Break

When formatting text into columns, Word automatically breaks the columns to fit the page. At times, you may want a column to break in a different location, or a column may break in an undesirable location. For example, a heading may appear at the bottom of the column, while the text that follows the heading begins at the top of the next column. You can insert a column break into a document to control where columns end and begin on the page. To insert a column break, position the insertion point where you want the new column to begin, then press Ctrl + Shift + Break; or choose Insert, Break, Column Break, then choose OK or press Enter.

DTP POINTERS
Make sure all column breaks are in appropriate locations.

If you insert a column break in the last column on a page, the column begins on the next page. If you want a column that is not the last column on the page to begin on the next page, insert a page break. To do this, press Ctrl + Enter or choose Insert, Break, Page Break.

If you want to "even out" or balance the text in columns, put a continuous section break at the end of the last column.

Moving the Insertion Point Within and Between Columns

To move the insertion point in a document using the mouse, position the arrow pointer where desired, then click the left mouse button. If you are using the keyboard, the up, down, left, and right arrows will move the insertion point in the direction indicated within the column. The up and down arrow keys will cause the insertion point to follow the snaking pattern of newspaper columns—down one column and then to the top of the next column. If you are using the arrow keys, the insertion point will not move to a second page until you have moved it all the way through the last column on the page. Consequently, the mouse is most often the preferred method to move the insertion point in text formatted into columns.

To move the insertion point between columns, you can use the mouse as stated above. If you are using the keyboard, press Alt + up arrow to move the insertion point to the top of the previous column, or press Alt + down arrow to move the insertion point to the top of the next column.

Creating a Dummy of a Three-Panel Brochure Using Columns

1. At a clear document screen, create a dummy similar to the one illustrated in figure 6.2 by completing the following steps:
   a. Change to the Page Layout viewing mode.
   b. Click File, then Page Setup.
   c. At the Page Setup dialog box, click the Paper Size tab.
   d. Make sure the Paper Size list box displays *Letter* and then select Landscape in the Orientation section.
   e. Click OK.
   f. Click Format, then Columns.
   g. At the Columns dialog box, change the Number of Columns to 3; or select Three (equal columns) in the Presets section of the Columns dialog box.

h. Click OK to close the dialog box.

2. Insert the panel labels by completing the following steps:
   a. Change the paragraph alignment to Center.
   b. Key **PANEL 1 (inside)** in the first panel (column 1).
   c. Choose Insert, then Break.
   d. At the Break dialog box, choose Column Break, then click OK.
   e. Repeat steps b through d until all six of the panels have been labeled.
3. Print the three-panel brochure dummy by completing the following steps:
   a. Position the insertion point on the first page by pressing Ctrl + Home.
   b. Choose File, then Print.
   c. At the Print dialog box, choose Current Page, then choose OK.
   d. Put the first printed page back in the printer so the second page can be printed on the back of the first page. (You may have to experiment with your printer to position the paper correctly.)
   e. Position the insertion point on the second page (panel 4, 5, or 6), then print the current page.
   f. Fold the dummy as you would for the real brochure and refer to the panel labels when creating the actual brochure to avoid confusion on the placement of text.
4. Save and name the dummy brochure as c06ex01, dummy.
5. Close c06ex01, dummy.

You can use a similar procedure to create a dummy using a table. Instead of creating three columns, insert a table with three columns and one row, label the panels, and then print as explained above.

A dummy can also be created with pencil and paper. Take a piece of the paper stock to be used and position it correctly (portrait or landscape). Fold the paper as the brochure will be folded, and label each panel as in figure 6.2.

You may create a paper size definition for paper stock that is different from the sizes available in the Paper Size drop-down list box. To do this, select Custom Size from the Paper Size drop-down list. Insert the correct width and height of your paper stock in the corresponding text boxes and then choose portrait or landscape orientation. Depending on your printer's capabilities, you may be able to directly insert different standard sizes of paper and envelopes into your printer. For example, your printer may adjust to holding letter, legal, and executive-size paper, as well as two standard-size business envelopes. However, your printer may not be able to hold and feed odd or custom-size papers even though you can create a custom-size paper definition in Word. If that is the case, print the custom-size document on standard-size paper of the desired stock. The document will be printed within the parameters of the custom paper size definition. However, since it will be printed on standard-size paper, measure the desired size and trim the document to the correct size or have it printed and trimmed professionally.

Using Reverse Text As A Design Element

Reverse Text: White text set against a solid 100% black background.

Reverse text usually refers to white text set against a solid (100% black) background, as shown in the first example in figure 6.4. Setting headings, subheadings, or other significant blocks of text in reverse type can be a very effective design element. Reversing text is most effective with single words or short phrases set in a larger type size. Impact can also be achieved by screening (shading with lighter shades of gray or color) the background or lettering. Solid areas of black, white, and varying shades of gray on a page give the visual effect of color, allowing you to achieve a dramatic effect with the use of only one color. In addition, interesting effects can be achieved by reversing color text out of a solid or screened colored background. As illustrated in figure 6.4, different variations of reverse type can be created. Keep these examples in mind when you are trying to provide focus, balance, contrast, and directional flow in a document.

FIGURE 6.4

Examples of Reverse Text

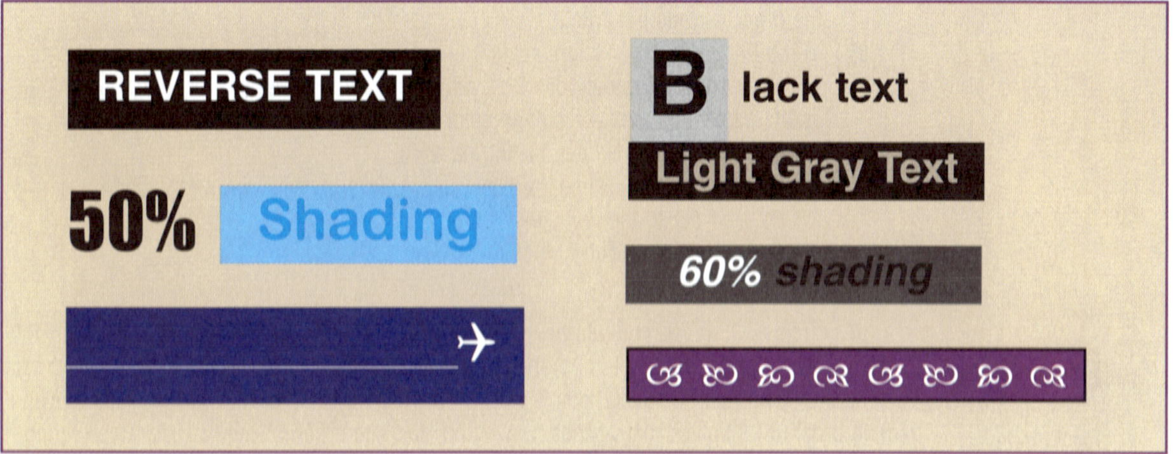

To create reverse text in Word using the Frame feature, you would complete the following steps:

1. Key and format the text (such as font type, font size, font style, or font color) that is to be placed in reverse text.
2. Select the text.
3. Choose Insert, then Frame.
4. Choose Format, then Borders and Shading.
5. At the Paragraph Borders and Shading dialog box, select the Shading tab.
6. Select the desired percentage of shading or pattern from the Shading list box.
7. Click once on the down-pointing triangle to the right of the Foreground list box and select a foreground color for the reverse text box.
8. Click once on the down-pointing triangle to the right of the Background list box to select a background color. If you want to create a lighter shade of the foreground color, select White (in addition to having selected a shading percentage in step 6) as the background color. To create other custom colors, select a shading percentage, a foreground color, and a different background color. For example, to create a purple color, select 50% as the pattern, select blue as the foreground color, and red as the background color.
9. Select the Borders tab if you want to place a border around the reverse text.
10. Click OK or press Enter.

Reverse text can also be created using the Text Box button from the Drawing toolbar. This method is useful when you want to place regular text next to reverse text, as illustrated in the *50% Shading* example in figure 6.4. To create reverse text using a text box, you would complete the following steps:

Text Box

1. Display the Drawing toolbar.
2. Click the Text Box button on the Drawing toolbar.
3. Position the crosshairs in the desired reverse text location, then click the left mouse button and drag the mouse to create a text box.
4. Key and format the text to be contained in the reverse text box, including the font color.
5. Choose Format, then Drawing Object.
6. At the Drawing Defaults dialog box, select the Fill tab.
7. In the Color section, select the desired fill color for the reverse text box.
8. In the Patterns section, select the desired percentage of shading or choose one of the other various patterns.
9. In the Pattern Color section, select the desired color of the pattern chosen in step 7. For example, if you choose Dk Cyan as the color, 50% as the pattern, and White as the pattern color, the resulting color will be a lighter shade of Dk Cyan (that is, Dk Cyan with a 50% white shading pattern).
10. Choose the Line tab or use the Line Color button on the Drawing toolbar if you want to add a border to the reverse text box.
11. Choose OK or press Enter when done.

DTP POINTERS
Desktop published documents involve many steps—SAVE as you work.

In exercises 2 and 3, you will have the opportunity to create a three-panel or letter-fold brochure using newspaper columns and other formatting features such as frames to create reverse text, color, and bulleted lists. A word of advice—**SAVE! SAVE! SAVE!** Creating even a simple brochure involves many steps. Save your document periodically as you are creating it to avoid any disasters—they happen to the best of us! Also, view your document frequently to assess the overall layout and design. Adjustments often need to be made that can affect other parts of the document not visible in the document window. In Word, click the arrow at the right of the Zoom Control button on the Standard toolbar (third button from the right). The Page Width and Full Page options are useful for viewing a brochure layout during the creation process.

Creating Panels 1, 2, and 3 of a Three-Panel Brochure Using the Columns Feature and Reverse Text

1. Use the dummy created in exercise 1 or create a new dummy following the directions in exercise 1 to guide you in the correct placement of text.
2. At a clear document screen, create the first three panels of a brochure, as shown in figure 6.5, by completing the following steps:
   a. Choose File, then Page Setup.
   b. At the Page Setup dialog box, select the Paper Size tab.
   c. Make sure *Letter* displays in the Paper Size list box, then select Landscape in the Orientation section.
   d. With the Page Setup dialog box still displayed, select the Margins tab. Change the top and bottom margins to 0.5 inches. Change the left and right margins to 0.67 inches. (The left and right margin settings were selected because of the unprintable zone that exists within the printer that was used to create and print the brochure in figures 6.5 and 6.6.)
   e. Choose OK or press Enter to close the dialog box.
   f. Display the Font dialog box, then select the Character Spacing tab.
   g. Choose Kerning for Fonts, key **14** in the Points and Above text box, then choose OK or press Enter.
   h. Choose Format, then Columns.

i. At the Columns dialog box, choose Three in the Presets section of the Columns dialog box, make sure Equal Column Width is selected, then choose OK or press Enter.
j. Insert the file containing the brochure text by completing the following steps:
   (1) Choose Insert, then File.
   (2) At the Insert File dialog box, double-click *ride safe four text* (located on your student data disk) in the Look in list box.
k. Press Ctrl + Home to move the insertion point to the beginning of the document.
l. Click the Show/Hide ¶ button on the Standard toolbar to display nonprinting characters, such as paragraph symbols and spaces.
m. Select the font for the whole document by completing the following steps:
   (1) Choose Edit, then Select All.
   (2) Change the font to 12-point Arial Rounded MT Bold.
   (3) Deselect the text.
n. Format the number *1* that displays at the top of the first panel (or column) of the brochure by completing the following steps:
   (1) Insert a space before and after the number *1*.
   (2) Select number *1* including the spaces before and after the number and the paragraph symbol.
   (3) Change the font to 72-point Arial Rounded MT Bold and change the color of the font to red. (If you do not have a color printer, you may use either gray or white.)
   (4) With the number, spaces, and paragraph symbol still selected, choose Insert, then Frame.
   (5) Choose Format, then Frame.
   (6) At the Frame dialog box, make the following changes:
      (a) Select None in the Text Wrapping section.
      (b) Make sure the Horizontal Position: is set at Left, Relative To: Column and the Vertical Position is set at 0 inches Relative To: Paragraph.
      (c) In the Size section, change the Width: to Exactly At: 1.15 inches.
      (d) Click OK or press Enter.
   (7) Insert the black fill behind the number by completing the following steps:
      (a) Select the frame if it is not already selected.
      (b) Choose Format, then Borders and Shading.
      (c) At the Paragraph Borders and Shading dialog box, select the Shading tab.
      (d) Make sure black (Auto) is selected as the Foreground color and then select *Solid (100%)* from the Shading list box.
      (e) Click OK or press Enter.
o. Format the lead-in text following the framed number by completing the following steps:
   (1) Select *Before entering the street from your driveway or sidewalk:*, change the font to 20-point Arial Rounded MT Bold Italic and change the Effects to Small Caps in the Font dialog box.
   (2) Position the insertion point to the left of *Stop* and press Enter two times.
p. Create the red bulleted list by completing the following steps:
   (1) Select the text that starts with *Stop* and ends with *Listen to be sure no traffic is approaching.* and change the font to 20-point Arial Rounded MT Bold.
   (2) With the text still selected, choose Format, then Bullets and Numbering.
   (3) At the Bullets and Numbering dialog box, select the Bulleted tab.
   (4) With the first bullet option selected, (first row, first column), click Modify.

(5) At the Modify Bulleted List dialog box, click the first box in the Bullet Character section. (A round bullet should be displayed in this box. If not, click Bullet and select a round bullet from the Symbol dialog box.)
(6) Change the Point Size to 32 points and change the Color to Red.
(7) Click OK or press Enter.

q. Adjust the spacing between the bulleted items by completing the following steps:
(1) With the bulleted list still selected, choose Format, then Paragraph.
(2) At the Paragraph dialog box, select the Indents and Spacing tab.
(3) Key **16 pt** in the After text box in the Spacing section.
(4) Click OK or press Enter.

r. If the number *2* is not positioned at the top of column two, position the insertion point to the left of *2* and insert a column break.

s. Format the text in panel 2 by completing the following steps:
(1) Format the number *2* by following steps 2n (1-7) above, except change the color of the number to yellow. (Be sure to select the spaces before and after the number and the paragraph symbol that follows.)
(2) Format the lead-in text below the frame by repeating steps 2o (1-2) above.
(3) Create the bulleted list by following steps 2p (1-4), then select the red Bullet Character (should display as the first choice in the Modify Bulleted List dialog box). Change the bullet color to yellow.

t. Follow the steps in 2q to adjust the spacing between the bulleted items.

u. Position the insertion point to the left of *3*, then insert a column break to position the number at the top of the third panel.

v. Format the text in panel 3 by completing the following steps:
(1) Format the number *3* by following steps 2n (1-7) above, except change the color of the number to green and format the frame to set the Horizontal Position to 7.7 inches Relative to: Page. (The change in the horizontal position in panel 3 allows for the frame to be positioned more appropriately in relation to the fold in the brochure.)
(2) Format the frame to set the Horizontal Position to 7.7 inches Relative To: Page and the Vertical Position to 0 inches Relative To: Paragraph.
(3) Format the lead-in text below the frame by repeating steps 2o (1 through 2) above.
(4) Create the bulleted list by following steps 2p (1-4), then select the yellow Bullet Character and change the bullet color to green.
(5) Follow the steps in 2q to adjust the spacing between the bulleted items.
(6) To accommodate the brochure fold, create more white space on the left side of panel 3 by completing the following steps:
(a) Select *Before turning, . . . to avoid an obstacle:*.
(b) Choose Format, then Paragraph.
(c) At the Paragraph dialog box, select the Indents and Spacing tab.
(d) Key **.28** in the Left box in the Indentation section.
(e) Click OK or press Enter.
(f) Select the bulleted list and repeat steps (b-e) above. (The bulleted list needs to be selected separately for the indentation to take effect.)
(7) Below the bulleted list, position the insertion point to the left of *4* and insert a column break.

3. Save the brochure and name it c06ex02, panels 1,2,3.
4. Print this exercise now or print after completing exercise 3.
5. Close c06ex02, panels 1,2,3.

FIGURE 6.5

BEFORE ENTERING THE STREET FROM YOUR DRIVEWAY OR SIDEWALK:

- Stop.
- Look left.
- Look right.
- Look left again.
- Listen to be sure no traffic is approaching.

AT STOP SIGNS, STOPLIGHTS, OR OTHER BUSY STREETS:

- Stop.
- Look left.
- Look right.
- Look left again.
- Listen and make sure the street is clear of traffic before crossing.

BEFORE TURNING, CHANGING LANES, OR SWERVING TO AVOID AN OBSTACLE:

- Look back over your shoulder.
- Be sure the road is clear of traffic.
- Signal.
- Look again.

In exercise 3, you will complete the brochure started in exercise 2. Remember to save your document every 10 to 15 minutes.

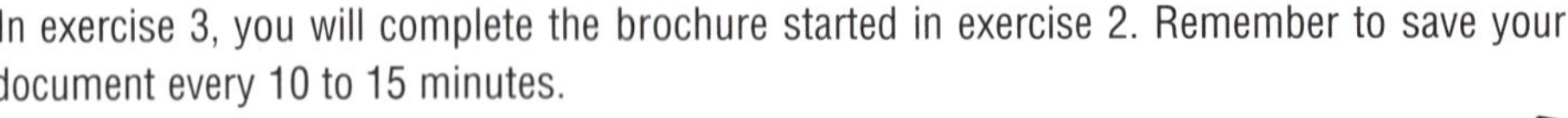

Creating Panels 4, 5, and 6 of a Three-Fold Brochure

1. At a clear document screen, open *c06ex02, panels 1,2,3.*
2. Save the document with Save As and name it c06ex03, ride safe brochure.
3. Create panels 4, 5, and 6 of a brochure as shown in figure 6.6 by completing the following steps:
   a. Format the text in panel 4 by completing the following steps:
      (1) Position the insertion point to the left of the number *4* located at the top of panel 4.
      (2) Format the number *4* by following steps 2n (1 through 7) in exercise 2. Change the color of the number to red. (Be sure to select the spaces before and after the number and the paragraph symbol that follows.)
      (3) Format the lead-in text below the frame by repeating steps 2o (1 through 2) in exercise 2.
      (4) Create the bulleted list by following steps 2p (1 through 4) in exercise 2, then select the green Bullet Character and change the bullet color to red.
      (5) Adjust the spacing between the bulleted items by following the steps in 2q in exercise 2.
      (6) Position the insertion point to the left of *Ride Safe is committed to educating children . . .* and insert a column break.
   b. Format the text in panel 5 by completing the following steps:
      (1) Press Enter five times.
      (2) Select the paragraph that begins with *Ride Safe is committed to educating children . . .* and change the type size to 10 points.
      (3) Position the insertion point to the left of the line that reads *We want everyone to RIDE SAFE!* and press Enter eight times.
      (4) Select the same line of text, change the type size to 18 points, change the color to green, turn on Italics, and change the paragraph alignment to center.
      (5) Select *Call us today at . . .* then choose Insert, then Frame.
      (6) In the same line of text, position the insertion point after the word *at*, delete the space and press Enter to force the phone number down to the next line.
      (7) Select *Call us today at 1-800-285-RIDE*, change the type size to 20 points, change the font color to yellow, and change the paragraph alignment to center.
      (8) Display the Frame dialog box, change the Horizontal Position to Center Relative to: to Column, and then change the Vertical Position to Bottom Relative to: Margin.
      (9) With the frame still selected, change the paragraph shading to solid (100%).
      (10) *THE RIDE SAFE FOUR* title should be at the top of panel 6. If it is not, insert a column break.
   c. Format the title in panel 6 (the cover) by completing the following steps:
      (1) Select the title *THE RIDE SAFE FOUR*, change the font to 36-point Arial Rounded MT Bold, and change the paragraph alignment to center.
      (2) Since the left column margin and the right margin of the page are uneven, adjust the title so that it will appear more centered on the cover panel by completing the following steps:
         (a) With the title already selected, choose Format, then Paragraph.
         (b) At the Paragraph dialog box, select the Indents and Spacing tab.
         (c) Key **.25** in the Left text box in the Indentation section.
         (d) Click OK or press Enter.
      (3) In the same line of text, position the insertion point after *THE*, delete the

space, and press Enter to force *RIDE* down to the next line.
(4) Select *RIDE* in the title and change the color to red.
(5) Select *SAFE* in the title and change the color to yellow.
(6) Select *FOUR* in the title and change the color to green.

d. Format the company name, address, and phone number by completing the following steps: (The traffic light image will be inserted last.)
   (1) Select *RIDE SAFE, INC.*, and change the type size to 14 points.
   (2) Select the company name, address, and phone number and change the paragraph alignment to center.
   (3) With the text still selected, choose Insert, then Frame.
   (4) Choose Format, then Frame.
   (5) At the Frame dialog box, make the following changes:
      (a) Change the Horizontal Position: to 7.5 inches, Relative To: Page.
      (b) Change the Vertical Position: to Bottom, Relative To: Margin.
      (c) Click OK or press Enter.
   (6) Choose Format, then Borders and Shading.
   (7) At the Paragraph Borders and Shading dialog box, select the Borders tab.
   (8) Choose None in the Presets section.
   (9) Click OK or press Enter.
   (10) Deselect the text.

e. Create the traffic light image by completing the following steps:
   (1) Choose Insert, then Frame.
   (2) Position the crosshairs below the cover title, then draw a rectangle below the title similar in size and shape to the traffic light on the brochure cover in figure 6.6.
   (3) Choose Format, then Frame.
   (4) At the Frame dialog box, make the following changes:
      (a) Select None in the Text Wrapping section.
      (b) In the Size section, change the Width to Exactly 1.2 inches and the Height to 2.73 inches.
      (c) In the Horizontal section, change the Position: to 8.4 inches Relative To: Page.
      (d) In the Vertical section, change the Position: to 3.4 inches Relative To: Page.
      (e) Click OK or press Enter.
   (5) Position the insertion point inside the frame, change the font to 60-point Arial Rounded MT Bold, change the color to red, and change the paragraph alignment to center.
   (6) Choose Insert, then Symbol.
   (7) At the Symbol dialog box, select the Symbols tab.
   (8) Change the Font to Wingdings, then select the round bullet in the third row, eighth column from the right.
   (9) Choose Insert, then Close.
   (10) Press Enter.
   (11) Repeat the same steps to insert yellow and green bullets, pressing Enter after each bullet.
   (12) Make sure the frame is selected, then choose Format, then Borders and Shading.
   (13) At the Paragraph Borders and Shading dialog box, select the Shading tab.
   (14) Select *Solid (100%)* from the Shading list box.
   (15) Click OK or press Enter.

4. Save the brochure again with the same name (c06ex03, ride safe brochure).
5. Print both pages of the brochure using both sides of the paper. Refer to the directions for printing in exercise 1, if necessary.
6. Close c06ex03, ride safe brochure.

FIGURE 6.6

EVERY TIME YOU GO BICYCLING OR IN-LINE SKATING:

- Wear an ANSI, ASTM, or Snell certified helmet.
- Wear appropriate protective gear!

Ride Safe is committed to educating children and their parents about bicycle safety and the importance of wearing helmets. In the last year, we've worked with over 1,200 PTAs/PTOs across the country to develop customized bicycle safety programs...and we'd like to work with you, too.

We want everyone to RIDE SAFE!

Call us today at 1-800-285-RIDE

THE RIDE SAFE FOUR

RIDE SAFE, INC.
1944 Hampton Drive
Wheaton, IL 60187-9900
1-800-285-RIDE

Designing A Brochure

As with letterheads, envelopes, and business cards, designing your own brochure can be a cost-saving measure. It eliminates the cost of paying a professional designer and the cost of committing to a minimum order. In addition, if the information in your brochure needs to be updated, it can be easily changed. Although not as cost effective, you can design your own brochure, print a master copy, and then take it to a professional printer to be duplicated on high-quality paper.

For a brochure to be noticed, it must be well designed, easy to read, and have some element that sets it apart from the pack. As with all publications, consider your target audience and start drawing some thumbnail sketches. Consider the content of the brochure; any illustrations or graphics that might be a required part of your brochure, such as a logo or a picture of a product or service; or any colors that might be associated with your company, organization, or topic.

The front cover of a brochure sets the mood and tone for the whole brochure. The front cover title must attract attention and let the reader know what the brochure is about. The typeface selected for the title must reflect the image and tone intended. For example, Arial Rounded MT Bold was the typeface used in the brochure cover title in exercise 3. The rounded, slightly juvenile nature of this typeface reflects the target audience. The use of red, yellow, and green in the title, along with the wording and stoplight image, reinforces the traffic safety theme of this brochure. If the same title had been set in Times New Roman, the mood or tone would be much more businesslike and conservative. Which do you think would be more appealing to a target audience of school-aged bicyclists?

A great deal of information is often contained within the confines of a brochure. Using one typeface for the brochure title, headings, and subheadings and another typeface for the body copy can provide visual contrast in your brochure. Do not use more than two typefaces or the brochure will appear crowded, cluttered, and more difficult to read. To provide contrast within the brochure text, vary the style of the typeface rather than changing typefaces. Text can be set in all caps, small caps, italics, reverse, bold, or color to achieve contrast. For example, Arial Rounded MT Bold was the only typeface used in the *Ride Safe Four* brochure shown in figures 6.5 and 6.6. The typeface was varied by using different type sizes, italics, small caps, all caps, and color.

DTP POINTERS
Vary the style of the typeface rather than changing typefaces.

While text set in color can be an effective contrasting element, use it sparingly. Use it for titles, headings, subheadings, and a small graphics element, if any. Remember to allow for white space between the headings and body copy and among separate sections of the body copy. For instance, in figure 6.5, extra white space exists between the lead-in statements and the bulleted lists in each panel, as well as within each bulleted list.

Several elements can be used to direct the reader's eyes through a brochure. Subheadings set in color or in reverse text can be useful directional tools. In figures 6.5 and 6.6, the numbers 1 through 4 are set in different colors on a solid black background (a variation of reverse text) to make them stand out. These numbered squares, which are actually frames with 100% solid black backgrounds, direct the reader to important points. A frame or text box with a specific border can also be used to place items of importance. Horizontal and vertical ruled lines can be used as visual separators. A screen (a shaded area behind a block of text) can be used to emphasize and separate a block of text. Bullets or special characters can be used to aid directional flow. For example, in figures 6.5 and 6.6, the round bullets (found in the Wingdings typeface character set) help to lead the reader's eyes down through the important points in each panel. Effective use of white space can be used to separate items on the page. White space makes the copy more appealing and easier to read.

Consistent elements are necessary to maintain continuity in a multipage brochure. Be consistent in the design and layout of your brochure. Do not mix landscape and portrait orientations within the same brochure. Format each panel in the same basic manner so the reader knows what to expect. Be consistent in the font used for headings, subheadings, and body copy. For example, the lead-in text in each brochure panel in figures 6.5 and 6.6 is set in 20-point Arial Rounded MT Bold Italic, small caps. The bulleted items are also set in the same font without italics and small caps.

DTP POINTERS
Use bullets to organize text and improve directional flow.

Continuity can be maintained by emphasizing the same theme or style throughout the brochure. The red, yellow, and green round bullets repeat the stoplight colors and signal shape, carrying the traffic safety theme from panel to panel in the brochure. Headers or footers can also make it easy to carry a theme or style throughout a document. In addition, consistent amounts of white space at the top and bottom of each panel and within each panel add to the continuity. When evaluating a brochure for continuity, open the brochure and view it the way your readers would. While the individual elements of each panel are important, viewing the design and layout as a whole unit is equally important. When you open a three-panel brochure, look at panels 1, 2, and 3 as a three-page spread. Does the design flow from one panel to the next? Do all three panels work together visually as a unit?

Copyright:
Exclusive legal ownership of a literary, musical, or artistic work.

A visual, such as a clip art image, an illustration, a photograph, or a drawing, can be a powerful tool. While a visual may attract attention, it also delivers an immediate message. It can turn a reader away before the intended message has even been read. What message does the stoplight image in figure 6.6 convey to you? When selecting visuals, select only those visuals that best enhance the intended message of the brochure. Always find out about *copyright* restrictions before using any artwork. Often clip art software owners are allowed to use and publish the images contained in the software package; however, the clip art may not be resold in any manner. If you intend to use a drawing, clip art, scanned art, or photograph, find out the source and request permission from the copyright owner.

Formatting With Styles

Documents created with desktop publishing features generally require a great deal of formatting. Some documents, such as company newsletters or brochures, may be created on a regular basis. These documents should contain formatting that maintains consistency in their appearance from issue to issue. The formatting should also be consistent within each issue and within any document that uses a variety of headings, subheadings, and other design elements.

To maintain consistency within a document, such as a brochure, newsletter, or report, you may find yourself frequently repeating formatting instructions for specific sections of text. For example, to create the brochure in figures 6.5 and 6.6, the formatting instructions for the framed numbers, the font for the lead-in statements and the bulleted items, and the spacing between the bulleted items had to be repeated in each panel. You can save time and keystrokes by using Word's Style feature to store repetitive formatting.

Style:
A group of defined formatting instructions that can be applied at one time to a whole document or to various parts of a document.

A *style* is a group of defined formatting instructions, such as margin settings, paper size, font, font size, and font style, that can be applied at one time to a whole document or to various parts of a document. Using styles assures that your formatting is uniform throughout your document, while at the same time being quick and easy. For example, a style can be created for the framed numbers in figures 6.5 and 6.6. Every time you are ready to format and key the numbers, you can quickly apply the specific style and save yourself the time of repeating the same keystrokes for each item. Because formatting instructions are contained within a style, a style can be edited, automatically updating any occurrence of that style within a document. For instance, if you applied a style for the framed numbers in all four panels of the brochure and then decided to change the background shading to 50% black, all you would need to do is edit the formatting instructions in the style and then all of the framed number boxes would be changed to 50% shading.

Understanding the Relationship Between Styles and Templates

As previously mentioned, a Word document, by default, is based on the *Normal.dot* template. The Normal template contains formatting instructions to set text in the default font (this may vary depending on the printer you are using or if another font has been selected as the default font), to use left alignment and single spacing, and to turn on Widow/Orphan control. These formatting instructions are contained in a style called the *Normal* style. When you access a clear document window, *Normal* will display in the Style list box located at the left side of the Formatting toolbar. The Normal style is automatically applied to any text that is keyed unless you specify other formatting instructions. If you click the down-pointing triangle to the right of the Style list box, you will see a total of five styles immediately available for your use as shown in figure 6.7. In addition to these styles, Word provides a large selection of other predesigned styles.

Normal Style: A set of formatting instructions automatically applied to any text that is keyed unless other formatting instructions are specified.

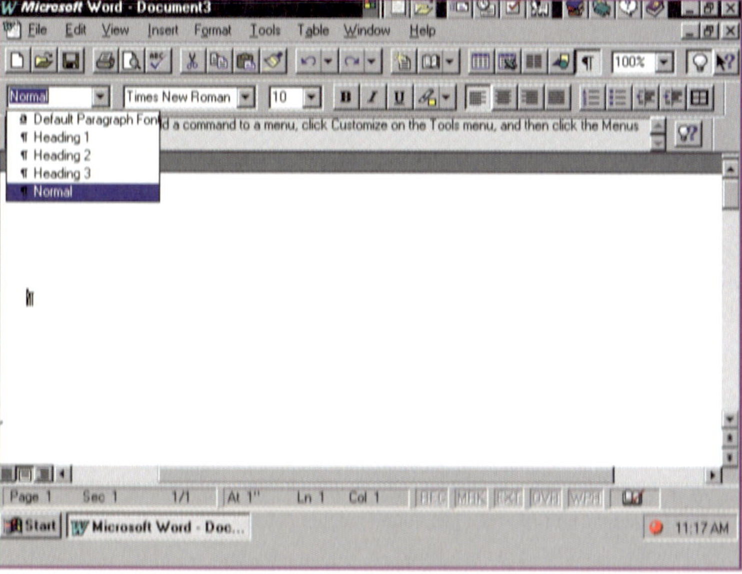

FIGURE 6.7

Style Drop-Down List

You can view all the styles that come with Word by choosing Format, and then Style. Click the down-pointing triangle in the List option and choose All Styles. Select any style name from the Styles list box and a description of the formatting instructions contained in that style will be displayed in the Description section of the Style dialog box. For example, if you select *Heading 7*, the description section displays the formatting instructions that are included in the Heading 7 style. The Heading 7 style includes all the formatting instructions contained in the Normal style. In addition, it also includes a font selection of Arial and a paragraph spacing setting that will provide 12 points of spacing before and 3 points of spacing after the paragraph to which this style is applied. An example of how the selected style will format text is also displayed in the Paragraph Preview box.

Most of Word's predesigned styles are available in any of its template documents. However, some of Word's template documents also contain additional styles depending on the type of document being created. For example, the memo templates, letter templates, and résumé templates used in previous chapters all contain their own set of specific styles. If you choose a different template document from the New dialog box, click the down-pointing triangle to the right of the Style list box on the Formatting toolbar to display the names of styles available for that particular template. If you access the Style dialog box and select *Styles in Use* from the List box, you will also see the names of styles available for that particular template.

You may print a list of all the styles contained in a particular template document. The list contains the names of the styles and all the formatting instructions included in each style. To print a list of the available styles in a document, you would complete the following steps:

1. Choose File, then Print.
2. At the Print dialog box, click the down-pointing triangle to the right of the Print What list box.
3. Choose Styles from the Print What drop-down list.
4. Click OK or press Enter.

Word contains some styles that are applied automatically to text when you use certain commands. For example, if you use the command to insert page numbers, Word applies a certain style to the page number text. Some other commands for which Word automatically formats text with styles include headers, footers, footnotes, endnotes, indexes, and tables of contents.

Using Word's Brochure Template

Word includes a three-panel brochure template called *Brochure*. This template is selected at the New dialog box with the Publications tab selected. When the brochure template document is displayed on the screen, it contains instructions and tips on how to create and customize the brochure. Printing these instructions first can be helpful so you can refer to them as you personalize and customize the brochure. After printing the instructional text, you can label the panels and use the printout as your dummy. The instructional text must be deleted when keying the actual brochure content.

The instructional text is formatted as text might appear in a brochure, including columns, headings, subheadings, cover title, and cover graphic image. The formatting instructions for these parts of the brochure are contained in styles that are available to the brochure template document. In exercise 4, you are instructed to create panels 1, 2, and 3 of a brochure using the *Brochure* template. You will insert a file containing the brochure text and then you will format specific sections of the text using some of the predefined styles provided in the brochure template.

To apply a style with the Style button on the Formatting toolbar, position the insertion point in the paragraph to which you want the style applied, or select the text, then click the down-pointing triangle to the right of the Style button. Click the desired style name in the list to apply the style to the text in the document.

Creating Panels 1, 2, and 3 of a Brochure Using the Brochure Template

1. Create panels 1, 2, and 3 of the brochure shown in figure 6.8 using the *Brochure* template by completing the following steps:
   a. Choose File, then New.
   b. At the New dialog box, select the Publications tab. Make sure Document is selected in the Create New section.
   c. Double-click *Brochure* in the Publications list box.
   d. Choose File, then Page Setup.
   e. At the Page Setup dialog box, select the Margins tab.

f. Change the left and right margin settings to 0.67 inches. Leave the top and bottom margins as set. (The left and right margin settings were selected because of the unprintable zone that exists on the printer that was used to print the brochure in figures 6.8 and 6.9. If your printer will accommodate the 0.5-inch margin settings that are set in the brochure template, you may leave them at this setting. Do not worry if your line endings do not match those in the figures. However, pay close attention to the placement of your text and make adjustments if necessary [in spacing or font size] so the same text is placed in each panel and the brochure maintains the same overall appearance.)
g. Print a copy of the brochure template instructional text by completing the following steps:
   (1) With the insertion point positioned anywhere on the first page of the brochure, choose File, then Print.
   (2) At the Print dialog box, choose Current Page, then OK.
   (3) Reinsert the copy of page one into the printer so that the second page of the brochure will print correctly on the back of the first page.
   (4) Position the insertion point anywhere on page 2 and then repeat steps (1) and (2). If a message displays telling you that the margins of page 2 are outside of the printable area of the page, choose No to continue. Display the Page Setup dialog box and change the left and right margin settings to .67 inches.
   (5) Read, fold, and label the brochure panels and use this as your dummy.
h. Choose Edit, then Select All.
i. Press the Delete key to remove all the instructional text. (This will also eliminate the second page; however, you will recreate the second page when needed.)
j. Click the Show/Hide ¶ button on the Standard toolbar so that nonprinting characters, such as paragraph symbols and style indicators, display on the screen. (A style indicator is a small black square that usually appears to the left of the text where a style has been applied.)
k. To insert the file containing the brochure text, complete the following steps:
   (1) Make sure the insertion point is located at the beginning of the document, then choose Insert, then File.
   (2) At the Insert File dialog box, double-click *volunteer text.*
l. Apply the predefined styles provided in the *Brochure* template document to specific sections of text in the first panel (or column) of the brochure by completing the following steps:
   (1) With the insertion point at the beginning of the document, choose Edit, then Select All.
   (2) Click the down-pointing triangle at the right side of the Style list box located on the Formatting toolbar, then select *Body Text* from the Style drop-down list. Use the vertical scroll bar in this drop-down menu to see all the style names listed in alphabetic order. (The Body Text style will change the font for all the text in the document to 12-point Garamond. Since the majority of text in this brochure is to be formatted as *Body Text,* this will eliminate the need to frequently reapply this style.)
   (3) Press Ctrl + Home, then position the insertion point anywhere within the line that reads *Giving Is Its Own Reward.*
   (4) Select *Heading 1* from the Style drop-down list as in step (2) above.
   (5) Select the title, *Giving Is Its Own Reward,* change the type size to 26 points, and turn on bold.
   (6) With the title still selected, click once in the style list box on the Formatting toolbar (*Heading 1* should be selected), then press Enter. Make sure "Redefine" the style using the selection as an example is selected, then choose OK to redefine the current style.

(7) Select the line that reads *As a volunteer, you will:*, and select *Emphasis* from the Style drop-down list.

(8) Select the list of items that begins with *Share your skills and talents* and ends with *Make a difference in other people's lives*, and select *List Bullet* from the Style drop-down list.

(9) To align the items in the list that are more than one line of text, complete the following steps:

(a) If the list of items is not already selected, select the bulleted list.

(b) Choose Format, then Paragraph.

(c) At the Paragraph dialog box, select the Indents and Spacing tab.

(d) Click the Special option list box in the Indentation section, then select *Hanging* from the drop-down list.

(e) Key **0.15** in the By: option text box, then click OK or press Enter.

(10) Position the insertion point at the beginning of the line of text that reads *What Do Volunteers Do?* and select *Heading 2* from the Style drop-down list.

(11) Select the same line of text and turn on bold.

(12) Redefine the *Heading 2* style by following steps similar to 1.1(6) above.

(13) To end panel 1 and to continue on to panel 2, position the insertion point at the beginning of the line of text that reads *Visitor Services*, then insert a column break.

m. Apply styles to format the text in panel 2 by completing the following steps:

(1) Position the insertion point anywhere in the line that reads *Visitor Services* and select *Heading 7* from the Style drop-down list.

(2) Position the insertion point anywhere in the line that reads *Patient Services* and select *Heading 7* from the Style drop-down list.

(3) To format the block of text at the bottom of panel two, complete the following steps:

(a) Position the insertion point anywhere within the line that reads *"Sharing Responsibility for Your Family's Health"* and select *Block Quotation* from the Style drop-down list.

(b) With the insertion point within the same line of text, change the paragraph alignment to center.

(c) Choose Format, then Borders and Shading.

(d) At the Paragraph Borders and Shading dialog box, select the Shading tab.

(e) Change the Shading to 20%, then choose OK or press Enter.

(f) Select and then bold the line of text.

(4) Place a column break, if necessary, after the shaded paragraph.

n. Apply styles to format the text in panel 3 by completing the following steps:

(1) At the top of panel 3, position the insertion point anywhere within the line that reads *Staff Services* and select *Heading 7* from the Style drop-down list.

(2) Position the insertion point anywhere within the line of text that reads *Who Can Volunteer?* and select *Heading 2* from the Style drop-down list.

(3) At the end of the paragraph that starts with *The volunteers at Edward Hospital . . .*, press Enter three times.

(4) Change the paragraph alignment to right, change the type size to 11 points, turn on italics, then key **(Continued on back panel)**.

(5) If the insertion point is not already located at the top of panel four on the second page, position the insertion point at the beginning of the line that reads *About Edward Hospital . . .* and insert a column break.

2. Save the brochure and name it c06ex04, panels 1,2,3.
3. You may either print the first page of your brochure now or wait and print it in exercise 5.
4. Close c06ex04, panels 1,2,3.

FIGURE 6.8

GIVING IS ITS OWN REWARD . . .

As an Edward Hospital volunteer, you will be involved in new experiences and challenges each day. Volunteering is a job that requires giving of yourself; your pay is in the form of personal reward.

As a volunteer, you will:

- Share your skills and talents
- Develop new interests
- Learn new skills
- Make new friends
- Grow in understanding and self-awareness
- Enjoy the satisfaction that comes from helping others
- Make a difference in other people's lives

WHAT DO VOLUNTEERS DO?

Edward Hospital offers volunteer opportunities in three different areas: visitor services, patient services, and staff services.

Visitor Services

At Edward Hospital, we stand by our motto, "Sharing Responsibility for Your Family's Health." We want to show our community that those are not just words, but the way Edward Hospital really operates. Often, a volunteer is the first and last person a hospital visitor encounters. We rely on our volunteers to provide accurate information while, at the same time, acting as goodwill ambassadors for the hospital.

Patient Services

Many volunteer positions involve direct interaction with patients. Many of our volunteers make a difference simply by lending a friendly ear or by performing a small favor when it is most needed and appreciated.

For those volunteers who are uncomfortable dealing directly with patients, there are many ways to help indirectly. Many Edward Hospital volunteers bring a smile to our patients' faces without ever seeing them. For instance, volunteers sew stuffed clowns to give to pediatric patients before surgery. We are always looking to our volunteers for new ideas to help make our patients' hospital stay as pleasant as possible.

"Sharing Responsibility for Your Family's Health."

Staff Services

Many volunteers draw on their past and present work experience to generously assist various hospital departments. Staff service volunteers play an important role in the hospital's team effort to provide cost-efficient, quality healthcare.

Volunteers offer their assistance in the following areas: Business Office, Central Distribution, Fitness Center, Women's Health Center, Employee Health, Human Resources, Laboratory, Edward Institute, Medical Library, Medical Records, Pharmacy, Preadmission Testing, and Surgery.

WHO CAN VOLUNTEER?

You must be at least 15 years of age to volunteer. We ask our volunteers to commit to a regular weekly schedule. It can be a few hours once a week or several hours each day. Volunteer opportunities are available seven days a week, days and evenings.

The volunteers at Edward Hospital range in age from teenagers to professionals to retirees, bringing a wealth of skill and experience to their volunteer positions.

(Continued on back panel)

In the following exercise, you will create panels 4, 5, and 6 to complete the brochure started in exercise 4. Remember to save periodically as you are creating the panels.

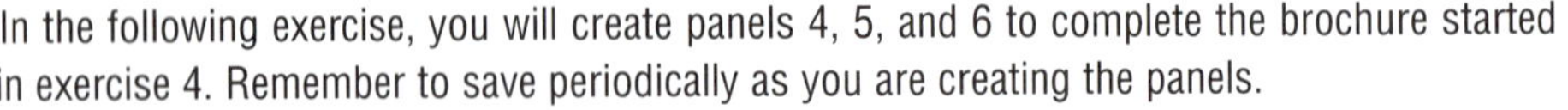

Creating Panels 4, 5, and 6 of a Brochure Using the Brochure Template

1. Open c06ex04, panels 1,2,3.
2. Save the document with Save As and name it c06ex05, volunteer brochure.
3. Create panels 4, 5, and 6 of the brochure shown in figure 6.9 by completing the following steps:
   a. Apply styles to format the text in panel 4 by completing the following steps:
      (1) Position the insertion point anywhere within the line of text that reads *About Edward Hospital . . .* (this should be located at the top of panel 4) and select *Heading 2* from the Style drop-down list.
      (2) Position the insertion point anywhere within the line of text that reads *Take The First Step . . .* and select *Heading 2* from the Style drop-down list.
      (3) In the last paragraph in panel 4 that starts with *For more information*, bold the text that reads *Cindy Bonagura, Volunteer Services Coordinator* and then bold the area code and phone number.
      (4) Position the insertion point at the beginning of the line that reads *You can make a difference at Edward Hospital* and insert a column break at this point.
   b. Apply styles to format the text in panel 5 by completing the following steps:
      (1) Press Enter three times.
      (2) Format the text in the shaded box by completing the following steps:
         (a) Position the insertion point anywhere within the text that reads *You can make a difference at Edward Hospital.* and select *Block Quotation* from the Style drop-down list.
         (b) Select the same line of text, then change the type size to 26 points, turn on bold, and change the paragraph alignment to center.
         (c) Choose Format, then Borders and Shading.
         (d) At the Paragraph Borders and Shading dialog box, select the Shading tab.
         (e) Change the Shading to 20%, then choose OK or press Enter.
      (3) Position the insertion point below the block quotation at the beginning of the first line of the address that reads *Edward Hospital*, then press Enter 7 times.
      (4) Select the hospital name and address, choose *Heading 7*, then change the paragraph alignment to center and the spacing after the paragraph (the selected text) to 0 points.
      (5) Select the name of the hospital and change the type size to 14 points.
      (6) Position the insertion point below the address at the beginning of the line that reads *Edward Hospital* and insert a column break to end panel 5.
   c. Apply styles and insert a picture to create the cover panel (panel 6) by completing the following steps:
      (1) Position the insertion point anywhere within the cover title that reads *Edward Hospital* and select *Title Cover* from the Style drop-down list.
      (2) Select *Edward Hospital*, change the paragraph alignment to center, then turn on bold. With the text still selected, display the Borders toolbar, then click the Top Border button.

(3) Position the insertion point anywhere within the text that reads *Volunteer Now . . . Giving Is Its Own Reward* and select *Subtitle Cover* from the Style drop-down list.
(4) Select the subtitle text, change the type size to 19 points, then change the paragraph alignment to center.
(5) Create the medical graphic image by completing the following steps:
   (a) Press Ctrl + End to position the insertion point after the subtitle.
   (b) Choose Insert, then Picture.
   (c) At the Insert Picture dialog box, double-click *Medstaff* in the Name list box.
(6) Scale and position the picture by completing the following steps:
   (a) Click once with the left mouse button inside the picture to select it.
   (b) Choose Format, then Picture.
   (c) At the Picture dialog box, change the Width to 115% and the Height to 175% in the Scaling section.
   (d) Click OK or press Enter.
   (e) Choose Insert, then Frame (so the picture can be positioned on the page).
   (f) Choose Format, then Frame.
   (g) At the Frame dialog box, change the Position: to Center and change the Relative To: option to Column in the Horizontal section.
   (h) In the Vertical section of the Frame dialog box, key **3.2** in the Position: text box and change the Relative To: option to Page.
   (i) Choose OK or press Enter to close the dialog box.
(7) If you were able to use 0.5 inch left and right margins, your text and picture will basically appear centered on the cover panel. If you changed your margins to match those mentioned in step 1f in exercise 4, complete the following steps to adjust the text and picture so that they appear more centered on the cover panel:
   (a) Position the insertion point at the beginning of the cover title text.
   (b) Select from this point to the end of the document, including all the cover text and the picture on the front cover panel.
   (c) Choose Format, then Paragraph.
   (d) At the Paragraph dialog box, select the Indents and Spacing tab.
   (e) In the Indentation section, key **.25** in the Left text box, then choose OK or press Enter.

d. View your brochure using the *Page Width* option located in the Zoom Control drop-down list, and then view the document using the *Whole Page* and Print Preview options. Carefully check your brochure for the correct placement of text and design elements. Make any adjustments if necessary.

4. Save the brochure again with the same name (c06ex05, volunteer brochure).
5. Print both pages of the brochure using both sides of the paper.
6. Close c06ex05, volunteer brochure.

FIGURE 6.9

ABOUT EDWARD HOSPITAL . . .

Edward Hospital was established 75 years ago as a respiratory disease sanitorium. Today, Edward Hospital operates as a full-service, not-for-profit hospital with 175 beds. Located on a 60-acre campus, Edward Hospital offers a state-of-the-art, all-private inpatient facility, as well as the Edward Cardiovascular Institute, the Women's Health Center, the Edward Health and Fitness Center, two satellite medical clinics, and Valley View Hospital—a private psychiatric facility. Over 1,500 employees work to make Edward Hospital a success.

TAKE THE FIRST STEP . . .

If you are interested in becoming a volunteer at Edward Hospital, you will need to schedule an interview. At the interview, your experience, skills, interests, and availability will be matched to those areas in need of volunteer support. An orientation will be scheduled before becoming an active volunteer. Once you start volunteering, you will receive on-the-job training from an experienced hospital employee.

For more information, please call **Cindy Bonagura, Volunteer Services Coordinator,** at: **(708) 555-3189**

You can make a difference at Edward Hospital.

Edward Hospital
801 South Washington Street
Naperville, IL 60540-9865

EDWARD HOSPITAL

Volunteer Now . . .
Giving Is Its Own Reward

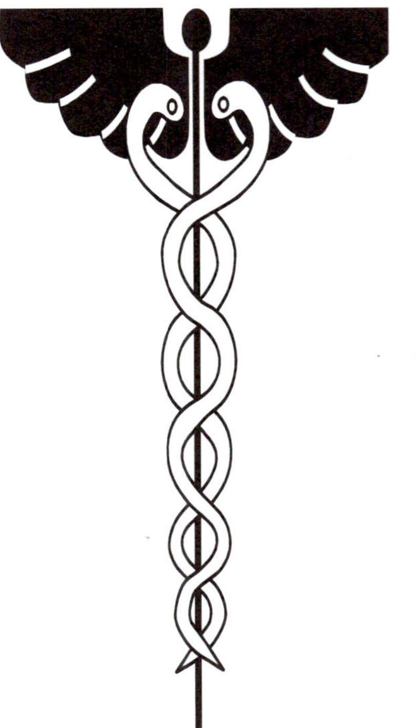

Character and Paragraph Styles

Two types of styles exist in Word—paragraph styles and character styles. A *paragraph style* applies formatting instructions to an entire paragraph, while a *character style* applies formatting to selected text only. Paragraph styles affect the paragraph that contains the insertion point or selected text. Word considers a paragraph as any text followed by a hard return. This means that even a short line with no punctuation is considered a paragraph. A paragraph style includes formatting instructions such as tabs, indents, borders, paragraph spacing, etc. Paragraph styles are useful for formatting headings, subheadings, and bulleted lists in a document.

Paragraph Style: A set of formatting instructions that is applied to an entire paragraph.

Character Style: A set of formatting instructions that applies to selected text only.

Character styles include options available at the Font dialog box such as font, font size, and font style such as bold, underlining, and italics. Character styles are useful for formatting single characters, words, or phrases.

In the Styles list (accessed through the Style dialog box or the Style button on the Formatting toolbar), paragraph styles are preceded by a ¶ symbol and character styles are preceded by an **a** character. When you used the brochure template document in exercises 4 and 5, the *Heading 1* style was a paragraph style and the *Emphasis* style was a character style. To find out if a particular style has been applied to text, position the insertion point within the line or paragraph, and the style name will display in the Style box on the Formatting toolbar. A character style can even be applied to selected text within a paragraph that has already been formatted with a paragraph style. If this is the case, you need to select the specific text first to see the character style name that has been applied to it.

Creating Styles

A style can be created in two ways. You can create a new style through the Style dialog box or you can create a style from existing text that already contains the formatting you desire. Creating a style from existing text is the easiest method.

When you create your own style, you must give the style a name. When naming a style, try to name it something that gives you an idea what the style will accomplish. Consider the following when naming a style:

- A style name can contain a maximum of 253 characters.
- A style name can contain spaces and commas.
- Do not use the backslash (\), braces ({}), or a semicolon (;) when naming a style.
- A style name is case-sensitive. Uppercase and lowercase letters can be used.
- Avoid using the names already used by Word.

To create a new style from existing text, you would complete the following steps:

1. Key a paragraph of text, such as a heading.
2. Format the text the way you want it to appear, such as changing the font, font size, applying color, etc.
3. Position the insertion point within the paragraph that contains the desired formatting; or select the text if you are creating a character style.
4. Click in the Style box on the Formatting toolbar to select the current style name.
5. Type a new name and then press Enter. The new style name is added to the list of styles available in that document.

The above method of inserting the style name in the Style text box on the Formatting toolbar automatically defines the style as a paragraph style. You must use the Style dialog box to create a character style. You can use the Style dialog box to create paragraph and character styles from existing text or from scratch. To create a new style using the Style dialog box, you would select text if necessary and then complete the following steps:

1. Choose Format, then Style.
2. At the Style dialog box, choose New.
3. At the New style dialog box, key a name for the style in the Name text box.
4. Select the Style Type option and specify whether you are creating a paragraph or character style.
5. Choose Format, then choose the desired formatting options.
6. When all formatting has been selected, make sure the correct formatting instructions display in the Description section of the dialog box.
7. If you want to assign the style to a keystroke combination, click Shortcut Key. Press the shortcut key combination in the Press New Shortcut Key text box and choose Assign.
8. If you want the style to be available to all new documents based on this template, click the Add to Template check box.
9. Choose OK or press Enter.
10. Choose Close at the Style dialog box.

When you choose Format at the New Style dialog box, a drop-down list displays with a variety of formatting options. These options, along with the formatting that can be selected with each option, are listed in Figure 6.10.

FIGURE 6.10

Formatting Options

Choose this:	To select this type of formatting instructions:
Font	Font, style, size, color, superscript, subscript, and character spacing.
Paragraph	Paragraph alignment, indentations, spacing, and line spacing. (Available for paragraph styles only.)
Tabs	Tab stop measurements, alignment, leaders, or clear tabs. (Available for paragraph styles only.)
Border	Border location, color, style, and shading. (Available for paragraph styles only.)
Language	Language that the spell checker, thesaurus, and grammar checker use for the current paragraph. (Available for paragraph styles only.)
Frame	Text wrapping, positioning, and sizing of frames. (Available for paragraph styles only.)
Numbering	Bulleted and Numbered paragraphs in various styles. (Available for paragraph styles only.)

You may also use an existing style as a base for creating a new style. The existing style is then known as the *base style*. The new style inherits all the formatting instructions included in the base style in addition to the formatting currently selected for the new style. If you make a change to the base style, the new style and any other related styles will reflect that change. For example, many of Word's predesigned styles are based on the *Normal* style. If you make a change to the Normal style, all styles based on the Normal style will be changed also. This may produce some unwanted results in your document if you applied any styles that were based on the Normal style. For this reason, **avoid making changes to the Normal style**.

Base Style: A preexisting style that is used as a base for creating a new style.

You can create your own base styles for different elements of your document. For example, suppose you want 14-point Impact headings and 12-point Impact Italic subheadings in your document. You could create a new style that contains an Impact font instruction that will serve as the base style. You could then create two separate styles for the headings and subheadings that include the specific font size and font style choices. Each style would be based on the base style that includes the Impact font selection. If in the future, you decide to change the font to Arial Rounded MT Bold, all you have to do is change the base style and the font will be changed in all the headings and subheadings.

Following One Style with Another

There are some situations where one set of formatting instructions is immediately followed by another set of formatting instructions. For instance, formatting for a heading is usually followed by formatting for body text. In Word, you can define one style to be immediately followed by another style. Pressing the Enter key after applying the first style will automatically apply the second style to the text that follows. For example, to define a heading style so that it is followed by a body text style, you would complete the following steps:

1. Create the body text style first using either the Style button on the Formatting toolbar or the Style option from the Format menu. (Creating the style that is to follow another style first is the easiest.)
2. Create the heading style using the Style option from the Format menu.
3. At the New Style dialog box, click the down-pointing triangle under the Style for Following Paragraph option, then select the body text style.
4. Choose OK or press Enter.
5. Choose Close at the Style dialog box.

Applying Styles

A style can be applied before you key text or it can be applied in a document with existing text. Applying styles to existing text is the most convenient method. How you apply a style to existing text depends on the style being used. To apply a character style to existing text, select the text first. If you are formatting a paragraph with a style, position the insertion point anywhere in the paragraph.

The most common methods of applying styles in Word include using the Style button on the Formatting toolbar and the Style command from the Format menu. To apply a style to existing text using the Style button on the Formatting toolbar, you would complete the following steps:

1. Position the insertion point in the paragraph to which you want the style applied, or select the text.
2. Click the down-pointing triangle to the right of the Style button on the Formatting toolbar.
3. Click the desired style name in the drop-down list to apply the style to the text in the document.

To apply a style using the Style command from the Format menu, you would complete the following steps:

1. Position the insertion point in the paragraph to which you want the style applied, or select the text.
2. Choose Format, then Style.
3. At the Style dialog box, choose List, then choose *All Styles*.
4. Double-click the desired style name or select the style name and click Apply.

If you want to apply the same style to different sections of text in a document, such as applying a heading style to all the headings, apply the style to the first heading. Then, move the insertion point to each of the remaining headings and press F4, Word's Repeat key.

To apply a style before text is keyed, position the insertion point where formatting is to begin and then display the Styles dialog box. From the Styles list, select the desired style and then choose Apply. You can also use the Style button on the Formatting toolbar to select a style name. If you apply a style before text is keyed, the style will affect any text you key after the style is applied, even if you begin a new paragraph. You must then apply a different style, such as the Normal style, to discontinue the first style.

In addition to applying styles with the Style button on the Formatting toolbar and the Style dialog box, you can use shortcut keys. To assign a style to a shortcut keystroke combination, refer to the Word 7 documentation.

Modifying an Existing Style

One of the advantages of using styles within a document is that a style can be modified and all occurrences of that style in the document are automatically updated. Once a style has been created, you can modify the style by changing the formatting instructions that it contains either with the Formatting toolbar or the Style dialog box. When you modify a style by changing the formatting instructions, all text to which that style has been applied is changed accordingly. To modify a style using the Formatting toolbar, you would complete the following steps:

1. Open the document that contains the style you want to modify.
2. Reformat text with the formatting instructions you want changed in the style.
3. Select the reformatted text.
4. Click the down-pointing triangle to the right of the Style button.
5. At the Styles drop-down list, click the style name you want to modify.
6. When Word asks if you want to redefine the style using the selection as an example, choose OK or press Enter.

You can also modify a style at the Style dialog box. To modify a style at the Style dialog box, you would complete the following steps:

1. Open the document containing the style you want to modify.
2. Choose Format, then Style.
3. At the Style dialog box, select the style name you want to modify in the Styles list box, then choose Modify.
4. At the Modify Style dialog box, add or delete formatting options by choosing Format, and then selecting the appropriate options.
5. When all changes have been made, choose OK or press Enter to close the Modify Style dialog box.
6. Choose Close to close the Style dialog box.

Additional formatting changes can be made to text even if a style has been previously applied to it. This is useful if you want to make a minor change to specific text without the need to redefine the whole style.

Copying Individual Styles from Other Documents and Templates

When you work on a document, you may want to use a style that already exists in one of Word's templates or in a document you may have created. For example, if you had to create some other promotional material for The Edward Cardiovascular Clinic, you could maintain consistency and reinforce the organization's identity by using the same heading and subheading styles that were created for the brochure in *c06ex06, panels 1,2.*

DTP POINTERS
Styles can help to maintain consistency and reinforce an organization's identity.

In Word, the Organizer feature lets you copy individual styles, in addition to macros, toolbars, and AutoText entries, from an existing document or template to another document or template.

For instance, to copy the *dk cyan heading* and the *dk magenta subhead* styles from *c06ex06, panels 1,2* to a fictitious document named *fact sheet* using the Organizer dialog box, as shown in figure 6.11, you would complete the following steps:

1. With the insertion point located in *fact sheet*, choose Format, then Style.
2. At the Style dialog box, click Organizer, and then select the Styles tab. By default, the name of the current document, *fact sheet*, displays above a list box on the left side of the Organizer dialog box. The list box shows a list of the styles available in the template attached to that particular document. By default, *Normal* will display as the file name on the right side of the dialog box and the list box below will display the styles available in the Normal template.
3. On the right side of the dialog box, click Close File to change the command button to Open File.
4. Click Open File.
5. Select *c06ex06 panels 1,2*, then click Open or press Enter.
6. In the right list box for *c06ex06, panels 1,2*, select *dk cyan heading*, hold down the Control key, then select *dk magenta subhead*. (Both style names should be selected.)
7. Click Copy. (The *dk cyan heading* and the *dk magenta subhead* styles will now be listed in the *fact sheet* list box on the left side of the dialog box.)
8. Click Close.

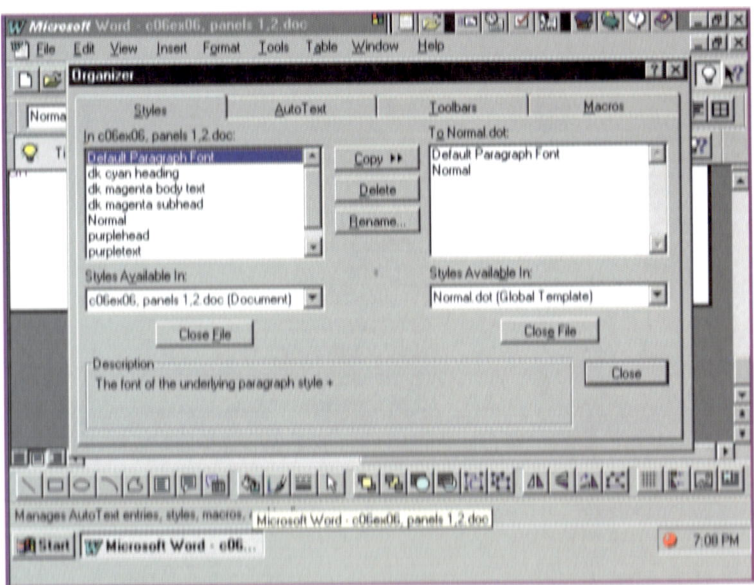

FIGURE 6.11

Style Organizer Dialog Box

A specific document does not have to be open for you to copy styles from one document or template to another. At the Organizer dialog box, you can select a different document name or template for each list box by clicking the Close File command button below either list box. This changes the command button to an Open File button. Click Open File and select the document or template you want to copy styles to or from.

The styles Organizer dialog box can be confusing because the Copy button displays triangles pointing to the right, making you think that styles must be copied from the left side to the right side. However, styles can be copied from either side. If you select a style in the list box on the right, the triangles on the Copy button change and point to the left, as do the labels above each list box.

Copying All Styles from a Template

Word's Style Gallery feature lets you copy all the styles from a template into the current document. To display the Style Gallery dialog box shown in figure 6.12, choose Format, then Style Gallery.

At the Style Gallery dialog box, the template documents are displayed in the Template list box. These are the same template documents that were mentioned in previous chapters, in addition to any you may have created on your own. The document currently open displays in the Preview of: section of the dialog box. With this section, you can choose a template name from the Template list box and see how the formatting from that template would be applied to the current document. If you accessed Style Gallery from a blank screen, the Preview box will be empty.

At the bottom of the Style Gallery dialog box, the Document option is selected in the Preview section. If you select a template name from the Template list box, and then choose Example from the Preview section, Word will insert a sample of the template document in the Preview of: section. Choosing Style Samples will cause the styles from the selected template to display in the Preview of: box.

To copy all the styles from a specific template into the current document, you would complete the following steps:

1. With the insertion point positioned in the current document, choose Format, then Style Gallery.
2. In the Template list box, select the template name that contains the styles you want to copy.
3. Choose OK or press Enter.

FIGURE 6.12

Style Gallery Dialog Box

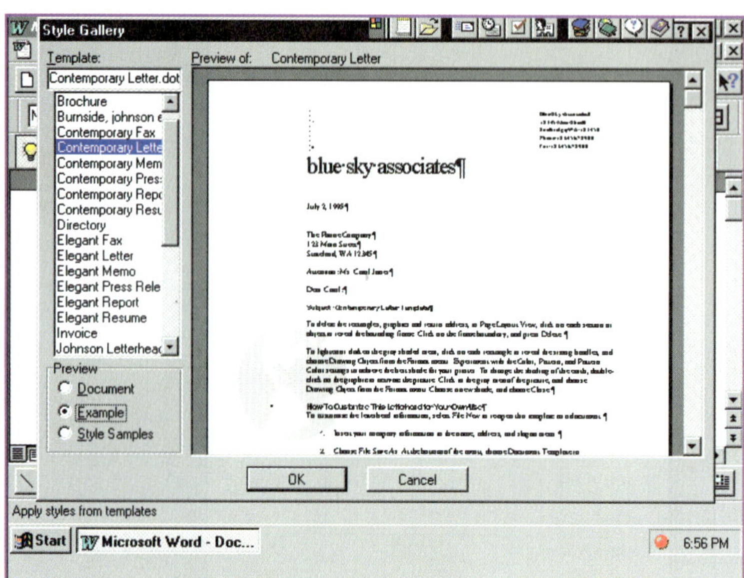

Removing a Style from Text

If you wish to remove a style immediately after applying it, click the Undo button on the Standard toolbar. When a style is removed, the style that was previously applied to the text is applied once again (usually this is the Normal style). Since only one style can be applied at a time to the same text, you can also remove a style from text by applying a new style. To remove a character style, select the text, then press Ctrl + Spacebar. The text will revert to the Normal style.

Using Drop Caps As A Design Element

In publications such as magazines, newsletters, or brochures, a graphics feature called drop cap can be used to enhance the appearance of text. A *drop cap* is the first letter of the first word in a paragraph that is set in a larger font size and set into a paragraph. Drop caps identify the beginning of major sections or parts of a document.

Drop Cap: The first letter of the first word in a paragraph, set in a larger font size and set into the paragraph.

Drop caps look best when set in a paragraph containing text set in a proportional font. The drop cap can be set in the same font as the paragraph text or it can be set in a complementary font. For example, a drop cap can be set in a sans serif font while the paragraph text is set in a serif font. A drop cap can be one character or the entire first word of a paragraph. The examples in figure 6.13 show some of the ways drop caps can be created and formatted.

FIGURE 6.13

This drop cap is set in Times New Roman, the same font as the body text. The drop cap was customized by selecting the Dropped position and setting the Lines to Drop to 2 lines in the Drop Cap dialog box. The Distance from Text is set at 0.05 inches.

This drop cap is set in Brush Script MT Italic, while the body text is set in Times New Roman. The drop cap was customized by selecting the In Margin position and setting the Lines to Drop to 3 lines in the Drop Cap dialog box. The Distance from Text was left at 0 inches. The drop cap was then selected and the font color was changed to red.

This drop cap is set in Kino MT Italic and the text is set in Garamond. The drop cap was customized by selecting the Dropped position and setting the Lines to Drop to 3 lines in the Drop Cap dialog box. The Distance from Text was set at 0.1 inches. The drop cap was selected and the text color changed to white. Shading of Solid (100%) black was then added to the frame through the Borders and Shading dialog box.

This drop cap is set in Wide Latin and the text is set in Book Antiqua. The drop cap was customized by selecting the Dropped position and setting the Lines to Drop to 2 lines in the Drop Cap dialog box. The Distance from Text was left at the default of 0 inches. The drop cap was then selected and the font color was changed to Dk Magenta.

This drop cap is set in Algerian and the text is set in Century Schoolbook Italic, Dk Blue. The drop cap was customized by selecting the Dropped position and the Lines to Drop to 4 lines in the Drop Cap dialog box. The Distance from Text was changed to 0.05 inches. A red shadow border, 3 points in weight, and Solid (100%) White shading were added to the frame. The drop cap was then selected and the font color was changed to Dk Blue.

This drop cap is set in Times New Roman, the same as the body text. The first word was formatted as a drop cap by selecting the word first and then choosing the Dropped position from the Drop Cap dialog box. The other options in the Drop Cap dialog box were not changed.

1 This drop cap is set in Arial, the same as the body text. The drop cap character is a symbol from the Wingdings character set. The symbol was inserted first and then it was selected before accessing the Drop Cap dialog box. The drop cap was customized by selecting the Dropped position and setting the Lines to Drop to 2 lines in the Drop Cap dialog box. The Distance from Text was left at the default of 0 inches. The drop cap was then selected and the font color was changed to Dk Cyan.

This drop cap was set in Arial Rounded MT Bold, the same font as the body text. The drop cap character is a symbol from the Wingdings character set. The symbol was inserted first and then it was selected before accessing the Drop Cap dialog box. The drop cap was customized by selecting the Dropped position and setting the Lines to Drop to 4 lines in the Drop Cap dialog box. The Distance from Text was left at 0 inches. The drop cap was then selected and the font color was changed to blue.

A drop cap can only be applied to existing text. To create a drop cap, you would complete the following steps:

1. Position the insertion point within the paragraph to be formatted with a drop cap. If a special symbol starts the paragraph, select the symbol first.
2. Choose Format, then Drop Cap.
3. At the Drop Cap dialog box, shown in figure 6.14, select Dropped in the Position section to create a drop cap that is set into the paragraph with the remaining text wrapping around it; or select In Margin to create a drop cap that is positioned in the margin to the left of the paragraph.
4. Choose Font in the Drop Cap dialog box to select the desired font for the drop cap letter only. This does not affect the remaining paragraph text.
5. Choose the Lines to Drop option to set the number of lines (from 1–10 lines) that the drop cap will be vertically set into the paragraph. This option affects both the height and width of the drop cap letter.
6. Choose Distance from Text to set the amount of distance the drop cap is positioned in relation to the paragraph text.
7. Choose OK or press Enter.
8. The drop cap is placed within a frame in your document. You can customize the drop cap letter by selecting the letter within the frame and changing the font color and font style. You can also apply other formatting, such as borders and shading, to the frame itself.

Customized drop caps can be an attractive addition to a design, as illustrated in figure 6.13. Practice restraint when using this design element.

FIGURE 6.14

Drop Cap Dialog Box

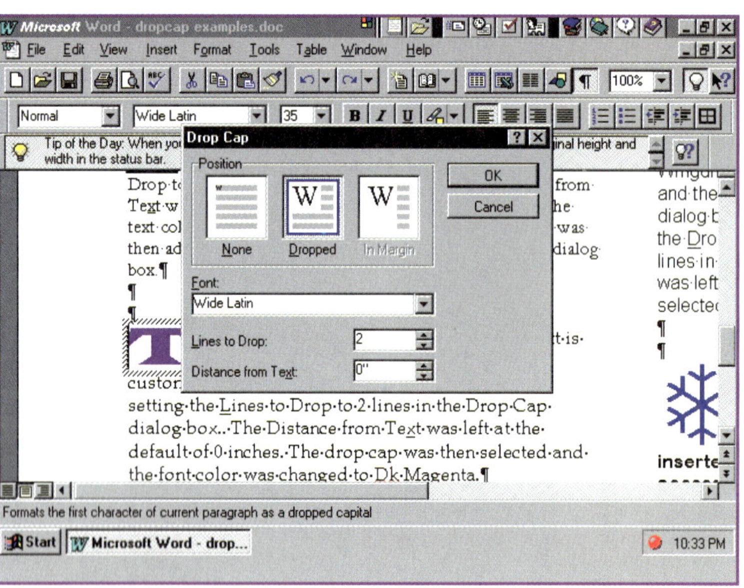

In exercise 6, you will create the inside panels of a single-fold brochure using various design and formatting techniques, including a drop cap and styles.

Creating the Inside Panels of a Single-Fold Brochure Using Styles and a Drop Cap

1. Create a dummy for a single-fold brochure using standard size 8½-by-11-inch paper in landscape orientation. Label the panels on one side of the page as Panel 1 (Inside) and Panel 2 (Inside). Label the panels on the other side as Panel 3 (Back) and Panel 4 (Cover). Refer to the dummy when creating the brochure to ensure that you are keying the appropriate text in the correct location. Remember to save your document periodically as you are working.

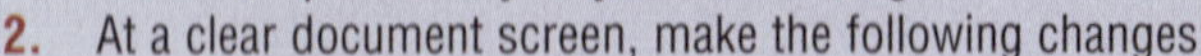

2. At a clear document screen, make the following changes:
   a. Change the paper orientation to Landscape. Make sure the paper size is Letter 8.5 by 11 inches.
   b. Change the top and bottom margins to 0.5 and the left and right margins to 0.67 inches.
   c. Choose Format, then Columns.
   d. At the Columns dialog box, change the number of columns to 2, then choose OK or press Enter.
   e. Display the Font dialog box, then select the Character Spacing tab. Turn on Kerning for Fonts at 14 Points and Above, then choose OK or press Enter to close the dialog box.
   f. Insert the file containing the text that is contained in the inside panels of the brochure shown in figure 6.15 by completing the following steps:
      (1) Choose Insert, then File.
      (2) At the Insert File dialog box, double-click *heart text* in the Look in list box. (The specific location of your student data disk files may vary.)
3. Create styles for the headings, subheadings, and body text, and format the text for the inside panels of the single-fold brochure shown in figure 6.15 by completing the following steps:
   a. Format the drop cap paragraph by completing the following steps:
      (1) Click the Show/Hide ¶ button on the Standard toolbar to display nonprinting symbols.
      (2) Select the first paragraph, then change the font to 16-point Arial Italic, Dk Magenta.
      (3) With the paragraph still selected, choose Format, then Paragraph.
      (4) At the Paragraph dialog box, select the Indents and Spacing tab.
      (5) Change the Line Spacing to 1.5 Lines, then click OK or press Enter.
      (6) Position the insertion point anywhere within the same paragraph, then choose Format, then Drop Cap.
      (7) At the Drop Cap dialog box, choose Dropped in the Position section.
      (8) Click the down-pointing triangle to the right of the Font list box, then select Impact as the font.
      (9) Make sure the Lines to Drop option displays 3.
      (10) Change the Distance from Text to 0.1 inches.
      (11) Choose OK or press Enter.
      (12) Make sure the frame around the drop cap is selected, then display the Font dialog box. At the Font dialog box, change the Font Style to Bold and the Color to Dk Cyan. Click OK or press Enter to close the dialog box.
      (13) Position the insertion point at the end of the same paragraph, then press Enter.
   b. Format the first heading, then create a style from the heading by completing the following steps:
      (1) Select *Diabetes: The Latest News* and change the font to 16-point Impact Bold, Dk Cyan.
      (2) Choose Format, then Paragraph, and then make the following changes at the Paragraph dialog box:

(a) Select the Indents and Spacing tab. In the Spacing section, click once on the up-pointing triangle to the right of the After list box to change the amount to 6 pt.

(b) Select the Text Flow tab. In the Pagination section, click the check box to the left of Keep with Next so that the heading will always stay with the paragraph that follows and will not be separated by a column break or a page break.

(c) Click OK or press Enter.

(3) Position the insertion point anywhere within the heading just formatted (the heading can still be selected). Click the Style list box on the Formatting toolbar to select the style name that is currently in the box.

(4) Key **dk cyan heading** and then press Enter. (This heading style will then be added to the list of styles available for this brochure.)

c. Format the first subheading (day, date, name, and title) and then create a style from the subheading by completing the following steps:

(1) Select **Tuesday, March 11, 1997** and **Katherine Dwyer, M.D.**

(2) Change the font to 12-point Arial Bold Italic, Dk Magenta.

(3) Choose Format, Paragraph, and then make the following changes at the Paragraph dialog box:

(a) Select the Indents and Spacing tab. Change the Left Indentation to 0.3 inches.

(b) Select the Text Flow tab. In the Pagination section, click the check box to the left of Keep with Next.

(c) Click OK or press Enter to close the dialog box.

(4) Position the insertion point anywhere within the subheading just formatted (the subheading can still be selected). Click the Style list box on the Formatting toolbar to select the style name that is currently in the box.

(5) Key **dk magenta subhead** and then press Enter. (This subheading style will then be added to the list of styles available for this brochure.)

d. Format the body text and then create a style for the body text by completing the following steps:

(1) Select the paragraph that begins with *One of the best ways* . . . and ends with . . .*new medical recommendations.*

(2) Change the font to 12-point Arial, Dk Magenta.

(3) Change the Left Indentation to 0.3 inches and make the spacing Before the paragraph 6 points and the spacing After 24 points.

(4) Position the insertion point anywhere within the paragraph just formatted (the paragraph can still be selected). Click the Style list box on the Formatting toolbar to select the style name that is currently in the box.

(5) Key **dk magenta body text** and then press Enter. (This body text style will then be added to the list of styles available for this brochure.)

e. Format the second heading by completing the following steps:

(1) Position the insertion point anywhere in the heading that reads *New Advances in Cardiac Surgery.*

(2) Click the down-pointing triangle to the right of the Style list box on the Formatting toolbar and select *dk cyan heading* from the Style drop-down list.

f. Format the second subheading by completing the following steps:

(1) Select *Tuesday, March 25, 1997* and *Christine Johnson, M.D.*

(2) Click the down-pointing triangle to the right of the Style list box on the Formatting toolbar and select *dk magenta subhead* from the Style drop-down list.

g. Format the second paragraph of body text by completing the following steps:

(1) Position the insertion point within the paragraph that begins with *Advances in minimally* . . . and ends with . . . *leads an informative discussion.*

(2) Click the down-pointing triangle to the right of the Style list box on the Formatting toolbar and select *dk magenta body text* from the Style drop-down list.

h. Apply the *dk cyan heading*, the *dk magenta subhead*, and the *dk magenta body text* styles to the remaining headings, subheads, and body text (up to but not including *All lectures: . . .)* in the brochure as illustrated in figure 6.15.

i. Select from *All lectures:* until the end of the document and change the font to 12-point Arial, Dk Cyan.

j. With the same text still selected, change the left indention to 0.3 inches.

k. Insert tabs to align the lecture information (time and location) as indicated in figure 6.15.

l. Position the insertion point after *Naperville, Illinois* and press Enter.

m. Select the last paragraph, change the font style to italics, and then change the paragraph alignment to center.

n. With the insertion point on page one, insert the watermark (yellow heart image) by completing the following steps:

(1) Click the Zoom Control button on the Standard toolbar and change the viewing mode to Whole Page.

(2) Display the Drawing toolbar.

(3) Click the Text Box button, position the crosshairs in the approximate location of the watermark, then draw a box. (This does not have to be exact.)

(4) Make sure the Fill Color and the Line Color of the text box is set to None.

(5) Choose Insert, then Picture. At the Insert Picture dialog box, double-click *Heart* in the Name list box. (Since the text box containing the heart image is in the drawing layer, the heart image will be on top of the text at this point.)

(6) Double-click inside the heart image to open the image in the Picture editing window.

(7) Click the Select Drawing Objects button on the Drawing toolbar. Position the mouse pointer outside, above, and to the left of the grid lines surrounding the heart. Click and drag the crosshairs to form an outline around the whole heart, including the grid lines. (The heart should display with selection handles within and on all four sides of the heart.)

(8) Choose Format, then Drawing Object. At the Drawing Object dialog box, select the Fill tab.

(9) Change the Color to yellow, select 50% from the Patterns drop-down list, and then select White as the Pattern Color.

(10) Click OK or press Enter to close the dialog box.

(11) Click Close Picture in the Picture dialog box to return to your document.

(12) Size and position the heart image by completing the following steps:

(a) Click once inside the heart to select it, and then use the sizing handles to widen and lengthen the heart image so that it resembles the heart in figure 6.15.

(b) With the picture still selected, choose Format, then Drawing Object. At the Drawing Object dialog box, select the Size and Position tab.

(c) In the Position section, make the Horizontal setting 4.2 inches From: Page and the Vertical setting 1.4 inches From: Page.

(d) With the picture still selected, click the Send Behind Text button on the Drawing toolbar. (The heart should appear as a watermark behind the existing text.)

4. Save panels 1 and 2 of the brochure and name it c06ex06, panels 1,2. (If the document contains a blank second page, delete it so that you are only saving the first page.)

5. Print and then close *c06ex06, panels 1,2*. (Panels 1 and 2 will also be printed as part of the next exercise.)

FIGURE 6.15

fit heart can contribute to a long, healthy life for you and the ones you love. Join experts at the Edward Cardiovascular Institute to learn how to keep yours beating strong.

Diabetes: The Latest News

Tuesday, March 11, 1997
Katherine Dwyer, M.D.

One of the best ways to manage any medical condition is to keep abreast of the very latest information. Join endocrinologist Katherine Dwyer, M.D., for an up-to-the-minute discussion of the latest diabetes clinical trials, revised treatment guidelines, and new medical recommendations.

New Advances In Cardiac Surgery

Tuesday, March 25, 1997
Christine Johnson, M.D.

Advances in minimally invasive surgical procedures are helping patients get back to active, healthy lives more quickly—and more safely—than ever. Today, cardiac surgical procedures are marked by shorter hospital stays and recovery times, and lower costs. Learn more about these advances as Christine Johnson, M.D., leads an informative discussion.

Exercise—Is It the Fountain of Youth?

Tuesday, April 8, 1997
Joan Polak, M.D.

Everyone knows that exercise is good for your heart. Now, learn from a cardiologist exactly why it is good for you and what exercises provide the greatest benefits. Learn the specifics behind the "Just Do It" philosophy from Dr. Joan Polak.

Setting Up a Heart-Healthy Kitchen

Tuesday, April 22, 1997
Kaitlin Anzalone, Registered Dietitian

A great start to beginning a heart-healthy diet is doing a heart-check of your kitchen. Join us for practical tips and suggestions for setting up your kitchen.

Diabetes and Cardiovascular Disease

Tuesday, May 6, 1997
Wilma Schaenfeld, M.D.

During this session, we will discuss the clinical features of heart disease in the diabetic, as well as what you can do to reduce the likelihood of future problems.

All lectures: 7:00 to 8:30 p.m.
Edward Cardiovascular Institute
120 Spalding Drive
Naperville, Illinois

The talk is FREE, but because space is limited, please register by calling (708) 555-4941.

In exercise 7, you will create the back and cover (panels 3 and 4) of the heart brochure started in exercise 6. This exercise involves editing the heart image to change the fill color, using text boxes to place text, and using WordArt to create the rotated return address.

Creating the Back (Panel 3) and Cover (Panel 4) of a Single-Fold Brochure

1. Open c06ex06, panels 1,2.
2. Save the document with Save As and name it c06ex07, heart brochure.
3. Press Ctrl + End to move the insertion point to the end of the document, then insert a next page section break.
4. Change the left paragraph indentation to 0 inches at the Paragraph dialog box.
5. Create the back (panel 3) and cover (panel 4) as illustrated in figure 6.16 by completing the following steps:
   a. Use WordArt to create the return mailing address in panel 3 by completing the following steps:
      (1) Choose Insert, then Object.
      (2) At the Object dialog box, select the Create New tab.
      (3) Double-click WordArt 2.0 or 3.0 in the Object Type list box.
      (4) In the text entry box, key the following text, ending lines where indicated and including a blank line between the company name and address:

      EDWARD
      CARDIOVASCULAR
      INSTITUTE

      One ECI Plaza
      120 Spalding Drive, Suite 102
      Naperville, IL 60540-9865

      (5) On the WordArt toolbar, make sure the Line and Shape button displays Plain Text, the Font button displays Arial, and the Font Size button displays Best Fit.
      (6) Click the Bold button on the WordArt toolbar to turn on bolding.
      (7) Click the Alignment button on the WordArt toolbar, then select Left.
      (8) Click the Special Effects button on the WordArt toolbar. At the Special Effects dialog box, change the rotation to 90%, then click OK or press Enter to close the dialog box.
      (9) Click the Shading button on the WordArt toolbar. At the Shading dialog box, click the down-pointing triangle to the right of the Foreground list box, then select Teal. Click OK or press Enter to close the dialog box.
      (10) Click in the document screen outside the text entry box to remove the text entry box.
   b. Position and format the frame containing the return address information by completing the following steps:
      (1) Choose Insert, then Frame.
      (2) Choose Format, then Frame.
      (3) At the Frame dialog box, change the Horizontal Position to 0.4 inches Relative To: Page and the Vertical Position to 6 inches Relative To: Page.
      (4) Choose OK or press Enter to close the dialog box.

(5) Use the Zoom Control option on the Standard toolbar and change the view to Whole Page so you can see the location of the return address. Continue to change the size of the viewing area as needed.
(6) With the WordArt text box still selected, choose Format, then Borders and Shading.
(7) At the Paragraph Borders and Shading dialog box, select the Borders tab.
(8) Click the Box option in the Presets section.
(9) In the Style section, select 4 ½ pt as the border thickness.
(10) In the Color section, select Dk Magenta for the border color.
(11) In the Border section, click once on the top and bottom borders to remove them from the frame. Leave the borders on the left and right sides.
(12) Click OK or press Enter when done.

c. Click outside the WordArt text box to deselect it. (Make sure the insertion point is positioned at the top of panel 3. You may want to change the zoom to whole page.)
d. With the insertion point positioned at the top of panel 3, insert a column break.
e. Create the heart image on the front cover by completing the following steps:
(1) With the insertion point positioned at the top of panel 4, choose Insert, then Picture.
(2) At the Insert Picture dialog box, double-click *Heart* in the Name list box.
(3) Change the color of the heart image by completing the following steps:
(a) Double-click inside the heart image to insert the image into Word's Picture editor.
(b) Click once in the upper left-hand corner of the heart to select the top half of the heart.
(c) On the Drawing toolbar, click the Fill Color button, then select Dk Cyan in the seventh row, second column.
(d) Click once in the bottom pointed area of the heart image to select the bottom half of the heart.
(e) Click the Fill Color button on the Drawing toolbar, then select Dk Magenta in the eighth row, second column.
(f) Click Close Picture in the Picture dialog box.

f. Size the heart by completing the following steps:
(1) Click inside the heart image to select it.
(2) Choose Format, then Picture.
(3) At the Picture dialog box, change the Width to 4.8 inches and the Height to 6.95 inches in the Size section.
(4) Click OK or press Enter.

g. Position the heart on the front cover by completing the following steps:
(1) Choose Insert, then Frame. (The image will move to the left side of the page; the position will be corrected in the following steps.)
(2) Choose Format, then Frame.
(3) At the Frame dialog box, change the Horizontal Position to Right Relative To: Margin and change the Vertical Position to Center Relative To: Page.
(4) Click OK or press Enter.

h. Create four separate text boxes (text boxes make positioning the text in a specific location easier) to hold the text inside the heart by completing the following steps:
(1) Display the Drawing toolbar.
(2) Click the Text Box button, then position the crosshairs in the upper left

portion of the heart. Draw a text box that will contain the word *for*. (Do not worry about the exact size or position at this time.)

(3) Click the Fill Color button on the Drawing toolbar and make sure None is selected. Click the Line Color button and make sure None is selected.

(4) Change the font to 24-point Impact, yellow.

(5) Key **for** then size and position the text box with the mouse, if necessary. (Check the position of this text box in figure 6.16.)

(6) Create a second text box that will contain the word *your* by following steps (2) through (5) above. Size and position the text box with the mouse, if necessary, so it appears as shown in figure 6.16.

(7) Create a third text box that will contain the word *Heart's* by following steps (2) through (5) above, except change the font size to 48-point Impact, yellow. Size and position the text box with the mouse, if necessary, so it appears as shown in figure 6.16.

(8) Create a fourth text box that will contain the word *sake* by following steps (2) through (5) above. Size and position the text box with the mouse, if necessary, so it appears as shown in figure 6.16.

i. Create a fifth text box to hold the *Presented by:* information by completing the following steps:

(1) Create a text box in the bottom left corner of the brochure cover. (Check the position of this text box in figure 6.16.)

(2) Change the font to 12-point Impact Italic, Dk Magenta.

(3) Key **Presented by:**.

(4) Press Enter once.

(5) Change the font to 16-point Impact Italic, Dk Cyan, Small Caps.

(6) Key **The Edward Cardiovascular Institute**, ending each line as illustrated in figure 6.16.

(7) Position the insertion point on any character in *Presented by:*, display the Paragraph dialog box, then change Spacing After the paragraph to 6 pt.

(8) Select *The Edward Cardiovascular Institute*, display the Paragraph dialog box, then change the Line Spacing to Exactly At 14 pt.

(9) Size and position the text box as needed.

j. Create a sixth text box that will contain the words *Spring 1997* by completing the following steps:

(1) Create a text box in the bottom right corner of the brochure cover. (Check the position of this text box in figure 6.16.)

(2) Change the font to 22-point Impact, Dk Cyan.

(3) Key **Spring 1997**.

(4) Size and position the text box as needed.

6. Save the document again with the same name (c06ex07, heart brochure).
7. Print both pages of the brochure using both sides of the paper. Refer to the directions for printing in exercise 1, if necessary.
8. Close c06ex07, heart brochure.

FIGURE 6.16

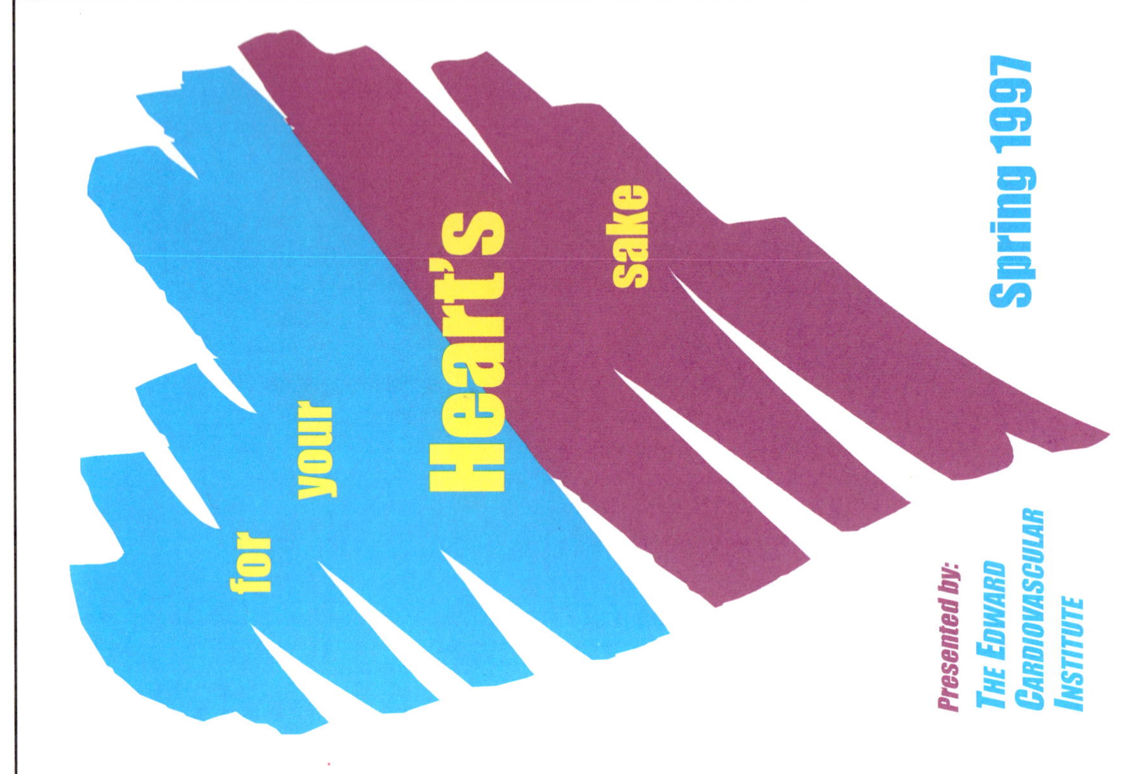
for
your
Heart's
sake
Spring 1997
Presented by:
The Edward
Cardiovascular
Institute
EDWARD
CARDIOVASCULAR
INSTITUTE
One ECI Plaza
120 Spalding Drive, Suite 102
Naperville, IL 60540-9865

Chapter Summary

- A brochure can be used to inform, educate, promote, or sell. It can also be used to establish an organization's identity and image.
- The manner in which a brochure is folded determines the order in which the panels are set on the page. Folds create distinct sections in which to place blocks of text. The most common brochure fold is called a letter fold.
- A dummy can be created to help determine the location of information on the brochure page layout.
- Consistent elements in a brochure are necessary to maintain continuity in a multipage brochure.
- The easiest method of creating a brochure page layout is to use the Columns feature.
- Column formatting can be varied within the same document by using section breaks to separate the different column formatting sections.
- Reverse text can be created in a document as a design element and usually refers to white text set against a solid black background. Reverse text can also be created with different colors for the text and the background as well as shading.
- The front cover of a brochure sets the mood and tone for the whole brochure. The front cover title must attract attention and let the reader know what the brochure is about.
- Formatting that applies to a variety of documents on a regular basis or that maintains consistency in a single publication can be applied to text using a style. A style can be edited and any occurrence of the style in the document is automatically updated to reflect the changes.
- The Normal style from the *Normal* template is automatically applied to any text that is keyed unless you specify other formatting instructions.
- Word provides two types of styles—*character* and *paragraph*. A character style applies formatting to selected text only. A paragraph style affects the paragraph that contains the insertion point or selected text.
- A style can be modified and all occurrences of that style in the document are automatically updated.
- A drop cap is a design element where the first letter of the first word in a paragraph is set in a larger font size and set into the paragraph.

Commands Review

	Mouse/Keyboard
Columns dialog box	Format, Columns
Insert a column break	Insert, Break, Column Break; or Ctrl + Shift + Enter
Insert a page break	Insert, Break, Page Break; or Ctrl + Enter
Move insertion point between columns	Position I-beam pointer at desired location, click left button; or Alt + Up arrow (top of previous column), Alt + down arrow (top of next column)

Character Spacing and Kerning	Format, Font, Character Spacing tab
Frame dialog box	Format, Frame
Paragraph Borders and Shading dialog box	Format, Borders and shading
Drop Cap dialog box	Format, Drop Cap
Insert Picture dialog box	Insert, Picture
Style dialog box	Format, Style
Style Organizer dialog box	Format, Style, Organizer, Styles tab
Style Gallery dialog box	Format, Style Gallery
Font dialog box	Format, Font; or click the font list box, type size list box, and/or character formatting buttons on the Formatting toolbar
Drawing Object dialog box	Format, Drawing Object
Display Drawing toolbar	Click Drawing button on Standard toolbar; or right-click Standard toolbar, select Drawing; or View, Toolbars, select Drawing, then press Enter
Borders toolbar	Click the Borders button on the Formatting toolbar; or right-click Standard toolbar, select Borders; or View, Toolbars, select Borders; press Enter
Draw a frame	Insert, Frame, position crosshairs and draw frame
Insert frame around selected text	Select text, choose Insert, Frame
Size and position a frame	Select frame, choose Format, Frame

Check Your Understanding

Terms: Match the terms with the correct definitions by writing the letter of the term on the blank line in front of the correct definition.

A.	Applying	**H.**	Paragraph style
B.	Style	**I.**	Parallel
C.	Character style	**J.**	Column Break
D.	Page Layout View	**K.**	Columns dialog box
E.	Drop cap	**L.**	Reverse text
F.	Dummy	**M.**	All Styles
G.	Panels	**N.**	Newspaper columns

_______ **1.** Folds in a brochure that all run in the same direction.

_______ **2.** The sections that divide a brochure page.

_______ **3.** A mock-up of a brochure.

_______ **4.** In this type of formatting, text flows from top to bottom in the first column, then to the top of the next column, and so on.

_______ **5.** Use this dialog box to create columns of unequal width.

_______ **6.** This viewing mode allows you to view columns as they will appear when printed.

_______ **7.** Insert this (or these) into a document to control where columns end and begin on the page.

_______ **8.** A set of formatting instructions saved with a name to be used repeatedly on different sections of text.

_______ **9.** Choose this at the Style dialog box to display all the available styles in Word.

_______ **10.** The name for the first letter of the first word in a paragraph that is set in a larger font size and set into the paragraph.

_______ **11.** The name for white text set against a black background.

Concepts: Write your answers to the following questions in the space provided.

1. What is the purpose of creating a dummy before creating a brochure?
2. What is the biggest advantage of using styles?
3. What is the difference between a paragraph style and a character style?
4. What styles could you create for the text in figure 6.5 to save time and keystrokes in the document creation process?
5. Explain the difference between using the Style Organizer versus the Style Gallery to use styles from other templates or documents.
6. How can drop caps and reverse text serve as design elements in a document?

Skill Assessments

Assessment 1

1. Create a dummy for a three-panel brochure using standard size 8½-by-11-inch paper in landscape orientation. Label the panels. Refer to the dummy when creating the brochure to ensure that you are keying the appropriate text in the correct location. Remember to save your document periodically as you are working.
2. At a clear document screen, create the brochure panels shown in figure 6.17 by completing the following steps (make any adjustments you feel necessary as you format the text in the brochure):
   a. Change the paper orientation to Landscape.
   b. Change the top and bottom margins to 0.5 and the left and right margins to 0.67 inches.
   c. Format the page for three equal width columns with 0.75 inches spacing between columns.
   d. Turn on kerning for fonts at 14 points and above.
   e. Insert *art text,* located on your student data disk. This file contains the brochure text displayed in figures 6.17 and 6.18.
   f. Format the first main heading, *SUPPORTING FINE ART*, and create a style from the existing formatting according to the following specifications:
      (1) Change the font to 15-point Garamond, Dk Magenta.
      (2) Change the spacing after the paragraph to 42 points.

(3) Change the alignment to center.
(4) Name the style *Dk Magenta heading.*

g. Format the first subheading, *Art League Offerings*, and create a style from the existing formatting according to the following specifications:
   (1) Change the font to 13-point Garamond, Bold Italic.
   (2) Change the spacing after the paragraph to 14 points.
   (3) Change the alignment to center.
   (4) Name the style *Black subhead.*
h. Format the first bullet, including the text that follows; create a style from the existing formatting; and apply the style according to the following specifications:
   (1) Select *Studio and Gallery Open to the Public.*
   (2) Display the Bullets and Numbering dialog box, select the Bulleted tab, then choose Modify.
   (3) Select the bullet—the quill pen symbol—from the Monotype Sorts character set (located in the first row, tenth column from the right).
   (4) Change the type size to 12 points.
   (5) Change the color to Dk Magenta.
   (6) Make sure the bullet is left aligned and indented 0.25 inches from the text.
   (7) Use the Font and Font Size button on the Formatting Toolbar to change the font to 12-point Garamond.
   (8) Change the spacing after the paragraph to 18 points and select a hanging indent of 0.25 inches.
   (9) Name the style *Quill bullet list.*
   (10) Select the remaining bulleted items in panel 1 and apply the *Quill bullet list* style.
i. Insert the paint splat image first and then edit, size, and position the picture as instructed. When you create the paint splat image at the bottom of panel 1, the default size of the picture will force it to the top of panel 2. When the size and position are adjusted, it will display at the bottom of panel 1. When changing the color of the image, use the Select Drawing Objects button on the Drawing toolbar first to select the whole image before changing the fill color.
j. When done creating the paint splat image, position the insertion point at the beginning of the text to be placed in the next panel and then insert a column break.
k. Insert column breaks where necessary. Use the previously created styles to format headings, subheadings, etc., as you proceed through the document.
l. When copying and pasting the paint splat image from panel 1 to panel 2, the image will display on top of the image in panel 1 because the position of the image is copied also. Follow the positioning specifications listed at the bottom of panel 2 in figure 6.17 to position the image correctly. This does not happen when copying the image from panel 2 to panel 3.
m. Insert column breaks where necessary. Use the previously created styles to format headings, subheadings, etc., as you proceed through the document.
n. Format the first heading in the shaded bordered box, *September 13 & 14, 1997*, and create a style from the existing formatting according to the following specifications:
   (1) Change the font to 12-point Garamond Bold and the alignment to center.
   (2) Name the style *Box heading.*
o. Format the first line of regular body text, *Four Corners Art League Art Fair,* and create a style from the existing formatting according to the following specifications:
   (1) Change the font to 12-point Garamond.
   (2) Name the style *Art body text.*
p. Apply the styles and format the remaining text in panels 2 and 3 as indicated by the handwritten instructions. When left indenting the text in panel 3, select the bulleted lists separately. Make any adjustments to spacing or positioning of text as you deem necessary.

3. Save the inside panels of the art gallery brochure and name it c06sa01, panels 1,2,3.
4. Print and then close *c06sa01, panels 1,2,3.*

FIGURE 6.17

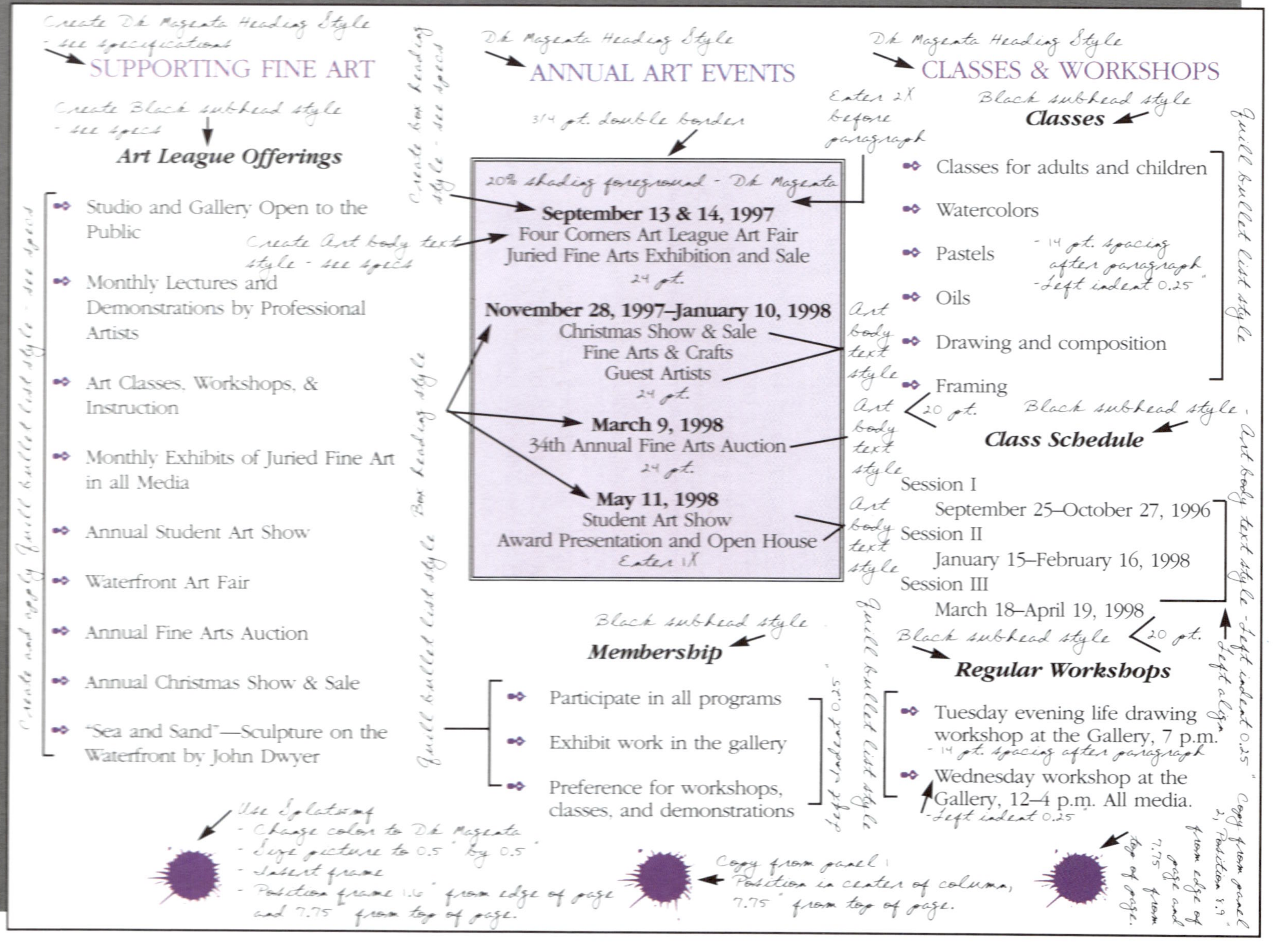
SUPPORTING FINE ART
Art League Offerings
Studio and Gallery Open to the Public
Monthly Lectures and Demonstrations by Professional Artists
Art Classes, Workshops, & Instruction
Monthly Exhibits of Juried Fine Art in all Media
Annual Student Art Show
Waterfront Art Fair
Annual Fine Arts Auction
Annual Christmas Show & Sale
"Sea and Sand"—Sculpture on the Waterfront by John Dwyer
ANNUAL ART EVENTS
September 13 & 14, 1997
Four Corners Art League Art Fair
Juried Fine Arts Exhibition and Sale
November 28, 1997–January 10, 1998
Christmas Show & Sale
Fine Arts & Crafts
Guest Artists
March 9, 1998
34th Annual Fine Arts Auction
May 11, 1998
Student Art Show
Award Presentation and Open House
Membership
Participate in all programs
Exhibit work in the gallery
Preference for workshops, classes, and demonstrations
CLASSES & WORKSHOPS
Classes
Classes for adults and children
Watercolors
Pastels
Oils
Drawing and composition
Framing
Class Schedule
Session I
September 25–October 27, 1996
Session II
January 15–February 16, 1998
Session III
March 18–April 19, 1998
Regular Workshops
Tuesday evening life drawing workshop at the Gallery, 7 p.m.
Wednesday workshop at the Gallery, 12–4 p.m. All media.
Create Dk Magenta Heading Style - see specifications
Create Black subhead style - see specs
Create and apply Quill bullet list style - see specs
Create box heading style - see specs
Create Art body text style - see specs
3/4 pt. double border
20% shading foreground - Dk Magenta
24 pt.
Enter 1X
Box heading style
Quill bullet list style
Dk Magenta Heading Style
Black subhead style
Art body text style
Enter 2X before paragraph
Left indent 0.25"
- 14 pt. spacing after paragraph
- Left indent 0.25"
20 pt.
Art body text style - Left indent 0.25"
Left align
Use Splatwing
- Change color to Dk Magenta
- Size picture to 0.5" by 0.5"
- Insert frame
- Position frame 1.6" from edge of page and 7.75" from top of page.
Copy from panel 1
Position in center of column, 7.75" from top of page.
Copy from panel 2, Position 8.9" from edge of page and 7.75" from top of page.

Assessment 2

1. Open c06sa01, panels 1,2,3.
2. Save the document with Save As and name it c06sa02, art brochure.
3. Referring to the dummy created in *c06sa01, panels 1,2,3*, create panels 4, 5, and 6 shown in figure 6.18 according to the following specifications:
   a. Format the text at the top of panel 4 as indicated by the handwritten instructions. When creating the lines in panel 4, set a right tab at the position where the line is to end. When you need to insert a line, turn on underlining, press the Tab key, and then turn underlining off. When creating the Zip and Phone lines, set a left tab where the Zip line is to end. Use underline as stated previously.
   b. Format the first check box bullet, including the text that follows; create a style from the existing formatting; and apply the style according to the following specifications:
      (1) Select *$5 Junior Membership (Jr./Sr. High).*
      (2) Display the Bullets and Numbering dialog box, then select the bullet—the check box symbol—from the Wingdings character set (located in the third row, fifth column from the right).
      (3) Change the type size to 12 points.
      (4) Make sure the bullet is black, left aligned, and indented 0.25 inches from the text.
      (5) Choose yes when asked if you want to replace the exising numbers with bullets.
      (6) Use the Font and Font Size buttons on the Formatting Toolbar to change the font to 12-point Garamond.
      (7) Change the spacing after the paragraph to 14 points.
      (8) Name the style *Check box bullet list.*
      (9) Select the remaining bulleted membership items in panel 4 and apply the *Check box bullet list* style.
   c. When creating the check boxes at the bottom of panel 4, insert the text into a two-column table. Be sure and delete any hard returns in the table. Change the spacing between columns to 0 inches. Apply the *Check box bullet list* style to all the text in the table.
   d. Format the remaining text in panels 4, 5, and 6 as indicated by the handwritten instructions. Make any adjustments to spacing or positioning of text as you deem necessary.
4. Save the brochure document again with the same name (*c06sa02, art brochure*).
5. Print the first page (panels 1, 2, and 3) of the brochure and then print the second page (panels 4, 5, and 6) on the back of the first page.
6. Close c06sa02, art brochure.

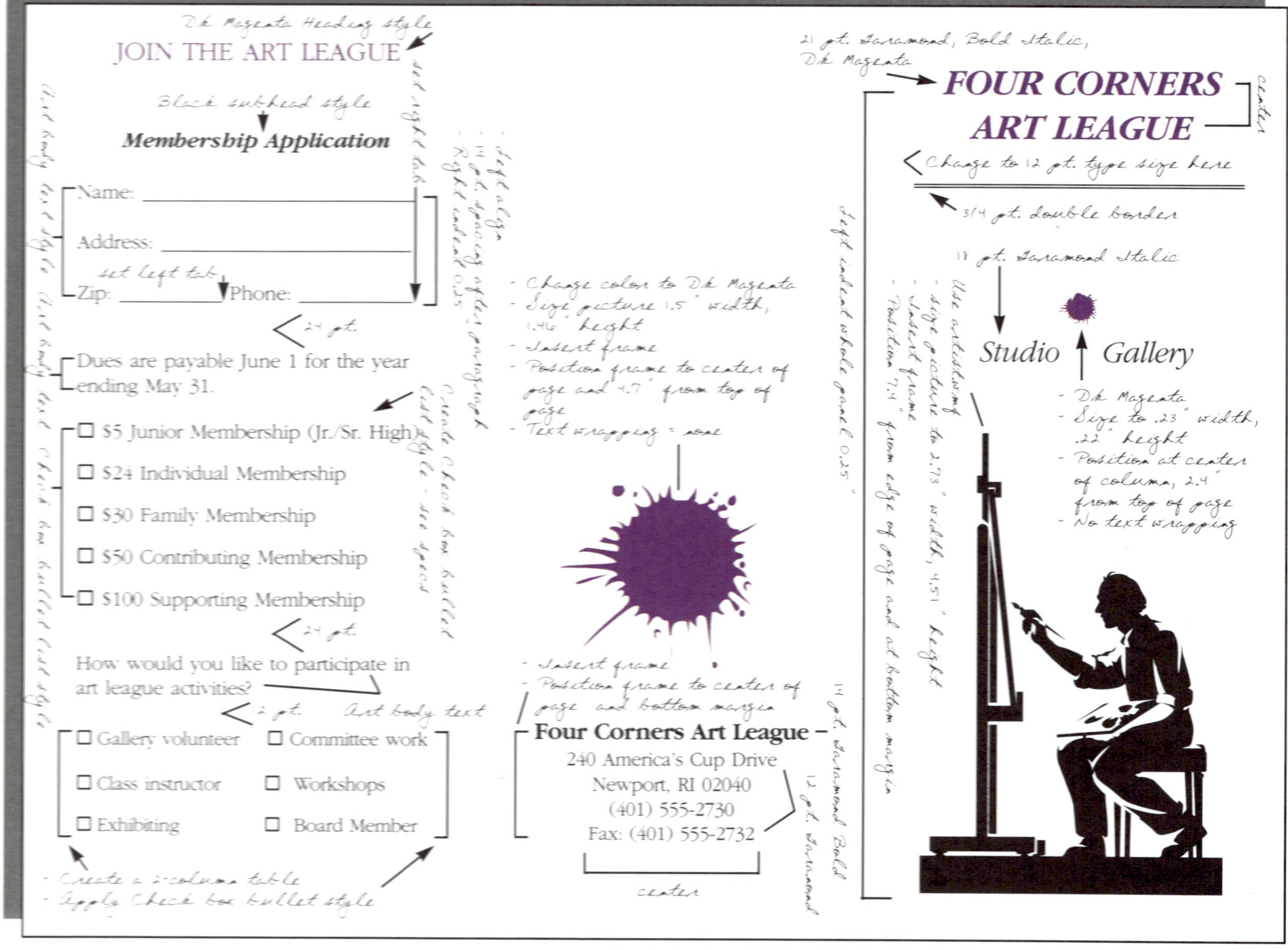

JOIN THE ART LEAGUE
Dk Magenta Heading style
Black subhead style
Membership Application
Name:
Address:
Zip:
Phone:
set left tab
set right tab
- Left align
- 12 pt. spacing after paragraph
- Right indent 0.25"
24 pt.
Dues are payable June 1 for the year ending May 31.
Create Check box bullet list style - see specs
☐ $5 Junior Membership (Jr./Sr. High)
☐ $24 Individual Membership
☐ $30 Family Membership
☐ $50 Contributing Membership
☐ $100 Supporting Membership
24 pt.
How would you like to participate in art league activities?
12 pt.
Art body text
☐ Gallery volunteer
☐ Committee work
☐ Class instructor
☐ Workshops
☐ Exhibiting
☐ Board Member
- Create a 2-column table
- Apply Check box bullet style
Art body text style
Art body text
Check box bullet list style
- Change color to Dk Magenta
- Size picture 1.5" width, 1.46" height
- Insert frame
- Position frame to center of page and 4.7" from top of page
- Text wrapping = none
- Insert frame
- Position frame to center of page and bottom margin
Four Corners Art League
240 America's Cup Drive
Newport, RI 02040
(401) 555-2730
Fax: (401) 555-2732
14 pt. Garamond Bold
12 pt. Garamond
center
Left indent whole panel 0.25"
21 pt. Garamond, Bold Italic, Dk Magenta
FOUR CORNERS
ART LEAGUE
center
Change to 12 pt. type size here
3/4 pt. double border
18 pt. Garamond Italic
Studio
Gallery
- Dk Magenta
- Size to .23" width, .22" height
- Position at center of column, 2.4" from top of page
- No text wrapping
Use artist.wmf
- Size picture to 2.73" width, 4.51" height
- Insert frame
- Position 7.4" from edge of page and at bottom margin

FIGURE 6.18

Assessment 3

1. You are a member of a fundraising committee for a local charity. Pick a charity, plan an event to raise money, and create a brochure that promotes the charity and advertises the event.
2. Open *document evaluation checklist* and print one copy.
3. Use the Document Evaluation Checklist to analyze your brochure. Label the exercise as c06sa04.
4. Attach the completed form to the back of your brochure.

Creative Activity

Visit a place where many brochures are displayed in a rack, such as a college, a chamber of commerce office, a travel agency, a doctor's office, a park district office, a hotel lobby, etc.

- Pick out two brochures that grab your attention. Use the *Document Evaluation Checklist* (open and print four copies of *document evaluation checklist*) to help you identify the elements that attracted you to pick up the two brochures. Write a short summary for each brochure explaining how these elements are successful.
- Pick out two brochures that failed to grab your attention. Use the *Document Evaluation Checklist* to help you identify what is wrong with the two brochures. Write a short summary for each brochure that analyzes the design problems and discusses how you would improve them.
- Divide into small groups in class and share your findings with your group.

7 CREATING SPECIALTY PROMOTIONAL DOCUMENTS

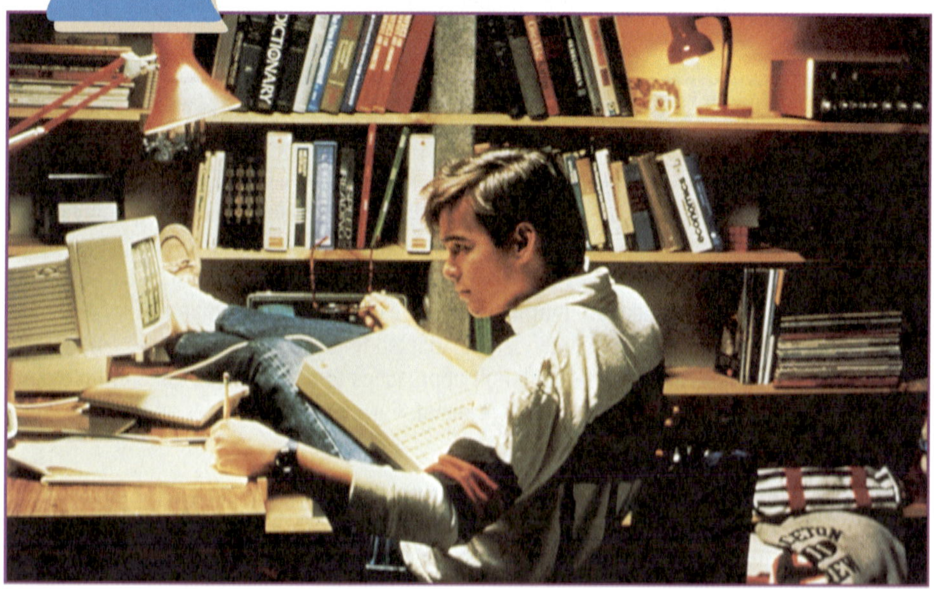

PERFORMANCE OBJECTIVE

Upon successful completion of chapter 7, you will be able to create specialty promotional documents, such as gift certificates, postcards, name tags, business greeting cards, and invitations.

DESKTOP PUBLISHING CONCEPTS

Templates	Em and en dashes	Balance
Landscape orientation	Layout and design	
Portrait orientation	Color	

WORD FEATURES USED

Tables	Mail Merge	Cut and paste
AutoText	Mail Merge Helper	Drag-and-Drop
Labels	Data Source	Special characters
Pictures	Main Document	Symbols
Borders		

Using Resources For Ideas In Desktop Publishing

By the time you reach this chapter, you will have accumulated a number of different examples of desktop publishing applications. As discussed in chapter 1, studying the work of others is a great way to pick up pointers on interesting uses of fonts, color, text, and graphics. Pick up the newspaper and study the layout of text. Pick up vacation flyers for advertising suggestions. Look at the flyers and the "junk mail" we all regularly receive. Published examples are all around you, and they can help show you how to apply what you have learned to applications in desktop publishing.

Another good source for useful ideas is *The Desktop Publisher's Idea Book* by Chuck Green. In this book, you will find project ideas, tips, and some hard-to-find sources for desktop publishing applications. Also, as mentioned in earlier chapters, paper supply companies offer predesigned papers that make all your communications look more professional.

Using Various Approaches To Creating Documents

You may have already realized that there are many different approaches to creating documents in Word. You must decide which approach is easiest for you to remember and apply. Getting good at a skill takes a lot of practice and experimentation. You may begin thinking of other ways of creating documents that are more efficient or easier to adapt to your setting. Any one of the exercises presented in this chapter can be adapted to just about any business situation. While we typically present one or two different approaches to creating a document, there are usually many other ways to achieve the same result. For instance, consider all the ways you can create a horizontal line in a document:

- Choose Format, then Font. At the Font dialog box, click Underline, then select single, double, or dotted lines. Press Tab as many times as necessary to draw a line of a desired length.
- Click the Underline button on the Formatting toolbar, then press Tab.
- Display the Borders toolbar, then select the top, bottom, left, or right line buttons.
- Click the Line button on the Drawing toolbar and drag to create a line. (Hold down the Shift key if you want to create a straight line.)
- Choose Format, Borders and Shading.
- Press Shift and the hyphen key on the keyboard.

Using Tables To Create Promotional Documents

DTP POINTERS
Well-organized and clearly written promotional documents inspire viewer confidence.

Besides flyers and announcements, other promotional documents include gift certificates, postcards, name tags, invitations, and greeting cards. They become promotional documents when a business or organization name is visible or an item is mentioned for sale in a document. Promotional documents are designed to advertise or promote an interest or sale.

Tables will be used in most of the exercises in this chapter. In Word, name cards and postcards are created using tables in the label feature. Greeting cards are formatted in tables in order to divide the paper into equal sections. A table is effective as a container for information as well as a means for copying the document.

Tables can be inserted anywhere in a document. A table can be framed as well as resized and positioned. Tables can hold text, numbers, pictures, or formulas in their cells. If you enter text in a cell, the text wraps to the next line based on the width of the cell. If you adjust the width of the cell, the text will adjust to the new cell width.

You can create a table by choosing Table, then Insert Table; or you can click the Insert Table button on the Standard toolbar. When you click the Insert Table button, Word automatically sets the width of each column. When you create a table from the menu command, you have control over setting the width of each column and the height of each row. Think about how many rows and columns will be needed before you create a table. However, you can insert and delete columns and rows by selecting options from the drop-down list of table commands.

Tables are helpful in desktop publishing because they offer you the chance to format several objects consistently and predictably. Tables can give you precise control over layout. If your document needs to be separated by lines or has several areas that share a common border, tables would be the most efficient choice for document layout. Tables require some planning before you can use them in the layout of your document. Like frames, cells in a table can be formatted choosing Format, then Borders and Shading. Like frames, tables exist in the text layer and text automatically wraps around them. Like text boxes, tables can hold paragraphs with different indents and alignments and still have the same border around them.

Additionally, cells are easier to copy to other locations, especially if there is a considerable amount of formatting within the cell, as compared to using a frame or text box as a container for text, graphics, etc. To copy a table, simply select the cell or cells you wish to duplicate by choosing Table, then selecting Row, Column, or Table from the menu list. Click the Copy button on the Standard toolbar, then position the insertion point in the desired location, and click the Paste button on the Standard toolbar. Copying in this manner saves the desktop publisher a considerable amount of time and energy.

However, when you place text, pictures, or objects (such as WordArt objects) in tables, you may encounter some difficulty in copying and moving text boxes using the cut and paste method. Text boxes will be used in many exercises in chapter 7, since they provide an excellent means for positioning elements in a document. However, remember that text boxes automatically position elements in the layer above or below the text layer. The cut and paste method of copying and moving will not consistently pick up the text boxes. Frames cannot be used in place of text boxes in a table format (this includes all the labels, which are actually created in tables), since the table format will not accept any frames within its cells.

Therefore, consider using the drag-and-drop method of copying and moving elements created in text boxes within tables. To use drag-and-drop complete the following steps:

1. Make sure the drag-and-drop feature has been turned on. Choose Tools, then Options. At the Options dialog box, select the Edit tab. Select the Drag-and-Drop Text Editing check box (an X should display in the check box). Choose OK or press Enter.
2. Select the information you want to copy or move. (You may want to click the Zoom Control button on the Standard toolbar; or click View, then Zoom; and select Whole Page or a lower percentage.)
3. To copy the information, hold down the Ctrl key, point to the selected information, and then hold down the mouse button. When the pointer displays with a small box and a + symbol, drag the pointer to the new location, and then release both the mouse button and the Ctrl key.
4. To move the information, point to the selected information, then hold down the mouse button. When the pointer displays with a small box below it, drag the pointer to the new location and release the mouse button.

The AutoText feature can also be used to copy elements, such as logos, pictures, and WordArt objects, into labels and other documents formatted in tables. This method will be discussed later in this chapter.

Creating Gift Certificates To Promote Business

In exercise 1, you will create a gift certificate template that will be used to create certificates in exercise 2 and in various skill and performance assessments later in this chapter. Gift certificates are excellent promotional documents that can be used for promoting further purchases or as rain checks, mini awards, "runner-up" prizes, or warranties. Predesigned and preperforated certificates can be purchased at most paper companies and may be used to accommodate your text. If you are using a predesigned form, you need to make wise decisions about formatting and laying out the text, logo, watermark, or graphics you have decided to use in your document. You may also consider using light-colored parchment paper or marbleized paper to make the certificate look more official.

DTP POINTERS
Use graphics to help emphasize text.

A table is being used for this template because of the ease in duplicating the cell to other locations. Using tables is just one approach to creating this type of document—other approaches include using text boxes or frames to build the framework for a gift certificate.

Consult your instructor on whether you should save the exercise as a template or as a document. If you save it to the hard drive as a template, be sure to give the template your name followed by a template name, for instance, *Smith, Gift Certificate Form.* Another option is to save the form as a document, open the document when needed, and name the newly created document by another name.

Creating a Gift Certificate Template

1. At a clean document window, create a gift certificate template by completing the following steps:
   a. Change the top, bottom, left, and right margins to 0.5 inches. (If a message displays regarding inappropriate margins, choose Fix to allow Word to increase the margin.)
   b. Choose Table, then Insert Table.
   c. At the Insert Table dialog box, change the Number of Columns to **2** and the Number of Rows to **1**. Choose OK or press Enter.
   d. With the insertion point positioned in the first cell, make the following changes:
      (1) Choose Table, then Cell Height and Width.
      (2) At the Cell Height and Width dialog box, choose the Row tab, then click the down-pointing arrow to the right of the Height of Row 1 text box and select *Exactly.* Key **210 pt** in the At text box. (One inch is equal to 72 points. To create a cell approximately 3 inches in height, multiply 72 x 3 = 216 pts. Using 210 points provides additional white space if adjustments need to be made for the unprintable zone.)
      (3) Key **0.2** in the Indent From Left text box. Make sure Left Alignment is selected. Deselect Allow Row to Break Across Pages.
      (4) Select the Column tab. Key **4.75** inches in the Width of Column 1 text box. Key **0** inches in the Space Between Columns text box.
      (5) Choose the Next Column button. Key **2.25** inches in the Width of Column 2 text box. Make sure **0** displays in the Space Between Columns text box. Choose OK or press Enter.
   e. Choose Table, then Gridlines to turn on this feature.
   f. Add a border around the cells by completing the following steps:
      (1) Display the Borders toolbar.
      (2) Position the insertion point inside the first cell, click the down-pointing arrow to the right of the Line Style text box on the Borders toolbar and

select the ¾ pt double line style at the drop-down list. Click the Top Border, Bottom Border, and Left Border buttons on the Borders toolbar.

(3) Position the insertion point inside the second cell, then click the Top Border, Bottom Border, and Right Border buttons on the Borders toolbar.

g. Position the insertion point in the first cell, choose Format, then Paragraph. At the Paragraph dialog box, select the Indents and Spacing tab. Change the Left and Right Indentations to **0.25** inches. Choose OK or press Enter.

h. With the insertion point still located in the first cell, press the space bar once, then press Enter. (This is necessary to insert an Enter code into the first cell.)

i. Position the insertion point in the second cell, then click the Center align button on the Formatting toolbar.

2. Save the certificate form as a template by completing the following steps: (Check with your instructor if you should save the certificate as a template to the hard drive or as a document to your student data disk.)
   a. Choose File, then Save As.
   b. At the Save As dialog box, click the down-pointing triangle to the right of the Save as type text box, then select *Document Template* from the drop-down list. Make sure *Templates* displays in the Save in text box.
   c. Double-click *Other Documents* in the folder list box. (Your template should appear in the New dialog box with the Other Documents tab selected.)
   d. Choose File name, then key **(Your Last Name), Gift Certificate Form.**
   e. Click the Save button.
3. Close (Your Last Name), Gift Certificate Form.

Creating a Gift Certificate Using the Template Created in Exercise 1

1. Create the gift certificate shown in figure 7.1 by completing the following steps:
   a. Choose File, then New; or if you saved the certificate form created in exercise 1 as a document on your student data disk, open **(Your Last Name), Gift Certificate Form**, then complete steps 1d and 1e.
   b. At the New dialog box, select the Other Documents tab.
   c. Double-click **(Your Last Name), Gift Certificate Form**.
   d. Choose File, then Save As.
   e. At the Save As dialog box, name your document c07ex02, gift certificate, then choose Save.
   f. Make sure the default font is 12-point Times New Roman.
   g. Turn on Kerning at 14 points.
   h. Create the text and fill-in lines appearing to the left of the certificate in figure 7.1 by completing the following steps:
      (1) Position the insertion point in the first cell (left side of the certificate), press the down-arrow key once, then key **Gift Certificate**. Press Enter twice.
      (2) Select *Gift Certificate*, then change the font to 30-point Brush Script MT. (Key 30 in the font text box, since it is not available in the drop-down list.)
      (3) Press the down-pointing arrow key twice.
      (4) Display the Ruler by choosing View, then Ruler. The ruler can help you in creating appropriate line lengths.

(5) Hold down the Ctrl key and press the Tab key 4 times, then key **Date** and a space. Create a horizontal line by holding down the Shift key and pressing the hyphen key on the keyboard. The line should be approximately 2.25 inches in length. (This line will copy in a table.)
(6) Press Enter twice.
(7) Key **This certificate entitles** and a space, then create a line similar to the line in step h4. (The line should end where the previous line ends.) Press Enter twice.
(8) Key **to** and a space, then create another line approximately 2 inches in length as shown in figure 7.1.
(9) Press the space bar once, then key **Dollars** and a space. Key **$** and a space, then create another line. Press Enter twice.
(10) Key **Presented by** and a space, then create a line that ends where the previous lines end. Press Enter twice.
(11) Hold down the Ctrl key and press the Tab key once, key **Authorized signature** and a space. Create a line that ends where the previous lines end.

i. Create the name and address in figure 7.1 by completing the following steps:
(1) Position the insertion point in the second cell (right side) of the certificate. Press Enter.
(2) Key the following:

Butterfield Gardens
29 W 036 Butterfield Road
Warrenville, IL 60555
(708) 555-1062
http://www.grower-2-you.com

(3) Select *Butterfield Gardens*, then change the font to 20-point Brush Script MT.
(4) Select the address in step 2, then change the font to 10-point Times New Roman. Deselect the text, then press Enter twice.

j. Include a graphic image in the certificate as shown in figure 7.1 by completing the following steps:
(1) With the insertion point positioned a double-space below the address, choose Insert, then Picture.
(2) At the Insert Picture dialog box, make sure Clipart displays in the Look in text box, then double-click *Buttrfly* in the Name list box. (If you need to resize the image, click on any one of the corner sizing handles and drag the image inward to reduce the size or outward to increase the size proportionately.)
(3) Deselect the image.

k. Copy the completed certificate to create two more certificates by completing the following steps:
(1) Position the insertion point anywhere in the certificate, choose Table, then Select Row.
(2) Click the Copy button on the Standard toolbar.
(3) Position the insertion point below the second certificate, then press Enter twice.
(4) Choose Edit, then Paste Cells.
(5) Position the insertion point below the certificate, then press Enter twice.
(6) Paste another copy of the certificate.

2. View the document in Print Preview. (Eliminate any unnecessary white space if the certificates interfere with the unprintable zone.)
3. Save the document again with the same name (c07ex02, gift certificate).
4. Print and then close c07ex02, gift certificate.

FIGURE 7.1

Gift Certificate

Date ____________________

This certificate entitles ____________________________

to ___________________________ Dollars $ _________

Presented by ____________________________________

Authorized signature ________________________

Butterfield Gardens
29 W 036 Butterfield Road
Warrenville, IL 60555
(708) 555-1062
http://www.grower-2-you.com

Gift Certificate

Date ____________________

This certificate entitles ____________________________

to ___________________________ Dollars $ _________

Presented by ____________________________________

Authorized signature ________________________

Butterfield Gardens
29 W 036 Butterfield Road
Warrenville, IL 60555
(708) 555-1062
http://www.grower-2-you.com

Gift Certificate

Date ____________________

This certificate entitles ____________________________

to ___________________________ Dollars $ _________

Presented by ____________________________________

Authorized signature ________________________

Butterfield Gardens
29 W 036 Butterfield Road
Warrenville, IL 60555
(708) 555-1062
http://www.grower-2-you.com

Creating Postcards To Promote Business

DTP POINTERS
Vary type size and style to add interest.

If you have a brief message to get across to prospective customers, postcards can be an appropriate means of delivering the message. Postcards are inexpensive to create and use. They can be used as appointment reminders, just-moved notes, return/reply cards, display cards, thank-you cards, or invitations. Consider purchasing predesigned printed postcards with attractive borders, color combinations, and sizes and weights that meet U.S. Post Office standards. You can purchase blank, prestamped 3½-inch by 5½-inch postcards from the U.S. Post Office at a cost of approximately 20 cents apiece. Or, you can use the Word label feature, which provides a predefined postcard sized at 4 inches by 6 inches. Two postcards will display on a standard-sized sheet of paper when you use Word's postcard label, Avery 5389

Most postcards are created on 100- to 110-pound uncoated cover stock paper. The paper weight or thickness should be strong enough to hold up in the mail. The front side of the postcard is used for your return address and the recipient's address along with an area reserved for the postage. On the back side, you may create a headline and use a graphic or watermark to emphasize the message. You will need to leave room for your message and optional signature.

Alternatively, use the Table feature in Word to produce four cells that represent four postcard-sized documents. You may want to save the postcards as a template before keying the text content. To create postcards using the Table feature as shown in figure 7.2, you would complete the following steps:

1. Change the top, bottom, left, and right margins to 0.5 inches.
2. Change the paper orientation to landscape.
3. Insert a table containing two columns and two rows.
4. Change the height of each row to 248 points and the width of each column to 5 inches. (These measurements will result in four postcards measuring 4 inches by 5 inches.)
5. Create the text content in the first cell, then copy this information to the remaining cells on the page.
6. The watermark was created in a text box and copied individually to each cell. (Text boxes do not copy well in cells.).

FIGURE 7.2

Creating Postcards Using the Table Feature in Word

A. G. Rowe & Sons, Inc. *Investments since 1902* Wendy Fausey and Elizabeth Krueper invite you to this FREE workshop ***Funding Your Child's Education*** Wednesday, November 7, 7:00 p.m. or Thursday, November 9, 7:00 p.m. Breckenridge Country Club 3400 Ridgeway Drive Baltimore, MD For reservations, call (410) 555-5132	*A. G. Rowe & Sons, Inc.* *Investments since 1902* Wendy Fausey and Elizabeth Krueper invite you to this FREE workshop ***Funding Your Child's Education*** Wednesday, November 7, 7:00 p.m. or Thursday, November 9, 7:00 p.m. Breckenridge Country Club 3400 Ridgeway Drive Baltimore, MD For reservations, call (410) 555-5132
A. G. Rowe & Sons, Inc. *Investments since 1902* Wendy Fausey and Elizabeth Krueper invite you to this FREE workshop ***Funding Your Child's Education*** Wednesday, November 7, 7:00 p.m. or Thursday, November 9, 7:00 p.m. Breckenridge Country Club 3400 Ridgeway Drive Baltimore, MD For reservations, call (410) 555-5132	*A. G. Rowe & Sons, Inc.* *Investments since 1902* Wendy Fausey and Elizabeth Krueper invite you to this FREE workshop ***Funding Your Child's Education*** Wednesday, November 7, 7:00 p.m. or Thursday, November 9, 7:00 p.m. Breckenridge Country Club 3400 Ridgeway Drive Baltimore, MD For reservations, call (410) 555-5132

Creating Postcards Using Word's Label Feature

1. At a clear document window, create two postcards based on the design in figure 7.3 by completing the following steps:
   a. Choose Tools, then Envelopes and Labels.
   b. At the Envelopes and Labels dialog box, select the Labels tab.
   c. Click the Options button. At the Labels Options dialog box, select *5389 - Postcard* in the Product Number list box. Choose OK or press Enter to close the Labels Options dialog box.
   d. At the Envelopes and Labels dialog box, click the New Document button.
   e. Change the Zoom Control to 75%.
   f. Turn on Kerning at 14 points.
   g. Make sure the default font is 12-points Times New Roman.
   h. Display the Drawing toolbar.
   i. Display the Borders toolbar.
   j. With the insertion point located in the first postcard, create a border around the postcard by completing the following steps:
      (1) Click the down-pointing arrow to the right of the Line Style text box on the Borders toolbar. Select the ¾ pt line style from the drop-down list.
      (2) Click the Outside Border button (third button from the right) on the Borders toolbar.
      (3) Position the insertion point in the second postcard (below the first one) and click the Outside Border button on the Borders toolbar.
   k. With the insertion point located in the first postcard, choose Insert, then Picture. At the Insert Picture dialog box, make sure Clipart displays in the Look in text box. Double-click *Notes* in the Name list.
   l. Click the Text Box button on the Drawing toolbar. Drag the crosshair into the label and to the right of the *Notes* picture. (See figure 7.3 for the placement of *Piano Tuning.*) Create the text box to measure approximately 0.75 inches in height and 2.5 inches in width. (You can verify the box size at the Drawing Object dialog box with the Size and Position tab selected.)
   m. With the insertion point positioned inside the text box created in step 1l, change the font to 38-point Brush Script MT. Key **Piano Tuning**. (If a border displays around the text box, select the text box, then click the Line Color button on the Drawing toolbar and choose None.)
   n. Position the insertion point below the note picture, then press the down-arrow key twice. (Press the Enter key instead of pressing the down-arrow keys if two Enters are not available below the text box—these Enters were created in the program label definition.)
   o. Click the Center align button on the Formatting toolbar.
   p. Key **Spring Special**, then press Enter twice.
   q. Key **$45**, then press Enter twice.
   r. Key **(Good until April 20, 1997)**, then press Enter twice.
   s. Select the following text and change the formatting according to the following specifications (do not select the paragraph symbols between the lines of text):

Spring Special	22-point Bookman Old Style
$45	36-point Bookman Old Style
(Good until April 20, 1997)	12-point Bookman Old Style

   t. Press the down-arrow key twice, then click the Align Left button on the Formatting toolbar.
   u. Choose Format, then Paragraph. At the Paragraph dialog box, select the Indent and Spacing tab and change the Left and Right Indentations to **0.25** inches. Choose OK or press Enter.

v. Change the font to 11-point Bookman Old Style, key **Robert Valecki**, then press Enter.
w. Key **Piano Lessons Available**.
x. Press Ctrl + Tab five times, then key **(312) 555-8765**.

2. Copy the postcard by completing the following steps:
   a. Position the insertion point below the Piano picture in the first formatted postcard, choose Table, then Select Row.
   b. Click the Copy button on the Standard toolbar.
   c. Position the insertion point in the second label (below the first one).
   d. Choose Edit, then Paste Rows.
   e. If the text box containing *Piano Tuning* did not copy into the second postcard, position the arrow pointer on the text box in the first label, select the box, then hold down the Ctrl key as you drag a copy of the box to the same location in the second postcard. Release the mouse, then deselect the text box.
3. Click File, then Print Preview. Make sure the elements are located in the postcards as shown in figure 7.3. Make any necessary editing changes. (If the bottom border line does not display, change the top and bottom margins.)
4. Save the document with the name c07ex03, postcard.
5. Print and then close c07ex03, postcard.

Optional: Save the postcard text as an AutoText entry by completing the following steps:

1. Create the postcard text as instructed in exercise 3, except create *Piano Tuning* in the text entry box in WordArt. (Creating the text in WordArt converts the text into an OLE object, which can be copied, even if it is placed inside a text box.)
2. When the postcard text is complete, choose Table, then Select Row.
3. Choose Edit, then AutoText.
4. At the AutoText dialog box, name the AutoText entry **Piano**.
5. Click the Add button at the AutoText dialog box.
6. Close the document window without saving.
7. Choose Tools, then Envelopes and Labels.
8. At the Envelopes and Labels dialog box, select the Label tab.
9. Click the Options button and select *5389 - Postcard* at the Product Number list box. Make sure the option Full Page of the Same Label is selected. Choose OK or press Enter.
10. Position the insertion point in the Address text box, key **Piano**, then press F3.
11. Choose the New Document button.
12. The postcard text, picture, and WordArt object should copy to both postcards in this label definition. (If a blank postcard displays between the two copies, choose Table, then Delete Rows.)

You can also copy the first postcard to other postcards using the cut and paste method of copying. Since *Piano Tuning* was created in WordArt and then inserted into a text box, it should copy when selected.

FIGURE 7.3

Spring Special

$45

(Good until April 20, 1997)

Robert Valecki
Piano Lessons Available **(312) 555-8765**

Using Mail Merge In Promotional Documents

Main Document: A form that receives the data.

Data Source: Contains variable data such as names and addresses.

Merge Fields: Special codes inserted into the main document instructing Word to collect information from the data source.

Mail Merge is the process of combining variable information with standard text to create personalized documents. Word's Mail Merge feature enables you to create form letters, envelopes, labels, and more. To do so, you merge a *main document*, which contains data such as the text of a form letter or the return address and picture on a postcard, with a *data source*, which contains varying data such as names and addresses. Special codes called *merge fields* in the main document direct Word to collect information from the data source and use it in the main document to create personalized documents. There are three basic processes involved in a mail merge:

- Create a new main document or edit and designate an existing main document as a main document.
- Create a new data source or choose an existing one.
- Perform the merge operation.

Word can create a merge from three different data sources. These sources are: a Word document formatted in a table, tab, or comma-delimited format; an imported application or database such as Microsoft Access, Excel, dBASE, Paradox, etc; and a shared office file such as the Personal Address Book, Schedule+, or Microsoft Network lists. You will create a data source formatted in a table.

Using the Mail Merge Helper

Word's Mail Merge Helper includes a series of dialog boxes that guide you through creating or identifying the main document and the data source, then through the merge of the main document and the data source. In exercise 4, you will use Mail Merge Helper to merge addresses onto the reverse side of the two postcards created in exercise 3.

Figure 7.4 illustrates the Mail Merge Helper dialog box, which lays out the three stages in creating a merged document—creating a main document, creating a data source, and completing a merge.

FIGURE 7.4

Mail Merge Helper Dialog Box

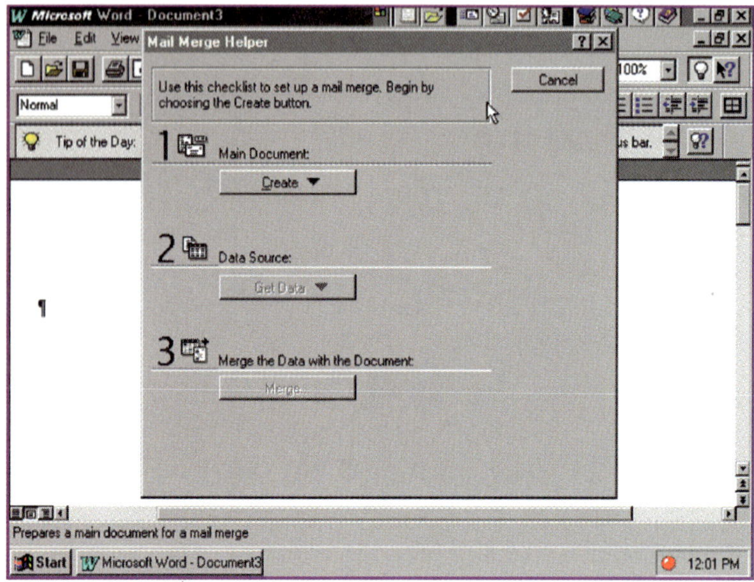

Creating a Data Source

When creating a data source, consider the present and future uses of this information. The data source contains the variable information about customers, clients, companies, etc. This may include such information as names, addresses, telephone numbers, and products. Information in a data source is usually laid out in a table. Each row of information is known as a *record.* If the data source contains names and addresses of clients, the record contains each individual's name, address, and any other specific information.

Record: Contains all the information for one unit (person, family, business).

Field: A specific section of variable information, such as title, first name, last name, etc.

Delimiters: Commas, tabs, and cells that separate each field of data.

Columns of information in a table used as a data source are known as *fields.* Each field, or column, contains one specific type of information about each client. For instance, one field may contain the state and another field may contain the zip code. Word understands commas, tabs, and cells in a table as *delimiters*, which separate each field of data. Variable information in a data source is saved as a record. A record contains all the information in one unit. A series of fields makes one record, and a series of records make a data source.

At the Mail Merge Helper, Word provides predetermined field names that can be used when creating the data source. Field names are used to describe the contents of each field in the data source as shown in figure 7.5. They are also used to indicate where information goes when it is taken from the data source and placed into a merged document. Field names are limited to 40 characters and they cannot contain spaces. Besides the predetermined field names, you have the option to create your own field names. You may delete any unwanted predetermined fields and insert your own fields at the Field Name text box in the Create Data Source dialog box.

When naming the data source file, you may want to add the letters *ds* to the name to identify it as a data source document.

Creating a Data Source

1. At a clear document window, create the data source shown in figure 7.8 and name it *Postcard ds* by completing the following steps:
   a. Choose Tools, then Mail Merge.
   b. At the Mail Merge Helper dialog box shown in figure 7.4, choose Create. From the drop-down list that displays, choose Mailing Labels.(You will later select the *5389 - Postcard* definition in the Label Options dialog box.)
   c. At the dialog box asking if you want to use the active document or a new document window, choose Active Window.

d. Choose Get Data, then, from the drop-down list that displays, choose Create Data Source.
e. At the Create Data Source dialog box shown in figure 7.6, the fields provided by Word are shown in the Field Names in Header Row list box. These fields are needed for the data source in this exercise: *Title*, *FirstName*, *LastName*, *Address1*, *City*, *State*, and *PostalCode*.
f. To remove *JobTitle* or any other unwanted fields, click the down-pointing triangle on the vertical scroll bar to the right of the Field Names in Header Row list box until *JobTitle* is visible. Click *JobTitle* in the list box, then click Remove Field Name. When *Job Title* is removed, it will display in the Field Name text box. Remove the following unwanted fields from the Field Names in Header Row list box: *Job Title, Company, Address2, Country, HomePhone*, and *WorkPhone*.
g. Choose OK or press Enter.
h. At the Save As dialog box, key **Postcard ds** in the File name text box, then choose Save or press Enter.
i. At the dialog box containing the warning that the data source contains no data, choose Edit Data Source. This displays the Data Form dialog box shown in figure 7.7.
j. At the Data Form dialog box, key the title **Mrs.** of the first customer shown in figure 7.5, then press the Enter key or the Tab key.
k. Continue keying the information in figure 7.5 for the customer, *Mrs. Peggy McSherry*, in the appropriate fields. Press the Enter key or the Tab key to move to the next field. Press Shift + Tab to move to the preceding field.
l. After entering all the information for *Mrs. Peggy McSherry*, choose Add New. This saves the information and displays a blank Data Form dialog box. Continue keying the information for each person in this manner until all records shown in figure 7.5 have been created.
m. After creating the last record for the data source, choose View Source and compare your document to figure 7.8.
n. At the data source document, choose File, then Save.

2. Close *Postcard ds*.
3. At the clear window, close the document without saving it.

Title	=	Mrs.
FirstName	=	Peggy
LastName	=	McSherry
Address1	=	3955 Kinzie Court
City	=	St. Louis
State	=	MO
PostalCode	=	50749
Title	=	Mrs.
FirstName	=	Kathleen
LastName	=	Nixon
Address1	=	409 Highland Drive
City	=	St. Louis
State	=	MO
PostalCode	=	50749

FIGURE 7.5

Data Source Client Information

Title	=	Mr. and Mrs.
FirstName	=	Eric
LastName	=	Gohlke
Address1	=	3740 North Orchard
City	=	St. Louis
State	=	MO
PostalCode	=	50750
Title	=	Ms.
FirstName	=	Margo
LastName	=	Godfrey
Address1	=	393 River Drive
City	=	St. Louis
State	=	MO
Postal Code	=	50750

FIGURE 7.6

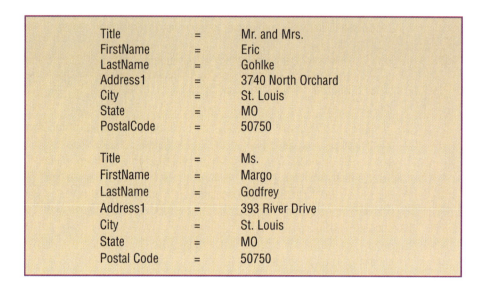

Create Data Source

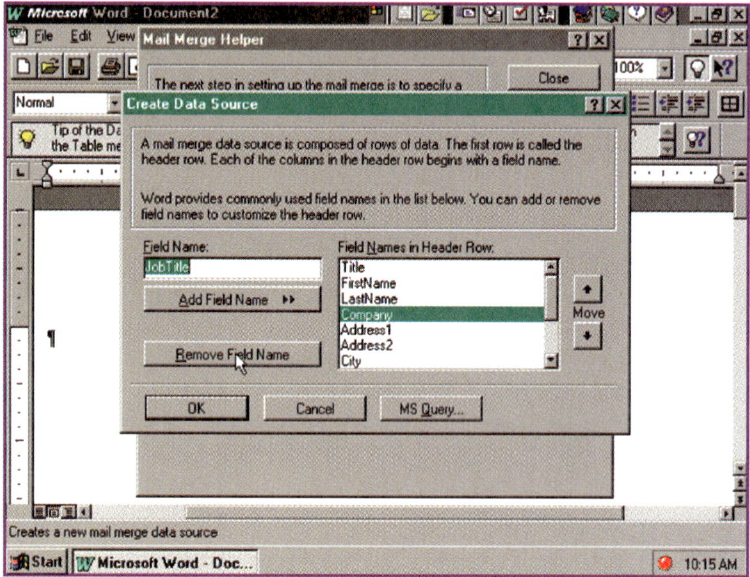

FIGURE 7.7

Data Form Dialog Box

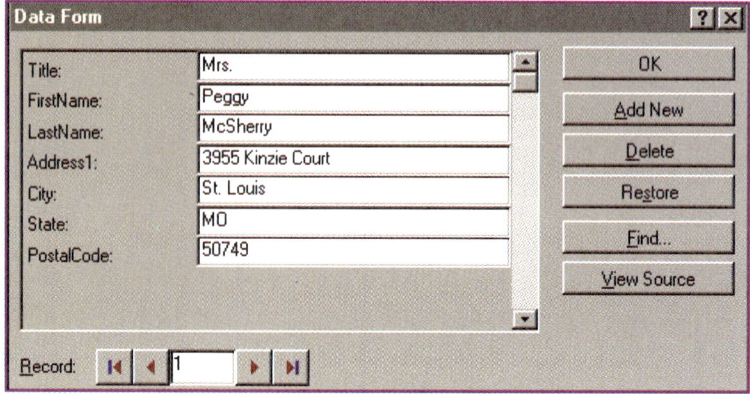

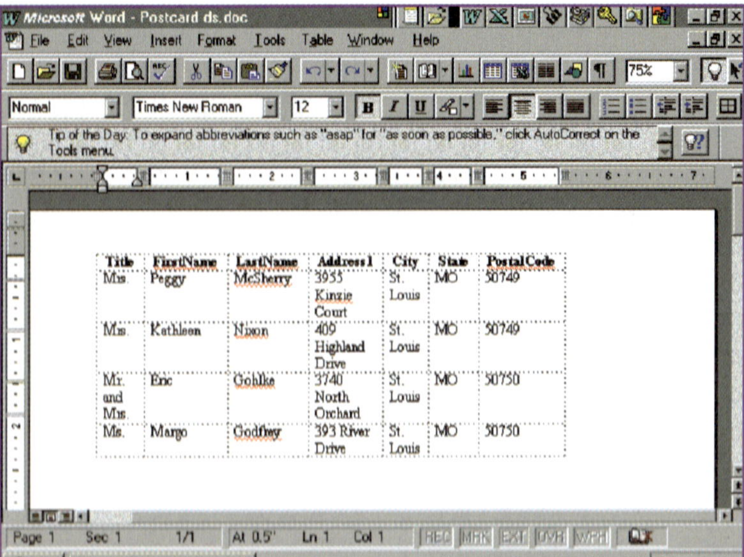

Title	FirstName	LastName	Address1	City	State	PostalCode
Mrs.	Peggy	McSherry	3955 Kinzie Court	St. Louis	MO	50749
Mrs.	Kathleen	Nixon	409 Highland Drive	St. Louis	MO	50749
Mr. and Mrs.	Eric	Gohlke	3740 North Orchard	St. Louis	MO	50750
Ms.	Margo	Godfrey	393 River Drive	St. Louis	MO	50750

FIGURE 7.8

Postcard ds

Creating the Main Document

The main document may be more than just a form letter; it may include a mailing list, catalog, mailing labels, letters, or more. In the next two exercises, you will merge a list of addresses to the back side of the postcard advertising a service for tuning pianos. When the main document is completed and the fields have been keyed into proper locations, your main document will look similar to figure 7.9. To create the main document shown in figure 7.9, complete exercise 5.

When naming a main document, you may want to add the initials *md* to indicate that the file is a main document. Insert spaces between the fields as you would key normal text. For instance, key a comma and space between the <City> field and the <State> field in an address.

Creating a Main Document

1. At a clear document window, create the main document shown in figure 7.9 and name it *Postcard md* by completing the following steps:
   a. Create the return address and the graphic image below it as shown in figure 7.9 as an AutoText entry that can be inserted in a postcard in a label definition by completing the following steps:
      (1) Key the following (make sure the default font is 12-point Times New Roman):

      Mr. Robert Valecki
      32 Lemon Creek Road
      St. Louis, MO 50477

      (2) Press Enter twice.
      (3) Choose Insert, then Picture.
      (4) At the Insert Picture dialog box, make sure Clipart displays in the Look in text box, then double-click *Flyace* in the Name list box.
      (5) Resize the picture by completing the following steps:
         (a) Select the picture.
         (b) Choose Format, then Picture.
         (c) At the Picture dialog box, change the Width to 2.25 inches and the Height to 0.70 inches in the Size section of the dialog box.
         (d) Choose OK or press Enter to close the Picture dialog box.

(6) Insert the text in the banner as shown in figure 7.9 by completing the following steps:
(a) Double-click the picture to access Microsoft Word Picture (graphic editor).
(b) Click the Text Box button on the Drawing toolbar which displays at the bottom of the screen.
(c) Drag the crosshairs into the banner section of the picture and create a box that fits inside this area. If a border or fill displays, click the Line Color and Fill Color buttons on the Drawing toolbar and select None.
(d) With the insertion point positioned inside the text box, change the alignment to Center and turn on bold. Key **Time to Tune!** in the text box. (Make any necessary spacing adjustments at the Paragraph dialog box with the Indents and Spacing tab selected. For instance, key **4** pt in the Before text box in the Spacing section.)
(e) Click the Close Picture button.
(7) Select the return address and the picture, then choose Edit, then AutoText.
(8) At the AutoText dialog box, key **Robert Valecki** in the Name text box, then click the Add button.
(9) Delete the address and picture from the document window.

b. Choose Tools, then Mail Merge.
c. At the Mail Merge Helper dialog box, choose Create (below Main Document).
d. At the drop-down list that displays, choose Mailing Labels.
e. At the question asking if you want to use the active document window or a new document, choose Active Window.
f. At the Mail Merge Helper dialog box, choose Get Data (below Data Source).
g. At the drop-down list that displays, choose Open Data Source.
h. At the Open Data Source dialog box, double-click *Postcard ds* in the list box.
i. At the Microsoft Word dialog box telling you that Word needs to set up your main document, choose Set Up Main Document.
j. At the Labels Options dialog box, make sure *5389 - Postcard* is selected in the Product Number list box, then click OK or press Enter.
k. With the insertion point positioned in the Sample Labels text box, press Enter.
l. Key **Robert Valecki** then press F3. (Robert Valecki's return address along with a picture of a banner and an airplane should display.)
m. Press Enter twice.
n. Insert the merge field codes into the Sample Label by completing the following steps:
(1) From the left edge of the Sample Label, press Ctrl + Tab five times.
(2) Click the Insert Merge Field button on the Mail Merge toolbar, select *Title* from the drop-down menu, then press the space bar once.
(3) Click the Insert Merge Field button on the Mail Merge toolbar, select *FirstName* from the drop-down menu, then press the space bar once.
(4) Click the Insert Merge Field button, select *LastName*, then press Enter. (The merge fields may wrap to the next line—do not be concerned!).
(5) Press Ctrl + Tab five times.
(6) Click the Insert Merge Field button, select *Address1*, then press Enter.
(7) Press Ctrl + Tab five times.
(8) Continue inserting the *City, State*, and *PostalCode* merge fields, including a comma between the city and state and using spaces as you would in regular address text.
(9) Click OK.
(10) Click Close at the Mail Merge Helper.

2. Choose File, then Save As. At the Save As dialog box, key **Postcard md** in the File name text box, then choose Save or press Enter.
3. Close *Postcard md.*

FIGURE 7.9

Mr. Robert Valecki
32 Lemon Creek Road
St. Louis, MO 50477

<<Title>> <<FirstName>> <<LastName>>
<<Address1>>
<<City>>, <<State>> <<Postal Code>>

Merging Information to a Postcard

Once the data source and the main document have been created and saved, they can be merged. Merged documents can be saved in a new document or sent directly to the printer. There are several ways to merge a data source with a main document. A main document and a data source can be merged with buttons on the Merge toolbar or options at the Merge dialog box. To merge a main document with a data source, open the main document, then click the Merge to New Document button (see figure 7.10—the fifth button from the right on the Mail Merge toolbar, which displays below the Tip Wizard Box).

When the main document is open, you can use buttons on the Mail Merge toolbar to view how the document will look after merging with the first record, the next record, the last record, or a specific record from the data source.

To merge to the printer, open the main document, then click the Merge to Printer button on the Mail Merge toolbar (the fourth button from the right).

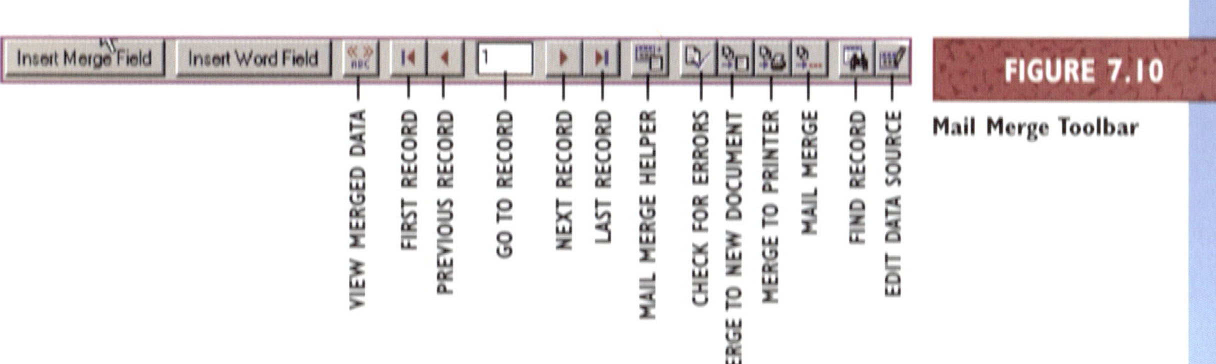

FIGURE 7.10

Mail Merge Toolbar

Merging Documents

1. Merge *Postcard md* with *Postcard ds* as shown in figure 7.11 by completing the following steps:
   a. Print two copies of c07ex03, postcard (four postcards should be the result.)
   b. Place the printed postcards from step 1a into your printer. (Be careful to position them correctly into the printer so the merge will occur on the back side of each postcard.)
   c. Open *Postcard md.*
   d. Click the Merge to New Document button on the Mail Merge toolbar (fifth button from the right). The Mail Merge toolbar will display below the Standard toolbar. (When the documents are merged, a partial section of a row may display in the document window at the bottom of the first page—do not be alarmed! The postcards should print correctly even though they may not view correctly.)
   e. When the main document is merged with the data source, save the document and name it c07ex06, merged postcards.
2. View the postcards in Print Preview.
3. Print and then close c07ex06, merged postcards.
4. Close *Postcard md* without saving the changes.

FIGURE 7.11

Spring Special

$45

(Good until April 20, 1997)

Robert Valecki
Piano Lessons Available **(312) 555-8765**

Mr. Robert Valecki
32 Lemon Creek Road
St. Louis, MO 50477

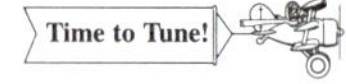

Mr. and Mrs. Eric Gohlke
3740 North Orchard
St. Louis, MO 50750

Spring Special

$45

(Good until April 20, 1997)

Robert Valecki
Piano Lessons Available **(312) 555-8765**

Mr. Robert Valecki
32 Lemon Creek Road
St. Louis, MO 50477

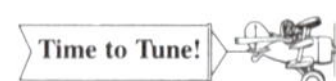

Ms. Margo Godfrey
393 River Drive
St. Louis, MO 50750

Creating Name Tags

A good name tag shows your name, your title, and the company or organization with which you are affiliated. The individual's name should be easy to read and the most dominant element on the name tag. Remembering a person's name is one of the biggest compliments you can pay to that person. However, if you are in a business where you meet a lot of people, remembering names can be difficult. Name tags can definitely reduce the embarrassment of forgetting someone's name.

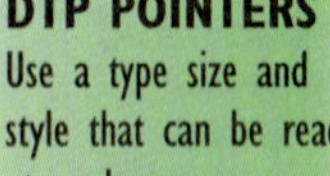

DTP POINTERS
Use a type size and style that can be read at a glance.

Word includes six name tag label definitions. The number of labels ranges from six labels to eight labels per sheet. The Avery name tags come in the following sizes: 2.17 inches by 3.5 inches, 2.33 inches by 3.38 inches, and 3 inches by 4 inches.

An alternative to choosing labels for name tags is to purchase name tag holders and insert a business card or name tag printed on heavier weight paper inside the holder. The holder is a clear plastic sleeve with a clip or pin on the back side. Holders are usually available through mail order paper companies or office supply companies.

Typically, more than one name tag is created at a time. If you are creating several tags for many different people, you may want to merge a data source to the label definition (main document) to efficiently produce this form. In exercise 7, you will use a data source that has already been prepared for you and saved to your student data disk—*Floral ds*.

Remember to plan your tags with a focal point in mind. The individual's name should be dominant. Choose a font and type size that emphasizes the name. Readability is important, so choose a font that is easy to read at a glance. Since this document is so small, consider using one font for the entire tag. Vary the type style and type size to add interest. Using an appropriate special character or logo with a touch of color will enhance the tag and increase its visual appeal.

Creating Name Tags Using Merge

1. At a clear document window, create the name tags in figure 7.13 by completing the following steps:
   a. Choose Tools, then Mail Merge.
   b. At the Mail Merge Helper dialog box, choose Create, then select Mailing Labels from the drop-down list. At the question asking if you want to use the active document window or a new document, choose Active Window.
   c. At the Mail Merge Helper dialog box, choose Get Data (below Data Source).
   d. At the drop-down list that displays, choose Open Data Source.
   e. At the Open Data Source dialog box, double-click *Floral ds* from your student data disk.
   f. At the Microsoft Word dialog box telling you that Word needs to set up your main document, click the Set Up Main Document button.
   g. At the Label Options dialog box, select *5095 - Name Tag* in the Product Number list box, then click OK.
   h. At the Create Labels dialog box, click OK. (You will not be keying text in the Sample Label text box.)
   i. At the Mail Merge Helper dialog box, click Edit under the Main Document section, then click Mailing Label: Document#.
   j. Format the name tag text and insert merge fields by completing the following steps:
      (1) Position the insertion point in the first cell and on the second paragraph symbol that displays. (Turn on Show/Hide ¶.)
      (2) Turn on Kerning at 14 points.

(3) Change the font to 16-point Britannic Bold and turn on small caps, then key **Midwest Floral Association**.
(4) Press Ctrl + Tab.
(5) Choose Insert, then Symbol. Select the Symbols tab, then change the Font to Wingdings. Select the symbol in the fifth row and the tenth column. Choose Insert, then Close.
(6) Press Enter.
(7) Select *Midwest Floral Association* and the symbol, then change the color to Dk Cyan at the Font dialog box.
(8) Display the Borders toolbar.
(9) With *Midwest Floral Association* still selected, change the Line Style to 1½ pt single line, then click the Bottom Border button on the Borders toolbar.
(10) Deselect the text.
(11) Press the down-pointing arrow key three times, then change the alignment to Center. (Press Enter three times if the down-pointing arrow key does not advance the insertion point.)
(12) Change the font to 20-point Britannic Bold.
(13) Click the Insert Merge Field button on the Mail Merge toolbar, then select *FirstName* as shown in figure 7.12.
(14) Press the space bar once, click the Insert Merge Field button, then select *LastName*.
(15) Change the font to 11-point Britannic Bold.
(16) Press Enter, then insert the *JobTitle* field.
(17) Press Enter four times, then change the alignment to Left.
(18) Insert the *Company* field.
(19) Create a right tab at approximately 3.25 inches on the Ruler.
(20) Press Ctrl + Tab, then insert *City* and *State* fields separated by a comma and space as shown in figure 7.12.
(21) Press Enter.

k. Insert the name tag text into AutoText so it can be inserted in the name tag label and saved as the main document by completing the following steps:
(1) Select and drag through the name tag text beginning with the Enter at the top of the cell and including the Enter at the bottom of the cell.
(2) With this text selected, choose Edit, then AutoText.
(3) At the AutoText dialog box, key **Midwest Floral** in the Name text box, then click Add.

l. Close the document window without saving.
m. At a clear document window, choose Tools, then Mail Merge.
n. At the Mail Merge Helper dialog box, choose Create, then select Mailing Labels. At the dialog box that displays, choose Active Window.
o. Choose Get Data, then choose Open Data Source from the drop-down menu. At the Open dialog box, double-click *Floral ds* on your student data disk.
p. Click the Set Up Main Document button.
q. Select *5095 - Name Tag* in the Product Number section of the Label Options dialog box, then click OK.
r. With the insertion point positioned in the Sample Label text box, key **Midwest Floral**, then press F3.
s. Click OK to close the Create Labels dialog box.
t. At the Mail Merge Helper dialog box, click Close.
u. Save the document with Save As and name it *Floral md.*
v. Click the Merge to New Document button on the Mail Merge toolbar (fifth button from the right).

2. Save the name tag document and name it c07ex07, name tags.
3. Print and then close c07ex07, name tags.
4. Close *Floral md* without saving changes.

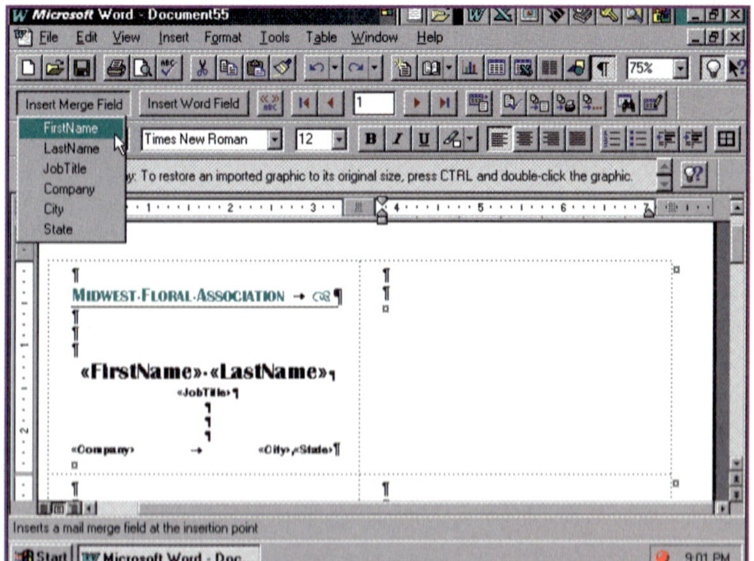

FIGURE 7.12

Insert Merge Field Button and Inserting Merge Codes into a Name Tag

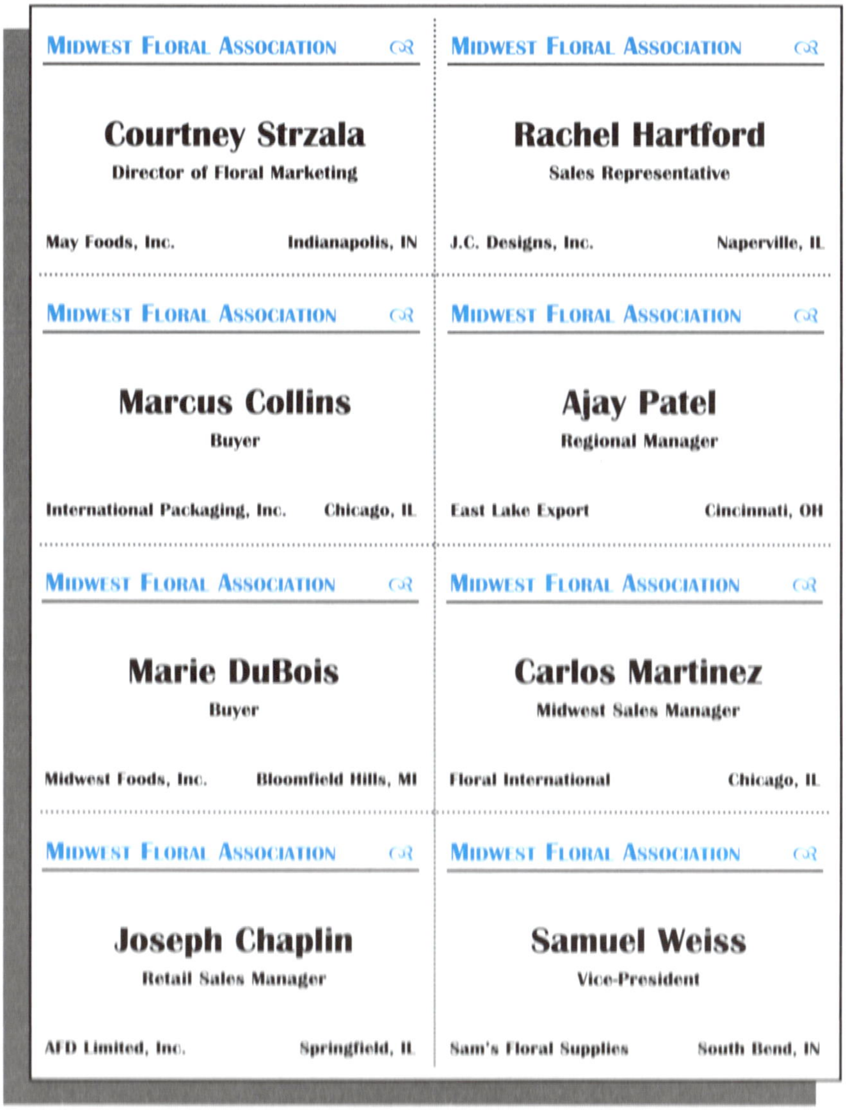

MIDWEST FLORAL ASSOCIATION

Courtney Strzala
Director of Floral Marketing
May Foods, Inc. — Indianapolis, IN

MIDWEST FLORAL ASSOCIATION

Rachel Hartford
Sales Representative
J.C. Designs, Inc. — Naperville, IL

MIDWEST FLORAL ASSOCIATION

Marcus Collins
Buyer
International Packaging, Inc. — Chicago, IL

MIDWEST FLORAL ASSOCIATION

Ajay Patel
Regional Manager
East Lake Export — Cincinnati, OH

MIDWEST FLORAL ASSOCIATION

Marie DuBois
Buyer
Midwest Foods, Inc. — Bloomfield Hills, MI

MIDWEST FLORAL ASSOCIATION

Carlos Martinez
Midwest Sales Manager
Floral International — Chicago, IL

MIDWEST FLORAL ASSOCIATION

Joseph Chaplin
Retail Sales Manager
AFD Limited, Inc. — Springfield, IL

MIDWEST FLORAL ASSOCIATION

Samuel Weiss
Vice-President
Sam's Floral Supplies — South Bend, IN

FIGURE 7.13

Using Tables To Create Invitations And Greeting Cards

DTP POINTERS
When sizing a graphic, use the corner selection handles to keep the image in proportion.

You will be using Word's Table feature to create a table that may be used to format holiday cards, business or personal invitations, seminar or open house announcements, personal notes, or even birth announcements. Figure 7.14 illustrates the result that will be achieved when a standard-sized sheet of paper is divided into four cells using a table, then folded to accommodate text and graphics. Each of the four panels (cells) in figure 7.14 has been identified with a panel number and marked with instructions for rotating text and graphics. In Word you can rotate a text box, but you cannot rotate the contents of the box unless you create the text in WordArt, where an option is available on the WordArt toolbar to rotate and/or slant text. While rotating your text in WordArt, you may consider enhancing your text further by using the line and shape palette, color, borders, shading, and more.

FIGURE 7.14

Guide for Creating an Invitation, Greeting Card, or Thank-You Card on One Sheet of Paper in Portrait Orientation

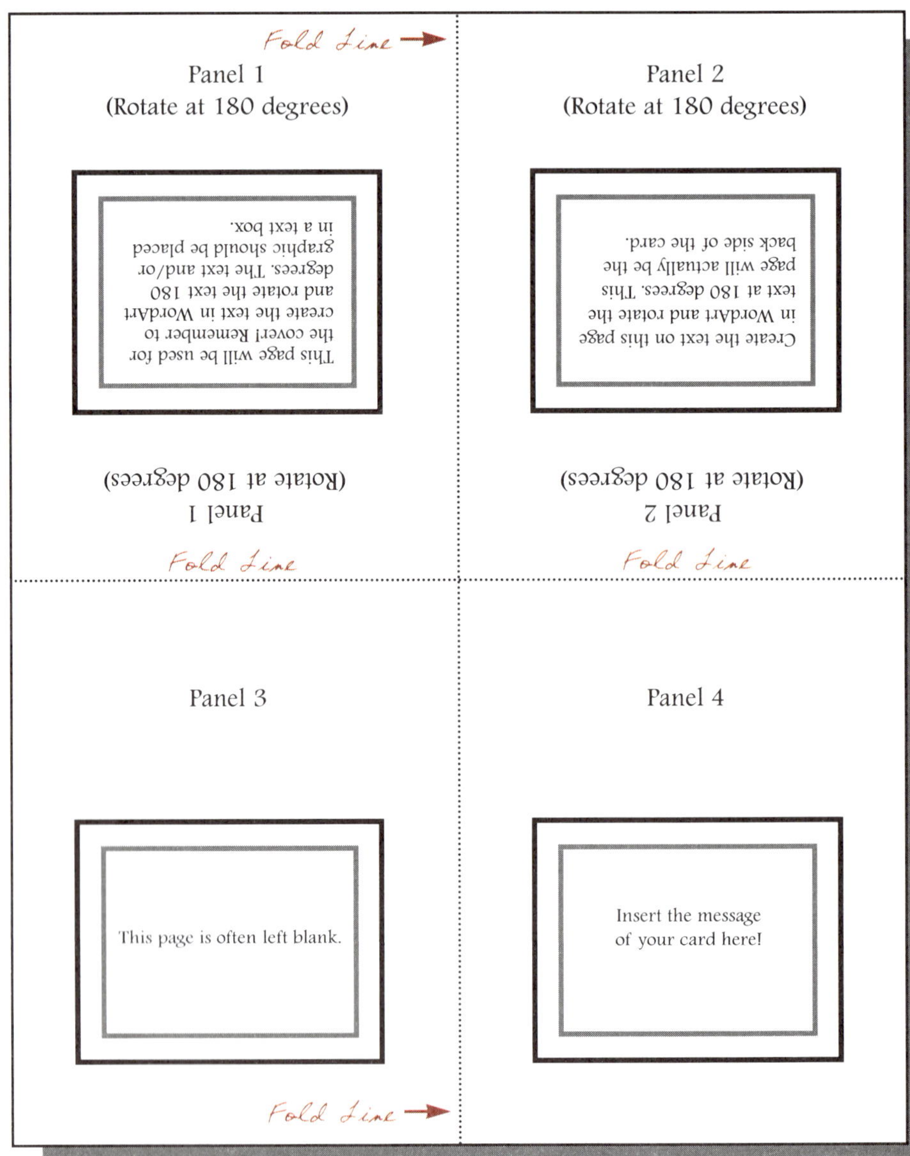

Alternatively, two invitations or greeting cards can be created on one sheet of paper by changing the paper orientation to landscape, then dividing the paper into four sections using cells in a table. You would then format and key the text and then print on one side. The paper is then reinserted in the printer and text is printed on the reverse side. The last step is to cut the paper in half, folding the top to meet the bottom (see figure 7.15).

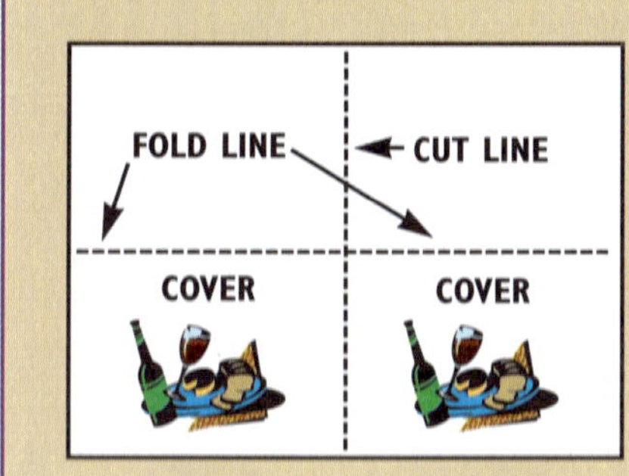

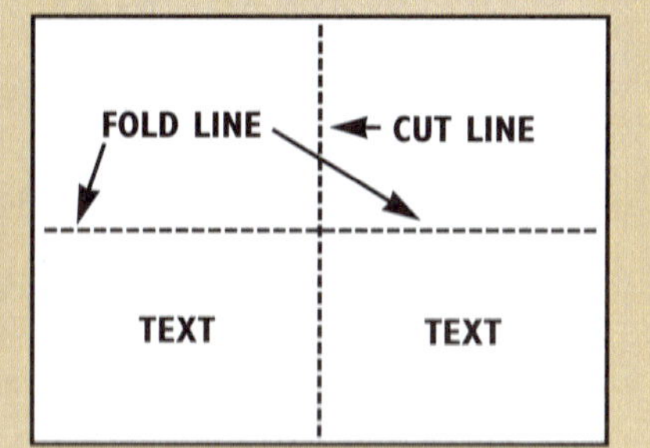

FIGURE 7.15

Guide for Creating Two Cards on One Sheet of Paper in Landscape Orientation

Planning and Designing Cards

In planning and designing your cards, consider focus, balance, proportion, contrast, and directional flow. Since you are working in a small area, remember to allow plenty of white space around design elements. If you are using a graphic image for focus, be sure that the image relates to the subject of the card. Shaded images (watermarks), symbols from the font special character sets, shapes, lines, and freeform designs add interest and individuality to your card design. Promote consistency through the use of color, possibly picking out one or two predominant colors from the graphic image used in your card. If the image appears in black and white, consider adding color to the image at Microsoft Word Picture. Select one or two fonts that match the tone of the document. For a formal invitation, consider using Brush Script MT Italic, Algerian, Colonna MT, or Desdemona. For bold and powerful text, consider Impact, Wide Latin, Braggadocio, or Arial MT Black.

DTP POINTERS
Pick out a color in a graphic to add color to accompanying text.

DTP POINTERS
Formal invitations often use a symmetrical design.

Your choice of paper is also important—consider using a heavier weight paper, such as 60- or 65-pound uncoated cover stock paper. Another possibility is to use marbleized paper or parchment paper for invitations and other types of cards. Predesigned papers or colored paper may add impact and interest to your document.

If you have a long list of guests, consider creating a master copy and taking it to a commercial printer to have it reproduced and machine folded. For a mass mailing of an invitation or a holiday card, consider creating a data source consisting of names and addresses of your guests, then merge this information onto envelopes or mailing labels.

Creating an Invitation Using a Table

1. At a clear document window, create the invitation shown in figure 7.16 by completing the following steps:
   a. Change the top, bottom, left, and right margins to 0.5 inches. (If a prompt regarding margins displays, click the Fix button to allow Word to increase the margin setting.
   b. Turn on Kerning at 14 points.
   c. Change the Zoom Control to 75%.
   d. Display the Drawing toolbar.
   e. Display the Borders toolbar.

f. Insert a table and include the following specifications:
   (1) Create a table with two columns and two rows.
   (2) With the insertion point positioned inside the table, choose Table, then Cell Height and Width.
   (3) At the Cell Height and Width dialog box, select the Row tab.
   (4) Change the Height of Rows 1–2: to *Exactly*, then key **350 pt** in the At text box. Make sure 0" displays in the Indent From Left text box and Left Alignment is selected. Deselect Allow Row to Break Across Page.
   (5) Select the Column tab.
   (6) Make sure the Width of Column 1 is 3.83 inches and the Space Between Columns measurement is 0.15 inches.
   (7) Click the Next Column button, then make sure the Width of Column 2 is 3.83 inches.
   (8) Choose OK to close the dialog box.

g. Create the text in the first cell of the first row of the table (Panel 1 as shown in figure 7.14) that contains the text, *Celebrating Books*, by completing the following steps:
   (1) With the insertion point located in the first cell, click the Text Box button on the Drawing toolbar, then drag the crosshair to create a text box that is approximately 1.25 inches in height and 3 inches in width. (If a fill and a border display around the text box, click the Fill Color and Line Color buttons on the Drawing toolbar and select None.)
   (2) Choose Insert, then Object.
   (3) At the Object dialog box, select the Create New tab, then double-click Microsoft WordArt 3.0 (2.0) in the Object Type list box.
   (4) Key **Celebrating Books** in the text entry box.
   (5) Choose Update Display.
   (6) Click the Line and Shape button (first button from the left) on the WordArt toolbar. Select the last shape in the fourth row (Wave 2).
   (7) Change the font to Britannic Bold.
   (8) Make sure Best Fit appears in the Font Size text box.
   (9) Click the Alignment button (sixth button from the right) and make sure Center is selected.
   (10) Click the Stretch button (seventh button from the right) on the WordArt toolbar.
   (11) Click the Special Effects button (fourth button from the right) and key **180** degrees in the Rotation text box. Choose OK or press Enter.
   (12) Click the Shading button (third button from the right) and select Purple at the Foreground text box. Make sure White displays in the Background text box. Choose OK or press Enter.
   (13) Click the Shadow button (second button from the right) and select the third shadow box from the left. Select Silver at the Shadow Color text box. Choose OK or press Enter.
   (14) Click in the document screen outside the text entry box to remove the text entry box.
   (15) At the document window, select the text box containing the WordArt object, increase the size by dragging the sizing handles, and move the object to a location similar to figure 7.16.

h. Create another text box that will hold the picture of the books as shown in figure 7.16 by completing the following steps:
   (1) Click the Text Box button on the Drawing toolbar and create a box that measures approximately 2 inches in height and 3 inches in width. (If a fill or border displays around the text box, click the Fill Color and Line Color buttons on the Drawing toolbar and select None.)

(2) With the insertion point located in the text box, choose Insert, then Picture.
(3) At the Insert Picture dialog box, make sure Clipart displays in the Look in text box, then double-click *Books*.

i. Edit the picture of the books by completing the following steps:
(1) Double-click the *Books* image to access Microsoft Word Picture.
(2) Position the arrow pointer on the ink bottle in the picture, then double click to select the bottle and access the Drawing Object dialog box. Select the Fill tab. Select the Dk Magenta color in the last row of the Color palette. Click OK or press Enter.
(3) Click the Select Drawing Object button (twelfth button from the left) on the Drawing toolbar. Beginning in the left corner of the grid that displays around the picture, drag and draw a dashed box around the entire image. When you release the mouse, the image should display in segments. (The image is ungrouped at this point.)
(4) Click the Group button (tenth button from the right) on the Drawing toolbar. (The image displays as one unit.)
(5) Click the Flip Vertical button (seventh button from the right) on the Drawing toolbar.
(6) Click the Flip Horizontal button (eighth button from the right) on the Drawing toolbar.
(7) Choose the Close Picture button to close Microsoft Word Picture.
(8) If necessary, select the text box containing the book picture and drag it to a location on the page as shown in figure 7.16.

j. Create the gray dashed line at the top and bottom of the first cell (panel 1) as shown in figure 7.16 by completing the following steps:
(1) Click the Line button (first button from the left) on the Drawing toolbar. Drag the crosshair into the first panel, hold down the Shift key, and draw a straight line at the top of panel 1 (the TextArt object and the book picture are upside down). The line should be positioned as shown in figure 7.16.
(2) Click the Line Color button on the Drawing toolbar and select Lt Gray in the eighth row and fourth column.
(3) Click the Line Style button (eleventh button from the left) on the Drawing toolbar and click More… at the bottom of the drop-down menu. At the Line tab, click the down-pointing arrow to the right of the Style text box and select the third line style from the top of the list. Click the down-pointing arrow to the right of the Weight text box and select 6 pt. Choose OK or press Enter.
(4) Select the gray, dashed line created in step l, then hold down the Ctrl key, and drag a copy of the line to the bottom of the panel as shown in figure 7.16.

k. Create the text in the second cell in the first row of the table (panel 2—see figure 7.14.) by completing the following steps:
(1) Position the insertion point inside panel 2. Click the Center align button on the Formatting toolbar.
(2) Click the Text Box button on the Drawing toolbar and create a box that is approximately 0.50 inches in height and 1.75 inches in width.
(3) Access WordArt 3.0 (2.0).
(4) Key **Created expressly for you** (press Enter) **by Arial Greetings, Ltd.** (press Enter) **1997** in the text entry box in WordArt.
(5) Change the font size to 8 points (key **8** in the Font Size box, since 8 is not available in the font drop-down list.) At the Font text box, select Times New Roman.
(6) Click the Special Effects button and key **180** degrees in the Rotation text box. Choose OK or press Enter.
(7) Click outside the text entry box to exit WordArt.

(8) Select the text box containing *Created expressly for...* and position it as shown in figure 7.16.

l. The first cell in the second row of the table (panel 3—see figure 7.14) will be blank.

m. Create the text in the second cell in the second row of the table (panel 4—see figure 7.14) by completing the following steps:

(1) Position the insertion point inside panel 4, then choose Insert, then File.

(2) At the Open dialog box, double-click *Panel 4, Invitation* located on your student data disk. (The text will display a little off center in the cell—when the paper is folded it should display properly.)

(3) Select the text box containing the card message, click the down-pointing arrow to the right of the Shading button on the Borders toolbar, then select 10% at the drop-down menu. Deselect the box.

2. View the document in Print Preview. Make sure all the design elements are positioned correctly as shown in figure 7.16.
3. Save the card as c07ex08, invitation.
4. Print, close, then fold c07ex08, invitation.

FIGURE 7.16

Optional: Create the four-paneled invitation form in portrait orientation and save it as a template. Create an invitation form in landscape orientation (see figure 7.14) and save it as a template.

Chapter Summary

- Besides flyers and announcements, other promotional documents include gift certificates, invitations, postcards, name tags, and invitations (or greeting cards). They become promotional documents when a business or organization name is visible or an item is mentioned for sale in a document. Promotional documents are designed to advertise or promote an interest or sale.
- The label definition formats your document so that you can print on designated label sheets.
- Use the AutoText feature to assist you in formatting documents created in Word's Label feature.
- Word includes a mail merge feature that you can use to create letters, envelopes, postcards, and much more, all with personalized information.
- A data source document and a main document are needed to perform a merge. A *data source* document contains the variable information. The *main document* contains the standard text along with identifiers showing where variable information is to be inserted. The identifiers are known as *field codes.*
- Any formatting codes you want applied to the merged document should be inserted in the main document.
- Use Word's Mail Merge Helper to assist you in creating the data source and the main document.
- Use WordArt to rotate text.
- Use Microsoft Word Picture (graphic editor) to group an image before flipping it vertically or horizontally.

Commands Review

	Mouse/Keyboard
Insert Table dialog box	Table, Insert Table
New dialog box	File, New
Envelopes and Labels dialog box	Tools, Envelopes and Labels
AutoText dialog box	Edit, AutoText
Mail Merge Helper dialog box	Tools, Mail Merge

Check Your Understanding

True/False: Circle the letter T if the statement is true; circle the letter F if the statement is false.

T F 1. A main document is a document that contains variable information about customers, clients, products, etc.

T F 2. Mail Merge is the process of combining information from a database to a data source.

T F 3. FirstName, JobTitle, and Address1 are examples of field names.

T F 4. The data source can be created in a table format or a tab format.

T F 5. The AutoText feature can be used to store text and graphics used to format a label.

T F 6. WordArt text can be sized at the Drawing Object dialog box.

T F 7. You can crop, scale, and size a picture to specific dimensions.

T F 8. Cells in a table can be formatted with options at the Paragraph Borders and Shading dialog box.

T F 9. Tables, like frames, exist in the text layer and text automatically wraps around them.

T F 10. A record contains all the information for one field.

Completion: In the spaces provided, indicate the correct term, command, or number.

1. At the ________________ dialog box, predetermined fields are provided by Word.
2. The data source and the main document can be merged to a new document or to the ____________________.
2. A series of ________________________ make a record.
3. FirstName, JobTitle, and Address1 are examples of ____________________ .
4. You can merge the source document to the main document by clicking the Merge to New Document button on the ________________________ toolbar.
5. To rotate text, you must create the text in ________________________.
6. To rotate a picture 180 degrees, click this button on the Drawing toolbar: ________________________.
7. The ________________________ document contains variable information about customers, etc.
8. Press ________________________ to insert a tab code within a table.
9. You can group or ungroup a graphic image at Word's graphic editor, which is known as ________________________.

Skill Assessments

Assessment 1

You are working part time at Hayden's Sporting Center while attending Western Michigan University in Kalamazoo. Your employer has asked you to prepare several $25 gift certificates to be used toward purchases in the store. Please prepare one certificate according to the following specifications. When completed, copy the certificate to fill a page (see figure 7.17).

1. Open the gift certificate template created in exercise 1.
2. Change the Zoom Control to 75%.
3. Turn on Kerning at 14 points.
4. Make sure the default font is 12-point Times New Roman.
5. Display the Drawing toolbar.
6. Position the insertion point inside the table (certificate form) and merge the two cells by completing the following steps:
   a. Choose Table, then Select Row.

b. Choose Table, then Merge Cells.

7. Choose Format, then Borders and Shading. Select the Borders tab, then select the Box in the Presets section and change the Line Style to 4½ pt. Click OK or press Enter.
8. With the insertion point positioned inside the table, change the alignment to Center. Press Enter once.
9. Change the font to Britannic Bold and key the text as shown in figure 7.17. Use the Shift and hyphen key to create the line (this type of line copies well in a table). Select the text and change the font sizes and colors. (You determine the appropriate font sizes and add color to the text.)
10. Click the Rectangle button on the Drawing toolbar. Drag to create a rectangle that is slightly smaller than the table cell (this box will form the inside border of the certificate). Click the Line Style button on the Drawing toolbar and select the fourth line from the top (4 pt) at the drop-down list. Click the Line Color button on the Drawing toolbar and select Dk Red in the last column of the seventh row. If a fill displays in the box, click the Fill Color button on the Drawing toolbar and select None.
11. Create a text box that is approximately 2 inches in height and 5 inches in width. (This box will contain the watermark image.) If a fill or border displays, click the Fill Color and Line Color buttons and select None at each.
12. Insert the picture *Tennis*. Resize the image if necessary to fit inside the certificate. Access Microsoft Word Picture and reduce the shading of the image at the Fill tab of the Drawing Object dialog box (do *not* group the entire picture, point to the black lines in the image and double-click on separate segments of the image, then change the shading to 15% or 20% of the color). Click the Close Picture button when completed.
13. If the watermark displays above the text in the certificate, select the watermark, then click the Send Behind Text button (eleventh button from the left) on the Drawing toolbar.
14. With the insertion point located in the table, choose Table, then Select Row.
15. Copy and paste the certificate twice. (Text boxes do not copy well in tables when you use the cut and paste features. Select the watermark [to select the watermark, click the Select Drawing Object button, the twelfth button on the Drawing toolbar, and position it on the watermark in the certificate and click to select the image], then hold down the Ctrl key and drag a copy of the certificate to the remaining two certificates. If the dk red border does not display in the certificates, select the border and while holding down the Ctrl key, drag a copy to each remaining certificate.)
16. Save the document as c07sa01, sports certificate.
17. Print and then close c07sa01, sports certificate.

FIGURE 7.17

Gift Certificate

Presented to ______________________________

This certificate entitles the bearer to $25 off any purchase at

Hayden's Sporting Center
3290 University Avenue
Kalamazoo, MI 49078

Gift Certificate

Presented to ______________________________

This certificate entitles the bearer to $25 off any purchase at

Hayden's Sporting Center
3290 University Avenue
Kalamazoo, MI 49078

Gift Certificate

Presented to ______________________________

This certificate entitles the bearer to $25 off any purchase at

Hayden's Sporting Center
3290 University Avenue
Kalamazoo, MI 49078

Assessment 2

You are working at Tuscany Realty and have been asked to prepare an announcement of an upcoming open house advertising the sale of a custom-built home on a golf course. The announcement is to be prepared as a postcard and mailed to prospective clients and all homeowners in this neighborhood. This promotional document makes the realtor's name visible to any homeowners in this neighborhood who may be thinking of selling their homes or buying a new one. The card will be reproduced at a printing company. Create two postcards similar to the ones shown in figure 7.18. Follow the guidelines given below.

1. Create the formatting and text for the postcard by completing the following steps:
   a. Choose the *Avery 5389 - Postcard* definition at the Labels dialog box.
   b. Click the New Document button at the Labels dialog box.
   c. Create the dots in the left corner and bottom corner of the postcard by inserting

the Wingding symbol found in the third row and the eighth column from the right. The small dots are also in the Wingding character set and located in the fifth row and the sixteenth column from the left. (Use F4, the repeat key, to save time in duplicating the dots.)

   d. The vertical line was drawn into the postcard using the Line button on the Drawing toolbar (be sure to hold down the Shift key as you draw the line).
   e. Create text boxes inside the label (table format) to hold the picture and formatted text. Even though text boxes do not consistently copy well using cut and paste, they provide an easier means for positioning pictures and text on a page.
   f. Create a text box to hold the WordArt text, *Tuscany Realty.* (WordArt can be accessed in the label feature.) Use the Deflate (Bottom) shape in the fifth row and the fourth column of the Line and Shape palette. Select the Wide Latin font and change the font color to purple.
   g. Insert the picture, *Realest* in a text box. Size the image as it appears in figure 7.18.
   h. Use Footlight MT Light for the office address and *Open House.* Use Times New Roman for the message text.

2. Copy the first postcard text to the second postcard in the label definition using the Drag-and-Drop method of copying.
3. Save the document as c07sa02, open house.
4. Print and then close c07sa02, open house.

Optional: Create a data source consisting of four of your friends, neighbors, co-workers, or relatives. Create a main document using your return address, the field codes for the data source, and any graphic or symbol that attracts attention and relates to the subject matter in assessment 2. Merge the data source to the main document and print the merged document to the reverse side of the postcards created in assessment 2.

FIGURE 7.18

Tuscany Realty

Sales Office

765 Sun Valley Drive
San Diego, CA 73021
(610) 555-9000

You are invited
to an

OPEN HOUSE

Sunday, April 21
from 1–4 p.m.

Come view an exquisite
custom-built home
overlooking
the seventh green at

1702 Granada Drive
Pebblestone Estate
San Diego

Tuscany Realty

Sales Office

765 Sun Valley Drive
San Diego, CA 73021
(610) 555-9000

You are invited
to an

OPEN HOUSE

Sunday, April 21
from 1–4 p.m.

Come view an exquisite
custom-built home
overlooking
the seventh green at

1702 Granada Drive
Pebblestone Estate
San Diego

Assessment 3

You are working for an accounting firm and have been asked to prepare name tags for your employer and five other employees who will be speaking at a banking conference. Design and create six name tags according to the following specifications:

- Choose the *Avery 5384 - Name Tag* definition at the Labels dialog box.
- Seminar name: **Northern Banking Association**
- Company name: **Rossi, DeLange Company**
- Create a company logo—use WordArt, symbols, graphics, or shapes, lines, etc. from the Drawing toolbar.
- Speakers' names are as follows:

  Frank B. Burton
  Rajendram Agtey
  Mary Jane Peterson
  Curtis Brown
  James McSherry
  Susan Howard

- Office is located in **Portland, ME**
- Save the document and name it c07sa03, name tags.
- Print and then close c07sa03, name tags.

Assessment 4

1. You are employed at First Bank and one of your responsibilities is to create an invitation to an *"Evening Out on the Town"* to be sent to several important bank clients. You may use Word's table feature and create the invitation in either landscape or portrait orientation. Refer to figures 7.14 and 7.15 in this chapter for two suggested layouts for your invitation. Add graphics, watermarks, lines, borders, symbols, or other enhancements to your document. Use the text and specifications listed below.

   On behalf of First Bank, we would like to cordially invite you to an "Evening Out on the Town" Thursday, May 22, 1997.

   Cocktails - 5:00 p.m.–5:30 p.m.
   Dinner - 5:30 p.m.–7:00 p.m.
   Trattoria 8
   15 North Dearborn Street
   Chicago, Illinois
   Theater - 7:30 p.m.
   Phantom of the Opera
   Chicago Theatre
   175 North State Street
   Chicago, Illinois

   First Bank management attending include:
   Jeffrey DeYoung, Executive Vice President; Michael H. Kapper, Executive Vice President; Gail S. Hartman, Senior Vice President; Gloria Martinez, Senior Vice President

   Please RSVP to Victoria Franz, (302) 555-3456 by April 25, 1996

Specifications:

- Consider your audience in creating an appropriate design.
- Prepare a thumbnail sketch.
- Use an appropriate font and vary the type size and type style.
- Change the character spacing in at least one occurrence.
- Use vertical and horizontal lines, or an appropriate graphic image, graphic border, or symbols to add interest and impact.
- Use special characters where needed—en or em dashes, bullets, etc.
- Change the leading if necessary.

2. Save the document and name it c07sa04, bank invitation.
3. Print and then close c07sa04, bank invitation.
4. Evaluate your invitation with the *Document Analysis Guide*.

Creative Activity

1. Create a promotional document of your own design or from an example you have saved or found in the mail, at a store, or from any other source. If you are using a sample document, first evaluate the document for good layout and design, clear and concise message, and proper use of other desktop publishing concepts as outlined in the *Document Analysis Guide*. Some possible promotional documents include the following examples:

    - Invitation to a new store opening
    - Bookmark
    - Name tag including a company or organization name or logo
    - Business greeting card
    - Postcard as a follow-up
    - Postcard used to promote a new business (coffee shop, party planner, attorney's office, computer services)
    - Membership card
    - Ticket with a company or organization name or logo
    - Gift certificate
    - Thank-you card
    - Employee retirement announcement
    - Company party invitation
    - Postcard advertising a sample sale
    - Raffle ticket for a charity
    - Postcard announcing the opening of a golf course
    - Postcard advertising services at a travel agency

2. Create a copy of the document with any necessary improvements. Try to find unusual, creative documents that were used to promote a business, organization, item, or event.
3. If the sample document was created on odd-sized paper, check to see if your printer can print it. You may need to recreate the document on a standard-sized paper then trim it to size.
4. Save the completed document and name it c07ca01, promotional.
5. Print and then close c07ca01, promotional. Attach the original document if one was used to c07ca01, promotional.

8 CREATING TABLES, CHARTS, AND PRESENTATION MATERIALS

PERFORMANCE OBJECTIVE

Upon successful completion of chapter 8, you will be able to define and create presentation materials, including transparencies/slides, tables, charts, and other supporting handouts using features in Word 7.0.

DESKTOP PUBLISHING CONCEPTS

Planning
Choosing a presentation visual medium
Kerning and tracking
Formatting a chart
Identity
Continuity
Color
Styles
Templates

WORD FEATURES USED

Page setup
Fonts
Frames
Character spacing
Pictures
Borders
Template
Tables
Microsoft Graph 5.0
Datasheet
Format
Chart Wizard
AutoFormat
Using styles
Modifying styles
Paragraph spacing
Bullets and numbering
Insert Sound Object

Defining Presentation Materials

Presentations are created and conducted for many different reasons. They are commonly used to:

- inform
- educate
- persuade
- motivate
- sell
- entertain

For example, a hospital needs to explain its new admission procedures to all patient admission staff; a financial consulting firm wants to sell its financial planning services and products; a large supermarket chain wants to entertain all management and celebrate 65 years of successful operation; a marketing representative from a packaging company wants to inform a current client's new buyer of its previous purchasing history; a coordinator of a community college office technology department wants to propose purchasing 20 computers and five color printers. As these examples indicate, presentations are not only for large audiences. They are often made to small- or medium-sized groups or presented one on one.

Presentation materials, such as transparencies, slides, graphs, flip charts, and handouts, are the supporting elements of a presentation. Handouts may include a history or introductory statement on letterhead, fact sheets, direct mail reply/response cards, testimonials, brochures, business cards, etc.

The concept of making a presentation and preparing presentation materials has been around for a long time. In the past, presentation materials were designed and created by outside sources, greatly adding to their cost. Today, advances in hardware and software make it possible to create most supporting presentation materials at your desktop, greatly reducing production costs.

DTP POINTERS
Creating presentation materials takes time, effort, practice, and patience.

In addition to production cost savings, creating your own presentation materials offers other advantages. You maintain total control over designing and producing the materials. Since you can easily make last minute changes, you can produce a top-quality product right up to the last minute. You have the flexibility of working around your own schedule, not the schedule of others. The only drawback of creating presentation materials on your own, as well as other desktop-published documents, is that it takes a great deal of time, practice, effort, and patience.

Planning A Presentation

The planning process for a presentation is basically the same as for other documents you have created in this textbook. In the planning stages:

- **Clearly define your purpose.** Do you want to inform? educate? sell? motivate? persuade? entertain?
- **Evaluate your audience.** Who will be listening to and watching your presentation? What is the age range? What is their educational level? What knowledge do they have of your topic? What image do you want to project to your audience? And what does your audience expect from your presentation?
- **Decide on content.** Decide on the exact content and organization of your message. Do not try to cover too many topics—this may strain the audience's attention or cause confusion.

Identifying the main point of the presentation will help you stay focused and convey a clear message.

- **Determine the medium to be used to convey your message.** Transparencies? slides? outlines? promotional fact sheets? To help decide the type of medium to be used, consider such items as the topic, availability of equipment, the size of the room where the presentation will be made, the number of people who will be attending the presentation, etc.

In this chapter, you will create presentation supporting materials for a company called Ride Safe, Inc. This company promotes and sells a bicycle and in-line skating safety program, along with bicycle helmets and other associated protective outerwear. To view the planning process in a more realistic way, consider the previous items in relation to a Ride Safe presentation.

Purpose: The purpose of a Ride Safe presentation is threefold. The company wants to *educate* audiences on bicycle and in-line skating safety and the importance of wearing protective outerwear to prevent serious injuries. The company wants to *motivate* the audience to take precautionary measures to prevent serious injuries. The company wants to *sell* its program and products.

Audience: Ride Safe presentations are most often made to adult audiences, although the safety program they sell is for children. The audience usually consists of parents, teachers, school administrators, or community program directors. This type of audience is usually well aware that bicycle and in-line skating accidents happen frequently—some serious, some not so serious. The educational levels and backgrounds of the audience members may vary. However, all the parents in the audience are naturally protective of their children and want to feel they are doing their best to protect them from harm.

Content: Content depends greatly on purpose. To achieve their goals, Ride Safe wants to include information about the company history and its goals. Statistics will be included on bicycle-related injuries and deaths. Additional information will be provided on why children have more accidents and why the company's program and protective equipment is the best choice. The company will also include information so individuals can request further information. Samples of the safety curriculum may be included.

Medium: Ride Safe prefers to use overhead transparencies as part of the presentation. Since the company's presentations often take place in schools, an overhead projector is readily available. Also, transparencies work well with their typical audience size of 50 people. Additionally, slides may be produced and then viewed using a slide projector; or an electronic slide presentation may be presented depending on the availability of presentation software, a computer, an overhead projector, and an LCD panel. Handouts, such as an introductory letter, a business card, and a return/reply postcard are also included in the presentation materials.

Selecting A Visual Medium

Selecting a visual medium depends on several factors: the topic, your style, your level of equipment-operating ability, audience size, location of presentation, equipment availability, lighting conditions, etc. Three common visual formats are overhead transparencies, 35mm slides, and electronic slide shows.

DTP POINTERS
Keep the text simple in transparencies and slides.

Transparencies are the most commonly used visual format for both formal and informal presentations. They work well with small- to medium-sized groups. Transparencies are preferred for many reasons. They allow for more interaction between audience and presenter; the lights stay on so the audience is able to take notes; equipment is readily available; overhead projectors are easy to use; additional points can be added or highlighted with a transparency marker; and they are fairly easy and inexpensive to produce. Laser and ink jet printers can print files you create on compatible transparency film. In addition, cardboard frames may be added to transparencies for ease in handling and as visual borders. Another piece of equipment, a transparency maker, can create a transparency from a printed copy of your document.

Thirty-five millimeter (35mm) slides are a popular visual format. Slides maintain high-quality color and can add visual impact to your presentation. Slide presentations work well with medium- to large-sized audiences. In order to produce slides, a special piece of equipment called a film recorder is necessary. This piece of equipment is attached to your computer and films the documents you want converted into slides. The film must then be taken to an outside service to be developed and made into slide images. Slide presentations tend to be more formal. The room needs to be darkened during a slide presentation, making it difficult for the audience to take notes or interact. Making last-minute changes to a slide presentation is difficult—they are more expensive to produce, and the equipment may be more difficult to operate.

Electronic slide shows are gaining popularity due to the array of presentation software on the market. Presentation software features let the user create "slides" for presentations. These slides, containing information and images created by you on the computer, do not have to be developed. The features of the presentation software enable the user to conduct a slide show from the computer screen. The ability to add animation and sound effects to presentations makes electronic slide shows especially attractive and effective. However, to conduct an electronic slide show, you must have a computer available, appropriate presentation software, an overhead projector, and a special computer projecting device called an LCD (liquid crystal display) panel. You also must be comfortable with the operation of the equipment and the software being used.

If you are using Microsoft Word 7.0 as part of the Microsoft Office suite (either Standard or Professional version) for Windows 95, you will be able to use Microsoft PowerPoint. PowerPoint is presented in the next chapter.

Creating Tables And Charts For Presentations

OLE:
Object linking and embedding.

Charts can be created with the *Microsoft Graph* application included in Word. Microsoft Graph is called an *applet*, which is a small application designed to work with Windows programs and contains Object Linking and Embedding (*OLE*) capability. OLE allows you to insert objects from one application into documents created with another application. OLE applications include Microsoft Excel, Microsoft Access, Windows Media Clip, Microsoft Graph 5.0, PowerPoint, and more. When you create a chart in Word 7.0, you are actually creating it in Microsoft Graph, Version 5.0, and embedding it in your document in Word.

In Word, a chart can be created from information created in a table in a Word document, keyed into Microsoft Graph's Datasheet, or imported from Microsoft Excel or other spreadsheet programs.

Tables can be used to illustrate data. While a table does an adequate job of representing data, a chart created from data in a table provides a more visual presentation. If a chart can represent the information you want to convey, then use a chart. Your audience can interpret information in a chart more quickly and easily than deciphering the same information in a table.

In the upcoming exercises, you will continue to prepare presentation materials for Ride Safe, Inc. You will first create a table; then, using the table, you will create a column chart with the help of ChartWizard and a pie chart using AutoFormat. These charts visually interpret statistical data that serve to inform, educate, and motivate Ride Safe's audience.

DTP POINTERS
Readers can interpret data in a chart more quickly and easily than in a table.

Creating Tables

Tables focus on data and present information in a concise, orderly manner. As discussed in earlier chapters, tables can be created by choosing Table, then Insert Table. At the Insert Table dialog box, select or key the number of rows and columns desired.

In exercise 1, you will create a table with data collected by the National Center for Health Statistics (NCHS) on death rates from bicycle injuries according to age and gender. These statistics are published by Johns Hopkins University Injury Prevention Center, 1993, sponsored by Snell Memorial Foundation, St. James, N.Y.

Since the table in exercise 1 is created for the sole purpose of creating a chart, formatting or customizing the table is not necessary. The table will be deleted after the chart is completed.

Creating a Table

1. At a clear document window, create the table shown in figure 8.1 by completing the following steps:
   a. Choose Table, then Insert Table.
   b. At the Insert Table dialog box, select or key **4** in the Number of Columns text box. Select or key **7** in the Number of Rows text box. (Auto should display in the Column Width text box.)
   c. Choose OK or press Enter.
   d. Key the data shown in the table in figure 8.1. Use the Tab key to move from one cell to the next. Use an en dash in the Ages column. (Choose Insert, Symbol, then select the Special Characters tab. From the Character list box, select En Dash; or press Ctrl + - [on the 10-key pad].)
2. Save the table and name it c08ex01, table.
3. Close c08ex01, table.

FIGURE 8.1

Ages	Male	Female	Total
1–4	29	10	39
5–9	243	55	298
10–14	348	66	414
15–19	270	29	299
20–24	160	25	185
25–34	227	39	266

Creating Charts

Graph: A picture of numeric data.

A chart communicates information quickly and clearly. A chart, sometimes referred to as a *graph*, is a picture of numeric data. Charts can enhance a presentation by translating numbers and values into images. Charts used in presentations can be shown in slides, transparencies, reports, fact sheets, or brochures. Additionally, presentation tools such as portable table-top easels with sheet protectors can be used when giving presentations on the go and to small audiences. The easels can hold and display charts and other presentation materials.

If you have a color printer, color can be added to enhance the information presented in the chart. For instance, data can be collected on the different colors of bike helmets sold by Ride Safe, and the colored bars in the chart can be made to coordinate with the colors of the helmets.

Creating a Chart from a Table

When you create a chart using the data from a Word table, you can include all the data in the table or you can include only parts of the table. Select only those table cells that contain the data from which the chart will be constructed. You can select an entire table by choosing Table, then Select Table, or by pressing Alt and the number 5 from the numeric keypad. To create a chart from data contained in a Word table, you would complete the following steps:

1. With the insertion point positioned within the table, choose Table, and then Select Table to select all the data in the table; or use the mouse to drag and select specific cells.
2. Choose Insert, then Object; or click the Insert Chart button if you have added this button to the Standard toolbar.
3. At the Object dialog box, select the Create New tab.
4. At the Object Type list box, double-click *Microsoft Graph 5.0*.

The data from the table is automatically inserted into a datasheet and a sample chart displays as shown in figure 8.2. The datasheet contains the text in cells as created in the table in the document. By default, Graph creates and displays a 3-D (three dimensional) Column chart, including a legend and some standard formatting. The chart is active by default. To make the datasheet active, click anywhere in the datasheet. To make the chart active, click anywhere in the chart.

FIGURE 8.2

Microsoft Graph Screen

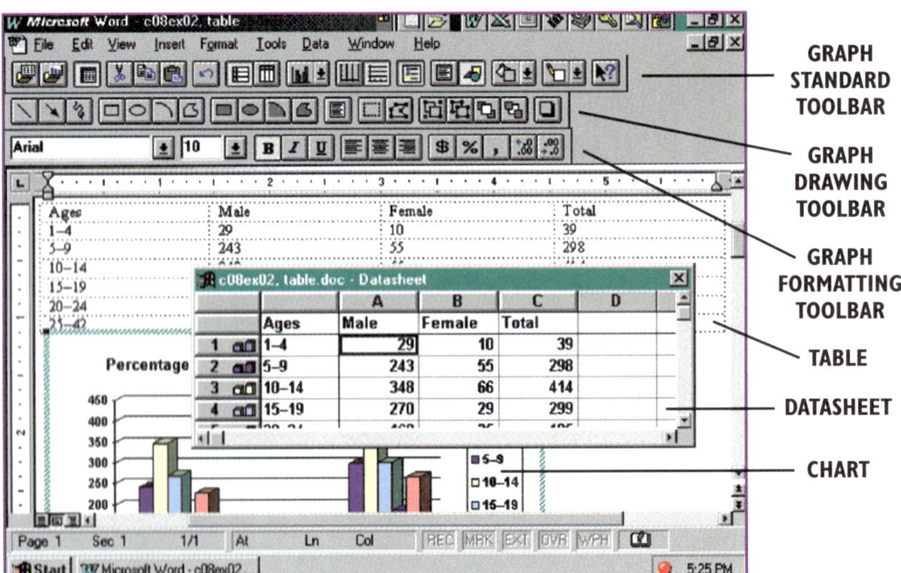

Displaying Microsoft Graph Toolbars

By default, the Microsoft Graph Standard toolbar displays below the menu bar at the top of the Graph screen as shown in Figure 8.2. Figure 8.3 illustrates the many features that can be applied to a chart through the use of the Microsoft Graph Standard toolbar.

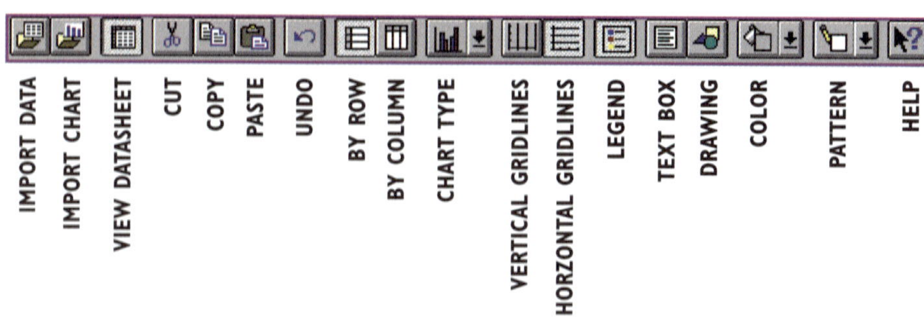

FIGURE 8.3

Microsoft Graph Standard Toolbar

The Drawing and Formatting toolbars, as displayed in figure 8.2, are provided in Graph to make designing and formatting a chart easier. To display these toolbars, position the mouse pointer within the Standard toolbar and click the right mouse button. Select *Drawing* and/or *Formatting* from the drop-down list. The Drawing and Formatting toolbars provide options similar to those in Word.

Adding the Insert Chart Button to the Standard Toolbar

Within this chapter, you will be creating charts to illustrate data for a Ride Safe presentation. For easy access to Microsoft Graph, you may want to add the Insert Chart button to the Standard toolbar as shown in figure 8.4.

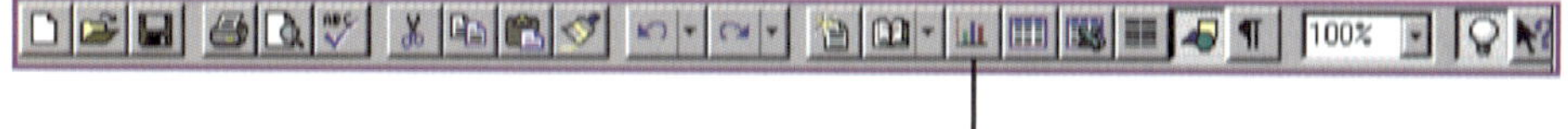

FIGURE 8.4

The Insert Chart Button Added to the Standard Toolbar

You would complete the following steps to add the Insert Chart button to the Standard toolbar.

1. Choose Tools, then Customize.
2. At the Customize dialog box, select the Toolbars tab.
3. In the Categories box, select Insert.
4. In the Buttons box, click the Insert Chart icon and drag it onto the Standard toolbar. (The icon looks like a chart with vertical bars as displayed in figure 8.4.)
5. Click Close at the Customize dialog box.
6. To start Microsoft Graph, click the Insert Chart button.

Identifying Datasheet Elements

Understanding the datasheet and chart terminology used by Microsoft Graph is necessary in order to use Graph efficiently and to customize charts to your specific needs. As mentioned earlier, information entered in a datasheet originates from one of three sources—data in a Word table, data in a spreadsheet from a program such as Excel, or data input directly into the

Datasheet:
A datasheet is a matrix of rows and columns that can be used to insert chart data instead of using a table or spreadsheet.

datasheet. A *datasheet*, similar to a spreadsheet or table, is a matrix of rows and columns that is commonly used to insert chart data instead of using a table or spreadsheet. As illustrated in figure 8.5, a datasheet has its own set of associated terminology.

FIGURE 8.5

Datasheet Elements

SELECT ALL BUTTON
COLUMN HEADING

Ch 08.doc - Datasheet

		A	B	C	D
		1st Qtr	2nd Qtr	3rd Qtr	4th Qtr
1	East	20.4	27.4	90	20.4
2	West	30.6	38.6	34.6	31.6
3	North	45.9	46.9	45	43.9
4					

ROW HEADING
DATA SERIES GRAPHIC
ACTIVE CELL

Editing the Datasheet

View Datasheet Button

Any time you access Graph to create a new chart in a document, the datasheet automatically displays. When you access an existing chart (by double-clicking inside the chart area), the datasheet is not visible. You can activate the datasheet anytime by choosing View, then Datasheet or by clicking on the View Datasheet button on the Graph Standard toolbar.

In a datasheet, the mouse pointer displays as a thick crossbar. To enter data in the Datasheet window, click in the desired cell and enter your data. As in a table or spreadsheet, you can move the insertion point to adjacent cells by using the arrow keys or by pressing Tab to move one cell to the right or Shift + Tab to move one cell to the left. To edit data in a cell, click the cell to make it active and enter the new information. You can select several cells at the same time by dragging the mouse over the desired cells. To select a whole row or column, click the column heading (labeled with A, B, C, etc.) or the row heading (labeled with 1, 2, 3, etc.). To select several rows or columns, drag the mouse over the desired row or column headings. To select all cells in the datasheet, click the Select All button in the top left corner as shown in figure 8.5.

If a data entry has too many characters to fit the current column width, the entry will display as a series of number symbols (#####). To solve this problem, position the insertion point on the vertical line to the right of the column heading (such as column B) until it displays as a double-pointed cross arrow. Click, hold, and drag the column border to the right to widen the column. When the column is wide enough to accommodate the data, the number signs will be replaced with the originally keyed data.

The quickest way to delete the contents of a cell, row, or column is to select the desired area and press the Delete key. The cell, row, or column will still exist but the contents will be deleted. To delete the contents and the row or column that contains the contents, select a cell in the desired row or column, and choose Edit, then Delete. Select Entire Row or Entire Column in the Delete dialog box. Use the Shift Cells Left option when you want to delete a cell(s) and shift the remaining cell contents to the left. Use the Shift Cells Up option when you want to delete a cell(s) and shift the remaining cell contents up.

Inserting a row or column in a datasheet is similar to inserting a row or column into a table. To insert a row, select a cell in the row that is to follow the new row. Choose Insert, Cells, and then select Entire Row. A new blank row will be inserted above the row that contains the selected cell. To insert a column, select a cell in the column that is to follow the new column.

Choose Insert, Cells, and then select Entire Column. A new blank column will be inserted to the left of the row that contains the selected cell.

You can format the contents of the datasheet by displaying and using the Formatting toolbar in Graph. The last five buttons on the Graph Formatting toolbar allow you to format the data as dollars or percentages, to use a comma style that includes a comma as a thousandths separator and two decimal places, and to increase or decrease the number of decimal places in the selected data.

Cells can be moved or copied the same way they are moved or copied in a table. Use the Cut, Copy, or Paste buttons on the Graph Standard toolbar or use the Cut, Copy, and Paste commands from the Edit menu.

Identifying Chart Elements

Like a datasheet, a chart created in Microsoft Graph has its own set of associated terminology. Figure 8.6 displays the parts of a 3-D Column chart, the default chart type. Corresponding definitions are displayed in Figure 8.7.

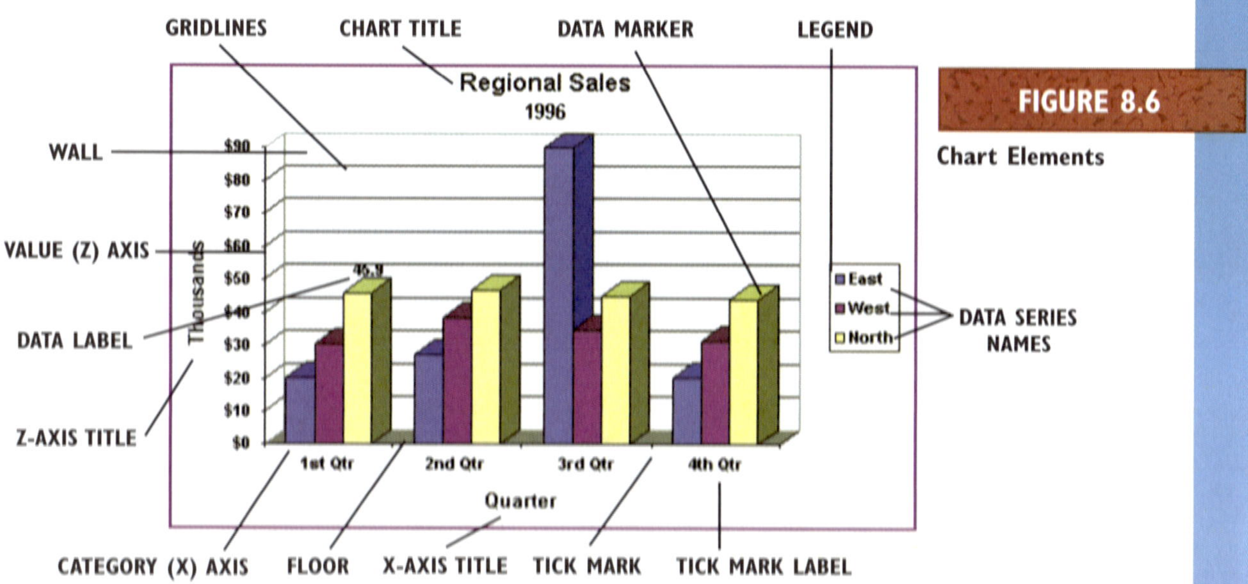

FIGURE 8.6

Chart Elements

Chart Title	The chart title is a name given to summarize the information in your chart. A chart title does not display by default.
Category (X) Axis	The category axis is the bottom horizontal line bordering the plot area of the chart and is known as the *x-axis.* By default, the x-axis displays the category names from the first row in the datasheet.
X-Axis Title	The x-axis title is a name given to summarize the category names displayed along the x-axis. An x-axis title does not display by default.

FIGURE 8.7

Chart Terminology

Value (Z) Axis	The vertical line that borders the left side of the chart. This line is known as the *z-axis* in a 3-D chart. By default, the z-axis displays a range of data values determined by the range of values in the datasheet.
Z-Axis Title (or Y-Axis Title in a 2-D Chart)	The z-axis title is a name given to the range of data values displayed along the z-axis. A z-axis title does not display by default.
Y-Axis	In a 2-D chart, the y-axis is the vertical line that borders the left side of the chart and displays a range of data values. When a specific 3-D Column Subtype chart is chosen, the y-axis displays along the right side of the chart floor and represents the data series names that are also shown in the legend.
Series Axis	This axis only displays in specific 3-D chart types and is known as the *y-axis*. By default, the data series names from the first column in the datasheet display along this axis.
Data Series	The data series is a series of values corresponding to the first row or column from the datasheet and plotted on the graph. The data series is identified in the datasheet by a chart graphic in the row or column heading.
Data Point	A data point is a value plotted in a chart corresponding to a single value in a datasheet cell. Data points are represented by a bar, column, slice, dot, etc.
Data Marker	A data marker is a bar, line, column, slice, dot, etc. representing a single value or data point in a data series.
Data Label	A data label is a data point value displayed on, above, or next to a data marker.
Legend	The legend displays the data series names. By default, the data series names are taken from the first column in the datasheet.
Tick Marks	Tick marks are the small lines that extend from an x-, y-, or z-axis.
Tick Mark Label	A tick mark label is a name for a category of data points.

Changing the Way Your Data Is Plotted

What you key in the first row and first column of a table and the *orientation* you choose determines how your data is plotted on a chart. By default, Microsoft Graph charts data in an orientation referred to as *Series in Rows*. With Series in Rows as the chosen orientation, Graph uses the text in the first column of the datasheet as the data series names, which Graph then uses as labels in the chart legend. Text in the first row of the datasheet becomes the category names that are displayed as tick mark labels below the x-axis (the horizontal axis). Figure 8.8 displays chart data plotted with a Series in Rows orientation.

FIGURE 8.8

Data Plotted Using Series in Rows Orientation

Document2 - Datasheet

		A	B	C	D
		1st Qtr	2nd Qtr	3rd Qtr	4th Qtr
1	East	20.4	27.4	90	20.4
2	West	30.6	38.6	34.6	31.6
3	North	45.9	46.9	45	43.9

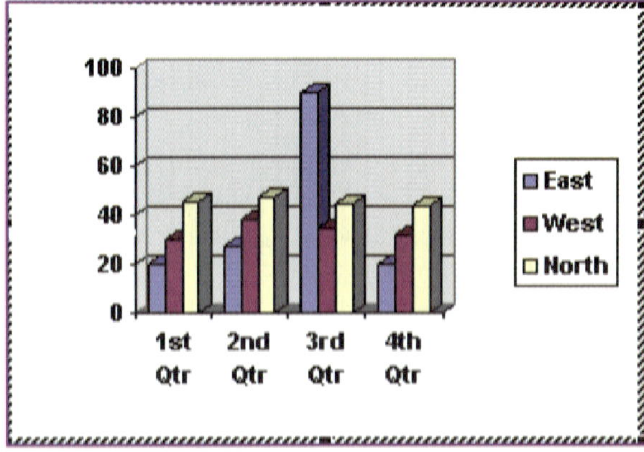

You can change the default method of plotting data by selecting *Series in Columns* orientation. When the orientation is changed to Series in Columns, text in the first row of the datasheet becomes the data series names, which Graph then uses as labels in the chart legend. Text in the first column of the datasheet becomes the category names, which Graph displays as tick mark labels below the x-axis. Figure 8.9 illustrates the same data used to create the chart in figure 8.8. However, the data displays differently because the orientation was changed to Series in Columns.

FIGURE 8.9

Data Plotted Using Series in Columns Orientation

Document3 - Datasheet

		A	B	C	D
		1st Qtr	2nd Qtr	3rd Qtr	4th Qtr
1	East	20.4	27.4	90	20.4
2	West	30.6	38.6	34.6	31.6
3	North	45.9	46.9	45	43.9

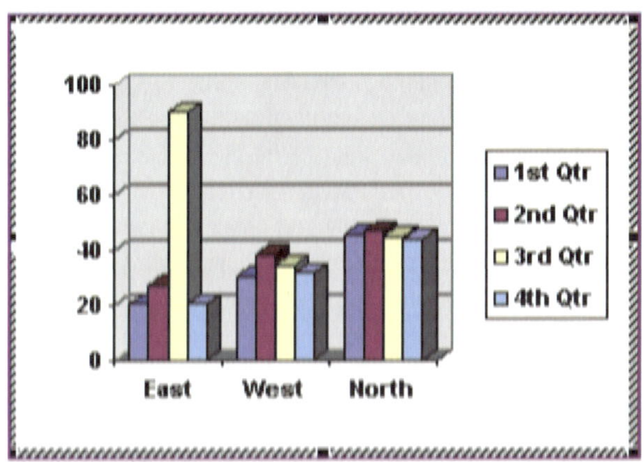

By Row

By Column

To change the chart orientation at the Microsoft Graph screen, click the By Row or By Column button on the Microsoft Graph Standard toolbar or choose Data from the menu bar, then select either Series in Rows or Series in Columns.

Which orientation is better? That decision is based on which method you think displays the data more clearly and concisely so that it is easily understood by the reader.

Adding Elements to a Chart

When a chart is created by Microsoft Graph, many elements are added by default. For example, the category names are automatically placed on the x-axis and the data series names are placed in the legend. In addition to these elements, you can include others such as a chart title; x-, y-, and z-axis titles; data labels; and gridlines.

To add or delete elements from a chart, choose Insert from the Graph menu bar. At the Insert drop-down menu, choose Titles, Data Labels, Legend, Axis, Gridlines, etc. to add or delete these particular items. For example, to add a chart title, an x-axis title, and a z-axis title to a chart, you would complete the following steps:

1. Display Microsoft Graph for the chart.
2. Choose Insert, then Titles.
3. At the Titles dialog box, click in the check boxes to the left of Chart Title, Value (Z) Axis, and Category (X) Axis to insert an X in each box. (To delete any of these items, click once to remove the X from the check box.)
4. Click OK or press Enter.

Follow similar steps to those above to add or delete data labels, a legend, axes labels, or gridlines.

Formatting Chart Elements

While in Microsoft Graph, some elements of a chart, such as the chart title, the axes titles, or the legend, can be selected and then moved. To select a chart element, position the arrow pointer on the element, then click the left mouse button one time. When a chart element is selected, selection handles (small black squares) display around the element. Depending on the element, the black squares may display within a shaded border or a single thin black border. To move a chart element, select the element, position the arrow pointer in the element, hold down the left mouse button, drag the element to the desired position, then release the mouse button.

Although only certain chart elements can be moved, all chart elements can be formatted. Two methods may be used to format chart titles. The first method involves using the Format option on the Graph menu bar. For example, to format the main chart title, click once in the title to select it, choose Format, and then Selected Chart Title. At the Format Chart Title dialog box, you can choose the Patterns, Font, or Alignment tab. The Patterns tab includes options to add a border to the chart title and to add color to the selected area behind the title. The Font tab contains options to change the font, font style, size, color, etc. The Alignment tab options let you align the title horizontally and vertically and change the orientation of the title. As a shortcut, you can double-click any chart title to directly access the formatting dialog box for that particular title. For instance, if you double-click an x-axis title, the Format Axis Title dialog box will display.

A second method of formatting chart titles is to click once in the title to select it and then apply any desired formatting using the options on the Graph Formatting toolbar. The formatting you choose will be applied to the whole title. You may replace a title in the same manner—select the title and key the replacement text. To format an individual item within a title, click the title once to select it and then click once again to display the I-beam pointer. Position the insertion point at the desired location, select the specific word, letter, or character in the title, and then apply formatting as desired using the options on the Graph Formatting toolbar. You can also insert and delete a word, letter, or character using this same method.

Some chart elements are grouped together, such as the data series. To select the whole data series, click any data marker belonging to the series. All of the data markers within that particular data series will display with selection handles. If the whole data series is selected, choose Format, and then Selected Data Series to display the Format Data Series dialog box. The options in this dialog box let you add a border and change the color/pattern of the data markers for the whole series and add data labels identifying the data point values. As a shortcut, double-click one of the data markers to quickly access the Format Data Series dialog box. To select a single data point within the series, select the whole data series (by clicking on any data marker within the series) and then click the specific data marker that represents the data point. Selection handles will display around that particular data marker only. Choose Format, then Selected Data Point to access the Format Data Point dialog box, which offers the same options as the Format Data Series dialog box.

Several other chart elements can be selected and formatted, such as the walls, floor, and gridlines. To select these elements, point to the element with the arrow pointer and follow the same procedure as with formatting other chart elements.

Two additional chart elements that can be formatted are the plot area and chart area. These elements are only visible when selected. The *plot area* includes the chart, the category names on the x-axis, the data point value range on the z-axis, the series names on the y-axis (if any), and the x-, y-, and z-axis labels (if any) as shown in figure 8.10. To select the plot area, click in the white space immediately surrounding the chart, such as to the immediate right of the chart or below the z-axis title. Experiment selecting the plot area to find the selection locations. Once the plot area is selected, you can add a border or a color/pattern to the selected area by choosing Format, then Selected Plot Area. As a shortcut, you can double-click the plot area to access the Format Plot Area dialog box.

The *chart area* includes the whole chart, and when selected, is identified by selection handles inside the border of the chart window as illustrated in figure 8.10. When the chart area is selected, you can choose Format, then Selected Chart Area to add a border or color to the chart area or to make font changes. This is useful when you want to change the font, font style, font size, and/or color of all the text in the chart at one time.

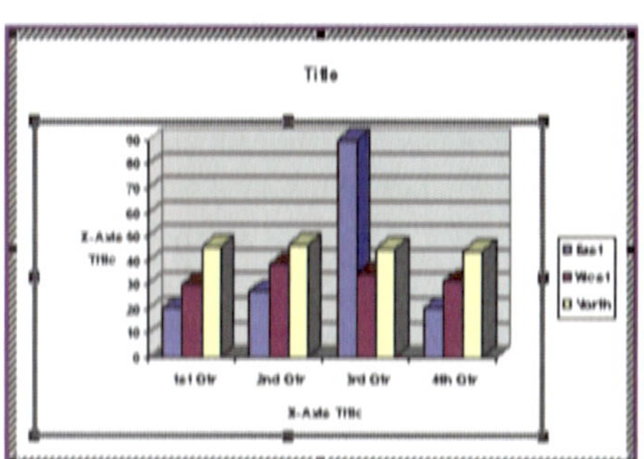

PLOT AREA SELECTED

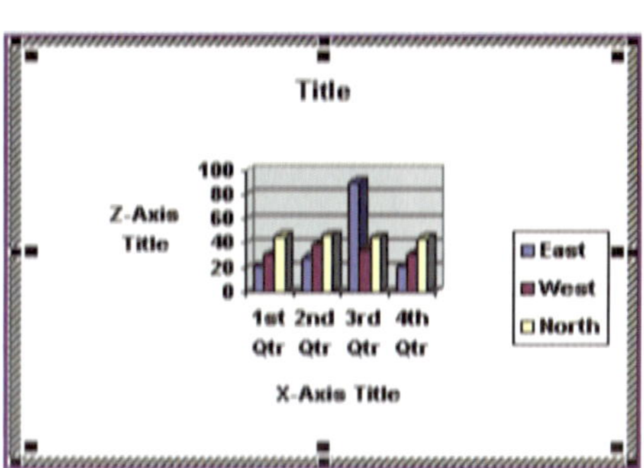

CHART AREA SELECTED

FIGURE 8.10

Plot Area and Chart Area

Updating a Chart

If you make changes to a value in a datasheet cell in the Microsoft Graph window, the chart will be updated as soon as you activate another cell or you click once inside the chart to activate the chart.

If data in a Word table used to create a chart is changed, the chart will not be updated automatically in Word or Graph. In this case, double-click in the chart to access Microsoft Graph and edit the table data in the datasheet.

Sizing and Framing a Chart

To change the size of a chart in the Microsoft Graph window, click and drag one of the side or corner sizing handles located on the slash-marked border. If you drag one of the corner sizing handles, the chart remains in proportion to its original dimensions.

If you want to size a chart to more specific measurements, you would complete the following steps:

1. Click outside of the Graph window to return to Word.
2. Click once inside the chart to select it.
3. Choose Format, Picture.
4. At the Picture dialog box, change the Width and Height in the Size section.
5. Click OK or press Enter.
6. Double-click on the chart to get back into Microsoft Graph.
7. Click outside the Graph window to return to Word and the size of the chart will be changed.

DTP POINTERS
Leave plenty of white space around a chart.

A chart can be framed like other graphic elements in a document. To frame a chart, change to the Page Layout viewing mode, select the chart, then choose Insert, Frame. When a chart is framed, it can be moved in the document. You can also customize the frame at the Frame dialog box and the Paragraph Borders and Shading dialog box.

Deleting a Chart

A chart displayed in the Word document screen can be deleted. To delete the chart, click once inside the chart to select it and then press the Delete key.

Using the ChartWizard to Create a Chart from a Table

ChartWizard: A Word feature that guides you through the chart creation process.

The *ChartWizard* displays dialog boxes that guide you through creating a chart as illustrated in figure 8.11. The ChartWizard lets you decide on the type of chart, the format, and how you want the data displayed. Depending on the task you are performing and the document in which you are working, the ChartWizard may or may not display when you access Microsoft Graph. The ChartWizard is not available for use with all applications that work in Microsoft Graph. The ChartWizard automatically displays in Graph when the source of the data is a table created in a Word document.

In exercise 2, you will use the ChartWizard to create a 3-D Column chart using data from the table created in exercise 1.

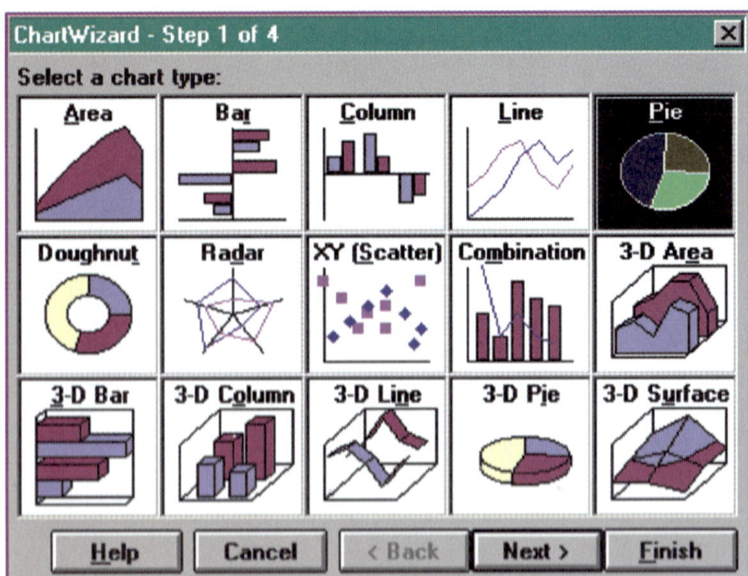

ChartWizard Dialog Box

Creating a Chart from a Table Using the ChartWizard

1. Open c08ex01, table.
2. Save the document with Save As and name it c08ex02, chart.
3. Change the paper orientation to Landscape.
4. Change the Top and Bottom margins to 1 inch. (The Left and Right margins should both be set at 1 inch.)
5. Turn on Kerning at 14 points and above.
6. Create the Column chart in figure 8.12 by completing the following steps:
   a. Select the entire table. To do this, position the insertion point inside the table, choose Table, then Select Table to select the entire table.
   b. Click the Insert Chart button on the Standard toolbar or choose Insert, Object, then Microsoft Graph 5.0.
   c. At the ChartWizard - Step 1 of 4 dialog box, make sure 3-D Column chart is selected, then click Next >.
   d. At the ChartWizard - Step 2 of 4 dialog box, make sure the fourth box is selected, then click Next >.
   e. At the ChartWizard - Step 3 of 4 dialog box, make sure the following items are selected: Data Series in Rows, first row as Category (X) Axis Labels, and first column Legend Text, then click Next >.
   f. At the Chart Wizard - Step 4 of 4 dialog box, make sure Yes is selected to Add a Legend. Click in the Chart Title text box, then key **Deaths from Bicycle-Related Injuries by Age and Gender, NCHS 1987–1988**. (Do not press Enter after Injuries—you will alter the title later.) Click in the Category (X) text box, then key **Gender and Total**. Click in the Value (Z) text box, then key **Deaths per 100,000**. Click Finish.
   g. Click the Close button in the upper right corner of the Datasheet to remove the Datasheet from the screen.
   h. If the chart does not fully display behind the Datasheet, select the chart, then drag the sizing handles to increase the size of the chart. (Specific measurements will be given in a later step.)
   i. Click outside the chart to return to the document—Microsoft Graph closes and

the Word toolbar reappears.

j. Click inside the table, choose Table, then Select Table. Choose Table again, then click Delete Rows. (This deletes the table.)

k. Click the chart then choose Insert, then Frame.

l. Size the chart (including the area around the chart along with the legend and title) by completing the following steps: (Alternatively, you can size a chart by dragging the sizing handles.)

  (1) With the chart selected, choose Format, then Picture.

  (2) At the Picture dialog box, select or key **8.75** inches in the Width text box and **6** inches in the Height text box.

  (3) Click the Frame button at the Picture dialog box.

  (4) At the Frame dialog box, change the Horizontal Position to *Center* and the Vertical Position to *Center*. Choose OK or press Enter.

m. Change the Zoom Control to 75 percent.

n. Double-click the chart to access Microsoft Graph.

o. Click the chart title to display the box with sizing handles. Position the insertion point after *Injuries*, click once, then press Enter.

p. Select the first line of the title, *Deaths from Bicycle-Related Injuries.* Choose Format, then Selected chart title. At the Font dialog box, change the font to 28-point Britannic Bold. Click the down-pointing triangle to the right of the Color text box and select the Teal box in the second row and sixth column of the color palette. Choose OK or press Enter. (If the chart appears too large, forcing the title to appear on the chart or out of proportion, click once to the left of the 450 tick mark on the z-axis to select the chart plot area. Then position the insertion point on the corner sizing handle in the upper left corner of the chart until the mouse pointer displays as a diagonal double-pointed arrow. Click and drag inward to reduce the size of the chart.)

q. Select the second line in the chart title, and change the font to 20-point Britannic Bold by choosing Format, then Selected chart title.

r. Click to select the z-axis label (the sizing handles should display), *Deaths per 100,000.* Choose Format, then Selected Axis Title.

s. At the Format Axis Title dialog box, select the Alignment tab.

t. Make sure Center is selected in the Text Alignment Horizontal section and Center is selected in the Vertical section.

u. In the Orientation section, select the second (middle) box.

v. Select the Font tab and change the font to 16-point Arial Bold. Choose OK or press Enter.

w. Click to select the Legend (the sizing handles should display). Choose Format, then Selected Legend. At the Format Legend dialog box with the Font tab selected, change the font to 14-point Arial Bold.

x. Select the Patterns tab and click inside the check box to turn on Shadow.

y. Select the Placement tab and make sure Right is selected in the Type box, then choose OK or press Enter. If the legend is not aligned as shown in figure 8.12, select and then drag it to the correct location.

z. Click to select the X axis title, *Gender and Total* (the sizing handles should display), then choose Format, then Selected Axis Title. Change the font to 20-point Britannic Bold.

7. Click outside the chart to return to the document window.
8. Choose File, then Print Preview. (Make sure the placement and size of the chart is similar to figure 8.12.)
9. Save the chart again with the same name c08ex02, chart.
10. Print and then close c08ex02, chart.

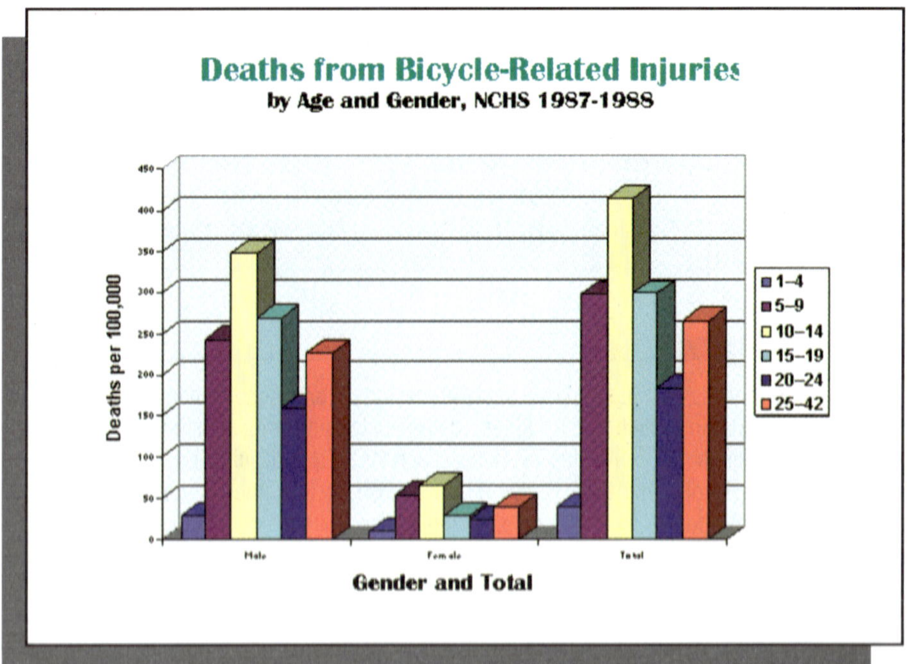

FIGURE 8.12

Customizing A Chart

Changing the Chart Type

You can choose from 15 chart types to present your data, as displayed in figure 8.11. Each chart type has several variations and combinations. While in Graph, you can change the chart type by clicking the Chart Type button (tenth button from the left) on the Microsoft Graph Standard toolbar, by making a selection from the first screen of the Chart Wizard, or by choosing Format, then Chart Type. Figure 8.13 summarizes each chart type.

DTP POINTERS
Select a chart type that most clearly and accurately represents your information.

Chart Type

Area (2D and 3D)	Shows trends and the amount of change over time.
Bar (2D and 3D)	Shows variations between data but not in relationship to the whole.
Column (2D and 3D)	Compares separate items as they vary over time.
Line (2D and 3D)	Shows trends and changes over time; can be used to display multiple data series.
Pie (2D and 3D)	Shows proportions and relationships of parts to the whole; can only display one data series.
Doughnut (2D)	Like the pie chart, shows proportions and relationships of parts to the whole; used to display more than one data series.
Radar (2D)	Shows changes of data series relative to a center point and to one another.

FIGURE 8.13

Types of Charts

Surface	Shows relationships between large amounts of data.
XY Scatter (2D)	Illustrates the interception points between x and y values; used primarily for scientific data.
Combination (2D)	Lays one chart over another; useful for comparing data of different types or data requiring different axis scales.

Using AutoFormat

AutoFormat: A feature that allows you to apply predesigned formats to a chart.

Choosing *AutoFormat* allows you to quickly apply predesigned formats to a chart. For instance, you can apply formatting such as gridlines, data labels, and more using AutoFormat. AutoFormat works much like templates or styles. Each AutoFormat selection is based on a chart type. To apply AutoFormat to an active chart, choose Format, then AutoFormat. In the Formats Used section, make sure Built-in is selected. In the Galleries section, select the chart type you want. In the Formats box, all built-in formats for the selected chart type are displayed. Choose the AutoFormat selection you want to apply to your active chart.

Creating a Pie Chart

A pie chart shows proportions and relationships of parts to the whole. Each slice (a data marker) in a pie chart represents a data point (a value from a cell in the datasheet, table, or spreadsheet). All the slices in a pie chart represent the values (data series) in a single category. The slices help the reader visualize how each slice (or data point) relates to the total for the whole data series.

A pie chart can only display one category and the values (data series) associated with that category. For example, in exercise 1, you created a table showing the number of deaths caused by bike-related injuries. This table includes statistics from three categories—males, females, and the total of males and females. To use a pie chart to represent all the information in the table, three tables or datasheets need to be created. One table or datasheet would be needed for the male statistics, one for the female statistics, and one for the total of males and females. Individual pie charts can then be made to display the information in each table or datasheet.

Some suggestions when creating pie charts for a presentation include the following:

- Limit the number of pie slices to a maximum of six; more than six is confusing.
- If you have more than six slices, try combining some of the smaller slices into an "Other" category, or consider making a second pie chart.
- Draw attention to an important slice by cutting and pulling a slice away from the chart—this is known as *exploding* a slice.
- Use plenty of white space around charts and accompanying text.
- Align the chart with any adjacent text columns.

Exploded Slice: To pull out a specific section of a pie chart for emphasis.

In exercise 3, you will create a pie chart using the Datasheet feature. You will key the data into the datasheet in Microsoft Graph. A pie chart will be created from the data in the datasheet. The pie slice representing the age category with the largest percentage of bicycle-related deaths will be exploded to call attention to this statistic. This data is important to your presentation because it validates the reason for selling helmets to children. In addition, you will use the AutoFormat feature in Graph to apply automatic predefined formatting to your chart.

Creating a Pie Chart Using a Datasheet

EXERCISE 3

1. At a clear document window, create the pie chart in figure 8.15 by completing the following steps:
   a. Change the Top, Bottom, Left, and Right margins to 0.75 inches.
   b. Turn on Kerning at 14 points.
   c. Click the Insert Chart button on the Standard toolbar if you have added this button to the Standard toolbar; or choose Insert, then Object, select the Create New tab, and double-click *Microsoft Graph 5.0.*
   d. Select all the cells in the datasheet by clicking the Select All button (as shown in figure 8.5).
   e. Choose Edit, Clear, then Contents; or press the Delete key.
   f. Key the following information in the first blank row (above row number 1) as shown in figure 8.14. (You cannot insert an en dash in the datasheet, therefore use "to" in place of an en dash to indicate a range.) Press Tab to advance to the next cell.

      Ages 1 to 4 5 to 9 10 to 14 15 to 19 20 to 24 25 to 34

   g. Key the following information beginning in cell A1 (the intersection of column A and row 1):

      39 298 414 299 185 266

Document2 - Datasheet

		A	B	C	D	E	F
	Ages	1 to 4	5 to 9	10 to 14	15 to 19	20 to 24	25 to 34
1	Pie 1	39	298	414	299	185	266
2							
3							
4							

FIGURE 8.14

Datasheet for c08ex04, pie chart

   h. With the datasheet displayed, click Format, then Chart Type.
   i. At the Chart Type dialog box, click 2-D in the Chart Dimension section, click the *Pie* box, then choose OK or press Enter.
   j. Choose Format, then AutoFormat.
   k. Select the sixth option in the Formats section, then choose OK or press Enter.
   l. Click the close box on the datasheet. (This box is located in the upper right corner of the datasheet—it has an X inside it.)
   m. Choose Insert, then Titles.
   n. At the Titles dialog box, click inside Chart Title text box, then choose OK or press Enter.
   o. Click once inside the chart title then click once again to position the insertion point so that a title may be keyed. Key **Percentage of Bicycle-Related Deaths by Age (1 to 34)**.
2. Increase the size of the chart by completing the following steps:
   a. Click outside the chart to return to the document screen. Change the view to Page Layout view, then change the Zoom Control to 50 percent.

b. Double-click on the chart to return to Microsoft Graph.
c. Click once to select the chart (the sizing handles should display). Make sure your chart displays in Page Layout view (a ruler should display above the document window as well as to the left of the document window.)
d. Position the arrow pointer on the middle right side sizing handle. When the arrow pointer becomes a horizontal double-headed arrow, drag it to the right side of the screen to the right margin setting that displays on the ruler where the white part of the ruler meets the dark part of the ruler. (If you hold down the Alt key and position the arrow pointer on the vertical line separating the white and dark parts of the ruler, 0.75 inches should display as the right margin.)
e. Position the arrow pointer on the bottom middle sizing handle. When the arrow pointer becomes a vertical double-headed arrow, drag the bottom border to the bottom margin as displayed on the left ruler in page layout view, then release. (The bottom border of the chart should display at the 0.75 bottom margin setting—this setting displays on the left ruler where the white part of the ruler meets the dark part of the ruler.)
f. Click outside the chart to exit Microsoft Graph and return to the document window.
g. Click to select the chart—all the sizing handles should display.
h. Choose Insert, then Frame.
i. Choose Format, then Frame.
j. At the Frame dialog box, click the down-pointing triangle to the right of the Position text box in the Horizontal section and select *Center*. In the Vertical section, change the Position to *Center*. Choose OK or press Enter.

3. Customize the chart at the Graph screen by completing the following steps:
   a. Double-click the chart to enter Microsoft Graph.
   b. Click to select the chart title, then choose Format, then Selected Chart Title. Select the Font tab, then change the font to 28-point Britannic Bold. Change the font Color to Teal, which is located in the second row and the sixth column of the color palette. Choose OK or press Enter.
   c. Click to select one of the percentages (the rest of the percentages should automatically become selected). Choose Format, then Selected Data Labels, then select the Font tab. Change the font to 14-point Arial Bold. Choose OK or press Enter.
   d. Click to select the Legend. Choose Format, then Selected Legend. At the Format Legend dialog box, select the Placement tab. Select the Bottom type. Select the Font tab and change the font to 16-point Arial Bold. Select the Patterns tab. Click inside the check box to turn on the Shadow option located in the Border section. (An X should display inside the box.) Choose OK or press Enter. Click to select the legend, then position the arrow pointer on one of the corner sizing handles. When the corner sizing handle becomes a diagonal double-headed arrow, drag the arrow inward causing the legend to display in two rows. Click the top center handle and drag outward to expand the width of the rows as shown in figure 8.15. Select the legend again and center it between the left and right margins.
   e. Click to select the yellow slice of the pie chart—the sizing handles should appear around the yellow slice only. Drag the yellow slice outward slightly to explode this piece—see figure 8.15.
   f. Click outside the chart to close Graph.

g. Choose File, then Print Preview. Make sure all the elements display similarly in size and location to the chart in figure 8.15. Make any necessary adjustments by first double-clicking to access Graph. (If the pie chart appears to display too low on the page, click once on the parameter of the pie chart to select it—a square box with sizing handles should display around the pie chart. Click again until the mouse pointer displays as a four-headed arrow, then drag the pie chart upward to center it vertically on the page. Also, you may need to drag the chart to the right slightly.)

4. Save and name the chart c08ex03, pie chart.
5. Print and then close c08ex03, pie chart.

FIGURE 8.15

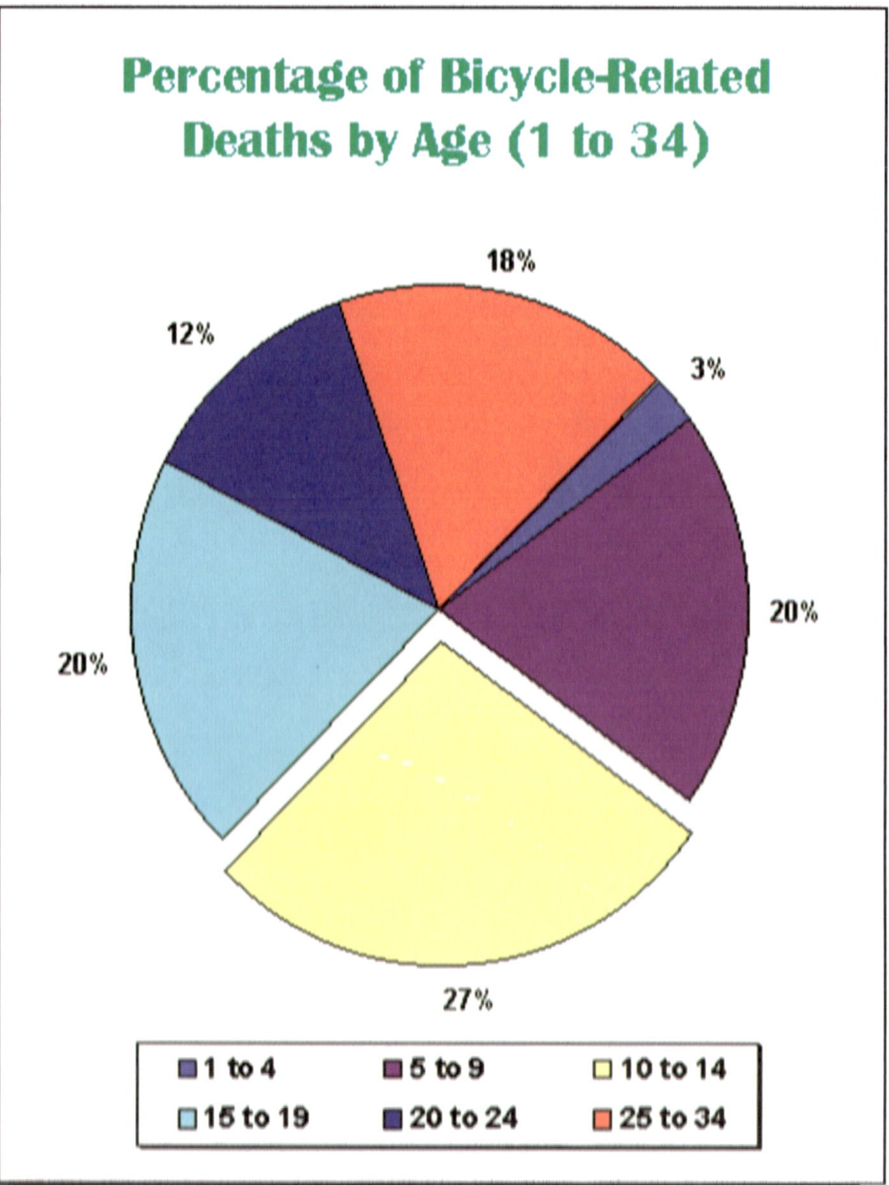

As mentioned earlier, different elements can be added to a chart and chart elements can be formatted in a variety of ways. In exercise 4, you will create a 3-D column chart and size the chart. You will then insert and format a chart title, subtitle, and data labels. In addition, you will change the color of the data markers, the thickness of the gridlines, the color of the walls, and the position and border of the legend.

Creating and Customizing a Chart

1. At a clear document screen, create the column chart shown in figure 8.16 by completing the following steps:
   a. Change the paper orientation to Landscape.
   b. Change the Top and Bottom margins to 1 inch. (Both the Left and Right margins should already be set at 1 inch.)
   c. Turn on Kerning at 14 points and above.
   d. Click the Insert Chart button on the Standard toolbar if you have added this button to the Standard toolbar; or choose Insert, then Object, select the Create New tab, and double-click *Microsoft Graph 5.0*.
   e. Insert data into the datasheet by completing the following steps:
      (1) Click the Select All button in the upper left corner of the datasheet to select all the cells in the datasheet.
      (2) Choose Edit, Clear, and then Contents; or press the Delete key.
      (3) Position the insertion point in the first cell in the first blank row and key the following information in the first column (widen the column to accommodate the text).

         Head
         Face
         Trunk
         Upper Extremity
         Lower Extremity
         Multiple
         Other

      (4) Key the following information in the second column:

         Total Number Admitted to Hospitals
         23052
         3977
         8098
         9342
         10789
         4646
         937

   f. Format the chart by completing the following steps:
      (1) With the datasheet still displayed, choose Format, then Chart Type.
      (2) At the Chart Type dialog box, make sure 3-D is selected in the Chart Dimension box, and the 3-D Column box in the first row of the chart type box is selected, then click OK or press Enter.
      (3) Choose Format, then AutoFormat.
      (4) At the AutoFormat dialog box, make sure 3-D Column has been selected in the Galleries list box, then select the fourth AutoFormat in the first row of the Format box. Choose OK or press Enter.
      (5) Click the By Row button (eighth button from the left) on the Graph Standard toolbar.

g. Click the close box in the upper right corner of the datasheet; or choose View, then Datasheet.
h. Click outside the chart to exit Microsoft Graph and return to the Word document screen.
i. At the Word screen, change the Zoom Control to 75 percent so the chart will be easier to work with.
j. Size and position the chart, including the area around the chart, along with the legend and title, by completing the following steps:
   (1) Select the chart at the document window.
   (2) Choose Format, then Picture.
   (3) At the Picture dialog box, select or key **8.75** inches in the Width text box and **6** inches in the Height text box. Choose OK or press Enter.
   (4) To activate the size change, double-click inside the chart to access Microsoft Graph.
   (5) Click outside the graph to return to the document window. (Change the Zoom Control to Whole Page to verify that the chart size has changed.)
   (6) Choose Insert, then Frame.
   (7) Choose Format, then Frame. At the Frame dialog box, change the Horizontal Position to *Center* and the Vertical Position to *Center*. Choose OK or press Enter.
   (8) Change the Zoom Control to 75 percent.
k. Insert and format the chart title by completing the following steps:
   (1) Double-click the chart to access Microsoft Graph.
   (2) Choose Insert, then Titles.
   (3) At the Titles dialog box, click inside the check box to select Chart Title.
   (4) Choose OK or press Enter.
   (5) Click once inside the chart title, select the heading, *Title*, then key **Number of Patients with Bicycle-Related Injuries**, press Enter, and then key **Admitted to Hospitals by Part of Body Injured**.
   (6) Select *Number of Patients with Bicycle-Related Injuries* and choose Format, then Font.
   (7) At the Format Chart Title dialog box, change the font to 22-point Britannic Bold and change the font Color to Teal (second row, sixth column of the color palette).
   (8) If the chart interferes with the heading, reduce the size of the chart by clicking to the left of *25000* in the upper left corner of the chart. Eight sizing handles should display around the chart defining the plot area. Click the top middle handle and when the arrow pointer becomes a vertical double-headed arrow, drag it downward to reduce the size of the chart plot area.
   (9) Select *Admitted to Hospitals by Part of Body Injured* and choose Format, and then Font.
   (10) Change the font to 16-point Britannic Bold Italic.
l. Format the legend by completing the following steps:
   (1) Click within the legend and choose Format, then Selected Legend.
   (2) Select the Font tab at the Format Legend dialog box and change the font to 12-point Britannic Bold Italic and the color to teal.
   (3) Select the Placement tab and choose Bottom from the Type section.
   (4) Select the Patterns tab and choose Custom in the Border section.
   (5) Click the down-pointing arrow to the right of the Weight list box, then select the third line from the top in the drop-down list.
   (6) Click OK or press Enter.
m. Format the x-axis title by completing the following steps:

(1) Click the x-axis to select it (the text *Total Number Admitted to Hospitals*).
(2) Choose Format, Selected Axis, then select the Font tab.
(3) Change the font to 10-point Britannic Bold.
(4) Choose OK or press Enter.

n. Insert and format data labels by completing the following steps:
(1) Choose Insert, Data Labels.
(2) At the Data Labels dialog box, select Show Value.
(3) Choose OK or press Enter.
(4) Click the first data label on the first data marker, and choose Format, Selected Data Labels.
(5) At the Format Data Labels dialog box, select the Alignment tab, then select Center as the Horizontal position and Top as the Vertical position in the Text Alignment section.
(6) Select the Patterns tab and choose Automatic in the Border section.
(7) In the Area section, make sure the Color selection is white. Click the down-pointing arrow to the right of the Patterns list box, then select the white square (first row, first column).
(8) Select the Number tab, then choose Number from the Category list box.
(9) Choose *#,##0* from the Format Codes list box.
(10) Click OK or press Enter.
(11) Follow steps (3) through (7) and format the remaining six data labels.

o. Format the data markers to display different colors by completing the following steps:
(1) Double-click the first data marker that represents head injuries and select the Patterns tab; or click the first data marker and choose Format, Selected Data Series, then select the Patterns tab.
(2) At the Format Data Series dialog box, click the down-pointing arrow to the right of the Pattern list box in the Area section.
(3) At the Color Palette in the Area section, select the purple color in the third row and the first column.
(4) Click OK or press Enter.
(5) Repeat steps (1) through (4) and change the colors of the remaining data markers as follows:
a. Second data marker—teal (second row, sixth column)
b. Third data marker—yellow (third row, third column)
c. Fourth data marker—blue (third row, fourth column)
d. Fifth data marker—purple (third row, fifth column)
e. Sixth data marker—red (third row, sixth column)
f. Seventh data marker—navy (second row, third column)

p. Change the color of the wall of the chart by completing the following steps:
(1) Double-click in any blank area of the wall of the chart; or click once and choose Format, Selected Walls.
(2) At the Format Walls dialog box, select Automatic in the Border section.
(3) In the Area section, select the light gray color in the fifth row, eighth column.
(4) Click OK or press Enter.

q. Change the thickness of the gridlines by completing the following steps:
(1) Double-click one of the chart gridlines; or click once on any chart gridline and choose Format, Selected Gridlines.
(2) Select the Patterns tab and click the down-pointing arrow to the right of the Weight list box. Select the third line down in the drop-down list.
(3) Click OK or press Enter.

r. Click outside of the chart area to return to the Word document window.

2. Save and name the chart c08ex04, chart.
3. Print and then close c08ex04, chart.

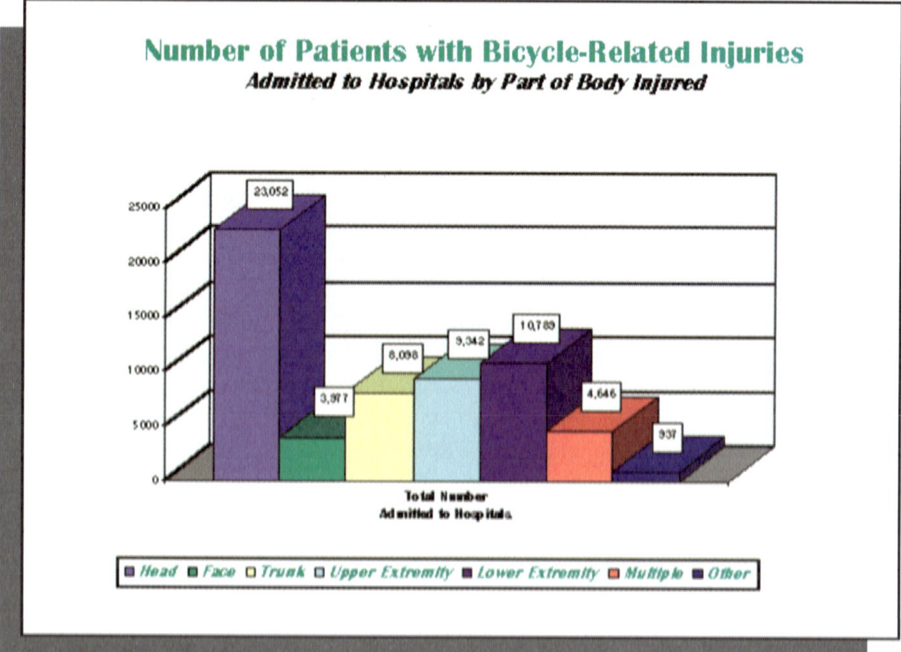

FIGURE 8.16

Creating Transparencies/Slides

When creating overhead transparencies or slides, consider these guidelines:

Purpose:	Ask yourself if the material you want to present clarifies and reinforces the topic being presented.
Typeface:	One typeface is fine; use two at the most. Instead of changing typefaces, try varying the type style, such as bold or italics. Legibility is of utmost importance.
Type size:	Eighteen points is the minimum. You want everyone in the room to be able to read what you have taken the time to prepare. Choose a thicker font or apply bold to increase the readability of the text.
Headings:	Keep titles short if possible; long headings are harder to read. Kern and track if necessary.
Organization:	Keep transparencies and slides simple and easy to read. Outline your message to organize ideas and then introduce one main topic or major point per transparency or slide. Each idea or supporting point needs its own line. Limit the number of words per line and the number of lines on a transparency to approximately seven.

Continuity: Be consistent in the design and layout of your transparencies or slides. Repeat specific design elements, such as logo, color, or type of bullets used, in all the transparencies/slides for a particular presentation. Consistent elements help to connect one transparency to the next and contribute to a cohesive presentation.

Color: Use restraint. Color must enhance the message, not detract from it. Color can be used to emphasize important points. Be consistent —if you decide to make a heading black text on a light yellow background, then make all headings black text on a light yellow background. If males are represented by the color green in a chart, then use the same color for males in any other charts. Colors used must look good together. Study pleasing color combinations in brochures, magazines, books, stores, etc.

Preparation: Plan and be ready for the unexpected. Will you be providing the audience with handouts? If so, what will they be? How many do you need? What about extras? What would you do if someone forgets the computer, you forget the presentation disk, or the lightbulb goes out in the overhead projector? Be prepared for all logical possibilities.

In the following exercises, you will create overhead transparencies that could be used for a group presentation. The same documents, printed on paper instead of transparency film, can add an impressive professional touch to a one-on-one presentation. In addition, the use of color, if not overdone, can provide visual impact.

DTP POINTERS
Be consistent when using color to represent facts in a presentation.

In exercises 5 and 6, you will create the two Ride Safe transparencies illustrated in figure 8.17 and 8.18. In exercise 5, styles will be created for the heading and bulleted text. The completed document will then be saved as a template so that it can be used over and over again to create other transparencies. In exercise 6, you will create a second transparency using the template created in exercise 5.

Creating an Overhead Transparency Using Styles

1. At a clear document window, create the transparency shown in figure 8.17 by completing the following steps:
   a. Change the paper size to Letter Landscape.
   b. Change the left, right, top, and bottom margins to 0.5 inches. (If Word displays a message that one or more margins are set outside of the printable area of the page, choose Fix. The right margin will most likely be changed. Due to the layout of the transparencies in this exercise, the left and right margins do not need to be exactly even. Choose OK or press Enter to accept the adjusted margin setting.)
   c. Turn on Kerning for 20 points and above.
   d. Key the following text:

      WHY RUN A BIKE/SKATING HELMET PROGRAM?
      Promotes children's health and safety.
      Teaches bike safety.
      Educates parents.
      Reduces serious injuries.
      Helps to overcome peer pressure.
      May save lives.

e. Insert the Ride Safe logo by completing the following steps:
   (1) Position the insertion point at the beginning of the first line of text.
   (2) Choose Insert, then Picture.
   (3) In the Look in: list box, change the directory to the location of the student graphic disk files.
   (4) Select *Ridesf2teal.bmp* from the Name list box, then click OK or press Enter.
f. Size the Ride Safe logo by completing the following steps:
   (1) Select the Ride Safe logo and choose Format, then Picture.
   (2) In the Size section of the Picture dialog box, change the Width to 1.74 inches and the Height to 1.72 inches.
   (3) Choose OK or press Enter.
g. Position the Ride Safe logo by completing the following steps:
   (1) Choose Insert, then Frame.
   (2) Choose Format, then Frame.
   (3) At the Frame dialog box, change the Horizontal Position to Left Relative To Margin and change the Vertical Position to Top Relative To Margin.
   (4) Choose OK or press Enter.
h. Change the Zoom Control to 50 percent.
i. Create the transparency heading by completing the following steps:
   (1) Select *WHY RUN A BIKE/SKATING HELMET PROGRAM?.*
   (2) Change the font to 42-point Britannic Bold and the color to Dk Cyan.
   (3) With the heading still selected, choose Format, then Paragraph.
   (4) At the Paragraph dialog box with the Indents and Spacing tab selected, change the Left indent to 0.5 inches and the Spacing After to 6 points.
   (5) Choose OK or press Enter.
j. Create a style from the heading by completing the following steps:
   (1) With the text still selected, click once in the Style list box on the Formatting toolbar.
   (2) Key **transhead** as the style name, then press Enter.
k. Position the insertion point at the beginning of the line that reads *Promotes children's health. . .* and press Enter.
l. Insert the graphic line by completing the following steps:
   (1) Move the insertion point up one line so that it is located to the left of the hard return just inserted.
   (2) Display the Borders toolbar.
   (3) Click the down-pointing arrow to the right of the Line Style list box and select the 4½ pt line.
   (4) Click the Top Border button on the Borders toolbar.
m. Adjust the spacing between the graphic border and the text that follows by completing the following steps:
   (1) With the insertion point in the same position, choose Format, Paragraph, and then select the Indents and Spacing tab.
   (2) Change the spacing Before the current paragraph to 20 points.
   (3) Click OK or press Enter.
n. Insert the teal triangular bullets by completing the following steps:
   (1) Position the insertion point at the beginning of the line that reads *Promotes children's health. . .*
   (2) Choose Format, then Bullets and Numbering.
   (3) At the Bullets and Numbering dialog box, select the Bulleted tab.

(4) Click Modify to display the Modify Bulleted list dialog box.
(5) Choose Bullet and then click the down-pointing arrow to the right of the Symbols From: list box. Select Monotype Sorts from the drop-down list.
(6) Select the triangle in the fourth row, first column and then click OK.
(7) At the Modify Bulleted List dialog box, choose Point Size, then change the size to 26 points.
(8) Change the Color option to Dk Cyan.
(9) Click OK or press Enter when done.

o. Format the bulleted text by completing the following steps:
(1) Select *Promotes children's health and safety.*
(2) Change the font to 36-point Britannic Bold.
(3) Choose Format, then Paragraph.
(4) At the Paragraph dialog box with the Indents and Spacing tab selected, change the Left Indentation to 1.9 inches, Special to Hanging, and By to 0.5 inches. Change the Spacing After to 14 points.
(5) Click OK or press Enter.

p. Create a style to include the formatting for the bulleted text by completing the following steps:
(1) With the first line of bulleted text still selected, click once in the Style list box on the Formatting toolbar.
(2) Key **tri-bullets** as the style name and press Enter.

q. Apply the style to the remaining text by completing the following steps:
(1) Select the remaining text.
(2) Click the down-pointing arrow to the right of the Style list box on the Formatting toolbar and select *tri-bullets* from the drop-down list.

2. Save the completed transparency document and name it c08ex05, trans1.
3. Print c08ex05, trans1.
4. Create a template out of the transparency by completing the following steps:
   a. Delete all the existing text by completing the following steps:
      (1) Position the insertion point at the beginning of the main heading, then select all the text from this point to the end of the document. (Do not include the Ride Safe logo.)
      (2) Press Delete.
   b. Save the document containing the Ride Safe logo and the styles as a template by completing the following steps:
      (1) Choose File, then Save As.
      (2) At the Save As dialog box, click the down-pointing arrow to the right of the Save as type list box and select *Document Template.*
      (3) Double-click the *Other Documents* folder.
      (4) In the File name text box, key **Ride Safe trans**.
      (5) Click Save or press Enter.
5. Close c08ex05, trans1.

FIGURE 8.17

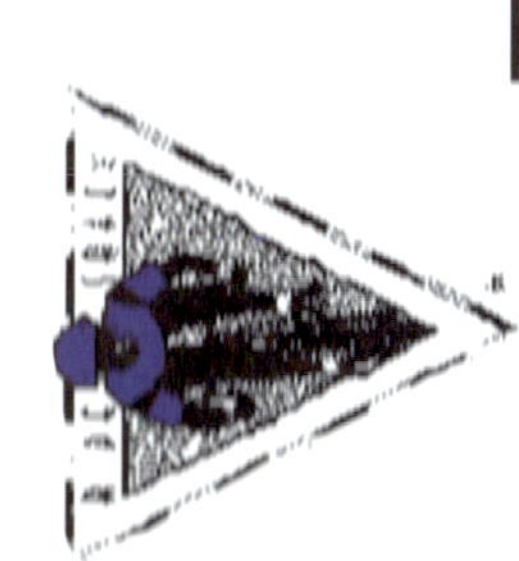

WHY RUN A BIKE/SKATING HELMET PROGRAM?

- Promotes children's health and safety.
- Teaches bike safety.
- Educates parents.
- Reduces serious injuries.
- Helps to overcome peer pressure.
- May save lives.

Using a Custom-Made Template to Create a Transparency

1. Create the transparency shown in figure 8.18 by completing the following steps:
   a. Open the transparency template created in exercise 5 by completing the following steps:
      (1) Choose File, then New.
      (2) At the New dialog box, select the Other Documents tab.
      (3) Double-click *Ride Safe trans.*
   b. Change the Zoom Control to 75 percent.
   c. Click outside of the Ride Safe logo, then change the style to Normal.
   d. Key the following text, using the Trademark symbol from the Special Characters tab at the Symbol dialog box:

      WHY USE THE SAFETY ON WHEELS™ PROGRAM?
      It's easy!
      Parents appreciate the support.
      Parents like the helmets.
      Children like the helmets.
      Success is easily measured.
      Ride Safe, Inc., provides promotional support.

   e. Raise the position of the trademark symbol by completing the following steps:
      (1) Select the trademark symbol and choose Format, then Font.
      (2) Select the Font tab, then click once in the Superscript check box in the Effects section.
      (3) Click OK or press Enter.
   f. Apply the *transhead* style to the main heading by completing the following steps:
      (1) Position the insertion point at the beginning of the title *WHY USE THE SAFETY ON WHEELS™ PROGRAM?*
      (2) Choose *transhead* from the Style drop-down list located on the Formatting toolbar.
   g. Position the insertion point at the beginning of the line that reads *It's easy!* and press Enter.
   h. Insert the graphic line by completing the following steps:
      (1) Move the insertion point up one line so that it is located to the left of the hard return just inserted.
      (2) Display the Borders toolbar.
      (3) Click the down-pointing arrow to the right of the Line Style list box and select the 4½ pt line.
      (4) Click the Top Border button on the Borders toolbar.
   i. Adjust the spacing between the graphic border and the text that follows by completing the following steps:
      (1) With the insertion point in the same position, choose Format, Paragraph, and then select the Indents and Spacing tab.
      (2) Change the spacing Before the current paragraph to 20 points.
      (3) Click OK or press Enter.
   j. Apply the *tri-bullets* style by completing the following steps:
      (1) Select the remaining text.
      (2) Select *tri-bullets* from the Style drop-down list located on the Formatting toolbar.
2. Save and name this transparency c08ex06, trans2.
3. Print and then close c08ex06, trans2.

FIGURE 8.18

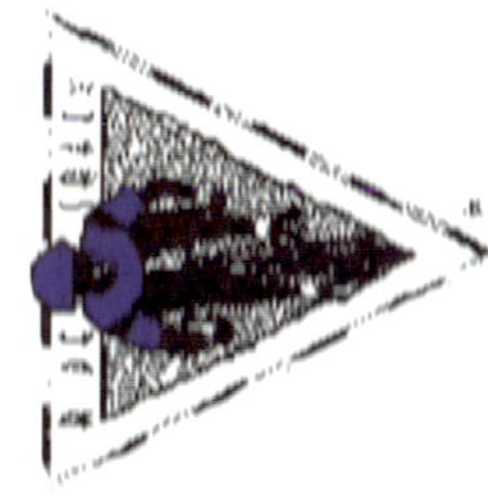

WHY USE THE SAFETY ON WHEELS™ PROGRAM?

- It's easy!
- Parents appreciate the support.
- Parents like the helmets.
- Children like the helmets.
- Success is easily measured.
- Ride Safe, Inc., provides promotional support.

Creating Supporting Handouts For A Presentation

DTP POINTERS
Use a logo picture, graphic line, bullets, and/or color as consistent elements in a presentation.

Presentation materials often include handouts for the audience. Handouts might contain an outline of the presentation topics and other supplementary information. Very often, supplementary materials include some type of a reply/response card, a fact sheet, a brochure, and a business card. The company or individual making the presentation may even provide a special folder for all of these materials with the organization's name and logo on the front cover. These materials make it easy for individuals to review the materials on their own time and to contact the company or presenter after the presentation is over. Refrain from handing out copies of the materials during your presentation as this can shift the listeners' attention from your presentation to reading ahead. Samples of supporting documents for a Ride Safe presentation can be found in figure 8.19.

FIGURE 8.19

Sample Documents for a Ride Safe Presentation

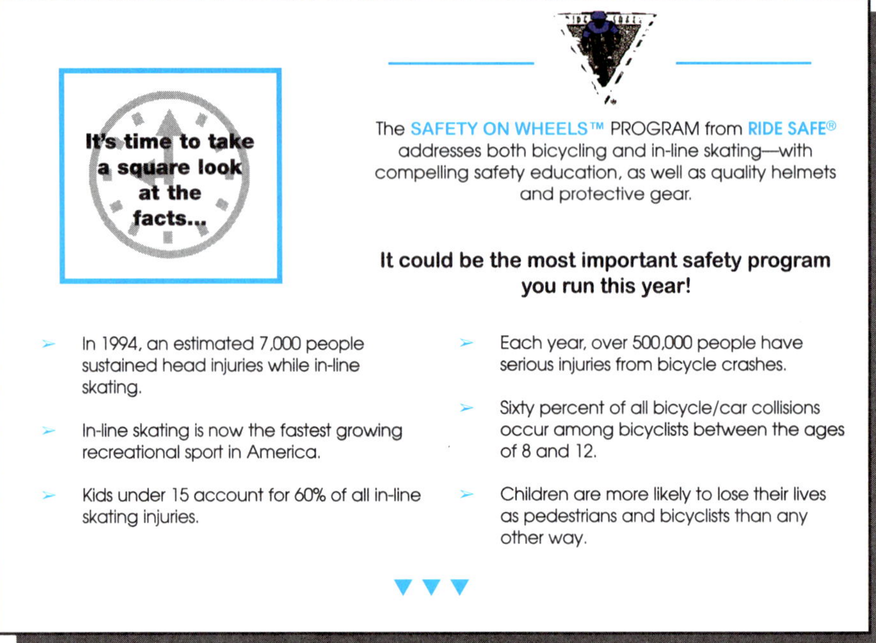

FACT SHEET

We are interested in the new Safety on Wheels Program™ from Ride Safe®. Please send us the following information.

- ❑ Safety on Wheels Program™ description and price list
- ❑ Bicycle safety trick shows
- ❑ In-line skating instruction programs
- ❑ Reflective sweatshirts and T-shirts

New Colors & Designs for '97

If you would like a sample helmet and Program Guide, or for *faster responses*, call 800-285-RIDE.

Name ______________________
Address ______________________
City ______________ State ________ ZIP ________
Phone ______________ Fax ______________
Organization Name ______________________
Phone ______________________

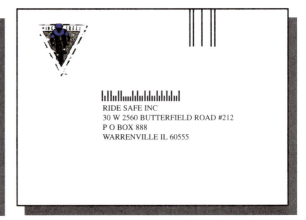

POSTCARD (FRONT AND BACK)

For Details, Contact:

Dane & Mary Beth Luhrsen
Ride Safe, Inc.
Phone 1-800-285-RIDE (7433)

Ride Safe, Inc.
30 W 260 Butterfield Road, #212
P.O Box 888
Warrenville, IL 60555
Phone 1-800-285-RIDE (7433)

Ride Safe News Release

Police Ticketing Program: Local Police to "Ticket" Children Wearing Bicycle Helmets

As part of the Main Street School PTA's BIcycle Safety Program, local police will be stopping and "ticketing" children who are wearing bicycle helmets when they are riding their bicycles.

Your Town, September 23, 1997: Should you keep your children off the streets? NO! These "tickets" are actually coupons that can be redeemed for free ice cream cones at Stewart's Ice Cream Parlor, free movie rentals from Star Video, and free pizza slices from Angelo's Pizzeria.

"The children are extremely excited about this program," said Mary Jones, PTA Health and Safety Coordinator from Main Street School. "We think children will start wearing their bicycle helmets because of the prizes and will continue wearing them because it has become a habit." According to statistics published by the National Safe Kids Coalition, more than 800 people die in bicycle accidents each year. Thousands more receive serious head and brain injuries. A recent study found that wearing a bicycle helmet could reduce the risk of head injuries by 85%.

"We want to do something before our community is faced with a tragic accident," says Ms. Jones. Ms. Jones would like to thank the local police, Stewart's Ice Cream Parlor, Star Video, and Angelo's Pizzeria for their support of the Program. Please call Mary Jones at 555-8974 if you have any questions about the program.

For Release 9 a.m. EDT
September 23, 1997

PRESS RELEASE

BUSINESS CARD

Ride Safe

Certificate of Achievement

Awarded to

Ride Safe Program Recipient

Congratulations on your outstanding achievement. Please remember the lessons that you have learned, alwyas wear your bicycle or in-line skating helmets whenever you ride your bike or in-line skates. RIDE SAFE!

Presented by

Ride Safe, Inc.

Thursday, September 25, 1997

PTA President | *School Principal*

Dane & Mary Beth Luhrsen, Ride Safe Owners | *Classroom Teacher*

CERTIFICATE

Optional: Adding A Sound Clip To A Word Document (Computer Sound Equipment Needed)

The Insert Object feature in Word for Windows 95 enables you to add sound to documents, providing your computer has sound equipment installed—sound board, microphone (to record sound), and speakers. In the next exercise, you will retrieve transparencies prepared for a presentation from your student data disk and insert prerecorded sound files from Windows 95 into specific locations within each transparency.

Windows 95 provides two different sound files that can be inserted and played in Word documents. One of the sound files uses the file format called MIDI (Musical Instrument Digital Interface). Windows 95 MIDI sound files include: Beethoven's 5th Symphony, Beethoven's Fur Elise, Mozart's Symphony No. 40, and more. These files end with the extension *.mid*, or *.rmi*. In addition to MIDI, Windows 95 includes Digital Audio sound files. Digital Audio files are saved with the extension *.wav*. These files digitize and store sound as a file; the files tend to be quite large.

If you have a microphone attached to your computer, you can record a Digital Audio (.wav) file and play it in a Word document. For example, you might decide to create a presentation or tutorial that includes sound. In order to use a Word document with a sound clip as part of a presentation, you would need a sound card, speakers, an LCD panel, and an overhead projector.

Inserting Windows 95 Sound Files into a Word Document

To add a Windows prerecorded MIDI sound file or an Digital Audio file to an active document, you would complete the following steps:

1. Position the insertion point in the document where you want the sound to play.
2. Choose Insert, then Object.
3. At the Object dialog box, select the Create New tab.
4. Click the down-pointing triangle to the right of the Object type list box and double-click Media Clip.
5. At the Media menu bar, choose Insert Clip, then select 3 Sound or 4 MIDI Sequencer.
6. If you choose 3 Sound, make sure the Media folder displays in the Look in: text box and Sound (*.wav) displays in the Files of type text box. Key a file name or select one of the sound files displayed in the Open list box, then choose Open. (A Media Clip icon with an on and off switch will display in the document at the insertion point. Right-click the mouse to access a quick menu with options to cut, copy, or paste; play, edit, or open; and add a border, shading, or a caption. Additionally, a frame can be selected from the quick menu and applied to the Media Clip icon—click and drag to another location.)
7. If you choose 4 MIDI Sequencer after choosing Insert Clip, make sure the Media folder displays in the Look in: text box and Midi Sequencer (*.mid, *.rmi) displays in the Files of type text box. Choose Open.

Playing a Sound Clip

To play a sound clip that has been inserted into a document, double-click on the title of the sound clip that appears at the bottom of the clip. To stop the music, click the Stop button (second button on the sound clip—it has a black box inside it).

Using Additional Sound Clip Features

The Sound Clip feature allows you to create customized sound clips through the recording option and the use of a microphone. You can also record an annotation (written or spoken comment) through Word's Annotation feature. See your Word reference manual for additional information on these features.

Inserting a Sound File into a Word Document

1. At a clear document window, open *Orchestra* from your student data disk and add a sound clip to the document as shown in figure 8.20 by completing the following steps:
   a. Save the document with Save As and name it c08ex07, sound clip.
   b. With the insertion point positioned at the top of the document, choose Insert, then Object.
   c. At the Object dialog box, select the Create New tab.
   d. Click the down-pointing triangle to the right of the Object type list box and double-click Media Clip.
   e. At the Media menu bar, choose Insert Clip, then select 4 MIDI Sequencer (might display as 3 MIDI Sequencer). Make sure the Media folder displays in the Look in: text box and Midi Sequencer (*.mid, *.rmi) displays in the Files of type text box. At the Open dialog box, double-click Beethoven's 5th Symphony. (A sound clip icon with a title will display in your document where the insertion point was located.)
   f. Click outside the sound clip to exit the Media screen and return to the document window.
   g. Click once on the sound clip to select it, then right-click to access a drop-down menu. At the drop-down menu, click the left mouse button on Frame Picture.
   h. Click to select the sound clip and drag it to the bottom left corner of the document.
2. Play the sound clip by completing the following steps:
   a. Press Ctrl + Home to move the insertion point to the top of the document.
   b. Choose View, then Full Screen.
   c. Double-click the sound clip to turn it on.
   d. Click the Stop button on the sound clip (second button on the sound clip) to turn off the sound. Double-click the sound clip to access the Play/Pause/Stop buttons. Press the Pause button. Press the Play button (first button on the sound clip) to turn on the sound again. Press the Stop button.
   e. Click the Full Screen button to return the document to the previous page layout view.
3. Save the document again with the same name, c08ex07, sound clip.
4. Print and then close c08ex07, sound clip.

FIGURE 8.20

Your contributions support...
Metropolitan Symphony
Orchestra

- Martin Music Education Center Building Fund
- 25th Anniversary Concert
- Russian/U.S.A. Exchange Program
- New Philharmonic

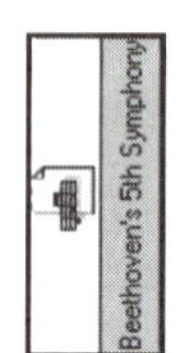

Chapter Summary

- Presentations are created and conducted to inform, educate, persuade, motivate, sell, and entertain.
- When planning a presentation, clearly define the purpose, evaluate the audience, decide on content, and determine the medium to be used to convey the message.
- A table can be created to illustrate data and present information in a concise, orderly manner.
- A chart, referred to as a *graph*, communicates information quickly and clearly, is a picture of numeric data, and shows relationships, comparisons, and/or trends. A chart can be created from data in a Word table or from data keyed directly into the datasheet.
- Fourteen types of charts can be created in Microsoft Graph 5.0—Area, Bar, Column, Line, Pie, Doughnut, Radar, XY (Scatter), Combination, 3-D Area, 3-D Bar, 3-D Column (default type), 3-D Line, 3-D Pie, and 3-D Surface.
- A variety of customizations can be made to a chart, such as:
    - adding a title
    - identifying the x- and y-axis
    - customizing the legend
    - changing options to a three-dimensional or two-dimensional appearance
    - changing how a data series is represented graphically
    - adding data labels
- The chart provides information along the x-, y-, and z-axis. The x-axis is the bottom horizontal line of a chart. The y-axis is the left vertical line of a 2-D Graph chart. The z-axis is the left vertical line of a 3-D Graph chart.
- A Series in Rows orientation displays the first row data (category names) on the x-axis as tick mark labels and the first column data as data series names in the legend.
- A Series in Columns orientation displays the first row data as data series names in the legend and the first column data on the x-axis as tick mark labels.
- When creating overhead transparencies, consider the following: typeface, type size, headings, organization, continuity, and color.
- Styles can be used in documents to provide continuity in the appearance of documents.
- Support materials for a presentation might include a reply/response card, a fact sheet, a brochure, and a business card.
- Windows 95 provides two different sound files that can be inserted and played in Word documents. One of the sound files uses the file format called MIDI (Musical Instrument Digital Interface); the other file format is known as Digital Audio.

Commands Review

	Mouse/Keyboard
Insert Picture dialog box	Insert, Picture
Create a frame	Insert, Frame, position crosshairs to draw frame
Create table with Standard toolbar	With arrow pointer on Insert Table button on Standard toolbar, hold down left mouse button, move arrow pointer down and right until desired table size displays, release button
Display Insert Table dialog box	Table, Insert Table
Display Microsoft Graph window	Insert, Object, select Create New tab, then select Microsoft Graph; or click the Insert Chart button on the Standard toolbar
Exit Microsoft Graph window	Click outside of the graph window
Insert Media Clip	Insert, Object, select Create New tab, then double-click Media Clip

Check Your Understanding

Parts of a Chart—3-D Column Chart: Insert the correct term that identifies each part of the chart displayed in figure 8.21 below. Use the terms included below the chart.

FIGURE 8.21

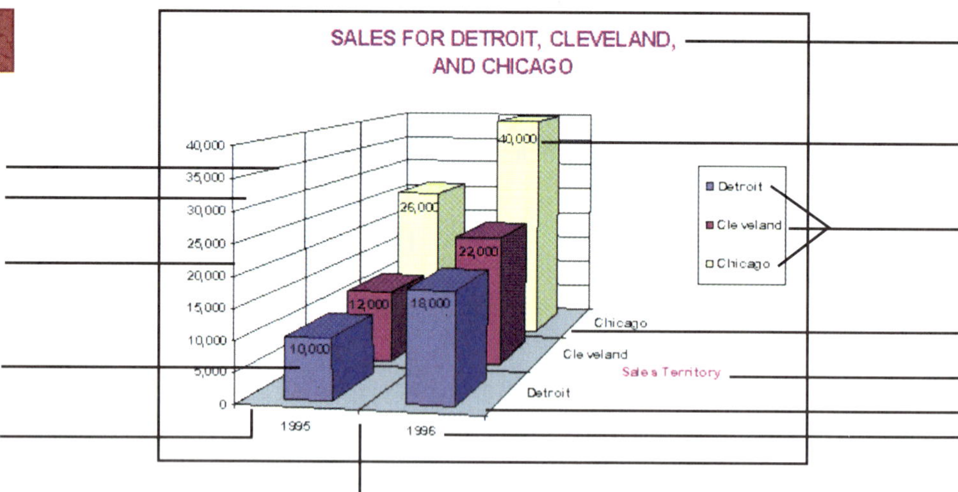

Chart Elements:

x-axis (data category)	tick mark
y-axis (data series)	chart title
z-axis (data value)	data label
data marker	y-axis title
tick mark label	data series names
legend	wall
gridline	floor

Terms: In the space provided at the right, indicate the correct term.

1. When a chart is created in Word, it is created using this application. ________________
2. This chart orientation uses text in the first row of the datasheet as data series labels in the chart legend and text in the first column of the datasheet as category names displayed below the x-axis. ________________
3. This chart orientation uses text in the first column of the datasheet as data series labels in the chart legend and text in the first row of the datasheet as category names displayed below the x-axis. ________________
4. To update the data in a chart, make changes to data in this Microsoft Graph element. ________________
5. This Word option displays dialog boxes that guide you through the creation of a chart. ________________
6. This type of chart shows variations between components but not in relationship to the whole. ________________
7. This type of chart shows proportions and relationships of parts to the whole. ________________
8. This feature allows you to apply predesigned formats to a chart. ________________

Concepts: Write your answers to the following questions in the space provided.

1. For what reasons are presentations created and conducted?

2. What are the basic steps for planning a presentation?

3. What type of medium may be used in a presentation?

4. When creating an overhead transparency, what guidelines should be considered in the organization of the transparency?

Skill Assessments

Assessment 1

Besides charting statistics for presentations, Ride Safe wants to chart sales of its own products to aid them in their equipment purchasing decisions. You need to create a Word table as your source of data, insert sales data for a particular model bicycle helmet by color and year sold, and then create a bar chart. (The sales figures used in this assessment are fictitious.) Complete this assessment according to the following instructions:

1. Change the paper orientation to Landscape.
2. Change the left, right, top, and bottom margins to 0.75 inches.
3. Turn on Kerning at 14 points and above.
4. Create the table shown in figure 8.22.
5. For future use, save and name the table c08sa01, table.
6. Create a horizontal bar chart (shown in figure 8.23) from the table by completing the following steps in ChartWizard:
   a. Change the chart type to bar chart.
   b. Select format 3 for the Bar chart.
   c. Choose Series in Rows orientation using the first row for category x-axis labels and the first column for the legend text.
   d. Include a legend in the chart.
   e. Title the chart **Sales of Model RS1000 Helmets 1990-1995**.
   f. Title the y-axis **Total Number of Model RS1000 Helmets Sold by Color**.
7. Click outside the chart to return to the Word screen and delete the table.
8. Size the chart to a width of 8.5 inches and a height of 6.5 inches. (Remember to size the chart at the Word Picture dialog box, access Microsoft Graph, then return to your Word document for the change to take effect.)
9. In Word, change the Zoom Control to 75% so the chart will be easier to work with when you access Graph.
10. Format the chart title as follows:
    a. Delete the space after *Helmets* in the title and then press Enter to place the range of years on a separate line.
    b. Select *Sales of Helmet Model RS1000*, change the font to 24-point Britannic Bold, and then change the color to teal (second row, sixth column).
    c. Select *1990–1995* and change the font to 18-point Britannic Bold Italic.
    d. If the title overlaps the top of the chart, select the plot area and use the top middle sizing handle to reduce the size of the chart to accommodate the title.
11. Format the y-axis title as follows:
    a. Change the font to 11-point Britannic Bold.
    b. Change the color to teal (second row, sixth column).
12. Format the y-axis as follows:
    a. Change the font to 10 points and leave the typeface and style as Arial Bold.
    b. Change the number format to thousands (#,##0).
13. Format the legend as follows:
    a. Change the font to 12-point Britannic Bold Italic.
    b. Use the mouse to position the legend as illustrated in figure 8.23.
    c. If necessary, use the mouse and sizing handles to adjust the size of the legend so that all of the legend text is visible.
    d. Change the legend border to shadow.
    e. Change the background color of the legend to white.
14. Change the color of each data series to match the color name of the series.

15. Click outside the chart to return to your Word document and format the chart as follows:
    a. Insert a frame around the chart.
    b. Format the frame so that it is centered horizontally and vertically on the page.
    c. Place a border around the chart using a 2¼-point line thickness.
16. Save the document with Save As and name the chart c08sa01, chart.
17. Print and then close c08sa01, chart.

Optional: Write a one paragraph summary analyzing the information in the chart you just created.

FIGURE 8.22

Model RS1000	1990	1991	1992	1993	1994	1995
Pink	235	487	1006	1498	2056	2125
Teal	280	715	1742	2214	2849	3005
White	115	320	569	1061	1489	1514
Black	400	850	2048	2685	3500	4243
Purple	290	776	1500	2128	2712	3572

FIGURE 8.23

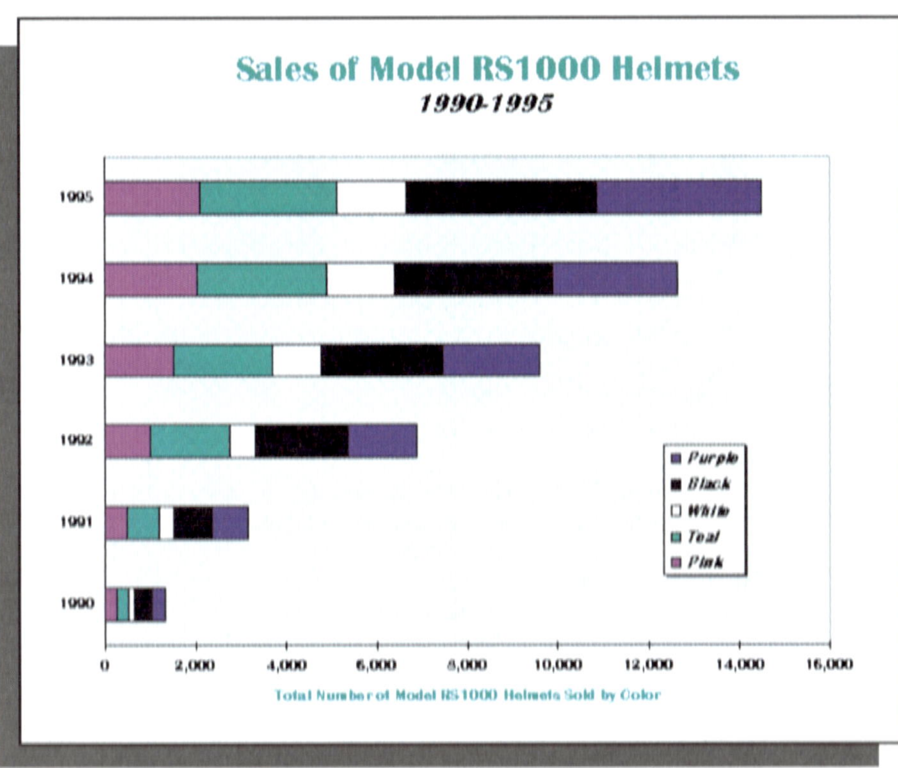

Assessment 2

Create the pie chart shown in figure 8.24 illustrating Ride Safe's 1995 total sales for all helmet models. (These figures are fictitious.) This chart tells the reader at a glance how each helmet model contributes to the total sales picture. You will insert the product sales figures into a datasheet and then create the pie chart. Complete this assessment according to the following specifications:

1. Change the paper orientation to Landscape.
2. Change the left, right, top, and bottom margins to 0.75 inches.
3. Turn on Kerning at 14 points and above.
4. Access Microsoft Graph.
5. Delete all the existing information in the datasheet.
6. Key the following information into the datasheet in the order indicated so the pie slices will display largest to smallest, clockwise:

Model #	**1995 Sales**
RS4000X	**25,783**
XSAir	**11,768**
RS1000	**62,352**

7. Format the chart as follows:
   a. Change the chart type to 3-D pie.
   b. Use AutoFormat and select format 6 (pie chart with % symbols).
   c. Change the chart orientation to Series in Columns.
8. Size the chart to a width of 8.5 inches and a height of 6.5 inches. (Remember to size the chart at the Word Picture dialog box, access Microsoft Graph, then return to your Word document for the change to take effect.)
9. In Word, change the Zoom Control to 75% so the chart will be easier to work with when you access Graph.
10. Insert and format the chart title as follows:
    a. Title the chart **1995 Total Helmet Sales**, press Enter, then key **Ride Safe, Inc.**
    b. Select *1995 Total Helmet Sales* and change the font to 36-point Britannic Bold and the color to teal (second row, sixth column).
    c. Select *Ride Safe, Inc.* and change the font to 22-point Britannic Bold and the color to black.
11. Insert and format a border around the title by completing the following steps:
    a. Select the title, choose Format, Selected Chart, and then select the Patterns tab.
    b. At the Format Chart Title dialog box, access the Style drop-down list in the Border section. Select the border style that is located second from the bottom.
    c. Access the Border Color option and select teal (second row, sixth column).
    d. Access the Border Weight option and select the last line weight option in the drop-down list.
    e. Activate the Border Shadow option.
    f. Click OK or press Enter.
12. Format, size, and position the legend as follows:
    a. Select the legend, hold down the left mouse button, and drag the legend to the approximate location shown in figure 8.28.
    b. Change the legend font to 16-point Britannic Bold.
    c. Use the mouse and the sizing handles to size the legend similar to figure 8.24.
    d. Insert a border around the legend using the same border selections as you used for the chart title in steps 11(a) through 11(f).
13. Insert and format the legend title as follows:
    a. Display the Drawing toolbar and use the Text Box button to draw a text box above the legend. Refer to figure 8.24 for the approximate size and position.
    b. Change the font to 18-point Britannic Bold Italic and the color to teal (second row, sixth column).
    c. Change the justification to Center.
    d. Key **Helmet Model Nos.**.
    e. Use the mouse and sizing handles to size and position the text box appropriately.
14. Format and move the data labels as follows:
    a. Click one of the data labels (*62%, 26%,* or *12%*) to select the whole data series.
    b. Change the font to 16-point Britannic Bold.

c. Select each of the data labels and use the mouse to drag each data label onto its corresponding pie slice as shown in figure 8.24.

15. Explode the pie slice representing XSAir sales as follows:
    a. Click once on the XSAir pie slice to select the whole data series.
    b. Click the pie slice again to select the XSAir data point.
    c. Click and drag the slice away from the pie the approximate distance as shown in figure 8.24.
16. Click outside the chart to return to your Word document and format the chart as follows:
    a. Insert a frame around the chart.
    b. Position the frame so that it is centered horizontally and vertically.
    c. Insert a shadow border around the entire chart using a 2¼-point Dk Cyan line style.
17. Save the chart and name it c08sa02, pie chart.
18. Print and then close c08sa02, pie chart.

Optional: Write a one paragraph summary interpreting the total sales in the chart you just created.

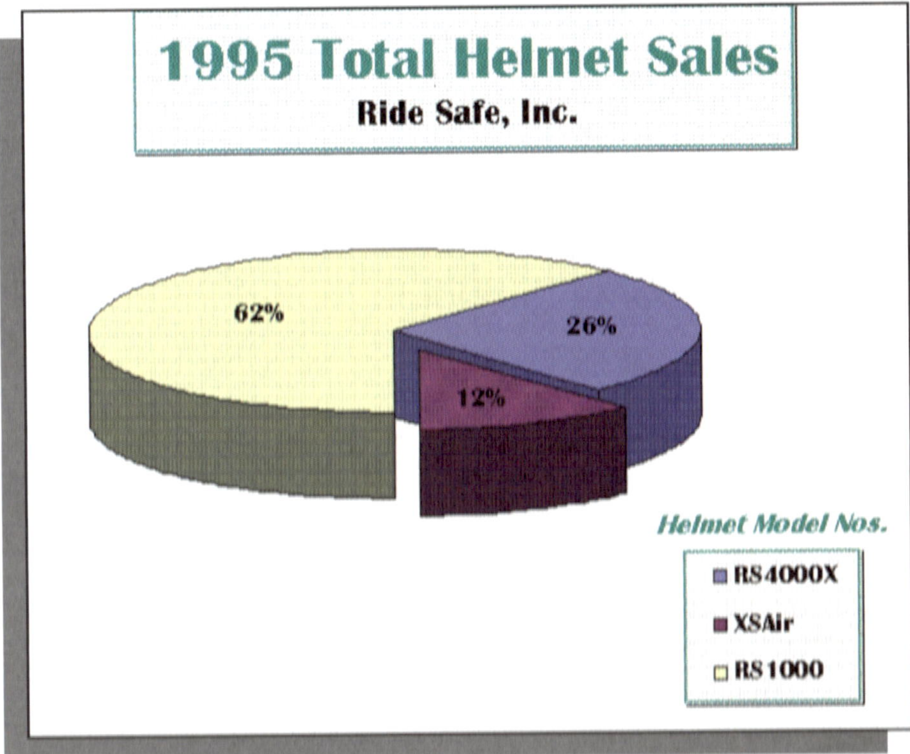

FIGURE 8.24

Creative Activity

Word has the ability to create several different types of charts. Find at least two examples of charts representative of two of the types mentioned in this chapter. Look for charts in books, the financial section of newspapers, investment magazines and newsletters, brochures, etc. Identify the following elements on the charts collected: data series names, title, subtitle, 2- or 3-dimensional layout, x-axis, y-axis, z-axis, axes titles, tick marks, tick mark labels, legend, data markers, data points, data labels, exploded slices, floor, wall, gridlines, fill color, and fill patterns. Also, note the use of any border attributes to the chart legend, titles, or frame. Identify each chart as c08ca01.

9 CREATING PRESENTATIONS USING POWERPOINT

PERFORMANCE OBJECTIVE

Upon successful completion of chapter 9, you will be able to create on-screen presentations, overhead transparencies (color or black and white), paper printouts, 35mm slides, notes, handouts, and outlines using PowerPoint's AutoContent Wizard, templates, and your own designs.

DESKTOP PUBLISHING CONCEPTS

Planning	Balance	White space
Designing	Proportion	Color
Focus	Contrast	Layout and design

POWERPOINT FEATURES USED

AutoLayout	Notes Pages View	Sound
Design Templates	Slide Show View	Slide Master
Slide View	AutoContent Wizard	Animation Effects
Outline View	Microsoft ClipArt Gallery	Build
Slide Sorter View	Slide Transitions	

Using PowerPoint To Create A Presentation

If you have access to Microsoft PowerPoint for Windows 95, you may continue with chapter 9. As discussed earlier in chapter 8, giving a successful presentation, whether using Word or PowerPoint, involves using visual aids to strengthen the impact of the message as well as organize the presentation. Visual aids may include transparencies, slides, photographs, or an on-screen presentation. Microsoft PowerPoint for Windows 95 is a complete presentation graphics program that lets you create on-screen presentations, overhead transparencies (color or black and white), paper printouts, 35mm slides, notes, handouts, and outlines.

In the following exercises, you will create several presentations based on Ride Safe information as presented in chapter 8. Each presentation will vary in content and method of delivery.

Planning A PowerPoint Presentation

DTP POINTERS
When giving a slide presentation, the first thing your audience should see is the first slide.

Suggestions for planning a presentation in Word are located in the beginning section of chapter 8. Refer to these same suggestions for planning a presentation in PowerPoint.

Creating A PowerPoint Presentation

PowerPoint provides several methods for creating a presentation. You can use PowerPoint's AutoContent Wizard, which asks questions and then chooses a presentation layout based on your answers. You can also create a presentation using predesigned templates. PowerPoint's templates provide a variety of formatting options for slides. If you want to apply all your own formatting to slides, you can start with a blank presentation screen.

The steps you follow to create a presentation will vary depending on the method you choose. There are, however, basic steps you will complete. These steps are:

DTP POINTERS
Introduce one concept per slide.

1. Load PowerPoint.
2. Choose a slide template, use PowerPoint's AutoContent Wizard, or choose a blank template if you want to apply your own formatting.
3. Key the text for each slide, adding additional elements as needed, such as graphic images.
4. Save the presentation.
5. Print the presentation as slides, an outline, and/or a handout.
6. Run the presentation.
7. Close the presentation.
8. Exit PowerPoint.

Understanding the PowerPoint Window

When PowerPoint has been loaded and you have chosen the specific type of presentation you want to create, you are presented with the PowerPoint window. What displays in the presentation window will vary depending on what type of presentation you are creating. However, the PowerPoint window contains some consistent elements.

Most of the elements in the PowerPoint window are similar to other Microsoft applications such as Word. The following PowerPoint window elements vary in comparison to the Word window: PowerPoint commands are grouped into options on the Menu bar; the Standard toolbar includes frequently used PowerPoint commands such as inserting clip art and adding animation effects; the vertical scroll box includes an elevator, which is used to quickly advance through slides; various view buttons display on the horizontal scroll bar; and the Status bar displays messages about certain PowerPoint features.

Understanding PowerPoint's Standard and Formatting Toolbars

Many buttons on PowerPoint's Standard toolbar remain consistent with Word and other Microsoft applications, but, as shown in figure 9.1, many buttons differ to represent specific PowerPoint features.

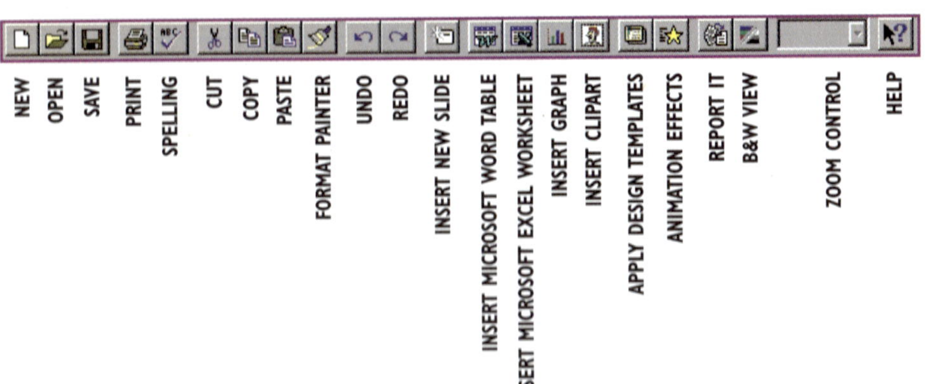

FIGURE 9.1

PowerPoint's Standard and Formatting Toolbars

The following buttons on the PowerPoint Standard toolbar differ from other Microsoft applications.

Select this button...	To perform this action:
Insert New Slide	Display the New Slide dialog box
Insert Microsoft Word Table	Insert a blank Microsoft Word Table with number of rows and columns you specify
Insert Microsoft Excel Worksheet	Add a blank Microsoft Excel Worksheet to your slide in slide view
Insert Graph	Embed a graph in a slide using specified data
Insert Clip Art	Insert a clip art image from the ClipArt Gallery
Apply Design Templates	Apply one of the PowerPoint design templates to a presentation
Animation Effects	Display the Animation Effects toolbar where you can create builds and animate text and objects for a slide show
Report It	Transfer contents of the current presentation to Microsoft Word
B&W View	Display a presentation in black and white (rather than color)

PowerPoint's Formatting toolbar includes a variety of options that are similar to other Microsoft applications, such as changing typeface and size, bold, italics, and underline, as shown in figure 9.2.

FIGURE 9.2

PowerPoint Formatting Toolbar

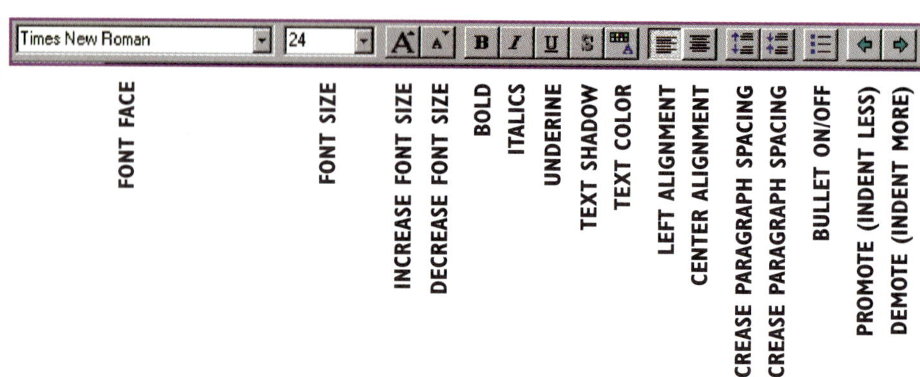

The following buttons on the Formatting toolbar activate specific PowerPoint features:

Select this button…	To perform this action:
Text Shadow	Add or remove a shadow to or from selected text
Text Color	Change color of selected text
Increase Paragraph Spacing	Increase spacing between selected paragraphs
Decrease Paragraph Spacing	Decrease spacing between selected paragraphs
Bullet On/Off	Add or remove bullets to or from selected text
Promote (Indent less)	Move selected text to the previous level (left) in an outline
Demote (Indent more)	Move selected text to the next level (right) in an outline

Viewing A Presentation

PowerPoint provides a variety of viewing options for a presentation. The presentation view can be changed with options from the View drop-down menu or with viewing buttons that display on the View toolbar located at the left side of the horizontal scroll bar as shown in figure 9.3.

FIGURE 9.3

View Toolbar

The viewing choices include:

Select this button…	To perform this action:
Slide View	Use the Slide view to display individual slides on the screen. This view is useful for determining the effectiveness of individual elements on slides. Editing can also be performed in this view.

Outline	The Outline view displays the organization of the presentation by headings and subheadings. Editing is probably easiest in Outline view since you simply click in the location you want to edit.
Slide Sorter	Choosing the Slide Sorter view causes several slides to display on the screen at one time. In this view, you can quickly and easily rearrange the order of slides by moving and dragging slides with the mouse.
Notes Pages	Some presenters provide a hard copy of the information covered in the presentation. With PowerPoint this can take the form of the slide printed at the top of the page with space available at the bottom of the page for the audience member to write notes. Change to the Notes Pages view to see how the slide will display on the page along with the space for taking notes.
Slide Show	Use the Slide Show view to run a presentation. When you choose this view, the slide fills the entire screen.

DTP POINTERS
Audiences appreciate handouts.

Previous Slide

Next Slide

In the Slide view and the Slide Sorter view, change slides by clicking the Previous Slide or Next Slide buttons located at the bottom of the vertical scroll bar. You can also change to a different slide by using the arrow pointer on the scroll box (called the *elevator*) on the vertical scroll bar. To do this, position the arrow pointer on the elevator, hold down the left mouse button, drag up or down until a yellow box displays with the desired slide number, then release the mouse button.

Elevator: The scroll box in the vertical scroll bar used to change to different slides.

The keyboard can also be used to change to a different slide. Press the Page Down key to display the next slide in the presentation or press the Page Up key to display the previous slide in the presentation.

Creating A Presentation Using A Template

When choosing a template for your slides, consider your audience, your topic, and the method of delivery. You wouldn't want to select a template with bright, vibrant colors for an audience of traditionally conservative bankers. Neither would you want to use a template with dark colors or patterns if you plan to photocopy printouts—the colors and patterns may blur.

In addition, studies on the psychology of color suggest that certain colors elicit certain feelings in an audience. For example, red backgrounds in presentations tend to heighten emotions in audiences. The color red evokes feelings of competition, desire, and passion. Red would be an effective color in a sales or marketing presentation. Darker shades of red, such as maroon or burgundy, are better choices for effective business presentations.

DTP POINTERS
Think about how your audience will respond to the colors in your presentation.

Blue backgrounds promote a conservative approach to the information presented and provide a general feeling of calmness. Blue tends to elicit feelings of loyalty and security. Yellow or white text against dark blue or indigo backgrounds are good combinations. Black backgrounds are effective in financial presentations. Black seems to show directness or forcefulness. Green backgrounds project an image of being direct, social, or intelligent. Green acts to stimulate interaction and is a good choice for use in training and educational presentations. Purple or magenta is appropriate in presentations that tend to entertain or represent less conservative or serious topics.

To create a presentation using a PowerPoint template, you would complete the following steps:

1. To load PowerPoint, click the Start button on the Windows Taskbar, choose *Programs*, then *Microsoft PowerPoint*.
2. When the Tip of the Day dialog box displays, read the tip, then choose OK or turn the feature off. (The tips include many helpful suggestions on desktop publishing!)
3. At the PowerPoint dialog box shown in figure 9.4, choose Template, then OK.
4. At the New Presentation dialog box shown in figure 9.5, select the Presentation Designs tab.
5. At the New Presentation dialog box with the Presentation Designs tab selected, click the desired template (the template displays in the Preview box at the right side of the dialog box), then choose OK. (The template names include: *Azure, Bedrock, Bevel, Blue Diagonal, Blue Green...)*
6. At the New Slide dialog box shown in figure 9.6, click the desired layout, then choose OK.
7. At the slide, key the desired text and/or insert the desired elements.
8. To create another slide, click the Insert New Slide button on the PowerPoint Standard toolbar or click the New Slide button located at the right side of the PowerPoint Status bar. Click the desired layout, then choose OK.
9. When all slides have been completed, save the presentation.

Apply Design Template

Additionally, you can apply a design template from Outline, Slide, or Slide Sorter view by clicking the Apply Design Template button (sixth button from the right) on the Standard toolbar. You may also access the design templates by choosing Format, Apply Design Template and then choose the template you want from the Format Design Template dialog box.

FIGURE 9.4

PowerPoint Dialog Box

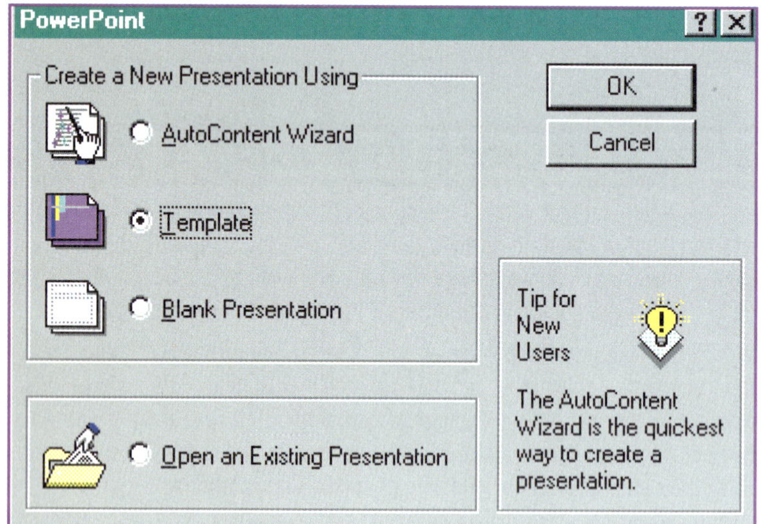

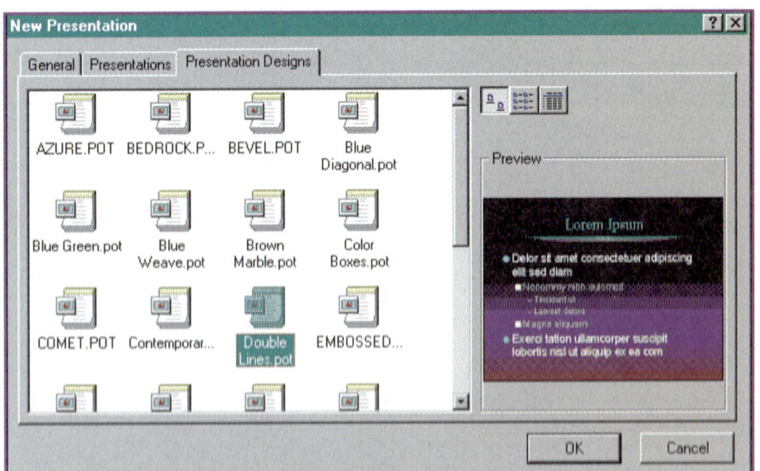

New Presentation Dialog Box

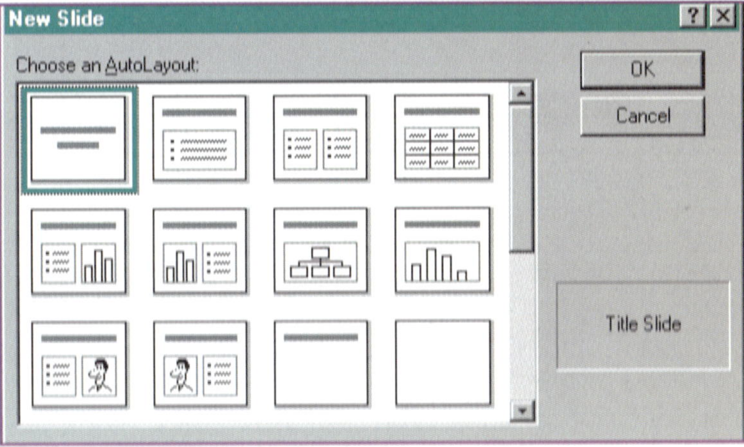

FIGURE 9.6

New Slide Dialog Box

Spell Checking A Presentation

Spelling

Unlike Microsoft Word, PowerPoint does not have a feature that will spell check your text automatically as you type. To run the spell checker in PowerPoint, position the insertion point at the beginning of the document, then click the Spelling button (fifth button from the left) on the Standard toolbar; or choose Tools, then Spelling; or press F7.

Printing A Presentation

A presentation can be printed in a variety of formats. You can print each slide on a separate piece of paper; print each slide at the top of the page, leaving the bottom of the page for notes; print all or a specific number of slides on a single piece of paper; or print the slide titles and topics in outline form. Use the Print what option at the Print dialog box to specify what you want printed. To display the Print dialog box, shown in figure 9.7, choose File, then Print, or press Ctrl + P. At the Print dialog box, click the down-pointing triangle at the right side of the Print what text box, then choose the desired printing format.

FIGURE 9.7

Print Dialog Box

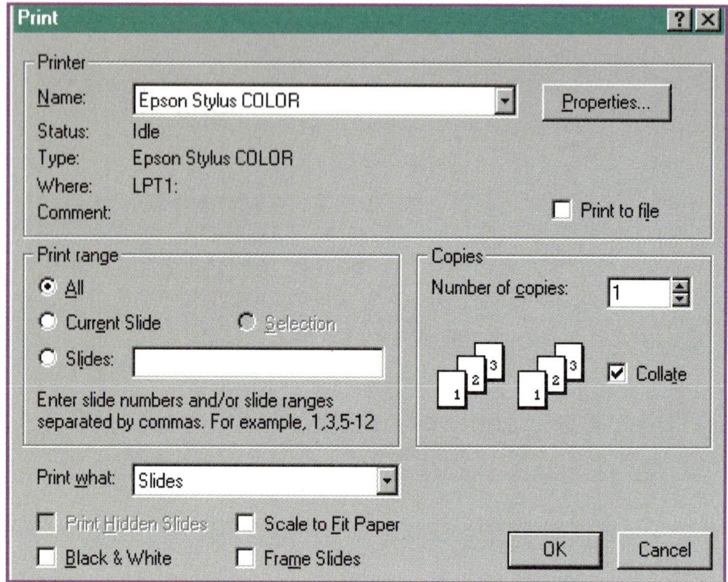

Creating A Presentation Using AutoLayout

When you choose an AutoLayout format, each slide will contain placeholders as shown in the New Slide dialog box in figure 9.6. A *placeholder* is a location on the slide where information is to be entered. For example, many slides contain a title placeholder. Click in this placeholder and then key the title of the slide. When text is entered into a placeholder, the placeholder turns into a text object.

You may replace an AutoLayout format previously selected for a slide by choosing Format, then Slide Layout. Make a selection from the Slide Layout dialog box, then choose the Reapply button.

An AutoLayout format may include some or all of the following placeholders:

- **Title:** Used to hold the title of the slide.
- **Bulleted List:** Used for a bulleted list of related points or topics.
- **Clip Art:** Holds a picture in a slide such as a clip art picture.
- **Graph:** Holds a graph, which is a visual representation of data.
- **Org Chart:** Used to display an organizational chart in a slide.
- **Table:** Used for a table that is inserted from Microsoft Word.
- **Object:** Holds an external object such as WordArt or a media clip or sound.

Creating and Printing a Presentation

1. Prepare a presentation that promotes membership in the Wheaton Bicycle Club sponsored by Ride Safe, Inc., as shown in figure 9.8, by completing the following steps:
   a. Load PowerPoint by clicking the Start button on the Windows Taskbar, choosing Programs, then *Microsoft PowerPoint.*
   b. When the Tip of the Day dialog box displays, read the tip, then choose OK or deselect Show Tips at Startup to turn this feature off.
   c. At the PowerPoint dialog box, choose Template, then choose OK.
   d. At the New Presentation dialog box, select the Presentation Designs tab.
   e. At the New Presentation dialog box with the Presentation Designs tab selected, double-click the *Azure* template.

f. At the New Slide dialog box, double-click the first layout in the list box (Title Slide).
g. At the slide, click in the text *Click to add title*, then key **Wheaton Bicycle Club**.
h. Select *Wheaton Bicycle Club* and change the font to 60-point Impact (use the Increase Font Size button on the Formatting toolbar).
i. Click in the text *Click to add sub-title*, then key the following:
   (1) Key **Sponsored by Ride Safe, Inc.**.
   (2) Press Enter, then key **Presented by:**.
   (3) Press Enter, then key **Your Name**.
   (4) Select *Sponsored by Ride Safe, Inc.* and change the font to 36-point Times New Roman Bold with Text Shadow. (Click the Increase Font Size button and the Bold button on the Formatting toolbar. The Text Shadow option is already active.)
   (5) Select *Presented by:* and change the font to 28-point Times New Roman with Text Shadow (click the Decrease Font Size button on the Formatting toolbar).
   (6) Select *Your Name* and change the font to 32-point Times New Roman Bold Italic with Text Shadow.
j. Create a second slide by completing the following steps:
   (1) Click the New Slide button located at the right side of the PowerPoint Status bar.
   (2) At the New Slide dialog box, double-click the second layout (Bulleted List) in the list box. (This inserts another slide on the screen.)
   (3) Key the following text inside the placeholders in the second slide:

Title	=	**Our Goal is Healthy Fun!**
Bullets	=	**Good friends**
	=	**Healthy exercise**
	=	**Great biking and social events**

   (4) Select *Our Goal is Healthy Fun!* and change the font size to 50-point Impact. Select the bulleted text, *Good friends...* and change the font to 36-point Times New Roman Bold with Text Shadow.
k. Create the remaining four slides by completing steps similar to steps j(1) through j(4). Key the text in each slide from the text shown in figure 9.8.

2. Click the Spelling button (fifth button from the left) on the Standard toolbar to spell check your slides.
3. Save the presentation by completing the following steps:
   a. Choose File, then Save.
   b. At the File Save dialog box, key **Bicycle Club Presentation**, then press Enter or choose Save.
4. View the presentation at various view screens by completing the following steps:
   a. To move the insertion point to the first slide, press Ctrl + Home, click the Previous Slide button, or click and drag the Elevator until the first slide displays.
   b. Choose View, then Outline or click the Outline View button on the View toolbar.
   c. Choose View, then Slide Sorter or click the Slide Sorter button on the View toolbar.
   d. Choose View, then Zoom. At the Zoom dialog box, change the setting to 100%. Choose OK or press Enter.
   e. Choose View, then Zoom, and change the setting back to 66%. Choose OK or press Enter.
   f. Choose View, then Notes Pages or click the Notes Pages View button on the View toolbar.
   g. Choose View, then Slides or click the Slide View button on the View toolbar.
   h. Choose View, then Black and White.

i. Click Black and White to deselect it and return the slides to color.
j. Choose View, then Slide Miniature.
k. Click the Close button in the upper right corner of Slide Miniature view (an X displays).

5. Print all six slides on the same page by completing the following steps:
   a. Choose File, then Print.
   b. At the Print dialog box, click the down-pointing triangle to the right of the Print what option, then click *Handouts (6 slides per page)* from the drop-down menu.
   c. Click OK.
6. Close Bicycle Club Presentation by choosing File, then Close.

FIGURE 9.8

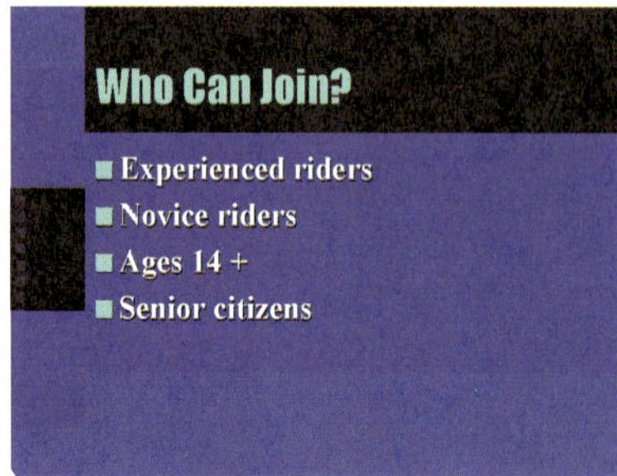

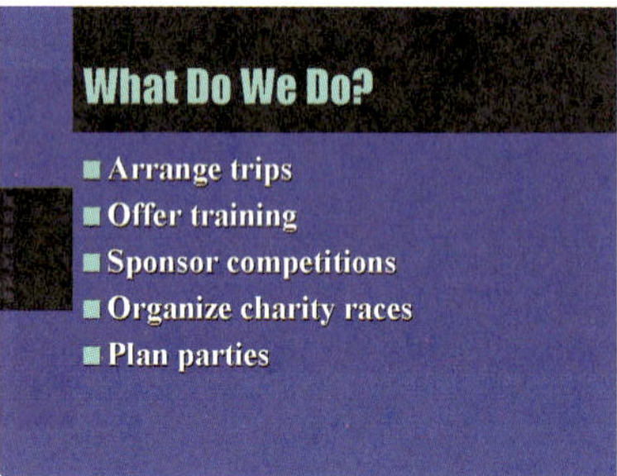

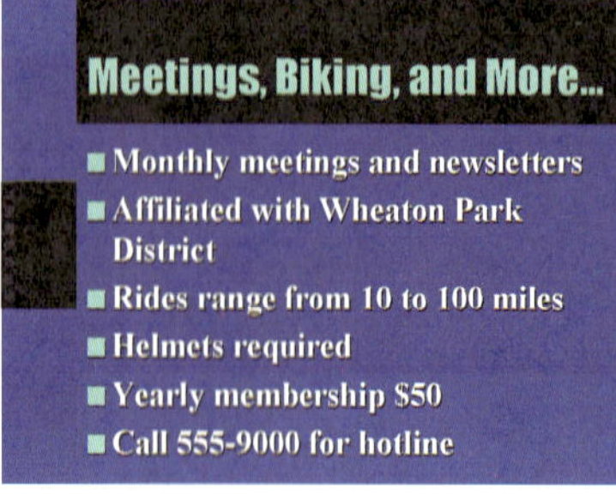

Adding Clip Art To A Slide

To enhance the visual impact of slides in a presentation, consider adding a Microsoft clip art image. Microsoft's clip art images cover a wide range of topics. A clip art image can be inserted into a slide in many different ways. One way is to use a slide layout that contains a clip art placeholder. A clip art placeholder displays in a presentation layout at the New Slide dialog box as a cartoon picture of a man. To insert an image in a clip art placeholder, display the desired layout, then double-click the clip art placeholder. This displays the Microsoft ClipArt Gallery dialog box as shown in figure 9.9. At this dialog box, choose the desired category, such as Business or People, then double-click a desired image in the Pictures list box.

A clip art image can also be inserted in a slide that does not contain a clip art placeholder. To do this, select the location in the slide where you want the clip art image inserted, then click the Insert Clip Art button on the Standard toolbar (seventh button from the right). Alternatively, you can choose Insert, then Clip Art. This displays the Microsoft ClipArt Gallery dialog box where you can choose the desired category and image.

Insert Clip Art

To insert graphic files from your student graphic disk into your PowerPoint slides, click once in the AutoLayout placeholder containing the clip art icon, then choose Insert, then Picture from the PowerPoint menu bar. You will need to size the image to fit the placeholder area. Size the image by holding down the Ctrl key as you drag a corner sizing handle inward to reduce the size and outward to increase the size proportionately. A graphic file from your student graphic disk may also be inserted without selecting a specific AutoLayout with a clip art placeholder. Decide where you want an image to display in your slide, then choose Insert, then Picture. Once the image is inserted into your slide, select the graphic image, then size and move it if necessary. It is recommended, however, to add the graphic files from your student graphic disk to Microsoft ClipArt Gallery for ease in retrieving and handling these images.

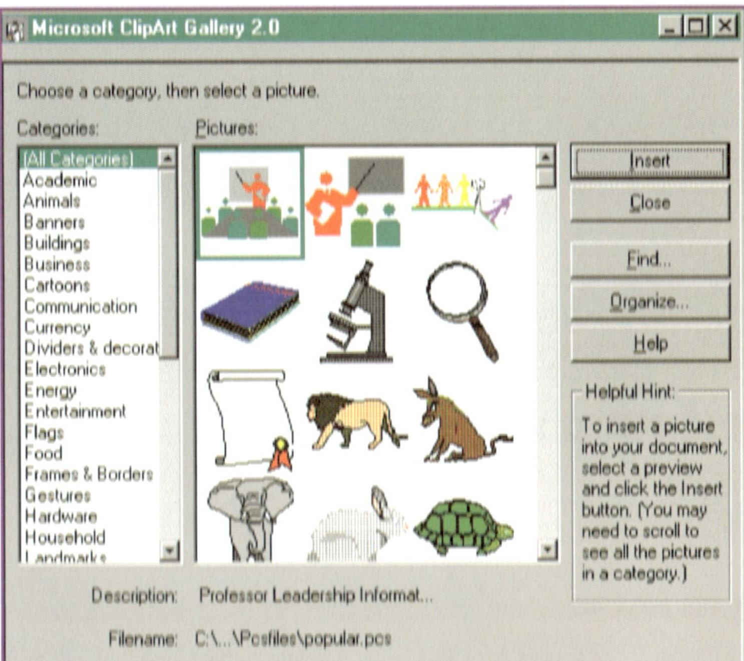

FIGURE 9.9

Microsoft ClipArt Gallery

Adding a Graphic Image to the ClipArt Gallery

If you frequently use a company logo or scanned image in slides, you may want to add these files to the ClipArt Gallery. To add other images to the ClipArt Gallery, complete the following steps:

1. Click the Insert Clip Art button (button with the cartoon man on it).
2. At the Microsoft ClipArt Gallery dialog box, click Organize.
3. At the Organize ClipArt dialog box, click Add Pictures.
4. Locate the file containing the image you want to add to the ClipArt Gallery, then click Open.
5. Select a category from the list in the Picture Properties dialog box. Key an optional description. (You can choose one or more categories for a picture, or you can choose to not categorize a picture at all.) Choose OK.
6. At the Microsoft ClipArt Gallery dialog box, choose Insert or Close depending on your desired action.

Inserting And Manipulating Graphics In PowerPoint Slides

Cropping an Image

Cropping: The process of trimming vertical and horizontal edges off a picture.

Once an image has been inserted, you may crop, scale, move, copy, or recolor it as you wish. *Cropping* is the process of trimming vertical and/or horizontal edges of a picture. Once an image has been cropped in PowerPoint, it can always be uncropped by using the same command. Photos are often cropped to focus attention on a particular area of a picture. To crop an image on a slide, complete the following steps:

1. Make sure the slide is in Slide view.
2. Select the image—eight sizing handles (small squares) should appear around the image.
3. Choose Tools, Crop Picture. The arrow pointer changes to the cropping tool. Or display the shortcut menu by right-clicking the mouse, then selecting Crop Picture.
4. Position the cropping tool over one of the handles.
5. Drag the handle. The original handles display, even though a dotted line also displays showing you the portion of the image that will appear on the slide.
6. When you are satisfied with the image, release the mouse button, then press Esc or click outside the selected area to turn off cropping.

Scaling (Resizing) an Image

Scaling: Reducing the size of an image without altering it proportionally.

To change the size of an image without changing its proportions, hold down the Ctrl key as you drag a corner handle. You can also proportionally scale an image by choosing Draw, Scale. Key the increment you would like, then click OK.

Moving an Image

To move an image, select it, click anywhere within the image, then drag it to a new location. The image will keep its original dimensions. You can also use the cut and paste buttons on the Standard toolbar or choose Edit, then Cut, position the insertion point where you want the image to appear, then click Paste.

In addition, you can move an image in very small increments in slide or notes view by selecting the image and then pressing an arrow key.

Copying an Image

You may duplicate an image to another slide by completing the following steps:

1. In Slide view, select the image you want to copy.
2. Choose Edit, then Copy or click the Copy button on the Standard toolbar.
3. Select Slide Sorter view, then double-click the slide to which you want to add the image.
4. Choose Edit, then Paste or click the Paste button on the Standard toolbar.

Additionally, you may use the Drag-and-Drop option to duplicate an image by completing the following steps:

1. Choose Tools, then Options.
2. At the Options dialog box, select the Edit tab, then click the Drag-and-Drop Text Editing check box to turn this feature on.
3. Select the image, hold down the Ctrl key and drag the copy to its new location.

Recoloring an Image

To recolor an image, complete the following steps:

1. In Slide view, select the image you want to recolor.
2. Choose Tools, then Recolor; or click the right mouse to access a shortcut menu and select Recolor.
3. At the Recolor Picture dialog box, select the color in the Original column that you would like to change, then click the down-pointing triangle in the New column and choose a new color.
4. Click Preview to see the color changes.
5. When you are satisfied with the results, click OK.

In exercise 2 you will open an existing presentation and add graphic images to enhance the presentation. Although it is unnecessary to insert an image in each slide, several graphics are added in exercise 2 to demonstrate various techniques in inserting and changing graphics. Too many graphics in a presentation may distract from the message of the presentation.

Steps are given in exercise 2 to insert graphic images from your student graphic disk. However, you may have added these images to the Microsoft ClipArt Gallery as discussed earlier. In that case, you may disregard these steps and insert the images by simply double-clicking on the cartoon man icon in the placeholder to access Microsoft ClipArt Gallery, then double-click on the desired image.

Inserting Graphic Images into a Presentation

1. Enhance a presentation with clip art images as shown in figure 9.10 by completing the following steps:
   a. Open *Basic Five Reasons* from your student data disk by completing the following steps:
      (1) If you are already in PowerPoint, choose File, then Open. If you have not yet entered PowerPoint, load PowerPoint, click OK at the Tip of the Day, then choose Open an Existing Presentation.

(2) At the File Open dialog box, make sure the drive or folder where your student data disk is located displays in the Look in: text box.
(3) Make sure Presentations (*.ppt) displays in the Files of type: text box.
(4) Select *Basic Five Reasons* from the Name list box.
(5) Choose Open.

b. Save the presentation with Save As and name it Five Reasons Presentation.

c. At the first slide, select *Your Name* and key your own name as the presenter. Click the Next Slide button at the bottom of the vertical scroll bar to advance to the second slide.

d. Insert a clip art image into the second slide by completing the following:
(1) Double-click the cartoon man icon located in the right section of the placeholder.
(2) At the Microsoft ClipArt Gallery, select *Science and Medicine* from the list displayed in the Categories section of the dialog box. (Choose All Categories if Science and Medicine is not available.)
(3) Continue clicking the down-pointing triangle to the right of the Pictures list box until a black and white picture of a medical staff displays, then double-click *medstaff*.
(4) Click outside the image to deselect it.
(5) Click the Next Slide button.

e. Insert a clip art image from your student graphic disk into the third slide by completing the following steps:
(1) Click once on the cartoon man icon located in the left section of the placeholder in the third slide. Eight sizing handles should display around the placeholder frame.
(2) Choose Insert, then Picture.
(3) Make sure the drive or folder where your student graphic disk is located displays in the Look in: text box.
(4) From the list box, double-click *certifct.cgm*.
(5) If the CGM Graphic Import dialog box displays, choose OK or press Enter. (The size of the graphic may be too large for the placeholder frame.)
(6) Size the image by holding down the Ctrl key and dragging one of the corner handles inward to reduce the image to an approximate size of the placeholder frame. You may need to drag the reduced image into the placeholder frame.
(7) Deselect the image.
(8) Click the Next Slide button.

f. Insert a graphic image into the fourth slide by completing the following steps:
(1) Double-click the cartoon man icon located in the right section of the placeholder.
(2) At the Microsoft ClipArt Gallery, select *Currency* from the list displayed in the Categories section of the dialog box. (Choose All Categories if Currency is not available.)
(3) At the Pictures list box, double-click the clip art image of a green bag of money with a dollar symbol in the center of the bag (*C:\...\Pcsfiles\popular.pcs*). The description of the graphic is *Reward Accounting*.
(4) With the clip art selected, right-click your mouse to access the shortcut menu.
(5) Click Recolor from the shortcut menu.
(6) At the Recolor dialog box, click the down-pointing arrow to the right of the dark green bar in the New section, then from the drop-down color palette that displays, select the bright yellow color in the first row. (A check mark will display in the check box to the left of the dark green box in the Original section.)

(7) Click the down-pointing arrow to the right of the bright green bar and from the color palette that displays, select the purple color in the second row.
(8) Choose OK or press Enter.
(9) Deselect the image.
(10) Click the Next Slide button.

g. Add a clip art image to the fifth slide by completing the following steps:
(1) Click once on the cartoon man icon located in the left section of the placeholder in the fifth slide.
(2) Choose Insert, then Picture.
(3) Make sure the drive or folder where your student graphic disk is located displays in the Look in: text box.
(4) From the list box, double-click *mntbike2.cgm.* (The image will take up most of the placeholder area.)
(5) Size the image by holding down the Ctrl key and dragging one of the corner handles inward to reduce the size to an approximate size of the placeholder frame.
(6) Drag the image into the placeholder frame.
(7) Crop the image as shown in figure 9.10 by completing the following steps:
(a) With the clip art selected, right-click your mouse to access the shortcut menu.
(b) Click Crop Picture from the shortcut menu. (The arrow pointer will display as a cropping tool.)
(c) Position the cropping tool on the lower middle sizing handle and drag the tool upward to eliminate the lower half of the image.
(d) Position the cropping tool on the left middle sizing handle and drag the tool to the right to eliminate part of the left side of the image.
(e) Position the cropping tool on the right middle sizing handle and drag the tool to the left and release the mouse near the cyclist's face.
(f) Increase the size of the image by dragging one of the corner handles outward to an approximate size of the placeholder frame as shown in figure 9.10. (The placeholder frame may not display at this point.)
(g) Deselect the image.

h. Spell check the presentation.

2. Save the presentation again with the same name, Five Reasons Presentation.
3. Print all six slides on the same page.
4. Close Five Reasons Presentation.

FIGURE 9.10

Five Reasons to Buy a Bicycle Helmet from Ride Safe, Inc.
Presented by: Your Name

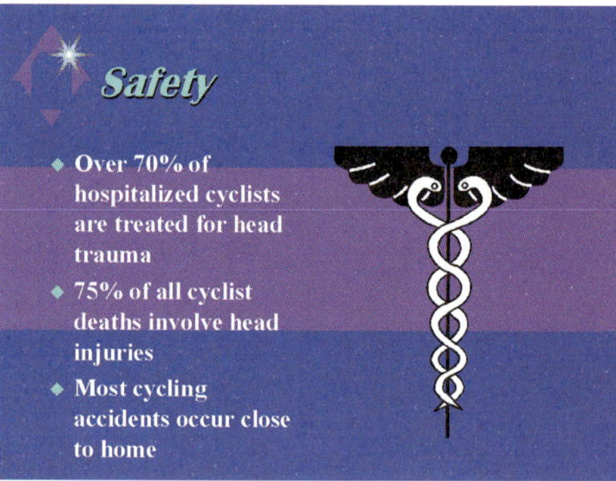
Safety
Over 70% of hospitalized cyclists are treated for head trauma
75% of all cyclist deaths involve head injuries
Most cycling accidents occur close to home

Safety Approvals
ANSI (American National Standards Institute)
Snell Memorial Foundation Impact Standards

Great Price
Soft shell helmets - $20
Microshells - $25
Extra covers - $5
$

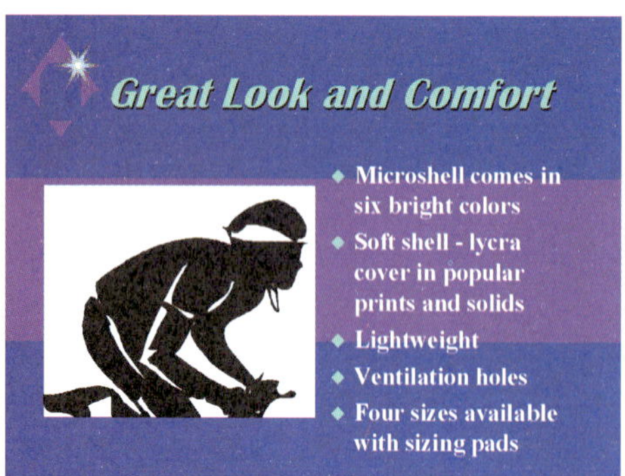
Great Look and Comfort
Microshell comes in six bright colors
Soft shell - lycra cover in popular prints and solids
Lightweight
Ventilation holes
Four sizes available with sizing pads

Safety Reminder
Helmets remind bicyclists that biking can be dangerous.
Bicyclists who wear helmets serve as good examples for others.
It is important to follow the rules of the road.

Planning A Presentation With The AutoContent Wizard

PowerPoint contains an AutoContent Wizard that will help you in the planning and organizing of a presentation. You respond to certain questions from the Wizard and, based on your responses, you are presented with slides containing information on what to include in your presentation and how to organize it. For example, suppose you are an employee of Ride Safe, Inc., and have been asked to prepare a presentation on selling bicycle and in-line skating helmets, you can use the AutoContent Wizard to help you organize this sales presentation. The Wizard also provides additional information on other types of presentations. Consider printing this information for help in creating other presentations.

AutoContent Wizard can be accessed at the PowerPoint dialog box as shown in figure 9.4. Alternatively, you can access AutoContent Wizard by choosing File, then New, then select the Presentations tab at the New Presentation dialog box, and double-click the AutoWizard icon.

DTP POINTERS
Use five to seven words per line on a slide.

DTP POINTERS
Use five to seven lines per slide.

Running A Slide Show

Several methods can be used to run a slide show. Slides created in PowerPoint can be converted to 35mm slides or transparencies; or the computer screen can display the slides, much like a slide projector. An on-screen presentation saves the expense of producing slides and lets you use the computer's color capability. However, you will need an overhead LCD projector if you are displaying a presentation to more than a few people.

If you are running a slide show in PowerPoint, there are several methods you can choose. You can run the slide show manually (you determine when to advance to the next slide), advance slides automatically, or set up a slide show to run continuously for demonstration purposes.

If you want to run a slide show manually, open the presentation, then click the Slide Show button on the View toolbar. You can also choose View, then Slide Show. At the Slide Show dialog box, choose Show. To control movement through slides in a slide show, refer to figure 9.11.

FIGURE 9.11

Commands for Controlling a Slide Show

To do this...	Perform this action:
Show next slide	Click left mouse button; or press one of the following keys: space bar, N, right arrow, down arrow, or Page Down
Show previous slide	Click right mouse button; or press one of the following keys: Backspace, P, left arrow, up arrow, or Page Up
Show specific slide	Key slide number, then press Enter
Toggle mouse on or off	Key A or equal sign (=)
Switch between black screen and current slide	Key B or period (.)
Switch between white screen and current slide	Key W or comma (,)
End slide show and return to PowerPoint	Press one of the following keys: Esc, hyphen (-), or Ctrl + Break

Using AutoContent Wizard for a Sales Presentation

1. Prepare slides to assist in organizing a presentation to sell bicycle and in-line skating helmets, as shown in figure 9.12, by completing the following steps: (If you have not yet loaded PowerPoint, follow the steps listed under step a. If you have already loaded PowerPoint, follow the steps listed under step b.)
   a. If you have not yet entered PowerPoint, complete the following steps:
      (1) Load PowerPoint by click the Start button on the Windows Taskbar, choosing Programs, then *Microsoft PowerPoint.*
      (2) If the Tip of the Day dialog box displays, read the tip, then choose OK.
      (3) At the PowerPoint dialog box, choose AutoContent Wizard, then choose OK.
   b. If you have already loaded PowerPoint, complete the following steps:
      (1) Choose File, then New.
      (2) At the New Presentation dialog box, select the Presentations tab.
      (3) Double-click the AutoContent Wizard icon.
   c. At the first AutoContent Wizard dialog box, read the information presented, then choose Next>.
   d. At the second AutoContent Wizard dialog box, key **Your Name** in the *What is your name?* text box. Key **Ride Safe Helmet Sales** in the *What are you going to talk about?* text box. Make sure the third and last box is empty. Then choose Next>.
   e. At the third AutoContent Wizard dialog box, choose Selling a Product, Service or Idea, then choose Next>.
   f. At the fourth AutoContent Wizard dialog box, choose Contemporary, choose 30 minutes or less, then choose Next.
   g. At the fifth AutoContent Wizard dialog box, choose On-screen presentation, choose No at *Will you print handouts?*, then choose Next>.
   h. At the sixth AutoContent Wizard dialog box, read the information presented, then choose Finish.
2. View the slides provided by Wizard by clicking the Next Slide button at the bottom of the vertical scroll bar. Continue reading the information on each slide until all slides have been read.
3. View the slides again using the elevator by completing the following step:
   a. Position the arrow pointer on the elevator (the scroll box) on the vertical scroll bar, hold down the left mouse button, drag the elevator to the top of the vertical scroll bar until a white box displays Slide 1 and the title of the slide, then release the mouse button. (This displays Slide 1 in the Presentation window.)
4. View the slides again using Slide Sorter view by choosing View, then Slide Sorter; or clicking the Slide Sorter View button on the View toolbar.
5. Run the slide presentation on the screen by completing the following steps:
   a. In Slide Sorter view, click once on Slide 1 or press Ctrl + Home. (This is to ensure that your slide show begins with the first slide.)
   b. Click the Slide Show button on the View toolbar (This should cause Slide 1 to display and fill the entire screen.)
   c. After viewing Slide 1, click the left mouse button. (This causes Slide 2 to display.)
   d. Continue viewing and then clicking the left mouse button until all eight slides have been viewed and the screen returns to the Slide Sorter view.
   e. After viewing the last slide (Slide 8), click the left mouse button again. (This returns the display to Slide Sorter view.)
6. Save the presentation by completing the following steps:
   a. Click the Save button on the Standard toolbar.
   b. At the File Save dialog box, key **Helmet Sales Presentation**, then press Enter or choose Save.

7. Print the information on the slides provided by the Wizard in outline view by completing the following steps:
   a. Choose File, then Print.
   b. At the Print dialog box, click the down-pointing triangle to the right of the Print what option, then click *Outline View* from the drop-down menu.
   c. Click OK.
8. Close Helmet Sales Presentation.

FIGURE 9.12

1 Ride Safe Helmet Sales

Your Name

2 Objective

- State the desired objective
- Use multiple points if necessary

3 Customer Requirements

- State the needs of the audience
- Confirm the audience's needs if you are not sure

4 Meeting the Needs

- List the products and features, and how each addresses a specific need or solves a specific problem
- This section may require multiple slides

5 Cost Analysis

- Point out financial benefits to the customer
- Compare cost-benefits between you and your competitors

6 Our Strengths

7 Key Benefits

- Summarize the key benefits provided by the product, service, or idea being promoted

8 Next Steps

- Specify the actions required of your audience

Running a Slide Show Automatically

Slides in a slide show can be advanced automatically after a specific number of seconds. To do this, specify the seconds at the Slide Transition dialog box shown in figure 9.13. To display this dialog box, open a presentation, change to the Slide Sorter view, select an individual slide or select all slides in the presentation, then choose Tools, then Slide Transition.

FIGURE 9.13

Slide Transition Dialog Box

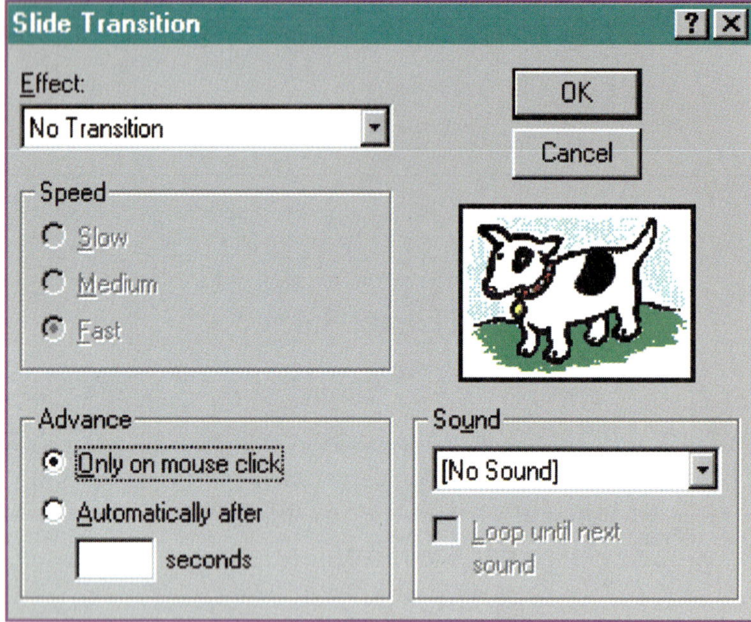

If you want to specify a time for an individual slide, select that slide first (by clicking it), then display the Slide Transition dialog box. If you want transition times to affect all slides in the presentation, select all the slides first and then display the Slide Transition dialog box. To select all slides in a presentation, display the slides in Slide Sorter view, hold down the Shift key, then click each slide. You can also select all slides by pressing Ctrl + A.

With the desired slides selected, make changes to the Slide Transition dialog box. To automatically advance slides, choose Automatically after (in the Advance section), then key the number of seconds. After making changes to the Slide Transition dialog box, choose OK to close the dialog box.

To automatically run the presentation, choose View, then Slide Show. At the Slide Show dialog box shown in figure 9.14, choose Use Slide Timings, then choose Show. This runs the presentation showing each slide on the screen the specified number of seconds.

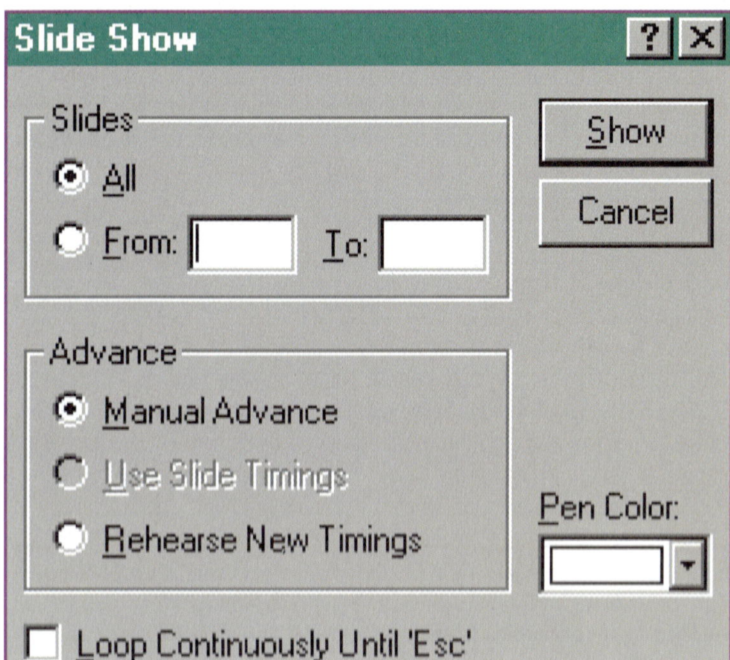

FIGURE 9.14

Slide Show Dialog Box

Running a Slide Show in a Continuous Loop

In a continuous-loop slide show, all the slides are viewed over and over again until you stop the show. This feature is especially effective when presenting a new product or service at a trade show or at a new store opening. To run a presentation in PowerPoint in a continuous loop, choose View, then Slide Show. At the Slide Show dialog box, click the check box to the left of Loop Continuously Until 'Esc'. When you're ready to run the presentation, choose Show.

When you're ready to end the slide show, press the Esc key on the keyboard. Click the check box to the left of Loop Continuously Until 'Esc' again at the Slide Show dialog box to turn the looping feature off.

Adding Transition and Sound Effects

At the Slide Transition dialog box shown in figure 9.13, you can enhance the presentation by adding transition effects and sound. *Transition* refers to what takes place when one slide is removed from the screen during a presentation and the next slide is displayed. Interesting transitions can be added such as blinds, boxes, checkerboards, covers, random bars, stripes, and wipes.

Transition: How one slide is removed from the screen and the next slide is displayed.

To add a transition effect, click the down-pointing triangle to the right of the Effect list box in the Slide Transition dialog box, then click the desired transition at the drop-down menu. When you click the desired transition, the transition is displayed at the right side of the dialog box (where the picture of the dog is located).

As a slide is removed from the screen and another slide is displayed, a sound can be added. To add a sound, click the down-pointing triangle to the right of the Sound list box, then click the desired sound. You can choose from a list of sounds such as camera, laser, screeching brakes, typewriter, and whoosh.

DTP POINTERS
Each slide can have a different transition effect.

When a time has been added to a slide (or slides), the time displays at the bottom of the slide (or slides) in Slide Sorter view. If a transition is added, a transition icon displays below the slide (or slides) at the bottom left side.

Setting and Rehearsing Timings for a Presentation

Setting a time at the Slide Transition dialog box sets the time for each selected slide. In some presentations, you may want to specify a different amount of time for each slide and then rehearse the presentation to ensure that the time set is appropriate. This can be accomplished with the Rehearse New Timings option at the Slide Show dialog box. To rehearse and set a time for each slide, you would complete these steps:

1. Open the presentation.
2. Change to the Slide Sorter view.
3. Choose View, then Slide Show.
4. At the Slide Show dialog box, choose Rehearse New Timings.
5. Choose Show. The first slide in the presentation displays along with a Rehearsal dialog box that displays at the bottom right corner of the screen. The Rehearsal dialog box shows the time for the current slide in the upper right corner and the entire time for the presentation in the upper left corner. The timer begins immediately.
6. Click the Next Slide button (displays at the bottom right side of the dialog box with a right-pointing triangle) when the desired time is displayed; choose the Pause button (displays with two thick vertical bars) to stop the timer and leave the slide on the screen; or choose the Repeat button if you want the time for the current slide to start over.
7. Continue in this manner until the time for all slides in the presentation has been specified.
8. After specifying the time for the last slide, a Microsoft PowerPoint dialog box displays with the total time of the presentation displayed and asks if you want to record the new slide timings. At this dialog box, choose Yes to save the new timings. (This returns the presentation back to the Slide Sorter view.)

Running a Presentation Automatically and Establishing Specific Times for Slides

1. Open the Bicycle Club Presentation. (This presentation was created in exercise 1.)
2. Save the presentation with Save As and name it Rehearsed Bicycle Club Presentation.
3. Add a graphic image to the slides as shown in figure 9.15 by completing the following steps:
   a. At the first slide, select the heading *Wheaton Bicycle Club*, and drag the text box containing the heading upward approximately one inch.
   b. Select the heading *Sponsored by Ride Safe...* and drag it downward approximately one-half inch. (Refer to figure 9.15 for correct placement.)
   c. Choose Insert, then Picture.
   d. At the Insert Picture dialog box, make sure the drive or folder where your student graphic files are located displays in the Look in: text box.
   e. Double-click *cycling.cgm* at the Name list box.
   f. If the CGM Graphics Import dialog box displays, choose OK or press Enter.
   g. Size the picture by dragging one of the corner sizing handles inward, then drag the picture to the middle of the slide as shown in figure 9.15.
   h. With the picture still selected, click the Copy button on the Standard toolbar. (This copies the image to the clipboard, so it may be pasted to other slides.)
   i. Click the Next Slide button to display the second slide.
   j. Click the Paste button on the Standard toolbar.

k. Drag to position the picture as shown in figure 9.15.
l. Continue copying the picture to the remaining slides by completing steps similar to 3(i) and 3(j).
m. Press Ctrl + Home to position the insertion point in the first slide.

4. Add transition sound effects, then run the presentation automatically by completing the following steps:
   a. Change to the Slide Sorter view.
   b. Hold down the Shift key then click each slide; or press Ctrl + A. (This selects all slides in the presentation.)
   c. Choose Tools, then Slide Transition; or click the Slide Transition button on the Slide Sorter toolbar (first button).
   d. At the Slide Transition dialog box, choose Automatically after, then key **5** in the Seconds text box.
   e. Add a transition effect by completing the following steps:
      (1) Click the down-pointing triangle to the right of the Effect list box (containing the text *No Transition*).
      (2) From the drop-down list that displays, click *Blinds Horizontal.*
   f. Make sure Fast is selected in the Speed section.
   g. Add a sound effect by completing the following steps:
      (1) Click the down-pointing triangle to the right of the Sound list box (containing the text *[No Sound]*).
      (2) From the drop-down list that displays, click *Camera.*
   h. Choose OK to close the dialog box.
   i. Specify that the presentation is to be run automatically by completing the following steps:
      (1) Choose View, then Slide Show.
      (2) At the Slide Show dialog box, choose Use Slide Timings.
      (3) Choose Show. (This runs the presentation automatically.)
5. When the presentation is done, the slides display in Slide Sorter view. (Notice the time and transition icons that display at the bottom of each slide as shown in figure 9.15.)
6. Set a different specific time for each slide by completing the following steps:
   a. Make sure all the slides are selected (press Ctrl + A) and displayed in Slide Sorter view, then choose View, then Slide Show; or click the Rehearse Timings button on the Slide Sorter toolbar (a clock displays on the button and it is the second button from the right).
   b. At the Slide Show dialog box, choose Rehearse New Timings.
   c. Choose Show.
   d. With the first slide displayed, wait until the timer at the right side of the Rehearsal dialog box displays 10 seconds, then click the Next Slide button. (The Next Slide button displays at the bottom right side of the dialog box and contains a right-pointing triangle.) If you miss 10 seconds, click the Repeat button at the bottom left side of the dialog box. This restarts the clock for that particular slide. (The middle button at the bottom of the Rehearsal dialog box will pause the timing.)
   e. With the second slide displayed, wait until the timer at the right side of the dialog box displays 8 seconds, then click the Next Slide button.
   f. Set 8 seconds for the third slide, and 5 seconds for the remaining three slides.
   g. After setting the time for the last slide, the Microsoft PowerPoint dialog box displays asking if you want to record the new timings. At this dialog box, choose the new timings. At this dialog box, choose Yes.

7. Run the presentation again by completing the following steps:
    a. Choose View, then Slide Show.
    b. At the Slide Show dialog box, choose Use Slide Timings in the Advance section.
    c. Make the slide show a continuous on-screen presentation by clicking in the check box to the left of Loop Continuously Until 'Esc'.
    d. Choose Show. (Let the slides change automatically; the first slide will display for 10 seconds, the second and third for 8 seconds, and the remaining three for 5 seconds.)
    e. Press the Esc key on the keyboard to end the loop.
8. Save the presentation again with the same name, (Rehearsed Bicycle Club Presentation).
9. Click to remove the check mark to the left of Loop Continuously Until 'Esc' at the Slide Show dialog box.
10. Print the presentation with six slides per page.
11. Close Rehearsed Bicycle Club Presentation.

FIGURE 9.15

Reharsed Timing Slide Show

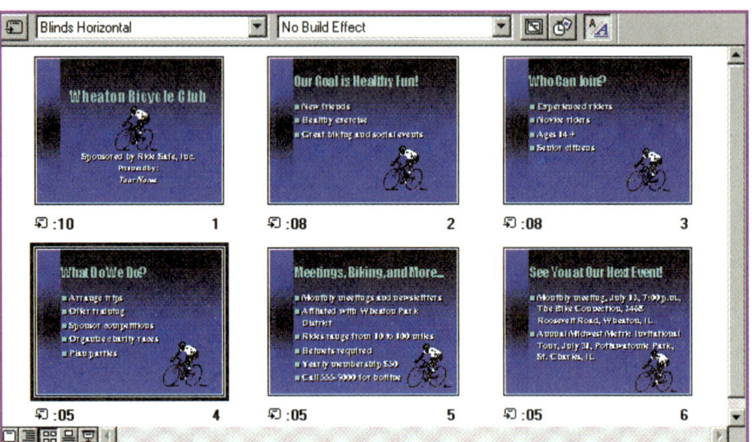

Preparing A Presentation In Outline View

In exercise 1, you created a short slide presentation using a PowerPoint template in which you inserted a small amount of text on each slide. If you are creating a longer presentation with more slides and text, consider using the Outline view to help organize the topics for the slides without the distractions of colorful templates, clip art, transition effects, or sound. To prepare a presentation in Outline view, you would complete the following steps:

1. Start the PowerPoint program.
2. If the Tip of the Day dialog box displays, choose OK.
3. At the PowerPoint dialog box, choose Template.
4. At the New Presentation dialog box, select the Presentation Designs tab, choose a specific template, then click OK.
5. At the New Slide dialog box, choose an AutoLayout format, then choose OK.
6. With the blank slide displayed on the screen, click the Outline View button on the View toolbar.

Outline View

7. Key the title of the first slide, then press Enter.
8. Click the Demote (Indent more) button on the Outlining toolbar or press the Tab key to move to the next tab stop, then key the first heading.
9. Continue keying the text for each slide in the presentation. Click the Demote (Indent more) button on the Outlining toolbar or press Tab to move the insertion point to the next tab stop (and automatically change the text formatting), or click the Promote (Indent less) button on the Outlining toolbar or press Shift + Tab to move the insertion point to the previous tab stop. Continue in this manner until all text is entered for the presentation.
10. When the presentation is completed, save it in the normal manner.

Demote

When keying text for a presentation in the Outline View mode, click the Demote (Indent more) button on the Outlining toolbar or press the Tab key to move the insertion point to the next tab stop. This moves the insertion point and also changes the formatting. The formatting will vary depending on the AutoLayout format you chose at the New Slide dialog box. For many AutoLayout formats, a slide title is set in 44-point Times New Roman Bold. Text keyed at the first tab stop will be set in a smaller point size such as 32-point Times New Roman.

Promote

To move the insertion point to a previous tab stop, click the Promote (Indent less) button on the Outlining toolbar or press Shift + Tab. This moves the insertion point and also changes text formatting. Moving the insertion point back to the left margin will begin another slide. These slides are numbered at the left side of the screen and are preceded by a slide icon.

In the Outline View, the Outlining toolbar displays at the left side of the screen. This toolbar contains the Promote and Demote buttons mentioned in the previous paragraphs along with other buttons as shown in figure 9.16.

FIGURE 9.16

Outlining Toolbar

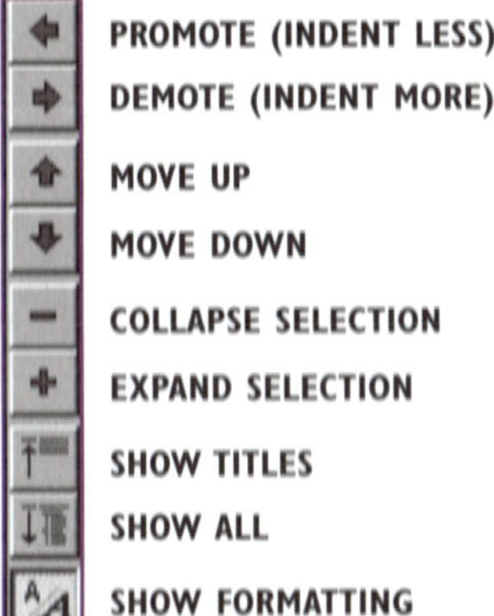

Editing Slides

Slides within a PowerPoint presentation can be edited. Text within individual slides can be inserted or deleted, slides can be deleted from the presentation, slides can be inserted into an existing presentation, and slides can be rearranged. Slides can be edited in several views—use the view that makes editing the easiest. For example, rearrange the order of slides in the Slide Sorter view; delete or insert text within slides in the Outline view or the Slide view.

DTP POINTERS
Don't clutter—use white space generously.

Inserting and Deleting Slides

An entire slide can be deleted from a presentation at the Slide Sorter or Outline view. To delete a slide from a presentation, display the presentation in Slide Sorter view, click the slide you want to delete, then press the Delete key. A slide can also be deleted in the Outline view. To do this, change to the Outline view, position the arrow pointer on the slide icon located next to the slide text you want to delete until the arrow pointer turns into a four-headed arrow, then click the left mouse button to select all of the text for the slide. With the text for the slide selected, press the Delete key.

A new slide can be inserted into an existing presentation at the Slide Sorter or Outline view. To add a slide to a presentation in the Slide Sorter view, you would follow these basic steps:

1. Open the presentation to which you want the slide added.
2. Change to the Slide Sorter view.
3. Click the slide that will immediately precede the new slide. (For example, if you want the new slide to immediately follow Slide 3, then click Slide 3.)
4. Click the New Slide button that displays in the Status bar toward the right side of the screen; or choose Insert, then New Slide.
5. At the New Slide dialog box, double-click the desired AutoLayout format.
6. At the Slide Sorter view, double-click the new blank slide. (This changes the presentation to the Slide view with only the new slide displayed in the Presentation window.)
7. Add the desired text to the new slide.
8. Save the presentation again.

Rearranging Slides

Collapse Selection

Expand Selection

Move Down

Move Up

Slides can be easily rearranged in Slide Sorter view. To do this, change to the Slide Sorter view, position the arrow pointer on the slide to be moved, hold down the left mouse button, drag the arrow pointer (with a square attached) to the desired position, then release the mouse button.

To move a slide created in Outline view, collapse the outline first. To collapse an outline, eliminate or hide all the details or levels of a slide. Click the Collapse Selection button (fifth button from the top) of the Outlining toolbar, and only the title of each slide will display. To expand the outline, click the Expand Selection button (sixth button from the top) of the Outlining toolbar and the titles and all bulleted points of the selected slide will display. The rest of the text is represented by a gray line below the text. Click anywhere in the title of the slide you want to move. Click on the Move Down button to move the slide down or click on the Move Up button to move the slide up. Each time you click the Move Up or Move Down button, the selected slide moves up or down one line at a time. Another way to move a slide in Outline view is to collapse the outline, then click the icon of the slide you want to move, drag the slide icon to the desired location (note that a black line appears at the slide's new position) and release the mouse button.

In several upcoming exercises, you will experiment with a variety of transitions and sounds. Most sources recommend that you refrain from using a different transition for each slide in a presentation. However, for demonstration purposes, you will add many transitions to the presentation in exercise 5. If you prefer to use several transitions, leave at least one consistent transition between all the slides. For example, make the transition for the heading the same for each slide.

Preparing a Presentation in Outline View then Rearranging Slides

1. Create a presentation in Outline view by completing the following steps: (If you have already entered PowerPoint, complete the steps listed under step a. If you have not yet entered PowerPoint, follow the steps listed under step b.)
    a. If you are already in PowerPoint, complete the following steps:
        (1) Choose File, then New.
        (2) At the New Presentation dialog box, select the Presentation Designs tab.
        (3) Double-click *International* at the list box.
        (4) At the New Slide dialog box, select the first layout in the list box (Title Slide). Choose OK or press Enter.

b. If you have not yet entered PowerPoint, complete the following steps:

(1) Load PowerPoint.

(2) If the Tip of the Day dialog box displays, read the tip, then click OK.

(3) At the PowerPoint dialog box, choose Template, then choose OK.

(4) At the New Presentation dialog box, select the Presentation Designs tab.

(5) At the New Presentation dialog box with the Presentation Designs tab selected, double-click *International* at the list box.

(6) At the New Slide dialog box, double-click the first layout in the list box (Title Slide).

c. With the first slide displayed, click the Outline View button on the View toolbar.

d. At the Outline screen, create the outline shown in figure 9.17 by completing the following steps:

(1) Key **Ride Safe, Inc.** in the first slide title shown in figure 9.17, press Shift + Enter, then key **presents**. Press Shift + Enter, then key **Elementary Traffic Education Program**, then press Enter. (Pressing Shift + Enter moves the insertion point to the next line without activating an outline level.)

(2) Key the second slide title shown in figure 9.17, **Curriculum Highlight #1**, then press Enter.

(3) Click the Demote (Indent more) button on the Outlining toolbar or press the Tab key, key the text after the first bullet in figure 9.17 that begins with **Presents positive images that focus on decision-making skills**, then press Enter.

(4) Click the Demote (Indent more) button on the Outlining toolbar or press the Tab key, then key the text after the hyphen bullet (-) that begins **De-emphasizes memorization of rules**, then press Enter.

(5) Continue keying the text as it displays in figure 9.17. Click the Demote (Indent more) button or press the Tab key to move the insertion point to the next tab stop. Click the Promote (Indent less) button or press Shift + Tab to move the insertion point back to a previous tab stop.

e. At Outline view, format the slide text by completing the following steps:

(1) Press Ctrl + Home to move the insertion point to the first slide.

(2) Select *Ride Safe, Inc.* and change the font to 60-point Times New Roman Bold.

(3) Select *presents* and change the font to 40-point Times New Roman Bold Italic.

(4) Select *Elementary Traffic Education Program* and change the font to 48-point Times New Roman Bold Italic.

(5) Select *Curriculum Highlight #1* and change the font to 54-point Times New Roman Bold.

(6) Select *Presents positive images that focus on decision-making skills* and change the font to 32-point Times New Roman Bold. With the text still selected, change the bullet symbol by completing the following steps:

(a) Choose Format, then Bullet.

(b) Click the down-pointing triangle to the right of the Bullets From text box and select Monotype Sorts.

(c) Select the circular symbol in the third row and the eighth column from the right in the list box. Choose OK or press Enter.

(7) Select the secondary bulleted text beginning with *De-emphasizes memorization...* and ending with *Role model demonstrations.* Change the font to 28-point Times New Roman Bold. Change the bullets to the small round bullet in the fifth row and sixth column of the [Normal Text] character set.

f. Format the remaining slides in outline view by copying the formatting in lines e(2) through e(7) using the Format Painter by completing the following steps:

(1) Select the formatted text you want to copy, including all levels and bullets.
(2) Double-click the Format Painter button on the Standard toolbar (ninth button).
(3) The arrow pointer now displays as a paintbrush. Drag the paintbrush over the text you want to format, then release the left mouse. Continue "painting" the formatting to other text.
(4) When finished, click the Format Painter button again to turn off this feature.

2. When all six slides have been created, save the presentation and name it Curriculum Outline 2.
3. If necessary, reposition the text in the first slide by completing the following steps:
   a. Press Ctrl + Home or click the Previous Slide button until the first slide displays.
   b. Change to Slide view by clicking the Slide view button on the View toolbar.
   c. Click to select the text box containing the text, *Click to add title* (the text box may display below the title text, in which case, click the right vertical side of the text box and the sizing handles should display around the text box). Click then drag the middle top sizing handle upward to expand the size of the text box to include the title text, *Ride Safe, Inc. presents....* Click to select the entire text box containing the title and drag the title downward to a location similar to figure 9.18. (The title text should display below the template globe.) Select then delete the sub-title box.
4. Rearrange some of the slides in the presentation by completing the following steps:
   a. Change to Slide Sorter view.
   b. Move Slide 5 (Highlight #4) before Slide 2 (Highlight #1). To do this position the arrow pointer on Slide 5, hold down the left mouse button, drag the arrow pointer (with a square attached) between Slides 1 and 2, then release the mouse button. (A vertical line will display between the two slides.)
   c. Move Slide 4 after Slide 2 by completing steps similar to those in step 4b.
   d. Use the Previous and Next Slide buttons to move between each slide and edit each slide by changing the title numbers until they are numbered consecutively —*Highlight #1, Highlight #2, etc.*
5. Move and copy text within and between slides by completing the following steps:
   a. With the slides still displayed in Slide Sorter view, click Slide 4 to select it.
   b. Click the Slide View button on the View toolbar or double-click Slide 4. (This displays only Slide 4 in the Presentation window.)
   c. In slide 4, move the first bulleted item *De-emphasizes...* to the end of the list by completing the following steps:
      (1) Position the I-beam pointer on any text in the bulleted items, then click the left mouse button. (This selects the object box containing the bulleted text.)
      (2) Position the mouse-pointer on the first small round yellow bullet until it turns into a four-headed arrow.
      (3) Hold down the left mouse button, drag the arrow pointer (turns into a double-headed arrow pointing up and down) to the bottom of the text box (a thin horizontal line displays with the double-headed pointer), then release the mouse button.
6. Add transitions and sound effects to the slides by completing the following steps:
   a. In Slide Sorter view, double-click the first slide.
   b. Choose Tools, then Slide Transition.
   c. At the Slide Transition dialog box, choose Effect, then choose *Dissolve* from the drop-down menu.
   d. Choose Sound, then choose *Drum Roll* from the drop-down menu.
   e. Choose OK to close the dialog box.
   f. Select each slide individually and apply the following transitions and sounds to each:

Slide No.	Transition	Sound
Slide 2 *(Highlight #1)*	Uncover Right Down	Chime

Slide 3 *(Highlight #2)*	Box Out	Laser
Slide 4 *(Highlight #3)*	Fade Through Black	Slide Projector
Slide 5 *(Highlight #4)*	Strips Left-Up	Camera
Slide 6 *(Highlight #5)*	Random Bars Vertical	Applause

7. Save the presentation again with Save As and name it Curriculum Presentation.
8. Run the presentation manually.
9. Print the six slides on one page by displaying the Print dialog box, then changing the Print what option to *Handout (6 slides per page).*
10. Close Curriculum Outline 2 and Curriculum Presentation.

FIGURE 9.17

1 Ride Safe, Inc.
presents
Elementary Traffic Education Program

2 Curriculum Highlight #1
- ✦ Presents positive images that focus on decision-making skills
  - De-emphasizes memorization of rules
  - Involves children in active play and discussion
  - Role model demonstrations

3 Curriculum Highlight #2
- ✦ Contains lessons that are developmentally appropriate
  - Constant repetition and reinforcement
  - Age appropriate

4 Curriculum Highlight #3
- ✦ Focuses on changing behaviors that may cause traffic mishaps
  - Young children's peripheral vision is about two-thirds that of adults'.
  - Children lack a sense of danger.
  - Children are often not patient enough to wait for traffic signals.
  - Children misjudge speed and distance.

5 Curriculum Highlight #4
- ✦ Taught in schools by trained, certified teachers
  - Regular school curriculum
  - Teacher's manual and video available
  - Seven to ten lessons per grade
  - Activities researched and tested

6 Curriculum Highlight #5
- ✦ Community involvement is encouraged
  - Parents and children
  - Teachers and school administrators
  - Police officers
  - Fun for all!

FIGURE 9.18

Curriculum Presentation

Curriculum Highlight #1

- Taught in schools by trained, certified teachers
  - Regular school curriculum
  - Teacher's manual and video available
  - Seven to ten lessons per grade
  - Activities researched and tested

Curriculum Highlight #2

- Contains lessons that are developmentally appropriate
  - Constant repetition and reinforcement
  - Age appropriate

Curriculum Highlight #3

- Presents positive images that focus on decision-making skills
  - Involves children in active play and discussion
  - Role model demonstrations
  - De-emphasize memorization of rules

Curriculum Highlight #4

- Focuses on changing behaviors that may cause traffic mishaps
  - Young children's peripheral vision is about two-thirds that of adults'.
  - Children lack a sense of danger.
  - Children are often not patient enough to wait for traffic signals.
  - Children misjudge speed and distance.

Curriculum Highlight #5

- Community involvement is encouraged
  - Parents and children
  - Teachers and school administrators
  - Police officers
  - Fun for all!

Using A Slide Master

If you use a PowerPoint template, you may choose to use the formatting provided by the template, or you may want to customize the formatting. If you customize formatting in a presentation, PowerPoint's slide master can be very helpful in reducing the steps needed to format all slides in a presentation. For instance, if you want to add a company logo or consistent formatting to all the slides in your presentation, a slide master will save you time and will make it easier to maintain a uniform appearance in your presentation. If you know in advance that you want to change the formatting of slides, display the slide master, make the changes needed, then create the presentation. If the presentation is already created, edit the presentation in a slide master. Any changes made to a slide master will affect all the slides in the presentation.

DTP POINTERS
Consistency is important in maintaining a uniform appearance.

To display the slide master, change to the Slide view, position the insertion point on the Slide View button on the View toolbar, hold down the Shift key, then click the left mouse. This displays a slide master similar to the one shown in figure 9.19. At this slide, make any desired changes, then click the Slide View button (do not hold down the Shift key this time) to exit the slide master. Changes made at a slide master will be reflected in the current slide displayed in addition to the remaining slides in the presentation. Alternatively, the slide master feature can be accessed by choosing View, Master, then Slide Master.

In exercise 6, you will use a slide master to create slides for a presentation.

FIGURE 9.19

Slide Master

Formatting Object Boxes

As mentioned earlier, placeholders in PowerPoint templates consist of object boxes containing specific formatting. Buttons on the Drawing toolbar can be used to customize these object boxes by changing such things as the background color or by adding a border. If you want changes to an object box to affect all slides in a presentation, make the changes at the Slide Master.

Inserting WordArt in PowerPoint

With WordArt, you can apply special effects to text. For instance, WordArt can be used to create interesting logos for a company or product. Like the results of Microsoft Graph and Microsoft Organization Chart, WordArt creations are objects. When a WordArt object is selected, the image is surrounded by handles. (Refer to chapter 4 for a review on WordArt.) You can create WordArt from either Slide view or the Slide Master. The advantage of creating WordArt in a slide master is that it will appear automatically on every slide in the presentation. To create WordArt in PowerPoint complete the following steps:

1. Open an existing slide.
2. Click Insert, then Object. (Make sure the Create New radio button is selected.)
3. Click Microsoft WordArt 3.0 (2.0) in the Object Type list. Choose OK.
4. Enter text in the Enter Your Text Here dialog box.
5. Click Update Display.
6. Modify your text with various WordArt features.
7. Close WordArt by clicking anywhere on the slide, then press Esc to deselect the WordArt object.

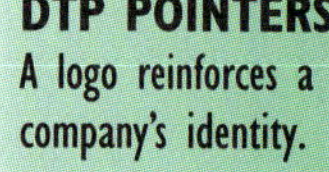
DTP POINTERS
A logo reinforces a company's identity.

EXERCISE
6

Formatting Objects and Creating a Logo in a Slide Master

1. Create the presentation on Ride Safe products as shown in figure 9.20 by completing the following steps (If you have already entered PowerPoint, complete the steps listed under step a. If you have not yet entered PowerPoint, follow the steps listed under step b.):
   a. If you are already in PowerPoint, complete the following steps:
      (1) Choose File, then New.
      (2) At the New Presentation dialog box, select the Presentation Designs tab.
      (3) Double-click *Multiple Bars* at the Name list box.
      (4) At the New Slide dialog box, select the first layout in the list box (Title Slide). Choose OK or press Enter.
   b. If you have not yet entered PowerPoint, complete the following steps:
      (1) Load PowerPoint.
      (2) If the Tip of the Day dialog box displays, read the tip, then click OK.
      (3) At the PowerPoint dialog box, choose Template, then choose OK.
      (4) At the New Presentation dialog box, select the Presentation Designs tab.
      (5) At the New Presentation dialog box with the Presentation Designs tab selected, double-click *Multiple Bars* at the Name list box.
      (6) At the New Slide dialog box, double-click the first layout in the list box (Title Slide).
   c. Create a slide master for the presentation by completing the following steps:
      (1) With the first slide displayed, hold down the Shift key as you position the arrow pointer on the Slide View button on the View toolbar (this turns the button into Title Master), then click the left mouse button. (This displays a slide master.)
      (2) With the slide master displayed, click anywhere in the text *Click to edit Master title style.*
      (3) Change the font to 48-point Impact.
      (4) Click the Italic button on the Formatting toolbar to turn this feature off. Leave the Text Shadow feature on.
      (5) Change the text color by clicking the Text Color button (eighth button from the right) on the Formatting toolbar and selecting the Lt. Gray color displayed in the palette (fourth color from the left in the first row).
      (6) Display the Drawing toolbar, then add fill color and shading to the object box containing the title text by completing the following steps:
         (a) Click the Fill Color button (tenth button from the top) on the Drawing toolbar.

(b) From the palette of color choices that displays, click the Red color (third color from the left in the first row).
(c) Click the Fill Color button again, then click the Shaded button below the color palette.
(d) At the Shaded Fill dialog box, make sure One Color is selected and the Color is red.
(e) Make sure Horizontal is selected in the Shade Style section.
(f) In the Variants section, select the second box in the first row. Choose OK or press Enter.

(7) Click anywhere in the text *Click to edit Master subtitle style.*
(8) Change the font to 40-point Times New Roman Bold with Text Shadow. Turn off the Italic feature.
(9) Add fill color and shading to the second object box by completing steps similar to steps 6(a) through 6(f). Change the object box fill color to blue (third color from the left in the second row of the Fill Color palette). Apply the same shading to the blue object box by completing steps 6(c) through 6(f)—however, use blue instead of red.
(10) With the blue text box still selected, drag the bottom middle sizing handle downward approximately one-half inch to increase the width of the box to accommodate text.
(11) Deselect the text box.
(12) Insert a logo for Ride Safe as a WordArt object in the slide master by completing the following steps:
(a) With the first slide displayed in Slide view, choose Insert, then Object.
(b) At the Insert Object dialog box, select Create New.
(c) At the Object Type list box, select Microsoft WordArt 3.0 (2.0). Choose OK.
(d) Key **Ride Safe, Inc.** in the text entry box, then click the Update Display button.
(e) Click the down-pointing arrow to the right of the Line and Shape button on the WordArt toolbar and select the sixth shape in the fourth row *(Wave 2).*
(f) Click the Shading button (third from right) on the WordArt toolbar. Click the down-pointing triangle to the right of the Foreground text box and select Red from the drop-down list. Choose OK.
(g) Click the Bold button on the WordArt toolbar.
(h) Click outside the text entry box to exit WordArt.
(i) At the Presentation window, size the WordArt object to look like the object in figure 9.20. (Hold the Ctrl key down as you drag a corner sizing handle inward.)
(j) Drag the sized logo to the position shown in figure 9.20.

(13) Insert the date and slide number by completing the following steps:
(a) Choose View, then Header and Footer.
(b) With the Slide tab selected, click Date and Time (make sure Update Automatically is selected).
(c) Click inside the check box to turn on Slide Number, but Footer should not be selected.
(d) Choose Apply to All.

d. Click the Slide View button on the View toolbar. (This removes the master slide and displays a slide with the formatted elements.)
e. Key the text in the first slide, as shown in figure 9.20, by completing the following steps:
(1) Click anywhere in the text *Click to add title.*

(2) Key **Ride Safe, Inc.**
(3) Click anywhere in the text *Click to add sub-title.*
(4) Key **New Biking and In-Line**, press Enter, then key **Skating Products**, press Enter, then key **for 1997**.

f. Click the New Slide button.
g. At the New Slide dialog box, double-click the first layout.
h. At the next slide, key the text shown in the second slide in figure 9.20.
i. Continue creating the remaining four slides shown in figure 9.20 by completing steps similar to those in e(1) through e(4).

2. Save the presentation and name it New Products Presentation.
3. Print all six slides on the same page.
4. Close New Products Presentation.

FIGURE 9.20

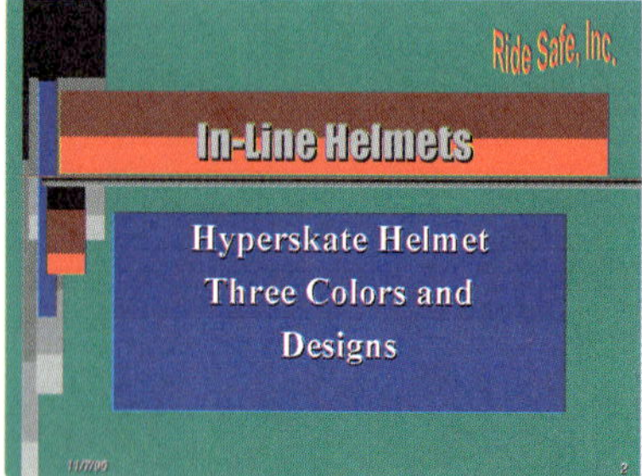

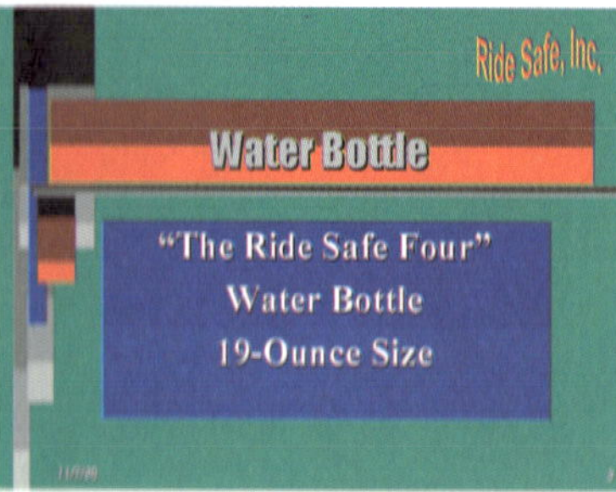

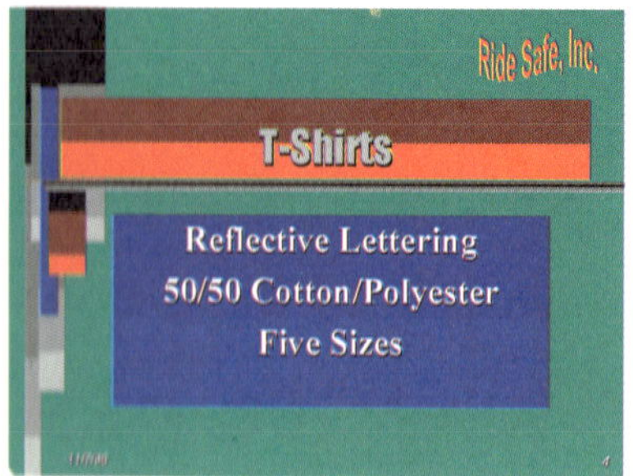

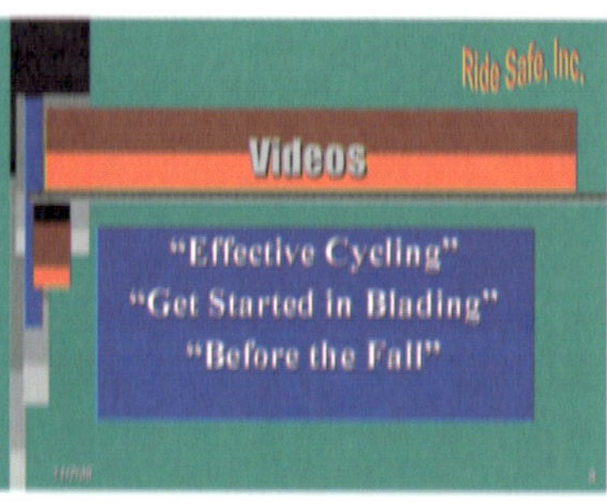

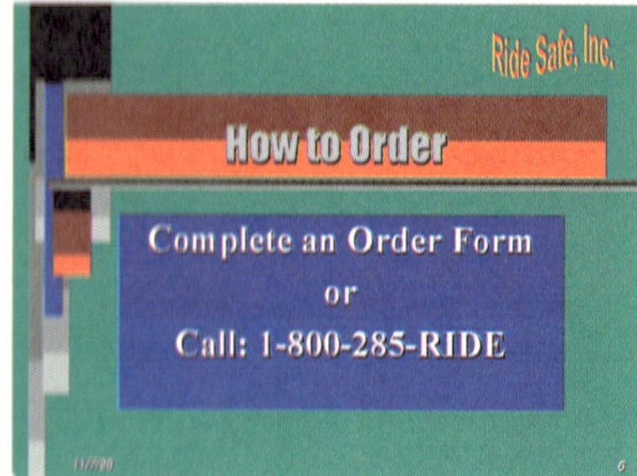

Adding Animation Effects To A Presentation

With options from the Animation Effects dialog box, you can add animation effects such as having an element fly or drive into a slide, display as a camera effect, or appear one step at a time during a slide show. To display animation choices, open a presentation, select the specific objects within a slide to which you want the animation added, then click the Animation Effects button on the Standard toolbar. This causes the Animation Effects toolbar to display as shown in figure 9.21.

Animation Effects

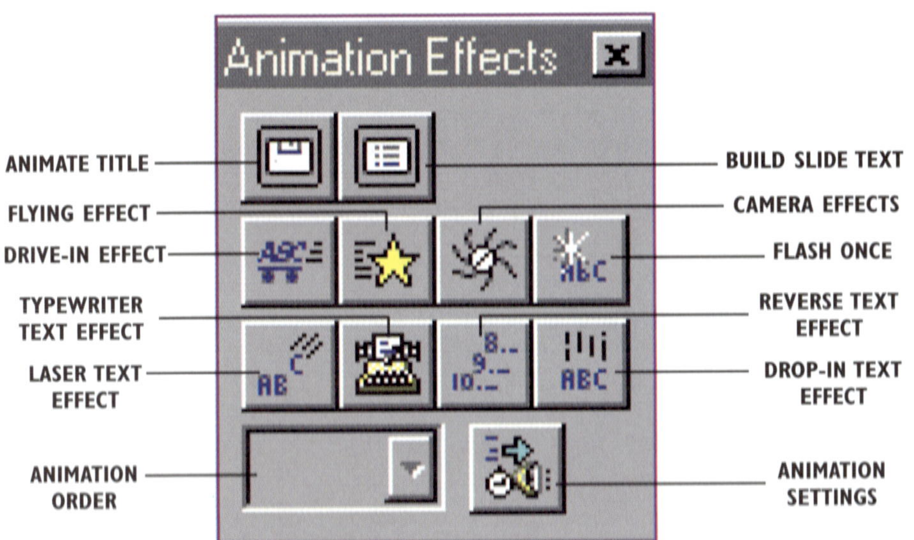

FIGURE 9.21

Animation Effects Toolbar

Select this button...	To perform this action:
Animate Title	Drop slide title from top of slide
Build Slide Text	Have body text appear one step at a time
Drive-in Effect	Make selected text or objects fly in from the right along with the sound of a car
Flying Effect	Have selected text or object fly in from the left with a whoosh sound
Camera Effect	Have selected text or object appear as if a camera shutter was opened
Flash Once	Make selected text or object flash once after last build
Laser Text Effect	Make selected text or object fly in from top right accompanied by the sound of a laser—if text is selected, it appears one letter at a time
Typewriter Text Effect	Make selected text or objects appear one character at a time accompanied by the sound of a typewriter
Reverse Text Build	Make selected text appear from the bottom up
Drop-In Text Effect	Make selected text or object drop in from the top of the slide. Text appears one word at a time.
Animation Order	Select order in which selected text or object appears
Animation Settings	Set options you want to use to build or play an inserted object

Adding A Build To A Slide Presentation

Build:
A feature that displays information (usually bulleted items) a little at a time.

With the buttons on the Animation Effects toolbar, you can display important points on a slide one point at a time, which is known as a build technique. The *build* technique helps the audience stay focused on the point being presented rather than reading ahead. The build technique is very effective in slides containing several points.

Options from the Animation Settings dialog box let you customize the build. To display this dialog box, open a presentation, display the desired slide, then click the Animation Effects button on the Standard toolbar. At the Animation Effects toolbar, click the Animation Settings button.

DTP POINTERS
To add a build effect to both text and graphics on a single slide, hold down the Shift key as you click each object.

With the Build Options, you can specify what items display during a build. You can specify that all items display at once or you can specify a level. At the Animation Settings dialog box, you can reverse the order of the build and have another build start when the previous build ends. With options in the Effects section, you can add a build transition effect such as flying, blinds, checkerboard, flash, or stripes; add sound such as a camera, laser, typewriter, or whoosh; or build by paragraph, word, or letter. With other options at the Animation Settings dialog box, you can specify whether the selected text is built first or second and also whether a previous build is dimmed when the next build is displayed.

You will be using a build technique in exercise 7 in addition to adding animation.

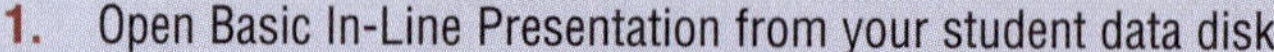

Adding Animation and Build to a Presentation

1. Open Basic In-Line Presentation from your student data disk.
2. Save the presentation with Save As and name it Animated In-Line Presentation.
3. Add a clip art image to each slide by completing the following steps:
   a. Change to Slide view. (Make sure the first slide is displayed in the Presentation window.)
   b. With the first slide displayed, choose Insert, then Picture.
   c. At the Insert Picture dialog box, make sure the drive or folder where your student graphic disk is located displays in the Look in: text box.
   d. Double-click *rollblde.cgm* at the list box. (Insert the graphic from Microsoft ClipArt Gallery if you added the graphic files from your student graphic disk to the gallery.)
   e. If the message *CGM Graphic Import* displays, click the OK button (this message may appear if you are retrieving a *.cgm* graphic file from your student graphic disk).
   f. Reduce the size of the image by dragging a corner sizing handle inward. Drag to reposition the image as shown in figure 9.22.
4. Add animation effects to the rollerblade image in each slide by completing the following steps:
   a. With the first slide displayed, click to select the rollerblade image.
   b. Click the Animation Effects button on the Standard toolbar (the button with a star on it).
   c. Click the Animation Settings button on the Animation Effects toolbar (last button in the last row).
   d. At the Animation Settings dialog box, click the down-pointing triangle to the right of *Don't Build* in the Build section, then select Build.
   e. Click the down-pointing triangle to the right of the Effects list box and select Fly From Left.
   f. Click the down-pointing triangle to the right of the Sound Effects list box (second list box below the text box containing *Fly From Left),* then select Screeching Brakes from the drop-down menu.

g. Choose OK or press Enter.
h. Click the Close button on the Animation Effects toolbar.
i. Click to select the image, then click the Copy button from the Standard toolbar. (You are copying the image to the clipboard so that it may be pasted to the other slides in this presentation.)

5. Paste the animated rollerblade image to each slide. (The image has been saved to the clipboard.) Move the image if necessary by selecting then dragging it to the location shown in figure 9.22.
6. Add a build effect to each slide by completing the following steps:
   a. With the first slide displayed, select the object box containing the title *International In-Line...Rules of the Road.*
   b. Click the Animation Effects button on the Standard toolbar.
   c. Click the Animate Title button on the Animation Effects toolbar (first button in the first row).
   d. Select the object box containing the text *Presented by...*, then click the Laser Text Effect button on the Animation Effects toolbar (the first button in the third row).
   e. Click the Next Slide button.
   f. With the second slide displayed, add the Animate Title effect to the title *Skate Smart* by completing steps similar to those in step 6a through 6c.
   g. With the second slide still displayed, add a build technique to the bulleted items on the slide by completing the following steps:
      (1) Click once in the bulleted text.
      (2) Click the Animation Settings button on the Animation Effects toolbar.
      (3) At the Animation Settings dialog box, click the down-pointing triangle to the right of the first list box in the Build Options section (contains the text *Don't Build*), then click *By 3rd Level Paragraphs* at the drop-down menu.
      (4) Click the down-pointing triangle in the first list box in the Effects section (contains the text *No Build Effect*), then click *Checkerboard Across* at the drop-down menu.
      (5) Click the down-pointing triangle in the last list box in the Effects section (contains the text [No Sound]), then click *Camera* at the drop-down menu.
      (6) Click the down-pointing triangle to the right of the After Build Step (contains the text *Don't Dim*), then click the blue color (last color in the second row).
      (7) Click OK to close the Animation Settings dialog box.
   h. Click the Next Slide button.
   i. With the third slide displayed, animate the title *Skate Alert* by completing steps similar to those in steps 6a through 6c.
   j. With Slide 3 still displayed, add a build technique to the bulleted text by completing steps similar to those in step 6g(1) through 6g(7).
   k. Format the remaining slides with the same title animation and build technique formatting.
   l. Click the Close button on the Animation Effects toolbar to remove it from the screen.
7. Display the presentation in Slide Sorter view, then click the first slide or press Ctrl + Home.
8. Run the presentation by clicking the Slide Show button on the View toolbar. Click the left mouse to advance each slide manually.
9. When the presentation is completed, save the presentation again with the same name, Animated In-Line Presentation.
10. Print the presentation with six slides on one page.
11. Close Animated In-Line Presentation.

Optional: Add different build and transition effects to each slide.

FIGURE 9.22

International In-Line Skating Association (IISA)

Rules of the Road

Presented by
Your Name Here

Skate Smart

- Always wear protective gear: helmet, wrist guards, elbow pads, and knee pads.
- Master the basics: moving, stopping, and turning.
- Keep your equipment in safe condition.

Skate Alert

- Control your speed.
- Watch for road hazards.
- Avoid water, sand, and oil.
- Avoid heavy traffic.

Skate Legal

- Observe all traffic regulations when on skates; you have the same obligations as any wheeled vehicle.

Skate Courteous

- Skate on the right, pass on the left; announce your intentions by saying "passing on your left."
- Always yield to pedestrians.
- Be a goodwill ambassador for in-line skating!

Chapter Summary

- A PowerPoint presentation can be created by using predesigned templates, the AutoContent Wizard, or a blank presentation screen.
- Slides in PowerPoint templates contain placeholders (object boxes) where specific text or objects are inserted.
- Placeholders (object boxes) can be customized by changing background color or adding a border or shadow.
- If you want changes made to a placeholder (object box) to affect all slides in a presentation, make the changes at the slide master.
- PowerPoint provides viewing options for presentations that include: Slide View, Outline, Slide Sorter, Notes Pages, and Slide Show.
- When choosing an AutoTemplate for your slides, consider your audience, the topic, and the method of delivery.
- AutoLayout formats may include placeholders that format a title, bulleted list, clip art, graph, organizational chart, table, or object.
- PowerPoint's AutoContent Wizard provides helpful information on planning and organizing a presentation based on the topic and purpose of the presentation.
- Slides in a slide show can be advanced manually or automatically at specific time intervals.
- Transition refers to what action takes place as one slide is removed from the screen during a presentation and the next slide is displayed.
- Preparing a presentation in Outline view helps to organize topics for each slide without the distractions of colorful templates, clip art, transitions, or sound. It is a good view to use when "brainstorming" the creation of a presentation.
- Sound effects and animation create impact in a slide show.
- PowerPoint's build technique displays important points one at a time on a slide.

Commands Review

Start PowerPoint	Start button on Taskbar, Program, Microsoft PowerPoint
Microsoft ClipArt Gallery	Insert, Clip Art; Insert, Object, Create New tab, Microsoft ClipArt Gallery; click Insert Clip Art button on Standard toolbar; or double-click clip art placeholder in Slide Layout
Run a slide show	View, Slide Show; or click Slide Show button
WordArt	Insert, Object, Create New tab, Microsoft WordArt 3.0
Slide Master	Click Slide View button while holding down Shift key; or View, Master, Slide Master

Check Your Understanding

True/False: Circle the letter T if the statement is true; circle the letter F if the statement is false.

T F 1. PowerPoint templates contain placeholders where specific text or objects are inserted.

T F 2. Slide view displays miniature versions of a presentation.

T F 3. PowerPoint automatically spell checks text as you key the text within a document.

T F 4. If you want changes made to placeholders to affect all slides in a presentation, make the changes at the slide master.

T F 5. At Slide Sorter view, the slide fills the entire screen.

T F 6. An AutoLayout format may contain a Graph placeholder.

T F 7. Scaling an image is the process of trimming vertical and/or horizontal edges of a picture.

T F 8. The AutoContent Wizard provides suggestions on how to plan and organize a presentation based on your responses.

T F 9. To run a presentation, choose Format, then Slide Show.

T F 10. You can rearrange slides in Slide Sorter view.

Terms: In the space provided, indicate the correct term(s).

1. Display the ____________________ toolbar to create builds and animate text and objects for a slide show.
2. Choose____________________ view to display several slides on a screen at one time.
3. Choose____________________ view to run a presentation.
4. ____________________ contains formatting that gives each slide in a presentation identical properties.

Skill Assessments

Assessment 1

As an instructor at the Van Buren Vocational Center, you are in charge of preparing a slide-show presentation promoting the Business Services and Technology Department. Your audience will include students, parents, teachers, school administrators, and school board members. Enhance last year's presentation by adding text color, clip art, transitions, and animation effects.

1. Enhance the Lawrence Vocational Center presentation as shown in figure 9.23 by completing the following steps:
   a. Load PowerPoint.
   b. Open Vocational Presentation from your student data disk.
   c. Save the presentation and name it Enhanced Vocational Presentation.
   d. Apply a design template to the presentation by completing the following steps:
      (1) With the first slide displayed, click the Apply Design Template button on the Standard toolbar.
      (2) Select the Presentation Designs folder and click the *Blue Diagonal* design template.
      (3) Choose Apply.

e. Add the following clip art images (Microsoft ClipArt Gallery) to each designated slide as listed below—refer to figure 9.23 as a guide. If any of the following graphic images are not available, substitute an appropriate image. Select All Categories in the Microsoft ClipArt Gallery, then scroll to locate the desired image.

	Filename
Slide 1	computer.wmf
Slide 2	office.wmf
Slide 3	lecture.wmf
Slide 4	supplies.wmf
Slide 5	disk.wmf
Slide 6	seminar.wmf

f. Size and position the clip art images in step e as shown in figure 9.23.
g. Select the title text in each slide and change the text color to yellow. (Use the Format Painter to copy the formatting to other slide titles or change the text color formatting in a slide master.)
h. Change the bullet symbols in each slide to a down-pointing triangle as found in the Monotype Sorts character set in the fourth row and first column of the list box. Change the symbol color to Red at the Special Color text box. (Use the Format Painter or a slide master to efficiently change the bullets in each slide.)
i. Apply a transition to at least 3 slides.
j. Apply a sound to at least 3 slides.
k. Select the clip art image in slide 1 and recolor the image by completing the following steps:
   (1) With the computer image selected, click Tools, then Recolor.
   (2) At the Recolor Picture dialog box, click the down-pointing triangle next to the second box from the top in the New section.
   (3) At the drop-down color palette that displays, select the red color. (A check mark will appear in the check box next to the Original gray box.)
   (4) Choose OK. (The people in the clip art image should display in red as shown in figure 9.23.)
l. Select Slide 6 and change the slide layout by choosing Format, then Slide Layout. At the Slide Layout dialog box, select the layout in the third row and second column (Clip Art & Text). Choose Apply.

2. Save the presentation again with the same name, Enhanced Vocational Presentation.
3. Run the Enhanced Vocational Presentation for a fellow student in your class and have the student summarize any good points and bad points about the presentation.
4. Print the Enhanced Vocational Presentation with six slides on one page.
5. Close the Enhanced Vocational Presentation.

FIGURE 9.23

BUSINESS SERVICES & TECHNOLOGY
Van Buren Vocational Center

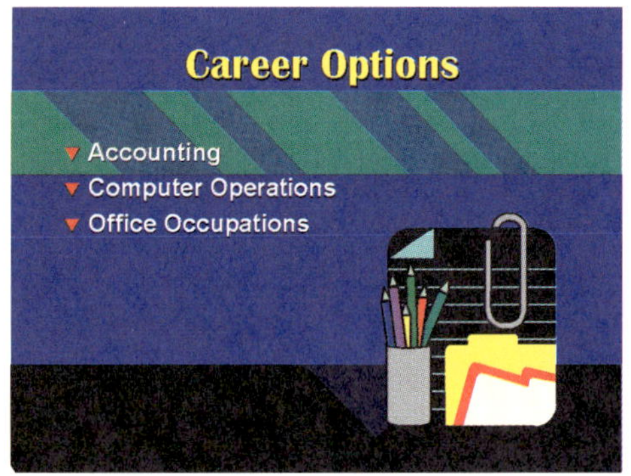
Career Options
Accounting
Computer Operations
Office Occupations

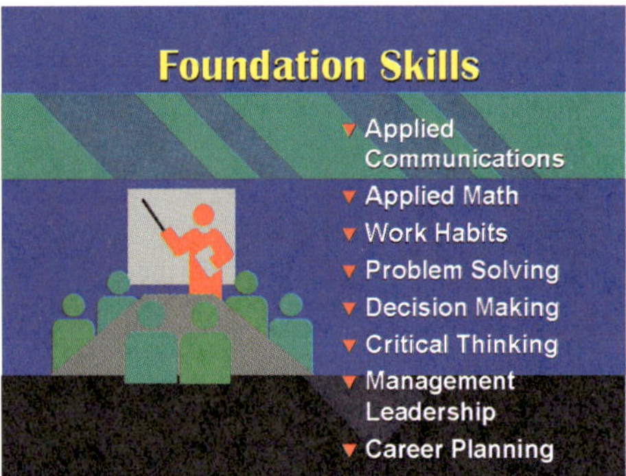
Foundation Skills
Applied Communications
Applied Math
Work Habits
Problem Solving
Decision Making
Critical Thinking
Management Leadership
Career Planning

Common Business Skills
Keyboarding
Computer Applications
Telephone Skills
Resource Management
Records Management
Study Skills

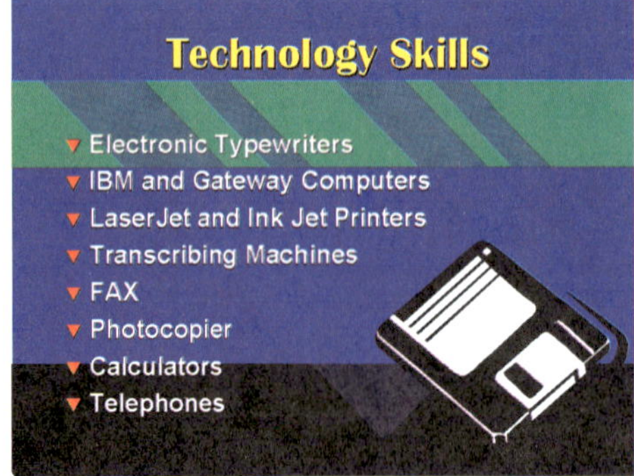
Technology Skills
Electronic Typewriters
IBM and Gateway Computers
LaserJet and Ink Jet Printers
Transcribing Machines
FAX
Photocopier
Calculators
Telephones

Earn College Credit
Lake Michigan College
SouthWestern Michigan College
Baker College
Davenport College
Kalamazoo Valley Community College

Assessment 2

You work for a travel vacation company named Paradise Vacations that specializes in selling vacation package plans to tropical locations. Your company is setting up a display booth at a well-attended travel trade show. You need to create an electronic slide show to be run continuously in your booth. Your target audience is travel consultants who sell vacation package plans to their clients. Your goal is to inform your audience of the travel plan benefits your company can offer to their travel clients, thereby motivating the travel consultants to promote your vacation packages when selling travel plans to their clients. Using specific text from your student data disk, create an on-screen presentation in PowerPoint according to the following specifications:

1. Access Microsoft Word. Print and read a copy of *paradise text* located on your student data disk.
2. Use the AutoContent Wizard to help you organize your presentation. Select Selling a Product, Service or Idea as the type of presentation you are going to give. (As you know, the AutoContent Wizard is automatically displayed when PowerPoint is loaded.) If PowerPoint is already open, choose File, New, select the Presentations tab, and then double-click the AutoContent Wizard icon, or, as an alternative, you can double-click *Selling a Product or Idea* at the Presentations tab to directly access the type of presentation you are going to give.
3. When the first slide displays, change to Outline View. Utilizing the information provided in *paradise text*, use the ideas supplied in the slide template to guide you in organizing your presentation. You may also edit the text to fit your needs.
4. Limit the length of your presentation to 8 slides.
5. After completing your presentation in Outline View, switch to Slide View.
6. Apply the design template labeled *Tropical.*
7. Use a build effect for the bulleted items. You decide on the bullet symbol to be used.
8. Apply transition effects to your slides. You decide if you want one type of transition for the whole presentation or if you want a different transition for each slide.
9. Time the slides to change every 8 seconds.
10. Make the slide show a continuous on-screen presentation by completing the following steps:
    a. Choose View, then Slide Show.
    b. At the Slide Show dialog box, select Use Slide Timings in the Advance section and click in the check box to the left of Loop Continuously Until 'Esc .
11. Save the presentation and name it Paradise Presentation.
12. Run the on-screen presentation for a classmate or your instructor.
13. Print and then close Paradise Presentation. (Check with your instructor about printing this presentation. One suggestion is to print six slides per page in Black and White to save on paper and printer ink.)

Optional: Add animation and sound effects to your Paradise Presentation.

UNIT 2 PERFORMANCE *Assessment*

Assume you are working for a well-known certified public accounting firm, named Winston & McKenzie, CPA. A relatively new department in your firm, Executive Search Services, offers other companies assistance in searching for individuals to fill executive positions. You have been asked to prepare various presentation materials that will be used to inform other partners (owners), staff members, and clients of the scope of this department.

First, you will create a fact sheet highlighting the services of the Executive Search Department and the qualifications of its consultants. Second, you will prepare a self-mailer brochure that lists the services of the Executive Search Department, the benefits to the reader, the way to obtain more information, and a mailing label section. Additionally, you will create a transparency presentation outlining the approach Executive Search Services uses when helping a company conduct an executive search. Finally, you will create a chart illustrating the growth of this department over the last nine quarters.

Think about the audience of an accounting firm in general, and then think more specifically about the audience that might use Executive Search Services. Before you begin, print *fact sheet text, W&McK text1,* and *W&McK text2* located on your student data disk. Read the text in these documents to familiarize yourself with the services offered by this company. Include some consistent elements in all your documents. Use a logo, a graphic image, a special character, ruled lines, borders, fill, or color to create unity among the documents. Incorporate design concepts of focus, balance, proportion, contrast, directional flow, color, and appropriate use of white space.

Assessment 1

Using the text in *fact sheet text*, create a fact sheet highlighting the services offered by Winston & McKenzie's Executive Search Services according to the following specifications:

1. Create a thumbnail sketch (experiment!) of your proposed page layout and design.
2. Create styles for repetitive formatting, such as for bulleted text or headings.
3. Design a simple logo using Microsoft Draw, WordArt, or other Word features.
4. Vary the fonts, type sizes, and type styles to emphasize the relative importance of items.
5. Use bullets to list the services offered. You decide on the character to be used as a bullet.
6. You may use any relevant picture, symbols, borders, colors, etc. in your fact sheet. You decide on the position, size, shading, border/fill, spacing, alignment, etc.
7. Save the document and name it u02pa01, fact sheet.
8. Print and then close u02pa01, fact sheet.
9. Print a copy of document evaluation checklist. Use the checklist to evaluate your fact sheet. Hand in both items.

■ Assessment 2

Using the text in *W&McK text1;W&McK text2;* and *W&McK text3* located on your student data disk, create a three-panel brochure according to the following specifications: (**Note:** Save periodically as you work through this assessment.)

1. Create a dummy of the brochure layout so you know exactly which panel will be used for each section of text. Use *W&McK text1* as the text in panel 1, *W&McK text2* as the text in panel 2, and *W&McK text3* as the text in panel 3. (Panel 3 is actually the information request side of a card the reader can send to the company for more information. The mailing address side, which is panel 4, will be created in step 5.)
2. Prepare a thumbnail sketch of your proposed layout and design.
3. Include the following formatting:
   a. Change the paper size to Letter Landscape.
   b. Change the top, bottom, left, and right margins to 0.5 inches (or as close to this as possible).
   c. Turn on Automatic Kerning.
4. Create the inside panels of the brochure according to the following specifications:
   a. Use the column feature to divide the page into panels.
   b. You decide on appropriate typeface, type size, and type style selections that best reflect the mood or tone of this document and the company or business it represents.
   c. Create a customized drop cap to be used at the beginning of each paragraph in panel 1. You decide on the color, position, the typeface, the number of lines to drop, and the distance from the text.
   d. Create any styles that will save you time and keystrokes, such as styles for headings, body text, and bulleted items.
   e. Itemize any lists with bullets. You decide on the bullet symbol, size, color, spacing, etc.
   f. Include ruled lines. You decide on the line style, thickness, placement, color, etc.
5. To make the brochure self-mailable, create the mailing address side of the request for information (created in panel 3) by completing the following steps in panel 4:
   a. Include the following text at the top of the panel:

      For More Information About Our Executive Search Services:
      Please call Janet Rankins at (317) 555-6342 or Bill Bush at (317) 555-8989 or complete the attached information request card.

   b. Create a dotted line from margin to margin to represent a cutting line or perforated line. Pay attention to the placement of this dotted line. If the reader were to cut the reply/request card on this line, are the items on the reverse side of the card (panel 3) placed appropriately? If not, make adjustments.
   c. Use Microsoft WordArt to create the mailing address. You decide on an appropriate font, type size, and color. Key the following address in the WordArt dialog box:

      Winston & McKenzie, CPA
      Executive Search Services
      4600 North Meridian Street
      Indianapolis, IN 46240

   d. Rotate the WordArt text box 90 degrees.

e. Insert a frame around the WordArt text box and use the mouse to drag the framed text to an appropriate mailing address position. You may also use the Frame dialog box to position the frame more precisely.
f. Follow steps 5c through 5d to create the return address. Use the same address as in step 5c. Position the framed text into an appropriate return address position.

6. Create the cover of the brochure by completing the following steps in panel 6:
   a. Key **You Can't Afford to Make the Wrong Hiring Decision!** as the title of the brochure.
   b. Use any appropriate graphic image you have available on the front cover of the brochure. You decide on the position, size, and border/fill, if any. (Word 7.0's business graphics selection is limited. Some suggestions might be *computer.wmf* or *speaker.wmf*. You could also use some contemporary designs such as *Celtic.wmf, Divider1.wmf, Divider2.wmf, Hplaque.wmf, Hpresbox.wmf., Lblkdiam.wmf, Ldiamond.wmf, Ornamnt4.wmf, Vberox.wmf, Vcontbox.wmf,* or *Vprisbox.wmf.*)
   c. Decide on an appropriate location and include the company name, address, and the following phone and fax numbers:

      Phone: **(317) 555-8900**
      Fax: **(317) 555-8901**

7. Save the brochure and name it u02pa02, brochure.
8. Print and then close u02pa02, brochure.
9. Print a copy of document evaluation checklist. Use the checklist to evaluate your brochure. Make any changes, if necessary. Hand in both items.

Optional: To save on mailing costs, you have to send out postcards to prospective clients. Rewrite and shorten the text in *W&Mc text1* so it highlights the pertinent points, but fits onto a 4-by-6-inch postcard. Include the company's name, address, phone, and fax numbers.

Assessment 3

Using the text provided in *W&McK transtext* located on your student data disk, prepare a transparency presentation highlighting the major steps Executive Search Services will take to aid a company in its search to fill executive positions according to the following specifications:

1. Use the *build* technique to present the major points listed in *W&McK transtext*. Use either of the build techniques illustrated in chapter 8, figures 8.20 or 8.21.
2. You decide on the margin settings.
3. Use a landscape orientation.
4. Turn on Automatic Kerning.
5. You decide on the design, layout, typeface, type size, and type style selections. Include any design element that will show some continuity among the documents previously created for this department.
6. Include reverse text.
7. Save, name, and print each document as you progress through the creation of the transparencies. Name the documents u02pa03, trans1; u02pa03, trans2; u02pa03, trans 3; etc.

Assessment 4

Prepare a chart highlighting the growth of Executive Search Services since its inception according to the following specifications:

1. Change the orientation to landscape.
2. Change all margins to 0.75 inches.
3. Turn on Automatic Kerning.

4. Create a Word table showing the number of searches performed per quarter by Executive Search Services. Include the following facts:

Quarter Ending	Number of Searches
11/93	4
3/94	11
7/94	9
11/94	18
3/95	15
7/95	6
11/95	10
3/96	12
7/96	16

5. Save the table.
6. Create a chart representing the table data according to the following specifications:
   a. You decide on the chart type. You may use a 2-D or 3-D perspective. Experiment to find the chart type that clearly represents your chart information.
   b. Select the chart orientation (Series in Rows or Series in Columns) that displays the quarter ending dates along the x-axis.
   c. Key **Number of Executive Searches Performed 11/93-7/96** as the chart title.
   d. Key **Per Quarter** as the x-axis title.
   e. Size the chart so that it could be readily used for a presentation. Make sure all elements of the chart are visible.
   f. To create a subtitle for the chart, delete the space after *Performed* in the title and then press Enter.
   g. Format the chart title, the x-axis title, the x-axis labels, and the y-axis labels. You decide on typeface, type size, type style, and border or area selections. Make selections that are appropriate, in proportion, and consistent. Try and tie in some consistent elements from the other documents created in previous assessments for this department.
   h. Change the color of the data series markers. Select a color(s) that is consistent with and coordinates with any colors used in the previous documents created for this department. If no additional color was used in previous documents, select a color(s) that reflects an accounting firm's image.
   i. Customize the chart legend as follows:
      (1) Decide on the typeface, type size, type style, border, or area selections. Make selections that are appropriate, in proportion, and consistent.
      (2) Use the mouse to position the legend in a location that is easily found by the reader and adds balance to the chart.
      (3) Size the legend in proportion to its importance and the other chart elements.
7. Return to the Word document screen and delete the table.
8. Change the Zoom Control to Whole Page to view your document. Make further adjustments to the chart's size and position if necessary.
9. At the Word document screen, include any other elements that you feel would enhance the presentation of your chart.
10. Save the chart and name it u02pa04, chart.
11. Print and then close u02pa04, chart.

Optional: In one paragraph, analyze the data presented in the chart you created.

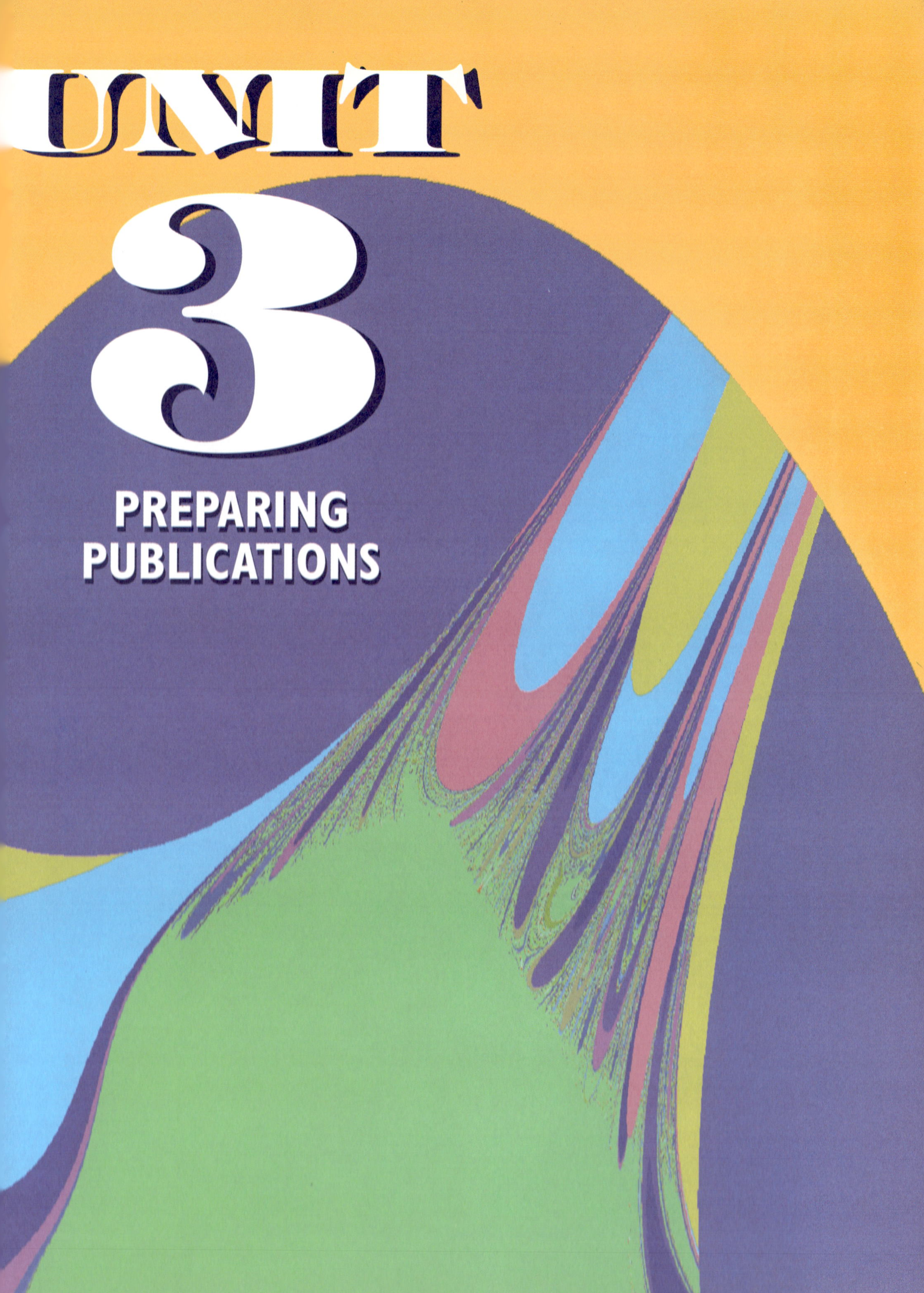
UNIT
3
PREPARING
PUBLICATIONS

In this unit, you will learn to create newsletters, reports, term papers, and manuals along with a variety of visual enhancements.

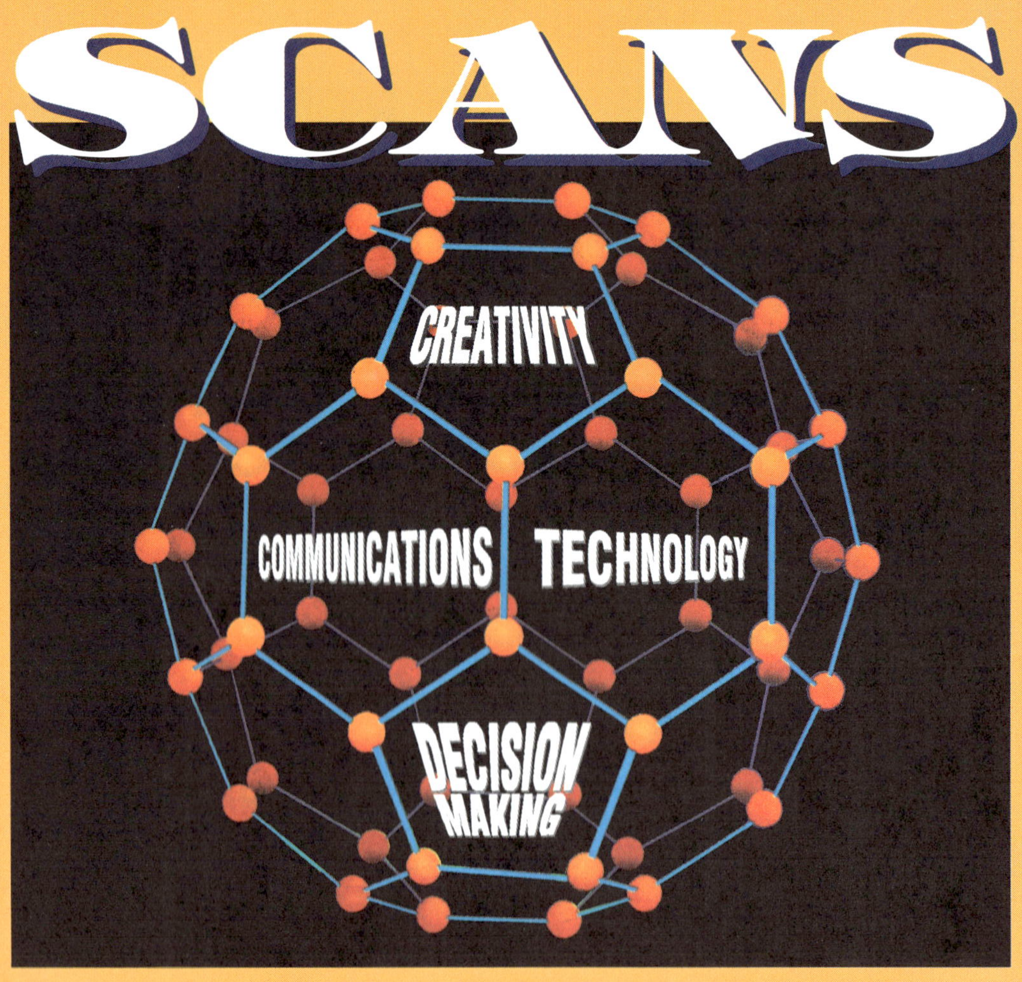

10 CREATING BASIC ELEMENTS OF A NEWSLETTER

PERFORMANCE OBJECTIVE

Upon successful completion of chapter 10, you will be able to create newsletters using Word's template feature and create your own designs based on desktop publishing concepts and Word features such as columns and styles. You will also be able to improve the readability of your newsletters by specifying line spacing, using kerning, adjusting character spacing, and changing alignment.

DESKTOP PUBLISHING CONCEPTS

- Template
- Layout and design
- Consistency
- Newsletter elements
- Readability
- Color

WORD FEATURES USED

- Newsletter template
- Styles
- Kerning
- Line spacing
- Character spacing
- Newspaper (snaking) columns
- Balanced and unbalanced columns
- Even and uneven columns
- WordArt
- Widow/orphan protection
- Paragraph indentation
- Em spaces
- Graphics images

The demand for newsletters in the private and business sectors has helped to promote the desktop publishing revolution. Affordable word processing and desktop publishing software, along with laser printers, significantly reduced the cost of producing professional-quality newsletters. Now users with limited budgets can create multipage documents in-house, providing organizations, businesses, or individuals with cost-effective means of communicating.

Newsletters are one of the most common means of communicating information and ideas to other people. Newsletters may be published by individuals, associations, clubs, churches, schools, businesses, consultants, service organizations, political organizations, and other establishments from all over the world.

Designing a newsletter may appear to be a simple task, but newsletters are more complex than they appear. Newsletters may be the ultimate test of your desktop publishing skills. Remember that your goal is to get the message across. Design is important because it increases the overall appeal of your newsletter, but content is still the most important consideration. Whether your purpose for creating a newsletter is to develop better communication within your company or to develop awareness of a product or service, your newsletter must give the appearance of being well-planned, orderly, and consistent. In order to establish consistency from one issue of a newsletter to the next, carefully plan your document.

Defining Basic Newsletter Elements

Successful newsletters contain consistent elements in every issue. Basic newsletter elements divide the newsletter into organized sections to help the reader understand the text, as well as entice the reader to continue reading. Basic newsletter elements usually include the items described in figure 10.1. Figure 10.2 illustrates the location of these basic elements on a newsletter page. Additional newsletter enhancements and elements are presented in chapter 11.

FIGURE 10.1

Basic Newsletter Elements

DTP POINTERS
Newsletter design should be consistent from issue to issue.

- *Nameplate*: The nameplate, or banner, consists of the newsletter's title and is usually located on the front page. Nameplates may include the company logo, a unique typeface, or a graphic image to help create or reinforce a company identity. A *logo* is a distinct graphic symbol representing a company.
- *Subtitle*: A subtitle is a short phrase describing the purpose or audience of the newsletter. A subtitle may also be called a *tagline*. The information in the subtitle is usually located below the nameplate near the folio.
- *Folio*: A folio is the publication information, including the volume number, issue number, and the current date of the newsletter. The folio usually appears near the nameplate, but it may also be displayed at the bottom or side of a page. In desktop publishing, *folio* may also mean page number.
- *Headlines*: Headlines are titles to articles that are frequently created to attract the reader's attention. The headline may be set in 22- to 72-point type or larger and is generally keyed in a sans serif typeface.
- *Subheads*: Subheads are secondary headings that provide the transition from headlines to body copy. Subheads break up the text into organized sections. Subheads are usually bolded and sometimes keyed in larger type sizes. There may be more space above a subhead than below.
- *Byline*: The byline identifies the author of the article.
- *Body Copy*: The main part of the newsletter is the body copy or text.
- *Graphic Image*: Graphic images are added to newsletters to help stimulate ideas and add interest to the document. They provide visual clues and visual relief from text-intensive copy.

FIGURE 10.2

Basic Elements of a Newsletter

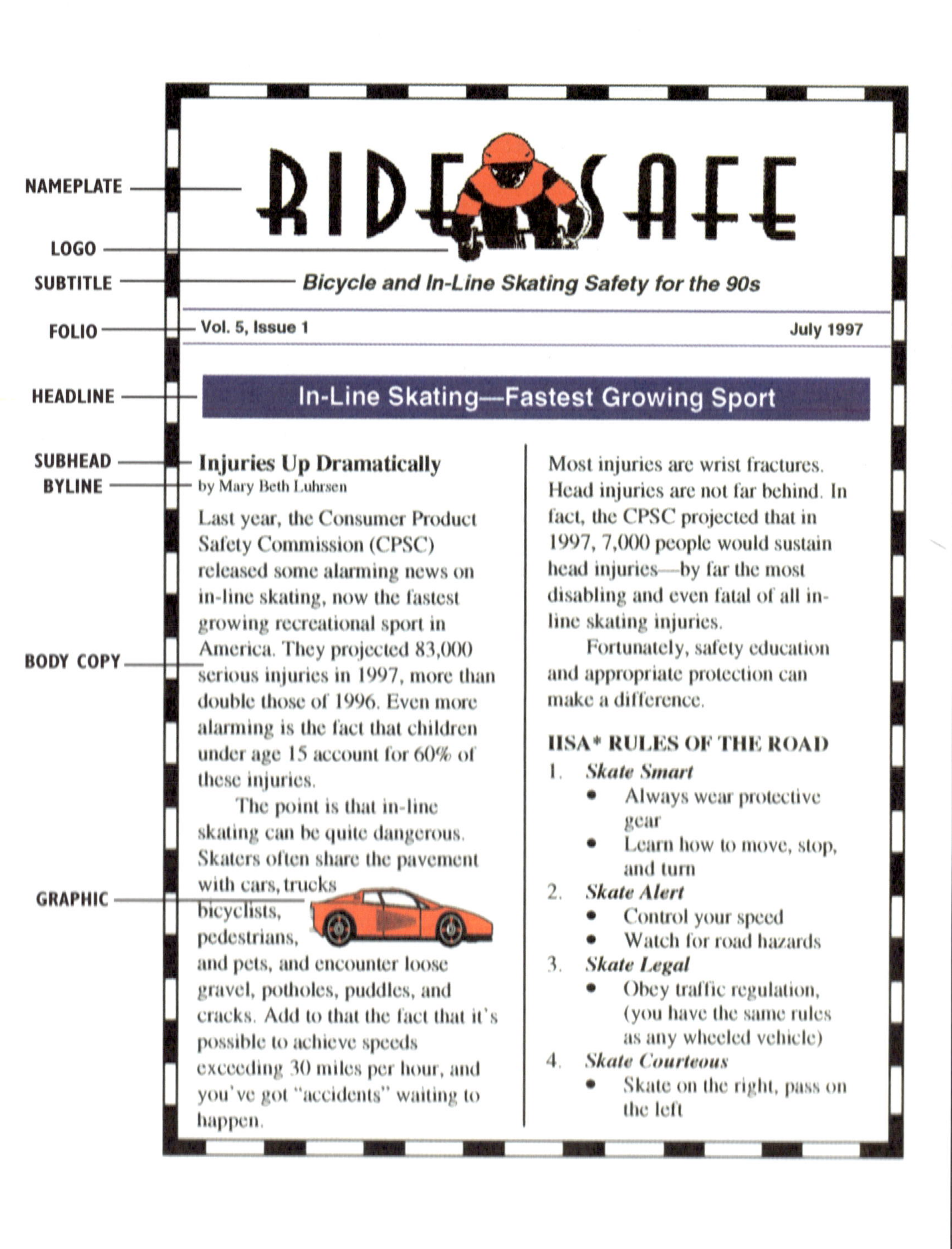

RIDE SAFE

Bicycle and In-Line Skating Safety for the 90s

Vol. 5, Issue 1 **July 1997**

In-Line Skating—Fastest Growing Sport

Injuries Up Dramatically
by Mary Beth Luhrsen

Last year, the Consumer Product Safety Commission (CPSC) released some alarming news on in-line skating, now the fastest growing recreational sport in America. They projected 83,000 serious injuries in 1997, more than double those of 1996. Even more alarming is the fact that children under age 15 account for 60% of these injuries.

The point is that in-line skating can be quite dangerous. Skaters often share the pavement with cars, trucks bicyclists, pedestrians, and pets, and encounter loose gravel, potholes, puddles, and cracks. Add to that the fact that it's possible to achieve speeds exceeding 30 miles per hour, and you've got "accidents" waiting to happen.

Most injuries are wrist fractures. Head injuries are not far behind. In fact, the CPSC projected that in 1997, 7,000 people would sustain head injuries—by far the most disabling and even fatal of all in-line skating injuries.

Fortunately, safety education and appropriate protection can make a difference.

IISA* RULES OF THE ROAD

1. ***Skate Smart***
   - Always wear protective gear
   - Learn how to move, stop, and turn
2. ***Skate Alert***
   - Control your speed
   - Watch for road hazards
3. ***Skate Legal***
   - Obey traffic regulation, (you have the same rules as any wheeled vehicle)
4. ***Skate Courteous***
   - Skate on the right, pass on the left

Planning A Newsletter

Before creating your newsletter, consider your target audience and your objective for providing the information. Is the goal of your newsletter to sell? inform? explain? or announce? What is the purpose of the newsletter? Companies and organizations often use newsletters to convey a sense of pride and teamwork among employees or members. When planning a company newsletter, consider the following suggestions:

- If a scanner is available, use pictures of different people from your organization in each issue.
- Distribute contributor sheets requesting information from employees.
- Keep the focus of the newsletter on issues of interest to employees.
- Make sure the focus of the newsletter is on varying levels of employment.
- Conduct regular surveys to see if your newsletter is providing relevant information.

If the aim of your newsletter is to promote a product, the focal point may be a graphic image or photograph of the product rather than more general company news. Your aim can also influence the selection of typefaces, type sizes, and visual elements and even the placement of all these elements.

DTP POINTERS
Look at as many publications as you can to get ideas for designs.

Also consider the following questions when planning your document: What is the image you want to project? How often will the newsletter appear? What is your budget? How much time can you devote to its creation? What items are likely to be repeated from issue to issue? And, will your newsletter accommodate ads, photographs, or clip art in its layout? After answering these questions, you are ready to begin designing your newsletter.

Designing A Newsletter

Desktop publishing concepts and guidelines discussed in previous chapters will provide you with a good starting point for your newsletter. These guidelines emphasize the use of consistency, balance, proportion, contrast, white space, focus, directional flow, and color. If you are designing a newsletter for a company, make sure the design coordinates with your firm's corporate identity by using the same logo, typefaces, type sizes, column arrangements, and color choices that are used in other corporate correspondence.

Applying Desktop Publishing Guidelines

One of the biggest challenges in creating a newsletter is balancing change with consistency. A newsletter is a document that is typically reproduced on a regular basis, whether monthly, bimonthly, or quarterly. With each issue, new ideas can be presented, new text created, and new graphics or photos used. However, for your newsletter to be effective, each issue must also maintain a consistent appearance. Consistency contributes to your publication's identity and gives your readers a feeling of familiarity.

DTP POINTERS
Many logos are trademarks. Before using them, find out whether you need permission.

When designing your newsletter, think about the elements that should remain consistent from issue to issue. Consistent newsletter features and elements may include: size of margins, column layout, nameplate formatting and location, logos, color, ruled lines, formatting of headlines, subheads, and body text. Later in the chapter, you will create styles to automate the process of formatting consistent elements.

Focus and balance can be achieved in a newsletter through the design and size of the nameplate, the arrangement of text on the page, the use of graphic images or scanned photographs, or the careful use of lines, borders, and backgrounds. When using graphic images or photos, use restraint and consider the appropriateness of the image. A single, large illustration is usually preferred over many small images scattered throughout the document. Size graphic images or photos according to their relative importance to the content. Headlines and subheads can serve as secondary focal points as well as provide balance to the total document.

White space around a headline creates contrast and attracts the reader's eyes to the headline. Surround text with white space if you want the text to stand out. If you want to draw attention to the nameplate or headline of the newsletter, you may want to choose a bold type style and a larger type size. Another option is to use WordArt to emphasize the nameplate title. Use sufficient white space throughout your newsletter to break up gray areas of text and to offer the reader visual relief.

DTP POINTERS
Use graphic accents with discretion.

Good directional flow can be achieved by using ruled lines that lead the reader's eyes through the document. Graphic elements, placed strategically throughout a newsletter, can provide a pattern for the reader's eyes to follow.

In figure 10.2, focus, balance, contrast, and directional flow were achieved through the placement of graphic images at the top and bottom of the document, the blue shaded text box with reverse text, and bolded headings.

If you decide to use color in a newsletter, use it sparingly. Establish focus and directional flow by using color to highlight key information or elements in your publication. The use of color as a newsletter enhancement will be discussed in chapter 11.

Creating A Newsletter Page Layout

Typically, page layout begins with size and orientation of the paper and the margins desired for the newsletter. Next, decisions on the number, length, and width of columns becomes imperative. Typefaces, type sizes, and type styles must also be considered. In addition, graphic images, ruled lines, and shading and coloring decisions must be made.

Choosing Paper Size and Type

One of the first considerations in designing a newsletter page layout is the paper size and type. This decision can be affected by the number of copies needed and the equipment available for creating, printing, and distributing the newsletter. Most newsletters are created on standard-size 8½-by-11-inch paper, although some are printed on larger sheets such as 11 by 14 inches. The most economical choice for printing is the standard 8½-by-11-inch paper. Also, consider that 8½-by-11-inch paper is easier to hold and read, cheaper to mail, and fits easily in standard file folders.

Paper weight is determined by the cost, the quality desired, and the graphics or photographs included. The heavier the stock, the more expensive the paper. In addition, pure white paper is more difficult to read because of glare. If possible, investigate other, more subtle colors. Another option is to purchase predesigned newsletter paper from a paper supply company. These papers come in many colors and designs. Several have different blocks of color created on a page to help separate and organize your text.

Creating Margins for Newsletters

After considering the paper size and type, determine the margins of your newsletter pages. The margin size is linked to the number of columns needed, the formality desired, the visual elements used, and the amount of text available. Keep your margins consistent throughout your newsletter. Listed here are a few generalizations about margins in newsletters:

DTP POINTERS
Be generous with your margins; don't crowd text.

- A wide right margin is considered formal. This approach positions the text at the left side of the page—the side where most readers tend to look first. If the justification is set at full, the newsletter will appear even more formal.
- A wide left margin is less formal. A table of contents or marginal subheads can be placed in the left margin giving the newsletter an airy, open appearance.
- Equal margins tend to create an informal look.

DTP POINTERS
Place page numbers on the outside edges when using mirror margins.

If you plan to create a multipage newsletter with facing pages, you may want to use Word's mirror margin feature, which accommodates wider inside or outside margins. Figure 10.3 and figure 10.4 illustrate mirror margins in a newsletter. Often the inside margin is wider than the outside margin; however, this may be dependent on the amount of space the binding takes up. To create facing pages with mirror margins, choose File, then Page Setup. At the Page Setup dialog box, select the Margins tab, then select the Mirror Margins option. If you plan to include page numbering, position the numbers on the outside edges of each page.

Gutter: Extra space added to the inside margin to accommodate the binding.

Also consider increasing the *gutter* space to accommodate the binding on a multipage newsletter. To add gutter space on facing pages, add the extra space to the inside edges; on regular pages, add space to the left edges. To add gutters, display the Page Setup dialog box with the Margins tab selected, then select or key a gutter width at the Gutter option. Gutters do not change the margins, but rather add extra space to the margins. However, gutters make the printing area of your page narrower.

FIGURE 10.3

Outside Mirror Margins in Facing Pages of a Newsletter

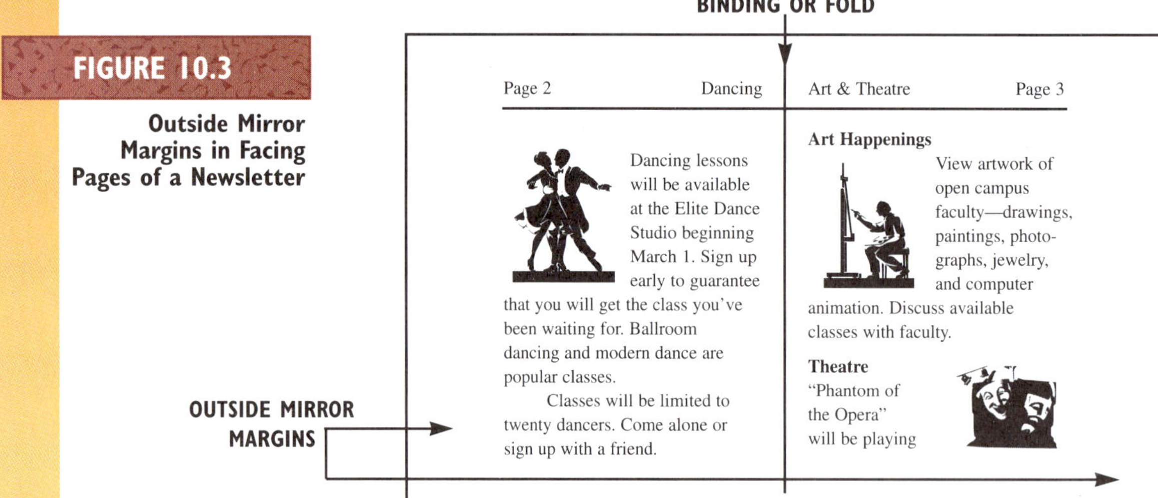

FIGURE 10.4

Inside Mirror Margins on Facing Pages

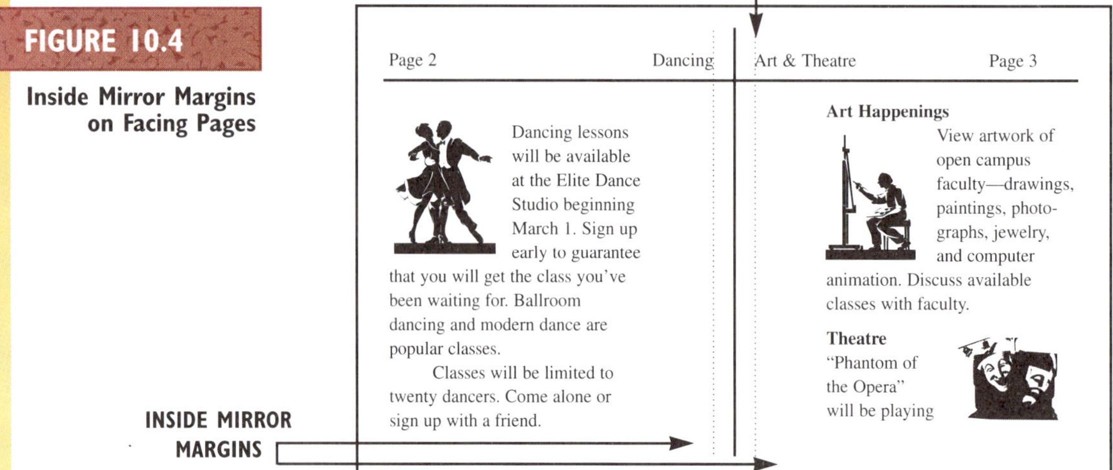

If you want to position text or graphics in the margins of a newsletter to add interest and emphasis, frame the text or object. Text in the newsletter will wrap around the framed object. More information will be provided in chapter 11 on creating text in frames—such as pull quotes, sidebars, and more.

Creating Newspaper Columns for Newsletters

When preparing newsletters, an important consideration is the readability of the document. *Readability* is the ease with which a person can read and understand groups of words. The line length of text in a document can enhance or detract from the readability of text. To improve readability of newsletters, you may want to set the text in columns.

Readability: The ease with which a person can read and understand a group of words.

Snaking Columns: Another name for newspaper columns where text flows up and down columns.

Newspaper columns in a newsletter promote the smooth flow of text and guide the reader's eyes. As discussed earlier in chapter 6, Word's newspaper column feature (also called *snaking columns*) allows text to flow up and down columns in the document. When the first column on the page is filled with text, the insertion point moves to the top of the next column on the same page. When the last column on the page is filled, the insertion point moves to the beginning of the first column on the next page.

As you know, newspaper columns can be created using the Columns button on the Standard toolbar or with options from the Columns dialog box. Columns of equal width are created with the Columns button on the Standard toolbar. To create columns of unequal width, use the Columns dialog box shown in figure 10.5. To display this dialog box, choose Format, then Columns. Notice the options selected in the Columns dialog box in figure 10.5—Three columns of equal width with 0.5-inch Spacing, Line Between, and Apply To: This Point Forward. Keying text first and then formatting it into newspaper columns is generally faster. The spacing in this instance refers to the gutter, or the space between columns. Word defaults to 0.5 inches for the gutter space.

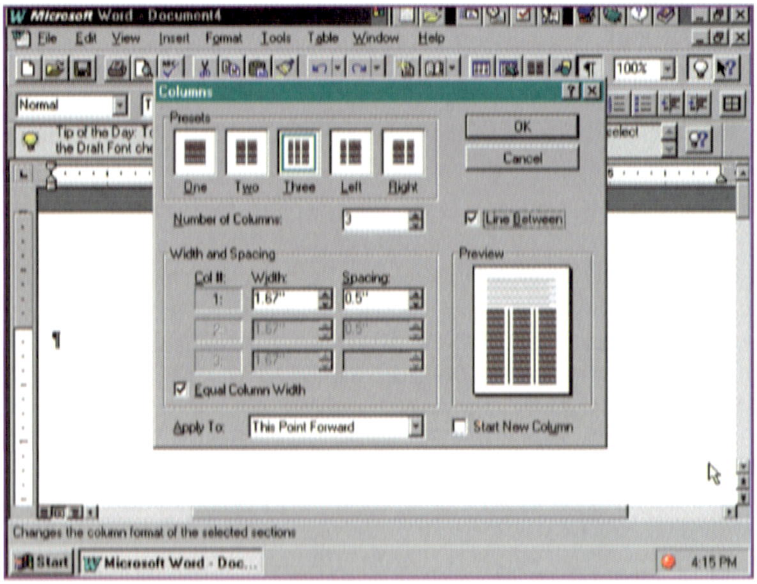

FIGURE 10.5

Columns Dialog Box

Using Balanced and Unbalanced Columns

Word automatically lines up (balances) the last line of text at the bottom of each column. On the last page of a newsletter, the text is often not balanced between columns. Text in the first column may flow to the bottom of the page, while the text in the second column may end far short of the bottom of the page. Columns can be balanced by inserting a section break at the end of the text by completing the following steps:

1. Position the insertion point at the end of the text in the last column of the section you want to balance.
2. Choose Insert, then Break.
3. At the Break dialog box, choose Continuous.
4. Choose OK or press Enter.

Figure 10.6 shows the last page of a document containing unbalanced columns and a page where the columns have been balanced.

FIGURE 10.6

Unbalanced and Balanced Columns

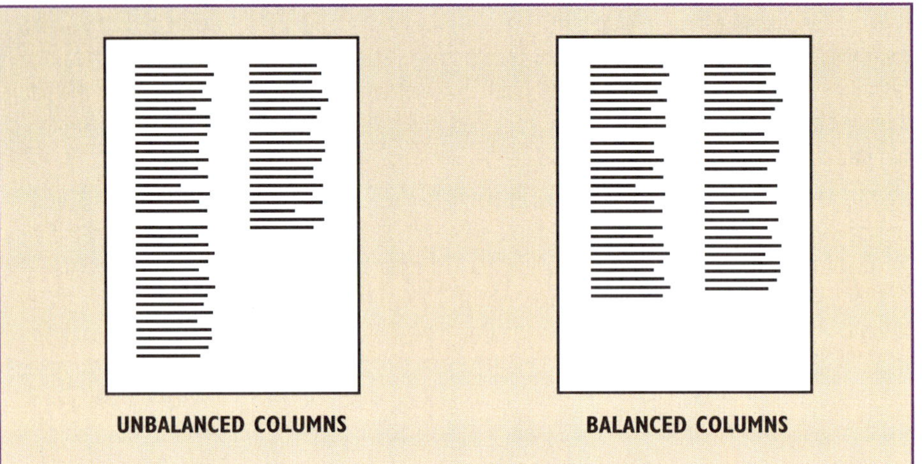

Determining Number of Columns

The number of columns used in newsletters may vary from one column to four or more columns. The size of the paper used, the font and type size selected, the content and amount of text available, and many other design considerations affect this decision.

One-column newsletters are easy to produce since the articles simply follow each other. If you do not have much time to work on your newsletter, this format is the one to use. The one-column format is the simplest to design and work with because it allows you to make changes and additions easily. You will want to use a large type size—usually 12 points—to accommodate the long line length of a one-column design. Be sure to use wide margins with this column layout. Also, keep in mind that an asymmetrically designed page is more interesting to look at than a symmetrical one, as shown in figure 10.7.

FIGURE 10.7

Asymmetrical and Symmetrical Design in Newsletters

XXXXXXXXXXXXXXXXXX
XXXXXXXXXXXXXXXXXX
Symmetrical Design
XXXXXXXXXXXXXXXXXX
XXXXXXXXXXXXXXXXXX
XXXXXXXXXXXXXXXXXX
XXXXXXXXXXXXXXXXXX
XXXXXXXXXXXXXXXXXX

The two-column newspaper format is the most frequently used selection for newsletters. It gives a formal look, especially if used with justified text. Use type sizes between 10 and 12 points when using a two-column layout. Be careful to avoid *tombstoning*, which occurs when headings display side by side in adjacent columns. Using an asymmetrical design in which one column is wider than the other and adding graphic enhancements will make this classic two-column format more interesting.

Tombstoning: When headings display side by side in adjacent columns.

A three-column format is successful if you avoid using too much text on the page. This popular format is more flexible for adding interesting design elements. You may use a smaller type size (9–11 points) and therefore fit more information on a page. You can also place headings, text, and graphics across one, two, or three columns to create a distinctive flow. Often, one column is reserved for a table of contents, marginal subheads, or a masthead (publication information), thus allowing for more white space in the document and more visual interest.

A four-column design gives you even more flexibility than the three-column layout; however, more time may be spent in putting this newsletter layout together. Leaving one column fairly empty with a great deal of white space to offset more text-intensive columns is a visually appealing solution. This format gives you many opportunities to display headings, graphics, and other design elements across one or more columns. You will need to use a small type size for your text—9 to 10 points.

Using Varying Numbers of Columns in a Newsletter

In Word, you can use newspaper columns in your whole document, or in sections. Section breaks can be used to vary the page layout within a single newsletter. For instance, you can use a section break to separate a one-column nameplate from text that can be created in three-columns as shown in figure 10.8.

There are three ways to insert section breaks into a document. One way is to use the Break dialog box. (To display this dialog box, choose Insert, then Break). Another way is to use the Columns dialog box and tell Word to format text into columns from This Point Forward from the location of the insertion point. The third way is to select the text first, then apply column formatting.

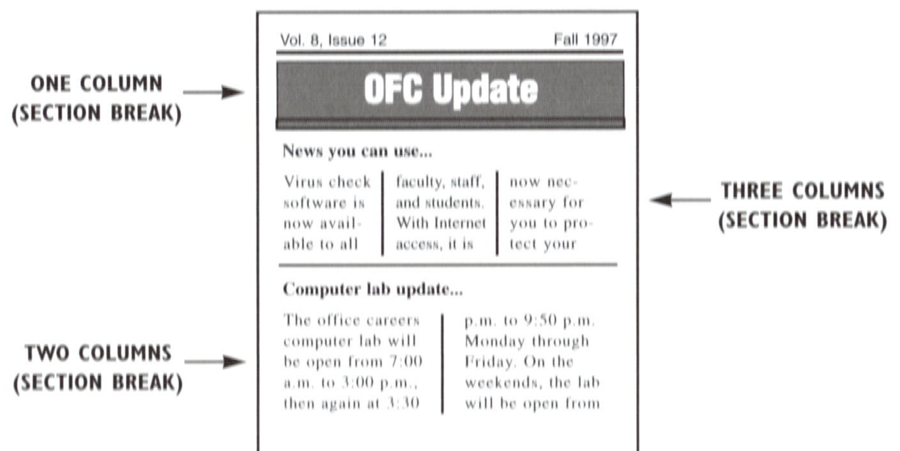

FIGURE 10.8

Section Breaks in Newsletters

As mentioned earlier in chapter 6, to move the insertion point between columns, you can use the mouse or you can press Alt + up arrow to move the insertion point to the top of the previous column, or Alt + down arrow to move the insertion point to the top of the next column.

Additionally, when formatting text into columns, Word automatically breaks the columns to fit the page. If a column break appears in an undesirable location, you can insert a column break into the document to control where the columns end and begin on the page. To insert a column break, position the insertion point where you want the new column to begin, then press Ctrl + Shift + Enter.

Be sure to switch to Page Layout viewing mode when working in columns. In Normal viewing mode, text will display in a single column at the left side of the document screen.

Preparing a Grid

As mentioned earlier in chapter 1, a grid is a valuable tool for organizing page elements and maintaining consistency in documents. This framework of lines guides the placement of margins, columns, visuals, headlines, subheads, and other elements in a newsletter. Once this layout is determined, it can be reused with slight alterations. Many desktop publishing programs have on-screen grids to help you visualize layout. However, many word processing programs, such as Word, do not have an on-screen grid feature.

Word does include a drawing grid that helps you align drawing objects, though the gridlines are not visible on the screen. Therefore, you will need to create a rough, penciled-in grid similar to that shown in figure 10.9. Not all columns on a page have to be the same width. For example, you can create a variation of the three-column grid with two uneven columns as shown in figure 10.10. However, this format must remain consistent from page to page as well as from issue to issue.

Pica: Measurement used to determine line length—1 pica is equal to 12 points, and there are 6 picas to a horizontal inch.

Typesetters and professional designers measure horizontal space on a page using *picas*. A *pica* is a measurement used for determining line length in desktop publishing; there are 6 picas in a horizontal inch. Pica, inch, and point equivalents are as follows:

1 inch	=	6 picas
1 pica	=	12 points
1 point	=	1/72 inch
12p6	=	12 picas and 6 points or roughly 2⅛ inches

FIGURE 10.9

Sketch of a Column Grid—("p" indicates picas)

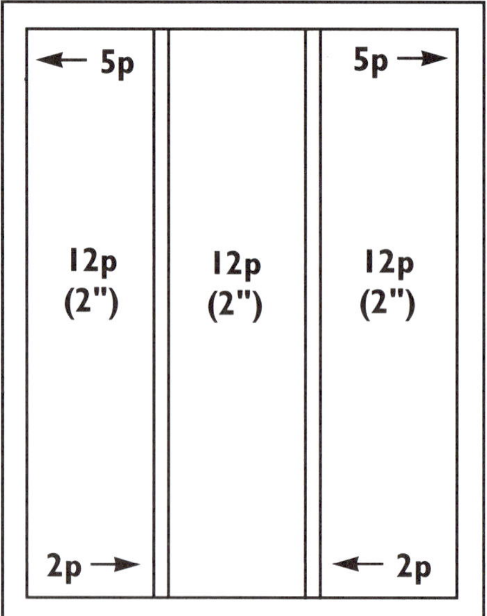

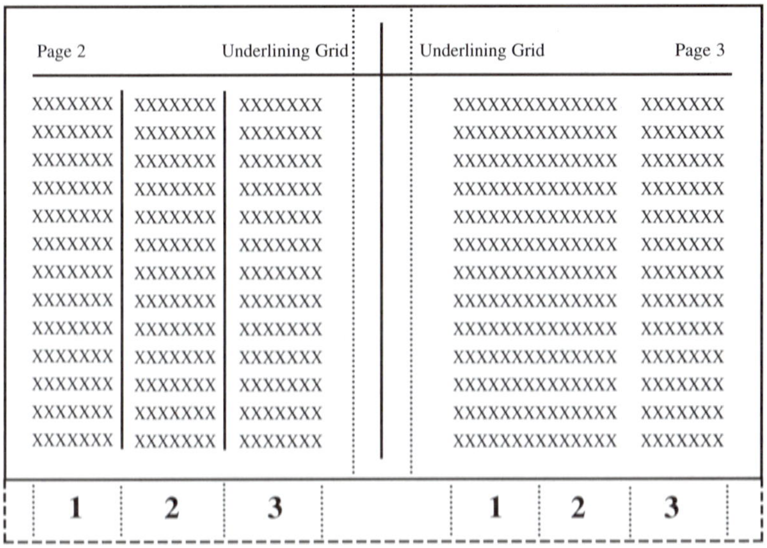

Page 2		Underlining Grid	Underlining Grid	Page 3
XXXXXXX	XXXXXXX	XXXXXXX	XXXXXXXXXXXXXX	XXXXXXX
XXXXXXX	XXXXXXX	XXXXXXX	XXXXXXXXXXXXXX	XXXXXXX
XXXXXXX	XXXXXXX	XXXXXXX	XXXXXXXXXXXXXX	XXXXXXX
XXXXXXX	XXXXXXX	XXXXXXX	XXXXXXXXXXXXXX	XXXXXXX
XXXXXXX	XXXXXXX	XXXXXXX	XXXXXXXXXXXXXX	XXXXXXX
XXXXXXX	XXXXXXX	XXXXXXX	XXXXXXXXXXXXXX	XXXXXXX
XXXXXXX	XXXXXXX	XXXXXXX	XXXXXXXXXXXXXX	XXXXXXX
XXXXXXX	XXXXXXX	XXXXXXX	XXXXXXXXXXXXXX	XXXXXXX
XXXXXXX	XXXXXXX	XXXXXXX	XXXXXXXXXXXXXX	XXXXXXX
XXXXXXX	XXXXXXX	XXXXXXX	XXXXXXXXXXXXXX	XXXXXXX
XXXXXXX	XXXXXXX	XXXXXXX	XXXXXXXXXXXXXX	XXXXXXX
XXXXXXX	XXXXXXX	XXXXXXX	XXXXXXXXXXXXXX	XXXXXXX
XXXXXXX	XXXXXXX	XXXXXXX	XXXXXXXXXXXXXX	XXXXXXX

1 2 3   1 2 3

FIGURE 10.10

Underlining Three-Column Grid

Determining Column Width

Column width, type size, and leading are related, in that altering one setting affects the settings of the others. As a general rule, narrow columns are easier to read than wide ones, but the number of words is important. Typically columns contain 5 to 15 words per line. In typesetting, the vertical line spacing, measured from the baseline of one line of text to the baseline of the next line of text, is referred to as *leading*. In general, short lines use minimal leading, whereas long lines require more leading.

Leading: Vertical line spacing measured from baseline to baseline.

One method for determining column width is based on the typeface and point size used. Use a typeface and type size you intend to use in the body text (choose a serif font in a type size between 10 and 12 points). Type a complete lowercase alphabet, print it, measure the length of the alphabet with a ruler, and multiply by 1.5 to determine the column width as shown in figure 10.11 (Use the desktop ruler attached to the back of this textbook.) Generally, line length should be approximately 1.5 to 2 alphabets or 39 to 52 characters.

Line length in typesetting is usually measured in picas. Since 6 picas equals 1 inch, a line length of 5 inches would be measured as 30 picas. A guideline in typesetting is that the line length measured in picas does not exceed twice the point size of the type. For instance, 12-point type looks best in a 20- to 23-pica column.

12-point Times New Roman	**12-point Palatia**
abcdefghijklmnopqrstuvwxyz	abcdefghijklmnopqrstuvwxyz
Measures: **2 inches**	Measures: **2.25 inches**
2 x 1.5 = **3 inches**	2.25 x 1.5 = **3.38 inches**
3 inches = 18 picas	**3.38 inches = 22.8 picas**

FIGURE 10.11

Determining Column Width

Creating a Thumbnail Sketch

DTP POINTERS
Position illustrations close to the text they illustrate.

One of the early steps in designing a newsletter is to plan the overall look of the document. As mentioned in chapter 1, a thumbnail sketch is a very basic, rough sketch used to visualize your design and layout as shown in figure 10.12. Your sketch need not be anything more than a penciled-in drawing on a sheet of paper. Most designers use wavy lines for headlines, straight lines for text, and large Xs for graphic images or photographs.

A thumbnail sketch is an excellent way to experiment with different layouts and designs. Look at the work of others for hints and suggestions on different layouts.

FIGURE 10.12

Thumbnail Sketch

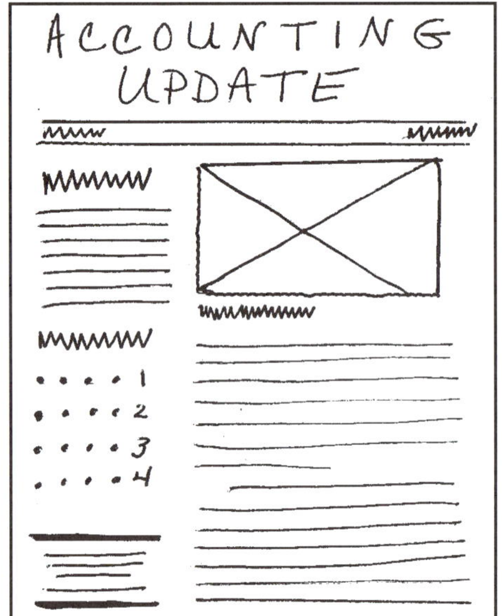

Using A Newsletter Template

Word includes one newsletter template and one newsletter wizard. You will use the newsletter template in this chapter and the newsletter wizard in chapter 11. The newsletter template banner is created in a one-column format and the body text is created in an asymmetrical, balanced, three-column layout. Figure 10.13 illustrates Word's newsletter template. The template includes a list of your newsletter highlights as well as a table of contents. To customize the template, replace the placeholder text with your text, then save the document as a template. To change a picture, click the picture, then choose Picture from the Insert menu. Double-click a new picture and the old picture will be replaced with your new choice. To re-size a picture, click it, then drag a corner handle. To "reshape" a picture, drag one of the middle handles. To crop a picture, hold down the Shift key and drag any handle.

FIGURE 10.13

Newsletter Template

Highlights

- Secrets To Creating a Professional Newsletter
- Newsletter Tips, Tricks, and Good Advice
- Complete Step-by-step Newsletter Instructions

Inside

1 How To Customize This Newsletter Template
2 How To Save Time in the Future
1 How To Improve Your Newsletter Print Quality

The Gazette

The Newsletter of Inspired Technologies
Volume 1 • Issue 7
September 1998

Home delivery service unites with retailers

Offers added value and convenience without increasing cost of goods; sales explode

To re-size a picture, click on it and drag a corner handle. To "re-shape" a picture, drag one of the middle handles. To crop a picture, hold the Shift key down and drag any handle.

How do we customize this design for our own use? I have a color printer and would like to print in color.

To change the shading of text borders, or to remove a ruling line, click your cursor on the paragraph, and, from the Format menu, choose Borders and Shading. Select a new option.

To change the color of text, select the paragraph, and choose Font from the Format menu. Choose a different color from the drop-down color list. Choose OK or Cancel to exit the dialog box.

Section breaks make it possible for various sections to have more than one column. To change the number of columns in any section, click your cursor in the section to be changed, and choose Format Column. Type a new number.

With the Break command, you can insert a page break, column, or section break. Assuming your nonprinting characters are turned on (in Tools Options View dialog box), you can identify breaks by the double, dotted lines. To insert a break, choose Break from the Insert menu. Select an option, and click OK to exit the dialog box.

To change/insert a picture, click on the picture, and choose Picture from the Insert menu. Choose a new picture, and click the Link to File box if you would like to save the art with the newsletter.

To change a picture color, double-click on the graphic to activate the drawing layer—where you can group or ungroup picture objects, and re-color or delete objects. Click on an object, and choose Drawing Object from the Format menu. Choose a new shade, and choose Close. To delete an object, press Delete.

Creating Newsletters

When you re-save the template with your changes, future document creation becomes easier. Select File New to re-open your template as a document.

1 With the template open, type your company text over the sample text.

2 Choose File Save As. In the menu, choose Document Template in the Save File as Type box. (The extension should change from .doc to .dot.) Save the file under a new name to protect the original, or use the same name to replace the existing version.

To create a newsletter from your newly saved template, select File New to re-open your template as a document. Your company information should now appear in place.

Style Names

There are three ways to view the preset Style names for this newsletter:

- In Normal view, choose Options from the Format menu. Click the View tab. In the Style Area Width box, type a number such as "6" (picas); or
- In Page Layout view, click on any paragraph and view the style name on the Formatting toolbar; or
- From the Format menu, choose Style Gallery. In the preview section, click on Example or Style Samples.

To change the picture background, double-click on the picture to activate the drawing. You'll see a blinking cursor and a paragraph mark. Experiment with that paragraph—alter Format Borders and Shading, and alter the spacing in Format Paragraph.

2 **THE GAZETTE** SEPTEMBER 1998

Inspired Questions & Answers

Readers Write

Q: I would like to darken some of the gray shading to improve the print quality. Can that be done?

A: Yes. To change the shading of the text or borders, click your cursor on the paragraph, and, from the Format menu, choose Borders and Shading to select a new option.

Q: Extra space seems to appear between the lines as I type sometimes? What's wrong?

A: Nothing. Depending on how fast you type, along with the speed of your computer, you may experience momentary lapses of proper linespacing. Not to worry, though—in just a few seconds, Word will redraw the screen.

Q: What's the best way to print this newsletter?

A: Print page 2 on the back of page 1. Fold like a letter (in thirds), and mail with or without an envelope. For best results, use a medium to heavyweight paper. If you're mailing without an envelope, seal with a label.

Q: I would like to mail my newsletter in an envelope. How do I remove the return address and indicia frames?

A: Click on the text to reveal the bounding border of the frame. Click on the frame border to highlight the frame handles, and press Delete. To save the frame for the future, click on the frame and choose AutoText from the Edit menu. Click Add, and OK.

Q: I would like to use my own clip art. How do I change the art without changing the design?

A: To change a picture, choose Picture from the Insert menu. Choose a new picture, and click the Link to File box to save your art with the template for future newsletters.

Q: How do I change the number of columns in this newsletter?

A: Click your cursor in the section to be changed and choose Columns from the Format menu. Choose a new option, and click OK.

Q: How do I remove the vertical column lines?

A: Click your cursor in the section to be changed, and choose Columns from the Format menu. Click the Line Between box to turn the column lines to the "off" position.

Q: Is it possible to have different column configurations on the same page?

A: Yes. Section breaks make it possible for various sections to have more than one column. To insert a section break, choose Break from the Insert menu. Select Continuous, and click OK. To change the number of columns in the section, click your cursor in the section to be changed, and choose Format Column. Type a new number and click OK to exit the dialog box.

The Q&A Styles use the Format Drop Cap command to create the large letters. Quickly copy and paste Styles using the Edit Copy or Edit Paste commands.

Inspired Technologies
12345 Main Street
Any City, State 12345

BULK RATE
UNITED STATES
POSTAGE PAID
PERMIT # 000
ANY CITY, ST

Inside: Great tips and techniques for creating a newsletter!

Creating a Newsletter Using Word's Newsletter Template

1. At a clear document window, create the newsletter shown in figure 10.14 by completing the following steps:
   a. Choose File, New, then select the Publications tab.
   b. Double-click Newsletter.dot.
   c. Print the newsletter template document and read the placeholder text for valuable information and tips about newsletters.
   d. With the newsletter template displayed, change to Page Layout view, turn on the nonprinting characters, and change the Zoom Control to 75%.
   e. Save the document with Save As and name it c10ex01, newsletter template.
   f. Select the entry table of contents section at the top of the newsletter, including the Highlights and Inside headings, bulleted list, numbered pages, and the End of Section code; then press Delete. (A table of contents is not needed on a one-page newsletter.)
   g. Customize the nameplate by completing the following steps:
      (1) Select *The Gazette* and key **Desktop Designs**. (The text will wrap to the next line.)
      (2) If a Reapply Style prompt displays, click the Cancel button to avoid changing the Document Label style.
      (3) To create a one-line nameplate, select *Desktop*, then change the font to 62-point Garamond. Select *Designs* and change the font to 64-point Arial in Dk Gray. (The nameplate was formatted with the *Document Label* style.)
   h. Customize the folio (located to the right of the nameplate) by completing the following steps:
      (1) Select the frame that contains the folio text and drag the frame upward to align it with the nameplate borders.
      (2) Select the year, then key **1997**.
      (3) Deselect the frame.
   i. Replace the existing graphic with a more appropriate graphic by completing the following steps:
      (1) Select the house picture located below the nameplate. Choose Insert, then Picture.
      (2) Make sure Clipart displays in the Look in text box, then double-click *Computer* in the Name list at the Insert Picture dialog box.

j. Size the picture by completing the following steps:
   (1) Select the picture and choose Format, then Picture.
   (2) In the Size section of the Picture dialog box, change the Width and Height to 1 inch.
   (3) Choose OK or press Enter.

k. Select *Home delivery...* and key **Keeping up with current trends**.

l. Select *Offers added value...* and key **Staying on the cutting edge of desktop publishing using Microsoft® Word for Windows 95**. (Use the Registered symbol in the Special Characters dialog box or key (R) and Word will replace (R) with ® if the Replace Text as you Type option has been turned on in AutoCorrect. Select the Registered symbol, then choose Superscript from the Font dialog box.

m. Create the headings and body text by completing the following steps:
   (1) Position the insertion point at the beginning of the first paragraph of placeholder text.
   (2) Click the Italic button on the Formatting toolbar to turn off the Italic feature.
   (3) Choose Insert, then File.
   (4) At the Insert File dialog box, change the directory in the Look in: box to the location of your student data disk.
   (5) Double-click *newsletter01*, text.
   (6) With the insertion point located at the end of the inserted text, press Ctrl + Shift + End to select the text from the insertion point to the end of the document. Press Delete to delete the rest of the placeholder text from the insertion point to the end of page 2. Only the first page of the newsletter will be created in this exercise.

n. Format the heading *Knowledge is Power!* as shown in figure 10.14 by completing the following steps:
   (1) Position the insertion point anywhere in the heading *Knowledge is Power!* (located at the beginning of the newsletter text).
   (2) Click the down-pointing arrow to the right of the Style text box and select the *Heading 1* style.
   (3) Select the heading *Training Techniques* in the third column of the newsletter, then apply the *Heading 1* style.
   (4) Edit the *Heading 1* style by completing the following steps:
      (a) Position the insertion point anywhere on the heading *Knowledge is Power!*, then choose Format, then Style.
      (b) At the Style dialog box, make sure *Heading 1* has been selected in the Styles list box.
      (c) Choose Modify.
      (d) At the Modify Style dialog box, choose the Format button, then Font.
      (e) Select Bold at the Font Style list box of the Font dialog box.
      (f) Choose OK or press Enter to close the Font dialog box.
      (g) Choose OK or press Enter to close the Modify dialog box.
      (h) Choose Apply at the Style dialog box.

o. Insert a graphic into the newsletter as shown in figure 10.14 by completing the following steps:
   (1) Position the insertion point at the beginning of the third paragraph in the first article, then choose Insert, then Picture.
   (2) At the Insert Picture dialog box, make sure Clipart displays in the Look in text box, then double-click *Books*.

2. Save the document again with the same name (c10ex01, newsletter template).
3. Print and then close c10ex01, newsletter template.

FIGURE 10.14

Document Label Style

Desktop Designs

The Newsletter of Inspired Technologies
Volume 1 • Issue 7
September 1997

Picture 2 Style *Title Style*

Keeping up with current trends

Subtitle Style

Staying on the cutting edge of desktop publishing using Microsoft® Word for Windows 95

Heading 1 Style *Body Text Style*

Knowledge is Power!

How can one have the up-to-date knowledge needed to keep on the cutting edge of desktop publishing? One way to have knowledge is to read some of the periodicals, newsletters, and books now available that address all aspects of desktop publishing.

Two basic types of periodicals are available. The first type is based on technological development to communication arts. These periodicals contain useful information about current and new products. The second type contains knowledge of technique, style, and applications.

Many newsletters and books are available. Listed below are some magazines, newsletters, and books that can help you as a desktop publisher.

Inside Microsoft® Word 95 by The Cobb Group is a monthly publication including helpful tips and techniques for using Microsoft Word for Windows 95 in creating everyday applications.

Working Smarter with Microsoft® Word—Your OneOnOne® Guide to Better Word Processing is an excellent bi-monthly newsletter, which includes sections on Quick Tips, Help Desk questions and answers, Test Your PC I.Q., and Instant Tutorial as well as helpful articles on how to use Word efficiently in day-to-day applications.

Publish is a monthly magazine with information of interest to those involved in all areas of print and multimedia productions. The focus is on print design and production and addresses emerging technologies.

PC Publishing covers information on desktop publishing and presentation graphics for those using IBM and compatibles. Each issue addresses specific subjects with in-depth discussion.

Desktop Communications covers hardware/software, design, typography, and useful tips. Industry professionals provide extensive knowledge from their experience.

Before and After, a bi-monthly newsletter, gives down-to-earth advice on graphic design and desktop typography.

Newsletters for the Desktop by Roger C. Parker has tips on saving time and money on design and layout of your newsletters. The book includes helpful tips and illustrations.

The Makeover Book: 101 Design Solutions for Desktop Publishing by Roger C. Parker includes design solutions for desktop publishers. "Before" and "After" examples are given to show you how to make your documents more interesting and persuasive. Basic design principles are reinforced in ads, brochures, flyers, and more.

The Desktop Publisher's Idea Book by Chuck Green offers something more than the usual newsletters, letterheads, and envelopes. There are a wealth of useful, eye-catching, and unusual projects perfectly suited to desktop publishing. You will find project ideas, tips, and hard-to-find sources available in this book.

Looking Good in Print—Guide to Basic Design for Desktop Publishing by Roger C. Parker is a book designed to show you how to produce attractive, effective newsletters, advertisements, brochures, manuals, correspondence, and more. The desktop publishing concepts of design, layout, balance, contrast, proportion, directional flow, consistency, and use of color are all introduced and reinforced throughout this book. Emphasis on organizational tools such as grids, thumbnails, columns, gutters, styles, bullets, and more are also discussed and illustrated throughout the chapters. An added feature includes checklists at the end of each chapter used by the document designer to verify the use of these concepts and tools. Additional new sections include photography and scanning.

Heading 1 Style

Training Techniques

Two types of training are available for those just beginning in desktop publishing.

The first type is a content-based program. This program is based on a typical college program and the information is presented in a classroom situation. Instructional books and videos are frequently utilized.

Skill-based training is another type of training. This training is useful to businesses as skill-based training produces capable people quickly.

Creating Your Own Newsletter

Using Styles in Newsletters

Styles are especially valuable in saving time, effort, and keystrokes in creating newsletters. Newsletters are typically one of the most frequently created desktop publishing documents. Additionally, certain newsletter elements must remain consistent from page to page as well as from issue to issue. Styles reinforce consistency in documents by saving repetitive formatting instructions with a name so they can be applied over and over. As shown in figure 10.14, Word's Newsletter template includes many styles.

In addition to predesigned system styles included in each Word template or wizard, you have the option to create your own customized styles either based on system styles or created from scratch as previously discussed in chapter 6. Throughout the creation of the newsletter in figure 10.16, you will use various predesigned system styles and customize them to certain specifications as well as create your own styles based on existing styles. Styles created in one document can be copied to another document by clicking Style on the Format menu and then clicking Organizer.

If you apply a style, then later decide you do not want the style applied to your text, you can modify any part of the style you find undesirable at the Style dialog box, or you can simply apply the Normal style, which will replace the previous style. To apply the Normal style, position your insertion point in the text you want to reformat, click the down-pointing arrow to the right of the Style list box on the Formatting toolbar, then select the Normal style from the Style drop-down list. Or, click the Undo button on the Formatting toolbar to undo the insertion of the style.

Word also includes the option to turn on the AutoFormat feature, which automatically applies formatting without your having to select a particular style from a list. AutoFormat analyzes a Word document to identify specific elements, and then formats the text by applying styles from the attached template. AutoFormat As you Type is an option you can turn on that will format headings, numbered and bulleted lists, borders, and numbers. To view the formatting that AutoFormat will automatically apply, choose Tools, then Options. At the Options dialog box, select the AutoFormat tab.

Adjusting Leading in Newsletters

DTP POINTERS
When line length increases, line spacing (leading) should also increase.

While creating newsletters, you will encounter areas where adjustments should be made to increase or decrease white space between lines. This may occur when creating a nameplate, headline, subhead, or body text. Insufficient leading makes the text difficult to read. Extra leading makes a page look less gray; however, too much leading or too little leading can make it difficult to find the beginning of the next line.

In Word, you can adjust leading by adjusting the line spacing—single, 1.5 lines, or double—or by specifying an exact amount at the At Least or Exactly settings. Or you can adjust line and paragraph spacing at the Paragraph dialog box. To adjust line and paragraph spacing, choose Format, then Paragraph. At the Paragraph dialog box, select the Indents and Spacing tab. Make selections at the Spacing section by selecting or keying a measurement Before or After your line of text. Be sure to include "pt" after keying an increment such as 4 pt.

Normal leading in Word is 120 percent of the type size being used. For example, a 10-point type has 12 points of leading. Large type size has an effect on leading. For instance, if a headline contains two lines both keyed at 30 points, the space between the two lines may be too wide. Reducing the leading will improve the appearance of the heading. Consider the following guidelines when determining leading:

- Large type requires more leading.
- Longer lines need more leading to make them easier to read.
- Sans serif type requires more leading because it does not have serifs that guide the eye along the line.
- Use styles to apply line spacing consistently in newsletters.

Adjusting Character Spacing in Newsletters

Letters in a nameplate can be altered so there is more or less space between the characters by adjusting character spacing at the Font dialog box. Figure 10.15 illustrates a nameplate that shows expanded and condensed character spacing. Kerning is usually applied to headlines and subheads.

 Expanded 3 points (Matura MT Script Capitals)	Desktop Publishing Condensed 1 point (Book Antiqua)

FIGURE 10.15

Adjusting Character Spacing

Throughout the remaining exercises in this chapter, you will continually build the newsletter shown in figure 10.16. Each exercise involves creating a style for each specific newsletter element. Each exercise builds on the previous one, finally resulting in a completed newsletter with embedded styles and saved as a template to help you create the next issue.

FIGURE 10.16

Sample Newsletter with Elements and Styles Marked

Volume 5, Issue 1 • June 1997 ← Folio Style

Subtitle → ***Bicycle and In-Line Skating Safety News for the 90s •***

IN-LINE SKATING—FASTEST GROWING SPORT ← Headline Style

Subhead Style

Injuries Up Dramatically

by Mary Beth Lubrsen ← By Line

Last year, the Consumer Product Safety Commission (CPSC) released some alarming news on in-line skating, now the fastest growing recreational sport in America. They projected 83,000 serious injuries in 1997, more than double those of 1996. Even more alarming is the fact that children under age 15 account for 60% of these injuries.

The point is that in-line skating can be quite dangerous. Skaters often share the pavement with cars, trucks, bicyclists,

pedestrians, and pets and encounter loose gravel, potholes, puddles, and cracks. Add to that the fact that it's possible to achieve speeds exceeding 30 miles per hour, and you've got "accidents" waiting to happen.

Most injuries are wrist fractures, followed by elbows or lower arm fractures. Head injuries are not far behind. In fact, the CPSC projected that in 1997, 7,000 people would sustain head injuries—by far the most potentially disabling and even fatal of all in-line skating injuries. ← Body Text Style

Fortunately, safety education and appropriate protection can make a difference. The International In-Line Skating Association (IISA) recommends helmets be certified to the ANSI, ASTM, or Snell bicycle helmet safety standards. Remember to think "Safety On Wheels" in 1997.

Subhead Style

A Message to Parents

by Mary Beth and Dane Lubrsen

For the past four years, Ride Safe has been committed to promoting safe bicycling and bicycle helmets. We started with our own four children (ages 2–8), who didn't want to wear helmets because their friends didn't wear them. We thought if we could offer "cool" looking helmets to a group of children, we could diminish this negative peer pressure. Our strategy worked, and the Ride Safe program has already convinced 200,000 people at over 2,000 schools to wear bicycle helmets.

In 1996, we expanded our program to include educational materials and protective gear for another very popular sport—in-line skating. Our new **Safety on Wheels**™ program includes safety gear made by Skating—In Line, "the choice of champions."

We are again offering helmets made in the USA by Bike Sports, Inc., the number one bicycle helmet maker in the world. We are especially proud of the new RS4000X helmet, which combines extended coverage in the back for extra in-line skating protection with a unique (H)Air Channel for ponytails.

We hope you will play an active role in your children's "Safety On Wheels" and give serious consideration to purchasing protective equipment for your entire family. If you have any questions about Ride Safe products and services, please call us at 800-285-RIDE.

Subhead Style

Our Ride Safe Guarantee

Ride Safe, Inc., guarantees 100% satisfaction. If anyone becomes dissatisfied with their Ride Safe product at any time, for any reason, it can be returned to Ride Safe for a refund.

DTP POINTERS

Text keyed in the same type size can vary from typeface to typeface.

Creating A Folio

Creating a folio for your newsletter will be the first step in building the Ride Safe newsletter. The folio will consist of information that will change from issue to issue, such as the volume number, issue number, and date. However, the formatting applied to the folio will remain consistent with each issue. To ensure consistency prepare a folio style and apply it to the new information keyed into the folio each month. Using this style will reduce time and effort.

Frequently, the folio is preceded or followed by a graphic line that sets the folio information apart from the rest of the nameplate. The folio can appear at the top of the nameplate as in this exercise, although it is more commonly placed below the nameplate. Reverse text can be added for emphasis and interest and text set in italics is often used.

Creating a Folio Style for a Newsletter

1. At a clear document window, create the folio for the newsletter in figure 10.16 by completing the following steps:
   a. Change the top and bottom margins to 0.50 and the left and right margins to 0.75.
   b. Change to Page Layout viewing mode, change the Zoom Control to 75%, and turn on the display of nonprinting characters.
   c. Format the folio by completing the following steps:
      (1) With the insertion point located at the beginning of the page, change the font to 13-point Impact and key **Volume 5, Issue 1**, then press the space bar three times.
      (2) Create the bullet symbol (•) as shown on the first line of the newsletter in figure 10.16, by completing the following steps:
         (a) Choose Insert, then Symbol.
         (b) At the Symbol dialog box, select the Symbols tab.
         (c) Select the *Wingdings* font, then select the symbol in the fifth row and the sixteenth column.
         (d) Click Insert, then Close.
      (3) Press the space bar three times, then key **June 1997**.
      (4) Press Enter.
      (5) Select *Volume 5...*, then choose Format, then Font.
      (6) Select the Character Spacing tab, then change the Spacing to Expanded By: 1 pt.
      (7) Turn on Kerning at 13 points, then choose OK or press Enter.
      (8) With the text still selected, choose Format, then Paragraph.
      (9) At the Paragraph dialog box, select the Indents and Spacing tab.
      (10) Change the Left indentation to 0.25 inches.
      (11) Key **5 pt** in the After text box located in the Spacing section.
      (12) Choose OK or press Enter.
      (13) Select the symbol between the issue and date, choose Format, then Font.
      (14) Select the Font tab, then change the Color to Blue at the Font dialog box. Choose OK or press Enter.
   d. Create a style from existing text by completing the following steps:
      (1) Position the insertion point anywhere in the folio text.
      (2) Click inside the Style box on the Formatting toolbar to select the current style name.
      (3) Key **Folio** and press Enter. (The *Folio* name is then added to the list of

styles available in this document.)

2. Save the document and name it c10ex02, folio.
3. Close c10ex02, folio. (You will not print until the entire newsletter has been created.)

Creating A Nameplate

After designing your newsletter, you will be ready to create a nameplate. A nameplate or banner is the first thing that captures the reader's eyes, and it provides immediate identification of the newsletter. A nameplate is the artwork (graphic, logo, scanned image, cropped image, etc.) or type, including the name of the publication, that is usually placed at the top of the first page of a newsletter. The choice of fonts, type sizes, and the design of the name are important since they are seen repeatedly by the reader. See figure 10.17 and examine the sample nameplate for varying locations for newsletter elements.

The nameplate in exercise 3 consists of the company's name and a logo bordered by two dotted lines created in the same color as the color used in the logo. Ride Safe, Inc., uses two different logo designs in most of their publications. The Ride Safe logos, however, may display in several different colors, such as blue, red, teal, orange, yellow, or purple. Most nameplates remain unchanged from issue to issue; therefore, it is not necessary to save it as a style. Moreover, the nameplate should be saved to a newsletter template.

Figure 10.17 illustrates several examples of nameplates. Looking at the work of others can help you develop your own skills in design and layout.

FIGURE 10.17

Sample Nameplates

August 1997

Naper News

NAMEPLATE USING AN ASYMMETRICAL DESIGN

FOCUS

Desktop Publishing

Volume 2 ◆ Issue 5 | News & Notes | March ◆ 1997

NAMEPLATE WITH LAYERED TEXT

Vol. 1, Issue 5 | July 1997

News & Views

For Desktop Publishers

Word 7.0 for Windows 95 is a Leader

NAMEPLATE USING WORDART, A FOLIO IN REVERSE TEXT, AND A HEADLINE

Technology Update | Volume 2 • Issue 6

August 1997

News

NAMEPLATE USING WORDART TO ROTATE TEXT, A GRAPHIC, AND REVERSED TEXT

Spring Issue 1997

29 W 036 Butterfield Road
Warrenville, IL 60555
(708) 555-1062
http://www.grower-2-you.com

NAMEPLATE WITH A COMPANY LOGO AND REVERSED TEXT

The Law Family Newsletter

1997 ❋ A Year in Review

NAMEPLATE USING WORDART TO ROTATE TEXT IN REVERSE

Creating a Nameplate for a Newsletter

1. At a clear document window, create a nameplate as shown in figure 10.16 by completing the following steps:
   a. Open c10ex02, folio.
   b. Save the document with Save As and name it c10ex03, nameplate.
   c. Change to Page Layout viewing mode, change the Zoom Control to 75%, and turn on the display of nonprinting characters.
   d. Format the nameplate by completing the following steps:
      (1) Position the insertion point on the paragraph symbol below the folio and choose Format, then Font.
      (2) At the Font dialog box, select the Font tab.
      (3) Change the font to 13-point Impact.
      (4) Change the font Color to Blue, then choose OK or press Enter.
      (5) Choose Insert, then Symbol.
      (6) At the Symbol dialog box, select the Symbols tab, then change the Font to Wingdings, and select the bullet symbol in the fifth row and the sixteenth column.
      (7) Click the Insert button, then click Close.
      (8) Continue pressing the F4 key until you have created an entire row of blue symbols.
      (9) Press Enter once.
   e. Insert the Ride Safe logo by completing the following steps:
      (1) Choose Insert, then Picture.
      (2) At the Insert Picture dialog box, change the directory in the Look in: box to the location of your student data disk files.
      (3) Make sure the Files of type list box displays *All Files (*.*)*, and then double-click *Ridesf1blue*.
      (4) With the image selected, click the Center button on the Formatting toolbar. Deselect the image.
      (5) Press Enter, then click the Align Left button on the Formatting toolbar.
      (6) Press Enter.
   f. Select, then copy the blue dotted line above the logo.
   g. Position the insertion point on the second paragraph symbol below the logo, then click the Paste button on the Standard toolbar.
2. Save the document again with the same name (c10ex03, nameplate).
3. Close c10ex03, nameplate. (You may want to wait and print the entire newsletter when it is completed.)

Creating A Subtitle

As the third step in building a newsletter, you will create a subtitle. Since the text in the subtitle will remain consistent from issue to issue, it is not necessary to create a style for the subtitle. A subtitle emphasizes the purpose of the newsletter and identifies the intended audience. The subtitle is usually keyed in a sans serif typeface in 14 to 24 points, and kerning should be turned on.

Creating a Subtitle in a Newsletter

1. At a clear document window, add a subtitle to the newsletter from exercise 3, as shown in figure 10.16, by completing the following steps:
   a. Open c10ex03, nameplate.
   b. Save the document with Save As and name it c10ex04, subtitle.
   c. Change to Page Layout viewing mode, change the Zoom Control to 75%, and turn on the display of nonprinting characters.
   d. Format the subtitle by completing the following steps:
      (1) Position the insertion point on the paragraph symbol below the dotted line, choose Format, then Font.
      (2) At the Font dialog box, select the Font tab.
      (3) Change the font to 13-point Impact Italic, and make sure the font Color displays in Black.
      (4) Select the Character Spacing tab.
      (5) Change the Spacing to Expanded By 1 pt.
      (6) Turn on the Kerning at 13 points. Choose OK or press Enter.
      (7) Choose Format, then Paragraph.
      (8) At the Paragraph dialog box, select the Indents and Spacing tab.
      (9) Change the Spacing Before to 5 pt, change the Spacing After to 12 pt, then click the Tabs button.
      (10) At the Tabs dialog box, key **6.75** inches in the Tab Stop Position text box, select Right Alignment, and choose OK or press Enter.
      (11) Press Tab.
      (12) Key **Bicycle and In-Line Skating Safety News for the 90s**.
      (13) Press the space bar three times, then click the Italic button on the Formatting toolbar to turn off this feature.
      (14) Choose Insert, then Symbol.
      (15) At the Symbol dialog box, select the Symbols tab, then change the Font to Wingdings, and select the bullet symbol in the fifth row and the sixteenth column.
      (16) Click the Insert button, then click Close.
      (17) Press Enter.
      (18) Select the symbol and change the font Color to Blue. Choose OK or press Enter.
2. Save the document again with the same name (c10ex04, subtitle).
3. Close c10ex04, subtitle. (You will print when the newsletter is complete.)

Creating A Headline

After completing the folio, nameplate, and subtitle, you will create a headline in exercise 5. Headlines organize text and help readers decide whether they want to read the article. To set the headline apart from the text, use a larger type size, heavier weight, and a different typeface than the body. When determining a type size for a headline, start with 18 points and increase the size until you find an appropriate one. As a general rule, you may want to choose a sans serif typeface for a headline. However, this is not a hard-and-fast rule.

Since the headline consists of text that will change with each issue of the newsletter, consider creating a style to format the headline.

DTP POINTERS
Avoid using all caps; small caps are easier to read.

Headlines often improve in readability and appearance if leading is reduced. The leading in a headline should be about the size of the type size used to create it. Using all caps (use sparingly) or small caps substantially reduces leading automatically, since capital letters lack descenders.

Headlines and subheads should have more space above than below. This indicates that the heading goes with the text that follows rather than the text that precedes the heading.

Creating a Headline Style for a Newsletter

1. At a clear document window, create a headline style for the newsletter in figure 10.16, by completing the following steps:
   a. Open c10ex04, subtitle.
   b. Save the document with Save As and name it c10ex05, headline.
   c. Change to Page Layout viewing mode, change the Zoom Control to 75%, and turn on the display of nonprinting characters.
   d. Format the headline by completing the following steps:
      (1) Position the insertion point on the second paragraph symbol below the subtitle.
      (2) Change the font to 24-point Britannic Bold.
      (3) Change the font Color to Dk Gray.
      (4) Turn on the Small Caps.
      (5) Change the Spacing to Expanded By 1.5 pt at the Character Spacing tab.
      (6) Turn on the Kerning at 14 points.
      (7) Key **In-Line Skating—Fastest Growing Sport**. (Use an em dash.)
      (8) Select *In-Line Skating...*, then choose Format, then Paragraph.
      (9) At the Paragraph dialog box, select the Indents and Spacing tab.
      (10) Change the Spacing at the Before text box to 6 pt and the Spacing After to 16 pt. Choose OK or press Enter.
      (11) Press Enter.
   e. Create a style from existing text by completing the following steps:
      (1) Position the insertion point anywhere in the headline text.
      (2) Click inside the Style box on the Formatting toolbar to select the current style name.
      (3) Key **Headline** and press Enter. (The *Headline* style is then added to the list of styles available in this document.)
2. Save the document again with the same name (c10ex05, headline).
3. Close c10ex05, headline. (You will print when the newsletter is complete.)

Formatting Body Text In A Newsletter

In exercise 6, you will format the body text for the newsletter you are building in this chapter. You will change the font and type size, turn on the Widow/Orphan feature, create em spaces for paragraph indentations, and turn on the columns feature. Before doing so, take a look at some of the formatting options that apply to body text.

Applying the Widow/Orphan Feature

Word's Widow/Orphan feature is on by default. This feature prevents the first and last lines of paragraphs from being separated across pages. A *widow* is a single line of a paragraph or heading that is pushed to the top of the next page. A single line of text (whether part of a paragraph or heading) appearing by itself at the end of a page is called an *orphan*. This option is located in the Paragraph dialog box with the Text Flow tab selected.

Widow: A single line of text pushed to the top of the next page.

Orphan: A single line of text appearing by itself at the end of a page.

Even with this feature on, you should still watch for subheadings that are inappropriately separated from text at the end of a column or page. If a heading displays inappropriately, insert a column break. To insert a column break, position the insertion point where you want a new column to begin, then press Ctrl + Shift + Enter or choose Insert, Break, then Column Break.

Aligning Text in Paragraphs in Newsletters

The type of alignment you choose for a newsletter influences the "color" or tone of your publication. Text within a paragraph can be aligned in a variety of ways. Text can be aligned at both the left and right margins (justified); aligned at the left or right; or centered on a line, causing both the left and right margins to be ragged.

Justified text is common in publications such as textbooks, newspapers, newsletters, and magazines. It is more formal than left-aligned text. For justified text to convey a professional appearance, there must be an appropriate line length. If the line length is too short, the words and/or characters in a paragraph may be widely spaced, causing "rivers" of white space. Remedying this situation requires increasing the line length, changing to a smaller type size, and/or hyphenating long words. Hyphenation will be discussed in greater detail in chapter 11. Text aligned at the left is the easiest to read. This alignment has become popular with designers for publications of all kinds. Center alignment should be used on small amounts of text.

Indenting Paragraphs with Em Spaces

In typesetting, tabs are generally measured by em spaces rather than inch measurements. An em space is a space as wide as the point size of the type. For example, if the type size is 12 points, an em space is 12 points wide. Generally, you will want to indent newsletter text one or two em spaces.

Em space indentations can be created in two ways. One way is to display the Paragraph dialog box with the Indents and Spacing tab selected, then select or key an inch or point increment at the Left or Right Indentation text boxes (be sure to include "pt" when keying a point increment). Or, you can create an em space at the Tabs dialog box. In exercise 6 you will change the default tab setting to 0.25 inches to create an em space indentation for each paragraph preceded with a tab code (0.25 inches is approximately 24 points or 2 em spaces if the text is keyed in 12 point type size).

Be sure to use em spaces for any paragraph indentations used in newsletters. Also, use em spaces for spacing around bullets and any other indented text in newsletters.

Generally, the first paragraph after a headline or subhead is not indented even though all remaining paragraphs will have an em space paragraph indentation. In figure 10.16 notice the paragraph formatting in the newsletter.

Creating a Body Text Style In a Newsletter

1. At a clear document window, create a body text style for the newsletter in figure 10.16 by completing the following steps:
   a. Open c10ex05, headline.
   b. Save the document with Save As and name it c10ex06, body text.
   c. Change to Page Layout viewing mode, change the Zoom Control to 75%, and turn on the display of nonprinting characters.
   d. Position the insertion point on the paragraph symbol below the headline text.
   e. Choose Insert, then File.
   f. At the Insert File dialog box, change the directory in the Look in: box to the location of your student data disk files.
   g. Make sure the Files of type list box displays *All Files (*.*)* or *Word Documents (*.doc)* and then double-click the file *Ride Safe.*
   h. Create a section break between the headline and the body text by completing the following steps:
      (1) Position the insertion point at the beginning of *Injuries Up Dramatically.*
      (2) Choose Insert, then Break.
      (3) At the Break dialog box, choose Continuous in the Section Breaks section.
      (4) Choose OK or press Enter.
   i. Turn on the columns feature by completing the following steps:
      (1) With the insertion point still positioned at the beginning of *Injuries Up Dramatically*, choose Format, then Columns.
      (2) At the Columns dialog box, select Three in the Presets section.
      (3) Click Line Between (this inserts a line between the columns).
      (4) Click Equal Column Width.
      (5) Click the down-pointing triangle to the right of the Apply To: text box, then select This Section from the drop-down list.
      (6) Choose OK or press Enter.
   j. Format the body text by completing the following steps:
      (1) Select all the text in the three columns beginning with *Injuries Up Dramatically*, then change the font to 11-point Garamond.
      (2) With the text still selected, Choose Format, then Paragraph. At the Paragraph dialog box, select the Indents and Spacing tab. Change the Line Spacing to At Least, then key **11 pt** in the At: text box.
      (3) Change the Spacing After to 4 pt.
      (4) To change the paragraph indentions to an em space, click the Tabs button at the Paragraph dialog box.
      (5) At the Tabs dialog box, key **0.25** in the Tab Stop Position text box and make sure Left is selected in the Alignment section.
      (6) Choose OK or press Enter to close the Tabs dialog box.
   k. Create a style to format the body text by completing the following steps:
      (1) Position the insertion point in one of the paragraphs in the body of the newsletter.
      (2) Click in the Style box on the Formatting toolbar to select the current name.
      (3) Key **RS Body Text** and press Enter. (The *RS Body Text* style is then added to the list of styles available in this document.)
2. Save the document with the same name (c10ex06, body text).
3. Close c10ex06, body text. (You will print when the newsletter is complete.)

Creating Subheads For Newsletters

At times a subhead may appear right after a headline, as is the case with this chapter's newsletter. Refer to figure 10.16 to view the subheads you will create in this exercise. Subheads organize text and expand upon headlines, giving readers more information or clues about the text. In addition, subheads also provide contrast to text-intensive body copy. Marginal subheads are sometimes placed in the left margin or in a narrow column to the left of the body text, providing an airy, open appearance. Subheads can be set in a larger type size, different typeface, or heavier weight than the text. They can be centered, aligned left, or aligned right and formatted in shaded boxes. In exercise 7, you will create a customized style based on an existing style. Figure 10.18 shows a newsletter created with marginal subheads.

DTP POINTERS
Do not use narrow typefaces in reverse text. Add bold to increase the thickness of the typeface.

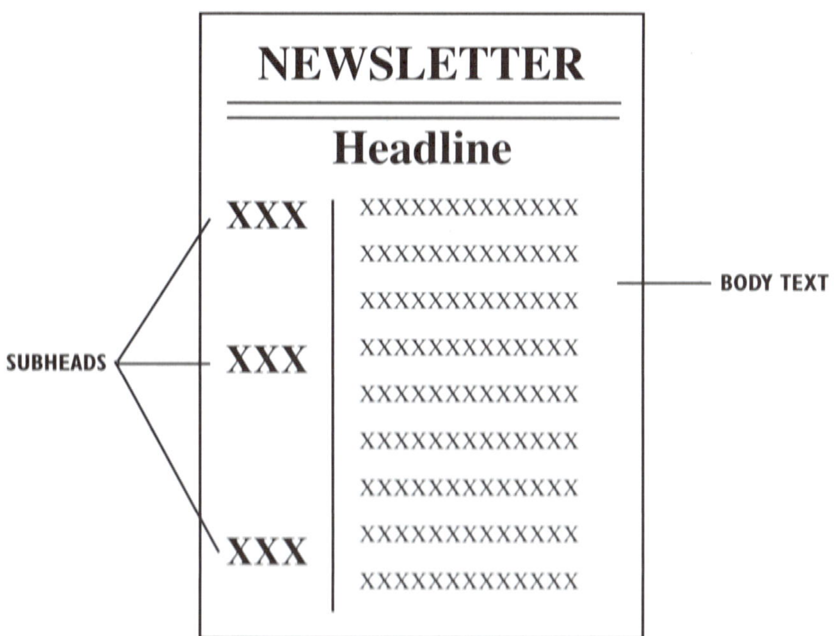

FIGURE 10.18

Marginal Subheads

Creating a Subhead Style

1. At a clear document window, create a subhead style for the newsletter in figure 10.16, by completing the following steps:
   a. Open c10ex06, body text.
   b. Save the document with Save As and name it c10ex07, subhead.
   c. Change to Page Layout viewing mode, change the Zoom Control to 75%, and turn on the display of nonprinting characters.
   d. Create a style to format the subhead in the newsletter in figure 10.16 based on an existing style by completing the following steps:
      (1) Select *Injuries Up Dramatically*, then select the Heading 1 style at the Style text box on the Formatting toolbar. (This will apply the Heading 1 style to the selected text.)
      (2) With *Injuries Up Dramatically* still selected, choose Format, then Style.
      (3) At the Style dialog box, make sure Heading 1 is selected in the Styles list box. Make sure All Styles displays in the List text box. Read the description of the style formatting.

(4) Choose the New button at the Style dialog box.
(5) At the New Style dialog box, key **Subhead** in the Name text box.
(6) Make sure that *Heading 1* displays in the Based On: text box.
(7) Choose the Format button, then select Font at the drop-down list.
(8) At the Font dialog box, change the font to 13-point Britannic Bold.
(9) Select the Character Spacing tab, then change the Spacing to Expanded By 0.5 pt.
(10) Select Normal at the Position text box.
(11) Turn Kerning on at 13 points, then choose OK or press Enter.
(12) Choose the Format button, then Paragraph.
(13) Select the Indents and Spacing tab, then change the Spacing Before to 12 pt and the After setting to 6 pt.
(14) Change the Alignment to Centered, then choose OK or press Enter.
(15) Choose OK or press Enter at the Modify Style dialog box.
(16) Choose Apply at the Style dialog box.

e. Apply the Subhead style to the other subheadings in the newsletter by completing the following steps:
(1) Position the insertion point on the heading *A Message to Parents*, located in the second column, then select *Subhead* in the Style list box on the Formatting toolbar. Delete the paragraph symbol before the subheading.
(2) Apply the *Subhead* style to the heading *Our Ride Safe Guarantee* in the third column. Delete the paragraph symbol before the subheading.

f. Position the insertion point in the first subhead *Injuries Up Dramatically*, choose Format, then Paragraph. Select the Indents and Spacing tab, then change the Spacing Before to 0 pt. Choose OK or press Enter. (This will eliminate the space before the first subhead at the beginning of the body text. The Subhead style remains unchanged.)

2. Save the document again with the same name (c10ex07, subhead).
3. Close c10ex07, subhead. (You will print when the newsletter is complete.)

Creating A Byline

The next step in the process of building your newsletter is to create the byline. The byline identifies the author of the article. Generally, the byline is set in italics, using the same typeface as the body text. The byline may be the same size as the body typeface, but it is usually set in a type size one or two points smaller.

The byline can be keyed below the headline or subhead depending on which is the title of the article. In addition, the byline can also be keyed as the first line of the body text if it follows a headline or subhead that spans two or more columns. The byline can be keyed at the left margin of a column or it can be keyed flush right in a column.

Creating a Byline Style in a Newsletter

1. At a clear document window, create a byline style for the newsletter in figure 10.16, by completing the following steps:
   a. Open c10ex07, subhead.
   b. Save the document with Save As and name it c10ex08, byline.
   c. Change to Page Layout viewing mode, change the Zoom Control to 75%, and turn on the display of nonprinting characters.
   d. Create a style to format the byline in the newsletter in figure 10.16 by

completing the following steps:
   (1) Select the byline *by Mary Beth Luhrsen* below the first subhead *Injuries Up Dramatically*.
   (2) Change the font to 10-point Garamond Italic.
   (3) At the Paragraph dialog box, change the Spacing Before to 0 pt and the Spacing After to 6 pt.
   e. Create a style from existing text by completing the following steps:
   (1) Position the insertion point anywhere in the byline text.
   (2) Click inside the Style box on the Formatting toolbar to select the current style name.
   (3) Key **Byline** and press Enter. (The *Byline* style is then added to the list of styles available in this document.)
   f. Apply the *Byline* style to the byline below *A Message to Parents*.
2. Save the document again with the same name (c10ex08, byline).
3. Close c10ex08, byline. (You will print when the newsletter is complete.)

Inserting Graphic Images In Newsletters

Clip art added to a newsletter should support or expand points made in the text. Use clip art so that it will give the newsletter the appearance of being well-planned, inviting, and consistent. You can modify clip art by altering it using Word's Draw program and Microsoft Word Picture graphic editor. Large and relatively inexpensive selections of clip art can be purchased on CD-ROM. In addition, you may want to scan predesigned company logos (with permission) or photographs that relate to the subject of your newsletter.

The image used in the nameplate in figure 10.16 was scanned professionally and copied to your student data disk in a file format that was compatible with Word 7.0. Because of the file format in which it was saved, you cannot alter this image in Microsoft Word Picture. To change the color of the scanned image, you must access Windows Paint. Optional steps for using Paint are provided at the end of exercise 9.

Inserting a Graphic Image into a Newsletter

1. At a clear document window, insert a graphic into the newsletter in figure 10.16 by completing the following steps:
   a. Open c10ex08, byline.
   b. Save the document with Save As and name it c10ex09, ride safe newsletter.
   c. Change to Page Layout view, change the Zoom Control to 75%, and turn on the display of nonprinting characters.
   d. Position the insertion point near the second sentence in the second paragraph near the text referring to a "car."
   e. Choose Insert, then Picture.
   f. At the Insert Picture dialog box, change the directory in the Look in: box to the location of your student data disk files.
   g. Make sure the Files of type list box displays *All Files (*.*)* and then double-click the file *Sprtscar*.
   h. Display the Drawing toolbar, select the graphic image, then click the Insert Frame button (first button from the right) on the Drawing toolbar.
   i. If necessary, select then drag the image to the location shown in figure 10.16.

2. View your newsletter in Print Preview. If the last column is unbalanced with the first and second columns, insert a continuous section break at the end of the last column. (This should result in three balanced columns.)
3. Save the document again with the same name (c10ex09, ride safe newsletter).
4. Print then close c10ex09, ride safe newsletter.

Optional steps to save the Ride Safe newsletter as a template:

To save time when creating future issues of your newsletter, save your newsletter as a template. To do this, delete all text, frames, pictures, objects, etc., that will not stay the same for future issues. Likewise, leave the nameplate and all text, pictures, symbols, frames, etc., that will remain the same in each issue of your newsletter. For example, to save the Ride Safe newsletter in exercise 9 as a template as shown in figure 10.19, leave the following items and delete the rest:

- Folio (the month and volume/issue numbers will change, but the titles will remain—use the folio text as placeholder text)
- Nameplate
- Subtitle
- Headline (the headline text will change, but the position and formatting will remain—use the headline text as placeholder text)
- Subheads (the subhead text will change, but the formatting will remain—use the subhead text as placeholder text)
- Byline (the byline text will change, but the position and formatting will remain—use the byline text as placeholder text)
- Body Text (the body text will change, but the formatting will remain—leave a paragraph as placeholder text)

Complete the following steps to save c10ex09, newsletter as a template as shown in figure 10.19:

1. Open c10ex09, ride safe newsletter.
2. Delete all text and newsletter elements that will change with each issue (refer to the bulleted items above).
3. Save the newsletter with Save As. At the Save As dialog box, select *Document Template (*.dot)* at the Save as type text box.
4. Double-click the Publications folder.
5. Key **Ride Safe Template** in the File name text box.
6. Choose the Save button.
7. Close the document on the screen.

Optional steps to access Windows Paint program to customize a graphic:

1. Click the Start button in the lower left corner.
2. At the Windows menu, select Programs.
3. Select Accessories at the Windows pop-up list.
4. Select Paint.
5. At the Paint screen, choose File, then Open.
6. At the Open dialog box, click the down-pointing arrow to the right of the Files of type text box and select All Files.
7. Click the down-pointing arrow to the right of the Look In text box and select the drive where your student data disk is located. Select *Ridesf1blue*. Click the Open button.
8. At the Paint dialog box, choose Image, then Attributes.
9. At the Attributes dialog box, select Colors in the Colors section. Choose OK or press Enter. (A color palette should display at the bottom of the screen.)

10. Click the Fill With Color button (jar of paint spilling) on the Paint tool palette. Click any color on the color palette. Position the insertion point inside the helmet area and left click. (The area should display in your chosen color.)
11. Repeat steps 9 and 10 to fill the shirt with the same color.
12. Save the picture with Save As and give the file a name.
13. Choose File, then Exit.

FIGURE 10.19

Ride Safe Template

Volume 5, Issue 1 • June 1997

Bicycle and In-Line Skating Safety for the 90s •

IN-LINE SKATING—FASTEST GROWING SPORT

Injuries Up Dramatically

by Mary Beth Luhrsen

Last year, the Consumer Product Safety Commission (CPSC) released some alarming news on in-line skating, now the fastest growing recreational sport in America. They projected 83,000 serious injuries in 1997, more than double those of 1996. Even more alarming is the fact that children under age 15 account for 60% of these injuries.

Chapter Summary

- Newsletter elements divide the newsletter into organized sections to help the reader understand the text. Basic newsletter elements include: nameplate, subtitle, folio, headline, subhead, byline, and body copy.
- Focus and balance can be achieved in a newsletter through the design and size of the nameplate, through the use of graphic images, or through careful use of lines, borders, and backgrounds.
- The margin size for a newsletter is linked to the number of columns needed, the formality desired, the visual elements used, and the amount of text available. Keep margins consistent in a newsletter.
- The line length of text in a newsletter can enhance or detract from the readability of text.
- Section breaks are used to vary the page layout within a single newsletter.
- Typesetters and professional designers measure horizontal space on a page using *picas.* A *pica* is equal to 12 points. One inch is equal to 6 picas.
- The underlying grid of a newsletter must remain consistent from page to page.
- Setting text in columns may improve the readability of newsletters.
- By default, column formatting is applied to the whole document.
- Change to Page Layout viewing mode to view columns as they will appear when printed.
- Word automatically lines up (balances) the last line of text at the bottom of each column. The last page of columns can be balanced by inserting a continuous section break at the end of the text.
- A challenge in creating a newsletter is how to balance change with consistency. Styles assist in maintaining consistency in recurring elements.
- When formatting instructions contained within a style are changed, all the text to which the style has been applied is automatically updated.
- Styles are created for a particular document and are saved with the document.
- A style can be applied using the Style button on the Formatting toolbar or the Style dialog box.
- Word's default leading is equal to approximately 120% of the type size used.
- Headlines and subheads should have more leading above than below.
- Set tabs in a typeset document by em spaces rather than inch measurements.
- An em space is a space as wide as the point size of the type.

Commands Review

Columns dialog box	Format, Columns; or double-click the Columns button on the Standard toolbar
Character Spacing dialog box	Format, Font, Character Spacing tab

Kerning	Format, Font, Character Spacing tab
Insert a column break	Insert, Break, Column Break; or Ctrl + Shift + Enter
Insert a section break	Insert, Break, Continuous
Leading	Format, Paragraph, Indents and Spacing tab, Spacing—Before and After
Style dialog box	Format, Style
Widow/orphan	Format, Paragraph, Text Flow
Windows Paint program	Start, Program, Accessories, Paint

Check Your Understanding

True/False: Circle the letter T if the statement is true; circle the letter F if the statement is false.

T F 1. A folio provides information that describes the purpose of the newsletter and/or the intended audience of the newsletter.

T F 2. Column formatting affects the entire document unless your document is divided into sections.

T F 3. Columns are separated by a default setting of 0.25 inches of space.

T F 4. A line length of 4 inches measures 28 picas.

T F 5. A guideline in typesetting is that line length measured in picas does not exceed two times the point size used in the body text of a newsletter.

T F 6. An em space indentation can be created at the Tabs dialog box and keyed in a point or inch increment.

T F 7. Extra leading can make a page look less gray.

T F 8. If a headline contains two lines both keyed in 36 points, the default spacing between the two lines (leading) should be increased to improve readability.

T F 9. One advantage of using styles in formatting a newsletter is that when formatting within a style is changed, the text to which it has been applied changes also.

T F 10. Once a style has been created, the only way to change the style is to rename it and create it again.

Terms: In the space provided, indicate the correct term, command, or number.

1. To create newspaper columns that are approximately equal or balanced, insert a ____________________ at the end of the text.
2. To divide different styles of columns in a document, divide the document into these ____________________.
3. Insert this (or these) into a document to control where columns end and begin on the page. ____________________
4. To insert a vertical line between columns, choose this at the Columns dialog box. ____________________
5. To set a tab at 2 em spaces in a newsletter set in 14-point Times New Roman, key this measurement at the Tabs Set dialog box: ____________________.
6. A set of formatting instructions that are saved with a name and can be used over and over are called a ____________________.

7. If you create a multipage newsletter with facing pages, you may want to use Word's ______________________________ margin feature, which accommodates wider inside or outside margins.
8. Avoid ______________________________, which occurs when headings display side by side in adjacent columns in a newsletter.
9. Word's ______________________________ feature prevents the first and last lines of paragraphs from being separated across pages; this feature is on by default.
10. The ______________________________ identifies the author of an article in a newsletter.

Skill Assessments

Assessment 1

1. Design and create two nameplates (including subtitle, folio, graphics, etc.) for two newsletters for organizations, schools, or a neighborhood to which you belong (real or fictional). Prepare thumbnail sketches of your designs and attach them to the back of your nameplates. Prepare one nameplate using an asymmetrical design. Also, include a graphic image, scanned image, or special character symbol in at least one of the nameplates.
2. Save and name the documents c10sa01a, nameplate and c10sa01b, nameplate.
3. Print and then close c10sa01a, nameplate and c10sa01b, nameplate.

Assessment 2

Your neighbor knows you are taking a desktop publishing class, and she would like you to help her create a family newsletter for the holidays. You are a person who cannot say no. Assume you designed the newsletter shown in figure 10.21, but you forgot to create styles and save it as a template. You know she will ask again next year, so you are going to recreate the newsletter and include styles for all future issues.

1. At a clear window, create the Law family newsletter in figure 10.21 by completing the following steps:
   a. Change the top, bottom, left, and right margins to 0.5 (or as close to 0.5 inches as your printer definition will allow).
   b. Turn on Kerning at 14 points.
   c. Change to the Page Layout viewing mode.
   d. Change the Zoom Control to 75%.
   e. Create the rotated nameplate by completing the following steps:
      (1) Choose Insert, then Object.
      (2) At the Object dialog box with the Create New tab selected, double-click Microsoft WordArt 3.0 (2.0).
      (3) Key **The Law Family Newsletter** in the text entry box.
      (4) Choose Update Display.
      (5) Change the font to 44-point Garamond Bold Italic.
      (6) Click the Special Effects button.
      (7) At the Special Effects dialog box, rotate the text 90 degrees.
      (8) Click the Shading button.
      (9) Change the Foreground color to White/Black and the Background color to White. Choose OK or press Enter.
      (10) Click in the document screen outside the text entry box to remove the text entry box.
   f. Select the WordArt text.
   g. Insert a Frame around the WordArt text.

h. Size the WordArt image in the size section of the Picture dialog box. Key or select **1** inch in the Width text box and **9.5** inches in the Height text box.

i. Create a text box approximately 0.75 inches square at the top of the WordArt image. Insert the snowflake symbol in the text box. This symbol is located in the third row and the thirteenth column of the Monotype Sorts font. Be sure to change the fill to Black and the font color to White. Copy this box and its contents to the bottom of the rotated text.

j. Click the Line button on the Drawing toolbar and draw a 3-point red vertical line to the right of the rotated text.

k. Create the headline by completing the following steps:
   (1) Choose Format, then Paragraph.
   (2) At the Paragraph dialog box, select the Indents and Spacing tab.
   (3) Change the Left Indentation to 1.25 inches.
   (4) Select or key **14 pt** in the Before text box in the Spacing section.
   (5) Choose OK or press Enter.
   (6) Change the font to 40-point Garamond.
   (7) Key **1996 ❄ A Year in Review**. (Use the same symbol as in step i.)
   (8) Create a style to format the headline by completing the following steps:
      (a) Position the insertion point in the headline.
      (b) Click in the Style box on the Formatting toolbar to select the current name.
      (c) Key **Family Headline** and press Enter.
   (9) Draw a 3-point Red line as shown in figure 10.20. (Use the Line button on the Drawing toolbar.)
   (10) Press Enter.

l. Insert a continuous section break.

m. Create two newspaper columns with the following specifications:
   (1) The Equal Column Width option is checked to indicate it is on.
   (2) Two columns have been selected.
   (3) The column Width is 2.73 inches.
   (4) The Spacing between columns is 0.3 inches.
   (5) At the Apply To: section, *This Section* is selected.
   (6) Choose OK or press Enter.

n. Insert the picture, *Dancers*, in the first column as shown in figure 10.20.

o. The picture should be sized to approximately 1.90 inches in Height and 1.44 inches in Width.

p. Center the picture in the middle of the first column.

q. Frame the picture and create a double red border.

r. Make sure the font defaults to 12-point Times New Roman, turn on bold, then center, and key **New Year's Eve 1996**.

s. Press Enter.

t. Choose Insert, then File.

u. Insert *Family Newsletter Text* from your student data disk.

v. Format the body text and create a body text style by completing the following steps:
   (1) Select the text in the columns, then change the font to 11-point Times New Roman.
   (2) With the text still selected, change the paragraph indentations to 2 em spaces (approximately 0.25 inches).
   (3) With the text still selected, create a style to format the body text and name it Family Body Text.

w. Create a drop cap for the first letter in the first paragraph of the newsletter. Choose Dropped in the Position section and select three lines as the number of Lines to Drop.

x. Insert the *Jet, Realest,* and *Divider 2* pictures as shown in figure 10.20.
y. Center, then change the last three lines to Brush Script MT in 20, 16, and 14 points, respectively.

2. Save the document and name it c10sa02, family newsletter.
3. Print and then close c10sa02, family newsletter.
4. Save the newsletter as a template at the publications tab.

FIGURE 10.20

The Law Family Newsletter

1996 ❄ A Year in Review

New Year's Eve 1996

We could have danced all night… and we did; what a way to kick off a new year. Now with the end of 1996 in sight and the holidays just around the corner, we have to wonder where 1996 has gone. Here are a few highlights of our year…

Emily will be 12 in January and now attends Junior High. She is a wonderful young lady and a great source of joy in our lives. We've had so much fun watching her grow from a little girl to a pre-teen—girl-friends coming over (and Mom taking them T.P.ing and participating a little, too), the phone ringing and it is always for her, crushes on a different boy every week—it doesn't seem that long ago that I was doing those things. It sure keeps us going and there never seems to be a dull or quiet moment—and if there is one (on a very rare occasion) you can bet you'll hear Grant yelling, "Mom, where are you?"

Grant is now 7 and he is a character. He is a typical little brother, bugging and teasing Emily and her friends. He really is a lively child and keeps us laughing with his performances. I don't know who is the bigger kid, Grant or Mike—they are forever pulling jokes on Mom.

We took a much needed vacation to Disney World and had an absolutely wonderful time. Mike (I think it was the accountant in him) had an agenda for us everyday and he took a lot of teasing from us about that—we wanted to buy him a clipboard and whistle!

Mike turned the big "40" this year. We had a great time surprising him with a 40th party celebrated by family and friends. Mike will be with Crowe 16 years this January. He has always enjoyed his work and he works with a great group of people. Mike is also our precinct Committeeman. He worked very hard on the fall campaign. The children were very involved in organizing and passing out literature, watching the debates, and learning about the election process.

Things have changed for Debbie with both the children in school full time. For those of you who knew me at Purdue you will be surprised (maybe shocked is a better word) that I am taking a real estate class at the local community college—and believe it or not I am not skipping classes.

Please let us know how you are doing. We think of our family and friends so often—we cherish the times we've shared with you and thank you for the wonderful memories—the best gift one could give another.

Happy Holidays

The Laws

Mike, Debbie, Emily, & Grant

Assessment 3

You are working in the office of a computer software company and have been asked to create the company's monthly newsletter. You recently replaced the individual who previously created the newsletters. You found handwritten specifications on a copy, which should help you get started with the task. Complete the following steps:

1. Complete the newsletter shown in figure 10.21 according to the specifications written on the front of the publication. Insert *Computer Newsletter Text* from your student data disk.
2. Use your knowledge of leading, character spacing, and type sizes to assist you in making the copy fit on a page.
3. Save the newsletter and name it c10sa03, computer newsletter.
4. Print and then close c10sa03, computer newsletter.

FIGURE 10.21

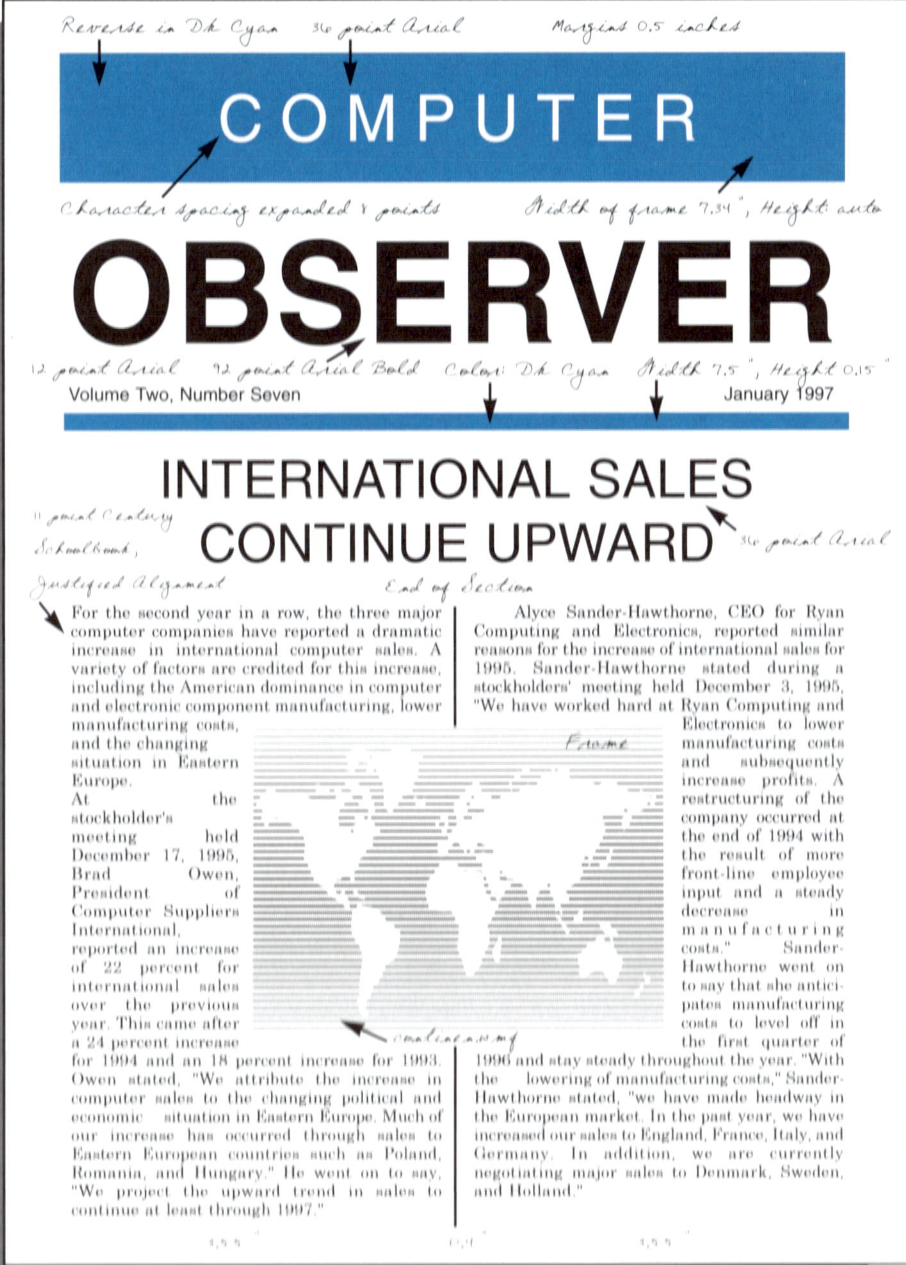

Reverse in Dk Cyan — 36 point Arial — Margins 0.5 inches

COMPUTER

Character spacing expanded 8 points — Width of frame 7.34", Height auto

OBSERVER

12 point Arial — 92 point Arial Bold — Color: Dk Cyan — Width 7.5", Height 0.15"

Volume Two, Number Seven — January 1997

INTERNATIONAL SALES CONTINUE UPWARD

11 point Century Schoolbook, Justified Alignment — End of Section — 36 point Arial

For the second year in a row, the three major computer companies have reported a dramatic increase in international computer sales. A variety of factors are credited for this increase, including the American dominance in computer and electronic component manufacturing, lower manufacturing costs, and the changing situation in Eastern Europe.

At the stockholder's meeting held December 17, 1995, Brad Owen, President of Computer Suppliers International, reported an increase of 22 percent for international sales over the previous year. This came after a 24 percent increase for 1994 and an 18 percent increase for 1993. Owen stated, "We attribute the increase in computer sales to the changing political and economic situation in Eastern Europe. Much of our increase has occurred through sales to Eastern European countries such as Poland, Romania, and Hungary." He went on to say, "We project the upward trend in sales to continue at least through 1997."

Alyce Sander-Hawthorne, CEO for Ryan Computing and Electronics, reported similar reasons for the increase of international sales for 1995. Sander-Hawthorne stated during a stockholders' meeting held December 3, 1995, "We have worked hard at Ryan Computing and Electronics to lower manufacturing costs and subsequently increase profits. A restructuring of the company occurred at the end of 1994 with the result of more front-line employee input and a steady decrease in manufacturing costs." Sander-Hawthorne went on to say that she anticipates manufacturing costs to level off in the first quarter of 1996 and stay steady throughout the year. "With the lowering of manufacturing costs," Sander-Hawthorne stated, "we have made headway in the European market. In the past year, we have increased our sales to England, France, Italy, and Germany. In addition, we are currently negotiating major sales to Denmark, Sweden, and Holland."

Frame

Optional: Apply AutoFormat to the newsletter created in c10sa03. Print the results of this method of formatting. Compare the automatically formatted document to the document you formatted in c10sa03. Write a short evaluation discussing likes and dislikes of each approach. Attach the evaluation to the back of the automatically formatted newsletter.

Assessment 4

Open and then print a copy of *Butterfield Gardens* from your student data disk. Assume you received this newsletter in the mail as a marketing device. The newsletter looks relatively neat and organized, but with closer inspection, you notice there are a few errors in spelling, formatting, and design and layout. Recreate the newsletter according to the following specifications:

1. Recreate the nameplate or create a nameplate (logo, subtitle, folio) of your own for this company.
2. Create a different design and layout for the newsletter using newspaper columns; use more than one column.
3. Prepare a thumbnail sketch of your design.
4. Correct all spelling and formatting errors.
5. You may use any graphics or scanned images that seem appropriate.
6. Create the recycling icon by inserting the Word picture, *Recycle*. Reduce the image by dragging the sizing handle in the lower right corner inward. Frame the image for ease in moving.
7. Use any newsletter elements and enhancements that improve the effectiveness and appeal of this newsletter.
8. Save and name your publication c10sa04, butterfield gardens.
9. Print and then close c10sa04, butterfield gardens. Attach the thumbnail sketch to the back of the newsletter.

Creative Activity

1. Bring in an example of a newsletter you may have collected, received in the mail, picked up at a local business, or received from an organization of which you are a member. Use the *Document Evaluation Checklist* (*document evaluation checklist.doc*) to evaluate the newsletter. Revise this newsletter using a completely different layout and design. Incorporate your own ideas and use graphics or scanned images if available. Remember to use consistent elements throughout the document. Create your own styles or use the system styles included in Word to aid in formatting your document. You may want to include this revision in your portfolio along with the original.
2. Save and name your publication c10ca01, newsletter.
3. Print and then close c10ca01. Attach the *Document Evaluation Checklist* and the original document to the back of your revised version.

Optional: Draw a thumbnail sketch of a different nameplate for this publication. Include the folio and subtitle in the sketch. Add specifications as to which typeface, colors, clip art, etc. should be used in this design.

11 INCORPORATING NEWSLETTER DESIGN ELEMENTS

PERFORMANCE OBJECTIVE

Upon successful completion of chapter 11, you will be able to define, create, and incorporate additional design elements into newsletters, such as headers/footers, tables of contents, mastheads, sidebars, pull quotes, kickers, end signs, jump lines, captions, and color.

DESKTOP PUBLISHING CONCEPTS

Spot color	Pull quotes	Adding graphics, illustrations, and photos
Headers/footers	Kickers	Mastheads
Sidebars	End signs	Captions
Tables of contents	Jump lines	Copy fitting

WORD FEATURES USED

Newsletter Wizard	Picture	Line spacing
Templates	Framed text	Character spacing
Newspaper columns	Borders and shading	AutoCaption
Headers/footers	Styles	Color
Special characters symbols	Paragraph spacing	Picture

Chapter 10 introduced you to the basic elements of a newsletter. Additional elements can be used to enhance the visual impact of a newsletter and to provide the reader with clues to the newsletter content. Newsletter enhancing elements, such as tables of contents, headers/footers, mastheads, pull quotes, kickers, sidebars, captions, ruled lines, jump lines, graphics, illustrations, photos, and end signs are discussed in this chapter.

Adding Visually Enhancing Elements To A Newsletter

The most effective newsletters contain an appealing blend of text and visual elements. As illustrated in figure 11.1, visual elements, such as a table of contents, pull quote, kicker, and sidebar, can be used as focal points to tempt the intended audience into reading more than just the nameplate. Visual elements such as headings, subheadings, tables of contents, headers/ footers, ruled lines, jump lines, and end signs can be used to indicate the directional flow of information in the document. Visual elements such as headings, subheadings, headers/footers, pull quotes, sidebars, and page borders can be used to provide balance, proportion, and contrast in a newsletter. All of these elements, if used in a consistent format and manner, can create unity within a single newsletter and among different issues of a newsletter.

FIGURE 11.1

Visually Enhancing Design Elements

From the Desktop

Volume 2, No.5 November 1997

SIDEBAR

Mark Your Calendar:

WORKSHOP:

Desktop Publishing Using Microsoft Word 7.0 for Windows 95

This workshop will help you learn how your students can meet today's demand for desktop publishing skills on the job using Word 7.0 for Windows 95.

PRESENTER:
Nancy Stanko, College of DuPage

WHEN:
Thursday, December 19, 1996
1–4 p.m.

WHERE:
Okemos Community College
Room 3067
2040 Mount Hope Road
Okemos, MI 47851

COST:
$50—includes materials and disk

To reserve your place, call:
(800) 555-6018

TABLE OF CONTENTS

What's Inside:

Two ways to learn: — KICKER

Training Techniques

Two types of training are available for those just beginning in desktop publishing.

The first type is a content-based program. This program is based on a typical college program and the information is presented in a classroom situation. Instructional books and videos are frequently utilized.

Skill-based training is another type of training. This training is useful to businesses because skill-based training produces capable people quickly. Productive skills are put to use on the type of job the person will be expected to fulfill.

Both types of training can produce workers with equal productivity and confidence. The best equipment is wasted if people are not trained to use it efficiently. Good training, regardless of which type, is essential to desktop publishing. ❑ — END SIGN

Knowledge Is Power!

How can one have the up-to-date knowledge needed to keep on the cutting edge of desktop publishing? One way to gain desktop publishing knowledge is to read, read, read! Read some of the periodicals, newsletters, and books now available that address all aspects of desktop publishing.

Two basic types of periodicals are available. The first type is based on technological development and communication arts. These periodicals contain useful information about current and new products. The second type contains knowledge of technique, style, and applications.

PULL QUOTE

One way to gain more desktop publishing knowledge is to read, read, read!

Some worthwhile desktop publishing resources to consider include the following:

Inside Microsoft® Word 95 by the Cobb Group is a monthly publication including helpful tips and techniques for using Microsoft Word for Windows 95 to create everyday applications.

Working Smarter with Microsoft® Word—Your OneOnOne Guide to Better Word Processing is an excellent bimonthly newsletter, which includes sections on Quick Tips, Help Desk question and answers, Test Your PC I.Q., and Instant Tutorial, as well as helpful articles on how to use Word efficiently in day-to-day applications.

JUMP LINE — (continued on page 2)

FOOTER — From the Desktop

Using the Newsletter Wizard

In addition to a newsletter template, Word also provides a newsletter wizard. This wizard, named *Newsletter Wizard.wiz*, offers two other newsletter template choices—*Classic* and *Modern*—which you may preview at the Newsletter Wizard dialog box. Other selections offered by the Newsletter Wizard include the number of columns desired, the name of the newsletter, and the number of pages. The wizard also offers you the option of including a table of contents, the date, the volume and issue number, and fancy first letters (drop caps for the first paragraph of an article). Any selections you make can always be edited at a later date. For example, if you selected four pages as the length of your newsletter and then later realize that your newsletter is only going to be two pages in length, you can easily delete the extra pages.

In exercise 1, you will create the first page of a newsletter using the *Newsletter Wizard.wiz* and the *Modern* template. The Modern template is already formatted to include styles for headlines and body text. If you instructed the Newsletter Wizard to include a table of contents, a large table of contents (created in a Word table) appears in the lower right corner of the first page. This template also includes a graphic image and a text box for a caption. The title of the newsletter is automatically filled in from information keyed at the Newsletter Wizard dialog box. You will insert article text, apply existing styles, and customize the template document by replacing the picture and changing type size.

Remember, a predefined template is often a perfect starting place for the creation of a document. Once the template framework is displayed on the screen, it becomes a Word document. You can customize it any way you want. You can then save and name it as a regular Word document, or you can save it as a new template document.

Creating a Newsletter Using the Newsletter Wizard

1. At a clear screen, create the first page of a newsletter, as shown in figure 11.2, by completing the following steps:
   a. Use the Newsletter Wizard to help you make the newsletter by completing the following steps:
      (1) Choose File, New, and then select the Publications tab.
      (2) Double-click the Newsletter Wizard.wiz icon.
      (3) In the Newsletter Wizard dialog boxes that display, make the following choices:

Template style	=	Modern
Page layout	=	Two columns
Newsletter name	=	From the Desktop
Newsletter length	=	1 page
Items to include:	=	Table of Contents
	=	Date
	=	Volume and Issue

      (4) Click Finish when done.
   b. Change to the Page Layout viewing mode, change the Zoom Control to 75%, and then turn on the display of nonprinting characters.
   c. Change the text in the folio by completing the following steps:
      (1) Position the insertion point in the reverse text folio.
      (2) Select the month and year and key the current month and year.
      (3) Select the volume number and key **2.3**.
   d. Click in the topic text box in the first column (contains the word TOPIC), select TOPIC, and then key **DESKTOP RESOURCES**.

e. Insert and format the first article headline by completing the following steps:
   (1) Select *Your Headline* and key **Knowledge Is Power**.
   (2) To create a one-line headline, select *Knowledge Is Power* and change the type size to 22 points.
f. Insert the first newsletter article by completing the following steps:
   (1) Select the text *Replace this text with text . . .* and delete it.
   (2) Insert the file *knowledge text,* located on your student data disk.
   (3) Select the text just inserted and apply the *Body Text* style from the Style list box located on the Formatting toolbar.
g. Replace the existing graphic of two people and a map with a more appropriate graphic by completing the following steps:
   (1) Position the arrow pointer inside the image and click once to select it.
   (2) Choose Insert, then Picture.
   (3) Double-click *Computer,* located in the Name list box.
h. Size the picture by completing the following steps:
   (1) Select the picture and choose Format, then Picture.
   (2) In the Size section of the Picture dialog box, change the Width to 2.16 inches and the Height to 1.85 inches.
   (3) Click OK or press Enter.
i. Size the frame to match the size of the picture and then position the frame by completing the following steps: (Matching the frame size to the picture size makes it easier to position the picture correctly.)
   (1) Select the frame and choose Format, then Frame.
   (2) In the Size section of the Frame dialog box, change the Width to Exactly 2.16 inches and the Height to Exactly 1.85 inches.
   (3) In the Horizontal section, change the Position to 5 inches Relative To: Page.
   (4) In the Vertical section, change the Position to 3 inches Relative To: Page.
   (5) Click OK or press Enter.
j. Position the caption text box by completing the following steps:
   (1) Select the text box that displays *YOUR CAPTION* and choose Format, Drawing Object, then select the Size and Position tab.
   (2) In the Position section of the Drawing Object dialog box, change the Horizontal position to 5.05 inches From: Page and the Vertical position to 4.96 inches From: Page.
   (3) Click OK or press Enter.
k. Select *YOUR CAPTION* in the text box and then key **KNOWLEDGE AND TRAINING**.
l. Click once immediately below the text box to position the insertion point and then insert the file *training text* located on your student data disk.
m. Format the second article by completing the following steps:
   (1) Position the insertion point anywhere within the heading *Training Techniques* and apply the *Headline* style.
   (2) Select *Training Techniques* and change the font to 22 points. (If too much white space exists above the heading, position the insertion point to the left of *Training Techniques* and press the Backspace key one time.)
   (3) Select the article text and apply the *Body Text* style.
n. Insert the table of contents text by completing the following steps:
   (1) Position the insertion point in the second row, second column (to the right of number 1) of the Word table that contains the table of contents.
   (2) Key **Knowledge Is Power**.
   (3) Position the insertion point in the third row, second column and key **Training Techniques**.

(4) Position the insertion point in the fourth row, second column and key **Newsletter Tips and Tricks**.

(5) Position the insertion point in the fifth row, second column and key **How to Save Time**.

(6) If a number five in a circle displays in the table of contents, position the insertion point to the left of the circle until the insertion point turns into a right-pointing arrow and click once to select the circle and number. Press Delete.

o. Position the insertion point at the top of the second page. Select from this point to the end of the newsletter and press Delete to delete the second page. Only the first page of the newsletter will be created in this exercise.

2. Save and name the newsletter c11ex01, desktop.
3. Print and then close c11ex01, desktop.

FIGURE 11.2

October '96 **Volume 2.3**

From the Desktop

DESKTOP RESOURCES

Knowledge Is Power

How can one have the up-to-date knowledge needed to keep on the cutting edge of desktop publishing? One way to gain desktop publishing knowledge is to read, read, read! Read some of the periodicals, newsletters, and books now available that address all aspects of desktop publishing.

Two basic types of periodicals are available. The first type is based on technological development and communication arts. These periodicals contain useful information about current and new products. The second type contains knowledge of technique, style, and applications.

Many newsletters and books are available. Your local library and bookstores can be good sources for resource material. Listed below are some newsletters and books that can help you as a desktop publisher.

Inside Microsoft®Word 95 by the Cobb Group is a monthly publication including helpful tips and techniques for using Microsoft Word for Windows 95 to create everyday applications.

Working Smarter with Microsoft® Word—Your OneOnOne Guide to Better Word Processing is an excellent bimonthly newsletter, which includes sections on Quick Tips, Help Desk questions and answers, Test Your PC I.Q., and Instant Tutorial, as well as helpful articles on how to use Word efficiently in day-to-day applications.

Publish is a monthly magazine with information of interest to those involved in all areas of print and multimedia productions. The focus is on print design and production and addresses emerging technologies.

PC Publishing covers information on desktop publishing and presentation graphics for those using IBM and compatibles. Each issue addresses specific subjects with in-depth discussion.

Desktop Communications covers hardware/ software, design, typography, and useful tips. Industry professionals provide extensive knowledge from their experience.

Before and After, a bimonthly newsletter, gives down-to-earth advice about graphic design and desktop typography.

Newsletters from the Desktop by Roger C. Parker has tips on saving time and money on design and layout.

The Makeover Book has 101 design solutions for desktop publishers. "Before" and "after" examples are given to show how to make your documents more interesting and persuasive.

KNOWLEDGE AND TRAINING

Training Techniques

Two types of training are available for those just beginning in desktop publishing.

The first type is a content-based program. This program is based on a typical college program and the information is presented in a classroom situation. Instructional books and videos are frequently utilized.

Skill-based training is another type of training. This training is useful to businesses because skill-based training produces capable people quickly. Productive skills are put to use on the type of job the person will be expected to fulfill.

Both types of training can produce workers with equal productivity and confidence. The best equipment is wasted if people are not trained to use it efficiently. Good training, regardless of which type, is essential to desktop publishing.

INSIDE

The newsletter created in exercise 1 uses a symmetrical nameplate and page layout. The table of contents is located in the bottom right corner of the page. It is easily identified since the type size used is so large, in addition to the table size and the gray-shaded background. This is definitely a more contemporary design and may not appeal to everyone. Remember, if a part of a template does not meet your needs, you can always customize it to your liking.

Using Spot Color

Spot Color: Using another color, in addition to black, as an accent color in a publication.

Spot color refers to using one other color, in addition to black, as an accent color in a publication. The more colors used in a publication, the more expensive it is to produce. Using spot color can be an inexpensive way to make a black-and-white publication more appealing. If you have a color printer, you can see the results of using a second color immediately. You can then take the newsletter to be professionally printed on high-quality paper.

Spot color can be applied to such elements as graphic lines, graphic images, borders, backgrounds, headings, special characters, and end signs. If your logo or organizational seal contains a particular color, use that color as a unifying element throughout your publication. Just as an all black-and-white page may have a gray look to it, using too much spot color can give the appearance of all one color, which defeats the purpose of using additional color. Variations of the spot color used can be obtained by *screening*, or producing a lighter shade of the same color. You can also apply spot color to the background in a reverse text box or to a drop cap. Refer to the two newsletter samples in figure 11.3 to see how spot color can really add to the visual appeal of a publication.

Screening: Decreasing the intensity of a color to produce a lighter shade.

In exercises 1 through 10, you will build a two-page newsletter, as shown in figure 11.18, adding visual enhancements as you proceed. In addition, you will use copy-fitting techniques and add spot color to the newsletter throughout the range of exercises.

FIGURE 11.3

Newsletter with and without Spot Color

Volume 5, Issue 2 • September 1997

RIDE SAFE

Bicycle and In-Line Skating Safety for the 90s •

In the **Helmet Habit**

"I don't quite know why my daughter, Kate, fell from her bike last July. Maybe she hit a small rock or just lost her balance. We found Kate lying on the ground. She was bleeding and had several cuts and bruises on her face and forehead. We called the paramedics and she began to lose consciousness just as they arrived. At the emergency room, we found out that Kate had a broken nose, a missing tooth, and four other loose teeth. Fortunately for all of us, Kate was wearing a bicycle helmet. Without even asking, three different doctors have told us that the helmet probably saved Kate's life. So many people tell me that their kids won't wear a helmet. I tell them to be firm—no helmet, no bike. Bicycle accidents can happen to anyone!"

Karen Brust
Boston, Massachusetts

In This Issue:

BICYCLE SAFETY: LET'S MAKE IT A PRIORITY!

Protect your child!

Did you know that each year over 1,200 people die and thousands more are seriously injured in bicycle accidents? According to the American Academy of Pediatrics, more than 500,000 emergency room visits annually in the U.S. are attributed to bicycle accidents.

Surprisingly, most of these accidents, especially those involving children, occur on quiet residential streets. Most do not involve cars. And many could be prevented with proper training and safety equipment.

Think about it. Before we're allowed to drive a car, we have to be a certain age and go through extensive training and testing. Yet many of us—children in particular—ride the very same roads on a bicycle with little or no training at all. Kids are especially vulnerable because of their undeveloped peripheral vision (about two-thirds that of adults), poor speed judgment, and lack of a sense of danger.

More than 500,000 trips are made to emergency rooms each year for bicycle-related injuries.

At Ride Safe, we believe bicycle safety education is crucial to our well-being and to that of our children. More and more states, including New York, New Jersey, Connecticut, Georgia, Tennessee, Oregon, and California are implementing legislation requiring bicycle helmets for children. As adults, we can teach our children safe riding habits, protect them from injury by purchasing bicycle helmets, and set a good example when we are riding our own bicycles.

The bottom line? *Bicycle safety is something we all need to make a priority!*

"ACCIDENTS" WAITING TO HAPPEN

The majority of bicycle/car "accidents" are not really accidents, but avoidable collisions. Most result from the bicyclist's failure to use proper riding techniques in a hazardous situation. Ironically, when asked, most children injured in traffic could describe the actual law they broke.

(continued on page 2)

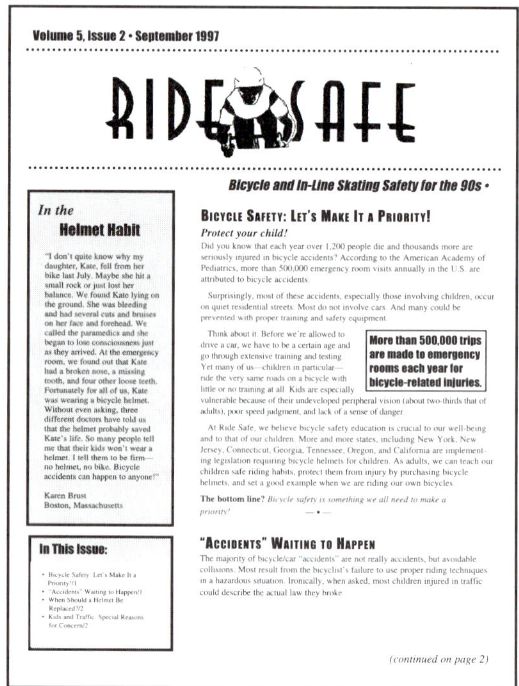

Volume 5, Issue 2 • September 1997

RIDE SAFE

Bicycle and In-Line Skating Safety for the 90s •

In the **Helmet Habit**

"I don't quite know why my daughter, Kate, fell from her bike last July. Maybe she hit a small rock or just lost her balance. We found Kate lying on the ground. She was bleeding and had several cuts and bruises on her face and forehead. We called the paramedics and she began to lose consciousness just as they arrived. At the emergency room, we found out that Kate had a broken nose, a missing tooth, and four other loose teeth. Fortunately for all of us, Kate was wearing a bicycle helmet. Without even asking, three different doctors have told us that the helmet probably saved Kate's life. So many people tell me that their kids won't wear a helmet. I tell them to be firm—no helmet, no bike. Bicycle accidents can happen to anyone!"

Karen Brust
Boston, Massachusetts

In This Issue:

- Bicycle Safety: Let's Make It a Priority!/1
- "Accidents" Waiting to Happen/1
- When Should a Helmet Be Replaced?/2
- Kids and Traffic: Special Reasons for Concern/2

BICYCLE SAFETY: LET'S MAKE IT A PRIORITY!

Protect your child!

Did you know that each year over 1,200 people die and thousands more are seriously injured in bicycle accidents? According to the American Academy of Pediatrics, more than 500,000 emergency room visits annually in the U.S. are attributed to bicycle accidents.

Surprisingly, most of these accidents, especially those involving children, occur on quiet residential streets. Most do not involve cars. And many could be prevented with proper training and safety equipment.

Think about it. Before we're allowed to drive a car, we have to be a certain age and go through extensive training and testing. Yet many of us—children in particular—ride the very same roads on a bicycle with little or no training at all. Kids are especially vulnerable because of their undeveloped peripheral vision (about two-thirds that of adults), poor speed judgment, and lack of a sense of danger.

More than 500,000 trips are made to emergency rooms each year for bicycle-related injuries.

At Ride Safe, we believe bicycle safety education is crucial to our well-being and to that of our children. More and more states, including New York, New Jersey, Connecticut, Georgia, Tennessee, Oregon, and California are implementing legislation requiring bicycle helmets for children. As adults, we can teach our children safe riding habits, protect them from injury by purchasing bicycle helmets, and set a good example when we are riding our own bicycles.

The bottom line? *Bicycle safety is something we all need to make a priority!*

"ACCIDENTS" WAITING TO HAPPEN

The majority of bicycle/car "accidents" are not really accidents, but avoidable collisions. Most result from the bicyclist's failure to use proper riding techniques in a hazardous situation. Ironically, when asked, most children injured in traffic could describe the actual law they broke.

(continued on page 2)

Creating Headers and Footers for a Newsletter

Headers and/or footers are commonly used in newsletters, manuscripts, textbooks, reports, and other publications. The term *header* refers to text that is repeated at the top of every page. Alternately, the term *footer* refers to text that appears at the bottom of every page. In figure 11.1, a horizontal, gray-shaded, ruled line and a small version of the nameplate text are included in a footer at the bottom of the page. In a newsletter, information such as page number, the name of the newsletter, the issue or date of the newsletter, and the name of the organization producing the newsletter are often included in a header or footer as illustrated in the header and footer examples in figure 11.4.

Header: Text repeated at the top of every page.

Footer: Text repeated at the bottom of every page.

TRAINING NEWS

Header Example

FINANCIAL SPOTLIGHT NOVEMBER 1997

Header Example

Winners wear helmets!

Header Example

Footer Example

Page 2 ***Fly with Sunshine Air***

Footer Example

Community News 3

Footer Example

3

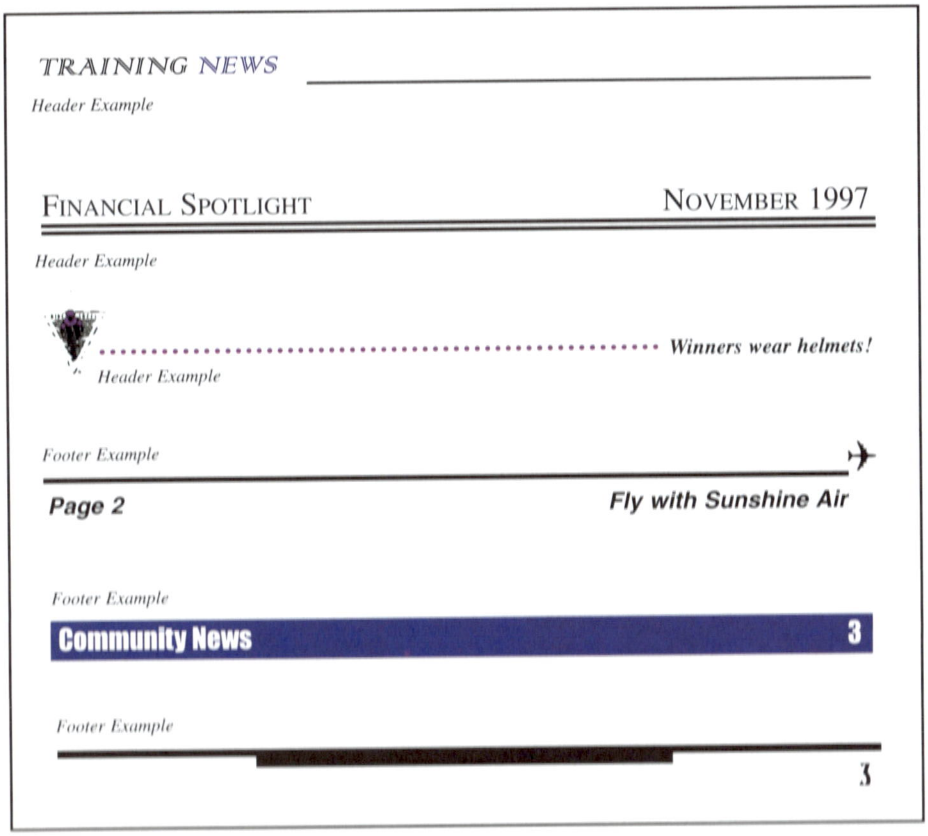

FIGURE 11.4

Examples of Headers and Footers

Since a header or footer is commonly repeated on every page starting with the second page, it provides the perfect place to reinforce the identity of a company or organization. For example, including the company or organization name, a very small version of the nameplate, or a logo in a header or footer can increase a reader's awareness of your identity. In figure 11.4 the Ride Safe header includes both the company logo and their slogan, while the Community News footer includes the newsletter name and the page number.

Headers or footers, consistently formatted, help to establish unity among the pages of a newsletter, as well as among different issues of a newsletter. In addition, they serve as landmarks for the reader, adding to the directional flow of the document.

Horizontal ruled lines are frequently placed in headers or footers. These serve as a visually contrasting element that clearly identifies the top or bottom of each page. Different effects can be achieved by varying the weight (thickness) of the line, the number of lines, and the arrangement of the lines.

DTP POINTERS

- Use a header or footer to reinforce company identity.
- Consistent formatting of a header/footer helps to establish unity in a publication.

To create a header or footer, you would complete the following steps:

1. Choose View, then Header and Footer.
2. Key the desired header text in the header pane. If you are creating a footer, click the Switch Between Header and Footer button on the Header and Footer toolbar, then key the desired footer text in the footer pane.
3. Click Close on the Header and Footer toolbar.

When you access the header and footer feature, Word automatically changes the viewing mode to Page Layout and your document text is dimmed in the background. After you insert text in the header and/or footer pane and then click Close on the Header and Footer toolbar, the document text is displayed in black and the header and/or footer is dimmed. If the Normal viewing mode was selected before the header and/or footer was created, you are returned to the Normal viewing mode. In the Normal viewing mode, a header or footer does not display on the screen. Change to Page Layout viewing mode to view the header or footer text dimmed, or use Print Preview to view how a header and/or footer will print.

Placing Headers/Footers on Different Pages

By default, Word will insert a header or footer on every page in the document. You can create different headers and footers in a document. For example, you can do the following:

- create a unique header or footer on the first page;
- omit a header or footer on the first page;
- create different headers or footers for odd and even pages; or
- create different headers or footers for sections in a document.

A different header or footer can be created on the first page of a document. To do this, position the insertion point anywhere in the first page, choose View, then Header and Footer. (If you are creating a footer, click the Switch Between Header and Footer button.) Click the Page Setup button on the Header and Footer toolbar. Make sure the Layout tab is selected, choose Different First Page, then choose OK or press Enter. Key the desired text for the first page header or footer. Click the Show Next button on the Header and Footer toolbar to open another header or footer pane. Key the text for the other header or footer that will print on all but the first page, then choose Close at the Header and Footer toolbar.

You can follow similar steps to omit a header or footer on the first page. Simply do not key any text when the first header or footer pane is opened.

The ability to place different headers and footers on odd and even pages is useful when numbering pages in a multipage newsletter. Odd page numbers can be placed on the right side of the page and even page numbers can be placed on the left side of the page. For example, in a four-page newsletter, a footer can be created that includes right-aligned page numbering that will appear on the odd pages only. Alternately, another footer can be created that contains left-aligned page numbering that will appear on even pages only.

To create a different header and/or footer on odd and even pages, choose View, then Header and Footer. (If you are creating a footer, click the Switch Between Header and Footer button.) Click the Page Setup button on the Header and Footer toolbar, and then select the Layout tab. Make sure there is no check mark in the Different First Page option. Choose Different Odd and Even, then choose OK or press Enter. Key the desired text at the header or footer pane. Click the Show Next button on the Header and Footer toolbar. At the even header or footer pane, key the desired text, then click the Close button on the Header and Footer toolbar.

Creating a Header and Footer in a Newsletter

1. At a clear document window, add a header and footer to the beginning stages of a newsletter, as shown in figure 11.5, by completing the following steps:
   a. Open *newsletter banner* located on your student data disk.
   b. Save the document with Save As and name it c11ex02, header&footer.
   c. Change to the Page Layout viewing mode, change the Zoom Control to 75%, and then turn on the display of nonprinting characters.
   d. Select the month and year in the folio and key the current month and year.
   e. Select one of the dotted lines in the banner and click the Copy button on the Standard toolbar. (This line will be pasted in the header later.)
   f. With the insertion point located at the beginning of the document, create a header that will start on the second page of the newsletter by completing the following steps:
      (1) Choose View, then Header and Footer.
      (2) With the insertion point in the Header pane, choose Insert, then Picture.
      (3) At the Insert Picture dialog box, change the directory in the Look in: list box to the location of your student data disk files.
      (4) Make sure the Files of type list box displays *All Files (*.*)*, and then double-click *Ridesf2teal*.
      (5) Select the image and choose Format, then Picture.
      (6) In the Scaling section of the Picture dialog box, change the scaled Width and Height to 35%, then click OK or press Enter.
      (7) Click once to the right of the image to deselect it.
      (8) Click the Paste button on the Standard toolbar to insert the dotted line. (The line length will be adjusted in future steps.)
      (9) Insert the slogan in the header by completing the following steps:
         (a) Position the insertion point at the end of the wrapped dotted line and change the font to 12-point Times New Roman Bold Italic Black.
         (b) Key **Winners wear helmets!**
      (10) Adjust the length of the dotted line by completing the following steps:
         (a) Position the insertion point in the dotted line to the left of the slogan.
         (b) Press the Backspace key as many times as necessary until the slogan moves up to the previous line and is aligned at the right side of the header pane. If you delete too much of the line, click the Undo button on the Standard toolbar and try again. (Do not be concerned that the header is displaying on the first page of the newsletter at this point.)
   g. Create the footer that will begin on the second page by completing the following steps:
      (1) Click the Switch Between Header and Footer button on the Header and Footer toolbar to switch to the footer pane.
      (2) Insert the round bullets by completing the following steps:
         (a) Change the justification to center.
         (b) Choose Insert, Symbol, then select the Symbols tab.
         (c) Change the Font to Wingdings and select the round bullet in the third row, twenty-first column.
         (d) Click Insert two times to insert two bullets, and then click Close.
         (e) Select the two bullets and change the font to 14-point Impact and the Color to Dk Cyan.
      (3) Insert and format automatic page numbering by completing the following steps:
         (a) Position the insertion point in between the two bullets.

(b) Click on the Page Numbers button on the Header and Footer toolbar to automatically insert a page number. (At this point, do not be concerned if the number 1 displays even though the footer is to begin on page 2.)

(c) Select the page number and change the font Size to 16-point Impact and change the Color to Black.

(d) Insert a space before and after the page number.

(4) Click the Page Setup button on the Header and Footer toolbar, then select the Margins tab. In the From Edge section, change the distance from the edge of the page to the Footer to 0.7". (Within the existing bottom margin setting, the footer would be partially cut off when printed, making this adjustment necessary.) Choose OK or press Enter.

(5) To insert the horizontal lines on each side of the bullets and page number, complete the following steps:

(a) Display the Drawing toolbar, and then click the Line button on the Drawing toolbar.

(b) Position the crosshairs to the left of the bullets and page number, hold the Shift key down, and draw a line the approximate length and in the approximate location indicated in figure 11.5.

(c) Repeat these same steps to draw the horizontal line on the right side of the bullets and page number.

(6) Format, position, and size the left horizontal line in the footer by completing the following steps:

(a) Double-click the horizontal line on the left to access the Drawing Object dialog box. Make sure the Line tab is selected.

(b) In the Line section, make sure the Line Style is a single line and the Color is black. Make sure there is no check mark in the Shadow option.

(c) Change the Line Weight to 2 points.

(d) Select the Size and Position tab. In the Position section, change the Horizontal position to 0.5 inches From the Page and the Vertical position to 10.2 inches From the Page.

(e) In the Size section, make sure the Height of the line is 0.1 inches and change the Width of the line to 3.4 inches.

(f) Click OK or press Enter.

(7) Format the right horizontal line in the footer by completing the following steps:

(a) Double-click the horizontal line on the right to access the Drawing Object dialog box. Make sure the Line tab is selected.

(b) Follow steps 6(b) through 6(e) above, except change the Horizontal position of the line to 4.6 inches From the Page.

h. To instruct Word to start the header and footer on page 2, complete the following the steps:

(1) Deselect the horizontal line, click the Page Setup button on the Header and Footer toolbar, and then select the Layout tab.

(2) In the Headers and Footers section, click in the check box to the left of Different First Page to activate this option.

(3) Click OK or press Enter. (The header and footer text will disappear from the first page.)

(4) Click Close on the Header and Footer toolbar.

(5) Press Ctrl + End to position the insertion point at the end of the document and press Ctrl + Enter to create a second page displaying the header and footer.

2. Save c11ex02, header&footer.
3. Position the insertion point on page 2 to print the page displaying the header and footer. Choose File, Print, and then select Current page in the Page range section of the Print dialog box. Click OK or press Enter.
4. Close c11ex02, header&footer.

FIGURE 11.5

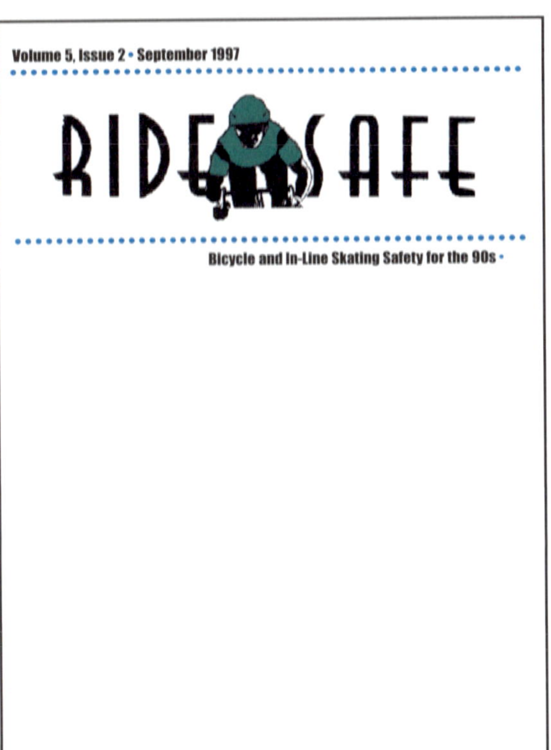

Look at a hard copy of c11ex02, header&footer, and notice how the triangular logo in the header repeats the image of the bicyclist in the nameplate. In addition, the dotted line in the header on page 2 is consistent in style and color with the dotted lines located within the nameplate on page 1 and the typeface used for the slogan matches that of the body text. The footer repeats the bullets found in the nameplate, the header, and the end sign which will later be used within the body copy to indicate the end of an article. As you can see, headers and footers can help to make separate pages a part of a whole unit.

Creating Sidebars in a Newsletter

A *sidebar* is a block of information or a related story that is set off from the body text in some type of a graphics box. In figure 11.1, a sidebar is included in the first column. A sidebar can also include a photograph or a graphic image along with the text. Frequently, the sidebar contains a shaded or *screened* background. A screened (lighter) version of the main color used

Sidebar: Information or a related story set off from the body text.

in a newsletter may serve as the background screen. The sidebar can be set in any position relative to the body text. In Word, sidebars can easily be created by creating a frame and inserting text. A text box can also be used.

In exercise 3, you will set up the column format for the newsletter created in exercise 2 and create a sidebar. The newsletter page layout will include two columns based on an underlying three-column grid. In later exercises, you will add more visually enhancing elements to the same newsletter.

Inserting a Sidebar in a Newsletter

1. At a clear document window, insert a sidebar in the newsletter from exercise 2, as shown in figure 11.6, by completing the following steps:
   a. Open c11ex02, header&footer.
   b. Save the document with Save As and name it c11ex03, sidebar.
   c. Change to the Page Layout viewing mode, change the Zoom Control to 75%, then turn on the display of nonprinting characters.
   d. Position the insertion point to the left of the Page Break on page 1 and press Delete to delete the empty page 2. (Working with one page is easier at this point.) Change the spacing after the paragraph to 0 points. (The spacing instruction was associated with the folio but is no longer needed.)
   e. Choose Insert, then Break. In the Section Breaks section of the Break dialog box, select Continuous, and then click OK or press Enter.
   f. Turn on Kerning for 14 Points and Above.
   g. Change the column format to two columns by completing the following steps:
      (1) Choose Format, then Columns.
      (2) Change the Number of Columns to two.
      (3) In the Width and Spacing section, change the Width of column 1 to 2.4 inches.
      (4) Change the Spacing in between columns to 0.25 inches.
      (5) Click in the Width text box for column 2 and make sure it displays 4.85 inches.
      (6) Choose OK or press Enter.
   h. Create the sidebar in the first column by completing the following steps:
      (1) Choose Insert, then File and double-click on *helmet habit text* located on your student data disk.
      (2) Select the text just inserted and change the font to 11-point Times New Roman (do not include the paragraph symbol below the last paragraph).
      (3) With the text still selected, choose Insert, then Frame.
      (4) Format the frame by completing the following steps:
         (a) Choose Format, then Frame.
         (b) Change the Width to Exactly At: 2.2 inches.
         (c) Change the Horizontal Position to Center Relative To: Column.
         (d) Change the Vertical Position to 3.19 inches Relative To: Page. (If this measurement forces the banner subtitle out of alignment, increase the amount in very small increments until the banner subtitle is in the original location.)
         (e) Click OK.
         (f) With the frame still selected, choose Format, then Borders and Shading, then select the Borders tab.
         (g) In the Presets section, select Box and make sure borders are displayed on all four sides in the Border preview box.
         (h) In the Border section, change the distance From Text to 3 points.

(This setting adjusts the distance from the border to the text inside the border.)

(i) Make sure ¾ pt is selected as the Line Style and then change the Line Color to Dk Cyan.

(j) Click OK or press Enter.

i. Format the title of the sidebar text by completing the following steps:
   (1) Change the Zoom Control to 100%.
   (2) Position the insertion point at the beginning of the title, *In the Helmet Habit*, and press Enter.
   (3) Select *In the*, and change the font to 12-point Times New Roman Bold Italic.
   (4) Position the insertion point after *In the*, delete the space, and then press Enter.
   (5) Select *Helmet Habit*, change the justification to center, then change the font to 14-point Impact and expand the character spacing to 1.2 points.
   (6) Position the insertion point after *In the,* and change the Italics Line Spacing to Exactly At: 10 points.
   (7) Position the insertion point after the word *Habit* and change the paragraph Spacing After to 6 points.

j. Adjust the spacing at the bottom of the sidebar by completing the following steps:
   (1) Position the insertion point after *...anyone!"* in the last line of the article text, press Delete to eliminate an extra hard return, and change the paragraph Spacing After to 6 points.
   (2) Position the insertion point after *Massachusetts* at the very bottom of the sidebar, and change the paragraph Spacing After to 6 points.

k. Insert a screened background in the frame by completing the following steps: (Since the screened background makes the text harder to read on the screen, this step is placed at this point in the exercise rather than in step h(4) above.)
   (1) With the frame still selected, choose Format, Borders and Shading, and then select the Shading tab.
   (2) In the Fill section, change the Foreground color to Dk Cyan.
   (3) Change the Background color to White and the Shading percentage to 30%, and then click OK.

2. Save c11ex03, sidebar.
3. Print and then close c11ex03, sidebar. (This newsletter continues to build throughout the remaining chapter exercises. Saving each exercise as a separate document takes up a tremendous amount of disk space. You will need three disks to save exercises 1 through 10 in this chapter. Consult with your instructor about saving each exercise as a separate document file. As an alternative, open c11ex03, sidebar and save the document with Save As and name the document c11newsletter. Continue completing the remaining exercises. However, do not save the document with Save As as instructed in each exercise. Instead, save the document with the same name (c11newsletter) as you progress through the exercises.)

FIGURE 11.6

Volume 5, Issue 2 • September 1997

Bicycle and In-Line Skating Safety for the 90s •

In the
Helmet Habit

"I don't quite know why my daughter, Kate, fell from her bike last July. Maybe she hit a small rock or just lost her balance. We found Kate lying on the ground. She was bleeding and had several cuts and bruises on her face and forehead. We called the paramedics and she began to lose consciousness just as they arrived. At the emergency room, we found out that Kate had a broken nose, a missing tooth, and four other loose teeth. Fortunately for all of us, Kate was wearing a bicycle helmet. Without even asking, three different doctors have told us that the helmet probably saved Kate's life. So many people tell me that their kids won't wear a helmet. I tell them to be firm—no helmet, no bike. Bicycle accidents can happen to anyone!"

Karen Brust
Boston, Massachusetts

Creating a Newsletter Table of Contents

In the previous chapter, you created a newsletter using a newsletter template as a framework. This newsletter template contained a table of contents. Since a *table of contents* is optional in a one- or two-page newsletter, it was deleted in the chapter 10 newsletter template exercise. However, in multipage newsletters, a table of contents is an important and necessary element. A table of contents lists the names of articles and features in the newsletter, along with their page numbers. The information in the table of contents greatly influences whether the reader moves beyond the front page of the newsletter, so the table of contents needs to stand out from the surrounding information. It must also be legible and easy to follow.

Table of Contents: A list of articles and features and their page numbers.

A table of contents is usually located on the front page of a newsletter. It is often placed in the lower left or right corner of the page. It can, however, be placed closer to the top of the page on either side, such as in the newsletter template used in chapter 10, or even within an asymmetrically designed nameplate. If a newsletter is designed to be a self-mailer, the table of contents can be placed in the mailing section so the reader is invited into the newsletter before it is even opened.

DTP POINTERS

The table of contents must:

- stand out from the surrounding text;
- be legible;
- be easy to follow;
- be consistent from issue to issue.

The table of contents in figure 11.1 is located in the lower left corner. The shadow box format and the background fill, or screen, make the table of contents easily identifiable while adding visual interest to the page. The table of contents, along with the shadow box above it, also add weight to the left side of the page. This added weight balances the heavier right side of the nameplate and the body copy below.

There are many ways to format a table of contents to make it easy to find and visually interesting. As illustrated in figure 11.7, a table of contents can easily be made by inserting text in a frame or text box and then adding various borders, screened backgrounds, fonts, graphics lines, reverse text, and special characters.

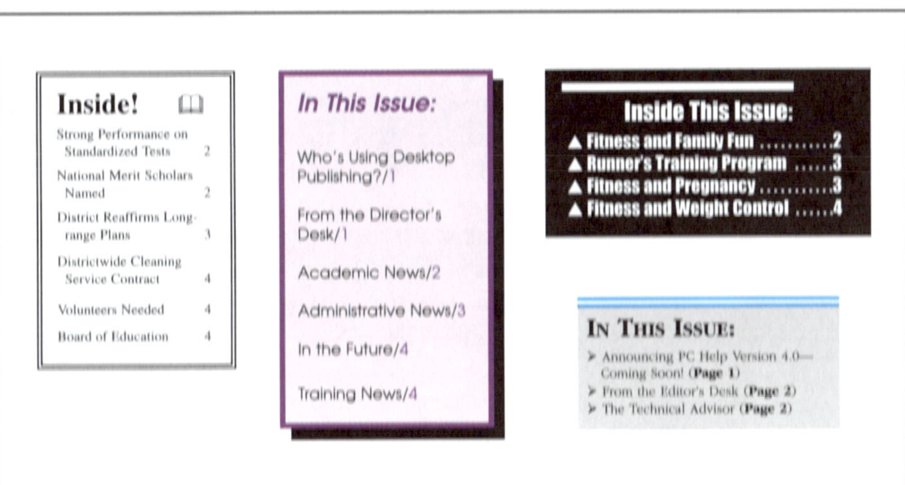

FIGURE 11.7

Examples of Tables of Contents

Inserting a Table of Contents in a Newsletter

1. At a clear document window, insert a table of contents to the newsletter from exercise 3, as shown in figure 11.8, by completing the following steps:
   a. Open c11ex03, sidebar.doc.
   b. Save the document with Save As and name it c11ex04, table of contents.
   c. Change to the Page Layout viewing mode, change the Zoom Control to 75%, then turn on the display of nonprinting characters.
   d. Press Ctrl + End to position the insertion point at the end of the document (below the sidebar) and press Enter.
   e. Insert the file *table of contents text* located on your student data disk.
   f. Select the table of contents text (do not include the paragraph symbol below the last line of text) and choose Insert, then Frame.
   g. Add a border to the frame by completing the following steps:
      (1) With the frame still selected, choose Format, Borders and Shading, and then select the Borders tab.
      (2) In the Presets section, select Box and make sure borders are displayed on all four sides in the Border preview box.
      (3) In the Border section, change the distance From Text to 3 points. (This setting adjusts the distance from the border to the text inside the border.)
      (4) Make sure ¾ pt is selected as the Line Style and then change the Line Color to Dk Cyan.
      (5) Click OK or press Enter.
   h. Size and position the framed table of contents text by completing the following steps:
      (1) With the frame selected, choose Format, then Frame.
      (2) At the Frame dialog box, make sure Around is selected in the Text Wrapping section.
      (3) In the Size section, change the Width to Exactly 2.2 inches.
      (4) In the Horizontal section, change the Position to Center Relative To: Column.
      (5) In the Vertical section, change the Position to 8.6 inches Relative To: Page.
      (6) Click OK or press Enter.
   i. Format the title in the table of contents by completing the following steps:
      (1) Change the Zoom Control to 100%.
      (2) Select *In This Issue:* (do not include the paragraph symbol) and change the font to 12-point Impact.
      (3) With the title still selected, choose Format, Font, and then select the Character Spacing tab. Change the Spacing to Expanded By: 1.2 points. Click OK or press Enter.
      (4) To create the screened background, complete the following steps:
         (a) With the frame still selected, choose Format, Borders and Shading, then select the Shading tab.
         (b) In the Fill section, change the Foreground color to Dk Cyan and the Background color to White.
         (c) Change the Shading percentage to 30%.
         (d) Click OK or press Enter.
      (5) Position the insertion point after the colon in *In This Issue:*, choose Format, Paragraph, and then select the Indents and Spacing tab. In the Spacing section, change the spacing After to 8 points. Click OK or press Enter.

j. Format the bulleted text in the table of contents by completing the following steps:
   (1) Select the remaining text below the title and change the font to 11-point Times New Roman.
   (2) Choose Format, Paragraph, and then select the Indents and Spacing tab. In the Spacing section, change the spacing After to 2 points. Click OK or press Enter.
   (3) With the text still selected, add bullets to each article name by completing the following steps:
      (a) Choose Format, Bullets and Numbering, and then select the Bulleted tab.
      (b) Select the first bulleted example and then click Modify.
      (c) In the Bullet Character section, change the Point Size to 14 points and change the Color to Dk Cyan.
      (d) Click Bullet, change the Symbols From: to Wingdings, and then select the round bullet in the fifth row, sixteenth column.
      (e) Click OK or press Enter to close the Symbol dialog box and then click OK again to close the Modify Bulleted List dialog box.
   (4) With the text still selected, change the Line Spacing to Exactly 10 points at the Paragraph dialog box.
   (5) Select the slash mark in each table of contents item and change the Color to Dk Cyan. (Hint: Change the color of the first slash mark, select the next slash mark, and press F4 to repeat the formatting.)
   (6) Bold the page number in each table of contents item.

k. For use in future issues, create a style for the bulleted items in the table of contents by completing the following steps:
   (1) Position the insertion point anywhere within the first bulleted item.
   (2) Click once in the Style list box on the Formatting toolbar to select the current style name.
   (3) Key **ToC bullets** as the new style name and press Enter.

l. To adjust the white space between the title and the table of contents, position the insertion point anywhere within the first bulleted item and change the spacing before the paragraph to 4 points.

2. Save c11ex04, table of contents.
3. Print and then close c11ex04, table of contents. (You may want to wait and print the whole newsletter when it is completed in exercise 10.)

FIGURE 11.8

Volume 5, Issue 2 • September 1997

Bicycle and In-Line Skating Safety for the 90s •

In the
Helmet Habit

"I don't quite know why my daughter, Kate, fell from her bike last July. Maybe she hit a small rock or just lost her balance. We found Kate lying on the ground. She was bleeding and had several cuts and bruises on her face and forehead. We called the paramedics and she began to lose consciousness just as they arrived. At the emergency room, we found out that Kate had a broken nose, a missing tooth, and four other loose teeth. Fortunately for all of us, Kate was wearing a bicycle helmet. Without even asking, three different doctors have told us that the helmet probably saved Kate's life. So many people tell me that their kids won't wear a helmet. I tell them to be firm—no helmet, no bike. Bicycle accidents can happen to anyone!"

Karen Brust
Boston, Massachusetts

In This Issue:

Creating Pull Quotes in a Newsletter

A *pull quote*, as illustrated in figure 11.1, acts as a focal point, helps to break up lengthy blocks of text, and provides visual contrast. A pull quote (also called a *pull out* or *call out*) is a direct phrase, summarizing statement, or important point associated with the body copy of a newsletter. Using pull quotes is an excellent way to draw readers into an article.

Pull Quote: A short, direct phrase, statement, or important point formatted to stand out from the rest of the body copy.

Effective pull quotes are interesting, brief, and formatted to stand out from the rest of the body copy. Keep in mind the following tips when creating pull quotes for a newsletter:

- Include relevant and interesting text in a pull quote. Edit any direct quotes so they will not be taken out of context when read individually as a pull quote.
- Pull quotes should be brief—approximately 10 to 15 words and never longer than a few lines.
- Choose a font that contrasts with the font used for the article text.
- Increase the type size.
- Vary the type style by bolding and/or italicizing the pull quote text.
- Set the pull quote off from the rest of the body text with ruled lines or a graphics box.
- Be consistent. Use the same format for other pull quotes throughout the newsletter and throughout future issues of the same newsletter.

DTP POINTERS
Pull quotes should be brief, be interesting, and stand out from the rest of the text.

The frames or text boxes displayed in figure 11.9 show some different ways that pull quotes can be customized to attract the reader's attention. This list of boxes is only a small representation of the methods for customizing pull quotes.

FIGURE 11.9

Pull Quote Examples

In design, function dictates form...

Pull Quote 1: Created in a frame, top and bottom borders in 4½ point line style, 30 percent fill, text in 14-point Arial MT Black, and center aligned. (Display the Borders toolbar to apply borders and fill.)

In design, function dictates form...

Pull Quote 1: Created in a frame, top and bottom borders in 2¼-point double-line style, clear fill, text in 14-point Kino MT, and center aligned. (Display the Borders toolbar to apply borders and fill.)

IN DESIGN, FUNCTION DICTATES FORM...

Pull Quote 1: Created in a text box with rounded corners in Dk Cyan, line weight 4-points, white fill color, text in 18-point Britannic Bold Italic in Dk Cyan, small caps, and center aligned.

In design, function dictates form...

Pull Quote 1: Created in a text box with a shadow, line weight 0.5 points, Dk Magenta fill color, text in 20-point Book Antigua Italic in white, and center aligned.

Creating Shortcuts to Formatting in a Newsletter

As mentioned several times previously, styles and templates can save you time and keystrokes. Knowing when to create a style or to save a document as a template is just as important as knowing how to create and use styles and templates.

Understanding style formatting limitations can help you determine when to make a style. Formatting selections from the following dialog boxes may be included in a style: Font, Paragraph, Tabs, Paragraph Borders and Shading, Language, Frame, and Bullets and Numbering. For example, you may include the formatting for a frame that surrounds a picture, but you cannot include the picture itself in the style. In addition, you may not save any text within a style. On the other hand, you may save a picture and/or text as part of a template document.

DTP POINTERS
Create styles for repetitive formatting.

In general, create styles for any repetitive formatting within a document. For example, a style can easily be created for article headings within a newsletter. Creating and applying an article heading style will assure you that all your headings will be consistently formatted the same. When creating a style for headings, include font selection, font size and style, font color, and any associated spacing before or after the paragraph symbol.

Other styles can be created for a newsletter banner, subtitle, folio, body copy, sidebar, pull quote, bulleted lists, frames containing images, etc. However, many times it may be more efficient to create certain styles and then to save a document as a template. Saving a newsletter as a template lets you save any formatting and/or text that does not change from issue to issue. For instance, a newsletter published on a regular basis includes some elements that remain the same from issue to issue, such as the newsletter banner and headers and footers. When saving a document as a template, omit any text or graphics that will change from issue to issue and leave all text, graphics, and formatting that will remain the same. Any styles created for other formatting in the newsletter will be saved along with the template.

In exercise 5, you will insert the first newsletter article, format the article heading and article text, and create a pull quote. Since these particular elements may be repeated throughout the newsletter, you will then create styles for these elements.

Creating Styles and a Pull Quote in a Newsletter

1. At a clear screen and using the newsletter from exercise 4, insert text and a pull quote and create styles, as shown in figure 11.10, by completing the following steps:
   a. Open c11ex04, table of contents.doc.
   b. Save the document with Save As and name it c11ex05, pull quote.
   c. Change to the Page Layout viewing mode, and then turn on the display of nonprinting characters.
   d. Insert the first newsletter article by completing the following steps:
      (1) Position the insertion point to the left of the second paragraph symbol at the top of the second column and choose Insert, then Break. In the Insert section, select Column Break. Click OK or press Enter.
      (2) Position the insertion point to the left of the Column Break and then insert the file *bicycle safety text* located on your student data disk.
   e. Format the first article heading by completing the following steps:
      (1) Select *Bicycle Safety: Let's Make It a Priority!*. At the Font dialog box, change the font to 18-point Impact, change the Color to Dk Cyan, and select Small Caps in the Effects section.
      (2) At the Font dialog box, choose the Character Spacing tab.
      (3) Change the Spacing to Expanded By: 1.2 points.
      (4) Choose Format, Paragraph, and then select the Indents and Spacing tab. Change the Spacing Before: to 8 points and After: to 6 points. Choose OK or press Enter.

(5) Select the paragraph symbol above the heading, then press Delete.

f. Create a style for future article headings by completing the following steps:
   (1) Make sure the insertion point is positioned within the article heading.
   (2) Click once in the Style list box located on the Formatting toolbar to select the current style name.
   (3) Key **article head** as the new style name and then press Enter.

g. Format the article text for the first article by completing the following steps:
   (1) Position the insertion point at the beginning of the line *Did you know . . .* and select all of the article text.
   (2) Change the font to 11-point Times New Roman.
   (3) Choose Format, Paragraph, and then select the Indents and Spacing tab. In the Spacing section, change the spacing After: to 3 points.
   (4) In the Indentation section, change the Special selection to First Line By: 0.2 inches to indent the first line of each paragraph.
   (5) Click OK or press Enter.

h. Create a style for the article text by completing the following steps:
   (1) With the article text still selected, click once in the Style list box located on the Formatting toolbar to select the current style name.
   (2) Key **article text** as the style name and then press Enter.

i. Create a style for the first paragraph of the article that eliminates the first line indentation by completing the following steps:
   (1) Position the insertion point within the first paragraph of article text.
   (2) Choose Format, Paragraph, then select the Indents and Spacing tab. In the Indentation section, change the Special option to (none).
   (3) Click once in the Style list box on the Formatting toolbar to select the current style name.
   (4) Key **1st paragraph** as the style name and then press Enter.

j. Insert a pull quote by completing the following steps:
   (1) Choose Insert, then Frame. Position the crosshairs on the right side of the third paragraph and draw a frame the approximate size and position of the pull quote in figure 11.10.
   (2) Change the font to 13-point Impact.
   (3) Key **More than 500,000 trips are made to emergency rooms each year for bicycle-related injuries.**

k. Format the pull quote frame by completing the following steps:
   (1) Choose Format, Borders and Shading, then select the Borders tab.
   (2) In the Presets section, select Box to apply borders to the frame.
   (3) In the Line section, change the Style to 2¼ point and the Color to Dk Cyan.
   (4) In the Border section, click the left and right sides of the box to eliminate borders on these sides, and then change the distance From Text to 3 points.
   (5) Click OK or press Enter.
   (6) Choose Format, Frame, then change the Width to Exactly 1.78". Change the Horizontal Position to Right Relative To: Margin and the Vertical Position to 0.1 Relative To: Paragraph.

l. Create a style for the pull quote by completing the following steps:
   (1) With the frame selected (make sure square black handles display on the frame), click once in the Style list box on the Formatting toolbar to select the current style name.
   (2) Key **pull quote** as the new style name and press Enter.

m. In the last paragraph, select and bold *The bottom line?*. Then select and italicize the last sentence.

2. Save c11ex05, pull quote.
3. Print and then close c11ex05, pull quote. (You may want to wait and print the whole newsletter when it is completed in exercise 10.)

FIGURE 11.10

Volume 5, Issue 2 • September 1997

Bicycle and In-Line Skating Safety for the 90s •

In the
Helmet Habit

"I don't quite know why my daughter, Kate, fell from her bike last July. Maybe she hit a small rock or just lost her balance. We found Kate lying on the ground. She was bleeding and had several cuts and bruises on her face and forehead. We called the paramedics and she began to lose consciousness just as they arrived. At the emergency room, we found out that Kate had a broken nose, a missing tooth, and four other loose teeth. Fortunately for all of us, Kate was wearing a bicycle helmet. Without even asking, three different doctors have told us that the helmet probably saved Kate's life. So many people tell me that their kids won't wear a helmet. I tell them to be firm—no helmet, no bike. Bicycle accidents can happen to anyone!"

Karen Brust
Boston, Massachusetts

Bicycle Safety: Let's Make It a Priority!

Protect your child!

Did you know that each year over 1,200 people die and thousands more are seriously injured in bicycle accidents? According to the American Academy of Pediatrics, more than 500,000 emergency room visits annually in the U.S. are attributed to bicycle accidents.

Surprisingly, most of these accidents, especially those involving children, occur on quiet residential streets. Most do not involve cars. And many could be prevented with proper training and safety equipment.

Think about it. Before we're allowed to drive a car, we have to be a certain age and go through extensive training and testing. Yet many of us—children in particular—ride the very same roads on a bicycle with little or no training at all. Kids are especially vulnerable because of their undeveloped peripheral vision (about two-thirds that of adults), poor speed judgment, and lack of a sense of danger.

More than 500,000 trips are made to emergency rooms each year for bicycle-related injuries.

At Ride Safe, we believe bicycle safety education is crucial to our well-being and to that of our children. More and more states, including New York, New Jersey, Connecticut, Georgia, Tennessee, Oregon, and California are implementing legislation requiring bicycle helmets for children. As adults, we can teach our children safe riding habits, protect them from injury by purchasing bicycle helmets, and set a good example when we are riding our own bicycles.

The bottom line? *Bicycle safety is something we all need to make a priority!*

In This Issue:

Creating Kickers and End Signs in a Newsletter

Additional elements, such as kickers and end signs, can also be used in a newsletter. A *kicker* is a brief sentence or phrase that is a lead-in to an article. Generally, it is set in a size smaller than the headline but larger than the body text. It is often stylistically distinct from both the headline and the body text. Kickers can be placed above or below the headline or article heading. In figure 11.1, a kicker is placed above the first article heading and serves as a lead-in to the first article.

Kicker: A lead-in phrase or sentence that precedes the beginning of an article.

Symbols or special characters used to indicate the end of a section of text are known as *end signs.* In figure 11.1, an end sign follows the last paragraph in the first article. It mimics the shadow boxes used for the sidebar, the table of contents, and the pull quote within the newsletter. Appropriate special characters or combinations of these characters, such as •, ■, ❑, ▼, ❖, ◆, ➢, and ✓ from the Monotype Sorts or Wingdings font selection, can be used as end signs.

End Sign: A symbol or special character indicating the end of an article.

In exercise 6, you will add a kicker and an end sign to the Ride Safe newsletter from exercise 5.

Creating a Kicker and an End Sign in a Newsletter

1. At a clear editing window, insert the kicker and end sign shown in figure 11.11 to the newsletter from exercise 5 by completing the following steps:
   a. Open c11ex05, pull quote.doc.
   b. Save the document with Save As and name it c11ex06, end sign.
   c. Change to the Page Layout viewing mode, change the Zoom Control to 75%, and then turn on the display of nonprinting characters.
   d. Create the kicker by completing the following steps:
      (1) Position the insertion point at the beginning of the first paragraph below the article heading.
      (2) Key **Protect your child!** and then press Enter.
      (3) Select *Protect your child!* and change the font to 14-point Times New Roman Bold Italic.
   e. Create a style for the kicker formatting by completing the following steps:
      (1) Position the insertion point anywhere within the kicker.
      (2) Click once in the Style list box on the Formatting toolbar to select the current Style name.
      (3) Key **kicker** and press Enter.
   f. Create the end sign by completing the following steps:
      (1) Position the insertion point at the end of the first article and delete any unnecessary hard returns, then press the tab key three times. (Make sure Italics is off.)
      (2) Choose Insert, Symbol, then select the Special Characters tab.
      (3) Double-click on the Em Dash selection, and then select the Symbols tab.
      (4) Change the Font selection to Wingdings, select and insert the round bullet in the third row, twenty-first column, and then select the Special Characters tab again.
      (5) Double-click on the Em Dash selection, then click Close.
      (6) Insert one space on each side of the bullet.
      (7) Select the end sign and change the font to 11-point Impact. (Remove Italic formatting, if any.)
      (8) Select the round bullet and change the color to Dk Cyan.
2. Save c11ex06, end sign.
3. Print and then close c11ex06, end sign. (You may want to wait and print the whole newsletter when it is completed in exercise 10.)

FIGURE 11.11

Volume 5, Issue 2 • September 1997

Bicycle and In-Line Skating Safety for the 90s •

In the Helmet Habit

"I don't quite know why my daughter, Kate, fell from her bike last July. Maybe she hit a small rock or just lost her balance. We found Kate lying on the ground. She was bleeding and had several cuts and bruises on her face and forehead. We called the paramedics and she began to lose consciousness just as they arrived. At the emergency room, we found out that Kate had a broken nose, a missing tooth, and four other loose teeth. Fortunately for all of us, Kate was wearing a bicycle helmet. Without even asking, three different doctors have told us that the helmet probably saved Kate's life. So many people tell me that their kids won't wear a helmet. I tell them to be firm—no helmet, no bike. Bicycle accidents can happen to anyone!"

Karen Brust
Boston, Massachusetts

In This Issue:

Bicycle Safety: Let's Make It a Priority!

Protect your child!

Did you know that each year over 1,200 people die and thousands more are seriously injured in bicycle accidents? According to the American Academy of Pediatrics, more than 500,000 emergency room visits annually in the U.S. are attributed to bicycle accidents.

Surprisingly, most of these accidents, especially those involving children, occur on quiet residential streets. Most do not involve cars. And many could be prevented with proper training and safety equipment.

Think about it. Before we're allowed to drive a car, we have to be a certain age and go through extensive training and testing. Yet many of us—children in particular—ride the very same roads on a bicycle with little or no training at all. Kids are especially vulnerable because of their undeveloped peripheral vision (about two-thirds that of adults), poor speed judgment, and lack of a sense of danger.

More than 500,000 trips are made to emergency rooms each year for bicycle-related injuries.

At Ride Safe, we believe bicycle safety education is crucial to our well-being and to that of our children. More and more states, including New York, New Jersey, Connecticut, Georgia, Tennessee, Oregon, and California are implementing legislation requiring bicycle helmets for children. As adults, we can teach our children safe riding habits, protect them from injury by purchasing bicycle helmets, and set a good example when we are riding our own bicycles.

The bottom line? *Bicycle safety is something we all need to make a priority!*

— • —

Creating Jump Lines in a Newsletter

A *jump line* in a newsletter indicates that an article or feature continues on another page. Jump lines enable the creator of a newsletter to feature the beginning of several articles on the front page, increasing the chances of attracting readers. A jump line also solves the problem of what to do with lengthy articles that might not fit on one page.

Jump Line: Text telling the reader that an article continues on another page.

As an aid in the directional flow of information in a document, a jump line must be distinguishable from surrounding text so the reader can easily find it. A jump line is commonly set in small italic type, approximately two points smaller than the body copy type. As an option, jump lines can also be enclosed in parentheses.

Creating a Jump Line in a Newsletter

1. At a clear editing window, add an article and a jump line to the newsletter from exercise 6 as shown in figure 11.12 by completing the following steps:
   a. Open c11ex06, end sign.
   b. Save the document with Save As and name it c11ex07, jump line.
   c. Change to the Page Layout viewing mode, and then turn on the display of nonprinting characters.
   d. Position the insertion point after the end sign and press Enter.
   e. To avoid having the table of contents pushed to the second page when the second newsletter article is inserted (step f), change the paragraph the table of contents is anchored to by completing the following steps:
      (1) Click once in the table of contents to select it. The anchor symbol will display by the paragraph the table of contents is anchored to.
      (2) Position the mouse pointer on the anchor until the pointer turns into a four-headed arrow.
      (3) Click and drag the anchor to the last paragraph in the first article. The anchor should then display to the left of the last paragraph.
   f. Press Ctrl + End again, then insert the file *accident text* located on your student data disk.
   g. Format the title of the second article by completing the following steps:
      (1) Position the insertion point anywhere within the title *"Accidents" Waiting to Happen.*
      (2) Click the down-pointing arrow to the right of the Style list box located on the Formatting toolbar and select *article head* from the Style drop-down list.
   h. Format the article text by completing the following steps:
      (1) Position the insertion point at the beginning of the line *The majority of bicycle/car "accidents"...* and select all of the article text, including any text on the second page (do not include the paragraph symbol or Column Break below the last paragraph).
      (2) Click the down-pointing arrow to the right of the Style list box located on the Formatting toolbar and select *article text* from the Style drop-down list.
      (3) Position the insertion point anywhere within the first paragraph and apply the *1st paragraph* style from the Style list box on the Formatting toolbar.
   i. Create the jump line by completing the following steps:
      (1) Position the insertion point at the end of the first paragraph and press Enter two times. (The insertion point should be located at the bottom of the page. If not, eliminate one of the hard returns.)
      (2) Change to right justification.
      (3) Key **(continued on page 2)**.
      (4) Select the jump line and change the font to 10-point Times New Roman Italic.
2. Save c11ex07, jump line.
3. Print the first page of the newsletter and then close c11ex07, jump line. (You may want to wait and print the whole newsletter when it is completed in exercise 10.)

FIGURE 11.12

Volume 5, Issue 2 • September 1997

Bicycle and In-Line Skating Safety for the 90s •

In the **Helmet Habit**

"I don't quite know why my daughter, Kate, fell from her bike last July. Maybe she hit a small rock or just lost her balance. We found Kate lying on the ground. She was bleeding and had several cuts and bruises on her face and forehead. We called the paramedics and she began to lose consciousness just as they arrived. At the emergency room, we found out that Kate had a broken nose, a missing tooth, and four other loose teeth. Fortunately for all of us, Kate was wearing a bicycle helmet. Without even asking, three different doctors have told us that the helmet probably saved Kate's life. So many people tell me that their kids won't wear a helmet. I tell them to be firm—no helmet, no bike. Bicycle accidents can happen to anyone!"

Karen Brust
Boston, Massachusetts

In This Issue:

Bicycle Safety: Let's Make It a Priority!

Protect your child!

Did you know that each year over 1,200 people die and thousands more are seriously injured in bicycle accidents? According to the American Academy of Pediatrics, more than 500,000 emergency room visits annually in the U.S. are attributed to bicycle accidents.

Surprisingly, most of these accidents, especially those involving children, occur on quiet residential streets. Most do not involve cars. And many could be prevented with proper training and safety equipment.

Think about it. Before we're allowed to drive a car, we have to be a certain age and go through extensive training and testing. Yet many of us—children in particular—ride the very same roads on a bicycle with little or no training at all. Kids are especially vulnerable because of their undeveloped peripheral vision (about two-thirds that of adults), poor speed judgment, and lack of a sense of danger.

More than 500,000 trips are made to emergency rooms each year for bicycle-related injuries.

At Ride Safe, we believe bicycle safety education is crucial to our well-being and to that of our children. More and more states, including New York, New Jersey, Connecticut, Georgia, Tennessee, Oregon, and California are implementing legislation requiring bicycle helmets for children. As adults, we can teach our children safe riding habits, protect them from injury by purchasing bicycle helmets, and set a good example when we are riding our own bicycles.

The bottom line? *Bicycle safety is something we all need to make a priority!*

— • —

"Accidents" Waiting to Happen

The majority of bicycle/car "accidents" are not really accidents, but avoidable collisions. Most result from the bicyclist's failure to use proper riding techniques in a hazardous situation. Ironically, when asked, most children injured in traffic could describe the actual law they broke.

(continued on page 2)

Inserting Graphics, Illustrations, and Photographs in a Newsletter

If used appropriately, headers, footers, sidebars, tables of contents, pull quotes, kickers, end signs, and jump lines can help to achieve focus, balance, proportion, contrast, directional flow, and consistency within a newsletter. Graphic images, illustrations, charts, diagrams, and photographs can help to achieve these same goals.

Graphics images include line art (black and white with no gray) and continuous-tone art (photographs or art with gray tones). Line art can be drawn with a graphics program or purchased as ready-made electronic clip art. A variety of clip art is available on the market that includes thousands of ready-made illustrations for almost any subject area. For example, you can purchase clip art for holidays, special events, occupations, sports, geography, entertainment, etc. Word includes approximately 100 predesigned graphic images in its program that you can insert into any document by choosing Insert, then Picture. Word graphics files are identified by a *.wmf* file extension.

In addition to using the clip art images provided, Word is compatible with most of the best-selling graphics programs. Graphics files with certain extensions such as those listed in figure 11.13 can be easily inserted into a Word document. To do this, choose Insert, then Picture as you normally would, and then change to the directory location of the desired graphic files.

FIGURE 11.13

Graphic File Extensions Compatible with Word

File Extension	Program Format
BMP	Windows Bitmap/Windows Paintbrush
CGM	Computer Graphics Metafile
CDR	CorelDRAW!
DXF	AutoCAD
DRW	Micrografx Designer/Draw
EPS	Encapsulated PostScript
GIF	CompuServe Graphics Interchange Format
HGL	HP Graphic Language
JPG	JPEG
PCD	Kodak Photo CD
PCX	PC Paintbrush
PIC	Lotus 1-2-3 Graphics
PCT	Macintosh PICT
PLT	AutoCAD Plot files
TIF	Tagged Image File Format
WMF	Windows Metafile
WPG	WordPerfect/DrawPerfect

Word uses graphic filters to import other graphic file formats such as those listed in figure 11.13. If you have any trouble importing graphic files with any of the above extensions, your system may be missing some graphic file filters. To determine which filters have been installed, choose Insert, then Picture, and check the List Files of Type list box. If all the extensions in figure 11.13 are not listed, you need to install additional graphic filters. Refer to the Word 7 reference manual to add filters.

Photographs can also be added to a newsletter. As the old saying goes, a picture is worth a thousand words, and sometimes just saying the words is not enough. Readers relate to the "realness" of photographs as opposed to clip art or computer-generated images. Photos best describe events or people because they can accurately depict a scene or an expressed emotion. Black-and-white photographs scan better than color photographs. Select only those photos that are clearly defined, in focus, and the correct exposure.

Some information is better understood in a visual format. Whenever possible, include illustrations, charts, tables, and diagrams when presenting technical, numerical, and detailed information.

Using Scanned Images in a Newsletter

Scanner: Converts a photograph, drawing, or text into a comparable digital file format that can be retrieved into specific programs.

Noncomputer-generated images, such as photographs, illustrations, and diagrams, can be included in a newsletter through the use of a scanner. A *scanner* converts a photograph, drawing, or text into a compatible digital file format that can be retrieved into a program such as Word.

In order to use a scanner, you must have an accompanying software program loaded into your computer to scan the image or text and to convert it into a compatible file format. Most scanners work in this manner:

1. Place the photograph or illustration face down on the image scanner.
2. Open the scanning software program.
3. Acquire the image.
4. Prescan the image.
5. Set the desired scanned image size.
6. Select the desired scan mode.
7. Select the desired resolution.
8. Execute the scan.
9. Save and name the file giving it a compatible file format extension, such as .bmp, .tif, or .wmf.
10. Exit the scanning software program.
11. Open Word.
12. Insert the scanned image into a Word document by choosing Insert, then Picture. Change to the directory location of the scanned image and select the desired file name.

DTP POINTERS
Find out about copyright restrictions on any images to be scanned and request permission, if necessary.

One very important factor to keep in mind is that you must get permission to use artwork, photos, or illustrations before you can legally scan them into a document. When you purchase clip art and stock photography, you generally buy the right to use it and even modify it, but you may not resell the images themselves as hard copy or computer images. When purchasing these items, read the copyright information provided in the front of the accompanying documentation.

When using photographs in a newsletter, you can scan the photographs, save them in a compatible graphic file format, and then insert them into your newsletter. Or you can insert a placeholder, such as a frame, in your newsletter. You can then print your newsletter, paste a photograph into the area reserved by the frame, and have a commercial printer duplicate your newsletter.

When trying to determine if your photographs should be professionally scanned, keep the following two points in mind:

- If you do not need high-quality output, using images scanned from a desk model scanner is acceptable.
- If you need high-quality output, use a service bureau to have your photos professionally scanned into your newsletter.

Inserting a Picture Placeholder in a Newsletter

1. At a clear screen, add a placeholder for a photograph and caption text to the second page of the newsletter from exercise 7, as shown in figure 11.14, by completing the following steps:
   a. Open c11ex07, jump line.
   b. Save the document with Save As and name it c11ex08, picture.
   c. Change to the Page Layout viewing mode, change the Zoom Control to 75%, and then turn on the display of nonprinting characters.
   d. Insert and format a title before the photo placeholder shown in figure 11.14 by completing the following steps:
      (1) Press Ctrl + End to position the insertion point at the top of the second column on page 2.
      (2) Key **Who Says Helmets Aren't Cool?**.
      (3) With the insertion point positioned anywhere in the title, apply the *article head* style from the Style drop-down list on the Formatting toolbar.
      (4) To align the title with the top of column one, place the insertion point anywhere within the title and change the paragraph Spacing Before: to 0 points.
   e. Insert a frame to serve as the photograph placeholder by completing the following steps:
      (1) Choose Insert, then Frame.
      (2) Position the crosshairs below the title and create a frame the approximate size of the frame in figure 11.14. (Do not be concerned if the title displays below the frame. Size and position adjustments will be made in the next few steps.)
   f. Size and position the frame to more exact specifications by completing the following steps:
      (1) Select the frame, and choose Format, then Frame.
      (2) In the Size section, change the Width to Exactly At: 4.8 inches and the Height to Exactly 2.12 inches.
      (3) In the Horizontal section, change the Position to Right Relative To: Margin.
      (4) In the Vertical section, change the Position to 1.82 inches Relative To: Page and change the Distance from Text: to 0.1 inches, then click OK or press Enter.
   g. Select the frame and insert a 1½ point Dk Cyan border around the frame.
   h. Click once inside the frame and change the justification to Center.
   i. Press Enter several times and key **Insert picture of children from Silverton, Oregon here.**
   j. Create the promotional text under the placeholder by completing the following steps:
      (1) Press Ctrl + End (the insertion point will be positioned after the title).
      (2) Press Enter and apply the *Normal* style from the Style drop-down list on the Formatting toolbar.
      (3) Insert the file *picture text* located on your student data disk.
      (4) Select the text just inserted and change the font to 10.5-point Times New Roman Bold Italic.
2. Save c11ex08, picture.
3. Position the insertion point on page 2. Print page 2 only and then close c11ex08, picture. (You may want to wait and print the whole newsletter when it is completed in exercise 10.)

FIGURE 11.14

Winners wear helmets!

Research indicates that 60% of all U.S. bicycle-car collisions occur among bicyclists between the ages of 8 and 12. Still, an average of only $1 is spent per child between birth and age 15 teaching traffic education. Children are permitted to travel with only a *"look both ways before you cross the street"* and *"make sure you stop at all stop signs"* warning. Obviously these "warnings" are not enough.

Who Says Helmets Aren't Cool?

Insert picture of children from Silverton, Oregon here.

Certainly not the children of Silverton, Oregon! One of the biggest reasons children don't wear bicycle helmets is because their friends don't wear them. By getting all the children in your school or neighborhood to order bicycle helmets at the same time, you can help turn this peer pressure from negative to positive. Suddenly wearing a bicycle helmet becomes the "cool" thing to do.

2

Creating a Newsletter Masthead

The *masthead* is a repeating element that can add consistency among newsletter issues. A masthead (see figure 11.15) usually contains the following information:

- the company or organization (and address) producing the newsletter
- the newsletter publication schedule, such as weekly, monthly, biannually, etc.
- the names of those contributing to the production of the newsletter, such as editor, authors, and graphic designers
- copyright information

The masthead can also contain a small logo, seal, or other graphic identifier. A masthead is commonly located on the back page of a newsletter, although you will sometimes find it on the first page. Wherever you decide to place the masthead, be consistent from issue to issue in the masthead's design, layout, and location.

Masthead: A list of all those contributing to the production of a newsletter

DTP POINTERS
Be consistent in the design and layout of the masthead from issue to issue.

FIGURE 11.15

Examples of Mastheads

From the ▫▫▫ Desktop

Editor: **Martha Ridoux**
Design and Layout:
Grace Shevick
Contributing Authors:
Jonathan Dwyer
Nancy Shipley
Christine Johnson
Published Monthly by:
DTP Training, Inc.
4550 North Wabash St.
Chicago, IL 60155
312 555-6840
Fax: 312 555-9366
http://www.dtp.com
©Copyright 1997 by:
DTP Training, Inc.
All rights reserved.

From the ▫▫▫ Desktop

Editor:
Martha Ridoux
Design and Layout:
Grace Shevick
Authors:
Jonathan Dwyer
Nancy Shipley
Christine Johnson
Published Monthly by:
DTP Training, Inc.
4550 North Wabash St.
Chicago, IL 60155
312 555-6840
Fax: 312 555-9366
http://www.dtp.com
©Copyright 1997 by:
DTP Training, Inc.
All rights reserved.

Creating a Newsletter Masthead

1. At a clear screen, add a masthead to the second page of the newsletter from exercise 8, as shown in figure 11.16, by completing the following steps:
   a. Open c11ex08, picture.
   b. Save the document with Save As and name it c11ex09, masthead.
   c. Change to the Page Layout viewing mode, change the Zoom Control to 75%, and then turn on the display of nonprinting characters.
   d. Insert an end sign at the end of the second article by completing the following steps:
      (1) Select the end sign located on page 1 and click the Copy button on the Standard toolbar.

(2) Position the insertion point on page 2 at the end of the article in the first column and press the space bar three times.
(3) Click the Paste button on Standard toolbar.

e. Position the insertion point to the left of the column break on page 2 and insert the file *masthead text* located on your student data disk.

f. To insert a frame around the masthead text, complete the following steps:
(1) Select the masthead text but **do not** include the last hard paragraph symbol in the selection.
(2) Choose Insert, then Frame.

g. Format the masthead text by completing the following steps:
(1) Select all of the masthead text and change to center justification.
(2) Select *Ride Safe* and change the font to 11-point Impact and expand the character spacing to 1.2 points.
(3) Select the remaining text and change the font to 9-point Times New Roman.
(4) Bold the following: *Editor:*, *Design and Layout:*, *Authors:*, *Published quarterly by:*, and *©Copyright 1994.*
(5) Apply Italics to the remaining text.

h. Adjust the paragraph spacing and line spacing (leading) by completing the following steps:
(1) Position the insertion point at the end of the *Ride Safe* heading and change the spacing After to 3 points at the Paragraph dialog box.
(2) Position the insertion point after the following items and change the spacing After to 1 point at the Paragraph dialog box: *Chris Urban*, *Cassie Lizbeth*, *Christine Pollistrini*, *Fax: . . .*, and *All rights reserved.* (Hint: Use F4 after you've formatted the first item to quickly repeat the formatting.)
(3) Select all of the masthead text, except for the heading, and change the Line Spacing to Exactly At: 10 points at the Paragraph dialog box.

i. Apply color to the framed text by completing the following steps:
(1) With the frame selected (deselect any selected text within the frame), choose Format, Borders and Shading, and then select the Borders tab.
(2) Choose Box in the Presets section and change the Line Color to Dk Cyan.
(3) Click OK or press Enter.
(4) Select the *Ride Safe* heading, choose Format, Borders and Shading, and then select the Shading tab.
(5) In the Fill section, change the Foreground color to Dk Cyan and change the Background color to white, 30% Shading.
(6) Click OK or press Enter.

j. Size and position the framed masthead by completing the following steps:
(1) Make sure the frame is selected (*Ride Safe* should be deselected) and choose Format, then Frame.
(2) In the Size section of the Frame dialog box, change the Width to Exactly At: 2 inches.
(3) In the Horizontal section, change the Position to Center Relative To: Column.
(4) In the Vertical section, change the Position to 7.2 inches Relative To: Page.
(5) Click OK or press Enter. (Use Print Preview to see the masthead displayed at the bottom of the first column.)

2. Save c11ex09, masthead.
3. Print page 2 only and then close c11ex09, masthead. (You may want to wait and print the whole newsletter when it is completed in exercise 10.)

FIGURE 11.16

Winners wear helmets!

Research indicates that 60% of all U.S. bicycle-car collisions occur among bicyclists between the ages of 8 and 12. Still, an average of only $1 is spent per child between birth and age 15 teaching traffic education. Children are permitted to travel with only a *"look both ways before you cross the street"* and *"make sure you stop at all stop signs"* warning. Obviously these "warnings" are not enough. — ● —

Who Says Helmets Aren't Cool?

Insert picture of children from Silverton, Oregon here.

Certainly not the children of Silverton, Oregon! One of the biggest reasons children don't wear bicycle helmets is because their friends don't wear them. By getting all the children in your school or neighborhood to order bicycle helmets at the same time, you can help turn this peer pressure from negative to positive. Suddenly wearing a bicycle helmet becomes the "cool" thing to do.

Ride Safe

Editor:
Chris Urban

Design and Layout:
Cassie Lizbeth

Authors:
Brandon Keith
Brian Stetler
Christine Pollistrini

Published quarterly by:
Ride Safe, Inc.
P.O. Box 888
Warrenville, IL 60555
800-285-RIDE
Fax: 630-653-9068

©Copyright 1994 by:
Ride Safe, Inc.
All rights reserved.

•2•

Using Captions

Think of all the times you pick up a newspaper, newsletter, or magazine. How many times do you look at a photograph and immediately read the accompanying explanation? Many graphics images can stand on their own; however, most photographs, illustrations, and charts need to be explained to the reader. Remember that your reader's eyes are automatically drawn to images or elements that stand out on the page. Adding an explanation to your image or photo quickly gives your reader an idea of what is going on. It may even entice your reader to read an accompanying article. Descriptions or explanations of graphics images, illustrations, or photographs are referred to as *captions*.

Caption:
A description or explanation of a graphics image, illustration, or photograph.

Captions should explain their associated images while at the same time establishing a connection to the body copy. Make the caption text different from the body text by bolding and decreasing the type size slightly. Legibility is still the key. Keep captions as short as possible and consistent throughout your document.

Word's AutoCaption feature automatically adds captions when certain elements are inserted into a document. These elements may include Microsoft ClipArt Gallery, Drawing, Graph, PowerPoint Slide, Word Picture, Word Table, or an Excel Worksheet. To use the AutoCaption feature, choose Insert, Caption, and then click AutoCaption at the Caption dialog box. At the AutoCaption dialog box, select the desired elements in the Add Caption When Inserting: list box. For example, if Microsoft Word Picture is selected, a numbered and labeled caption, such as *figure 1*, will automatically be added every time you insert a Microsoft Picture. (See figure 11.17.) The caption numbers will increase automatically as additional Microsoft Pictures are added to a document.

Word's Caption feature is useful because it automatically numbers the desired elements in sequence. In addition, if one element is deleted or moved, the numbering method of the remaining elements is automatically updated. If you want to add captions to all items of a specific type, such as all tables or all figures in a document, the AutoCaption feature can save you a lot of time.

If elements do not have to be numbered, such as photographs in a newsletter, the easiest way to create a caption is to position the insertion point below the element and key and format the desired caption as you did in exercise 8. Another possibility is to insert a frame around the caption text so that you can size and position the caption more precisely.

If you move any element that has a caption, including those created by the AutoCaption feature, the caption and the element will not automatically stay together. To avoid separating the two, select the picture, table, chart, etc. and the caption, and choose Insert, then Frame. You can then drag the frame to the desired location.

FIGURE 11.17

Caption Examples

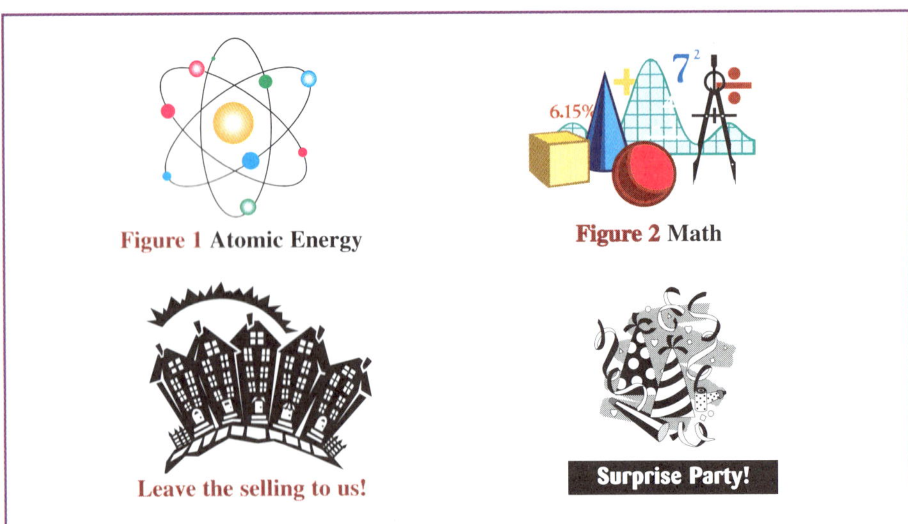

Using Additional Enhancements for Starting Paragraphs

In a previous chapter, you learned about the Drop Cap feature. This design element can be used to indicate the beginning paragraph of a new article. Other types of paragraph enhancements can also be included in a newsletter. The following is a short list of paragraph enhancements—you may think of many more:

- Set the first few words of the beginning paragraph in all caps.
- Set the first line of the beginning paragraph in all caps.
- Set the first word of the beginning paragraph in small caps.
- Set the first line of the beginning paragraph in color.
- Use a larger type size with more leading in the first line of the beginning paragraph.

Understanding Copy Fitting

Publications such as magazines and newsletters contain information that varies from issue to issue. Though there is structure in how the articles or stories are laid out on the page (such as the uneven two-column format in the Ride Safe newsletter), there may be times when more or less text is needed to fill the page. Making varying amounts of text or typographical enhancements fit in a fixed amount of space is referred to as *copy fitting*. Some copy-fitting suggestions include the following:

Copy Fitting: Fitting varying amounts of text or typographical enhancements into a fixed amount of space.

To create more space:

- Change the margins.
- Change the justification.
- Use hyphenation.
- Change the typeface, type size, or style. Limit body type size to a minimum of 9 points.
- Reduce the spacing between paragraphs.
- Condense the spacing between characters.
- Reduce the leading (line spacing) in the body copy.
- Reduce the spacing before and after paragraphs (or hard returns) to reduce the spacing around the nameplate, headlines, subheads, frames, or text boxes.
- Remove a sidebar, pull quote, kicker, or end sign.
- Edit the text, including rewriting and eliminating sections.

To fill extra space:

- Adjust margins.
- Change justification.
- Change font size. Limit body type size to a maximum of 12 points.
- Increase the spacing between paragraphs.
- Adjust the character spacing.
- Increase the leading (line spacing) in the body copy.
- Increase the spacing around the nameplate, headlines, subheads, frames, or text boxes.
- Add a sidebar, pull quote, kicker, end sign, graphic lines, clip art, photo, etc.
- Add text.

DTP POINTERS
Copy fitting adjustments are less noticeable when done uniformly throughout the whole document.

Be consistent when making any copy-fitting adjustments. For example, if you increase the white space after a headline, increase white space after all headlines. Or, if you decrease the type size of the body copy in an article, decrease the point size of all body copy in all articles. Adjustments are less noticeable when done uniformly. Also, adjustments often can be very small. For instance, rather than reducing type size by a whole point, try reducing it a half or quarter point. In addition, Word includes a Shrink to Fit feature that automatically "shrinks" the contents of the last page in a document onto the previous page if there is only a small amount of text on the last page. To access this copyfitting feature, choose File, then Print Preview, then click the Shrink to Fit button (seventh button from the left) on the Print Preview toolbar. Word will automatically reduce the point size in order to fit the text on the previous page. Carefully check your document after using the Shrink to Fit feature, the results are not always desirable.

In the Ride Safe newsletter created in the previous exercises, adjustments were made to the typeface, type size, type style, spacing above and below the article headings, spacing between paragraphs, spacing within the paragraphs (leading), and size and position of framed text.

In the next exercise, you will add two more articles to the second page of the Ride Safe newsletter, apply styles, and insert a clip art image. These articles are selected and adjusted to "fit" into the remaining space.

Employing Copy-Fitting Techniques

1. At a clear screen, add two articles to the second page of the newsletter from exercise 9, as shown in figure 11.18, by completing the following steps: (Make your own minor adjustments if necessary to fit the articles in their respective locations.)
   a. Open c11ex09, masthead.
   b. Save the document with Save As and name it c11ex10, copyfit.
   c. Change to the Page Layout viewing mode, change the Zoom Control to 75%, and then turn on the display of nonprinting characters.
   d. Insert an article in the space above the masthead in the newsletter from exercise 9, as shown in figure 11.18, by completing the following steps:
      (1) On page 2, position the insertion point on the line below the end sign at the end of the article in column one.
      (2) Insert the file *light bulb test* located on your student data disk.
   e. Apply styles to the article text just inserted by completing the following steps:
      (1) Position the insertion point anywhere in the title *The Light Bulb Test*, and apply the *article head* style.
      (2) Position the insertion point within the first paragraph, and apply the *1st paragraph style.*
      (3) Position the insertion point within the second paragraph, and apply the *article text* style.
   f. Insert a frame for the light bulb image by completing the following steps:
      (1) Choose Insert, then Frame.
      (2) Position the crosshairs within the first paragraph, and draw a small frame in the approximate location of the light bulb image in figure 11.18.
   g. Size and position the frame by completing the following steps:
      (a) Make sure the frame is selected, and choose Format, then Frame.
      (b) In the Size section, change the Width to Exactly At: 0.42 inches and change the Height to Exactly At: 0.5 inches.
      (c) In the Horizontal section, change the Position to Left Relative To: Margin.
      (d) In the Vertical section, change the Position to 0" Relative To: Paragraph.
      (e) Click OK or press Enter.

h. Insert the light bulb image into the frame by completing the following steps:
   (a) Make sure the frame is selected, then choose Insert, and Picture.
   (b) At the Insert Picture dialog box, double-click *lightblb* from the Name list box.
i. Scroll down through the article and make sure all the article text fits in the space available and that the text in column two has not been displaced. If necessary, delete any extra hard returns that may exist between the Light Bulb article and the masthead. If that fails, try adjusting the vertical position of the masthead.
j. Copy the end sign and space from the previous article and paste it at the end of the lightbulb article.
k. Save c11ex10, copyfit.
l. Insert an article in the space below the picture placeholder, as shown in figure 11.18, by completing the following steps:
   (1) Press Ctrl + End to position the insertion point at the end of the document below the picture caption.
   (2) Insert the file *replace helmet text.*
m. Apply styles to the article text just inserted by completing the following steps:
   (1) Position the insertion point anywhere in the title *When Should A Helmet Be Replaced?*, and apply the *article head* style.
   (2) Select all the paragraph text, and apply the *1st paragraph style.*
n. Position the insertion point anywhere within the article heading and change the spacing before the paragraph to 12 points to increase the white space between the caption and the heading.
o. Insert the bullet and bold the text at the beginning of each paragraph by completing the following steps:
   (1) With the insertion point positioned at the beginning of the first paragraph, select all of the article text.
   (2) Choose Format, Bullets and Numbering, and then select the Bulleted tab.
   (3) Select the first bulleted example and then click Modify.
   (4) In the Bullet Character section, change the Point Size to 11 points and change the Color to Dk Cyan.
   (5) In the Bullet Position section, make sure there is a check mark in the Hanging Indent check box.
   (6) Click Bullet, change the Symbols From: to Wingdings, and then select the round bullet in the third row, twenty-first column.
   (7) Click OK or press Enter to close the Symbol dialog box and then click OK again to close the Modify Bulleted List dialog box.
   (8) Select the phrase *After a crash.* and change the font to 11-point Impact.
   (9) Repeat step (8) to format the three remaining phrases at the beginning of each bulleted item. (A style could be created for this formatting, if desired; otherwise, press F4 to repeat the formatting.)
p. Scroll down through the article and make sure all the article text fits in the space available. If not, make some copy-fitting adjustments.
q. Copy the space and end sign at the end of the *Light Bulb Test* article and paste it at the end of the last article on page 2.

2. Save c11ex10, copy fit.
3. Print both pages of the Ride Safe newsletter and then close c11ex10, copy fit.

FIGURE 11.18

Volume 5, Issue 2 • September 1997

Bicycle and In-Line Skating Safety for the 90s •

In the
Helmet Habit

"I don't quite know why my daughter, Kate, fell from her bike last July. Maybe she hit a small rock or just lost her balance. We found Kate lying on the ground. She was bleeding and had several cuts and bruises on her face and forehead. We called the paramedics and she began to lose consciousness just as they arrived. At the emergency room, we found out that Kate had a broken nose, a missing tooth, and four other loose teeth. Fortunately for all of us, Kate was wearing a bicycle helmet. Without even asking, three different doctors have told us that the helmet probably saved Kate's life. So many people tell me that their kids won't wear a helmet. I tell them to be firm—no helmet, no bike. Bicycle accidents can happen to anyone!"

Karen Brust
Boston, Massachusetts

In This Issue:

Bicycle Safety: Let's Make It a Priority!

Protect your child!

Did you know that each year over 1,200 people die and thousands more are seriously injured in bicycle accidents? According to the American Academy of Pediatrics, more than 500,000 emergency room visits annually in the U.S. are attributed to bicycle accidents.

Surprisingly, most of these accidents, especially those involving children, occur on quiet residential streets. Most do not involve cars. And many could be prevented with proper training and safety equipment.

Think about it. Before we're allowed to drive a car, we have to be a certain age and go through extensive training and testing. Yet many of us—children in particular—ride the very same roads on a bicycle with little or no training at all. Kids are especially vulnerable because of their undeveloped peripheral vision (about two-thirds that of adults), poor speed judgment, and lack of a sense of danger.

More than 500,000 trips are made to emergency rooms each year for bicycle-related injuries.

At Ride Safe, we believe bicycle safety education is crucial to our well-being and to that of our children. More and more states, including New York, New Jersey, Connecticut, Georgia, Tennessee, Oregon, and California are implementing legislation requiring bicycle helmets for children. As adults, we can teach our children safe riding habits, protect them from injury by purchasing bicycle helmets, and set a good example when we are riding our own bicycles.

The bottom line? *Bicycle safety is something we all need to make a priority!*

— • —

"Accidents" Waiting to Happen

The majority of bicycle/car "accidents" are not really accidents, but avoidable collisions. Most result from the bicyclist's failure to use proper riding techniques in a hazardous situation. Ironically, when asked, most children injured in traffic could describe the actual law they broke.

(continued on page 2)

Research indicates that 60% of all U.S. bicycle-car collisions occur among bicyclists between the ages of 8 and 12. Still, an average of only $1 is spent per child between birth and age 15 teaching traffic education. Children are permitted to travel with only a *"look both ways before you cross the street"* and *"make sure you stop at all stop signs"* warning. Obviously these "warnings" are not enough. — • —

The Light Bulb Test

To illustrate the effectiveness of a bicycle helmet, try the following. Wrap a light bulb in plastic wrap, seal the bottom with a rubber band and place it in a bicycle helmet. Secure the light bulb with tape and drop the helmet onto a flat, hard surface from above your head. The light bulb will not break. In most cases, it will even still light. Now, drop the light bulb without the protection of the helmet. The light bulb will produce a sick thud as it breaks. Helmets *can* make a difference.

Caution: Parents, this experiment is meant to be done by you or under your close supervision. — • —

Ride Safe

Editor:
Chris Urban
Design and Layout:
Cassie Lizbeth
Authors:
Brandon Keith
Brian Stetler
Christine Pollistrini
Published quarterly by:
Ride Safe, Inc.
P.O. Box 888
Warrenville, IL 60555
800-285-RIDE
Fax: 630-653-9068
©Copyright 1994 by:
Ride Safe, Inc.
All rights reserved.

Who Says Helmets Aren't Cool?

Insert picture of children from Silverton, Oregon here.

Certainly not the children of Silverton, Oregon! One of the biggest reasons children don't wear bicycle helmets is because their friends don't wear them. By getting all the children in your school or neighborhood to order bicycle helmets at the same time, you can help turn this peer pressure from negative to positive. Suddenly wearing a bicycle helmet becomes the "cool" thing to do.

When Should a Helmet Be Replaced?

- **After a crash.** Almost all bicycle helmets are designed to absorb the impact of a crash so that your head is protected. This damages the foam liner and reduces its ability to protect in the future. If you are involved in a crash and your helmet hits the pavement, it should be carefully inspected and/or replaced. Most manufacturers offer free inspection services and sometimes even free crash replacement policies.
- **When it doesn't fit.** Bicycle helmets must fit correctly to offer the intended protection. See your owner's manual for information on how to achieve a correct fit.
- **After three to five years.** The Snell Memorial Foundation recommends that you replace your helmet after five years. Due to advances in technology and performance, we suggest your helmet be evaluated after three years. Normal wear and tear due to drops and exposure gradually reduces a helmet's strength and protection capabilities. Helmets that receive extremely rough treatment should be considered for replacement even earlier. Does you child carefully hang up his/her helmet or is it tossed in the corner?
- **When it isn't being worn.** For whatever reason (not comfortable, too hot, too heavy, too old, doesn't match the new hat or coat, etc.), it may be time for a new helmet. Manufacturers have made dramatic improvements in style, weight, ventilation and cost over the last few years. If you and your children are not wearing helmets, there is nothing like a brand-new one to renew your interest and commitment. — • —

• 2 •

Saving Your Newsletter as a Template

To save time when creating future issues of your newsletter, save your newsletter as a template document. To do this, delete all text, frames, pictures, objects, etc. that will not stay the same for future issues. Likewise, leave all text, pictures, symbols, frames, headers and footers, etc. that will remain the same in each issue of your newsletter. For example, to save the Ride Safe newsletter as a template, leave the following items and delete the rest:

- Folio
- Nameplate
- Headers and footers
- Sidebar with the title since this will be a feature article every month; delete the sidebar article text; press the Enter key to leave placeholders for future text
- Table of Contents and heading; delete the table of contents text; press the Enter key to leave placeholders for future text
- Masthead

Once you have deleted the text and elements that will change every month, save the newsletter with Save As. At the Save As dialog box, click the down-pointing arrow to the right of the Save as type list box and select *Document Template (*.dot)* as the file type. Double-click the Publications folder, key a name for your newsletter template, and then click OK. To use the newsletter template, choose File, New, then select the Publications tab. Double-click the name of your newsletter template. The stripped-down version of your newsletter will display on the screen. Select and replace the month, date, and volume number in the folio. Key article headings and text to complete your newsletter. Delete any placeholder hard returns when necessary. Remember to update the authors' names in the masthead. Save your completed newsletter with a new name, such as RideSafe Oct newsletter. See figure 11.19 for an example of how the Ride Safe newsletter might look if saved as a template.

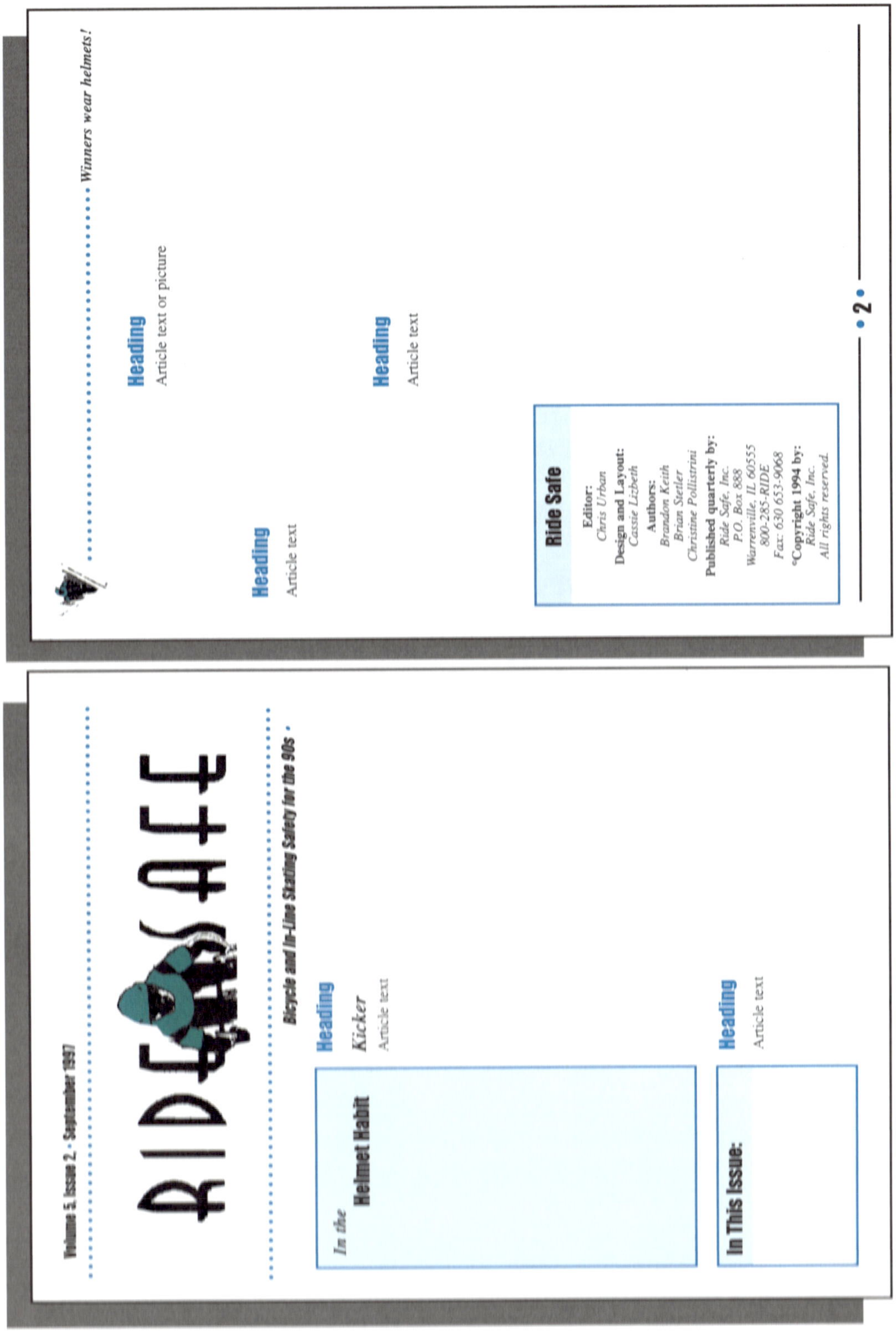

FIGURE 11.19

Sample of Ride Safe Newsletter Saved as a Template

Volume 5, Issue 2 • September 1997

RIDE SAFE

Bicycle and In-Line Skating Safety for the 90s •

In the
Helmet Habit

Heading

Kicker
Article text

In This Issue:

Heading

Article text

Winners wear helmets!

Heading

Article text or picture

Heading

Article text

Heading

Article text

Ride Safe

Editor:
Chris Urban
Design and Layout:
Cassie Lizbeth
Authors:
Brandon Keith
Brian Stetler
Christine Pollistrini
Published quarterly by:
Ride Safe, Inc.
P.O. Box 888
Warrenville, IL 60555
800-285-RIDE
Fax: 630 653-9068
©Copyright 1994 by:
Ride Safe, Inc.
All rights reserved.

• 2 •

Chapter Summary

- Elements can be added to a newsletter to enhance the visual impact, including tables of contents, headers and/or footers, mastheads, pull quotes, kickers, sidebars, captions, ruled lines, jump lines, page borders, and end signs.
- Use spot color—a color in addition to black— in a newsletter as an accent to such features as graphics lines, graphics images, borders, backgrounds, headings, and end signs.
- Headers and footers are commonly used in newsletters. Headers/footers can be placed on specific pages, only odd pages, or only even pages, and horizontal ruled lines can be added for visual contrast.
- A sidebar is set off from the body text in a graphics box and can include a photograph or graphics image along with text.
- In multipage newsletters, a table of contents is an important element and is generally located on the front page in the lower left or right corner.
- A pull quote acts as a focal point, helps to break up lengthy blocks of text, and provides visual contrast.
- A masthead is a repeating element that usually contains the company address, newsletter publication schedule, names of those contributing to the production, and copyright information. It is generally located on the back page of a newsletter.
- A kicker is generally set in a smaller type size than the headline but larger than the body text and is placed above or below the headline or article heading.
- Symbols or special characters used to indicate the end of a section of text are called end signs.
- In a newsletter, a jump line is a continuation of an article or feature to another page and enables the creator of the newsletter to feature the beginning of several articles on the front page.
- Graphics images, illustrations, charts, diagrams, and photographs can add focus, balance, proportion, contrast, directional flow, and consistency to a newsletter. Graphics images include line art and continuous-tone art.
- Noncomputer-generated images such as photographs and illustrations can be scanned and then inserted in a newsletter.
- Captions can be added to images to establish a connection to the body copy. Bold caption text and set it in a smaller point size to make it different from the body text.
- Copy fitting refers to making varying amounts of text or typographical enhancements fit in a fixed amount of space.

Commands Review

	Mouse/Keyboard
New dialog box to access a template	File, New, select desired tab
Newsletter Wizard	File, New, Publications tab
Insert File dialog box	Insert, File
Insert Picture dialog box	Insert, Picture
Headers and Footers	View, Header and Footer; click Switch Between Header and Footer to display Header or Footer pane
Display Drawing toolbar	Click Drawing button on Standard toolbar; or right-click Standard toolbar, select Drawing; or View, Toolbars, select Drawing, then press Enter
Draw a frame	Insert, Frame, position crosshairs and draw frame
Insert frame around selected text	Select text, choose Insert, Frame
Format Picture	Select picture; Format, Picture
Format Frame	Select frame; Format, Frame
Format Drawing Object	Select drawing object; Format, Drawing Object
Paragraph Borders and Shading dialog box	Format, Borders and Shading
Size and position a frame	Select frame, choose Format, Frame
Kerning (Character Spacing of specific pairs of characters)	Format, Font, Character Spacing tab, Kerning for Fonts, enter specific amount of Points and Above to be kerned
Tracking (Character spacing)	Format, Font, Character Spacing tab, Spacing, Expand or Condense or Normal, enter point By: amount in point increments
Insert special characters	Insert, Symbol
Style dialog box	Format, Style
Insert a Column Break	Insert, Break, Column Break
Bullets and Numbering	Format, Bullets and Numbering

Check Your Understanding

Terms: Match the terms with the correct definitions by writing the letter of the term on the blank line in front of the correct definition.

A. Caption
B. Copy fitting
C. End sign
D. Footer
E. Header
F. Jump line
G. Kicker
H. Masthead
I. Pull quote
J. Scanner
K. Sidebar
L. Spot color

_______ 1. A repeating element that can add consistency among newsletter issues and contains the company address, newsletter publication schedule, names of those contributing to the production of the newsletter, and copyright information.

_______ 2. Description or explanation of a graphics image, illustration, or photograph.

_______ 3. Text that is repeated at the top of every page.

_______ 4. A block of information or a related story that is set off from the body text in a graphics box.

_______ 5. A color in a newsletter, other than black, used as an accent.

_______ 6. A brief direct phrase, summarizing statement, or important point associated with the body copy of a newsletter.

_______ 7. A symbol or special character used to indicate the end of a section of text.

_______ 8. Indicates a continuation of an article or feature to another page.

_______ 9. A brief sentence or phrase that is a lead-in to an article.

_______ 10. A piece of equipment that converts a photograph, drawing, or text into a compatible digital file format.

Concepts: Write your answers to the following questions in the space provided.

1. What are at least five tips to consider when creating a pull quote?

2. What graphics file extensions are compatible with Word? (List at least ten.)

3. What are at least six copy-fitting ideas to create more space in a document?

4. What are at least six copy-fitting ideas to fill extra space in a document?

5. What are at least four paragraph enhancements that can be included in a newsletter?

Skill Assessments

Assessment 1

1. Find two newsletters from two different sources. Review the newsletters for the items listed below. Label those items that you find in each newsletter.

   Nameplate
   Subtitle
   Folio
   Headlines
   Subheads

Table of contents
Masthead
Header
Footer
Sidebar
Pull quote
Kicker
End sign
Jump line
Caption
Spot color

Optional: Write a summary explaining which of the two newsletters is the most appealing and why.

Assessment 2

In this assessment, you are to redesign the first page of a newsletter located on your student data disk. Two pages of text are provided. You only need to redesign the first page, but you may use any of the text on the second page for copy-fitting purposes.

1. Redesign a basic newsletter named *redesign text.doc* located on your student data disk according to the following specifications:
   a. Create a new nameplate, subtitle, and folio. Experiment with thumbnail sketches.
   b. Create the body of the newsletter using an asymmetrical column layout.
   c. Include the following:

      Header and footer
      Table of contents
      Sidebar
      Pull quote
      Graphic with caption
      Spot color (or varying shades of gray)

   d. Use a kicker, end signs, jump line, clip art, frame for a photo, etc. if desired or needed for copy fitting.
   e. Use tracking (character spacing), leading (line spacing), paragraph spacing before and after, frames, etc., to set the body copy attractively on the page.
2. Save and name the new newsletter as c11sa02, redesign nwsltr.
3. Print and then close c11sa02, redesign nwsltr.
4. In class, edit each other's newsletters by completing the following steps:
   a. Independently choose an editor's name for yourself and do not share it with the rest of the class. (This is your chance to be really famous!)
   b. Your instructor will collect all the newsletters and randomly distribute a newsletter to each class participant.
   c. Sign your individual editor's "name" on the back of the newsletter and make editorial comments addressing such items as: target audience, visual appeal, overall layout and design, font selection, graphics image selection, focus, balance, proportion, contrast, directional flow, consistency, and use of color.
   d. Rotate the newsletters so that you have an opportunity to write editor's comments on the back of each newsletter, identified by your individual editor's name only.

e. Review the editor's comments on the back of your own newsletter and redo your newsletter.

5. Save and name the revised version of your newsletter c11sa02, revised.
6. Print c11sa02, revised.
7. Evaluate your redesigned newsletter with the *Document Evaluation Checklist* (*document evaluation checklist.doc)*.

Assessment 3

Assume that you are an employee of Ride Safe, Inc., and are responsible for creating their newsletter. You have already completed an issue of this newsletter in c11ex10, and now you have to create the next issue. Using articles from your student data disk and the Ride Safe newsletter already created, create the next issue of the RideSafe newsletter according to the following specifications:

1. Print *RideSafe issue2 text.doc* located on your student data disk.
2. Review the printout of possible articles to be used for the second issue of your newsletter. Decide what articles you would like to include. Save the rest for possible fillers.
3. Make a thumbnail sketch of a possible layout and design. Be consistent in column layout and design elements used. Include the following items:

   Masthead
   Sidebar
   Pull quote
   End sign
   Caption
   Picture
   Spot color

4. Open c11ex10, ride safe newsletter.doc.
5. Save the document with Save As and name it c11sa03, ride safe issue2, then move the insertion point to page 2. For the masthead, use your instructor's name as the editor and your name for the design and layout.
6. Use the *article head* style for the article headings.
7. You decide on the order and placement of articles. You may use bullets, bold, italics, reverse, etc., if appropriate to the design and layout of the next issue of your newsletter.
8. Make any copy-fitting adjustments as necessary.
9. Save, print, and then close c11sa03, ride safe issue2.
10. Evaluate your newsletter with the *Document Evaluation Checklist* (*document evaluation checklist.doc*).

Optional: Rewrite and redesign all the article heads to be more clever, interesting, and eye-catching.

Creative Activity

With a partner, find a poor example of a newsletter and redesign the first page, including the nameplate. Use a different column layout and copy-fitting techniques to produce a newsletter that entices people to actually read your publication. Rewrite the text copy to make it more interesting. Recreate, save, and print c11ca01, then close it. In class, break up into small groups of four to six students and present the before and after versions of your newsletter. Give a brief explanation of the changes made, problems encountered, and solutions found. Vote on the most creative copy and the most creative design.

12 PREPARING REPORTS AND MANUALS

PERFORMANCE OBJECTIVE

Upon successful completion of chapter 12, you will be able to prepare reports, term papers, manuals, and forms containing elements such as a cover page, table of contents, title page, and index.

DESKTOP PUBLISHING CONCEPTS

Cover	Back matter	Directional flow
Front matter	Back cover	Balance
Body text	Consistency	

WORD FEATURES USED

Templates	Picture	Frame
Styles	Borders and Shading	Headers and Footers
Insert File	Index and Tables	Drop Cap
Format Drawing Object	Page Numbering	Tables

Structured publications such as reports, manuals, and directories are text-intensive, multipage documents containing repeating elements, such as headers or footers, and consistently styled title and text pages. Structured publications may contain all or some of the following elements in the order shown:

Cover
Front matter
Title page
Copyright page

Preface
Table of contents
Body text
Sections/chapters
Back matter
Appendix
Bibliography
Glossary
Index
Back cover

Not all structured publications contain each element. The elements are determined by the contents, length, and type of document. For example, a company manual may contain a title page, table of contents, index, and appendix, while a company catalog may contain all elements. Each element is described as follows:

Cover: The cover of a report, manual, or booklet is generally the first thing a reader notices. It should be attractively designed and draw a person's interest and attention. A cover may be multicolored while the inside text is printed in one color. It may be designed and produced by the desktop publisher or sent to a graphic designer for production. For some projects a cover is printed on the same stock as the other pages, while for others a heavier stock is used.

Title Page: The title page of a structured publication generally contains the full title of the publication (including any subtitles), the full name of the author, editor, and publisher, and possibly the publisher's address. If the structured publication is bound, the title page is printed on a right-hand page.

Copyright Page: A copyright page generally includes elements such as copyright dates, copyright permissions, name of the country where the structured publication is published, Library of Congress Cataloging-in-Publication (CIP) data, and the International Standard Book Number (ISBN). A copyright page is generally printed on the reverse of the title page.

Preface: A preface is a statement by the author about the publication and may include acknowledgments. A preface usually begins on an odd-numbered page. A preface is sometimes referred to as the *foreword* and may be eliminated in technical or short publications.

Table of Contents: The table of contents for a report, manual, or booklet contains the name of each chapter or section and the page number on which each begins. The first page of a table of contents is generally designed like the first page of a chapter or section and begins with an odd-numbered page. Page numbers in a table of contents can be placed immediately after an item, separated by a comma, or separated from an item by leaders. Leaders are characters (generally periods) that print from the item to the page number, which is aligned at the right side of the page. The leaders help guide the reader's eyes across the page to the proper page number.

Body Text: When creating body text for a structured publication, consider such elements as the font, margin widths, running headers/footers, and page numbering. Set body text in approximately 11- or 12-point size and use a serif typeface for easy readability. Set headings and subheadings in a larger point size and consider using a typeface that complements the typeface used for the body text. Add a type style such as bold and/or italics to enhance headings and/or subheadings.

Appendix: Appendices include information that is not essential to the text but may help clarify the information presented. Appendices appear after the body text and usually begin on an odd-numbered page. The beginning page of an appendix is designed in the same manner as the first page of chapters or sections.

Preparing A Report

A report is a structured publication containing consistently styled title and text pages. Word provides three report templates to help you create a formatted report. The three report templates are labeled Contemporary Report, Elegant Report, and Professional Report. Word formats the pages of each of these reports using fonts and design enhancements similar to those in the memo, letter, and newsletter templates carrying the same descriptive names.

DTP POINTERS
Organize the content and graphic images of a report ahead of time.

In exercise 1, you will prepare a report using the Contemporary Report template. This template contains the formatting for a cover page, a chapter or section title page, headings, body text, and more. Instructions on how to use and customize the report template are included in the template. The instructional text is formatted using many of the styles saved with this template, enabling you to visualize the formatting options available in this template. One suggestion when using any of the report templates is to print a hard copy of the template and read the instructional text before creating your own document from the template. Another suggestion is to scroll through the template document as it is displayed on the screen, click any paragraph, and view the style name in the Style list box on the Formatting toolbar. Then write the style names next to the corresponding text on the hard copy of the template document. This way, when you delete the instructional text, you will know what styles were applied to specific sections of text. In exercise 1, you will insert text and use the Contemporary Report template's styles to format the text into a report layout.

Creating a Report Using the Contemporary Report Template

1. Prepare a report using the Contemporary Report template, as shown in figure 12.1, by completing the following steps:
   a. Choose File, then New.
   b. At the New dialog box, select the Reports tab and then double-click the Contemporary Report icon.
   c. Print a copy of the report template document and read the instructional text.
   d. Insert the company name and address by completing the following steps:
      (1) With the insertion point located in the framed text in the upper right corner of the title page (*Return Address* should display in the Style list box on the Formatting toolbar), select all of the existing text in the frame.
      (2) Key the following:

      Global Communications, Inc.
      73 West 22nd Street
      Oak Brook, IL 60555
      Phone: (630) 555-5647
      Fax: (630) 555-6521

   e. Insert the company name, cover title, and subtitle by completing the following steps:
      (1) Select *blue sky associates* (*Company Name* should display in the Style list box on the Formatting toolbar), then key **global communications, inc.**
      (2) Scroll down and select the cover title, *Film Watch Division Marketing Plan* (*Title Cover* should display in the Style list box on the Formatting toolbar), then key **Communications Systems**.
      (3) Scroll down and select the cover subtitle, *Trey's Best Opportunity to Dominate Market Research for the Film Industry*, excluding the End of Section and Page Break identifiers. (*Subtitle Cover* should display in the Style list box on the Formatting toolbar).

(4) Key the following, pressing Shift + Enter as indicated:

Prepared by: (Shift + Enter)
Your name (Shift + Enter)
Current date

f. On page two, insert the title, subtitle, and the first heading by completing the following steps:
   (1) Select the title, *FilmWatch Division Marketing Plan* (*Title* should display in the Style list box on the Formatting toolbar), then key **Communications Systems**.
   (2) Select the subtitle, *Trey's Best Opportunity to Dominate Market Research for the Film Industry*, (*Subtitle* should display in the Style list box on the Formatting toolbar), then key **Telecommunications at Work**.
   (3) Select the first heading, *How To Use This Report Template*, (*Heading 1* should display in the Style list box on the Formatting toolbar), then key **Ergonomics**.
g. Insert the first section of report text by completing the following steps:
   (1) Position the insertion point at the beginning of the first paragraph of instructional text located below the heading *Ergonomics*.
   (2) Select the remaining text and press the Delete key.
   (3) Press Enter.
   (4) Insert the file *report text1* located on your student data disk.
h. Format the report text and headings by completing the following steps:
   (1) Select all of the report text just inserted and apply the *Body Text* style from the Style list box located on the Formatting toolbar.
   (2) Position the insertion point anywhere within the following headings and apply the *Heading 2* style from the Style list box located on the Formatting toolbar:

Ergonomic Features
Information Formats
The Work Station as a Focal Point

i. Emphasize specific items in the report text with bullets by completing the following steps:
   (1) In the section titled *The Work Station as a Focal Point*, select the two lines that read *the realization that the microcomputer can be used for multiple business purposes;* and *the anticipation of a one-to-one ratio of workers to PCs.*
   (2) Apply the *List Bullet* style from the Style list box located on the Formatting toolbar.
   (3) In the same section, select *how the information is created;* and *how the information is delivered.*
   (4) Repeat step (2) or press F4.
j. Press Ctrl + End to position the insertion point at the end of the document.
k. Press Ctrl + Enter to insert a hard page break.
l. To maintain consistency from the first section title page to the second title page, copy the vertical dotted line by completing the following steps:
   (1) At the top of page two, position the insertion point in the vertical dotted line until it displays as an arrow with a four-headed arrow attached, then click once to select the text box containing the dotted line. Make sure the black selection handles display around the box.
   (2) Click the Copy button on the Standard toolbar.

(3) Position the insertion point at the top of page 4, then click the Paste button on the Standard toolbar.
(4) Click outside of the text box to deselect it.
(5) Press the Enter key until the status line displays 1.6 inches.

m. Insert and format the section subtitle by completing the following steps:
(1) Key **Communications Equipment**, then press Enter.
(2) Position the insertion point on any character within the subtitle, Communications Equipment, then apply the *Subtitle* style from the Style list box located on the Formatting toolbar.

n. Insert and format the first heading by completing the following steps:
(1) Position the insertion point a line below the subtitle, then key **Multimedia PC**, and then press Enter.
(2) Position the insertion point on any character within the heading, Multimedia PC, then apply the *Heading 1* style from the Style list box located on the Formatting toolbar.

o. With the insertion point located a line below the heading, insert the file *report text2* located on your student data disk.

p. Format the report text and headings by completing the following steps:
(1) Select all of the report text just inserted and apply the *Body Text* style from the Style list box located on the Formatting toolbar.
(2) Position the insertion point anywhere within the following headings and apply the *Heading 2* style from the Style list box located on the Formatting toolbar: (After the first style has been applied, you can easily repeat the style by pressing F4 at each heading location.)

Hardware
Software
Telecommunications Links
Local Area Networks
Wide Area Networks
Applications of Multimedia PC

q. Select and apply the *List Bullet* style from the Style list box located on the Formatting toolbar to the following items:
(1) In the section titled *Hardware* on page 4, all the items following *In designed information... include a PC with:*.
(2) In the section title *Software* on pages 4 and 5, all the items following *The software... environment includes:*.
(3) In the section titled *Telecommunications Links* on page 5, all the items following *The following questions... basic options:*.
(4) In the section titled *Local Area Networks* on page 5, all the items following *Consider the following... area networking:*.

r. In the section title *Wide Area Networks* on page 5, select and apply the *List Number* style from the Style list box located on the Formatting toolbar to the two paragraphs following *The alternatives... service providers:*.

s. In the same section, emphasize the two categories identified by the numbers by completing the following steps:
(1) Select *Media*, the first word after the number one.
(2) Apply the *Emphasis* style from the Style list box located on the formatting toolbar.
(3) Select *Service providers*, the first two words after the number two, then repeat step (2).

2. Save and name the report c12ex01, report.
3. Print and then close c12ex01, report.

FIGURE 12.1

[illegible]
Fax: (630) 555-6521

global communications, inc.

Communications Systems

Prepared by.
Your name
Current date

Communications Systems

Telecommunications at Work

Ergonomics

Upon your arrival at work today, you seat yourself at the ergonomically designed work station where most of your activities are conducted. *Ergonomics* is the science of helping individuals interface with their immediate office environment so they can function at their highest levels.

Ergonomic Features

Features that contribute to productivity are chairs that are comfortable and that offer good back support, sufficient lighting to minimize eye strain, panels that provide visual privacy, and sufficient space to do the jobs required. Another component of your work station is a multifunction display terminal that can generate, store, transmit, and receive voice, data, word, image, and video information. A terminal should have a filter to eliminate glare from windows or lighting systems, and the top of the screen should be at eye level.

Information Formats

Not all the information you receive at work arrives in an electronic format. You use a laser scanner—another component of your work station—to convert information into an electronic format so it can be acted upon, distributed to others, or stored for future reference.

Documents and information that you create are dictated to your voice-actuated display terminal. Words appear on your terminal display for editing and revision. This activity can be done on your keyboard or with an electronic pointer device that allows you to make changes orally. Once the document is completed, you direct the system to check for spelling, grammar, and syntax errors. For example, if you had dictated a sentence starting with "You is," which is grammatically incorrect, the system would change it to "You are." And when you dictated that "too few people were involved in the activity," the system would use the correct "too," and not "to" or "two."

The completed document or information can now be distributed via electronic mail to one or more individuals anywhere in the world. An electronic copy of what you created is automatically stored in the optical digital disk storage system. If the document or information has legal value, you store it using Wrote Once Read Many (WORM) optical disk technology. Otherwise, the information is stored on the erasable optical disk system so it can be purged when no longer of value.

The Work Station as a Focal Point

The microcomputer has entered its second decade. The dynamic changes that took place in microcomputers in the first decade were astonishing. The power, speed, capacity, and applications of these systems increased tenfold. By all indications, the PC's second decade will be even more dramatic than the first. Here are two reasons:

2

- the realization that the microcomputer can be used for multiple business purposes;
- the anticipation of a one-to-one ratio of workers to PCs.

Two basic factors that determine the effectiveness of business information systems are

- how the information is created;
- how the information is delivered.

Historically, voice, data, and video applications have been generated by separate devices and, when appropriate, brought together to be telecommunicated. While the integration of voice, data, and video telecommunications will continue to function in this fashion, another alternative has emerged: integration of these technologies using the microcomputer. The microcomputer equipped with the appropriate hardware and software components can be used to create voice, data, and video information.

3

Communications Equipment

Multimedia PC

With a single source as the generating device, the process of telecommunication becomes less complicated because all information is converted to a digital format. The term *multimedia PC* describes a microcomputer that has the capacity to integrate voice, data, and video into signals that can be telecommunicated.

Hardware

In designed information systems that incorporate voice, data, and video technologies for business, the hardware components required include a PC with:

- hard drive (600 megabytes or more);
- fast processor (32-bit cycling at 50 million or more hertz);
- CD-ROM drive (for accessing stored voice, data, and/or video information);
- sound board (to generate and receive voice and other forms of sound);
- analog to digital converter (a component that not only converts analog signals to digital signals—e.g., video signals from a camcorder—but also compresses them to reduce storage and telecommunications costs);
- high-resolution color monitor to enhance onscreen graphics, video, and animation;
- serial port or a network-interface card for local and wide area networking;
- mouse device for working with screen graphics.

Software

The software required to function in a multimedia environment includes:

- a work station operating system (examples include DOS, OS/2, and UNIX);
- communications software (for local area networking or wide area networking);
- device driver software (e.g., disk drivers, mouse drivers, etc.);

4

- graphical user interface software (e.g., Windows);
- applications software packages (must be suited for the environment, e.g., packages designed for particular operating systems, graphical user interfaces, networking).

Telecommunications Links
Once the information to be communicated is digitized and compressed, where appropriate, the next step is telecommunications. The deciding factor is distance. The following questions will help you choose among basic options:

- Will the telecommunications be internal so that a local area network is the only consideration?
- Will the telecommunications be external, requiring the services of a wide area network?
- Will the telecommunications be a combination of the two?

Local Area Networks
Consider the following alternatives for local area networking:

- cable-based or wireless transmission (wireless transmission featuring radio-wave communications may be appropriate, but the number of work stations required and obstacles associated with building construction and location could be obstacles);
- network media (while twisted pair wire and coaxial cable may be sufficient, in cable-based systems, fiber optics offers the highest speed and bandwidth capacities);
- baseband/broadband (baseband can be used effectively for transmitting the integrated information; while broadband provides multiple channels for communications, it requires more hardware and is a more complex operation involving frequency division multiplexing).

Wide Area Networks
The alternatives for wide area networking can be divided into two categories, media and service providers:

1. **Media** (since the information to be transmitted is in a digital format and, where appropriate, compressed, the available media includes twisted pair wire, coaxial cable, optical fiber, microwave, satellite, and laser). Consider cost, ease of use, distance, distribution, security required, and availability in making a media choice.
2. **Service providers** (*common carriers*—telephone companies; *value added carriers*—companies that provide special features; *bypass*—company sets up its own communication links to avoid the continuing costs of local and long distance services).

5

Applications of Multimedia PC
There are numerous applications for the multimedia PC. Think for a moment of a computer manufacturer that has multiple U.S. locations. Assume that this organization's research and development division produces new components for use in their computers and corrects problems encountered in the manufacturing process.

Through the use of multimedia PC, an e-mail message that incorporates data, video, and voice could be sent to all plant locations. The data would be the text stating a computer component change. The video would be a picture of the current component that has been recorded on CD-ROM disk. A copy of the picture can be extracted from the CD-ROM disk and added to the memo. The voice could be a voice message explaining what has been changed.

A video camera can be used to show the new component, and the installation process can be videotaped. The video signals can be compressed using the analog-to-digital conversion/compression card in the multimedia PC. This information is also added to the e-mail message. Through an uplink satellite dish, the e-mail message containing voice, data, and video information is transmitted to a satellite transponder, then downlinked to satellite dishes at each plant location.

Projected uses of multimedia PC are limited only by imagination. Currently, multimedia PCs are popularly used to develop and telecommunicate training materials to local or distant sites. Whether the information to be télecommunicated comes from a single source, such as a multimedia PC, or from a variety of devices, knowing the alternatives available and the features and benefits of each will help you make the right choice.

6

The Contemporary Report template uses several consistent elements to contribute to a unified appearance. The cover title and the report headings are set in 36-point Arial, while the subtitles are set in Times New Roman. The body text of the report is set in 10-point Times New Roman, which is a serif typeface—an appropriate choice for such a text-intensive document. The vertical dotted line at the top of the cover page is repeated at the top of the section title page (page two) and a horizontal variation of the dotted line is included in the middle of the cover page. The shaded text boxes located at the top and bottom of the cover page are repeated in the form of paragraph shading in the *Heading 1* style. A miniature version of the shaded text box is also included at the top of the section title page.

Customizing A Report

The report templates let you easily and quickly create a very professional-looking report. However, if you do not like all the formatting choices included in a specific template, or if you want a more customized report, you can use a report template as a base and then modify it to fit your needs or liking. For example, if you created the report in exercise 1, you might like to replace the globe with a different image or exclude the image completely. Or maybe you would like to use a different typeface for the report headings, add color to the shaded boxes, or move the horizontal dotted line on the front cover. All of these revisions can be easily made, including modifying styles, while still maintaining the initial framework of the report template. In addition, you can include other report elements such as a preface, table of contents, or index.

DTP POINTERS
Use a template as a base and modify it to fit your needs.

Customizing a Report Created with a Report Template

1. Customize the cover and section title pages of the report created in exercise 1, as shown in figure 12.2, by completing the following steps:
   a. Open c12ex01, report.
   b. Use Save As and name the report c12ex02, custom report.
   c. Add color to the shaded text box that contains the company name by completing the following steps:
      (1) On the cover page (page 1), position the insertion point in the shaded text box containing *global communications, inc.* until it turns into a pointer arrow with a four-headed arrow attached, then double-click in the text box to quickly access the Drawing Object dialog box.
      (2) Select the Fill tab.
      (3) In the Color: section, select Dk Blue in the seventh row, first column.
      (4) Change the Patterns: to 70% and the Pattern Color: to White.
      (5) Choose OK to close the dialog box.
   d. Scroll down and select *Prepared by:*, then change the type size to 16 points.
   e. Add color to the globe by completing the following steps:
      (1) Position the insertion point inside the globe image until it displays as a pointer arrow with a four-headed arrow attached, then double-click to display the image in Word Picture.
      (2) In Microsoft Word Picture, double-click the left side of the globe to display the Drawing Object dialog box.
      (3) Select the Fill tab.
      (4) In the Color: section, select Dk Blue in the seventh row, first column.
      (5) Change the Patterns: to 70% and the Pattern Color: to White.
      (6) Choose OK to close the dialog box.
      (7) Double-click the right side of the globe and repeat steps (3) through (6) to add color to the remaining part of the globe.
      (8) In the Picture dialog box, click Close Picture.
   f. Double-click in the shaded text box located at the bottom of the title page and follow steps c(2) through c(5) above to add blue shading to this text box.
   g. Move the text box containing the horizontal dotted line, located between the cover title and cover subtitle, by completing the following steps:
      (1) Position the arrow pointer either at the beginning or at the end of the dotted line, then click once to select the text box containing the dotted line. (This line is difficult to select other than at the beginning or the end.)
      (2) Position the pointer arrow on the text box border, then double-click to access the Drawing Object dialog box.
      (3) At the Drawing Object dialog box, select the Size and Position tab.
      (4) Change the Horizontal Position to 0.5 inches From: Page, then change the Vertical Position to 9 inches From: Page.
      (5) Choose OK to close the dialog box.
   h. On page 2, select the shaded text box located in the top right corner of the page, then press Delete. (This element seems out of place.)
   i. On page 2, add color to the paragraph shading surrounding the heading *Ergonomics* by completing the following steps:
      (1) Position the insertion point anywhere within the heading *Ergonomics*.
      (2) Display the Borders and Shading dialog box, then select the Shading tab.
      (3) Change the Foreground fill color to White, change the Background fill color to Dk Blue, then select 70% as the level of Shading.
      (4) Choose OK to close the dialog box.
   j. On page 4, add color to the paragraph shading surrounding the heading *Multimedia PC* by completing the following steps:

(1) Position the insertion point anywhere within the heading *Multimedia PC.*
(2) Press F4 to repeat the shading formatting. (The style could also be redefined, if desired.)

2. Save the customized report with the same name, c12ex02, custom report.
3. Print and then close c12ex02, custom report.

FIGURE 12.2

Pages 1, 2, and 4

Global Communications, Inc.
73 West 22nd Street
Oak Brook, IL 60555
Phone: (630) 555-5647
Fax: (630) 555-6521

global communications, inc.

Communications Systems

Prepared by:
Your name
Current date

Communications Systems

Telecommunications at Work

Ergonomics

Upon your arrival at work today, you seat yourself at the ergonomically designed work station where most of your activities are conducted. *Ergonomics* is the science of helping individuals interface with their immediate office environment so they can function at their highest levels.

Ergonomic Features

Features that contribute to productivity are chairs that are comfortable and that offer good back support, sufficient lighting to minimize eye strain, panels that provide visual privacy, and sufficient space to do the jobs required. Another component of your work station is a multifunction display terminal that can generate, store, transmit, and receive voice, data, word, image, and video information. A terminal should have a filter to eliminate glare from windows or lighting systems, and the top of the screen should be at eye level.

Information Formats

Not all the information you receive at work arrives in an electronic format. You use a laser scanner—another component of your work station—to convert information into an electronic format so it can be acted upon, distributed to others, or stored for future reference.

Documents and information that you create are dictated to your voice-actuated display terminal. Words appear on your terminal display for editing and revision. This activity can be done on your keyboard or with an electronic pointer device that allows you to make changes orally. Once the document is completed, you direct the system to check for spelling, grammar, and syntax errors. For example, if you had dictated a sentence starting with "You is," which is grammatically incorrect, the system would change it to "You are." And when you dictated that "too few people were involved in the activity," the system would use the correct "too," and not "to" or "two."

The completed document or information can now be distributed via electronic mail to one or more individuals anywhere in the world. An electronic copy of what you created is automatically stored in the optical digital disk storage system. If the document or information has legal value, you store it using Write Once Read Many (WORM) optical disk technology. Otherwise, the information is stored on the erasable optical disk system so it can be purged when no longer of value.

The Work Station as a Focal Point

The microcomputer has entered its second decade. The dynamic changes that took place in microcomputers in the first decade were astonishing. The power, speed, capacity, and applications of these systems increased tenfold. By all indications, the PC's second decade will be even more dramatic than the first. Here are two reasons:

2

Communications Equipment

Multimedia PC

With a single source as the generating device, the process of telecommunication becomes less complicated because all information is converted to a digital format. The term *multimedia PC* describes a microcomputer that has the capacity to integrate voice, data, and video into signals that can be telecommunicated.

Hardware

In designed information systems that incorporate voice, data, and video technologies for business, the hardware components required include a PC with:

- hard drive (600 megabytes or more);
- fast processor (32-bit cycling at 50 million or more hertz);
- CD-ROM drive (for accessing stored voice, data, and/or video information);
- sound board (to generate and receive voice and other forms of sound);
- analog to digital converter (a component that not only converts analog signals to digital signals—e.g., video signals from a camcorder—but also compresses them to reduce storage and telecommunications costs);
- high resolution color monitor to enhance onscreen graphics, video, and animation;
- serial port or a network interface card for local and wide area networking;
- mouse device for working with screen graphics.

Software

The software required to function in a multimedia environment includes:

- a work station operating system (examples include DOS, OS/2, and UNIX);
- communications software (for local area networking or wide area networking);
- device driver software (e.g., disk drivers, mouse drivers, etc.);

4

Preparing A Table Of Contents

A report, manuscript, book, or textbook often includes sections such as a table of contents, index, and table of figures. Creating these sections in a document can be accomplished quickly and easily with Word's automated features. As mentioned earlier, a table of contents appears at the beginning of a report, manuscript, or book and contains headings and subheadings with corresponding page number locations.

To create a table of contents in Word, you must first mark or identify all the items in your document that you want to include in your table of contents. Then Word must be instructed to compile the table of contents from the marked text. Text to be included in a table of contents can be marked or identified using one of three methods. You can apply Word's built-in heading styles to the text you want to be included in the table of contents, you can apply your own custom styles to those items you want included in a table of contents, or you can mark items for a table of contents as field entries.

Using Styles to Mark Table of Contents Entries

When instructed to compile a table of contents, Word automatically includes any items formatted by its built-in heading styles (labeled *Heading 1* through *Heading 9*). Word uses the heading style numbers to determine what level the item will occupy in the table of contents. For example, an item formatted with a *Heading 1* style will be formatted as a level one heading in the table of contents. An item formatted with a *Heading 2* style will be formatted as a level two heading in the table of contents, and so on, as illustrated in figure 12.3. The advantage of using styles to mark text for a table of contents is that it is quick and easy. The disadvantage is that the appropriate heading styles must be applied to the desired items in your document for this feature to work. In addition, the document will display with the formatting applied by the styles.

FIGURE 12.3

Sample Table of Contents

TABLE OF CONTENTS

LEVEL ONE HEADING 1
LEVEL TWO HEADING 1
Level Three Heading 1
Level Three Heading 2
Level Three Heading 2

To apply styles for a table of contents you would complete these steps:

1. Position the insertion point on any character in the text you want included in the table of contents.
2. Click the down-pointing triangle to the right of the Style button on the Formatting toolbar, then click the desired style name, such as *Heading 1*.
3. Continue applying the appropriate numbered heading styles to the remaining items to be included in your table of contents.

To compile a table of contents from Word's built-in heading styles you would complete these steps:

1. After the necessary heading styles have been applied, position the insertion point where you want the table of contents to appear.
2. Choose Insert, Index and Tables, and then select the Table of Contents tab.
3. In the Formats list box, select one of the table of contents formats.
4. Choose OK to close the dialog box.
5. Word compiles the table of contents and then inserts it at the location of the insertion point with the formatting selected at the Index and Tables dialog box.

When you select a format, you can view how your table of contents will be formatted in the Preview box. You can also vary the selected table of contents format by changing the options located at the bottom of the dialog box. These options include showing page numbers, right aligning page numbers, showing a specific number of levels, and using dot leaders. The settings for these options may vary, depending on which format you have selected for your table of contents.

If you want the table of contents to print on a page separate from the document text, position the insertion point in the desired location (commonly the bottom of the cover page), choose Insert, then Break. Select Next Page to insert a section break that begins a new page between the cover or title page and the body of the document. Use section breaks instead of regular page breaks between different sections of your document such as the cover, table of contents, chapters, etc., to accommodate the different page numbering formats that may be necessary in your document. Since a table of contents is generally numbered with lowercase Roman numerals, the page numbering method must be changed for that specific page. In addition, the starting page number for the body of the report should be counted as page 1; however, the number is usually not printed on the first page of a publication.

DTP POINTERS
A table of contents is usually numbered with Roman numerals.

If you position the insertion point within the table of contents, the whole table displays with a gray background. When Word compiles a table of contents, the whole table is actually a field; hence, the gray background. The gray background does not mean the table of contents is selected. You can select, insert, delete, and format any of the text as normal.

Creating a Customized Style List to Mark Table of Contents Entries

By default, Word uses the built-in heading styles *(Heading 1* through *Heading 9)* to compile a table of contents automatically. In many instances, however, styles with different names other than *Heading 1*, *Heading 2*, etc., can be applied to text in a document that you want to include in a table of contents. You can customize the list of styles Word uses to build a table of contents in a document. For instance, if a style named *Subtitle* is applied to text that you would like to be included in a table of contents as a level one heading, you can instruct Word to recognize the *Subtitle* style as a level one heading.

To customize the list of styles Word uses to build a table of contents you would complete these steps:

1. Position the insertion point where you want the table of contents to appear.
2. Choose Insert, then Index and Tables, then select the Table of Contents tab.
3. Select the desired table of contents format from the Formats list box.
4. Make any desired changes to the available formatting options, such as Show Page Numbers, Right Align Page Numbers, Show Levels, and Tab Leader.
5. Choose Options. The Table of Contents Options dialog box lists all the styles available in your document, as shown in figure 12.4. The list of styles will vary depending on what document is displayed on the screen.

6. Find the style name that you want to be included as a level one heading in your table of contents and key **1** in the corresponding TOC Level text box.
7. Find the style name that you want to be included as a level two heading in your table of contents and key **2** in the corresponding TOC Level text box.
8. Repeat this process for each style you want Word to use when it compiles a table of contents. (Make sure the TOC Level text box is empty for any style you do not want to be included.)
9. If your table of contents is to be compiled completely from styles, make sure the Styles check box displays with a check mark and the Table Entry Fields check box is empty. If your table of contents is to be compiled from a combination of styles and field entries, select the Table of Entry Fields check box to insert a check mark.

FIGURE 12.4

Table of Contents Options Dialog Box

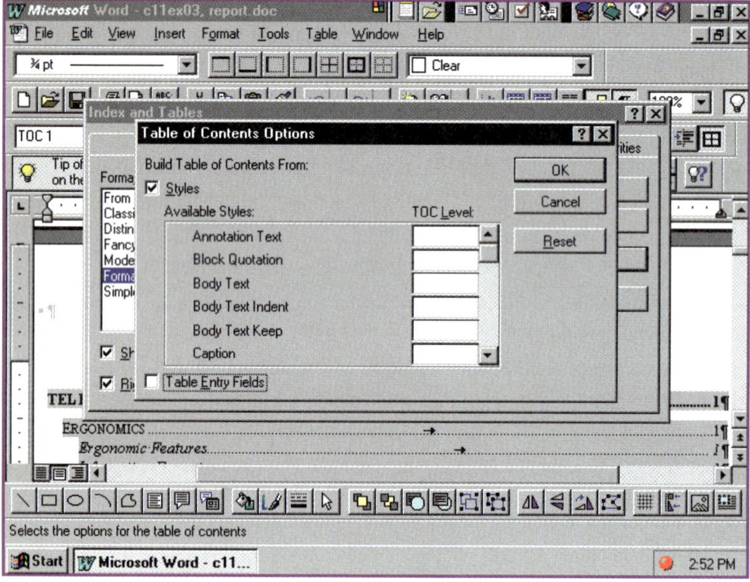

Using Fields to Mark Table of Contents Entries

If you do not want style formatting to be applied to the title, headings, or subheadings in a document, but you do want to include a table of contents, manually mark text for the table as fields. When text is marked for a table of contents as a field, a field code is inserted in the document. For example, a field code entry for a heading such as *Telecommunications at Work* would look like *{TC "Telecommunications at Work"\l1}* in your document. The backslash and the lowercase L are referred to as a *switch*. This switch tells Word that the character after the switch is the heading level for the table of contents, in this case, a level one. Word can then be instructed to compile a table of contents from text entry fields rather than from styles. This method takes more time than the style method but can be useful when you want to eliminate style formatting in your document or when you want to include text in the table of contents that has been formatted by styles other than the built-in heading styles.

To mark text as a field in a table of contents you would complete these steps:

1. Select the text you want included in the table of contents, or position the insertion point at the beginning of the text to be included.
2. Press Alt + Shift + O to access the Mark Table of Contents dialog box.

3. If the text was selected first, it will appear in the Entry text box, along with any character formatting. If the text was not selected first, key the text to be included in the table of contents in the Entry text box.
4. Make sure the Table Identifier displays *C*. (This tells Word the marked entry belongs in a table of contents, versus a table of figures or a table of authorities.)
5. Key or select a table of contents heading Level.
6. Choose Mark to close the dialog box.

To compile a table of contents from entries marked as fields you would complete these steps:

1. Follow the same steps you would take to compile a table of contents from heading styles.
2. Before closing the dialog box, select Options at the Index and Tables dialog box.
3. In the Table of Contents Options dialog box, select the Table Entry Fields check box to insert a check mark.
4. Remove the check mark from the Styles check box.
5. Choose OK to close the dialog box, then choose OK again to close the Index and Tables dialog box.

Using a Table of Contents to Access Parts of a Document

When you use Word to automatically compile a table of contents in a document, you can quickly access parts of your document through the table of contents. To do this, open the file containing your document that includes a table of contents. Position the insertion point on the table of contents page and double-click any of the page numbers displayed in the table of contents. Word will then display the specific location associated with that page number. This feature is especially useful when trying to access sections of a lengthy document to make revisions.

Updating a Table of Contents

Creating the table of contents should be the last step in creating any publication. Try to make all changes that affect pagination before you compile the table of contents. However, if you make changes to a document after compiling a table of contents, you can either update the existing table of contents or replace the entire table of contents with a new one.

Since the table of contents is actually a field, you can update the table of contents by updating the field. To do this, position the insertion point anywhere within the current table of contents (this causes the table of contents to display with a gray background), then press F9, the Update Field key. At the Update Table of Contents dialog box shown in figure 12.5, choose Update Page Numbers Only if the only changes occur to the page numbers, or choose Update Entire Table if changes were made to headings or subheadings within the table. Choose OK or press Enter to close the Update Table of Contents dialog box.

If you make extensive changes to the document, you may want to replace the entire table of contents. To do this, position the insertion point anywhere within the current table of contents (this causes the table of contents to display with a gray background), then choose Insert, then Index and Tables. At the Index and Tables dialog box, make sure the Table of Contents tab is selected, then choose OK or press Enter. At the prompt asking if you want to replace the existing table of contents, choose Yes.

Deleting a Table of Contents

A table of contents that has been compiled in a document can be deleted. To do this, select the entire table of contents using the mouse or the keyboard, then press the Delete key. (Even though the table of contents displays with a gray background when the insertion point is positioned within it, the contents still need to be selected in the normal manner.)

FIGURE 12.5

Update Table of Contents Dialog Box

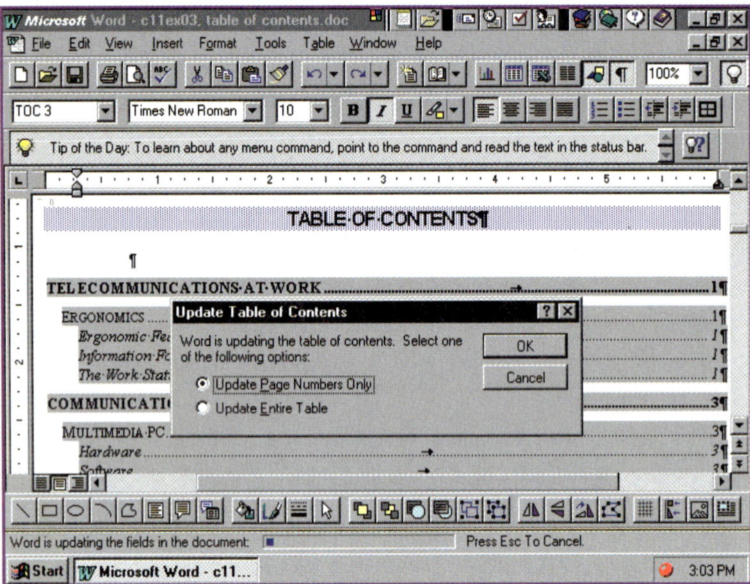

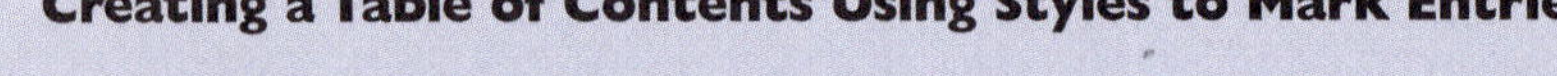

Creating a Table of Contents Using Styles to Mark Entries

1. Open c12ex02, custom report.
2. Save the document with Save As and name it c12ex03, table of contents.
3. Create the table of contents shown in figure 12.6 by completing the following steps:
   a. Insert and format a blank page for the table of contents by completing the steps:
      (1) Position the insertion point at the beginning of page 2.
      (2) Choose Insert, Break, and then Next Page to insert a section break.
      (3) Choose OK or press Enter.
      (4) Position the insertion point at the top of the blank page (page 2), and then key **TABLE OF CONTENTS**.
      (5) Press Enter, then change the paragraph alignment back to left.
   b. Compile and insert a table of contents from a custom list of styles by completing the following steps:
      (1) Choose Insert, then Index and Tables.
      (2) At the Index and Tables dialog box, choose the Table of Contents tab.
      (3) Choose *Formal* in the Formats list box.
      (4) Choose Options.
      (5) At the Table of Contents Options dialog box, make sure there is a check mark in the Styles check box.
      (6) Make sure there is no check mark in the Table Entry Fields check box.
      (7) In the Available Styles list box, use the vertical scroll bar to display the *Subtitle* style name.

(8) Key **1** as the level in the *Subtitle* style's corresponding TOC Level text box.
(9) Use the vertical scroll bar to display the *Heading 1* style name.
(10) Select any existing number in the Heading 1 style's corresponding TOC Level text box, then key 2.
(11) Display the Heading 2 style name.
(12) Select any existing number in the Heading 2 style's corresponding TOC Level text box, then key 3.
(13) Display the Heading 3 style name.
(14) Delete the number in Heading 3 style's corresponding TOC Level text box.
(15) Make sure the TOC Level text boxes are empty for all styles you do not want to be included.
(16) Click OK to close the Table of Contents Options dialog box, then click OK again to close the Index and Tables dialog box.

c. Adjust the page numbering in the report to accommodate the table of contents by completing the following steps:
(1) With the insertion point positioned anywhere in the Table of Contents page, choose Insert, then Page Numbers.
(2) At the Page Numbers dialog box, choose Format.
(3) At the Page Number Format dialog box, choose Number Format, then choose *i, ii, iii, ...* from the drop-down list.
(4) Choose Start At. (This inserts *i* in the Start At text box.)
(5) Choose OK or press Enter to close the Page Number Format dialog box.
(6) At the Page Numbers dialog box, choose OK or press Enter.
(7) Scroll to the bottom of the page. The page number should display as *ii.* The cover page is counted as the first page.)
(8) Scroll through the rest of your document to check the page numbering. The first page of the report will be counted as page number 1; however, by default, page numbering is not displayed on the first page. The second page of the report should display with a number 2 and so on.)
(9) Check the table of contents items and make sure the correct page numbers are being displayed.

d. Format the table of contents heading by completing the following steps:
(1) Position the insertion point anywhere within the title *TABLE OF CONTENTS.*
(2) Apply the *Heading 1* style from the Style list box located on the Formatting toolbar.
(3) Display the Paragraph dialog box, then select the Indents and Spacing tab.
(4) In the Indentation section, change the Special option to (none).
(5) Choose OK to close the dialog box.
(6) With the insertion point still positioned within *TABLE OF CONTENTS,* change the justification to center.
(7) Display the Borders and Shading dialog box, then select the Shading tab.
(8) Change the Foreground fill color to White, then change the Background fill color to Dk Blue, and then select 70% as the level of Shading.
(9) Choose OK to close the dialog box.

4. Save the report again with the same name, c12ex03, table of contents.
5. Print the table of contents page. (Check with your instructor to see if you should print the other pages of the document.)

FIGURE 12.6

Table of Contents Page

TABLE OF CONTENTS

Preparing A Manual

Many companies prepare publications for employees and/or customers. These publications may include policies and procedures manuals, benefits manuals, training manuals, and product and client information. A manual is a structured publication that may include some or all of the elements described earlier such as a cover, title page, table of contents, headers/footers, page numbering, glossary, and index.

Preparing a Manual Cover

When planning a cover, consider the contents of the manual. Choose a layout that is appealing and attractive. Choose a font that complements or harmonizes with the contents of the manual. Consider using a picture or graphic image on the cover. Remember all graphic images or clip art need to be relevant to the subject matter. Use large type with one or two words. Text lines set at a 90-degree angle can add visual appeal to a cover. Consider the desktop publishing concepts presented in chapter 1 when designing a cover. Determine the focus (such as a photograph, graphic image, or large display type); create a logical directional flow; maintain consistency with inside elements; and provide contrasting elements. Figure 12.7 illustrates some sample cover designs.

In exercise 4, you will create a manual cover page and title page for a Word 7.0 training manual using Word's Manual template. In exercise 5, you will prepare the body text for the manual; in exercise 6, you will create a concordance file for an index; in exercise 7, you will create an index for the manual; and, in exercise 8, you will compile a table of contents for the manual.

FIGURE 12.7

Cover Designs

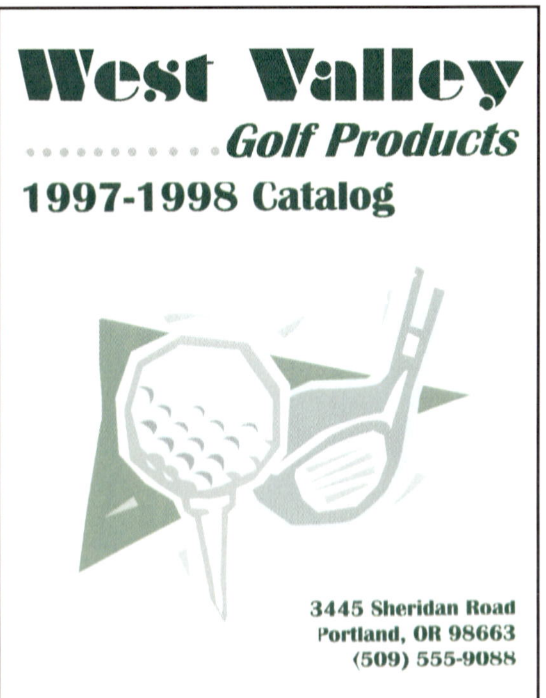

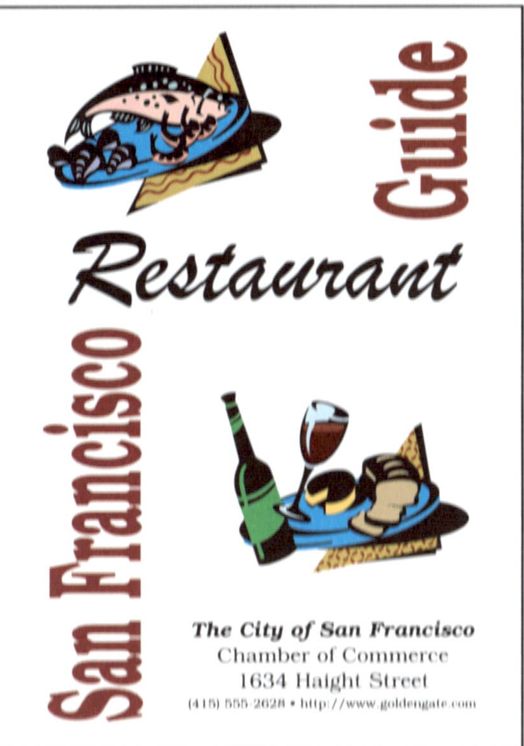

Creating a Manual Cover Page and Title Page

1. Create a manual cover page and title page using the Manual template, as shown in figure 12.8, by completing the following steps:
   a. Choose File, then New.
   b. Select the Publications tab, then double-click the Manual icon.
   c. Print and read a copy of the manual template document.
   d. Scroll through the template document. Click any paragraph, view the style name in the Style list box on the Formatting toolbar, then note the style names on the hard copy.
   e. Change the Zoom Control to Page Width. Continue to adjust the viewing mode as needed as you progress through this exercise.
   f. Replace the framed text on the cover page with a picture by completing the following steps:
      (1) With the insertion point positioned within the framed text *(Volume 3)* in the upper right corner of the cover page (use the horizontal scroll bar to see this portion of the screen), select the frame border, then press Delete.
      (2) Choose Insert, then Frame.
      (3) Position the crosshairs in the upper right corner of the cover page and draw a frame approximately 1.5 inches by 1.5 inches. (Do not be concerned if the frame overlaps the horizontal line below the title.)
      (4) Choose Insert, then Picture.
      (5) At the Insert Picture dialog box, double-click *Computer* from the Name list box.
      (6) Size the picture by completing the following steps:
         (a) Click once in the picture to select it.
         (b) Choose Format, then Picture.
         (c) At the Picture dialog box, change the Scaling Width and Height to 110%.
         (d) Choose OK to close the dialog box.
      (7) Position the frame by completing the following steps:
         (a) Choose Format, then Frame.
         (b) At the Frame dialog box, change the Text Wrapping to None.
         (c) Change the Horizontal Position to *Right* Relative To: *Margin*, then change the Vertical Position to *Top* Relative To: *Margin*.
         (d) Choose OK to close the dialog box.
   g. Insert the company name, the cover subtitle, and the cover title by completing the following steps:
      (1) Scroll down and select *INSPIRED TECHNOLOGIES* and key **WINSTON & MCKENZIE, CPA** as the company name. (The style includes All Caps as a formatting instruction, so the text may be keyed in lower case, if desired.)
      (2) Select *Corporate Graphics and Communications* and key **Corporate Training and Support Services** as the cover subtitle.
      (3) Scroll toward the bottom of the cover page, then select *Administrative Stylesheet Guide*, and then key **Word 7.0 Desktop Training Manual** as the cover title.
      (4) Display the Paragraph Borders and Shading dialog box, then change the Shading to 20%.
   h. Adjust the character spacing of the cover title (the *Title Cover* style includes a formatting instruction to condense the text by 9 points) by completing the following steps:

(1) Select the cover title, then choose Format, then Font.
(2) At the Font dialog box, select the Character Spacing tab.
(3) Change the Spacing to Condensed By 4.2 points, then click OK or press Enter.

i. Customize the title page (page 2) by completing the following steps:
(1) Position the insertion point on page 2.
(2) Select *CORPORATE GRAPHICS AND COMMUNICATIONS*, then key **CORPORATE TRAINING AND SUPPORT SERVICES** as the title page subtitle.
(3) Select *Administrative Stylesheet Guide*, then key **Word 7.0 Desktop Training Manual** as the title for the title page.
(4) Scroll down and select the company name and address, then key:

Winston & McKenzie, CPA
2100 North Meridian Street
Indianapolis, IN 46240

2. Save and name the document c12ex04, manual cover&title page.
3. Print the cover page and the title page only and then close c12ex04, manual cover&title page.

FIGURE 12.8

WINSTON & MCKENZIE
Corporate Training and Support Services

Word 7.0 Desktop Training Manual

CORPORATE TRAINING AND SUPPORT SERVICES
Word 7.0 Desktop Training Manual

Winston & McKenzie, CPA
2100 North Meridian Street
Indianapolis, IN 46240

In exercise 5, you will insert the body text for the manual started in exercise 4. You will apply styles included in the manual template to various sections of the inserted text.

Inserting and Formatting the Body Text for a Manual

1. Open c12ex04, manual cover&title page.
2. Save the document with Save As and name it c12ex05, manual.
3. Customize the framed chapter label on the first page of Section 1 of the report, as shown in figure 12.9, by completing the following steps:
   a. On the fourth physical page (labeled as page 4 in the status line but labeled as page 1 in the footer), position the insertion point in the framed text (*Chapter 1*) in the upper right corner of the page.
   b. Select *Chapter*, then key **Section**.
4. Edit the header text by completing the following steps:
   a. Choose View, then Header and Footer.
   b. At the Header pane, select *DESIGN CUSTOMIZATION*, then key **WORD 7.0**.
   c. Click Close on the Header and Footer toolbar.
5. Position the insertion point to the left of *Seven Keys to Creating*, select all the instructional text, including the index, and then press Delete.
6. Insert the manual text for Section 1 by completing the following steps:
   a. With the insertion point located at the left margin below the framed *Section 1* text, select *Normal* from the Style list box on the Formatting toolbar.
   b. Insert the file named *manual text1* located on your student data disk.
   c. Select the text just inserted and apply the *Body Text* style.
7. Format the section title and subtitle by completing the following steps:
   a. Position the insertion point on any character within the title *Using Word's Letterhead Templates*, then apply the *Chapter Title* style from the Style list box on the Formatting toolbar.
   b. Position the insertion point on any character within the subtitle, *Using Word's letterhead templates is an easy way for you to establish identity and consistency among both your internal and external business documents.*, then apply the *Chapter Subtitle* style from the Style list box.
8. Change the first letter of the first paragraph into a drop cap by completing the following steps:
   a. Position the insertion point to the left of *Word* in the first paragraph.
   b. Choose Format, then Drop Cap.
   c. At the Drop Cap dialog box, choose Dropped in the Position section.
   d. Choose OK to close the dialog box.
9. Below the first paragraph, select *Letter Wizard...* through *Professional Letter*, then apply the *List Bullet 3* style.
10. Position the insertion point on any character within the following headings, then apply the *Heading 1* style to each heading:

    Understanding Template Styles
    Using the Letter Wizard
    Using the User Info Feature

11. Press Ctrl + End to position the insertion point at the end of the document.
12. Choose Insert, then Break. At the Break dialog box select Next Page in the Section Breaks section, then click OK or press Enter.
13. With the insertion point positioned on the first page of Section 2 (displayed as page 6 in the status bar), insert the file *manual text2* located on your student data disk.
14. Select the text just inserted and apply the *Body Text* style.
15. Adjust the page numbering so that it is continuous from Section 1 to Section 2 by completing the following steps:
    a. With the insertion point positioned on the first page of Section 1 (displayed as page 4 in the status bar), choose Insert, then Page Numbers.
    b. At the Page Numbers dialog box, make sure the Position text box displays *Bottom of Page (Footer)*.
    c. Display the Alignment drop-down list, then select Center.
    d. Make sure there is no check mark in the Show Number on First Page check box.
    e. Choose Format.

f. At the Page Number Format dialog box, make sure Start At: is selected and a number one displays in the text box.
g. Choose OK to close the dialog box.
h. Position the insertion point on the first page of Section 2 (displayed as page 6 in the status bar), choose Insert, then Page Numbers.
i. Make sure the Position displays *Bottom of Page (Footer)* and the Alignment displays *Center.*
j. Click in the Show Number on First Page check box so that a check mark displays.
k. Choose Format, then select Continuous from Previous Section.
l. Choose OK to close the Page Numbers dialog box.
m. Check the page numbering in both sections of the report. Sections 1 and 2 should be numbered consecutively from one through eight. A page number should not display on the first page of Section 1.

16. Position the insertion point to the left of the first heading *(Styles)* and create the framed section number by completing the following steps:
    a. Key **Section** and then press Enter.
    b. Select *Section*, then apply the *Part Title* style. (*Section* will then be displayed in a frame in the upper right corner of the page.)
    c. Click once in the frame to deselect the text.
    d. Position the insertion point at the end of the word *Section*, then press Enter.
    e. Key **2**. (The *Part Title* style contains an instruction that it should automatically be followed by the *Part Label* style; hence, you do not have to manually apply a style to the section number.)
17. Position the insertion point on any character within the section title, *Styles*, then apply the *Chapter Title* style.
18. Position the insertion point on any character within the subtitle *You can save time... repetitive formatting.*, then apply the *Chapter Subtitle* style.
19. Position the insertion point on any character within the following headings, then apply the *Heading 1* style to each heading. (Note: after applying the style to the first heading, you can press F4 at each heading location to repeat the style.)

    Understanding the Relationship Between Styles and Templates
    Character and Paragraph Styles
    Creating Styles
    Applying Styles
    Modifying an Existing Style
    Removing a Style from Text

20. Position the insertion point to the left of *Documents*, the first word in the first paragraph of section two, then repeat steps 8(b) through 8(d) to create a drop cap.
21. Apply bullets to a list of items by completing the following steps:
    a. Find the heading *Creating Styles.* (Hint: Use the Find feature.)
    b. In the text that follows this heading, select the five items that follow *Consider the following when naming a style:.*
    c. Apply the *List Bullet* style.
22. Select the following items and apply the *List Number* style to:
    a. In the *Creating Styles* section, the five steps following *To create a new style from existing text, you would complete the following steps:.*
    b. In the *Creating Styles* section, the ten steps following *To create a new style using the Style dialog box, you would select text if necessary and then complete the following steps:.*
    c. In the *Applying Styles* section, the three steps following *To apply a style to existing text using the Style button on the Formatting toolbar, you would complete the following steps:.*
    d. In the *Applying Styles* section, the four steps following *To apply a style using the Style command from the Format menu, you would complete the following steps:.*
    e. In the *Modifying an Existing Style* section, the six steps following *To modify a style using the Formatting toolbar, you would complete the following steps:.*

f. In the *Modifying an Existing Style* section, the seven steps following *To modify a style at the Style dialog box, you would complete the following steps:*.

23. In the last sentence of the last paragraph of the *Creating Styles* section, select *avoid making changes to the Normal template,* then apply the *Emphasis* style.
24. Save the manual with the same name, c12ex05, manual.
25. Print and then close c12ex05, manual. (Check with your instructor before printing this document. You may want to postpone printing until the table of contents and index have been created in the next two exercises.)

FIGURE 12.9

Exercise 5 Sample Pages

WORD 7.0

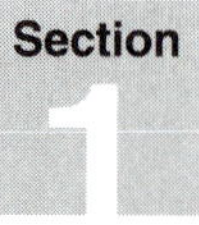

Using Word's Letterhead Templates

Using Word's letterhead templates is an easy way for you to establish identity and consistency among both your internal and external business documents.

Word includes a variety of predesigned template documents, including letterheads. At the New dialog box, select the Letters & Faxes tab to display the following Word letterhead templates:

- Letter Wizard
- Contemporary Letter
- Elegant Letter
- Professional Letter

This is an easy way for you to establish identity and consistency among both your internal and external business documents. For example, select Professional for your memo, fax, and letter template choices and all your documents will have matching elements. Even though you can view a template in the Preview box at the New dialog box, printing samples of your template documents lets you see firsthand what is available. The body of the template document also contains some valuable user information.

Understanding Template Styles

A template may include several components, such as styles, text, graphics, AutoText entries, and macros. Word automatically bases a new document created at a blank screen on the *Normal.dot* template. This template initially contains five styles, including one called the Normal style. The *Normal* style contains formatting instructions to use 10-point Times New Roman as the font, English (US) as the language, flush left alignment, single spacing, and Widow/Orphan Control. Word automatically applies

1

WORD 7.0

Styles

You can save time and keystrokes by using Word's Style feature to store repetitive formatting.

Documents created with desktop publishing features generally require a great deal of formatting. Some documents, such as company newsletters or brochures, may be created on a regular basis. These documents should contain formatting that maintains consistency in their appearance from issue to issue. The formatting should also be consistent within each issue and within any document that uses a variety of headings, subheadings, and other design elements.

You can save time and keystrokes by using Word's Style feature to store repetitive formatting. A *style* is a group of defined formatting instructions, such as margin settings, paper size, font, font size, and font style, that can be applied at one time to a whole document or to various parts of a document. Using styles is quick and easy, and it assures that your formatting is uniform throughout your document. Because formatting instructions are contained within a style, a style can be edited, automatically updating any occurrence of that style within a document.

Understanding the Relationship Between Styles and Templates

A Word document, by default, is based on the Normal.dot template. The Normal template contains formatting instructions to set text in the default font (this may vary depending on the printer you are using or if another font has been selected as the default font), to use left alignment and single spacing, and to turn on Widow/Orphan control. These formatting instructions are contained in a style called the Normal style. When you access a clear document window, Normal will display in the Style list box located on the left in the Formatting toolbar. The Normal Style is automatically applied to any text that is keyed unless you specify other formatting instructions. If you click on the down-pointing arrow to the right of the Style list box, you will see a total of five styles immediately available for your use. In addition to these styles, Word provides a large selection of other predesigned styles.

3

WORD 7.0

paragraph that has already been formatted with a paragraph style. If this is the case, you need to select the specific text first to see the character style name that has been applied to it.

Creating Styles

A style can be created in two ways. You can create a new style through the Style dialog box or you can create a style from existing text that already contains the formatting you desire. Creating a style from existing text is the easiest method.

When you create your own style, you must give the style a name. When naming a style, try to name it something that gives you an idea what the style will accomplish. Consider the following when naming a style:

- A style name can contain a maximum of 253 characters.
- A style name can contain spaces and commas.
- Do not use the backslash (\), braces ({}), or a semicolon (;) when naming a style.
- A style name is case-sensitive. Uppercase and lowercase letters can be used.
- Avoid using the names already used by Word.

To create a new style from existing text, you would complete the following steps:

1. Key a paragraph of text, such as a heading.
2. Format the text the way you want it to appear, such as changing the font, font size, applying color, etc.
3. Position the insertion point within the paragraph that contains the desired formatting; or select the text if you are creating a character style.
4. Click in the Style box on the Formatting toolbar to select the current style name.
5. Type a new name and press Enter. The new style name is then added to the list of styles available in that document.

The above method of inserting the style name in the Style text box on the Formatting toolbar automatically defines the style as a paragraph style. You must use the Style dialog box to create a character style. You may use the

5

Preparing An Index Using Word

As mentioned earlier, an index lists the topics covered in a publication and the pages where those topics are discussed. Word lets you automate the process of creating an index in a manner similar to that used for creating a table of contents. When creating an index, you mark a word or words that you want included in the index. Creating an index takes some thought and careful planning. You must determine what text will be used as main entries and what text will be used as subentries listed under main entries. In doing this, plan your index around the needs of your readers. Does the index need to be extremely detailed? Do you want to cross-reference index items for your readers? How many levels (nine maximum) do you want to include in the index? An index can include such items as the main idea of a document, the main subject of a chapter or section, variations of a heading or subheading, and abbreviations. Figure 12.10 shows an example of an index. In Word, the items located at the left margin in figure 12.10 are known as main entries. The items indented from the left margin under specific main entries are known as subentries.

DTP POINTERS
An index requires thought and careful planning.

There are two ways to mark text for inclusion in an index. Text can be marked automatically using a concordance file or text can be marked manually. The most efficient way to create an index would be to first create a concordance file to mark text for an index and then manually mark any remaining items that you may have missed.

FIGURE 12.10

Sample Index

INDEX

A
Alignment, 12, 16
ASCII, 22, 24, 35
    word processing, 39
    data processing, 41

B
Backmatter, 120
    page numbering, 123
Balance, 67-69
Banners, 145

C
Callouts, 78
Captions, 156
Color, 192-195
    ink for offset printing, 193
    process color, 195

D
Databases, 124-128
    fields, 124
    records, 124
Directional flow, 70-71

Marking Text Using a Concordance File

The quickest and easiest way to mark text as index entries is to create a *concordance file.* A concordance file is a regular Word document containing a single, two-column table with no text outside the table, as shown in figure 12.11. In the first column of the table, you enter the word(s) you want to index. The words listed in this column must be the exact words from your document, including capitalization and punctuation. For example, if you want to index the word *software* on one page and *Software* on another page, you must include them as two separate entries in your concordance file because of the difference in capitalization. If you want the item in the first column to be a main entry in your index, key the item in the second column exactly the way you want it to appear in the index. (See the main entry *Hardware* in figure 12.11.) If you want the item in the first column to be a subentry of a main entry, key the main entry item in the second column followed by a colon. Then key the subentry item exactly as you want it to appear in your index. (See *Multifunction display* in figure 12.11.)

Concordance File:
A file containing words and/or phrases used in marking text for an index.

In the concordance file shown in figure 12.11, the text as it appears in the document is inserted in the first column. The second column contains the text as you want it to appear in the index, specifying whether it is a main entry or subentry.

Remember to spellcheck and proofread the concordance file before using it to mark your document.

To mark text for an index using a concordance file you would complete these steps:

1. Open the document containing text you want marked for the index.
2. Choose Insert, then Index and Tables.
3. At the Index and Tables dialog box, choose AutoMark.
4. At the Open Index AutoMark File dialog box, select the concordance file name in the File Name list box.
5. Choose Open or press Enter.

FIGURE 12.11

Concordance File

Multifunction display	Terminal: multifunction display
voice-activated	Terminal: voice-activated
pointer	Electronic: pointer
copy	Electronic: copy
digital	Optical Disk: digital
erasable	Optical Disk: erasable
voice	Applications: voice
Hardware	Hardware
hard drive	Hardware: hard drive
processor	Hardware: processor
sound board	Hardware: sound board
CD-ROM	Hardware: CD-ROM
software	Software
Software	Software

Marking Text Manually

Even though using a concordance file is a quick and efficient method of creating an index, there may be times when text needs to be marked manually. For instance, a concordance file marks every occurrence of an item listed in the first column, even though you may not want every occurrence marked. To avoid this, the text to be included in the index may need to be marked manually. In addition, manually marking text allows you to add some remaining items to the index that may have been missed in the concordance file.

A selected word or words can be marked for inclusion in an index. To manually mark text for an index, you would complete the following steps:

1. Select the word or words you want included in the index.
2. Choose Insert, then Index and Tables.
3. At the Index and Tables dialog box, choose the Index tab, and then choose Mark Entry.
4. At the Mark Index Entry dialog box, the selected word(s) display in the Main Entry text box. If the text is a main entry, leave it as displayed. If the text is a subentry,

key the text in the Subentry text box, then key the appropriate main entry in the Main Entry text box.

5. Choose Mark.
6. Choose Close to close the Mark Index Entry dialog box.

When you choose Mark Entry, Word automatically turns on the display of nonprinting characters and displays the index field code, as shown in the example in figure 12.12.

The main entry and subentry do not have to be the same as the selected text. You can select text for an index, type the text the way you want it to display in the Main Entry or Subentry text box, then choose Mark.

At the Mark Index Entry dialog box, you can apply bold and/or italic formatting to the page numbers that will appear in the index.

The Options section of the Mark Index Entry dialog box contains several options, with Current Page as the default. At this setting, the current page number will be listed in the index for the main and/or subentry. If you choose Cross-reference, you would key the text you want to use as a cross-reference for the index entry in the Cross-reference text box. Choose the Mark All button at the Mark Index Entry dialog box to mark all occurrences of the selected text in the document as index entries.(This option performs the same function as a concordance file.) Word marks only those entries whose uppercase and lowercase letters exactly match the index entry.

A·template·may·include·several·components,·such·as·styles·{·XE·"Templates:·styles"·},· text,·graphics,·AutoText·entries,·and·macros.·Word·automatically·bases·a·new·document· created·at·a·blank·screen·on·the·*Normal.dot*·template{·XE·"Templates:·normal.dot· template"·}.·This·template·initially·contains·five·styles,·including·one·called·the·*Normal*· style{·XE·"Styles:·normal·style"·}.·The·Normal·style·contains·formatting·instructions·to·

FIGURE 12.12

Sample of Document Index Codes

Compiling an Index

After all entries have been marked for the index, establish the location of the index in the document. An index should appear at the end of a document, generally on a page by itself. To establish the index location, position the insertion point at the end of the document, then insert a page break. With the insertion point positioned below the page break, key **INDEX** centered and bolded, then press the Enter key. With the insertion point positioned at the left margin, you are now ready to compile the index.

To compile an index you would complete the following steps:

1. Choose Insert, then Index and Tables.
2. At the Index and Tables dialog box, choose the Index tab.
3. Select the desired index formatting, such as indented subentries, predesigned index formats, page number alignment, number of columns, and tab leaders.
4. Choose OK or press Enter.

Word compiles the index then inserts it at the location of the insertion point with the formatting selected at the Index and Tables dialog box. Word also inserts a section break above and below the index text.

Updating or Replacing an Index

If you make changes to a document after inserting an index, insert or delete the desired entries in the concordance file and then save the concordance file with the changes. Repeat the original steps to mark the text for an index using a concordance file. As an alternative, you can manually mark or remark any new or revised entries in your document. You can then either update the existing index or replace the index with a new one. To update an index, position the insertion point anywhere within the index (displays with a gray background), then press F9.

Replace an index in the same manner as you would replace a table of contents. To do this, position the insertion point anywhere within the current index (index displays with a gray background), then choose Insert, then Index and Tables. At the Index and Tables dialog box, make sure the Index tab is selected, then choose OK or press Enter. At the prompt asking if you want to replace the existing index, choose Yes.

Deleting an Index

An index that has been compiled in a document can be deleted. To delete an index, select the entire index using either the mouse or the keyboard, then press the Delete key.

Creating a Concordance File

1. At a clear screen, create a concordance file with the text shown in figure 12.13, for the manual created in exercise 5, by completing the following steps:
   a. Create a two-column table by completing the following steps:
      (1) Choose Table, then Insert Table.
      (2) At the Insert Table dialog box, choose OK to accept the default of two columns and two rows.
   b. Key the text in each cell as shown in figure 12.13. Press the Tab key in the last cell of the table to create new rows as you need them. Pay careful attention to capitalization and punctuation.
   c. Save and name the concordance file c12ex06, concordance.
   d. Close c12ex06, concordance.

FIGURE 12.13

Templates	Templates
letterhead	Templates: letterhead
Styles	Styles
styles	Templates: styles
Normal template	Templates: normal.dot template
Normal style	Styles: normal style
Letter Wizard	Letter Wizard
Letter Wizard	Templates: letter wizard
User Info	User Info
User Info	Letter Wizard: user info
paragraph style	Paragraph Style
paragraph style	Styles: paragraph style
character style	Character Style
character style	Styles: character style
Creating a style	Style: creating styles
Style dialog box	Styles: style dialog box
naming a style	Styles: naming styles
base style	Styles: base style
Applying Styles	Styles: applying styles
Style command	Styles: style command
Modifying an Existing Style	Styles: modifying styles
Removing a Style from Text	Styles: removing styles

In exercise 7, you will use the concordance file created in exercise 6 to compile an index for the *Word 7.0 Desktop Training Manual* created in previous exercises.

Creating an Index Using a Concordance File

1. Open c12ex05, manual.
2. Use Save As and name the document c12ex07, index.
3. Create an index for the *Word 7.0 Desktop Training Manual* using a concordance file, as shown in figure 12.14, by completing the following steps:
   a. Prepare a separate page for the index by completing the following steps:
      (1) Press Ctrl + End to position the insertion point at the end of the document.
      (2) Press Enter, then press Ctrl + Enter to insert a page break.
      (3) Key **Index**, then press Enter.
      (4) Position the insertion point anywhere within the *Index* heading, then apply the *Section Label* heading.
   b. Mark text as index entries by completing the following steps:
      (1) Choose Insert, then Index and Tables.
      (2) At the Index and Tables dialog box, select the Index tab.
      (3) Choose AutoMark.
      (4) At the Open Index AutoMark File dialog box, display the location of c12ex06, concordance, in the Look in list box.
      (5) Select c12ex06, concordance, then choose Open. (If you scroll through your document, all of the automatically inserted index codes will display in your document; these codes will not print or affect the placement of text in your document.)
   c. Compile the index by completing the following steps:
      (1) With the insertion point located at the left margin below the *Index* heading, choose Insert, then Index and Tables.
      (2) In the Formats section, make sure *From Template* is selected.
      (3) Click OK to compile the index.
   d. Position the insertion point at the left margin below the heading, then change the column format to one column. (The two columns display because of a column formatting instruction in the original template.)
   e. Check the index displayed on the screen for all entries listed in figure 12.13. If any entries are missing, complete the following steps:
      (1) Open c12ex06, concordance and make any necessary revisions.
      (2) Save and then close c12ex06, concordance.
      (3) With the compiled index displayed on the screen, repeat steps 3 b(1) through (5) to re-mark the text for index entries.
      (4) Position the insertion point anywhere within the index (displays with a gray background), then press F9 to update the index.
   f. Save the document with the same name, c12ex07, index.
   g. With the insertion point positioned on the Index page, display the Print dialog box, then select Current Page to print the Index page.
   h. Close c12ex07, index.

FIGURE 12.14

WORD 7.0

Index

10

In exercise 8, you will create a table of contents for the *Word 7.0 Desktop Training Manual*. As part of the original Manual template, a table of contents already occupies the third physical page of the manual created in exercises 4 through 7. The original table of contents needs to be deleted before a new table of contents for the manual can be compiled. The table of contents will be compiled from a customized style list that designates the *Chapter Title* style as a level one table of contents heading, the *Heading 1* style as a level two heading, and *Heading 2* as a level three heading. After the table of contents is compiled, you will manually insert section headings, and you will modify the *Heading 2* style to include a left indent formatting instruction. Since a table of contents page is usually numbered using lowercase Roman numerals, you will adjust the page numbering to display and print a Roman numeral *i* at the bottom of the table of contents page.

Compiling a Table of Contents for a Manual

1. Open c12ex07, index.
2. Use Save As and name the document c12ex08, table of contents.
3. Create a table of contents for the *Word 7.0 Desktop Training Guide* as displayed in figure 12.15 by completing the following steps:
   a. Prepare the table of contents page as follows:
      (1) Display the page titled *Table of Contents* (displays as page 3 in the status bar).
      (2) Under the *Table of Contents* title, position the insertion point to the left of *Introduction.*
      (3) From this point forward, select all the text on this table of contents page. Since this text is formatted into two newspaper columns, it is easier to select the text by holding down the Shift key and using the arrow keys to select the text in both columns. Do not include the End of Section break in the selection.
      (4) Press the Delete key.

b. With the insertion point positioned below the heading at the left margin, compile the table of contents by completing the following steps:
   (1) Choose Insert, then Index and Tables.
   (2) At the Index and Tables dialog box, select the Table of Contents tab.
   (3) Make sure *From Template* is selected in the Formats list box.
   (4) Choose Options.
   (5) At the Table of Contents Options dialog box, make sure there is a check mark in the Build Table of Contents From Styles check box.
   (6) Make sure there is no check mark in the Table Entry Fields check box.
   (7) In the Available Styles list box, use the vertical scroll bar to display the *Chapter Title* style name.
   (8) Key **1** as the level in the *Chapter Title* style's corresponding TOC Level text box.
   (9) Use the vertical scroll bar to display the *Heading 1* style name.
   (10) Select any existing number in the *Heading 1* style's corresponding TOC Level text box, then key **2**.
   (11) Display the *Heading 2* style name.
   (12) Select any existing number in the *Heading 2* style's corresponding TOC Level text box, then key **3**.
   (13) Display the *Heading 3* style name.
   (14) Delete the number in *Heading 3* style's corresponding TOC Level text box.
   (15) Make sure the TOC Level text boxes are empty for all styles you do not want to be included.
   (16) Click OK to close the Table of Contents Options dialog box, then click OK again to close the Index and Tables dialog box.

c. Adjust the page numbering in the manual to accommodate the table of contents by completing the following steps:
   (1) With the insertion point positioned anywhere in the Table of Contents page, choose Insert, then Page Numbers.
   (2) Change the Alignment to Center.
   (3) At the Page Numbers dialog box, choose Format.
   (4) At the Page Number Format dialog box, make sure *i, ii, iii,...* displays in the Number Format list box.
   (5) In the Page Numbering section, select Start At: and key or display *iii* in the list box.
   (6) Choose OK or press Enter to close the Page Number Format dialog box.
   (7) At the Page Numbers dialog box, choose OK or press Enter.
   (8) Scroll to the bottom of the page. The page number should display as *iii*. (The cover page is counted as the first page and the title page is counted as the second page even though no page numbers display on these pages.) If the *iii* does not display, display the footer pane, delete the existing number, if any, then click the Page Numbers button on the Header and Footer toolbar.
   (9) Scroll through the rest of your document to check the page numbering. The first page of the report should be counted as number *1*. The second page of the report should display with a number *2* and so on.
   (10) Check the table of contents items and make sure the correct items and corresponding page numbers are being displayed.

d. Modify the *TOC 2* style so that all items at this level are indented by completing the following steps:
   (1) Choose Format, then Style.
   (2) At the Styles dialog box, select *TOC 2* from the Styles list box.
   (3) Choose Modify.

(4) At the Modify Style dialog box, choose Format.
(5) From the Format drop-down list, choose Paragraph.
(6) At the Paragraph dialog box, select the Indents and Spacing tab.
(7) In the Indentation section, display or key **0.1** in the Left text box.
(8) Choose OK to close the Paragraph dialog box.
(9) Choose OK to close the Modify Style dialog box.
(10) Choose Close to close the Style dialog box. (Any table of contents item formatted by the *TOC 2* style should now be indented.)

e. Include section titles in the table of contents by completing the following steps:
(1) Position the insertion point to the left of the first table of contents entry, *Using Word's Letterhead Templates.*
(2) Key **section 1**, then press Enter.
(3) Position the insertion point anywhere within *section 1*, then apply the *Section Heading* style.
(4) Position the insertion point to the left of the word *Styles.*
(5) Key **section 2**, then press Enter.
(6) Position the insertion point anywhere within *section 2*, then apply the *Section Heading* style.

f. Save the document with the same name, c12ex08, table of contents.

g. Print c12ex08, table of contents. (Check with your instructor about printng the whole manual or just printing the table of contents page.)

h. Close c12ex08, table of contents.

FIGURE 12.15

Table of Contents

SECTION 1	
Using Word's Letterhead Templates	1
Understanding Template Styles	2
Using the Letter Wizard	2
Using the User Info Feature	2
SECTION 2	
Styles	4
Understanding the Relationship Between Styles and Templates	4
Character and Paragraph Styles	5
Creating Styles	6
Applying Styles	8
Modifying an Existing Style	9
Removing a Style from Text	10

222

Binding Publications

The final finishing process for a publication is binding. A wide variety of bindings can be used. Some can be finished in the office and others can be finished with more sophisticated options at commercial binders. In the office, binding can include stapling the publication or three-hole punching the paper for use in a ring notebook or report cover.

Chapter Summary

- Structured publications such as reports, manuals, and booklets are text-intensive, multipage documents containing repeating elements, such as headers or footers, and consistently styled title and text pages.
- Structured publications can contain all or some of the following elements: a front cover; front matter such as a title page, copyright page, preface, and table of contents; body text; back matter such as an appendix, bibliography, glossary, and index; and a back cover.
- Word provides three report templates—Contemporary, Elegant, and Professional.
- When creating a table of contents in Word, two basic steps are completed: the title, headings, and subheadings are marked automatically or manually in the document; then the table of contents is compiled.
- When creating an index in Word, two basic steps are completed: the words or phrases are marked automatically or manually as main entries or subentries, then the index is compiled.
- Words or phrases that appear frequently in a document can be entered into a Word table and saved as a concordance file. This file is then used when creating the index.
- When including a table of contents or index, adjust page numbering in your document to accommodate these items.
- A table of contents and an index compiled by Word are considered fields and can be updated.

Commands Review

	Mouse/Keyboard
New dialog box to access a template	File, New, select desired tab
Insert File dialog box	Insert, File
Drawing Object dialog box	Select drawing object, Format, Drawing Object
Word Picture	Double-click the picture
Borders and Shading dialog box	Format, Borders and Shading
Index and Tables dialog box	Insert, Tables and Index

Table of Contents Options dialog box	Insert, Index, Tables and Index, Table of Contents tab, Options
Mark Table of Contents dialog box	Alt + Shift + 0
Update Table of Contents dialog box	Position insertion point within table, press F9
Page Numbers dialog box	Insert, Page Numbers
Insert a frame	Insert, Frame, position crosshairs, draw frame
Format Frame dialog box	Select frame, Format, Frame
Insert Picture dialog box	Insert, Picture
Headers and Footers	View, Header and Footer
Drop Cap dialog box	Format, Drop Cap
Mark Index dialog box	Insert, Index and Tables, Index tab, Mark Entry
Insert a table	Table, Insert Table

Check Your Understanding

Terms: Match the terms with the correct definitions by writing the letter of the term on the blank line in front of the correct definition.

A. Appendix
B. Bibliography
C. Copyright page
D. Glossary
E. Index
F. Preface
G. Table of Contents
H. Title page

_____ **1.** A statement by the author about the publication that may include acknowledgments.

_____ **2.** Information that is not essential to the text but may help clarify the information presented.

_____ **3.** The full title of the publication (including any subtitles) and the full name of the author, editor, and publisher.

_____ **4.** A set of definitions for specialized terms used in the publication.

_____ **5.** A list of topics contained in the publication with the pages on which those topics are discussed.

_____ **6.** A list of sources or suggestions for further reading.

_____ **7.** A list of the names of each chapter or section and the page number on which each begins.

Concepts: Write your answers to the following questions in the space provided.

1. Name the three report templates provided by Word.

2. By default, what styles does Word use to automatically compile a table of contents?

3. Name the file that can be created that contains words or phrases in a Word table to be included in an index.

4. Explain the steps necessary to update or replace a table of contents or an index.

5. An index appears at this location in a publication.

6. Name the two basic steps to follow when creating a table of contents or an index for a document using Word.

Skill Assessments

Assessment 1

1. At a clear editing window, prepare a report using the Elegant Report template. You may want to print and read the report instructional text first. You may also want to note the style names used on the hard copy.
2. Click in the prompt *CLICK **HERE*** AND TYPE COMPANY NAME and key **Communications Solutions, Inc.** (An All Caps formatting instruction is included in the style.)
3. Individually select the title and subtitle, and then replace with the following:

Title	Alternative Services
Subtitle	Prepared by: (Your name here) (press Shift + Enter) Current date

4. Insert the *continen.wmf* picture on the cover. Size and position the picture appropriately.
5. On the first page of the report, select the title *PROPOSAL AND MARKETING PLAN,* then key **Teleports**.
6. Delete *Blue Sky's Best Opportunity For East Region Expansion.*
7. Select *How To Customize This Report* and key **A "One-Stop Shopping" Telecommunications Solution**.
8. Delete the text in the report from the paragraph that begins *Change the information...* to the end.
9. Press Enter to place the insertion point below the heading.
10. Insert the file named *chapter1 text* located on your student data disk into the report.
11. Select the text just inserted and apply the *Body Text* style.
12. Apply the *Heading 2* style to the following headings:

    Evolution of Teleports
    Types of Teleports
    Teleport Services

13. Apply the *List Bullet* style to the following items:
    a. At the end of the first paragraph, the five items following *There are a number of reasons for unacceptable service:.*
    b. In the *Types of Teleports* section, the two items following *There are two types of teleports:.*
    c. In the *Teleport Services* section, the six items following *Here are some examples of the services provided by teleports:.*
14. Move the insertion point to the end of the document, then press Enter.
15. Choose Insert, then Break. Choose Next Page in the Section Breaks section.
16. With the insertion point positioned at the top of page 5, key **Integrated Services Digital Network** as the title, then press Enter.
17. Apply the *Title* style to the title keyed in step 16.
18. Position the insertion point at the left margin below the title, key **An Alternative Source for Transmitting Communications**, then press Enter.
19. Apply the *Heading 1* style to the heading keyed in step 18.
20. Position the insertion point below the heading, then insert the file named *chapter2 text* located on your student data disk into the report.
21. Select the text just inserted and apply the *Body Text* style.
22. Apply the *Heading 2* style to the following headings:

    ISDN Services
    ISDN Operations
    ISDN Benefits

23. In the *ISDN Benefits* section, apply the *List Bullet* style to the seven items following *ISDN implementation has many potential benefits:.*
24. Adjust the page numbering so that the first page of the report (titled *Teleports*) starts numbering with *1* (although it will not display), the second page of the report displays a number *2*, and so on. Make the page numbering continuous from the first section (*TELEPORTS*) of the report to the second section (*INTEGRATED SERVICES DIGITAL NETWORK*). Display the Page Setup dialog box, select the Layout tab, then remove the check mark from Different Odd and Even in the Headers and Footers section.

25. Create a table of contents according to the following specifications:
    a. Insert a next page section break at the end of the cover page to create a separate page for the table of contents between the cover page and the first page of the report.
    b. Title the page *Table of Contents.* (The *Title* style will be applied to this heading after the table of contents is compiled to eliminate it from being included as an entry in the table of contents.)
    c. Mark the text for a table of contents using a customized style list. Use the *Title* style as a first level table of contents heading, the *Heading 1* style as a second level table of contents heading, and the *Heading 2* style as a third level table of contents heading. Remove *Heading 3* from the table of contents level listing.
    d. Choose *Formal* as the table of contents format.
    e. Compile the table of contents.
    f. Select the page numbers in each item formatted by the *TOC 3* style, then remove the italics.
    g. Adjust the page numbering to include a Roman numeral *ii* at the bottom of the table of contents page. (The Roman numeral will display in small caps since the footer style includes a small caps formatting instruction.)
    h. Check the page numbers listed in the table of contents for accuracy; update the table of contents if necessary.
    i. Select the table of contents, then change the font to 11-point Garamond.
    j. Apply the *Title* style to the table of contents heading.
26. Check all page numbering in the document; make adjustments if necessary.
27. Save the report and name it c12sa01, communications report.
28. Print and then close c12sa01, communications report.

Optional: Write a one-paragraph summary of the report.

Assessment 2

1. Prepare a concordance file to be used in creating an index for the report created in assessment 1 by completing the following steps:
    a. Create a two-column table.
    b. Mark the following words in the concordance file as main entries and subentries as indicated:

        voice (subentry; main entry = *communication*)
        data (subentry; main entry = *communication*)
        video (subentry; main entry = *communication*)
        technology (subentry; main entry = *communication*)
        market potential (subentry; main entry = *communication*)
        fiber optic (subentry; main entry = *communication*)
        coaxial cable (subentry; main entry = *communication*)
        microwave (subentry; main entry = *communication*)
        satellite (subentry; main entry = *communication*)
        common (subentry; main entry = *carrier*)
        value-added (subentry; main entry = *carrier*)
        facility-based (subentry; main entry = *teleports*)
        real estate-based (subentry; main entry = *teleports*)
        digital data reception (subentry; main entry = *transmission*)
        encryption (subentry; main entry = *transmission*)

protocol (subentry; main entry = *transmission*)
conversion (subentry; main entry = *transmission*)
analog (subentry; main entry = *transmission*)
digital (subentry; main entry = *transmission*)
services (subentry; main entry = *Integrated*)
operations (subentry; main entry = *Integrated*)
benefits (subentry; main entry = *transmission*)

c. Save and name the file c12sa02, concordance.
d. Close c12sa02, concordance.
e. Open c12sa01, communications report and save as c12sa02, index.
f. Create an index by completing the following steps:
   (1) Move the insertion point to the end of the document, insert a page break, then create a title for the index.
   (2) Apply the *Title* style to the index title.
   (3) Position the insertion point below the title, then mark the text to be included in the index using the concordance file, c12sa02, concordance.
g. Update the table of contents to include the Index just created by completing the following steps:
   (1) Position the insertion point within the table of contents (should display with a gray background).
   (2) Press F9 (Update Field key) to update the field.
   (3) At the Update Table of Contents dialog box, choose Update Entire Table, then click OK.
h. Save the document again with the same name, c12sa02, index.
i. Print c12sa02, index. (Check with your instructor to see if you should print the entire document or just the table of contents page and the index pages.)

Assessment 3

1. At a clear editing window, format body text for a Bicycle Helmet Program Resources manual by completing the following steps:
   a. Open *manual text6* located on your student data disk. (The text in this file is divided into three sections. Each section contains a Word table, providing a side-by-side column layout for this manual.)
   b. Save the document with Save As and name it c12sa03, bicycle manual.
   c. Select all the text in the third column in each table and change the font to 11-point Garamond.
   d. Format the first section title in 16-point Arial Bold, then create a style named *section heading* from this formatting. (This could also be done with Format Painter. However, using styles for the formatting makes compiling a table of contents for the document easier.)
   e. Apply the section heading style to the remaining section titles.
   f. Format the headings (left column) in 14-point Arial Bold, then create a style named *side heading* from this formatting.
   g. Create a footer that prints at the bottom of each page, with the following specifications:
      (1) Display the Footer pane.
      (2) At the Footer pane, create a single horizontal line with a weight of 4½ points.

(3) Position the insertion point below the line, change the font to 10-point Arial Bold, then key BICYCLE HELMET PROGRAM RESOURCES.
(4) Set a right tab to align text with the right side of the horizontal line.
(5) Press Tab, key **Page**, press the space bar once, then click the Page Number button on the Header and Footer toolbar.

h. Check page numbering throughout the whole document. The first page of Section 1 should be counted as page number 1 but the page number should not display. The second page of Section 1 should display with a page number 2, and so on. Make the page numbering continuous from one section to another.
i. Create a header that prints a 2¼ point horizontal line on all pages except the beginning page of each section. *(Hint: Refer to Page Setup, Layout, Different First Page in Header and Footer section.)*
j. Check page breaks in the document and, if necessary, make adjustments.

2. Save the document with the same name, c12sa03, bicycle manual.
3. Create a table of contents according to the following specifications:
   a. Create a separate page for the table of contents.
   b. Key **Table of Contents** as the title. (It will be formatted later.)
   c. With c12sa03, bicycle manual still displayed on the screen, mark and compile the text for a table of contents using the *section heading* style as a level one table of contents heading and the *side heading* style as a level two table of contents heading.
   d. Apply the *section heading* style to the table of contents heading.
4. Save the document again with the same name, c12sa03, bicycle manual.
5. Print and then close c12sa03.

Optional: Write a notice to all students at your local elementary school telling them why wearing a bicycle helmet is important.

Assessment 4

1. Create a cover for the Bicycle Helmet Program Resources manual prepared in assessment 3 according to the following specifications:
   a. Use any of the Ride Safe logo graphics included on your student graphic disk or any appropriate graphic image that you may have available to you.
   b. Create thumbnail sketches to formulate your design and layout.
   c. Title the manual BICYCLE HELMET PROGRAM RESOURCES.
   d. You decide on an appropriate font, font size, and font style. *(Hint: Remember to be consistent with the elements that you have already established in the manual.)*
   e. You may incorporate graphic lines, color, WordArt, rotated text, reverse text, etc.
2. When the cover is completed, save the document and name it c12sa04, cover.
3. Print and then close c12sa04, cover.
4. Evaluate your booklet by using the *Document Evaluation Checklist* found on your student data disk.

Creative Activity

Find two examples of a report, manual, booklet, etc. Use the *Document Evaluation Checklist* located on your student data disk to evaluate the two examples. Hand in the checklists along with a list of suggested improvements for each of the documents.

UNIT 3 PERFORMANCE Assessment

Assessment 1

At a clear document window, create a one-page newsletter by completing the following instructions. This newsletter may be a holiday, personal, or family newsletter that you would like to duplicate and mail to your friends or relatives. Write four or five short paragraphs describing the highlights of this year and your expectations for next year. You may include items about your accomplishments, awards, talents, skills, hobbies, or any vacations you may have taken. Use the thesaurus and spelling features to assist you. Also, be sure to create your own styles, use any appropriate system styles, or use the Format Painter to assist you in repetitive formatting.

1. Create a thumbnail sketch of your newsletter.
2. Incorporate the following in your newsletter:
   - Use appropriate typefaces and type sizes for all of the elements in your newsletter.
   - Use em spaces for any indented text.
   - The nameplate should include your last name (e.g., Smith Family Newsletter).
   - Create a subtitle.
   - Create a folio.
   - Use appropriate column numbers and widths.
   - Apply the desktop publishing concepts of focus, balance, proportion, contrast, directional flow, and consistency to your newsletter design and layout.
   - Use kerning and character spacing.
   - Use appropriate leading (paragraph spacing) before and after the headline and all subheads.
   - Use a graphic, symbol, WordArt object, clip art, or a scanned picture. (A photograph would add a nice personal touch!)
   - Be creative.
3. Save and name the newsletter u03pa01, newsletter.
4. After completing *u03pa01, newsletter*, exchange newsletters in the classroom and evaluate them using the Document Evaluation Checklist *(doeval)*. Write any additional comments or suggestions, discussing weaknesses and strengths, on the bottom of the second page of the evaluation form.

Optional: As the President of the United States, you have the task of writing and creating a newsletter for the White House describing the highlights of the year and your expectations for next year. Research the actual accomplishments of the First Family for the year, but use your creativity when writing about next year's expectations.

■ Assessment 2

In chapter 11, skill assessment 2, you redesigned the first page of an accounting firm's newsletter. In this assessment, you will create a two-page newsletter using the same text from your student data disk.

1. At a clear document window, open *redesign text.* (This document is located on your student data disk.)
2. Save the document with Save As and name it u03pa02, disclosures.
3. Redesign *both* pages of the newsletter and include the following items:
   a. Nameplate
   b. Folio
   c. Heading and subheading styles
   d. Header and footer
   e. Table of contents
   f. Sidebar
   g. Pull quote
   h. Graphic with caption
   i. Spot color
   j. Use a kicker, end signs, and jump lines, if desired or needed for copy fitting.
   k. Use tracking, leading (paragraph spacing), etc., to set the body copy attractively on the page.
   l. Use any design elements necessary to achieve consistency and unity between the two pages.
4. When completed, save the document again with the same name (u03pa02, disclosures).
5. Print and then close u03pa02, disclosures. (Ask your instructor about printing each page separately or printing the pages back to back.)
6. Evaluate your own work using the Document Evaluation Checklist *(doceval.doc.)* located on your student data disk. Revise your document if any areas need improvement.

■ Assessment 3

1. At a clear document window, create a cover for your portfolio with the following specifications:
   a. Create a thumbnail sketch of your cover.
   b. Use at least one graphic element such as ruled lines, a graphic image, or a scanned image.
   c. Consider balance, focus, contrast, directional flow, and proportion when creating the cover.
2. Save the completed cover and name it u03pa03, cover.
3. Print and then close u03pa03, cover.

Optional: Create a new cover for your portfolio. Assume you are applying for a government position or for a job in a comedy gallery and try to convey a tone that's appropriate to your purpose.

■ Assessment 4

1. Prepare a benefits manual for Grant County Medical using the document *benefits manual* that is located on your student data disk. Format the manual with the following specifications:
   a. Set the body text in a serif typeface and in a point size appropriate for a text-intensive document.
   b. Set the section headings and side headings in a sans serif typeface in a size larger than the body text.
   c. Create styles for the section headings and side headings.
   d. Create appropriate headers and/or footers.
   e. Include page numbering (this can be part of a header or footer).
   f. Prepare a table of contents using a customized style list, including the styles you created for the section headings and side headings. (*Hint:* When creating a separate page for the table of contents, use a next page section break.)
   g. Adjust page numbering format to include Roman numerals for the table of contents page. (Check the page numbering in the remainder of your document to make sure the pages are numbered correctly.)
2. Save the manual and name it u03pa04, manual.
3. Print and then close u03pa04, manual.

■ Assessment 5

1. At a clear document window, create a manual cover for the manual created in assessment 4. Consider these elements when creating the cover:
   a. Balance
   b. Directional flow
   c. Focus (use lines, fonts, and/or a graphic image as a focal point)
   d. Color
   e. Include the following text in the cover:
      Grant County Medical
      Benefits Plan
      Beginning January 1, 1998
2. Save the completed cover and name it u03pa05, benefits cover.
3. Print and then close c03pa05, benefits cover.

Optional: Read the manual and write a memo telling your employees what information this manual provides and why they should keep it readily available.

■ Assessment 6

As a volunteer for the *Spotlight on the Arts* membership and fundraising campaign, you have been assigned the responsibility of creating a slide show presentation to be viewed by patrons and possible contributors. Plan, design, and create a presentation consisting of five slides.

Your presentation should include the following:

- Text—open *Spotlight Outline.ppt* from your student data disk
- A title slide with your name as the presenter
- An appropriate template as the background for the slides
- Appropriate clip art images

- The date and slide number at the bottom of each slide
- Bullets to organize important points
- Text color and appropriate text size to emphasize the text
- Appropriate transition effects, builds, animations, or sounds

Complete the following tasks after creating your presentation:

- Spell check your slides before printing.
- Run your presentation for a classmate or your instructor.
- Ask your classmate or teacher to summarize all the good points and bad points about your presentation.
- Make any necessary changes as recommended by your classmate or teacher.
- Print your presentation with six slides per page.
- Save your presentation and name it Spotlight on the Arts Presentation.
- Close Spotlight on the Arts Presentation.

INDEX

A

B

C

D

E

F

G

H

I

J

K

L

M

N

O

P

T

U

V

X

Y

Z

Cut Along This Line

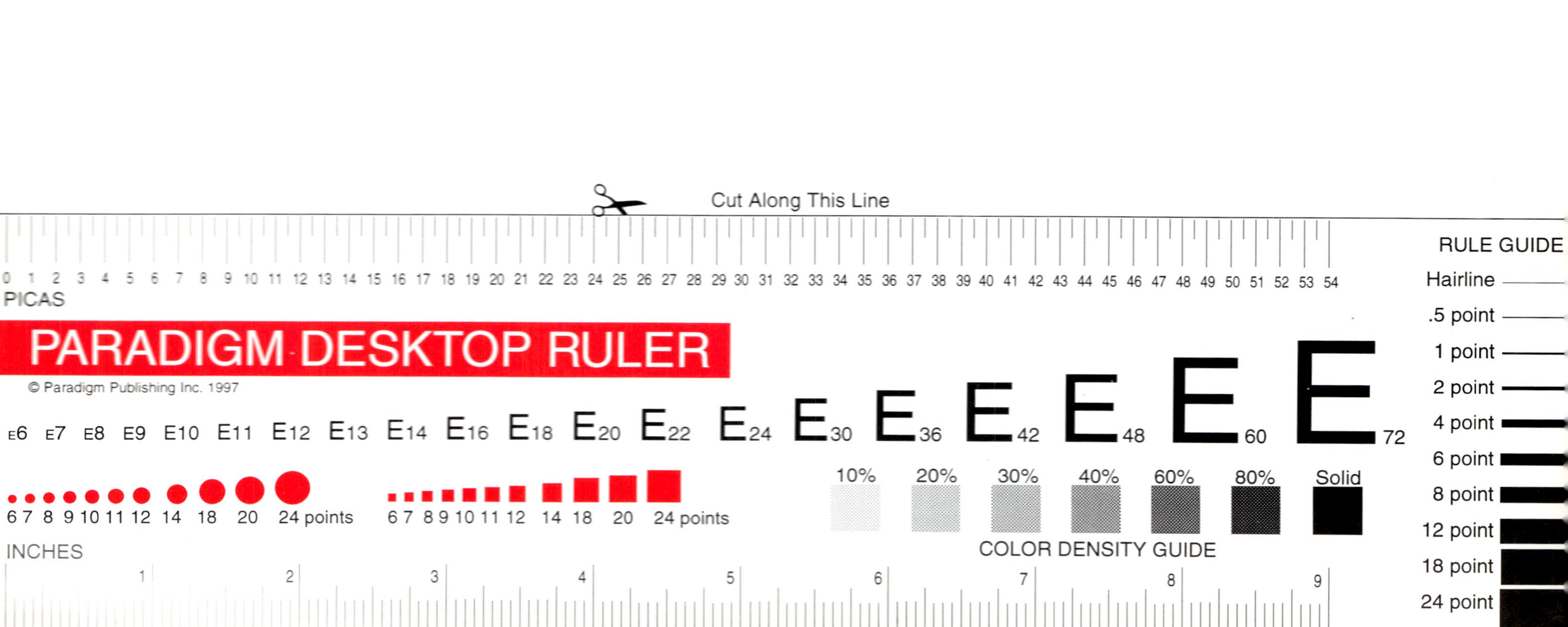